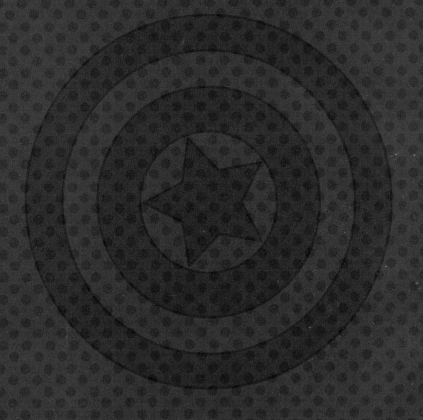

CAPTAIN AMERICA

OPERATION REBIRTH

CAPTAIN AMERICA

OPERATION REBIRTH

Writer: Mark Waid
Penciler: Ron Garney with Pino Rinaldi
Inkers: Scott Koblish, Mike Sellers, Denis Rodier & Mike Manley
Colorists: John Kalisz & Paul Becton
Color Separations: Malibu
Letterer: John Costanza
Editor: Ralph Macchio & Bobbie Chase

Front Cover Art: Ron Garney

Collection Editor: Mark D. Beazley
Assistant Editors: John Denning & Cory Levine
Editor, Special Projects: Jennifer Grünwald
Senior Editor, Special Projects: Jeff Youngquist
Production: Jerron Quality Color, Nelson Ribeiro & Jerry Kalinowski
Senior Vice President of Sales: David Gabriel

Editor in Chief: Joe Quesada
Publisher: Dan Buckley

INTRODUCTION

When I came to the job, I wanted to do Tom Clancy. Once I got into it – thanks in n
small part to the astounding Ron Garney – I ended up with a lot more Jackie Chan, an
quite frankly, I think we were all the better for it.

More than any other action hero, Captain America thrives on Impossible Odds.
honestly believe that Cap's brain is incapable of registering the concept of defeat. If h
weren't twenty times smarter than I am, I wouldn't even be entirely convinced he coul
spell it. No matter how I stacked the deck against him... despite the fact that I shackle
him with his worst enemy and hammered him with his ex-girlfriend... he raced toward
victory like a red, white and blue freight train, and there wasn't anything in this worl
I could throw in his path that had any serious chance of slowing him down.

– Mark Waid

First off, let me say that I do my own stunts. Other people have told me that I was born
to do the character, but you're only as good as the creative team you're a part of... I wa
very lucky. CAP was the most fun I've ever had, and I'm sure that from now until th
day that I'm wormfood, my career will most likely be defined by this most wonderfu
series. Thanks, guys... let's do it again soon.

– Ron Garney

For one brief, shining moment... A glistening phrase that nicely sums up my feeling
on the wondrous Waid/Garney collaboration that energized CAPTAIN AMERICA
#445-448, "Operation: Rebirth." At last, here was the story that was begging to b
told! It was the shield-slinger getting the chance to do the one thing he'd been denie
in his decades-long existence as a super hero: stopping Adolf Hitler himself! An
with Mark Waid's superb storytelling skills on full display, and Ron Garney penciling
the character he was born to illustrate, I knew we were on our way to an instant Ca
Classic! Followed by the equally compelling "Man Without A Country" arc serving a
a bookend, it was time to just sit back and savor the magic. This was a rare teaming of
eminently compatible talents and it was a pleasure to see the creative sparks fly betwee
them. To both of you, Mark and Ron, my sincerest thanks for giving me one of the most
thoroughly satisfying runs I've had on any title as a Marvel editor. Let's do it again
guys, sometime soon.

– Ralph Macchio

WHAT HAS GONE BEFORE...

He was the greatest hero America had known.

Created to be the ultimate soldier, *Steve Rogers* became something much greater. During the darkest days of World War II, he was a symbol of hope to a troubled world... the Sentinel of Liberty... the living legend known as *Captain America!*

For five long years, he battled the vile Axis powers – saving thousands of lives – and inspiring still more. But in the closing days of history's greatest conflict, he disappeared.

Presumed dead for decades, he returned – phoenix-like – to renew his mission for a world in desperate need. It seemed no foe – not even time itself – could overcome the fierce will of Captain America.

Until now.

For the very thing that allowed Steve Rogers to become the perfect human fighting machine – the never-duplicated *super-soldier serum* – began to decay, leaving mankind's finest physical specimen a near-invalid. Unwilling to relinquish his role as freedom's defender, Rogers donned a specially-designed suit of armor that would allow him to continue fighting. It could only last so long...

Captain America died.

The nation – and the world – now mourns the loss of a man who embodied all that was good in humanity, while sinister forces plan a campaign that will create global chaos, and *destroy* that which Captain America fought and died for...

...liberty, freedom, and justice...

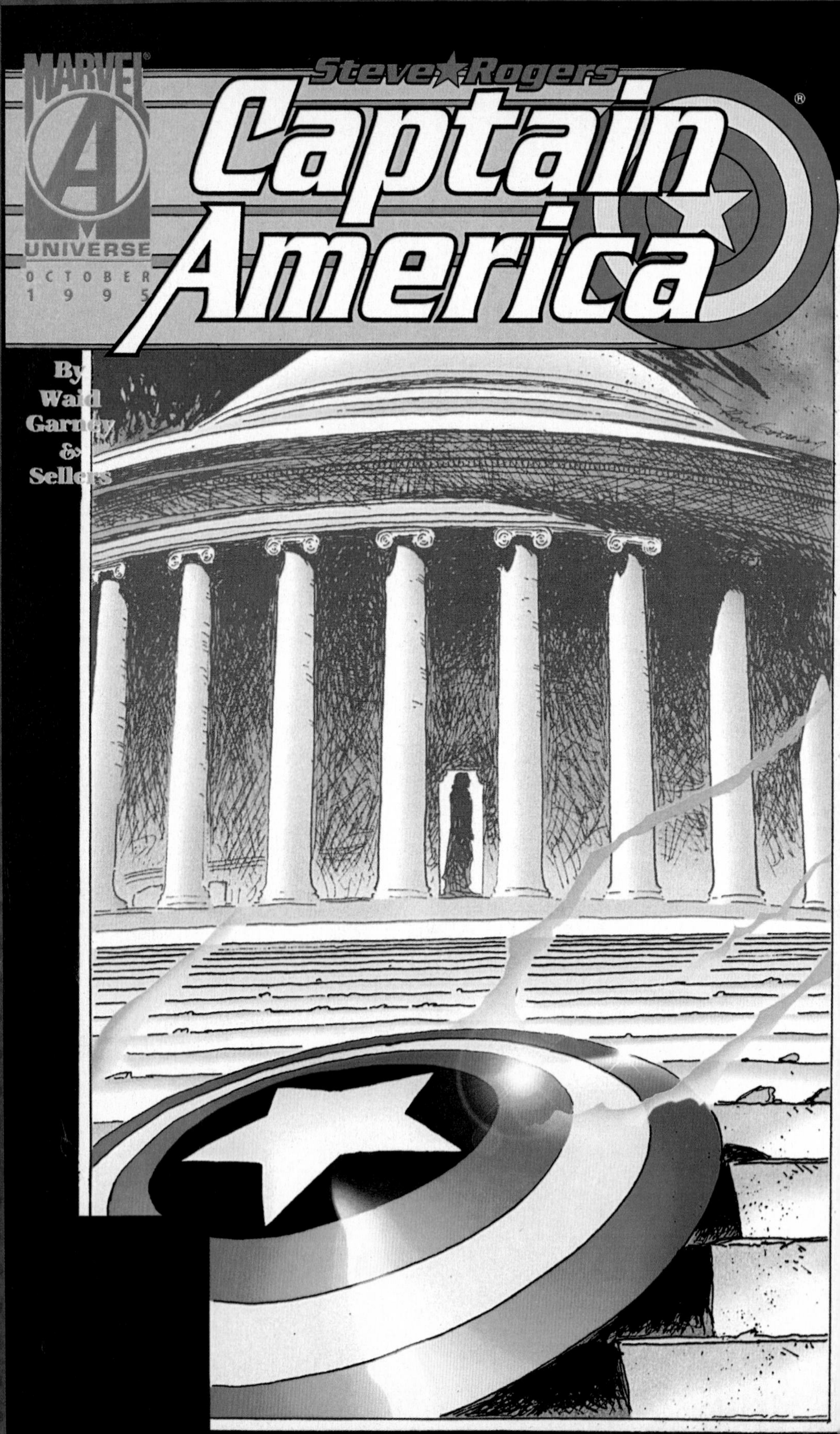
MARVEL
UNIVERSE
OCTOBER
1995
Steve★Rogers
Captain America
By
Waid
Garney
&
Sellers

HE'LL BE HERE.
YOU'D BETTER HOPE SO.

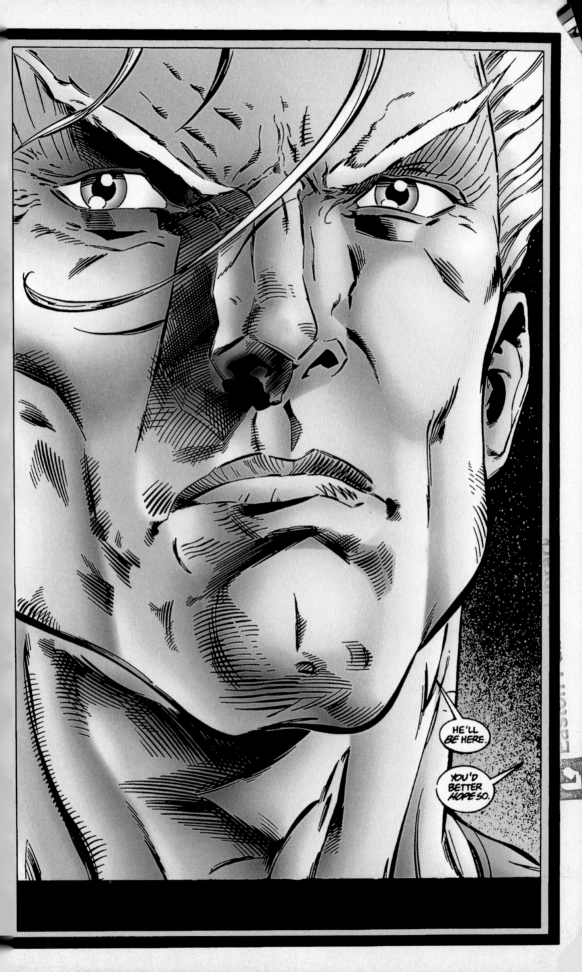

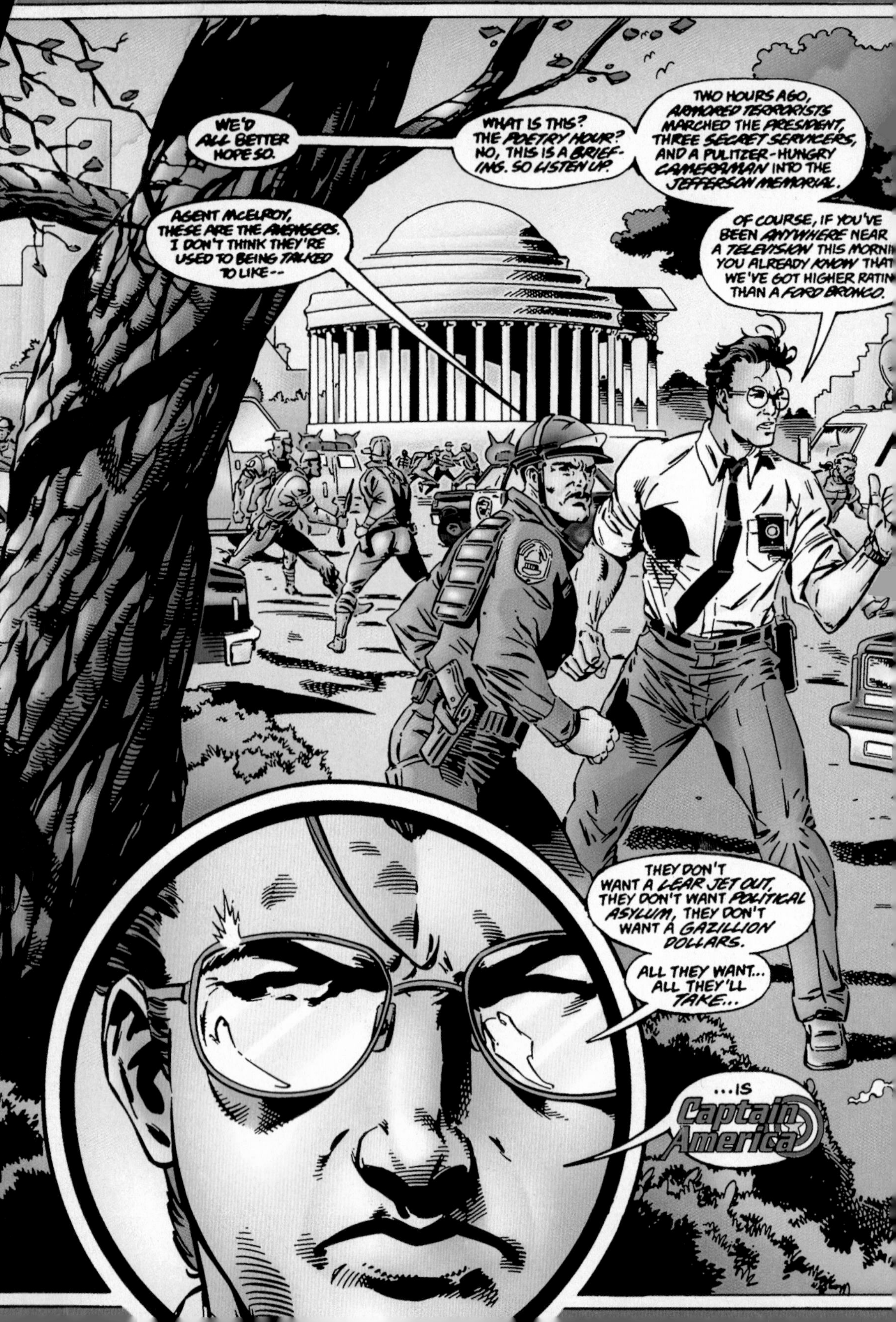
WE'D ALL BETTER HOPE SO.
WHAT IS THIS? THE POETRY HOUR? NO, THIS IS A BRIEF-ING. SO LISTEN UP.
TWO HOURS AGO, ARMORED TERRORISTS MARCHED THE PRESIDENT, THREE SECRET SERVICERS, AND A PULITZER-HUNGRY CAMERAMAN INTO THE JEFFERSON MEMORIAL.
AGENT MCELROY, THESE ARE THE AVENGERS. I DON'T THINK THEY'RE USED TO BEING TALKED TO LIKE--
OF COURSE, IF YOU'VE BEEN ANYWHERE NEAR A TELEVISION THIS MORNIN YOU ALREADY KNOW THAT WE'VE GOT HIGHER RATIN THAN A FORD BRONCO.
THEY DON'T WANT A LEAR JET OUT, THEY DON'T WANT POLITICAL ASYLUM, THEY DON'T WANT A GAZILLION DOLLARS.
ALL THEY WANT... ALL THEY'LL TAKE...
...IS Captain America

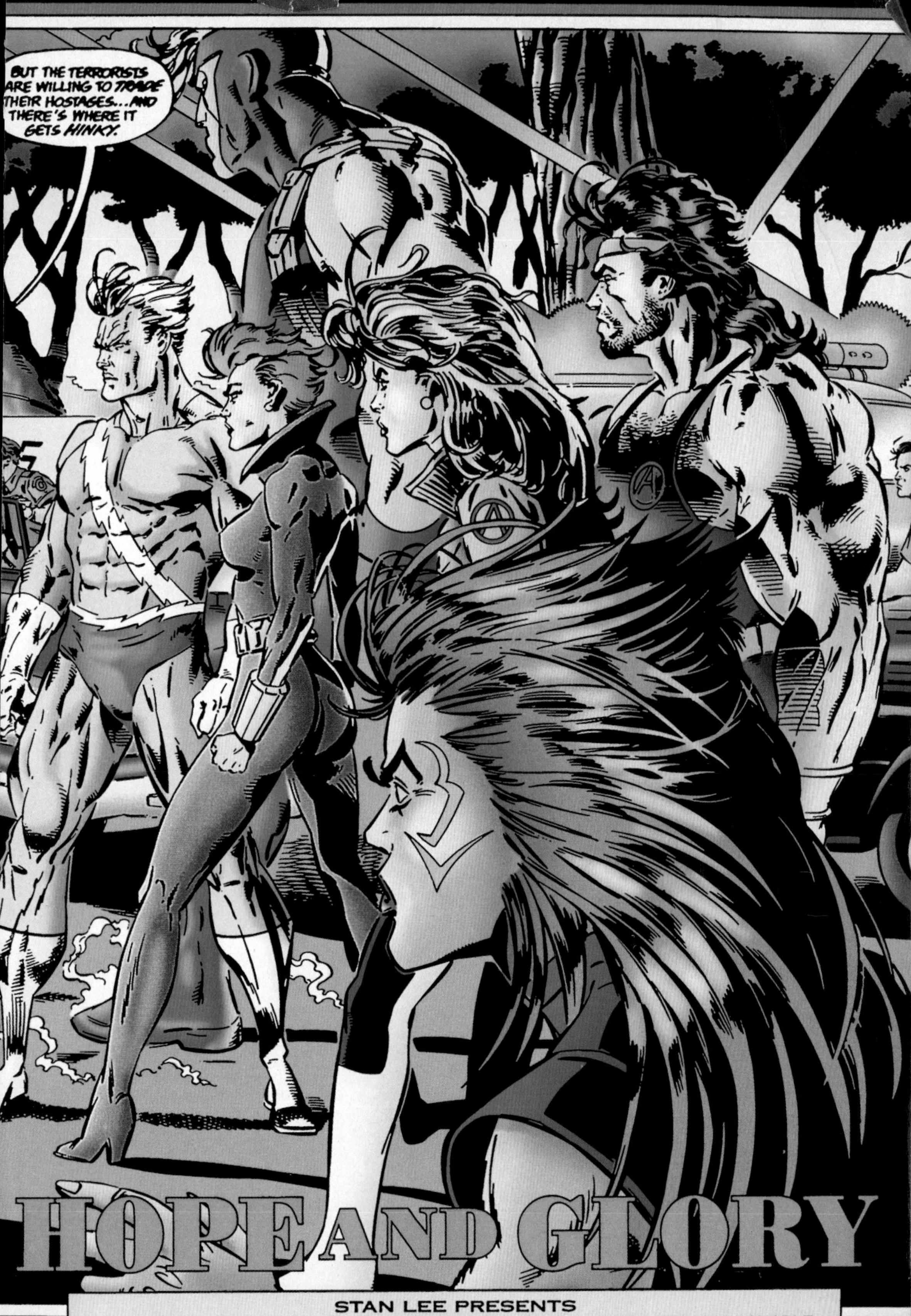
BUT THE TERRORISTS ARE WILLING TO *TRADE* THEIR HOSTAGES... AND THERE'S WHERE IT GETS *HINKY.*
HOPE AND GLORY

STAN LEE PRESENTS

THE BEGINNING OF A NEW ERA OF GREATNESS! BROUGHT TO YOU WITH PARDONABLE PRIDE BY:

MARK WAID STORY · RON GARNEY PENCILS · MIKE SELLERS INKS · JOHN KALISZ COLORS

JOHN COSTANZA LETTERS · RALPH MACCHIO EDITOR · MARK GRUENWALD EDITOR IN CHIEF

COMPUTER COLOR BY: MALIBU

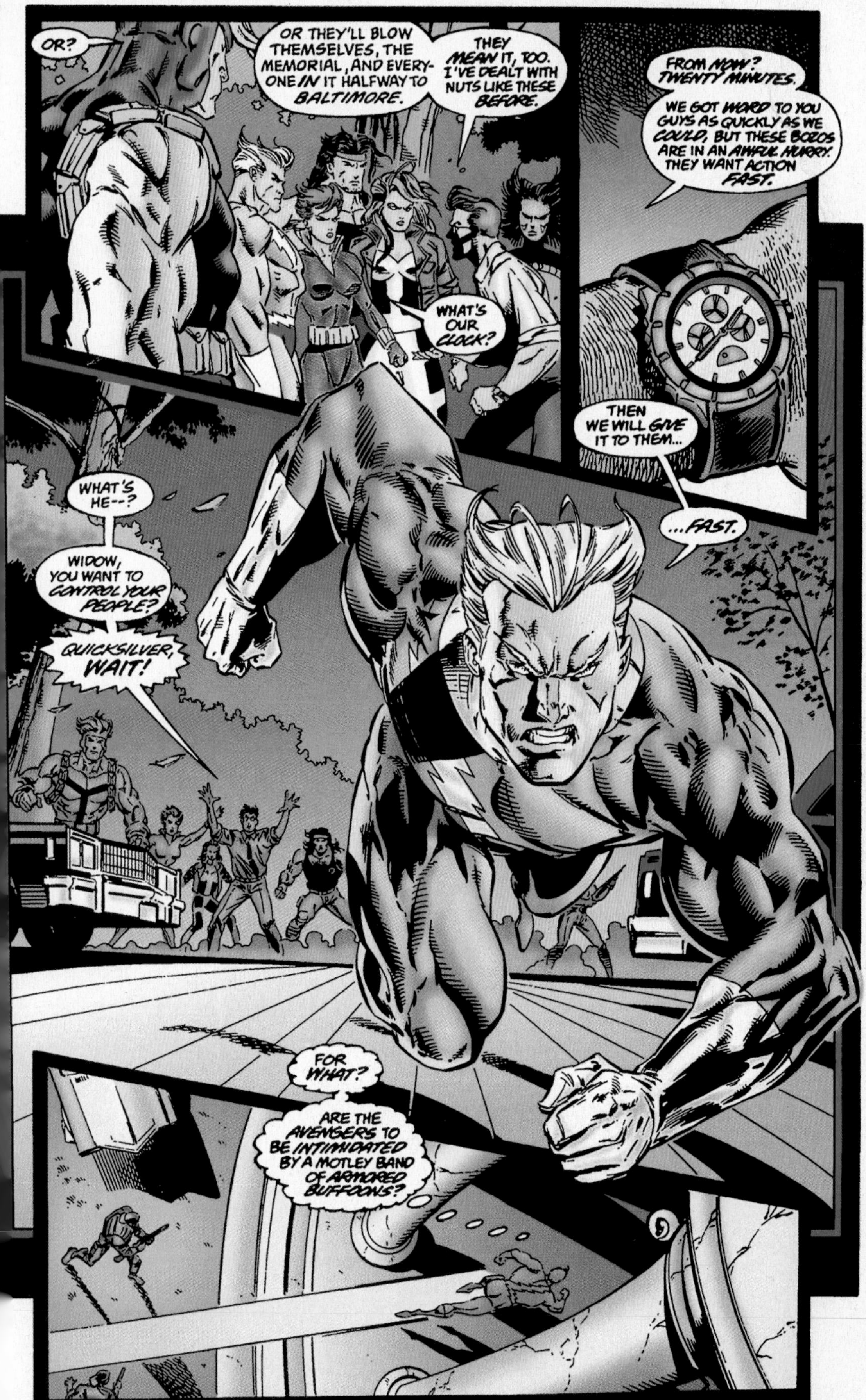
OR?
OR THEY'LL BLOW THEMSELVES, THE MEMORIAL, AND EVERYONE IN IT HALFWAY TO BALTIMORE.
THEY MEAN IT, TOO. I'VE DEALT WITH NUTS LIKE THESE BEFORE.
WHAT'S OUR CLOCK?
FROM NOW? TWENTY MINUTES.
WE GOT WORD TO YOU GUYS AS QUICKLY AS WE COULD, BUT THESE BOZOS ARE IN AN AWFUL HURRY. THEY WANT ACTION FAST.
THEN WE WILL GIVE IT TO THEM...
...FAST.
WHAT'S HE--?
WIDOW, YOU WANT TO CONTROL YOUR PEOPLE?
QUICKSILVER, WAIT!
FOR WHAT?
ARE THE AVENGERS TO BE INTIMIDATED BY A MOTLEY BAND OF ARMORED BUFFOONS?

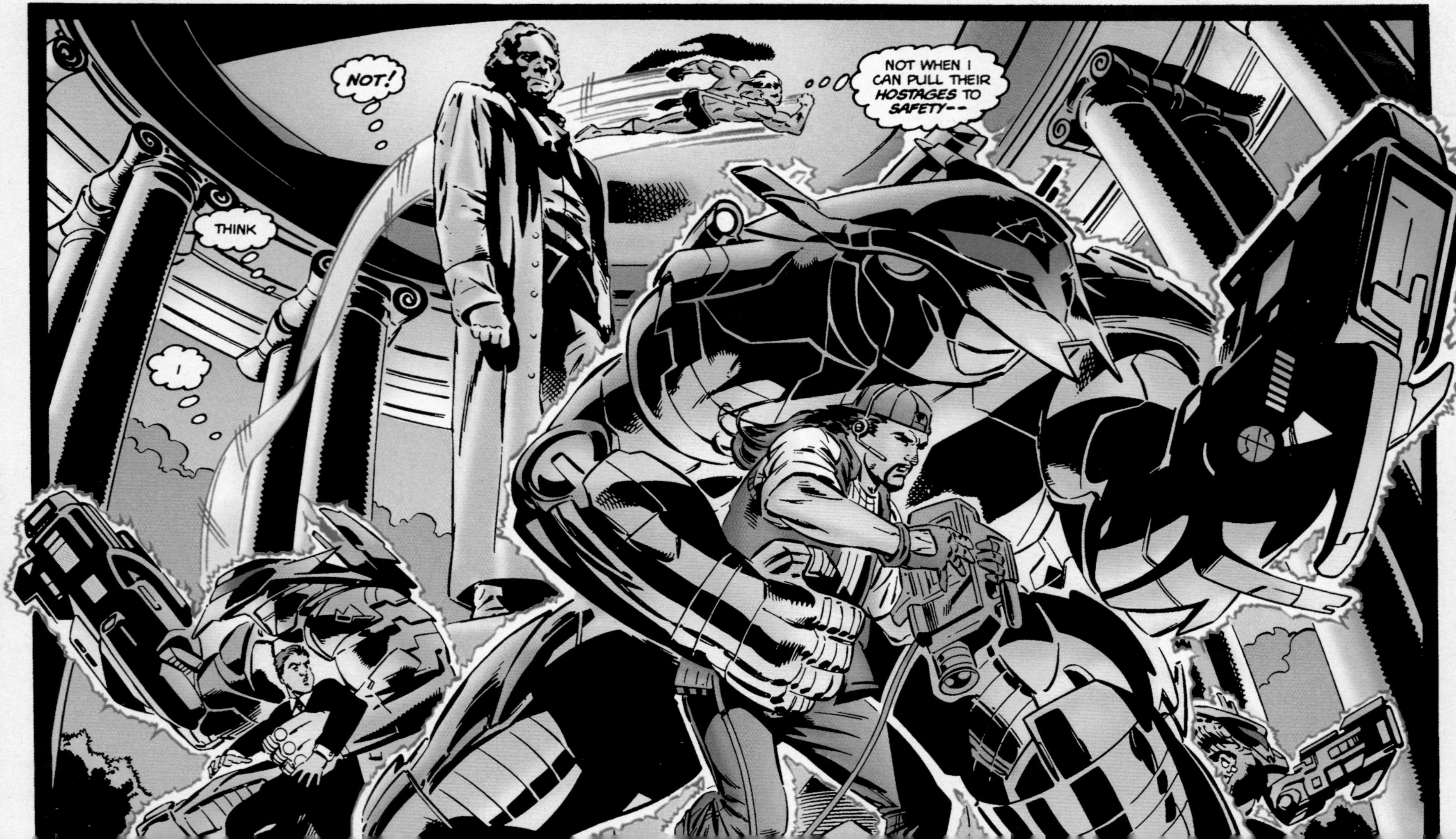
I
THINK
NOT!
NOT WHEN I CAN PULL THEIR HOSTAGES TO SAFETY--

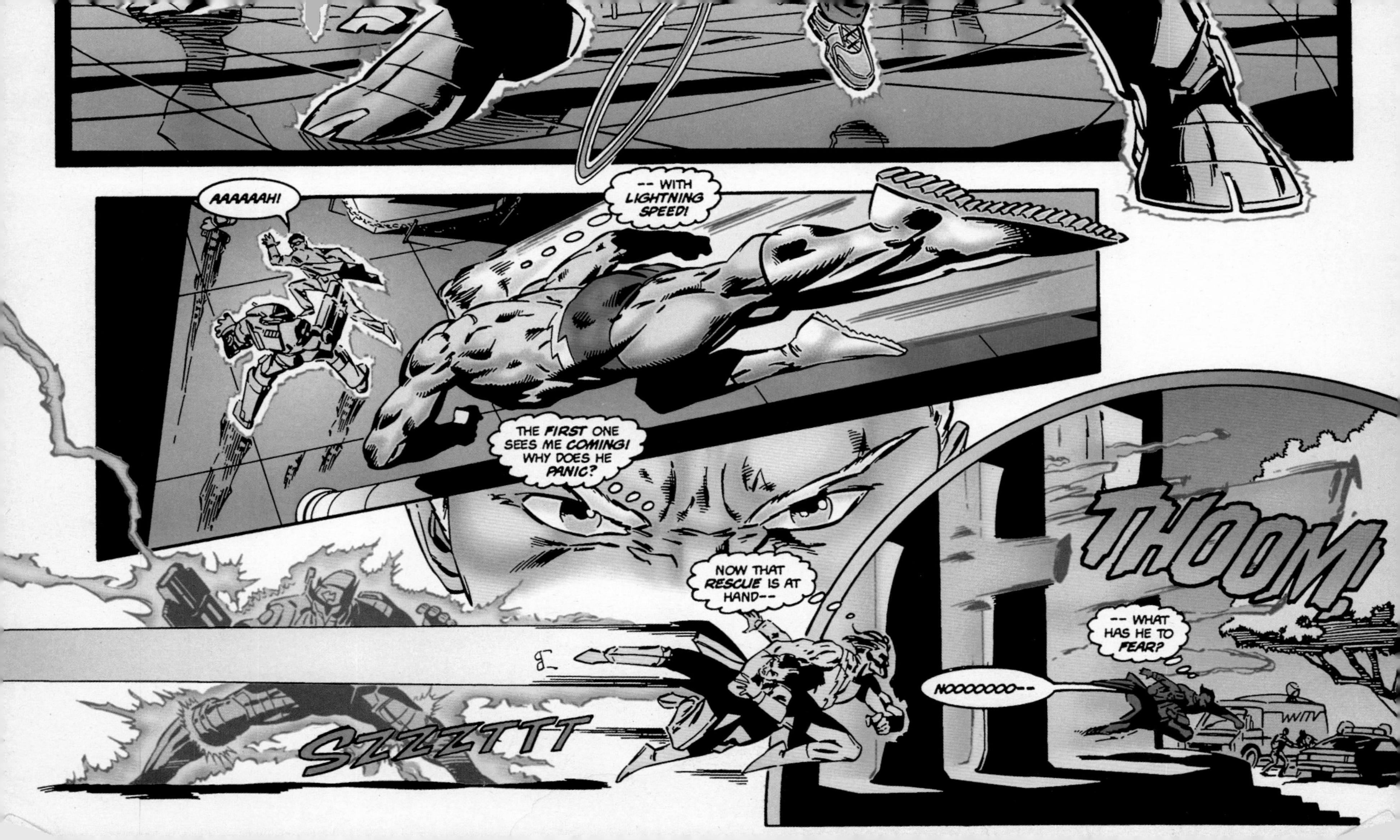
AAAAAAH!
-- WITH LIGHTNING SPEED!
THE FIRST ONE SEES ME COMING! WHY DOES HE PANIC?
NOW THAT RESCUE IS AT HAND--
THOOM!
-- WHAT HAS HE TO FEAR?
NOOOOOOO--
SZZZTTT

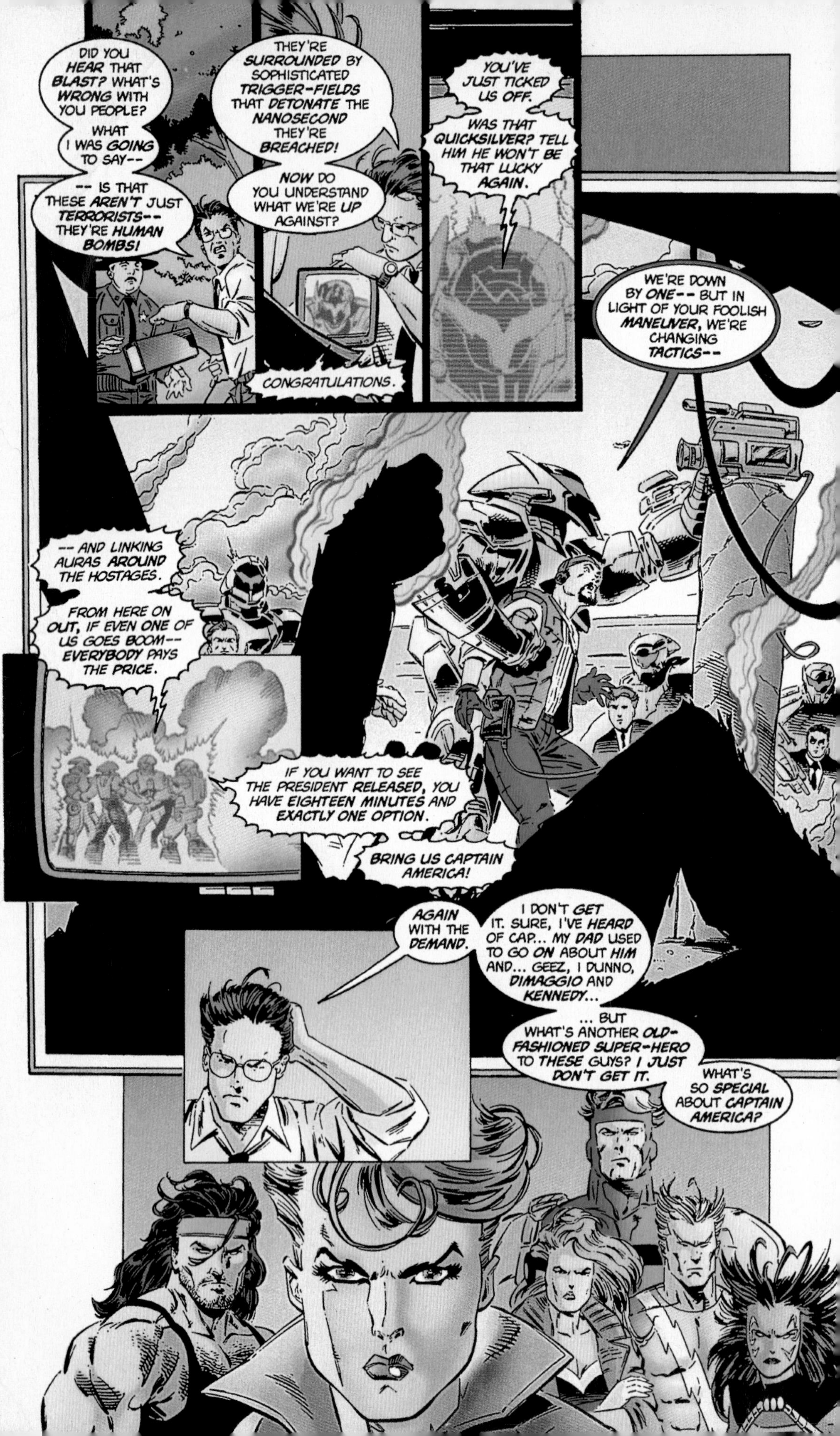
DID YOU HEAR THAT BLAST? WHAT'S WRONG WITH YOU PEOPLE?
WHAT I WAS GOING TO SAY--
-- IS THAT THESE AREN'T JUST TERRORISTS-- THEY'RE HUMAN BOMBS!
THEY'RE SURROUNDED BY SOPHISTICATED TRIGGER-FIELDS THAT DETONATE THE NANOSECOND THEY'RE BREACHED!
NOW DO YOU UNDERSTAND WHAT WE'RE UP AGAINST?
CONGRATULATIONS.
YOU'VE JUST TICKED US OFF.
WAS THAT QUICKSILVER? TELL HIM HE WON'T BE THAT LUCKY AGAIN.
WE'RE DOWN BY ONE-- BUT IN LIGHT OF YOUR FOOLISH MANEUVER, WE'RE CHANGING TACTICS--
-- AND LINKING AURAS AROUND THE HOSTAGES.
FROM HERE ON OUT, IF EVEN ONE OF US GOES BOOM-- EVERYBODY PAYS THE PRICE.
IF YOU WANT TO SEE THE PRESIDENT RELEASED, YOU HAVE EIGHTEEN MINUTES AND EXACTLY ONE OPTION.
BRING US CAPTAIN AMERICA!
AGAIN WITH THE DEMAND.
I DON'T GET IT. SURE, I'VE HEARD OF CAP... MY DAD USED TO GO ON ABOUT HIM AND... GEEZ, I DUNNO, DIMAGGIO AND KENNEDY...
... BUT WHAT'S ANOTHER OLD-FASHIONED SUPER-HERO TO THESE GUYS? I JUST DON'T GET IT.
WHAT'S SO SPECIAL ABOUT CAPTAIN AMERICA?

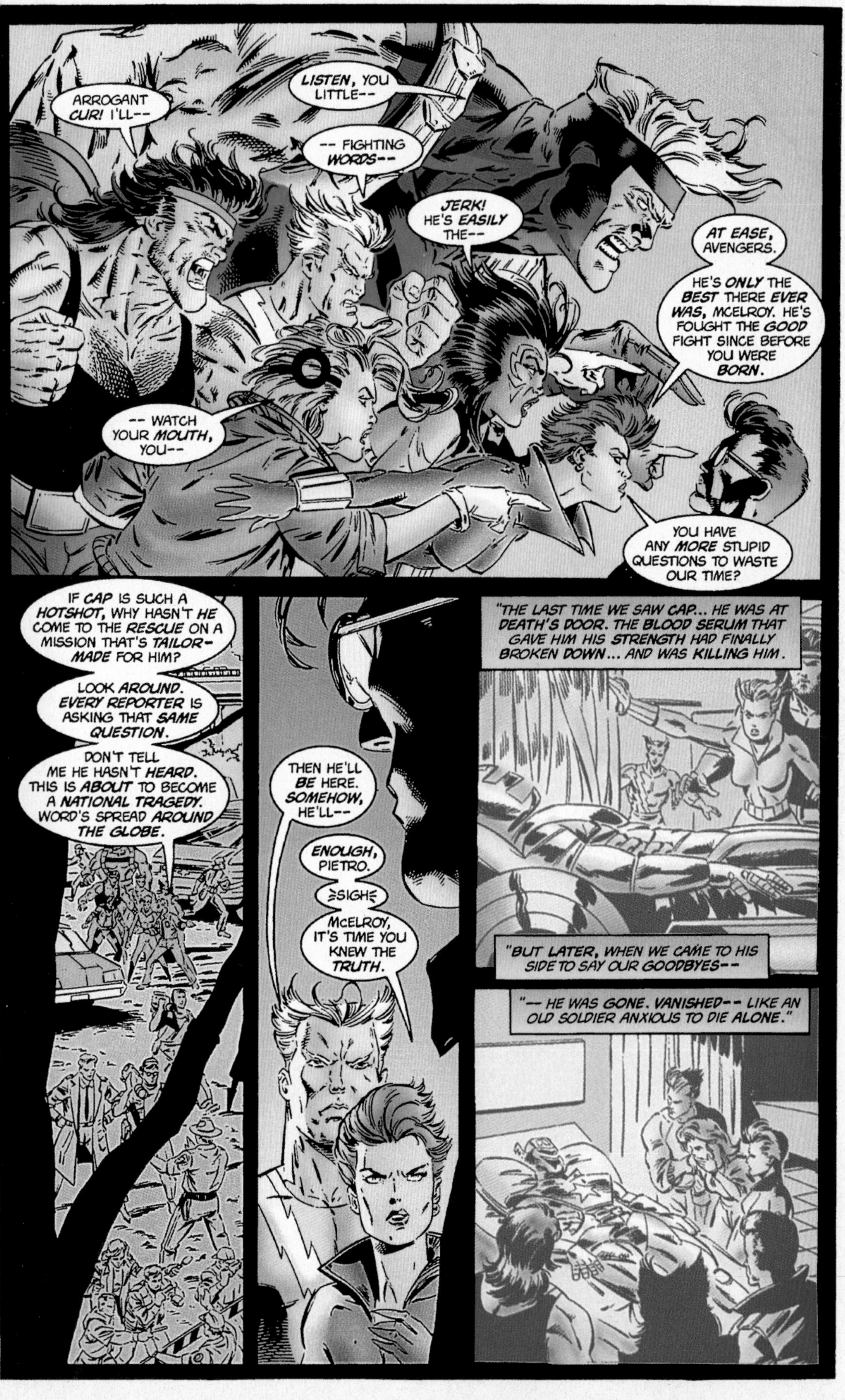

ARROGANT CUR! I'LL--
LISTEN, YOU LITTLE--
-- FIGHTING WORDS--
JERK! HE'S EASILY THE--
AT EASE, AVENGERS.
HE'S ONLY THE BEST THERE EVER WAS, MCELROY. HE'S FOUGHT THE GOOD FIGHT SINCE BEFORE YOU WERE BORN.
-- WATCH YOUR MOUTH, YOU--
YOU HAVE ANY MORE STUPID QUESTIONS TO WASTE OUR TIME?
IF CAP IS SUCH A HOTSHOT, WHY HASN'T HE COME TO THE RESCUE ON A MISSION THAT'S TAILOR-MADE FOR HIM?
LOOK AROUND. EVERY REPORTER IS ASKING THAT SAME QUESTION.
DON'T TELL ME HE HASN'T HEARD. THIS IS ABOUT TO BECOME A NATIONAL TRAGEDY. WORD'S SPREAD AROUND THE GLOBE.
THEN HE'LL BE HERE. SOMEHOW, HE'LL--
ENOUGH, PIETRO.
SIGH
MCELROY, IT'S TIME YOU KNEW THE TRUTH.
"THE LAST TIME WE SAW CAP... HE WAS AT DEATH'S DOOR. THE BLOOD SERUM THAT GAVE HIM HIS STRENGTH HAD FINALLY BROKEN DOWN... AND WAS KILLING HIM.
"BUT LATER, WHEN WE CAME TO HIS SIDE TO SAY OUR GOODBYES--
"-- HE WAS GONE. VANISHED-- LIKE AN OLD SOLDIER ANXIOUS TO DIE ALONE."

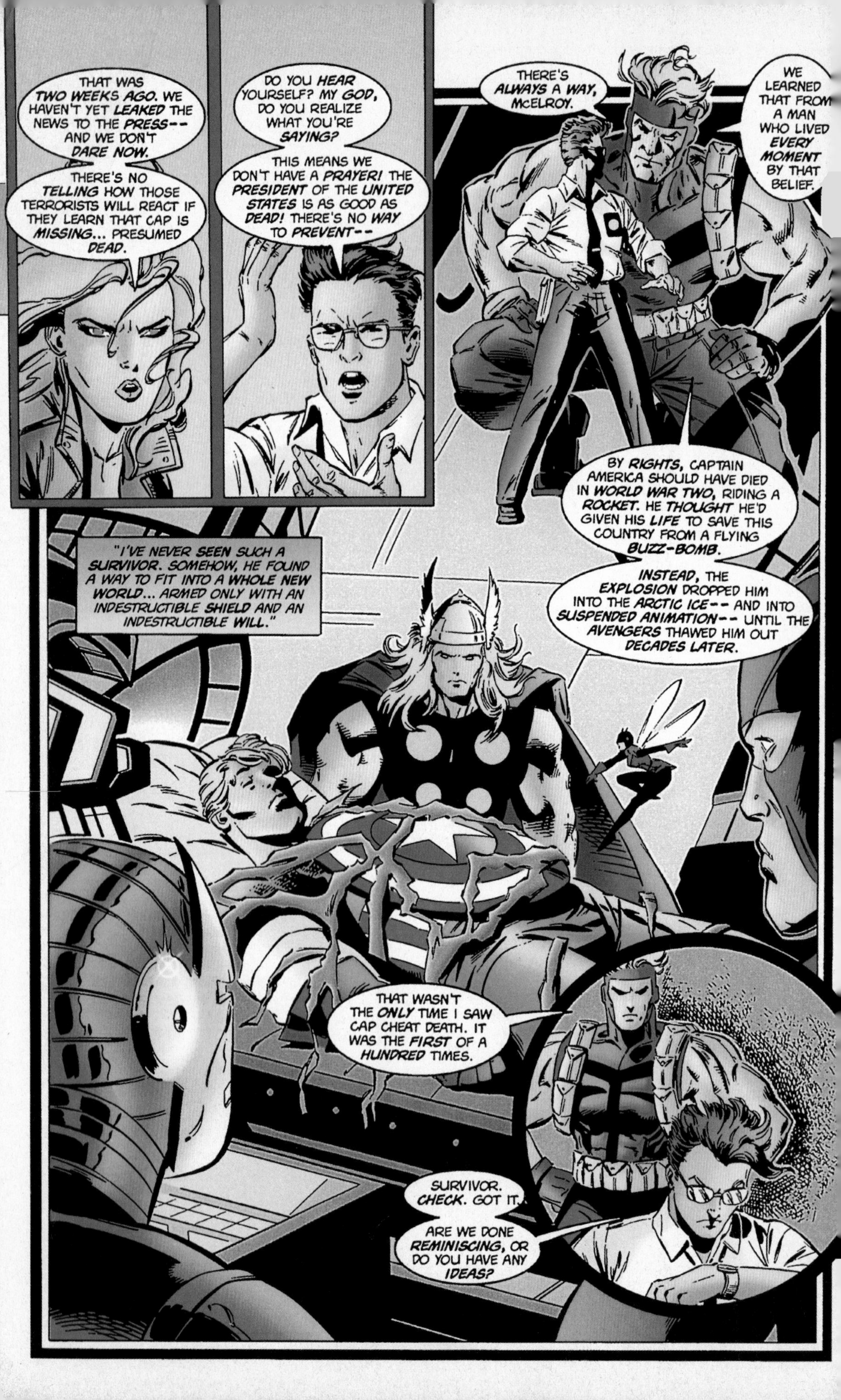

THAT WAS TWO WEEKS AGO. WE HAVEN'T YET LEAKED THE NEWS TO THE PRESS-- AND WE DON'T DARE NOW.
THERE'S NO TELLING HOW THOSE TERRORISTS WILL REACT IF THEY LEARN THAT CAP IS MISSING... PRESUMED DEAD.
DO YOU HEAR YOURSELF? MY GOD, DO YOU REALIZE WHAT YOU'RE SAYING?
THIS MEANS WE DON'T HAVE A PRAYER! THE PRESIDENT OF THE UNITED STATES IS AS GOOD AS DEAD! THERE'S NO WAY TO PREVENT--
THERE'S ALWAYS A WAY, McELROY.
WE LEARNED THAT FROM A MAN WHO LIVED EVERY MOMENT BY THAT BELIEF.
BY RIGHTS, CAPTAIN AMERICA SHOULD HAVE DIED IN WORLD WAR TWO, RIDING A ROCKET. HE THOUGHT HE'D GIVEN HIS LIFE TO SAVE THIS COUNTRY FROM A FLYING BUZZ-BOMB.
INSTEAD, THE EXPLOSION DROPPED HIM INTO THE ARCTIC ICE-- AND INTO SUSPENDED ANIMATION-- UNTIL THE AVENGERS THAWED HIM OUT DECADES LATER.
"I'VE NEVER SEEN SUCH A SURVIVOR. SOMEHOW, HE FOUND A WAY TO FIT INTO A WHOLE NEW WORLD... ARMED ONLY WITH AN INDESTRUCTIBLE SHIELD AND AN INDESTRUCTIBLE WILL."
THAT WASN'T THE ONLY TIME I SAW CAP CHEAT DEATH. IT WAS THE FIRST OF A HUNDRED TIMES.
SURVIVOR. CHECK. GOT IT.
ARE WE DONE REMINISCING, OR DO YOU HAVE ANY IDEAS?

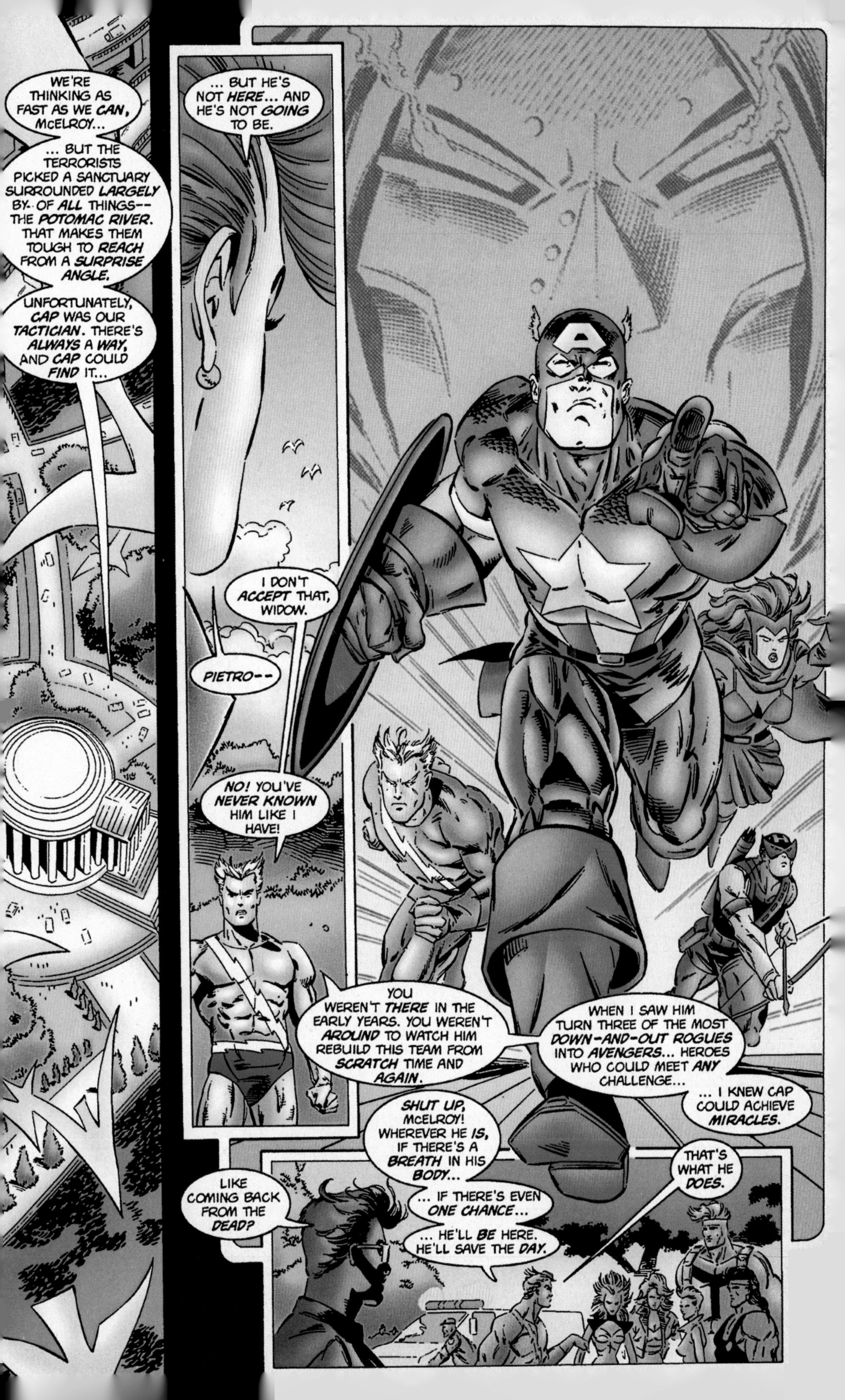
WE'RE THINKING AS FAST AS WE CAN, McELROY...
... BUT THE TERRORISTS PICKED A SANCTUARY SURROUNDED LARGELY BY-- OF ALL THINGS-- THE POTOMAC RIVER. THAT MAKES THEM TOUGH TO REACH FROM A SURPRISE ANGLE.
UNFORTUNATELY, CAP WAS OUR TACTICIAN. THERE'S ALWAYS A WAY, AND CAP COULD FIND IT...
... BUT HE'S NOT HERE... AND HE'S NOT GOING TO BE.
I DON'T ACCEPT THAT, WIDOW.
PIETRO--
NO! YOU'VE NEVER KNOWN HIM LIKE I HAVE!
YOU WEREN'T THERE IN THE EARLY YEARS. YOU WEREN'T AROUND TO WATCH HIM REBUILD THIS TEAM FROM SCRATCH TIME AND AGAIN.
WHEN I SAW HIM TURN THREE OF THE MOST DOWN-AND-OUT ROGUES INTO AVENGERS... HEROES WHO COULD MEET ANY CHALLENGE...
... I KNEW CAP COULD ACHIEVE MIRACLES.
LIKE COMING BACK FROM THE DEAD?
SHUT UP, McELROY! WHEREVER HE IS, IF THERE'S A BREATH IN HIS BODY...
... IF THERE'S EVEN ONE CHANCE...
... HE'LL BE HERE. HE'LL SAVE THE DAY.
THAT'S WHAT HE DOES.

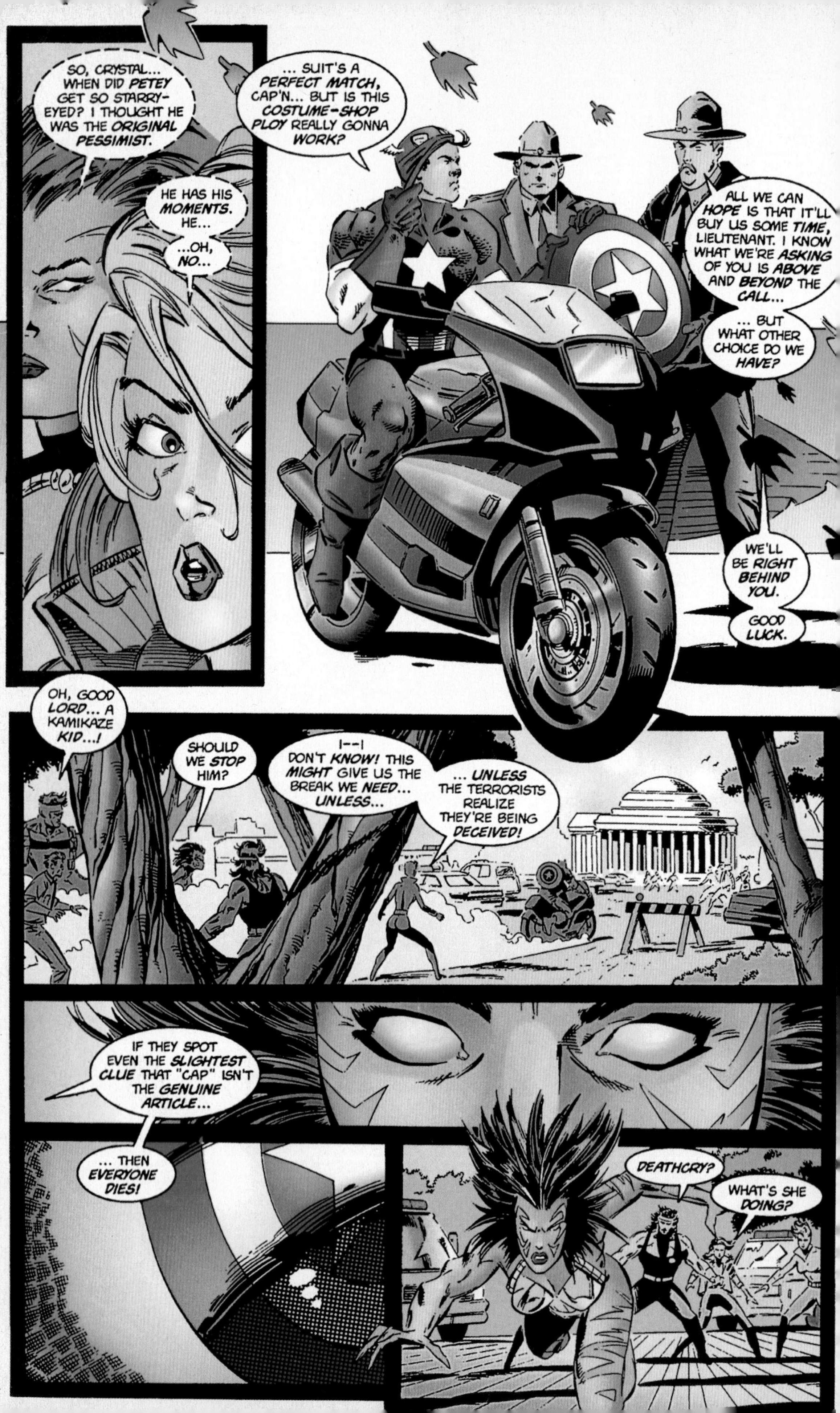
SO, CRYSTAL... WHEN DID PETEY GET SO STARRY-EYED? I THOUGHT HE WAS THE ORIGINAL PESSIMIST.
HE HAS HIS MOMENTS. HE...
...OH, NO...
... SUIT'S A PERFECT MATCH, CAP'N... BUT IS THIS COSTUME-SHOP PLOY REALLY GONNA WORK?
ALL WE CAN HOPE IS THAT IT'LL BUY US SOME TIME, LIEUTENANT. I KNOW WHAT WE'RE ASKING OF YOU IS ABOVE AND BEYOND THE CALL...
... BUT WHAT OTHER CHOICE DO WE HAVE?
WE'LL BE RIGHT BEHIND YOU.
GOOD LUCK.
OH, GOOD LORD... A KAMIKAZE KID...!
SHOULD WE STOP HIM?
I--I DON'T KNOW! THIS MIGHT GIVE US THE BREAK WE NEED... UNLESS...
... UNLESS THE TERRORISTS REALIZE THEY'RE BEING DECEIVED!
IF THEY SPOT EVEN THE SLIGHTEST CLUE THAT "CAP" ISN'T THE GENUINE ARTICLE...
... THEN EVERYONE DIES!
DEATHCRY?
WHAT'S SHE DOING?

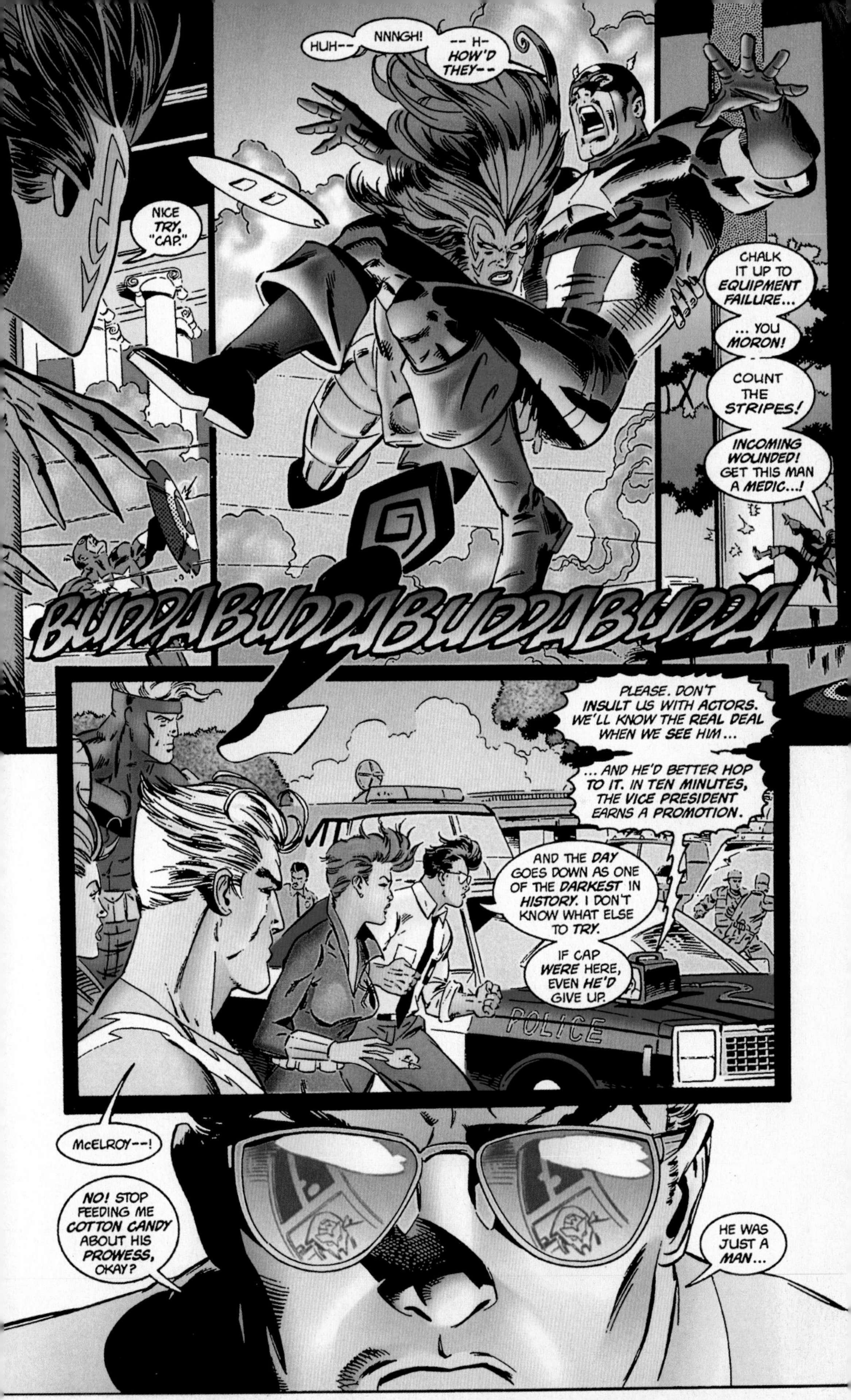
HUH--
NNNGH!
-- H-
HOW'D
THEY--
NICE
TRY,
"CAP."
CHALK
IT UP TO
EQUIPMENT
FAILURE...
... YOU
MORON!
COUNT
THE
STRIPES!
INCOMING
WOUNDED!
GET THIS MAN
A MEDIC...!
BUDDABUDDABUDDABUDDA
PLEASE. DON'T
INSULT US WITH ACTORS.
WE'LL KNOW THE REAL DEAL
WHEN WE SEE HIM...
... AND HE'D BETTER HOP
TO IT. IN TEN MINUTES,
THE VICE PRESIDENT
EARNS A PROMOTION.
AND THE DAY
GOES DOWN AS ONE
OF THE DARKEST IN
HISTORY. I DON'T
KNOW WHAT ELSE
TO TRY.
IF CAP
WERE HERE,
EVEN HE'D
GIVE UP.
POLICE
McELROY--!
NO! STOP
FEEDING ME
COTTON CANDY
ABOUT HIS
PROWESS,
OKAY?
HE WAS
JUST A
MAN...

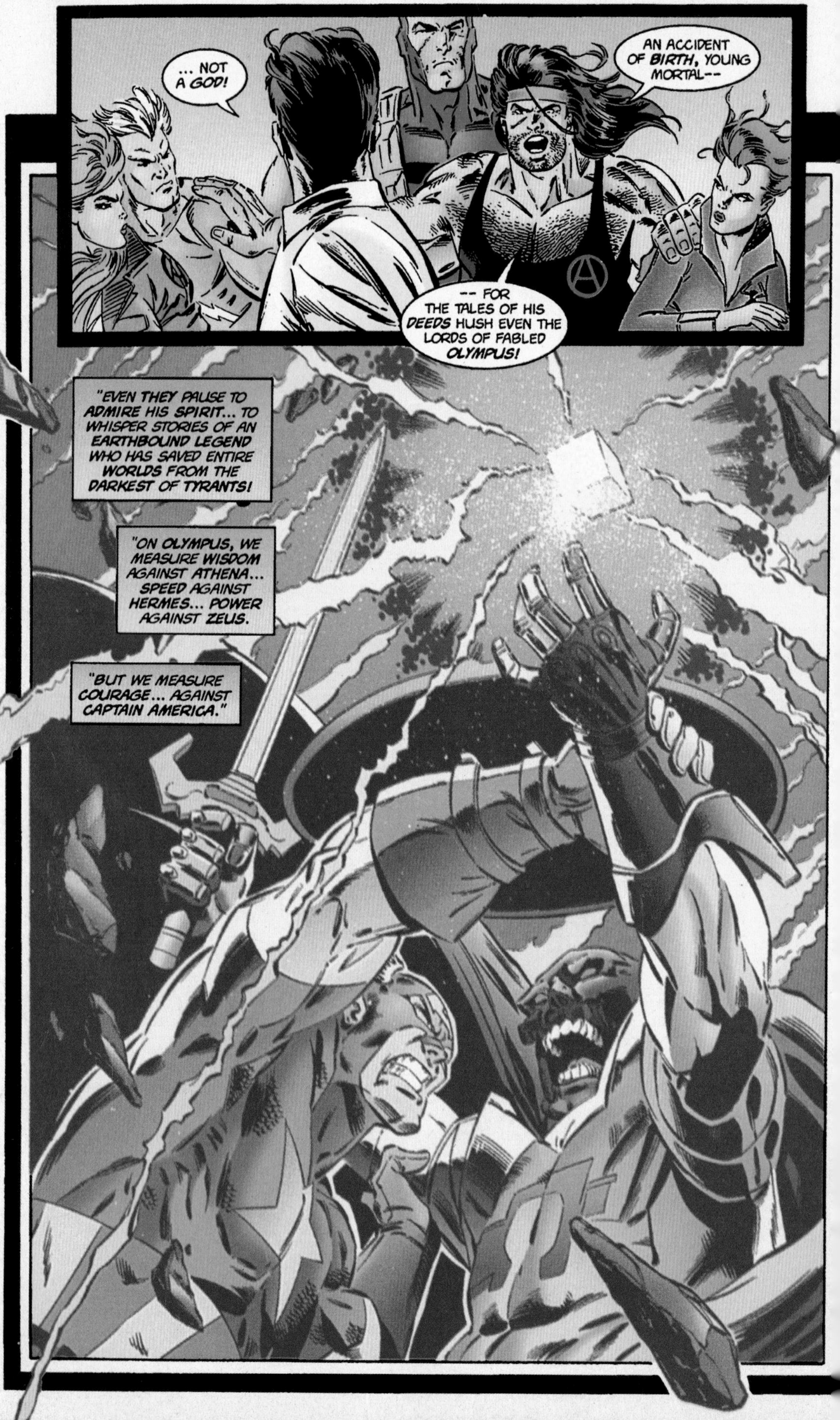

... NOT A GOD!
AN ACCIDENT OF BIRTH, YOUNG MORTAL--
-- FOR THE TALES OF HIS DEEDS HUSH EVEN THE LORDS OF FABLED OLYMPUS!
"EVEN THEY PAUSE TO ADMIRE HIS SPIRIT... TO WHISPER STORIES OF AN EARTHBOUND LEGEND WHO HAS SAVED ENTIRE WORLDS FROM THE DARKEST OF TYRANTS!
"ON OLYMPUS, WE MEASURE WISDOM AGAINST ATHENA... SPEED AGAINST HERMES... POWER AGAINST ZEUS.
"BUT WE MEASURE COURAGE... AGAINST CAPTAIN AMERICA."

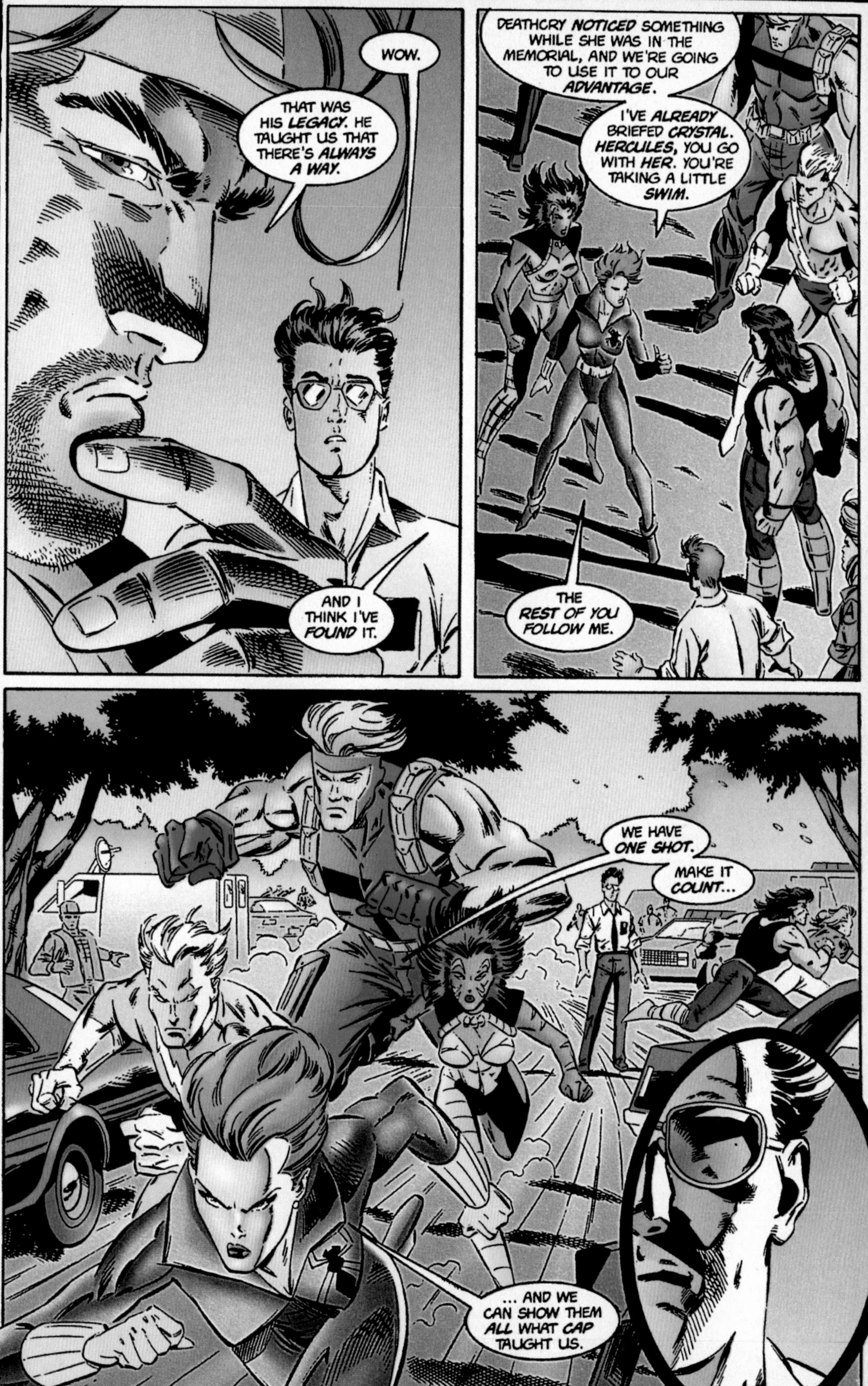
WOW.
THAT WAS HIS LEGACY. HE TAUGHT US THAT THERE'S ALWAYS A WAY.
AND I THINK I'VE FOUND IT.
DEATHCRY NOTICED SOMETHING WHILE SHE WAS IN THE MEMORIAL, AND WE'RE GOING TO USE IT TO OUR ADVANTAGE.
I'VE ALREADY BRIEFED CRYSTAL. HERCULES, YOU GO WITH HER. YOU'RE TAKING A LITTLE SWIM.
THE REST OF YOU FOLLOW ME.
WE HAVE ONE SHOT.
MAKE IT COUNT...
... AND WE CAN SHOW THEM ALL WHAT CAP TAUGHT US.

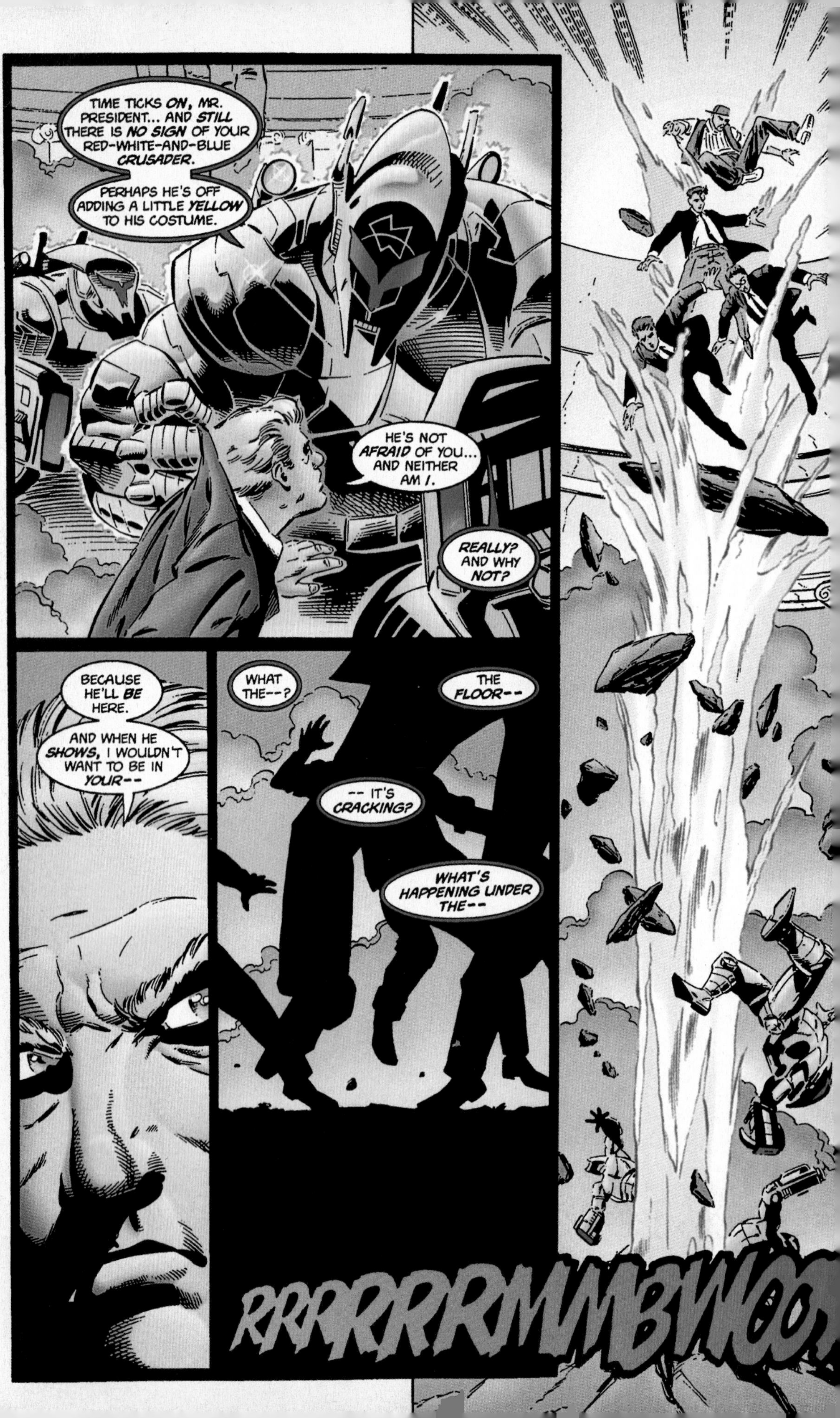
TIME TICKS ON, MR. PRESIDENT... AND STILL THERE IS NO SIGN OF YOUR RED-WHITE-AND-BLUE CRUSADER.
PERHAPS HE'S OFF ADDING A LITTLE YELLOW TO HIS COSTUME.
HE'S NOT AFRAID OF YOU... AND NEITHER AM I.
REALLY? AND WHY NOT?
BECAUSE HE'LL BE HERE.
AND WHEN HE SHOWS, I WOULDN'T WANT TO BE IN YOUR--
WHAT THE--?
THE FLOOR--
-- IT'S CRACKING?
WHAT'S HAPPENING UNDER THE--
RRRRRRRMMMBWOO

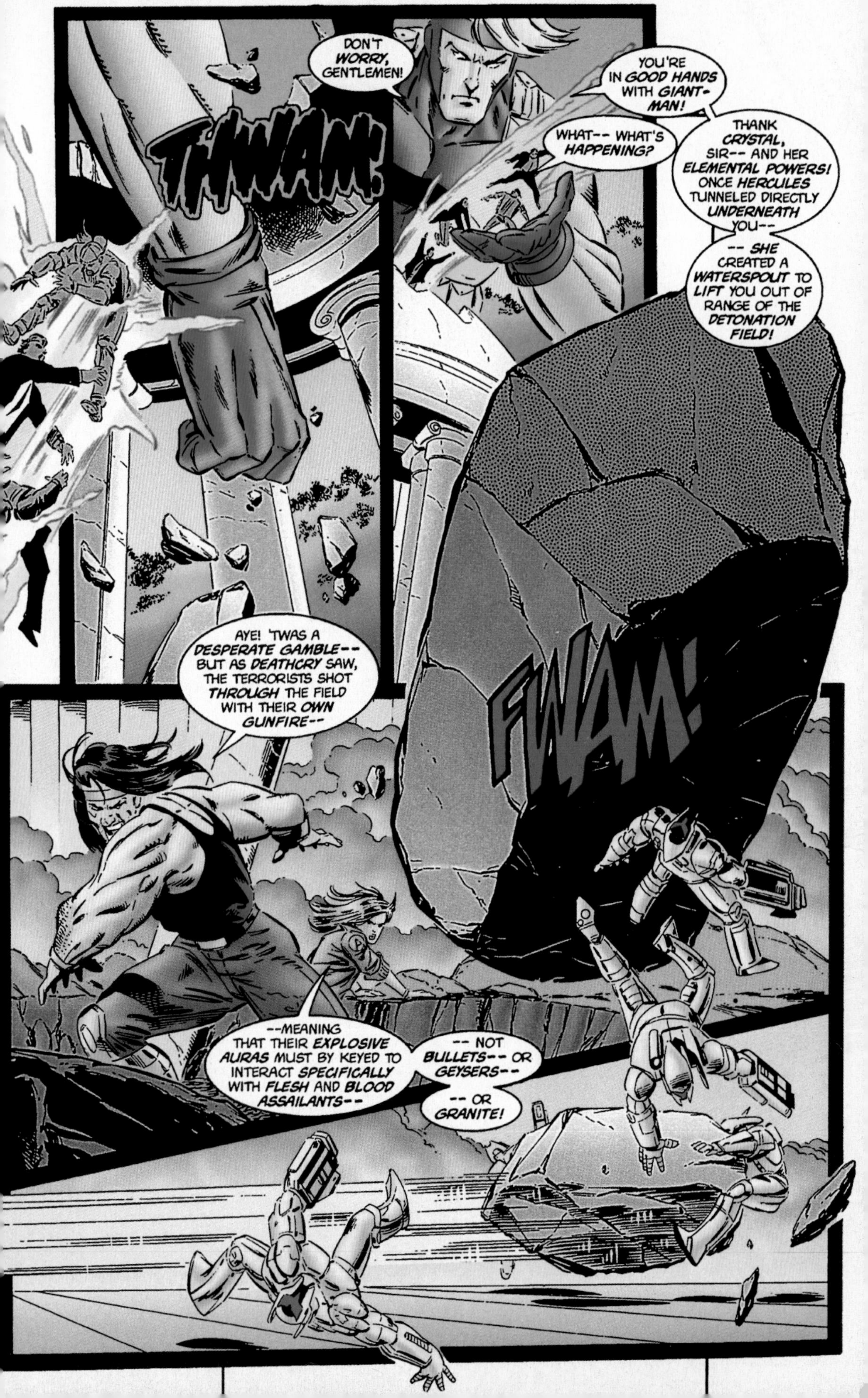
THWAM!
DON'T WORRY, GENTLEMEN!
YOU'RE IN GOOD HANDS WITH GIANT-MAN!
WHAT-- WHAT'S HAPPENING?
THANK CRYSTAL, SIR-- AND HER ELEMENTAL POWERS! ONCE HERCULES TUNNELED DIRECTLY UNDERNEATH YOU--
-- SHE CREATED A WATERSPOUT TO LIFT YOU OUT OF RANGE OF THE DETONATION FIELD!
AYE! 'TWAS A DESPERATE GAMBLE-- BUT AS DEATHCRY SAW, THE TERRORISTS SHOT THROUGH THE FIELD WITH THEIR OWN GUNFIRE--
FWAM!
--MEANING THAT THEIR EXPLOSIVE AURAS MUST BY KEYED TO INTERACT SPECIFICALLY WITH FLESH AND BLOOD ASSAILANTS--
-- NOT BULLETS-- OR GEYSERS--
-- OR GRANITE!

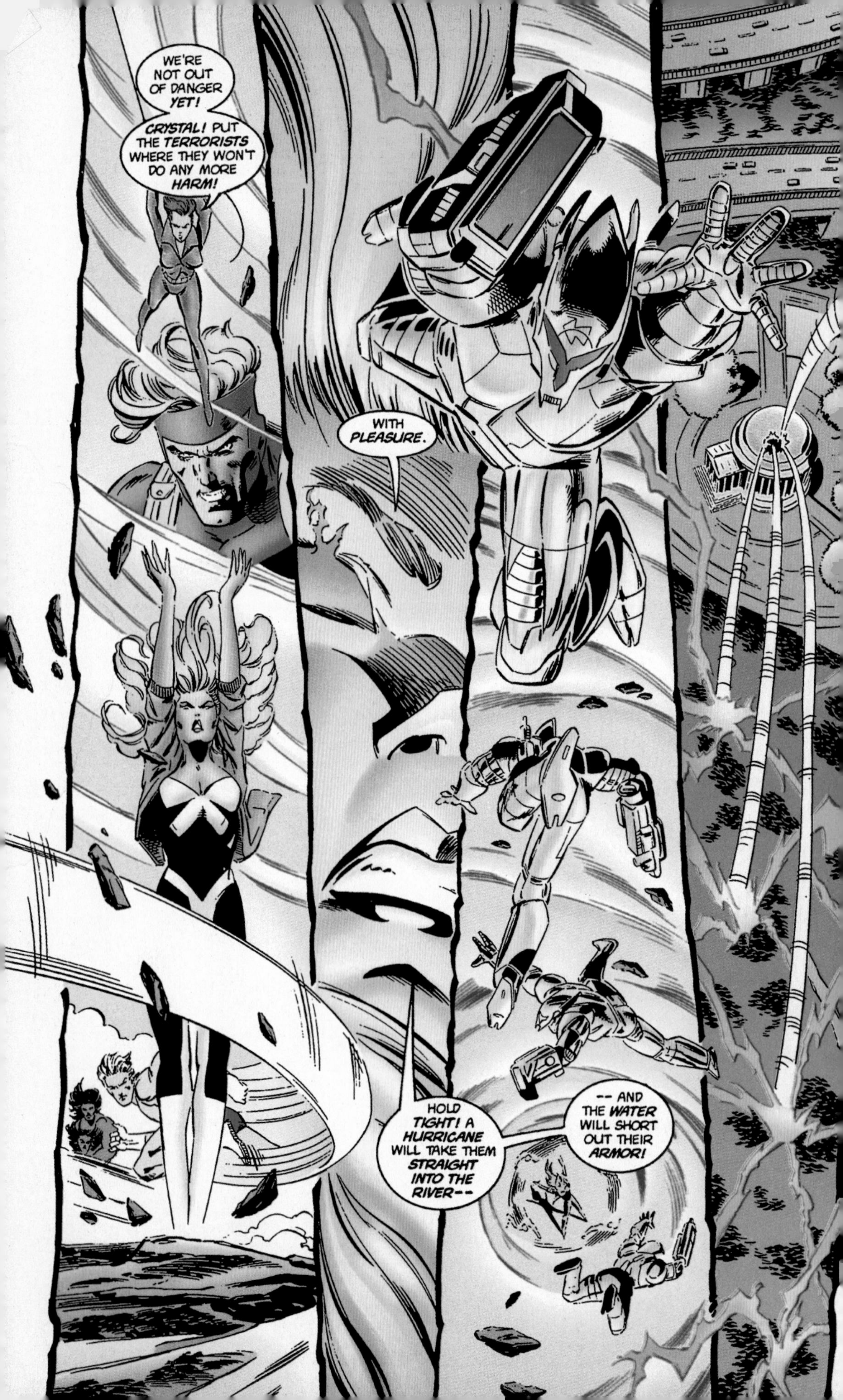
WE'RE NOT OUT OF DANGER YET!
CRYSTAL! PUT THE TERRORISTS WHERE THEY WON'T DO ANY MORE HARM!
WITH PLEASURE.
HOLD TIGHT! A HURRICANE WILL TAKE THEM STRAIGHT INTO THE RIVER--
-- AND THE WATER WILL SHORT OUT THEIR ARMOR!

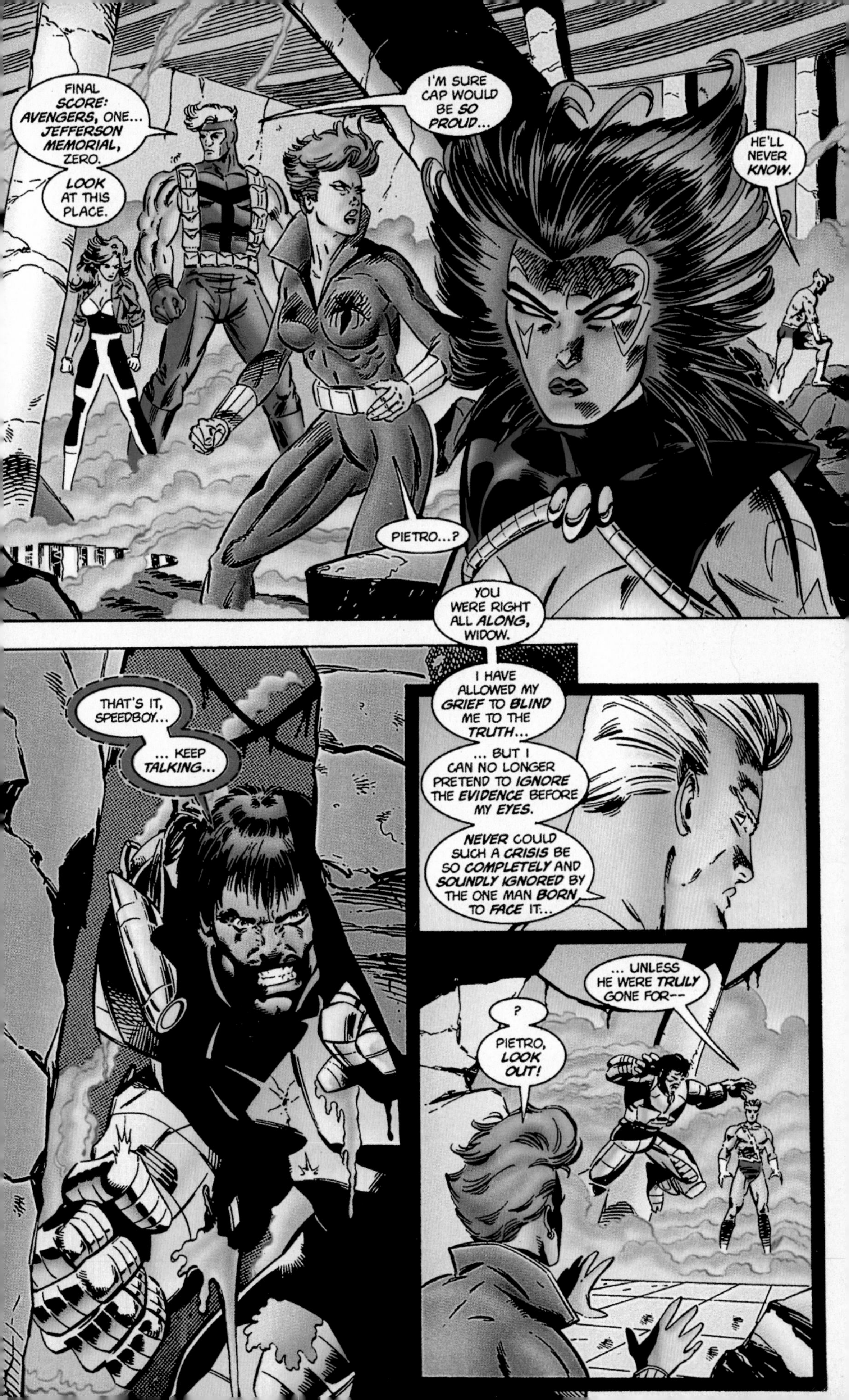

FINAL SCORE: AVENGERS, ONE... JEFFERSON MEMORIAL, ZERO.
LOOK AT THIS PLACE.
I'M SURE CAP WOULD BE SO PROUD...
HE'LL NEVER KNOW.
PIETRO...?
YOU WERE RIGHT ALL ALONG, WIDOW.
THAT'S IT, SPEEDBOY...
... KEEP TALKING...
I HAVE ALLOWED MY GRIEF TO BLIND ME TO THE TRUTH...
... BUT I CAN NO LONGER PRETEND TO IGNORE THE EVIDENCE BEFORE MY EYES.
NEVER COULD SUCH A CRISIS BE SO COMPLETELY AND SOUNDLY IGNORED BY THE ONE MAN BORN TO FACE IT...
... UNLESS HE WERE TRULY GONE FOR--
?
PIETRO, LOOK OUT!

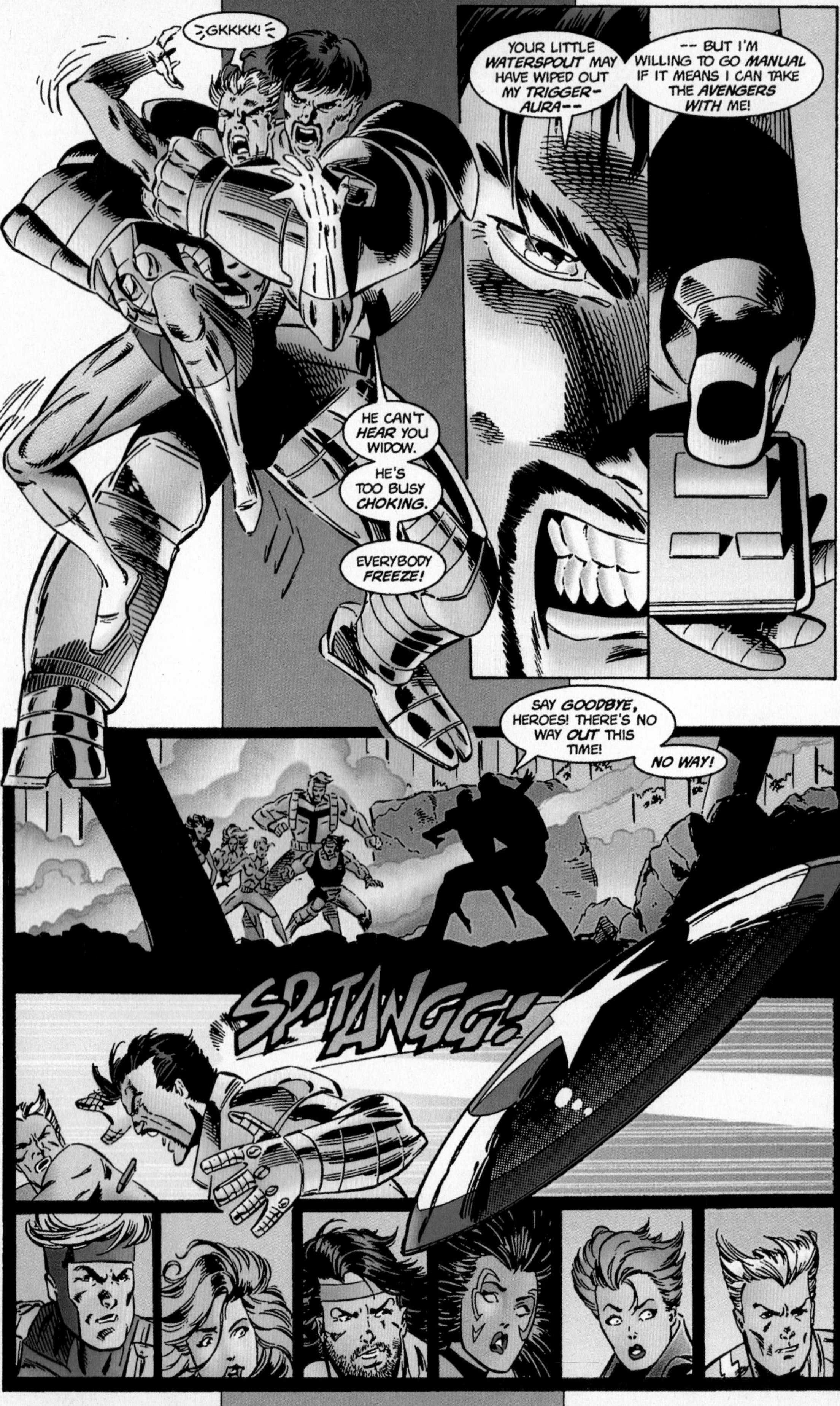
GKKKK!
YOUR LITTLE WATERSPOUT MAY HAVE WIPED OUT MY TRIGGER-AURA--
-- BUT I'M WILLING TO GO MANUAL IF IT MEANS I CAN TAKE THE AVENGERS WITH ME!
HE CAN'T HEAR YOU WIDOW.
HE'S TOO BUSY CHOKING.
EVERYBODY FREEZE!
SAY GOODBYE, HEROES! THERE'S NO WAY OUT THIS TIME!
NO WAY!
SP-TANGG!

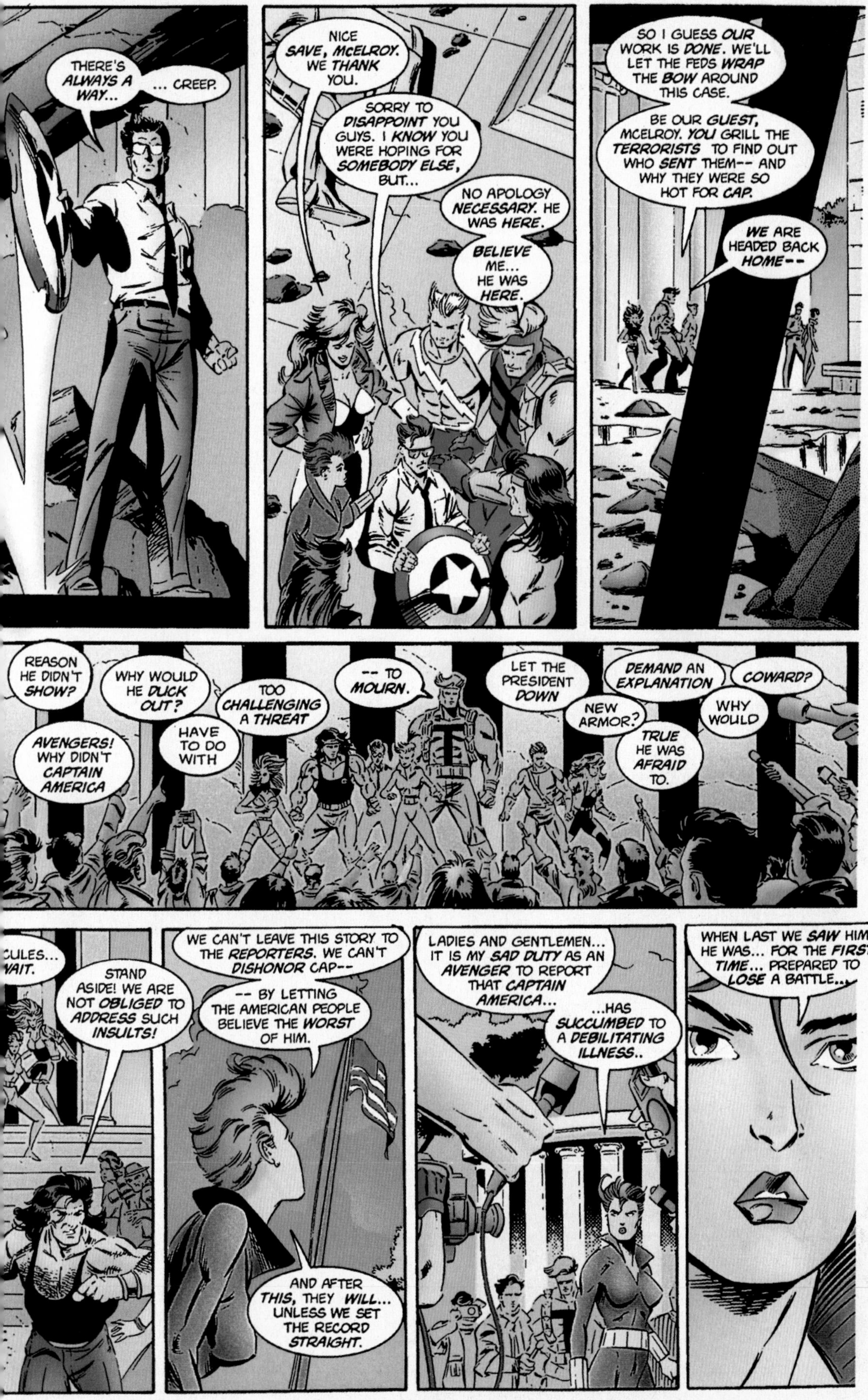

THERE'S ALWAYS A WAY...
... CREEP.
NICE SAVE, McELROY. WE THANK YOU.
SORRY TO DISAPPOINT YOU GUYS. I KNOW YOU WERE HOPING FOR SOMEBODY ELSE, BUT...
NO APOLOGY NECESSARY. HE WAS HERE.
BELIEVE ME... HE WAS HERE.
SO I GUESS OUR WORK IS DONE. WE'LL LET THE FEDS WRAP THE BOW AROUND THIS CASE.
BE OUR GUEST, McELROY. YOU GRILL THE TERRORISTS TO FIND OUT WHO SENT THEM-- AND WHY THEY WERE SO HOT FOR CAP.
WE ARE HEADED BACK HOME--
REASON HE DIDN'T SHOW?
AVENGERS! WHY DIDN'T CAPTAIN AMERICA
WHY WOULD HE DUCK OUT?
HAVE TO DO WITH
TOO CHALLENGING A THREAT
-- TO MOURN.
LET THE PRESIDENT DOWN
NEW ARMOR?
DEMAND AN EXPLANATION
TRUE HE WAS AFRAID TO.
WHY WOULD
COWARD?
CULES... WAIT.
STAND ASIDE! WE ARE NOT OBLIGED TO ADDRESS SUCH INSULTS!
WE CAN'T LEAVE THIS STORY TO THE REPORTERS. WE CAN'T DISHONOR CAP--
-- BY LETTING THE AMERICAN PEOPLE BELIEVE THE WORST OF HIM.
AND AFTER THIS, THEY WILL... UNLESS WE SET THE RECORD STRAIGHT.
LADIES AND GENTLEMEN... IT IS MY SAD DUTY AS AN AVENGER TO REPORT THAT CAPTAIN AMERICA...
...HAS SUCCUMBED TO A DEBILITATING ILLNESS..
WHEN LAST WE SAW HIM HE WAS... FOR THE FIRST TIME... PREPARED TO LOSE A BATTLE...

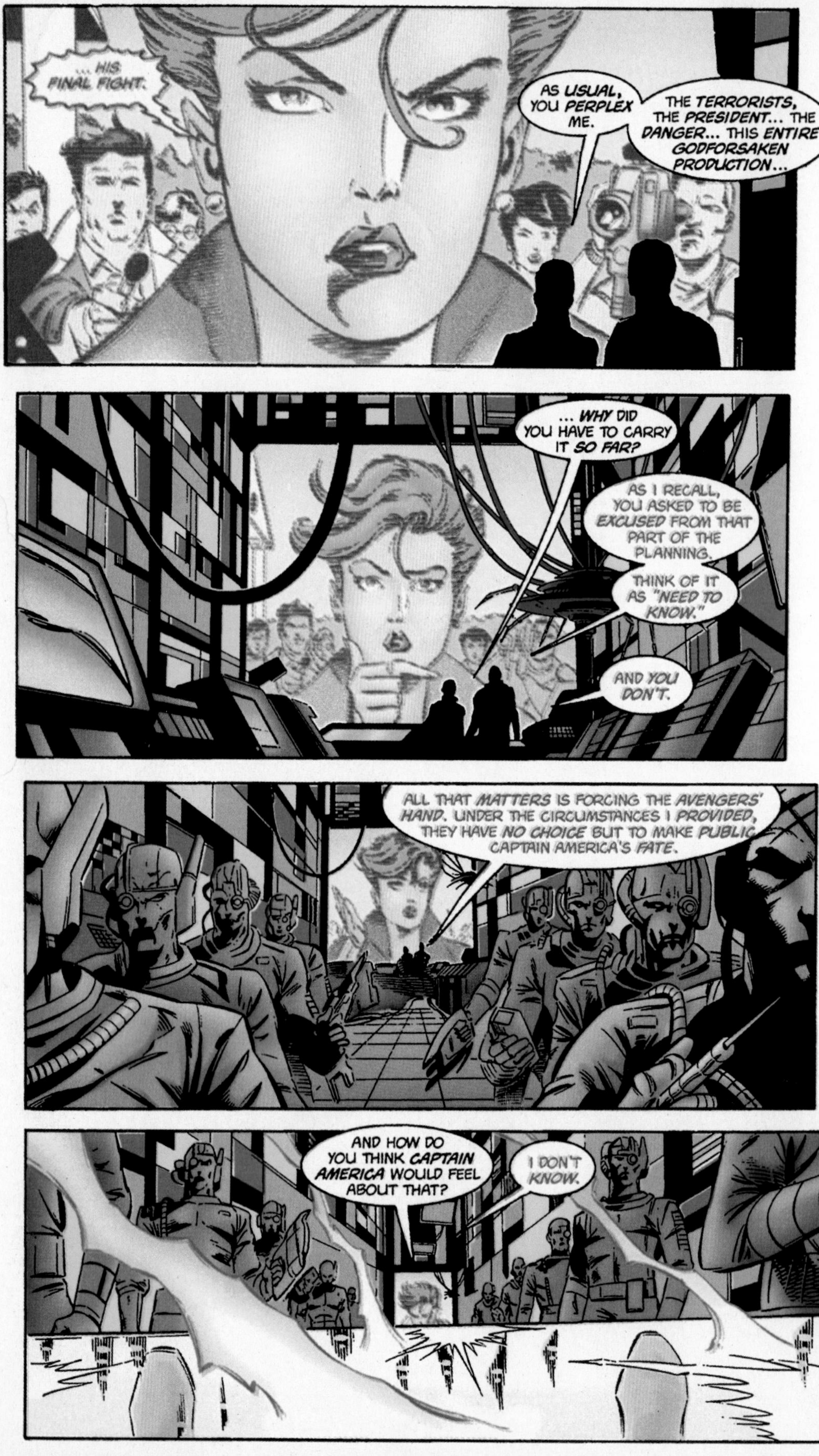
... HIS FINAL FIGHT.
AS USUAL, YOU PERPLEX ME.
THE TERRORISTS, THE PRESIDENT... THE DANGER... THIS ENTIRE GODFORSAKEN PRODUCTION...
... WHY DID YOU HAVE TO CARRY IT SO FAR?
AS I RECALL, YOU ASKED TO BE EXCUSED FROM THAT PART OF THE PLANNING.
THINK OF IT AS "NEED TO KNOW."
AND YOU DON'T.
ALL THAT MATTERS IS FORCING THE AVENGERS' HAND. UNDER THE CIRCUMSTANCES I PROVIDED, THEY HAVE NO CHOICE BUT TO MAKE PUBLIC CAPTAIN AMERICA'S FATE.
AND HOW DO YOU THINK CAPTAIN AMERICA WOULD FEEL ABOUT THAT?
I DON'T KNOW.

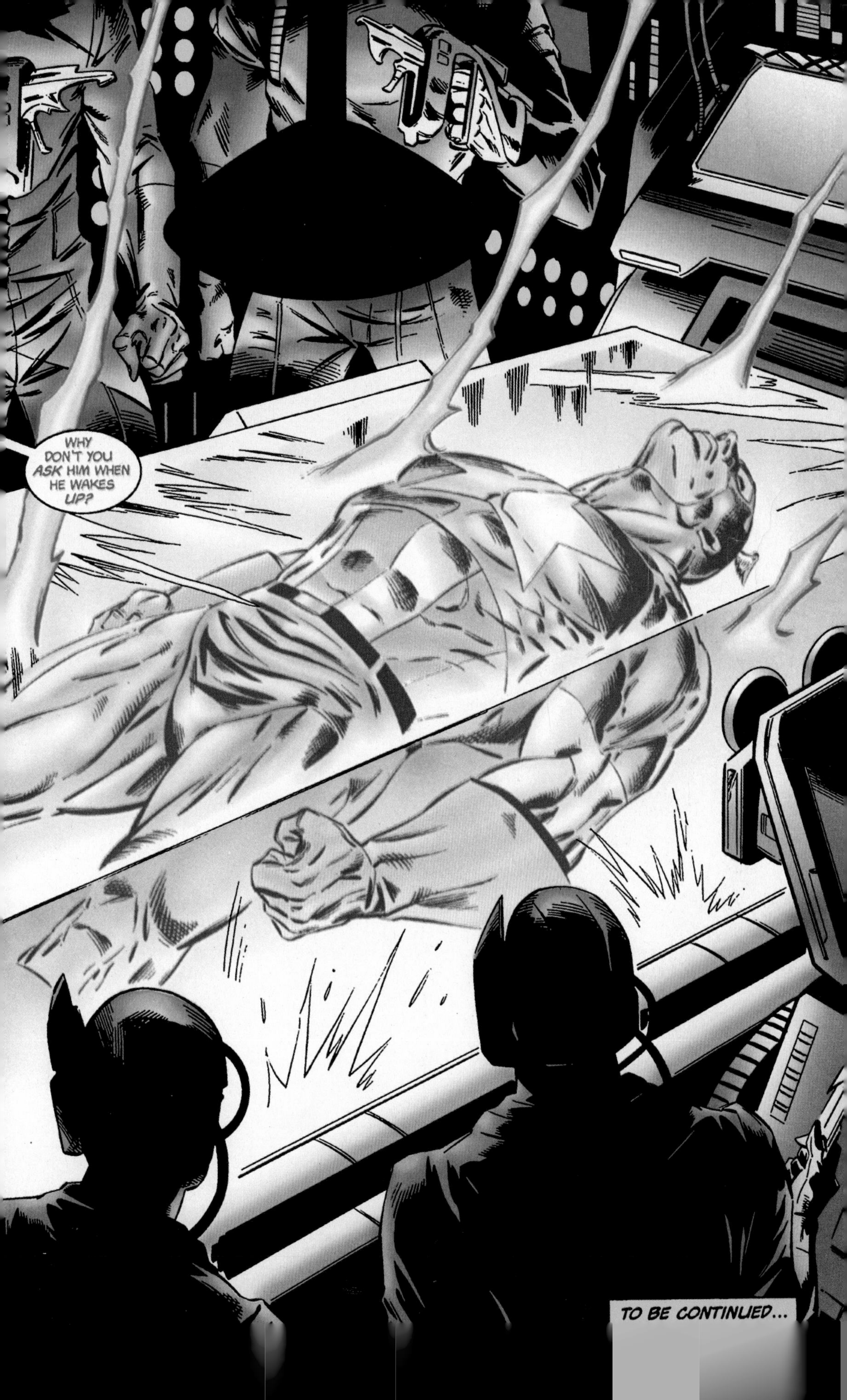
WHY DON'T YOU ASK HIM WHEN HE WAKES UP?
TO BE CONTINUED...

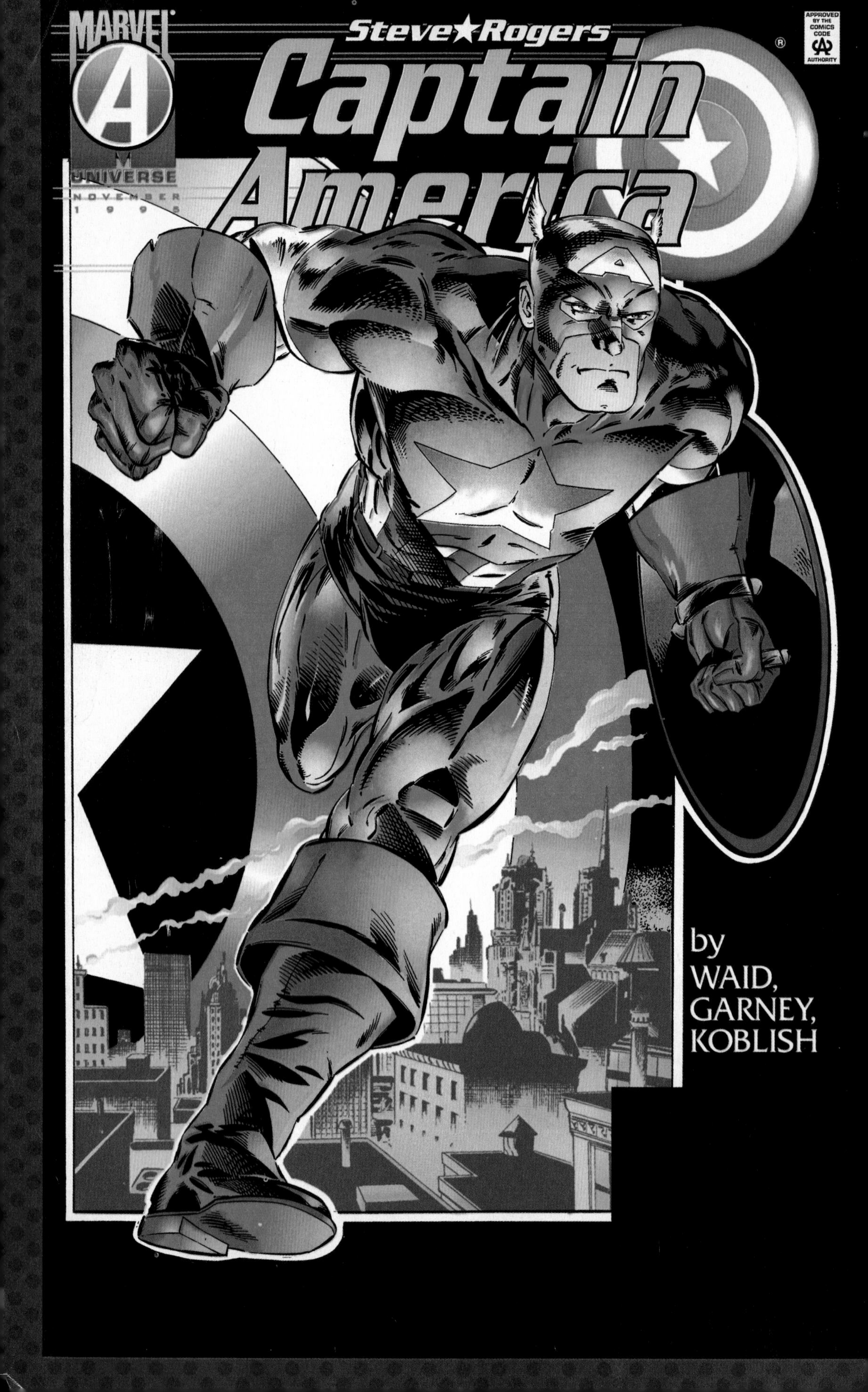
MARVEL
A
UNIVERSE
NOVEMBER 1995
Steve★Rogers
Captain America
APPROVED BY THE COMICS CODE AUTHORITY

by
WAID,
GARNEY,
KOBLISH

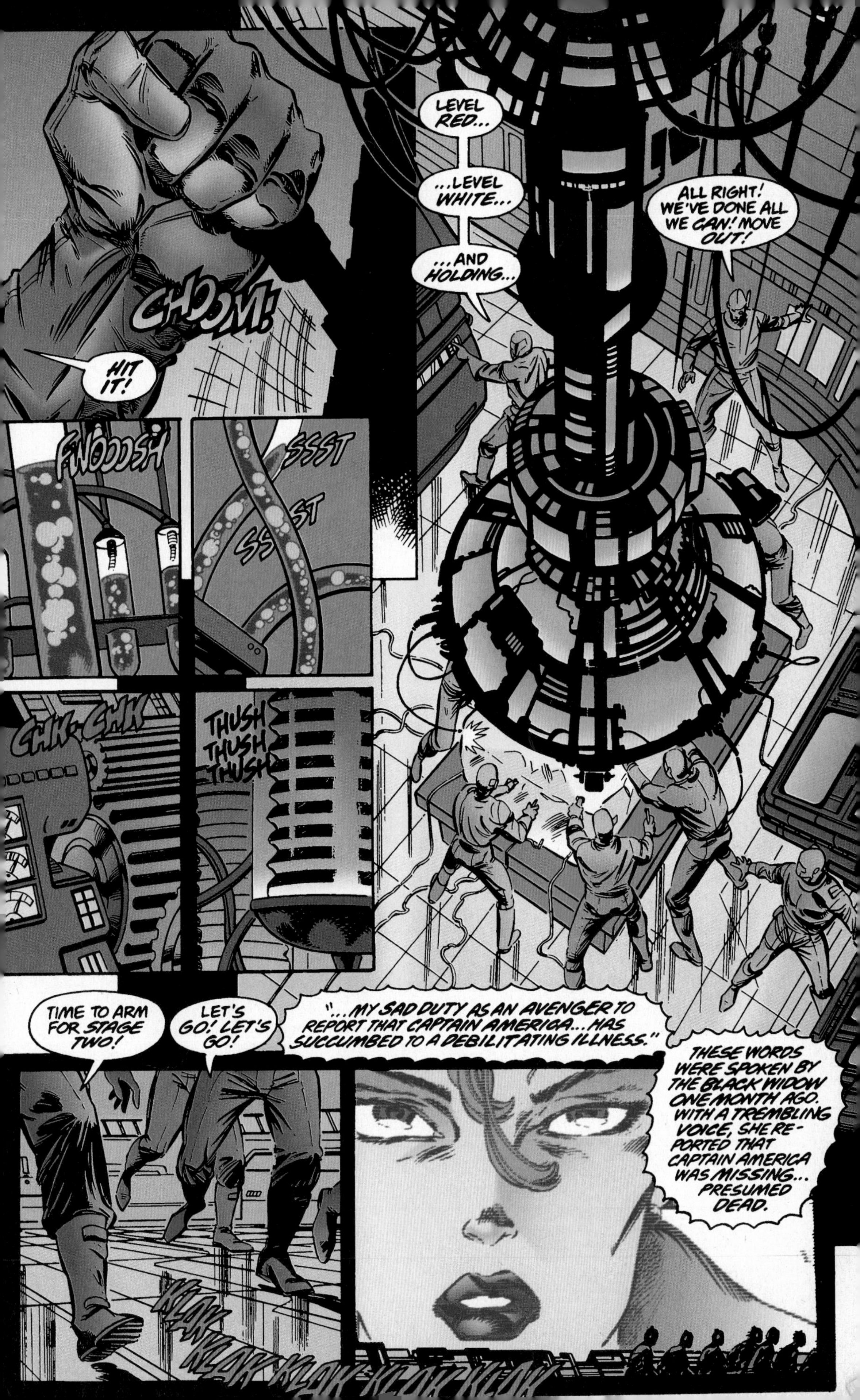
CHOOM!
HIT IT!
LEVEL RED...
...LEVEL WHITE...
...AND HOLDING...
ALL RIGHT! WE'VE DONE ALL WE CAN! MOVE OUT!
FWOOOOSH
SSSST
SSSST
CHK-CHK
THUSH THUSH THUSH
TIME TO ARM FOR STAGE TWO!
LET'S GO! LET'S GO!
"...MY SAD DUTY AS AN AVENGER TO REPORT THAT CAPTAIN AMERICA... HAS SUCCUMBED TO A DEBILITATING ILLNESS."
THESE WORDS WERE SPOKEN BY THE BLACK WIDOW ONE MONTH AGO. WITH A TREMBLING VOICE, SHE REPORTED THAT CAPTAIN AMERICA WAS MISSING... PRESUMED DEAD.
KLAK KLAK KLAK KLAK KLAK

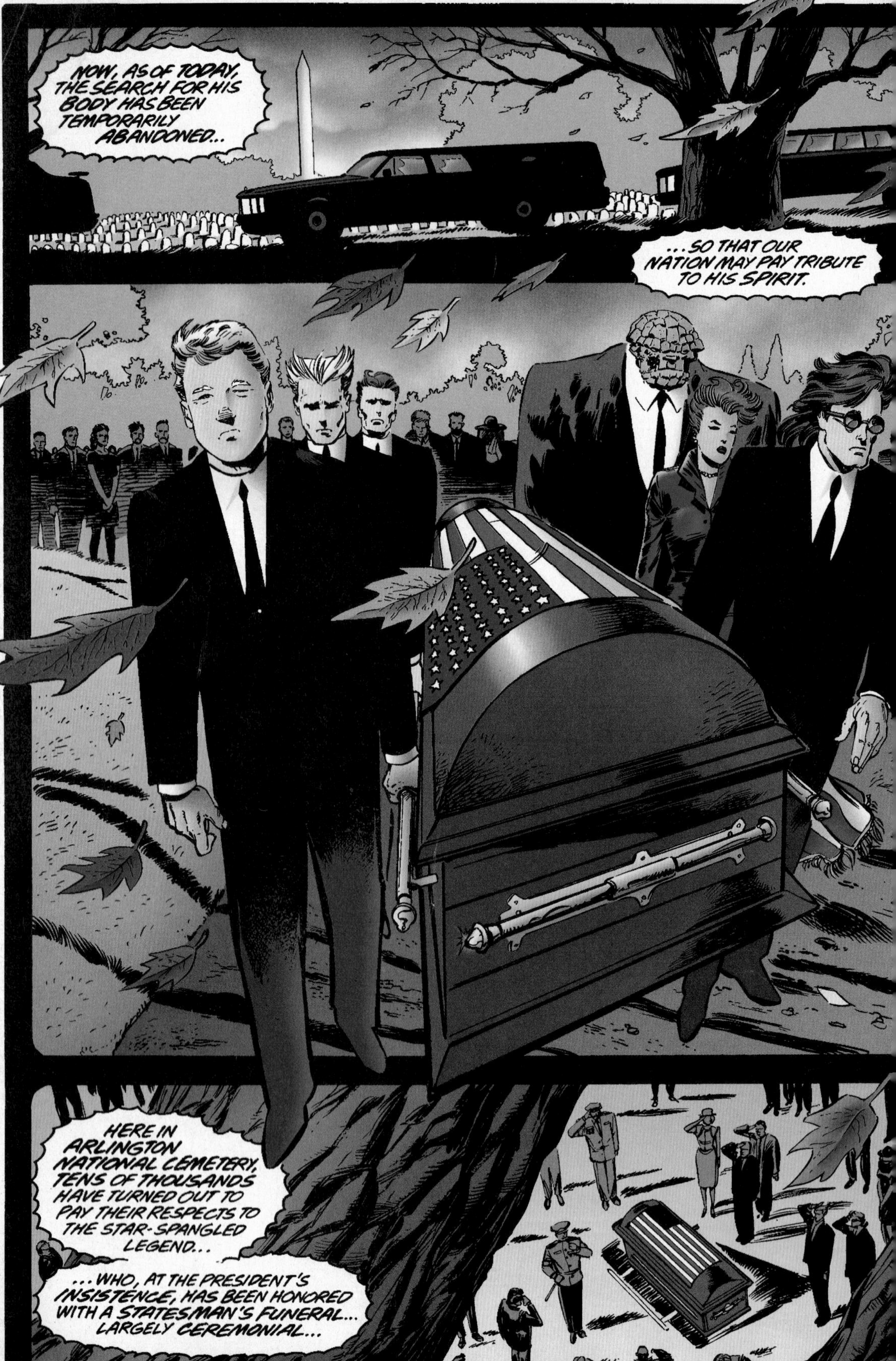
NOW, AS OF TODAY, THE SEARCH FOR HIS BODY HAS BEEN TEMPORARILY ABANDONED...
...SO THAT OUR NATION MAY PAY TRIBUTE TO HIS SPIRIT.
HERE IN ARLINGTON NATIONAL CEMETERY, TENS OF THOUSANDS HAVE TURNED OUT TO PAY THEIR RESPECTS TO THE STAR-SPANGLED LEGEND...
...WHO, AT THE PRESIDENT'S INSISTENCE, HAS BEEN HONORED WITH A STATESMAN'S FUNERAL... LARGELY CEREMONIAL...

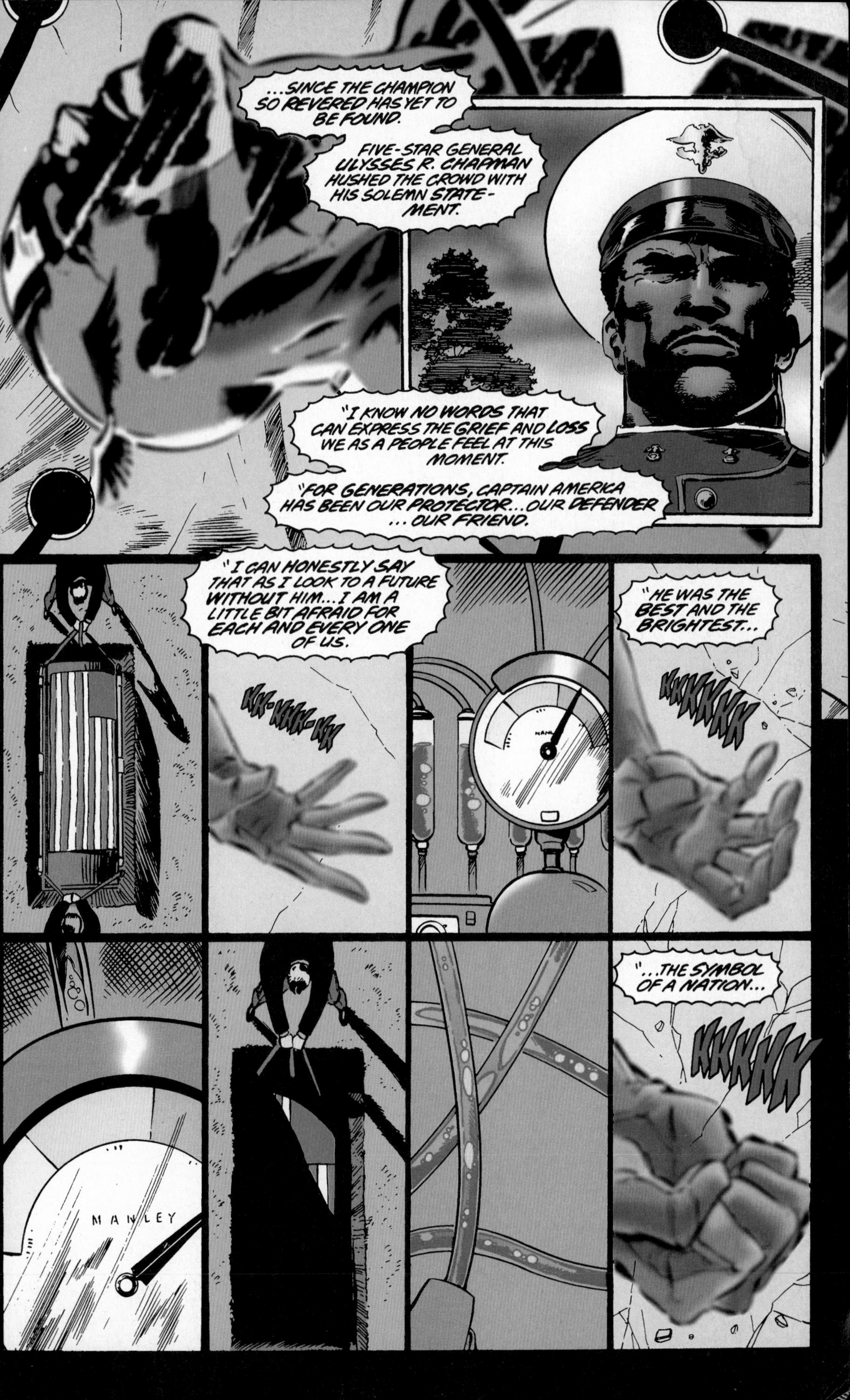

...SINCE THE CHAMPION SO REVERED HAS YET TO BE FOUND.
FIVE-STAR GENERAL ULYSSES R. CHAPMAN HUSHED THE CROWD WITH HIS SOLEMN STATEMENT.
"I KNOW NO WORDS THAT CAN EXPRESS THE GRIEF AND LOSS WE AS A PEOPLE FEEL AT THIS MOMENT.
"FOR GENERATIONS, CAPTAIN AMERICA HAS BEEN OUR PROTECTOR... OUR DEFENDER ... OUR FRIEND.
"I CAN HONESTLY SAY THAT AS I LOOK TO A FUTURE WITHOUT HIM... I AM A LITTLE BIT AFRAID FOR EACH AND EVERY ONE OF US.
KK-KKK-KK
"HE WAS THE BEST AND THE BRIGHTEST...
KKKKKK
"...THE SYMBOL OF A NATION...
KKKKK
MANLEY

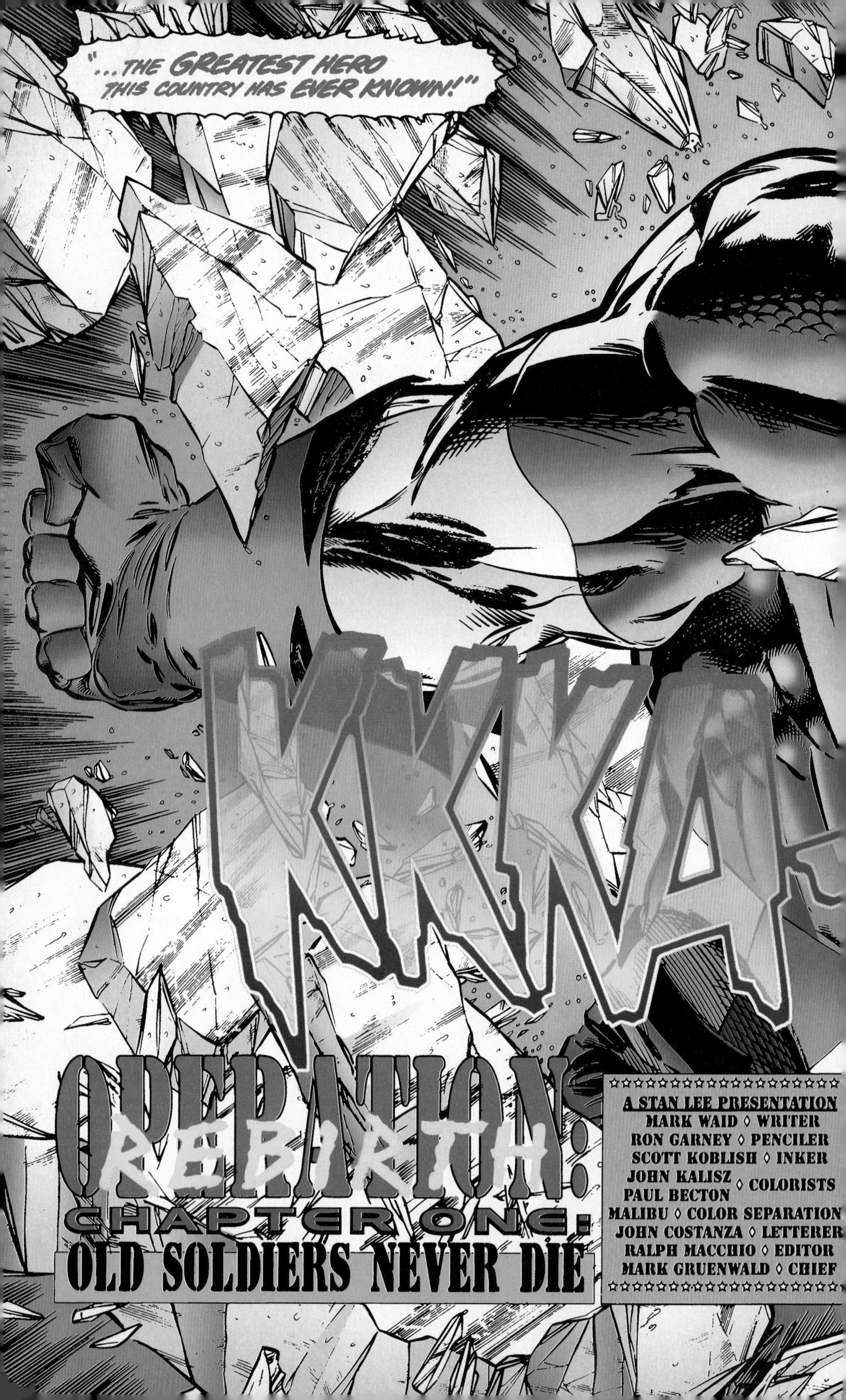
"...THE GREATEST HERO THIS COUNTRY HAS EVER KNOWN!"
KKWA
OPERATION: REBIRTH
CHAPTER ONE:
OLD SOLDIERS NEVER DIE
A STAN LEE PRESENTATION
MARK WAID ◊ WRITER
RON GARNEY ◊ PENCILER
SCOTT KOBLISH ◊ INKER
JOHN KALISZ
PAUL BECTON ◊ COLORISTS
MALIBU ◊ COLOR SEPARATION
JOHN COSTANZA ◊ LETTERER
RALPH MACCHIO ◊ EDITOR
MARK GRUENWALD ◊ CHIEF

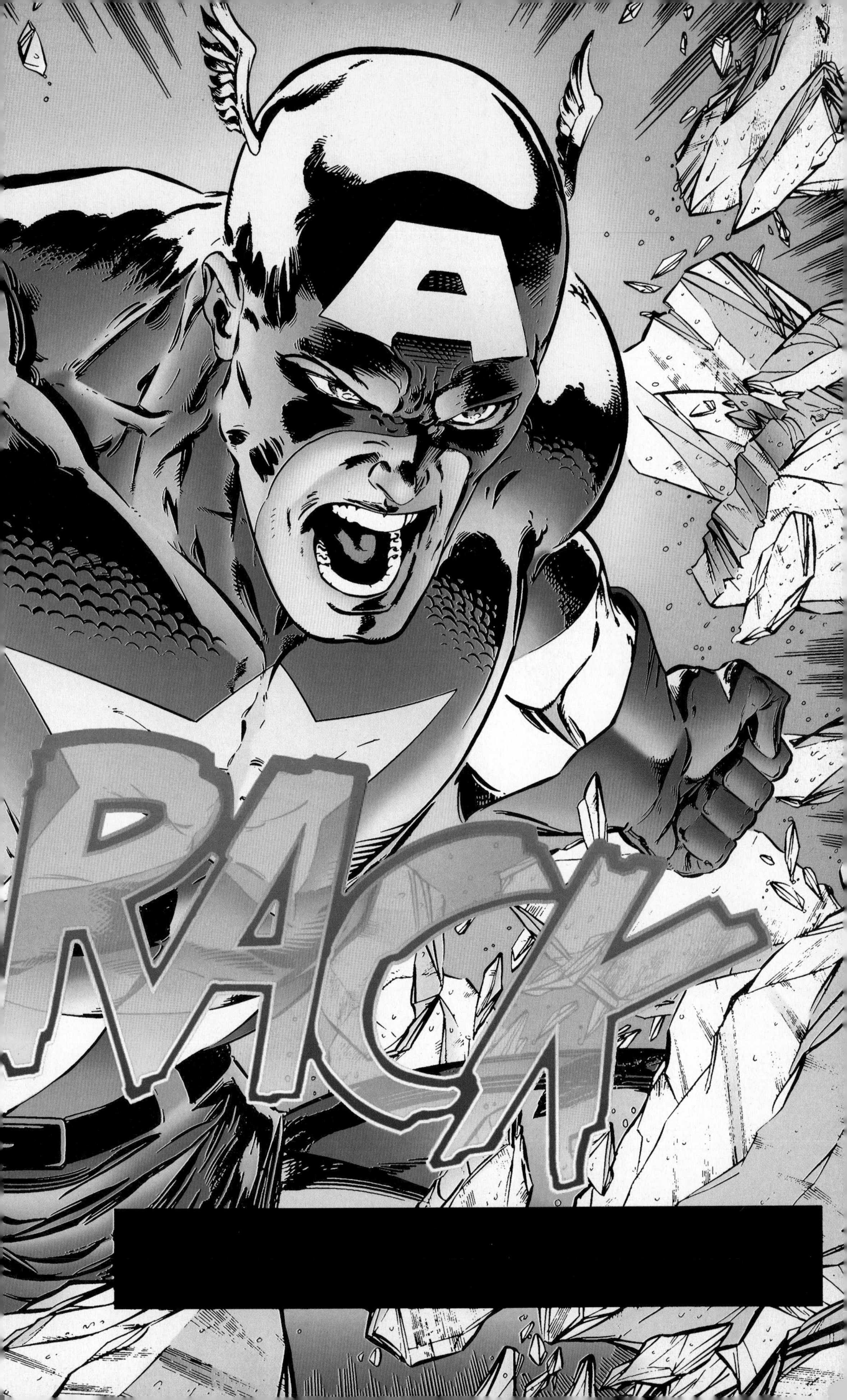
RACK
[redacted]

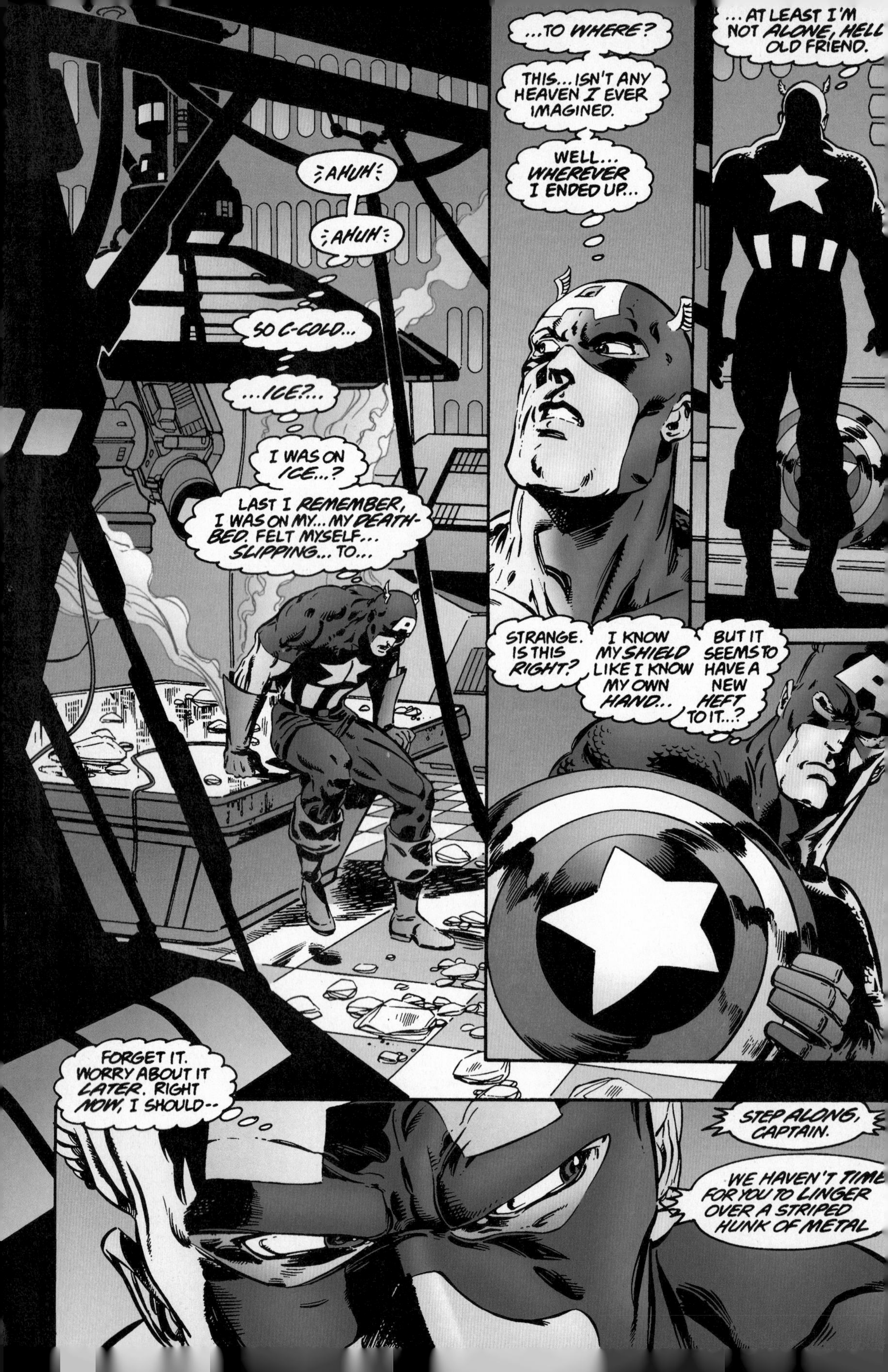
AHUH
AHUH
SO C-COLD...
...ICE?...
I WAS ON ICE...?
LAST I REMEMBER, I WAS ON MY... MY DEATH-BED. FELT MYSELF... SLIPPING... TO...
...TO WHERE?
THIS... ISN'T ANY HEAVEN I EVER IMAGINED.
WELL... WHEREVER I ENDED UP...
... AT LEAST I'M NOT ALONE, HELL OLD FRIEND.
STRANGE. IS THIS RIGHT?
I KNOW MY SHIELD LIKE I KNOW MY OWN HAND...
BUT IT SEEMS TO HAVE A NEW HEFT TO IT...?
FORGET IT. WORRY ABOUT IT LATER. RIGHT NOW, I SHOULD--
STEP ALONG, CAPTAIN.
WE HAVEN'T TIME FOR YOU TO LINGER OVER A STRIPED HUNK OF METAL

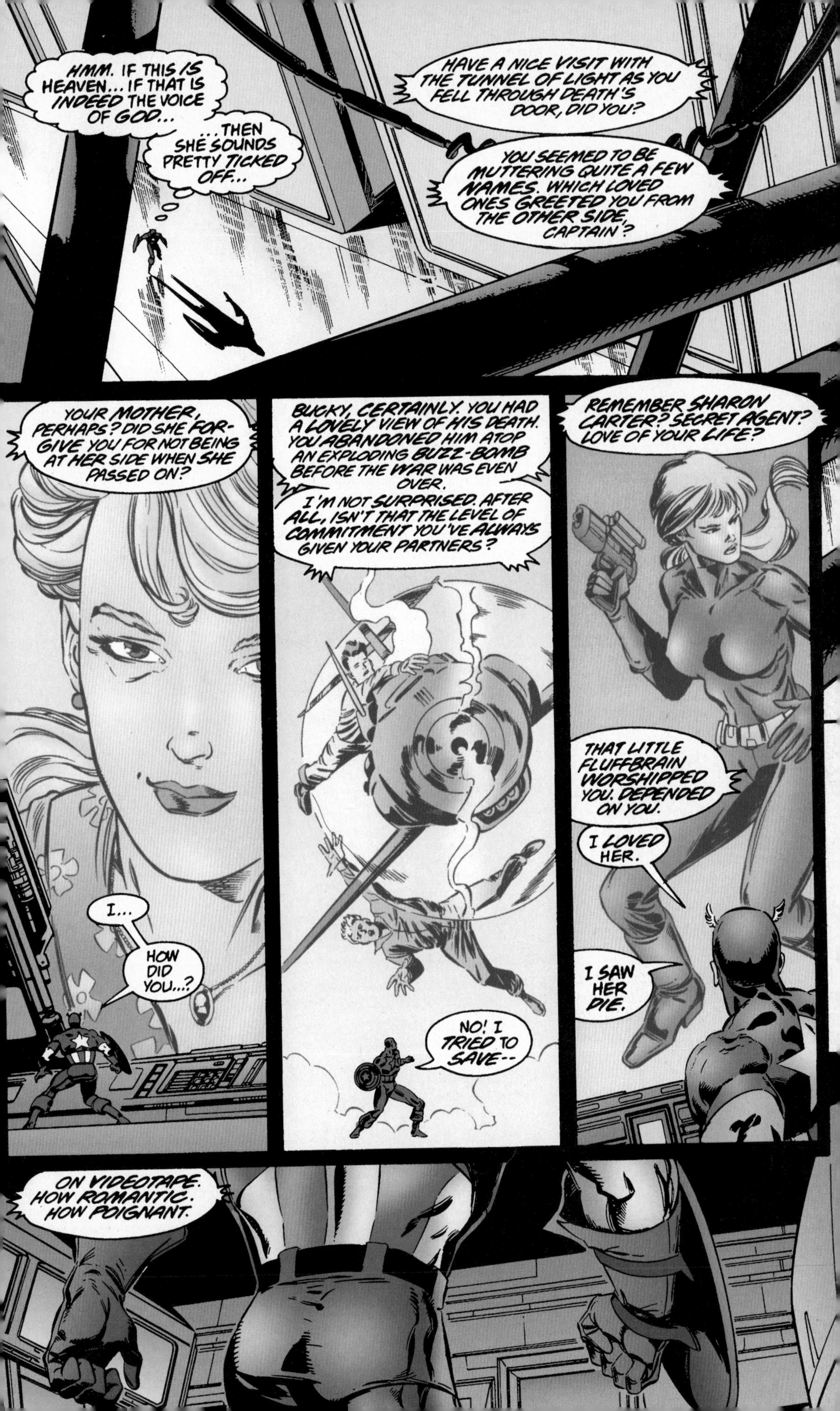
HMM. IF THIS IS HEAVEN... IF THAT IS INDEED THE VOICE OF GOD...
...THEN SHE SOUNDS PRETTY TICKED OFF...
HAVE A NICE VISIT WITH THE TUNNEL OF LIGHT AS YOU FELL THROUGH DEATH'S DOOR, DID YOU?
YOU SEEMED TO BE MUTTERING QUITE A FEW NAMES. WHICH LOVED ONES GREETED YOU FROM THE OTHER SIDE, CAPTAIN?
YOUR MOTHER, PERHAPS? DID SHE FORGIVE YOU FOR NOT BEING AT HER SIDE WHEN SHE PASSED ON?
I...
HOW DID YOU...?
BUCKY, CERTAINLY. YOU HAD A LOVELY VIEW OF HIS DEATH. YOU ABANDONED HIM ATOP AN EXPLODING BUZZ-BOMB BEFORE THE WAR WAS EVEN OVER.
I'M NOT SURPRISED. AFTER ALL, ISN'T THAT THE LEVEL OF COMMITMENT YOU'VE ALWAYS GIVEN YOUR PARTNERS?
NO! I TRIED TO SAVE--
REMEMBER SHARON CARTER? SECRET AGENT? LOVE OF YOUR LIFE?
THAT LITTLE FLUFFBRAIN WORSHIPPED YOU. DEPENDED ON YOU.
I LOVED HER.
I SAW HER DIE.
ON VIDEOTAPE. HOW ROMANTIC. HOW POIGNANT.

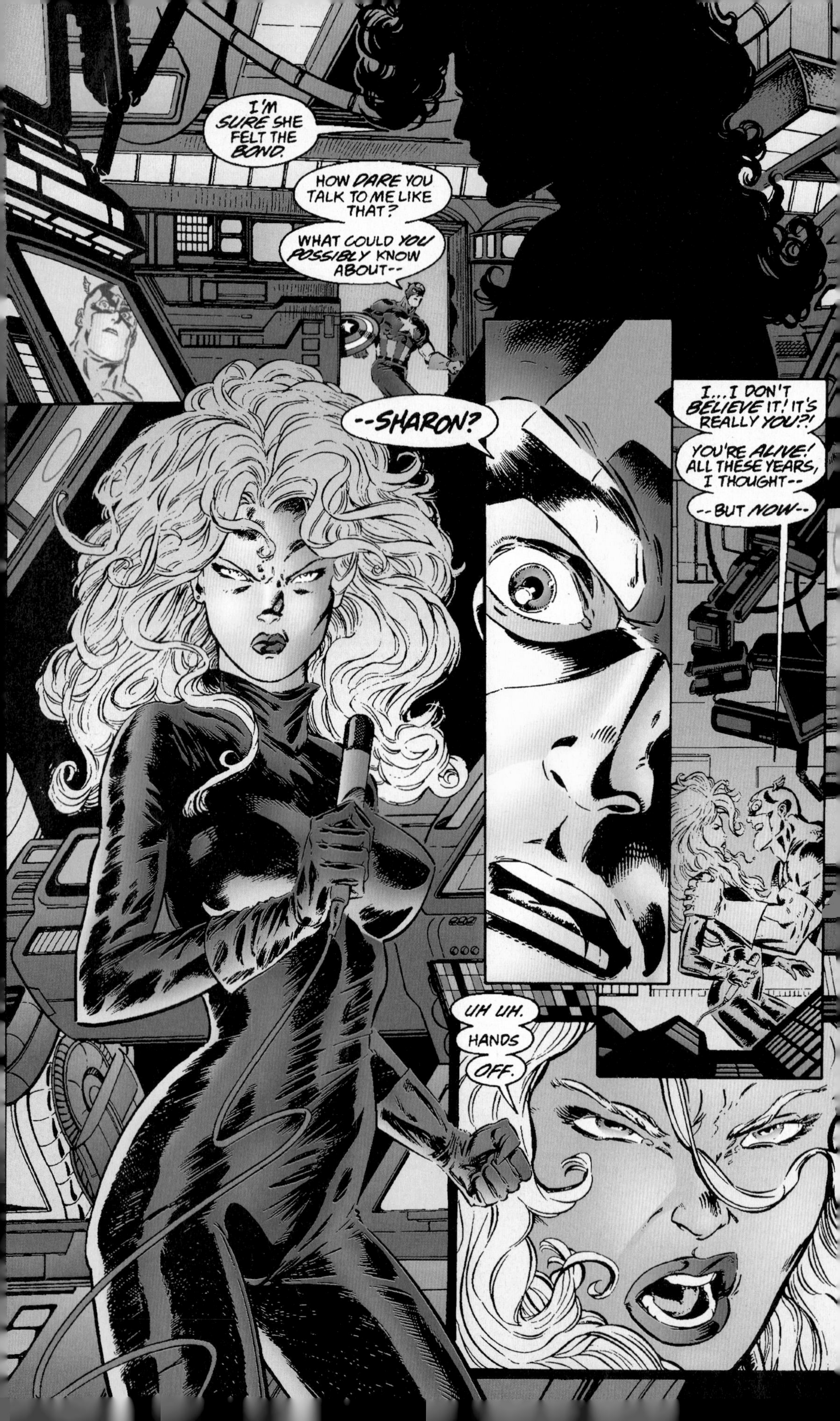
I'M SURE SHE FELT THE BOND.
HOW DARE YOU TALK TO ME LIKE THAT?
WHAT COULD YOU POSSIBLY KNOW ABOUT--
--SHARON?
I... I DON'T BELIEVE IT! IT'S REALLY YOU?!
YOU'RE ALIVE! ALL THESE YEARS, I THOUGHT--
--BUT NOW--
UH UH.
HANDS
OFF.

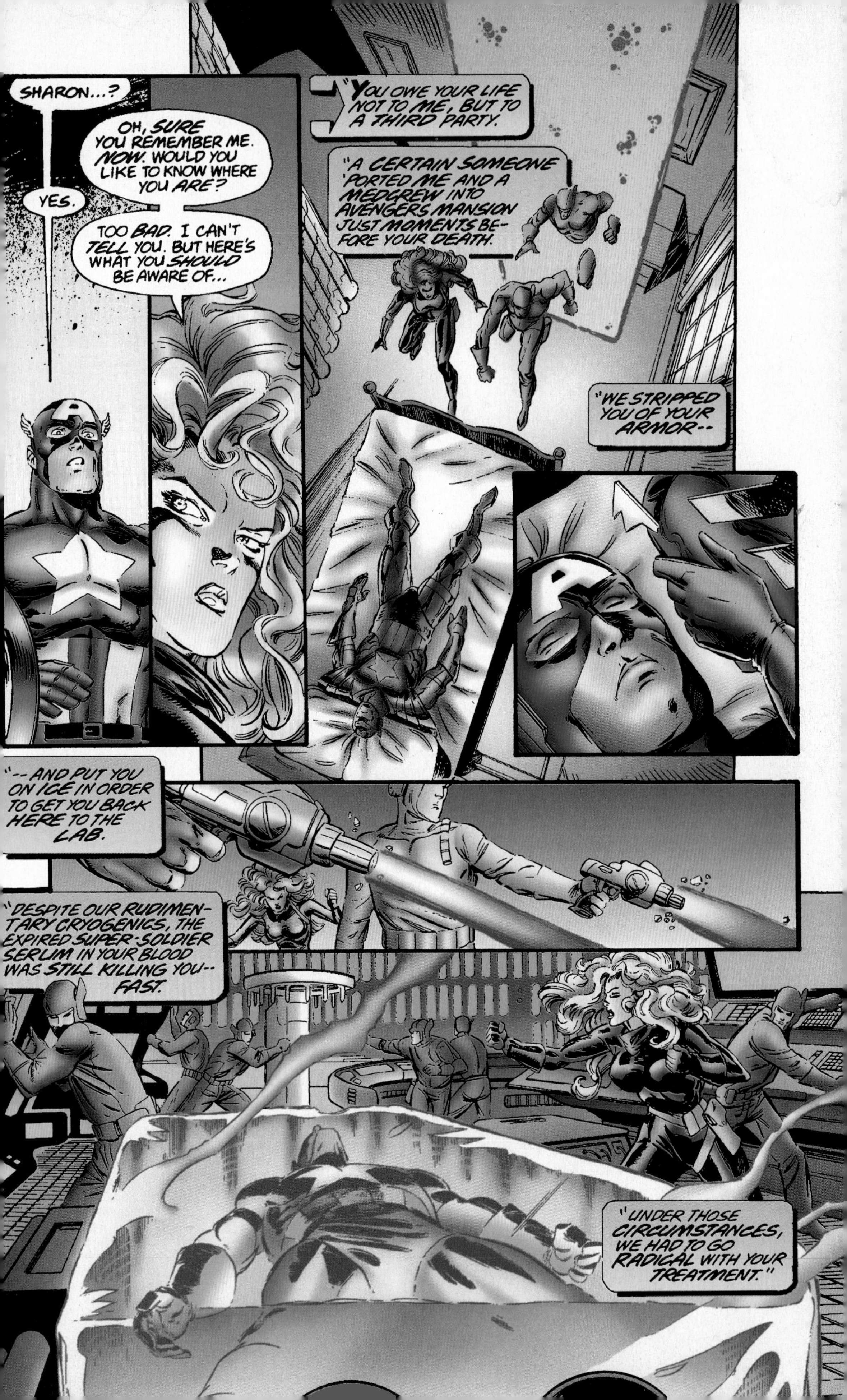
SHARON...?
OH, SURE YOU REMEMBER ME. NOW. WOULD YOU LIKE TO KNOW WHERE YOU ARE?
YES.
TOO BAD. I CAN'T TELL YOU. BUT HERE'S WHAT YOU SHOULD BE AWARE OF...
"YOU OWE YOUR LIFE NOT TO ME, BUT TO A THIRD PARTY.
"A CERTAIN SOMEONE 'PORTED ME AND A MEDCREW INTO AVENGERS MANSION JUST MOMENTS BEFORE YOUR DEATH.
"WE STRIPPED YOU OF YOUR ARMOR--
"--AND PUT YOU ON ICE IN ORDER TO GET YOU BACK HERE TO THE LAB.
"DESPITE OUR RUDIMENTARY CRYOGENICS, THE EXPIRED SUPER-SOLDIER SERUM IN YOUR BLOOD WAS STILL KILLING YOU--FAST.
"UNDER THOSE CIRCUMSTANCES, WE HAD TO GO RADICAL WITH YOUR TREATMENT."

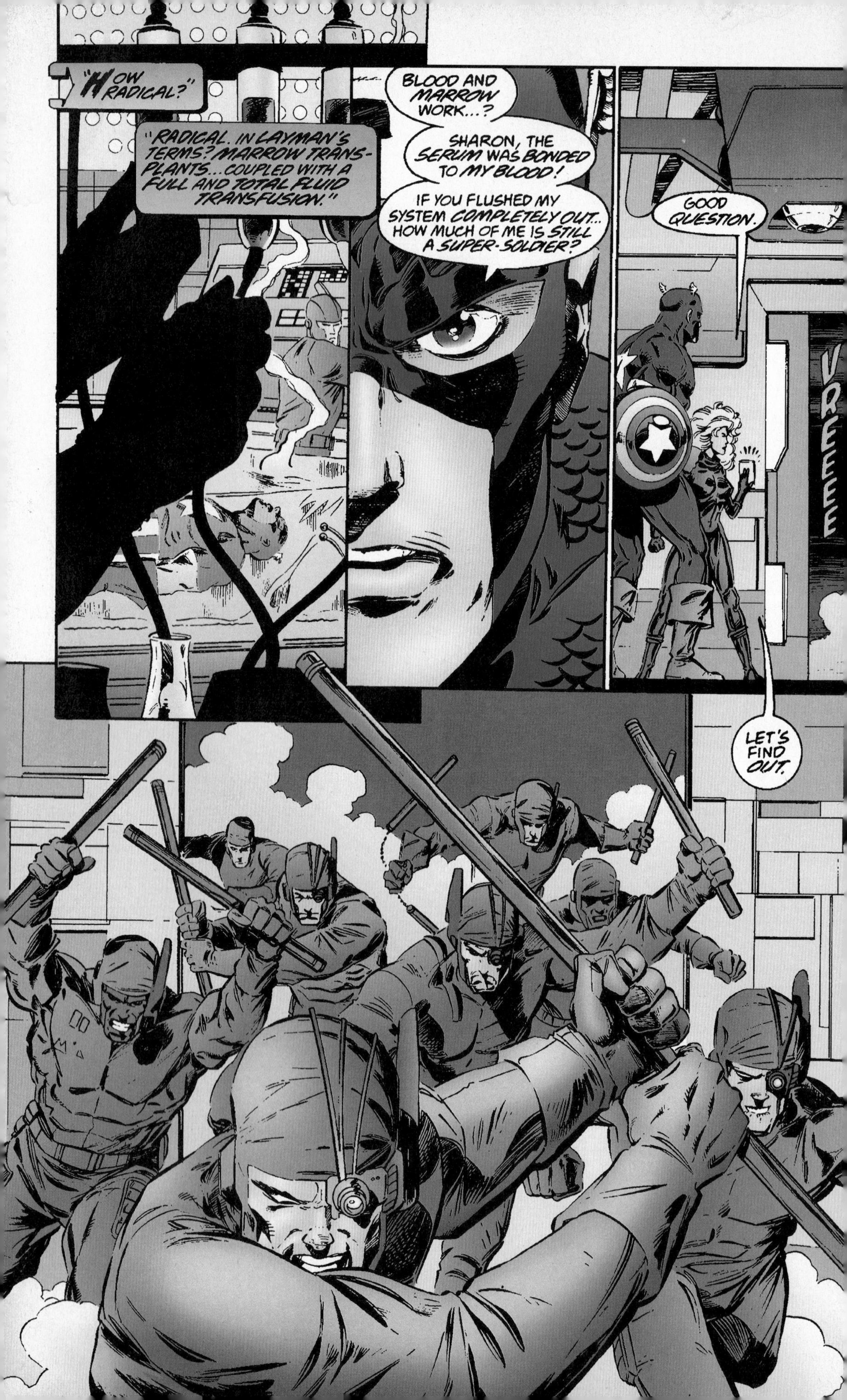
"HOW RADICAL?"
"RADICAL. IN LAYMAN'S TERMS? MARROW TRANS-PLANTS...COUPLED WITH A FULL AND TOTAL FLUID TRANSFUSION."
BLOOD AND MARROW WORK...?
SHARON, THE SERUM WAS BONDED TO MY BLOOD!
IF YOU FLUSHED MY SYSTEM COMPLETELY OUT... HOW MUCH OF ME IS STILL A SUPER-SOLDIER?
GOOD QUESTION.
VREEEE
LET'S FIND OUT.

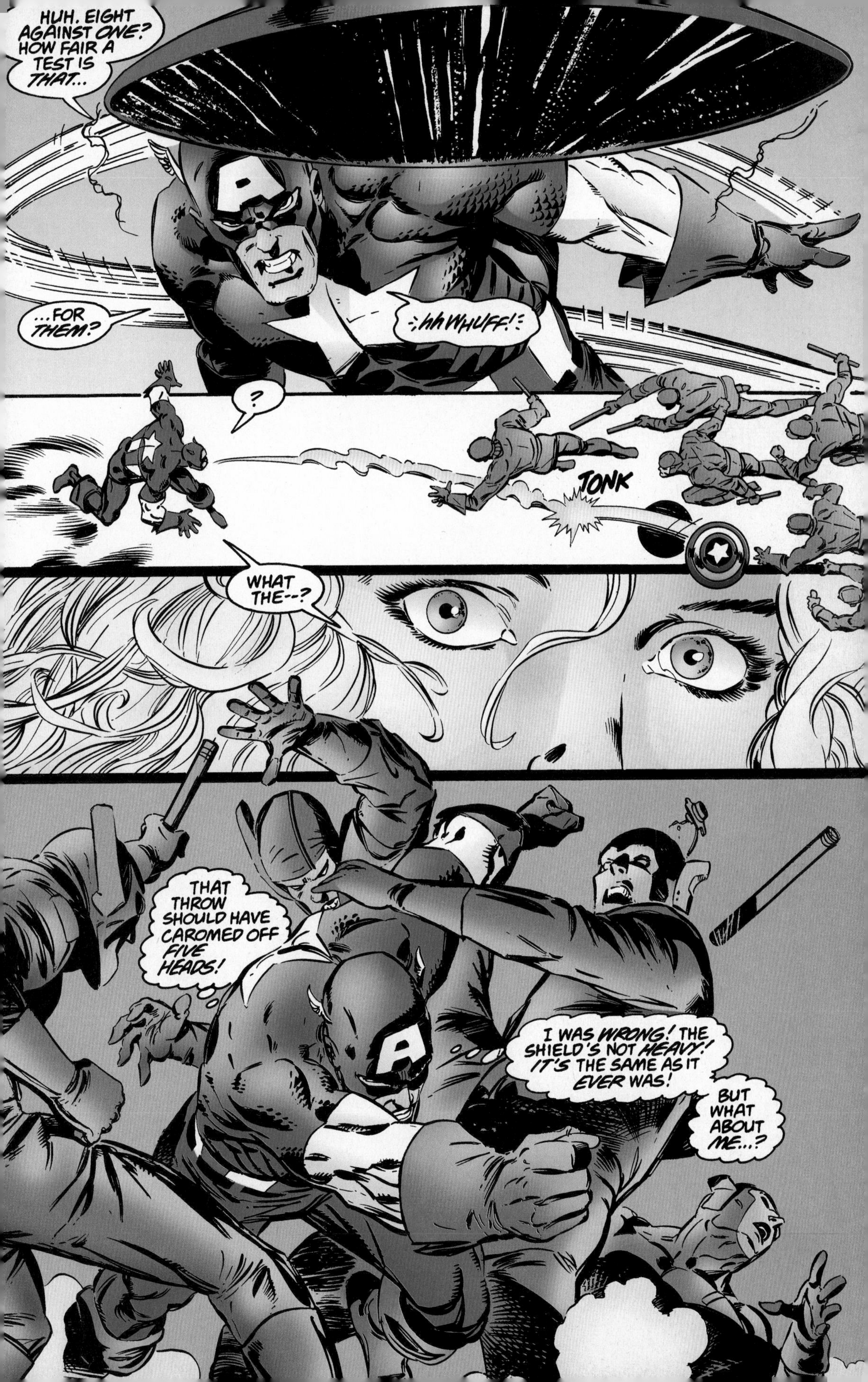
HUH. EIGHT AGAINST ONE? HOW FAIR A TEST IS THAT...
...FOR THEM?
:hh WHUFF!:
?
TONK
WHAT THE--?
THAT THROW SHOULD HAVE CAROMED OFF FIVE HEADS!
I WAS WRONG! THE SHIELD'S NOT HEAVY! IT'S THE SAME AS IT EVER WAS!
BUT WHAT ABOUT ME...?

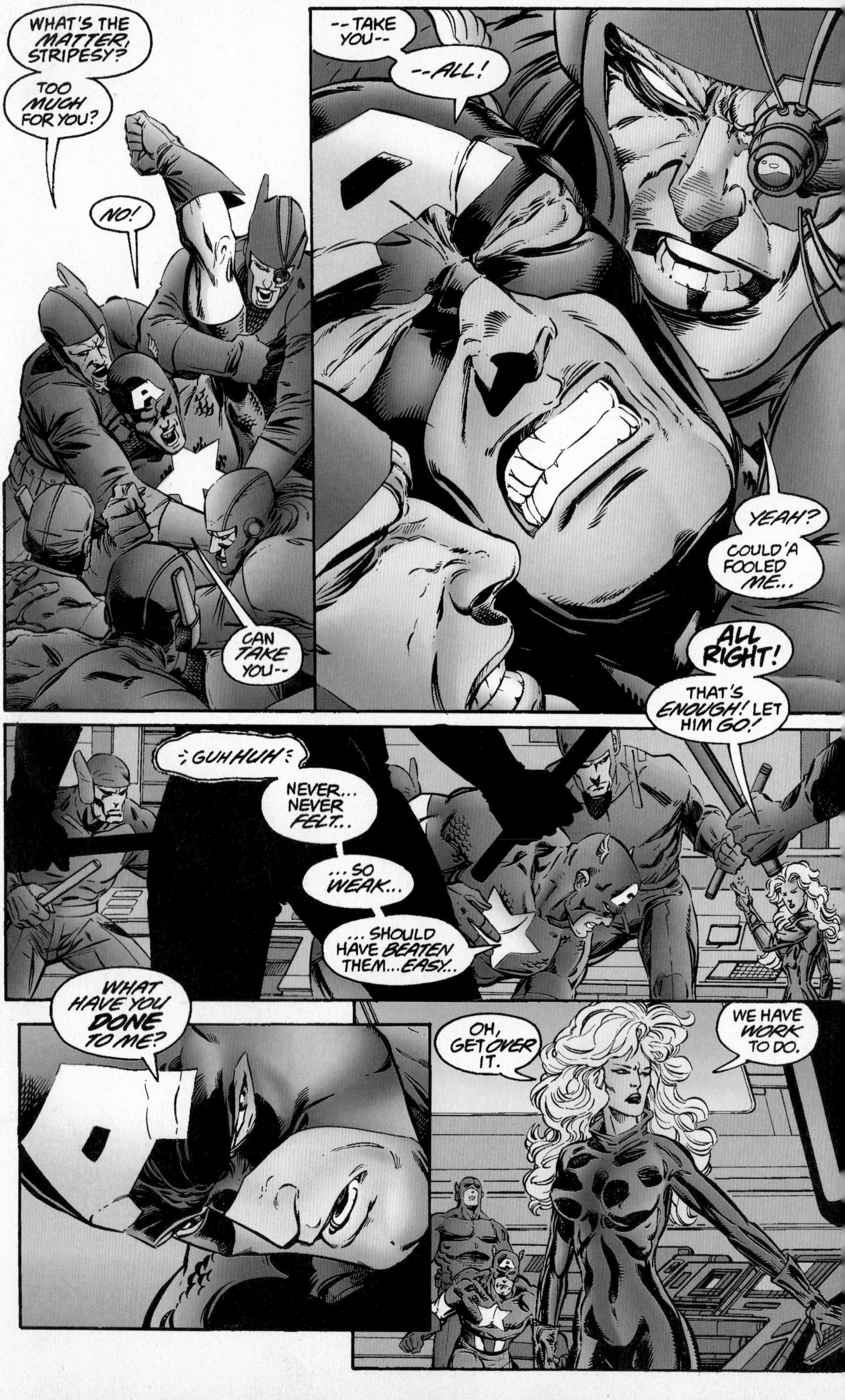
WHAT'S THE MATTER, STRIPESY?
TOO MUCH FOR YOU?
NO!
CAN TAKE YOU--
--TAKE YOU--
--ALL!
YEAH?
COULD'A FOOLED ME...
ALL RIGHT!
THAT'S ENOUGH! LET HIM GO!
GUHHUH
NEVER... NEVER FELT...
...SO WEAK...
...SHOULD HAVE BEATEN THEM...EASY...
WHAT HAVE YOU DONE TO ME?
OH, GET OVER IT.
WE HAVE WORK TO DO.

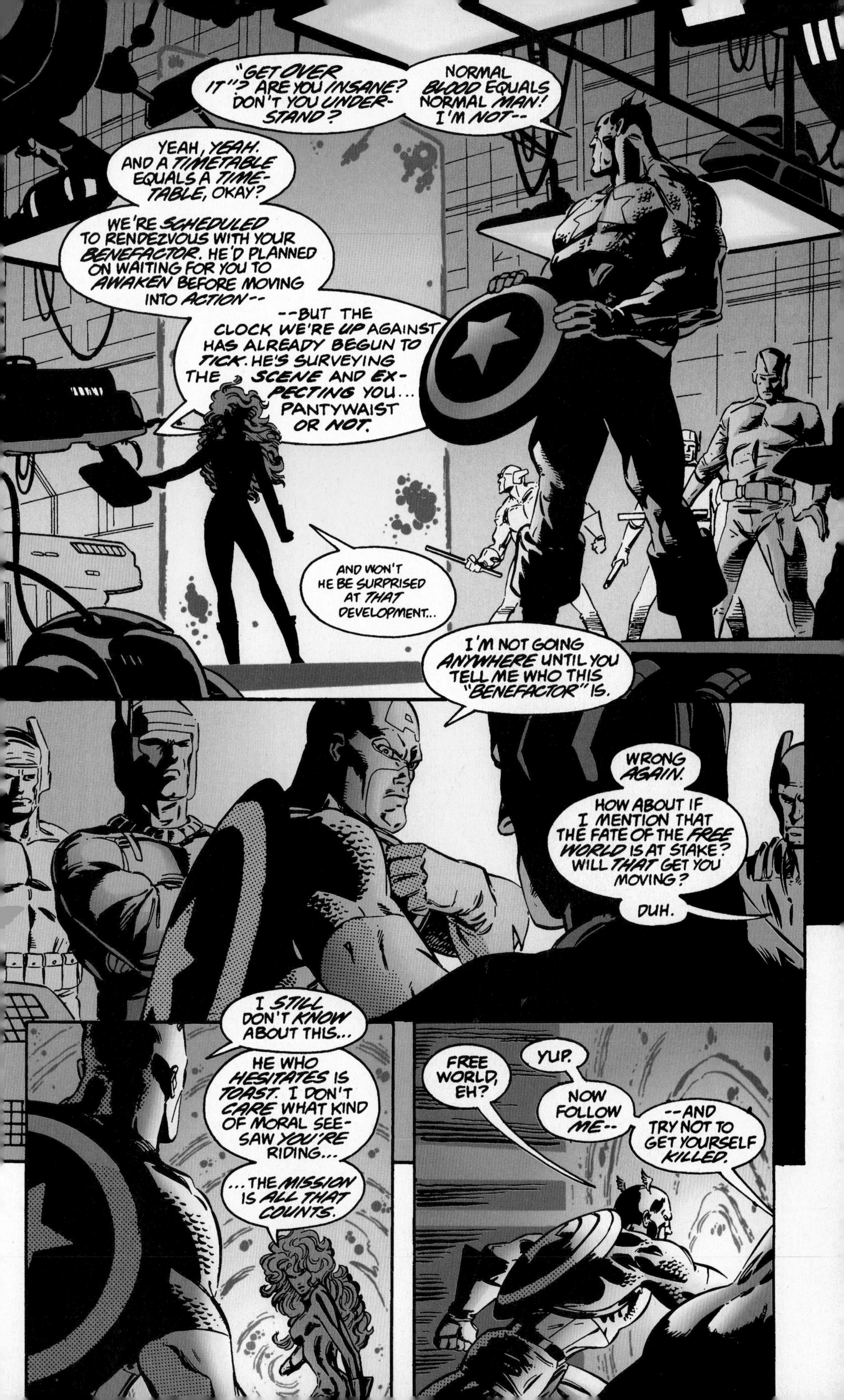
"GET OVER IT"? ARE YOU INSANE? DON'T YOU UNDERSTAND?
NORMAL BLOOD EQUALS NORMAL MAN! I'M NOT--
YEAH, YEAH. AND A TIMETABLE EQUALS A TIMETABLE, OKAY?
WE'RE SCHEDULED TO RENDEZVOUS WITH YOUR BENEFACTOR. HE'D PLANNED ON WAITING FOR YOU TO AWAKEN BEFORE MOVING INTO ACTION--
--BUT THE CLOCK WE'RE UP AGAINST HAS ALREADY BEGUN TO TICK. HE'S SURVEYING THE SCENE AND EXPECTING YOU... PANTYWAIST OR NOT.
AND WON'T HE BE SURPRISED AT THAT DEVELOPMENT...
I'M NOT GOING ANYWHERE UNTIL YOU TELL ME WHO THIS "BENEFACTOR" IS.
WRONG AGAIN.
HOW ABOUT IF I MENTION THAT THE FATE OF THE FREE WORLD IS AT STAKE? WILL THAT GET YOU MOVING?
DUH.
I STILL DON'T KNOW ABOUT THIS...
HE WHO HESITATES IS TOAST. I DON'T CARE WHAT KIND OF MORAL SEE-SAW YOU'RE RIDING...
...THE MISSION IS ALL THAT COUNTS.
FREE WORLD, EH?
YUP.
NOW FOLLOW ME--
--AND TRY NOT TO GET YOURSELF KILLED.

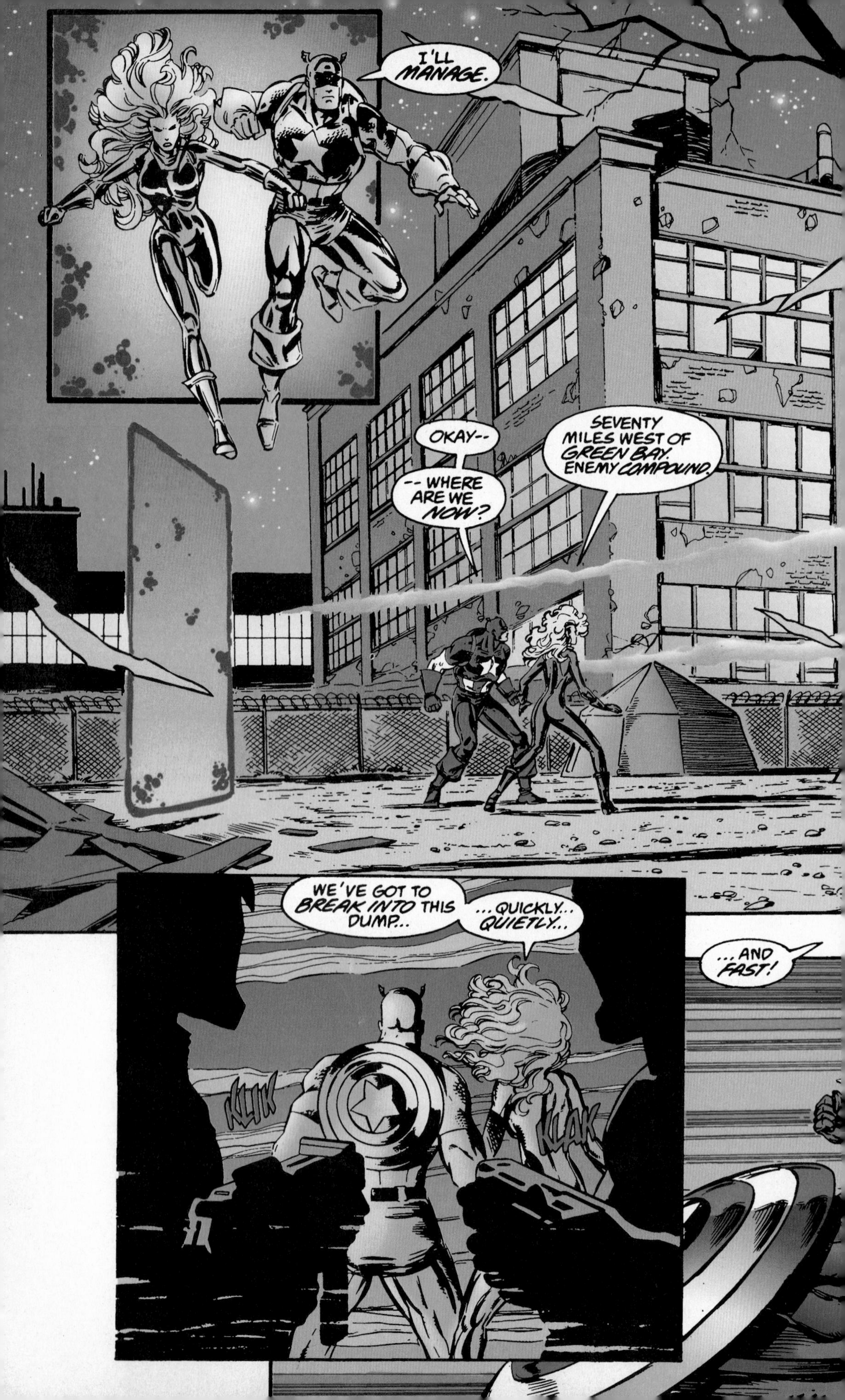
I'LL MANAGE.
OKAY--
--WHERE ARE WE NOW?
SEVENTY MILES WEST OF GREEN BAY. ENEMY COMPOUND.
WE'VE GOT TO BREAK INTO THIS DUMP...
...QUICKLY... QUIETLY...
...AND FAST!
KLIK
KLAK

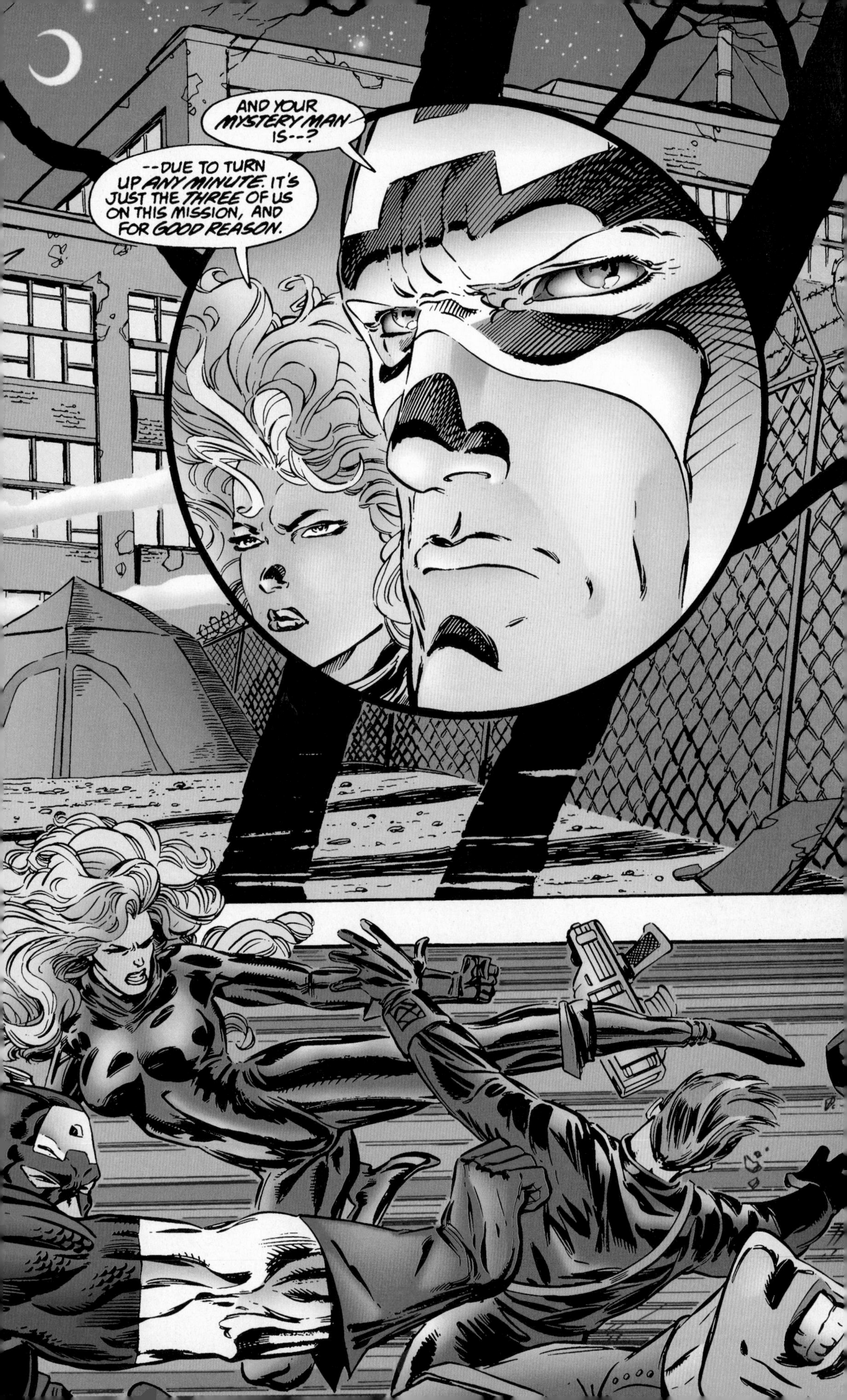
AND YOUR MYSTERY MAN IS--?
--DUE TO TURN UP ANY MINUTE. IT'S JUST THE THREE OF US ON THIS MISSION, AND FOR GOOD REASON.

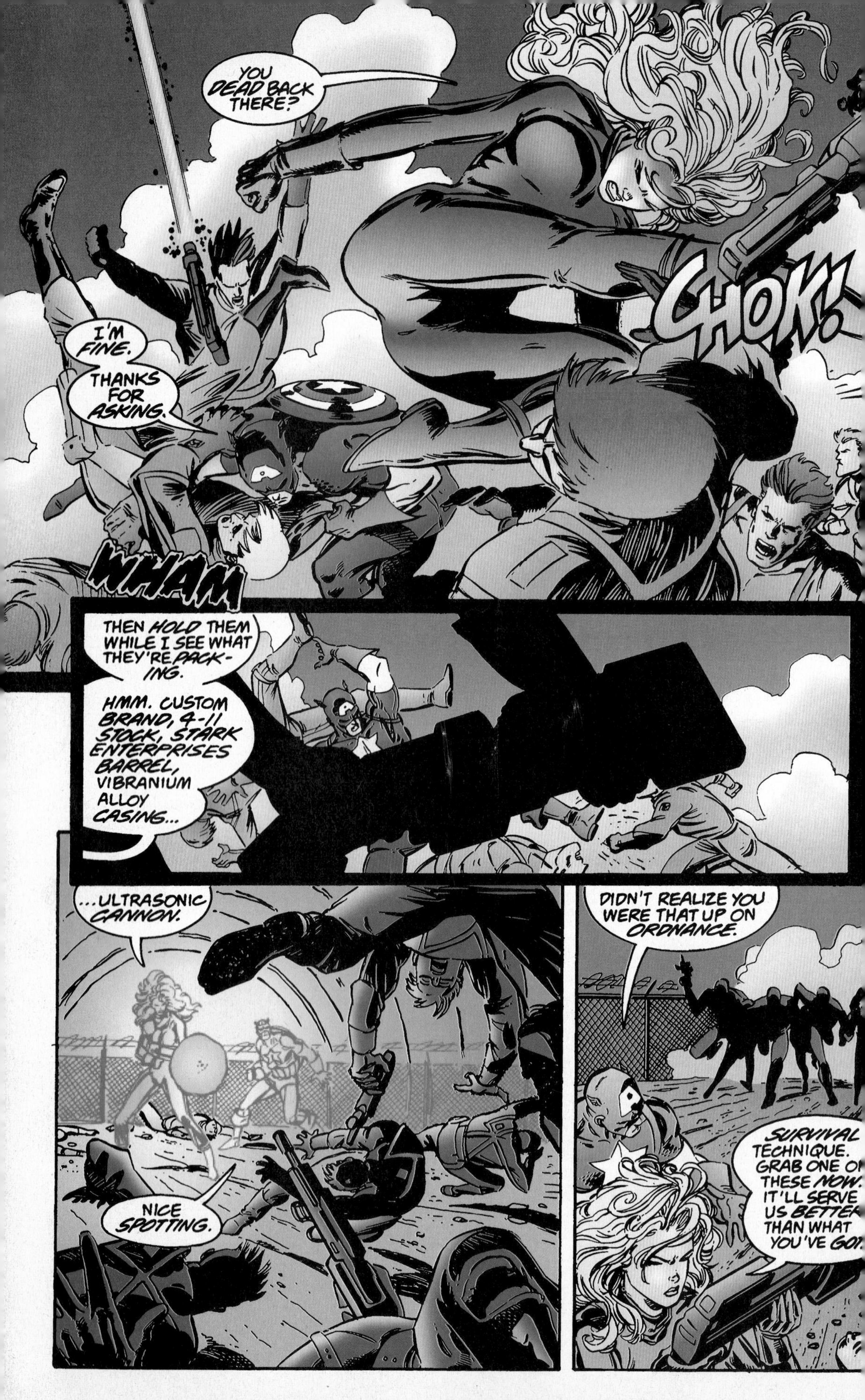
YOU DEAD BACK THERE?
CHOK!
I'M FINE.
THANKS FOR ASKING.
WHAM
THEN HOLD THEM WHILE I SEE WHAT THEY'RE PACK-ING.
HMM. CUSTOM BRAND, 4-11 STOCK, STARK ENTERPRISES BARREL, VIBRANIUM ALLOY CASING...
...ULTRASONIC CANNON.
NICE SPOTTING.
DIDN'T REALIZE YOU WERE THAT UP ON ORDNANCE.
SURVIVAL TECHNIQUE.

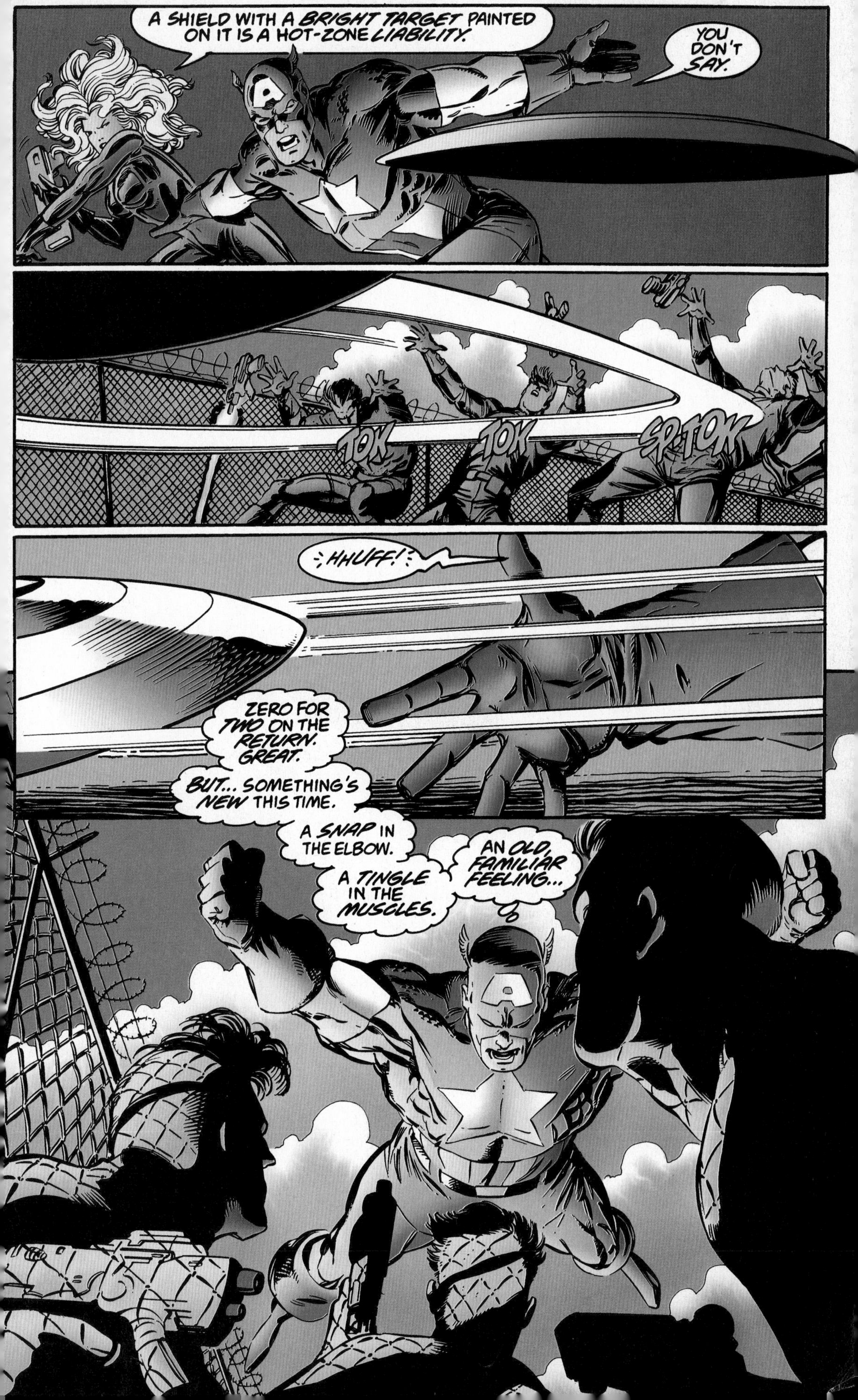
A SHIELD WITH A BRIGHT TARGET PAINTED ON IT IS A HOT-ZONE LIABILITY.
YOU DON'T SAY.
TOK
TOK
SP-TOK
HHUFF!
ZERO FOR TWO ON THE RETURN. GREAT.
BUT... SOMETHING'S NEW THIS TIME.
A SNAP IN THE ELBOW.
A TINGLE IN THE MUSCLES.
AN OLD, FAMILIAR FEELING...

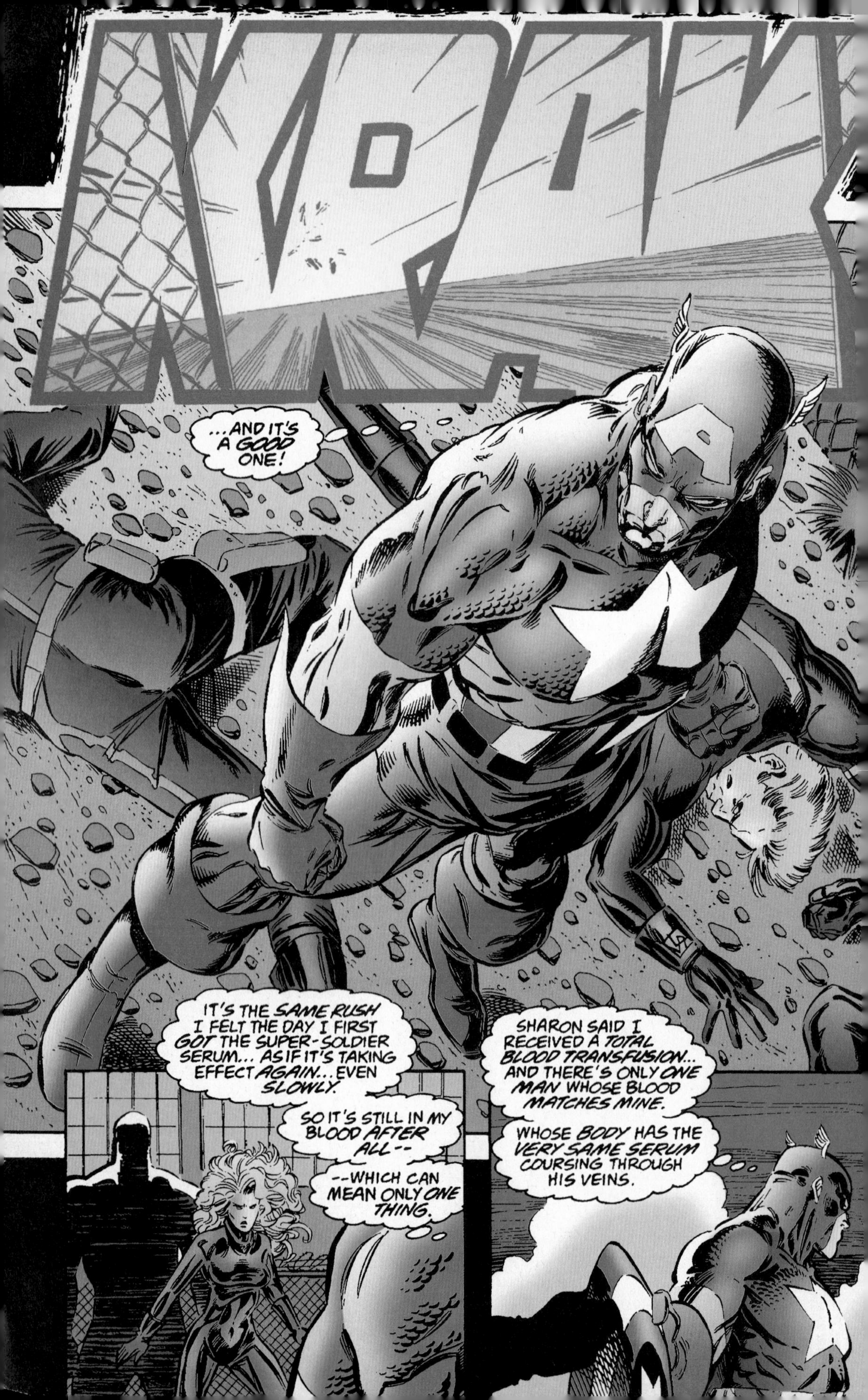
KRAK
...AND IT'S A GOOD ONE!
IT'S THE SAME RUSH I FELT THE DAY I FIRST GOT THE SUPER-SOLDIER SERUM... AS IF IT'S TAKING EFFECT AGAIN... EVEN SLOWLY.
SO IT'S STILL IN MY BLOOD AFTER ALL--
--WHICH CAN MEAN ONLY ONE THING.
SHARON SAID I RECEIVED A TOTAL BLOOD TRANSFUSION... AND THERE'S ONLY ONE MAN WHOSE BLOOD MATCHES MINE.
WHOSE BODY HAS THE VERY SAME SERUM COURSING THROUGH HIS VEINS.

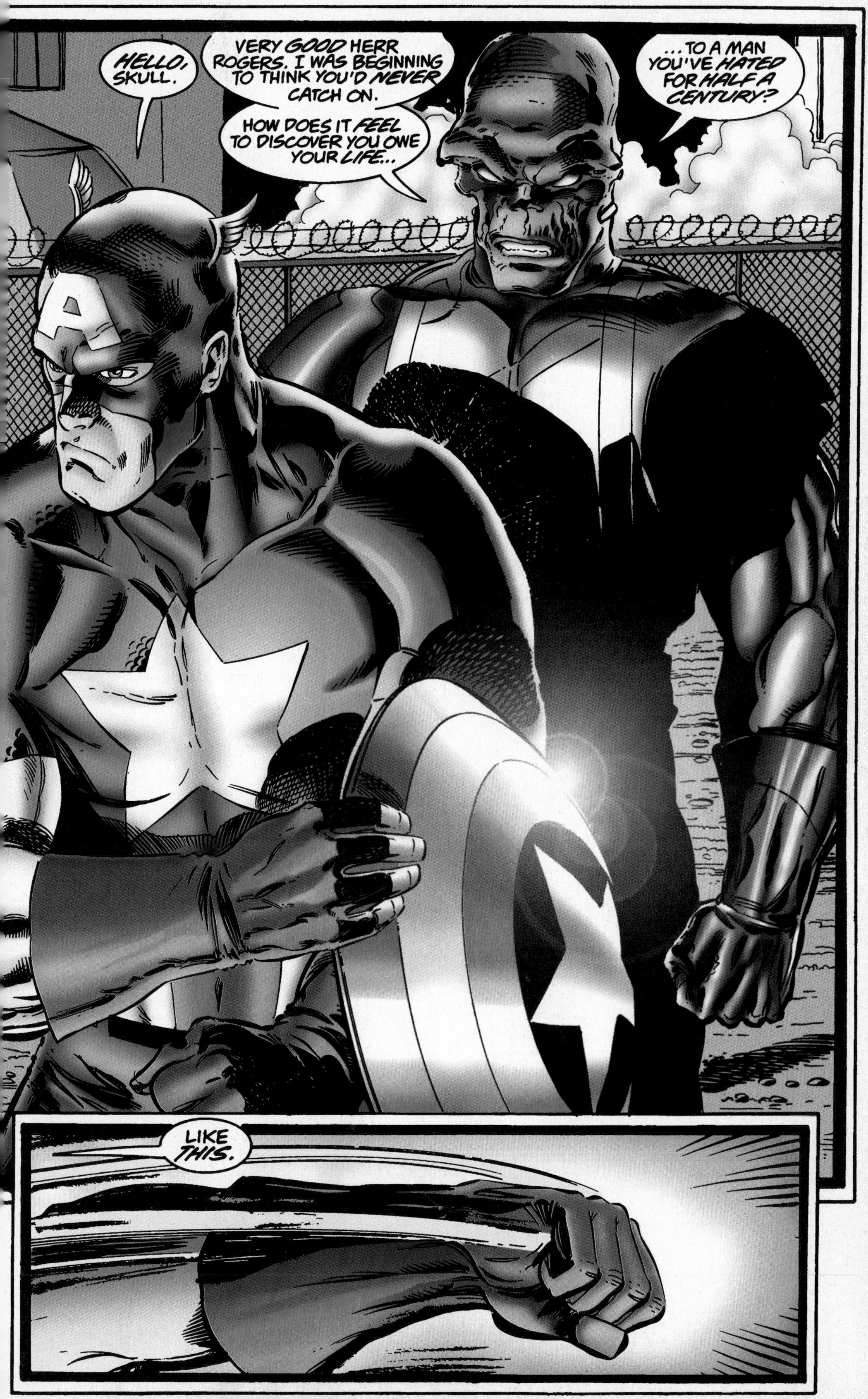
HELLO, SKULL.
VERY GOOD HERR ROGERS. I WAS BEGINNING TO THINK YOU'D NEVER CATCH ON.
HOW DOES IT FEEL TO DISCOVER YOU OWE YOUR LIFE...
...TO A MAN YOU'VE HATED FOR HALF A CENTURY?
LIKE THIS.

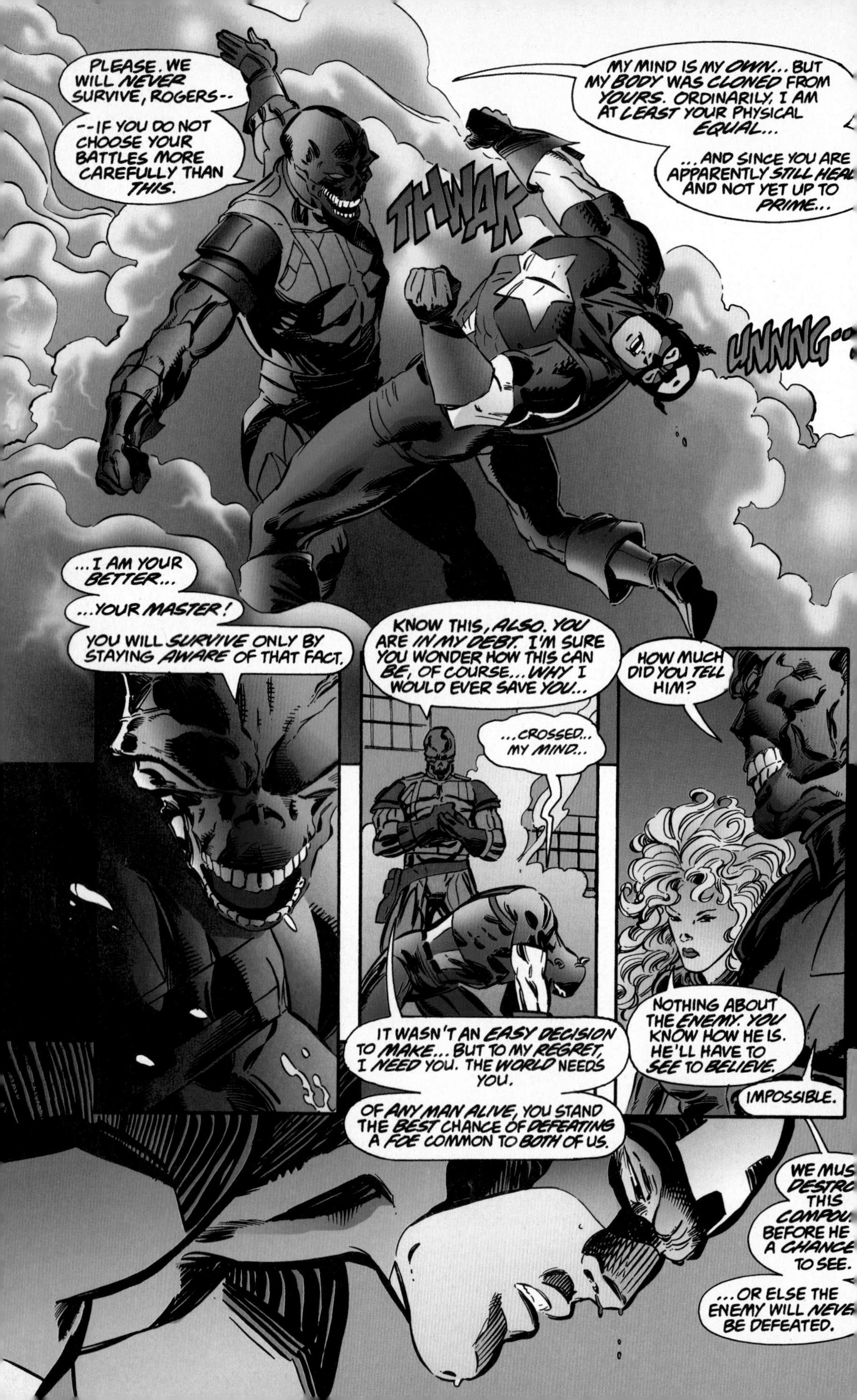
PLEASE. WE WILL NEVER SURVIVE, ROGERS--
--IF YOU DO NOT CHOOSE YOUR BATTLES MORE CAREFULLY THAN THIS.
MY MIND IS MY OWN... BUT MY BODY WAS CLONED FROM YOURS. ORDINARILY, I AM AT LEAST YOUR PHYSICAL EQUAL...
...AND SINCE YOU ARE APPARENTLY STILL HEAL AND NOT YET UP TO PRIME...
THWAK
UNNNG
...I AM YOUR BETTER...
...YOUR MASTER!
YOU WILL SURVIVE ONLY BY STAYING AWARE OF THAT FACT.
KNOW THIS, ALSO. YOU ARE IN MY DEBT. I'M SURE YOU WONDER HOW THIS CAN BE, OF COURSE... WHY I WOULD EVER SAVE YOU...
...CROSSED... MY MIND...
IT WASN'T AN EASY DECISION TO MAKE... BUT TO MY REGRET, I NEED YOU. THE WORLD NEEDS YOU.
OF ANY MAN ALIVE, YOU STAND THE BEST CHANCE OF DEFEATING A FOE COMMON TO BOTH OF US.
HOW MUCH DID YOU TELL HIM?
NOTHING ABOUT THE ENEMY. YOU KNOW HOW HE IS. HE'LL HAVE TO SEE TO BELIEVE.
IMPOSSIBLE.
WE MUS DESTRO THIS COMPOU BEFORE HE A CHANCE TO SEE.
...OR ELSE THE ENEMY WILL NEVE BE DEFEATED.

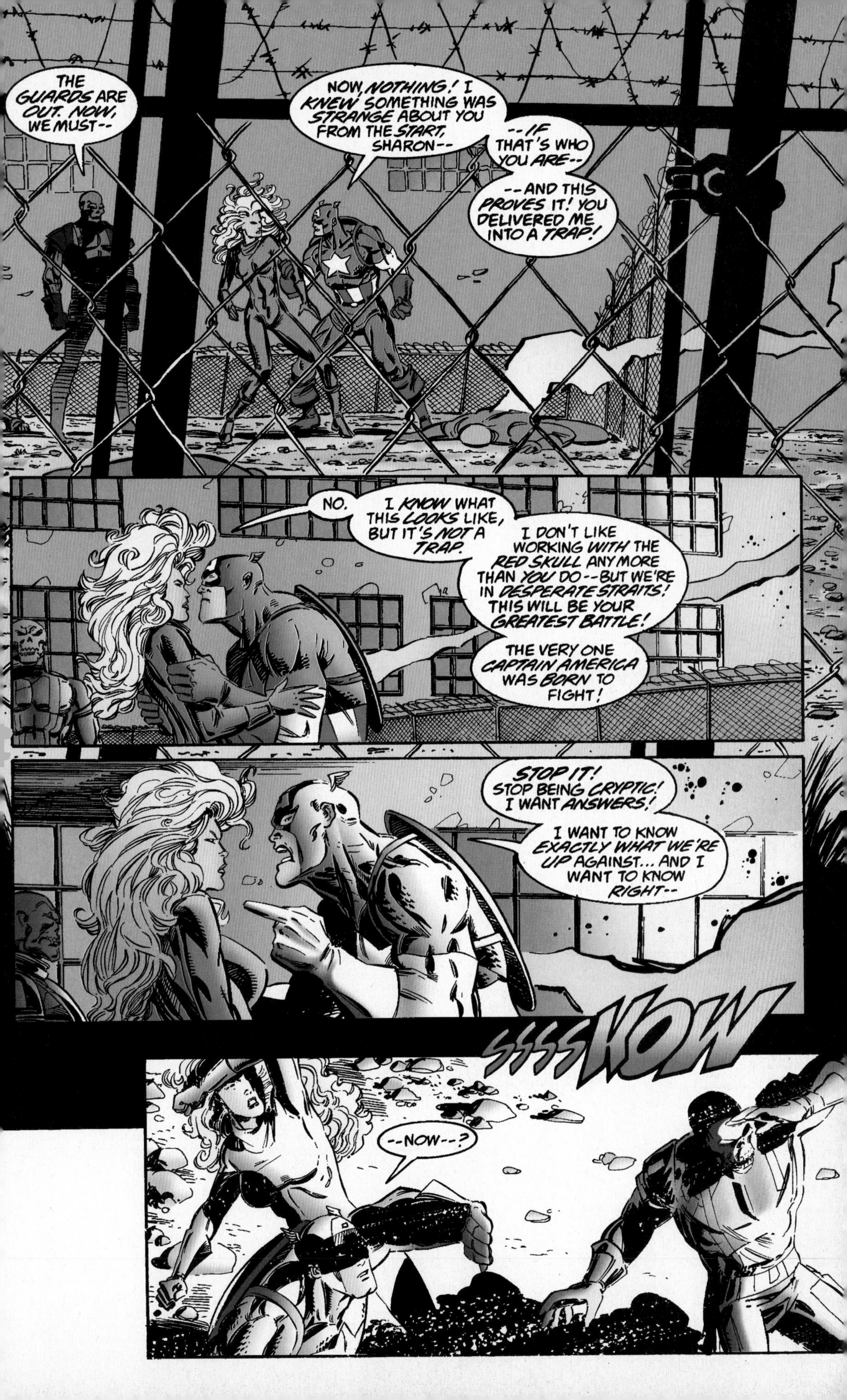
THE GUARDS ARE OUT. NOW, WE MUST--
NOW, NOTHING! I KNEW SOMETHING WAS STRANGE ABOUT YOU FROM THE START, SHARON--
--IF THAT'S WHO YOU ARE--
--AND THIS PROVES IT! YOU DELIVERED ME INTO A TRAP!
NO.
I KNOW WHAT THIS LOOKS LIKE, BUT IT'S NOT A TRAP.
I DON'T LIKE WORKING WITH THE RED SKULL ANY MORE THAN YOU DO--BUT WE'RE IN DESPERATE STRAITS! THIS WILL BE YOUR GREATEST BATTLE!
THE VERY ONE CAPTAIN AMERICA WAS BORN TO FIGHT!
STOP IT! STOP BEING CRYPTIC! I WANT ANSWERS!
I WANT TO KNOW EXACTLY WHAT WE'RE UP AGAINST... AND I WANT TO KNOW RIGHT--
SSSSKOW
--NOW--?

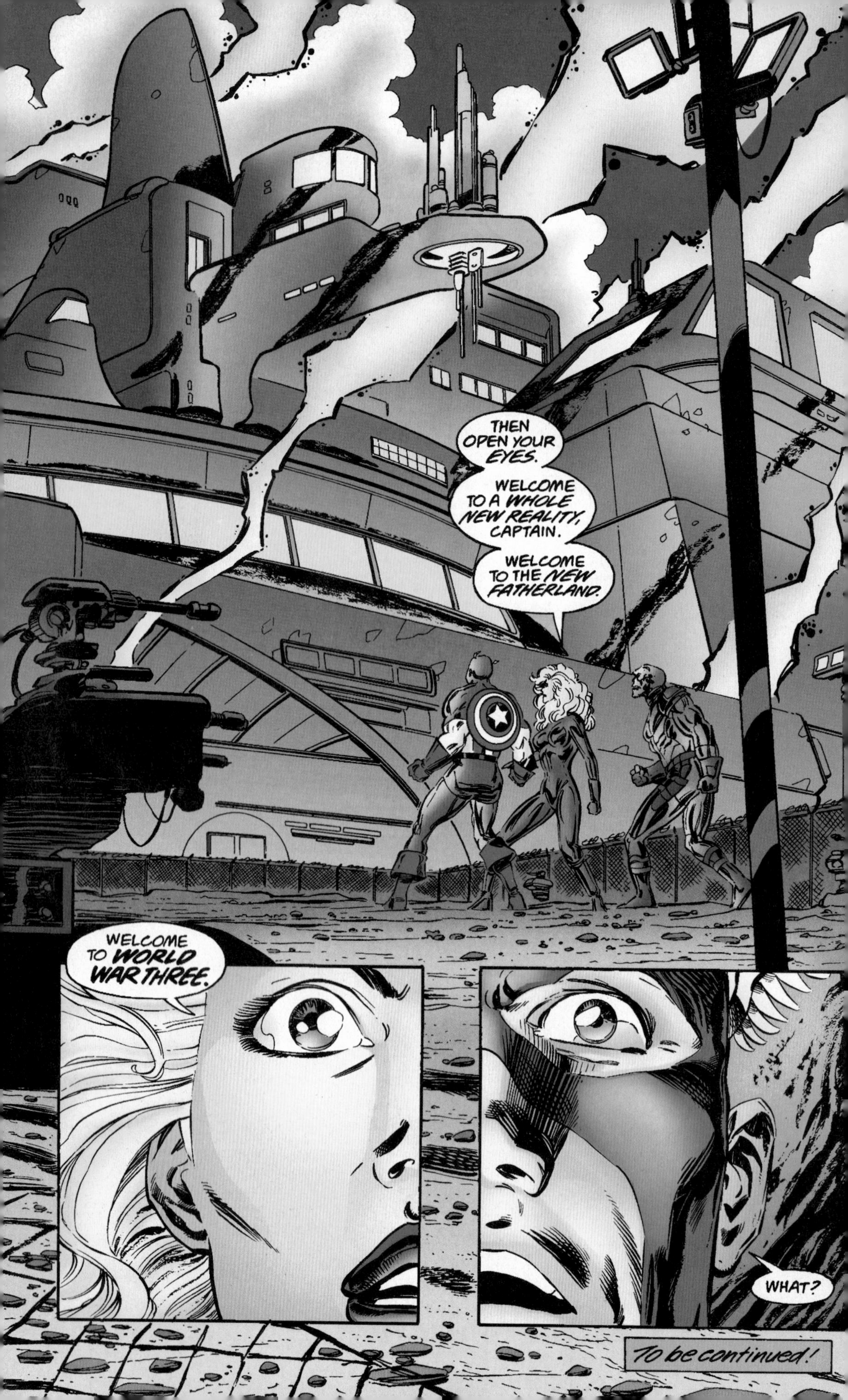
THEN OPEN YOUR EYES.
WELCOME TO A WHOLE NEW REALITY, CAPTAIN.
WELCOME TO THE NEW FATHERLAND.
WELCOME TO WORLD WAR THREE.
WHAT?
To be continued!

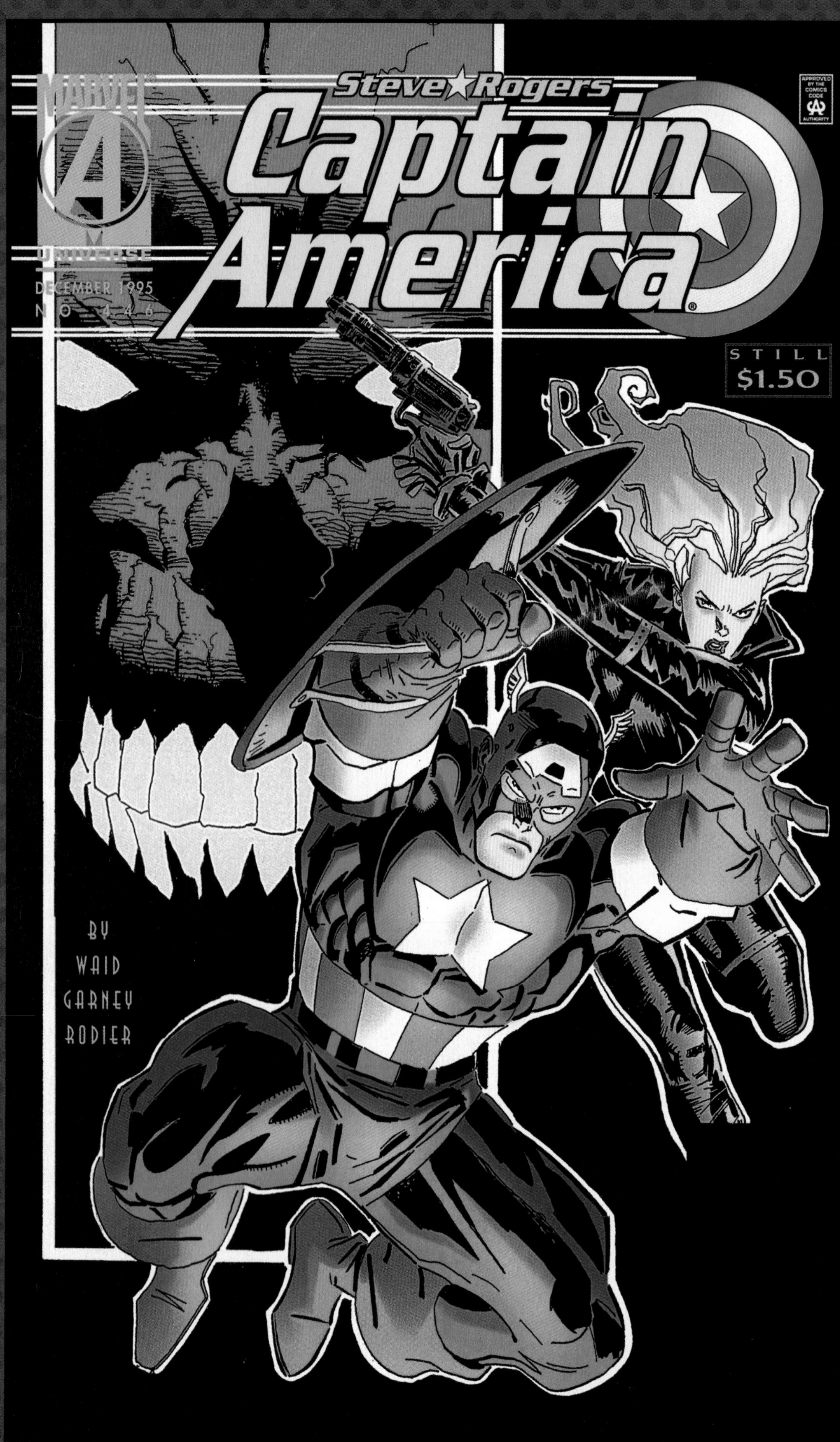
MARVEL UNIVERSE
DECEMBER 1995
NO 446
Steve★Rogers
Captain America
APPROVED BY THE COMICS CODE AUTHORITY
STILL $1.50
BY
WAID
GARNEY
RODIER

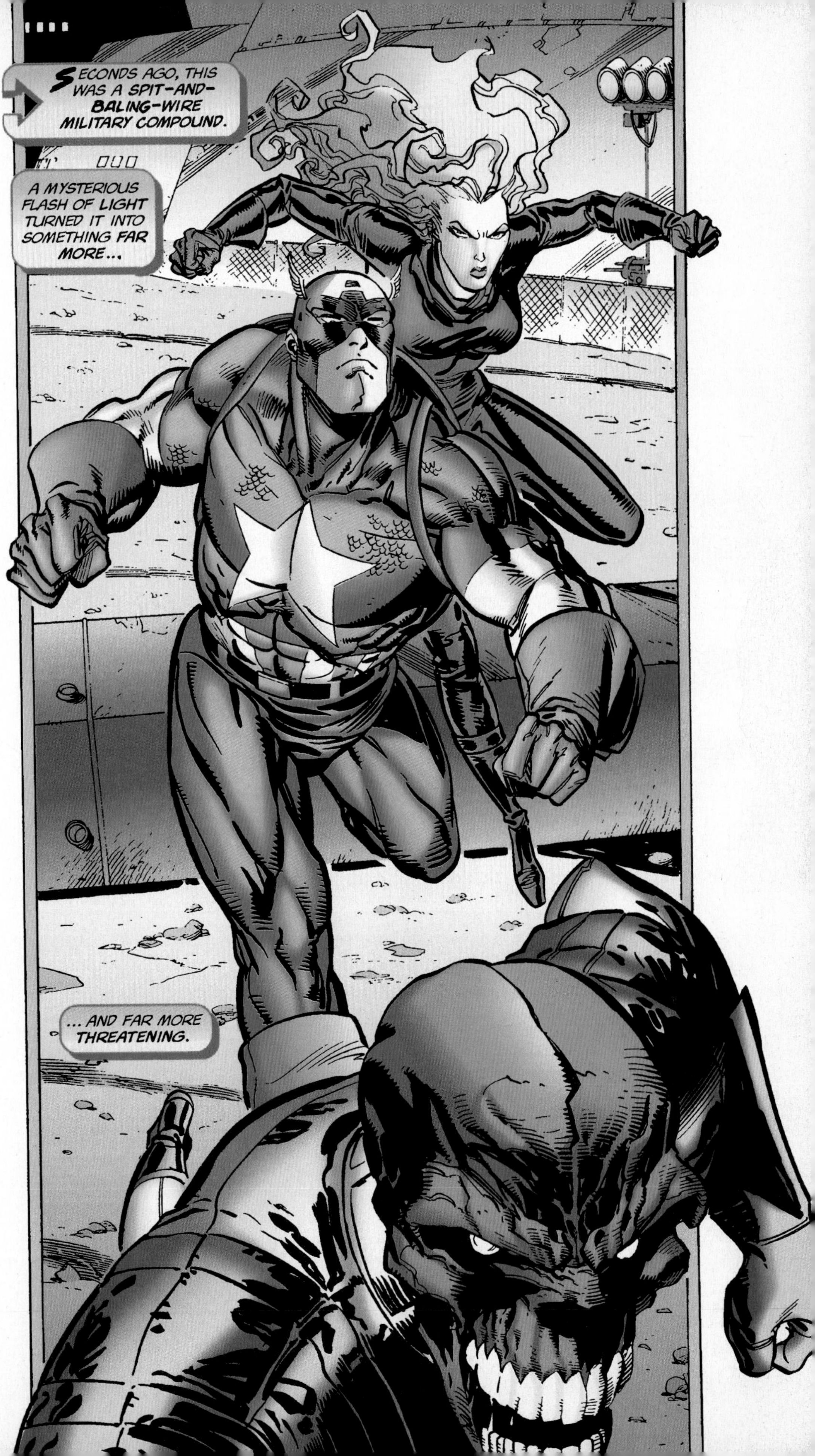
SECONDS AGO, THIS WAS A SPIT-AND-BALING-WIRE MILITARY COMPOUND.
A MYSTERIOUS FLASH OF LIGHT TURNED IT INTO SOMETHING FAR MORE...
...AND FAR MORE THREATENING.

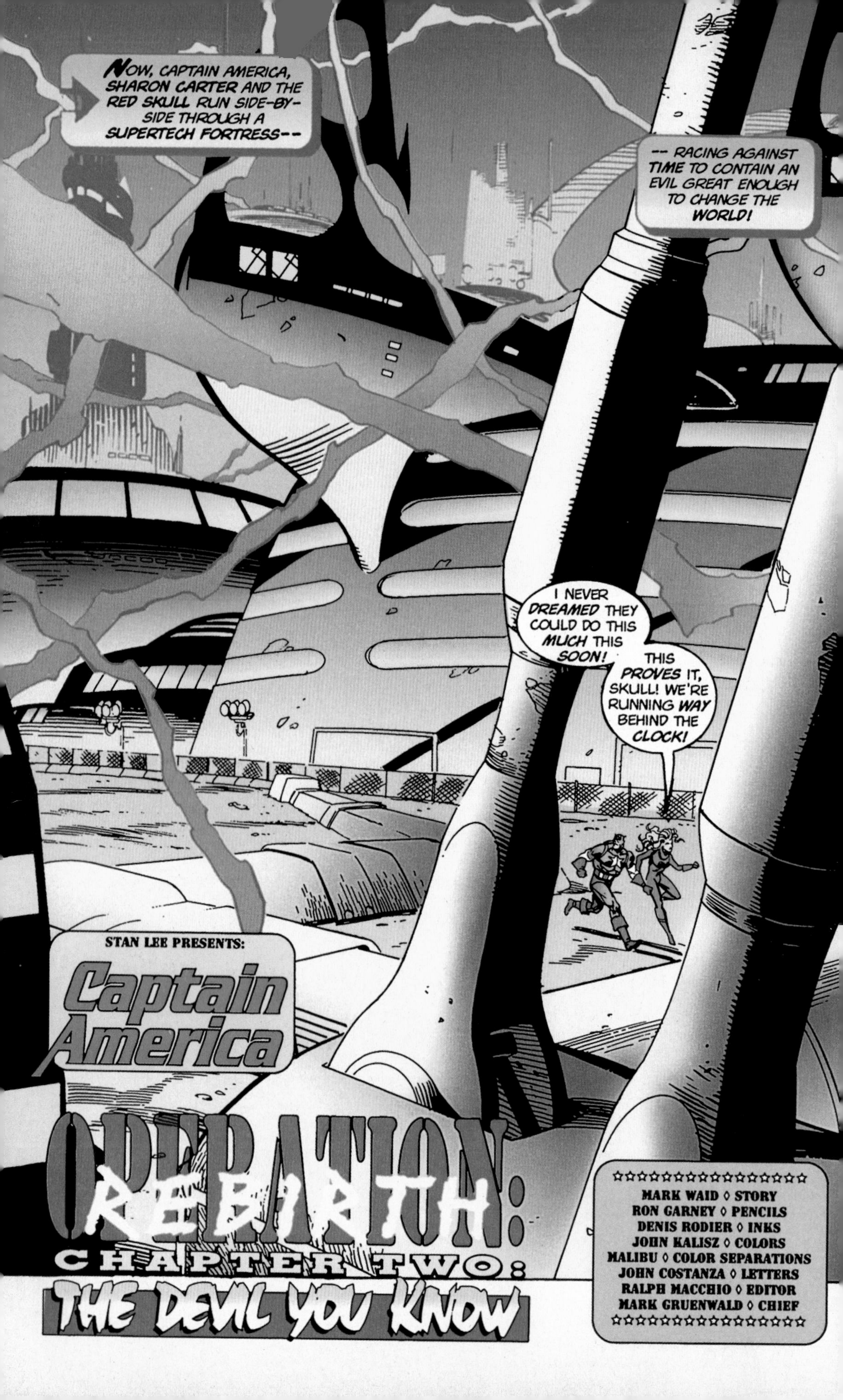

NOW, CAPTAIN AMERICA, SHARON CARTER AND THE RED SKULL RUN SIDE-BY-SIDE THROUGH A SUPERTECH FORTRESS--
-- RACING AGAINST TIME TO CONTAIN AN EVIL GREAT ENOUGH TO CHANGE THE WORLD!
I NEVER DREAMED THEY COULD DO THIS MUCH THIS SOON!
THIS PROVES IT, SKULL! WE'RE RUNNING WAY BEHIND THE CLOCK!
STAN LEE PRESENTS:
Captain America
OPERATION: REBIRTH
CHAPTER TWO:
THE DEVIL YOU KNOW
MARK WAID ◊ STORY
RON GARNEY ◊ PENCILS
DENIS RODIER ◊ INKS
JOHN KALISZ ◊ COLORS
MALIBU ◊ COLOR SEPARATIONS
JOHN COSTANZA ◊ LETTERS
RALPH MACCHIO ◊ EDITOR
MARK GRUENWALD ◊ CHIEF

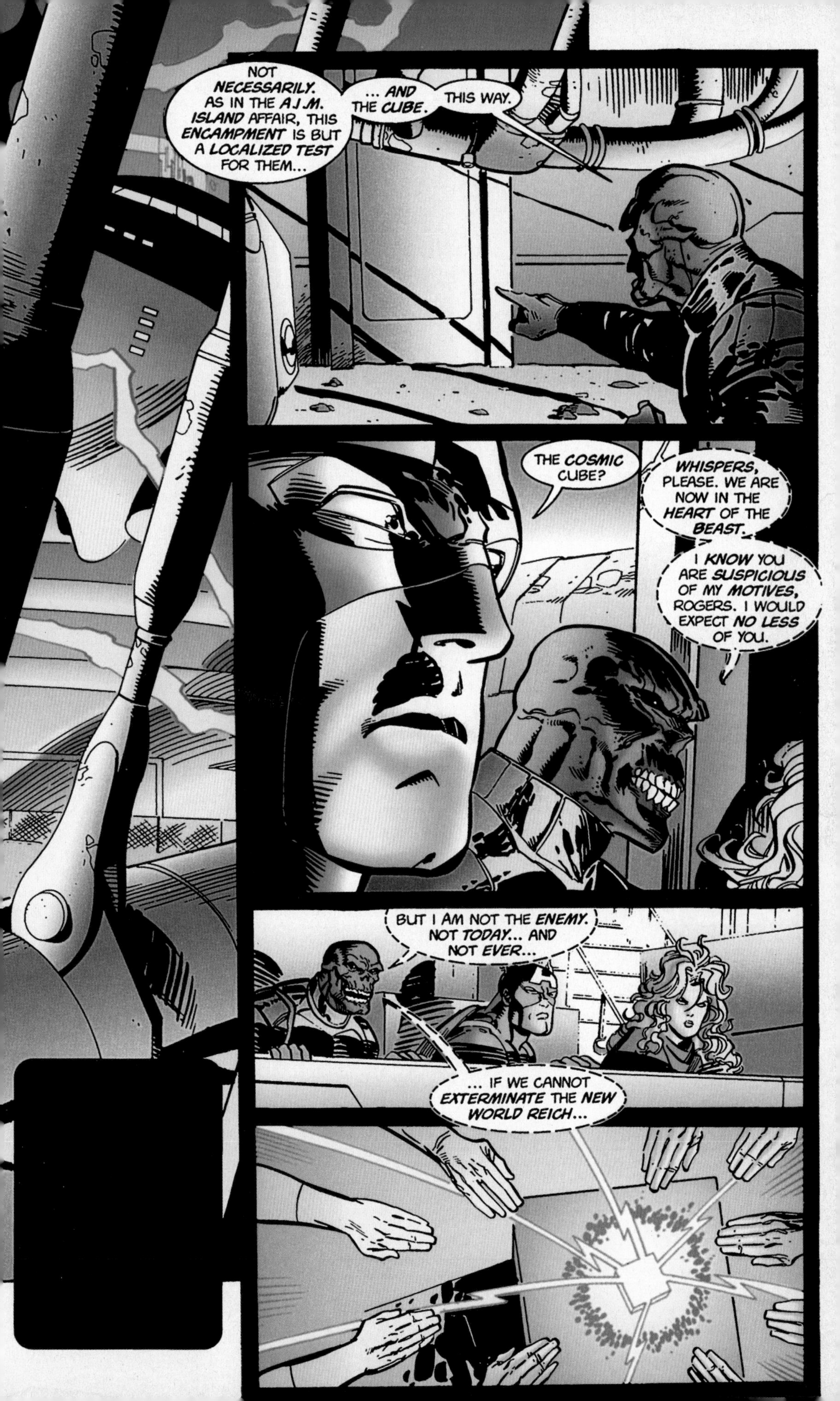

NOT NECESSARILY. AS IN THE A.I.M. ISLAND AFFAIR, THIS ENCAMPMENT IS BUT A LOCALIZED TEST FOR THEM...
... AND THE CUBE.
THIS WAY.
THE COSMIC CUBE?
WHISPERS, PLEASE. WE ARE NOW IN THE HEART OF THE BEAST.
I KNOW YOU ARE SUSPICIOUS OF MY MOTIVES, ROGERS. I WOULD EXPECT NO LESS OF YOU.
BUT I AM NOT THE ENEMY. NOT TODAY... AND NOT EVER...
... IF WE CANNOT EXTERMINATE THE NEW WORLD REICH...

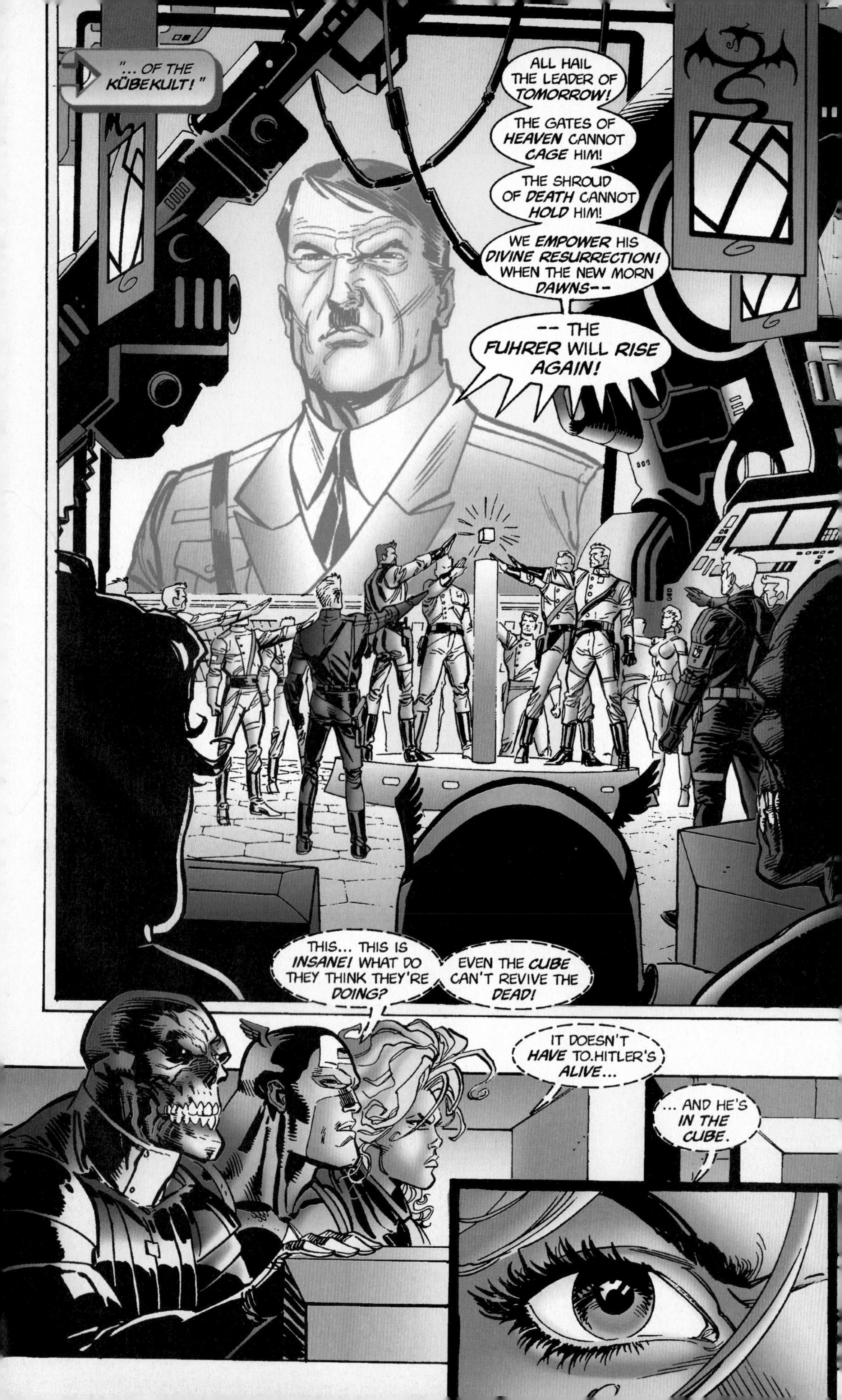
"... OF THE KÜBEKULT!"
ALL HAIL THE LEADER OF TOMORROW!
THE GATES OF HEAVEN CANNOT CAGE HIM!
THE SHROUD OF DEATH CANNOT HOLD HIM!
WE EMPOWER HIS DIVINE RESURRECTION! WHEN THE NEW MORN DAWNS--
-- THE FUHRER WILL RISE AGAIN!
THIS... THIS IS INSANE! WHAT DO THEY THINK THEY'RE DOING?
EVEN THE CUBE CAN'T REVIVE THE DEAD!
IT DOESN'T HAVE TO. HITLER'S ALIVE...
... AND HE'S IN THE CUBE.

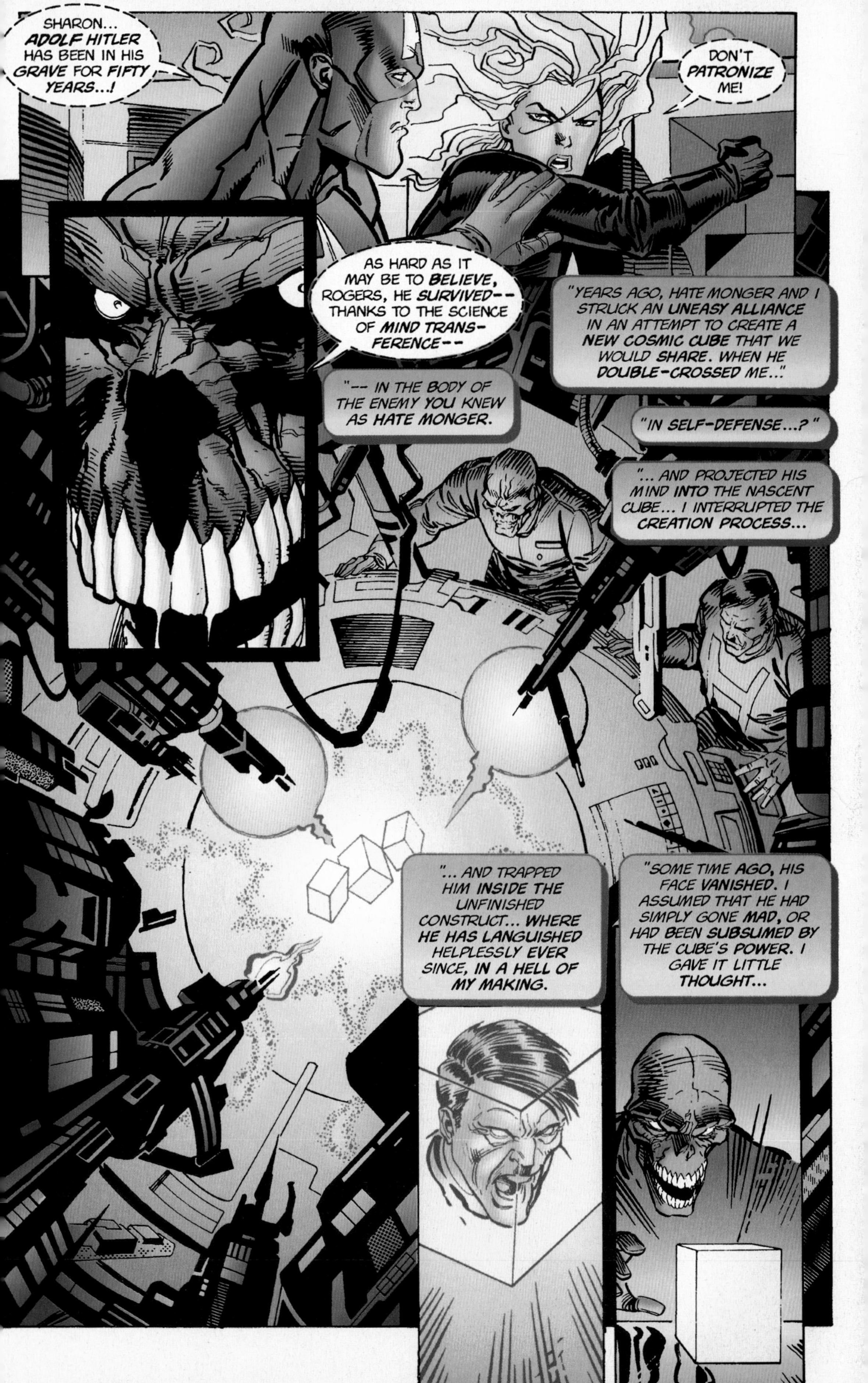

SHARON... ADOLF HITLER HAS BEEN IN HIS GRAVE FOR FIFTY YEARS...!
DON'T PATRONIZE ME!
AS HARD AS IT MAY BE TO BELIEVE, ROGERS, HE SURVIVED-- THANKS TO THE SCIENCE OF MIND TRANS-FERENCE--
"-- IN THE BODY OF THE ENEMY YOU KNEW AS HATE MONGER.
"YEARS AGO, HATE MONGER AND I STRUCK AN UNEASY ALLIANCE IN AN ATTEMPT TO CREATE A NEW COSMIC CUBE THAT WE WOULD SHARE. WHEN HE DOUBLE-CROSSED ME..."
"IN SELF-DEFENSE...?"
"... AND PROJECTED HIS MIND INTO THE NASCENT CUBE... I INTERRUPTED THE CREATION PROCESS...
"... AND TRAPPED HIM INSIDE THE UNFINISHED CONSTRUCT... WHERE HE HAS LANGUISHED HELPLESSLY EVER SINCE, IN A HELL OF MY MAKING.
"SOME TIME AGO, HIS FACE VANISHED. I ASSUMED THAT HE HAD SIMPLY GONE MAD, OR HAD BEEN SUBSUMED BY THE CUBE'S POWER. I GAVE IT LITTLE THOUGHT...

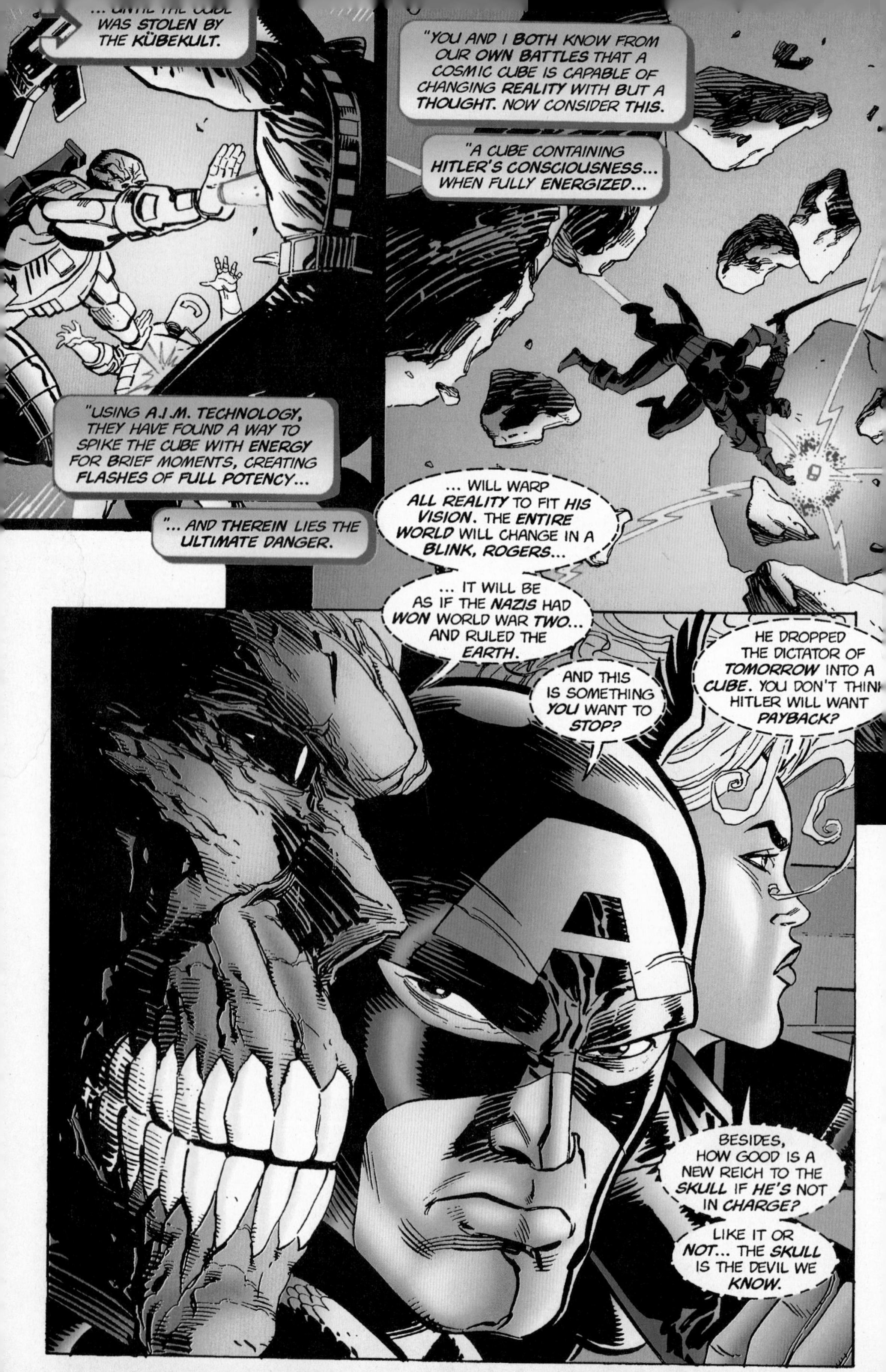

WAS STOLEN BY THE KÜBEKULT.
"YOU AND I BOTH KNOW FROM OUR OWN BATTLES THAT A COSMIC CUBE IS CAPABLE OF CHANGING REALITY WITH BUT A THOUGHT. NOW CONSIDER THIS.
"A CUBE CONTAINING HITLER'S CONSCIOUSNESS... WHEN FULLY ENERGIZED...
"USING A.I.M. TECHNOLOGY, THEY HAVE FOUND A WAY TO SPIKE THE CUBE WITH ENERGY FOR BRIEF MOMENTS, CREATING FLASHES OF FULL POTENCY...
"... AND THEREIN LIES THE ULTIMATE DANGER.
... WILL WARP ALL REALITY TO FIT HIS VISION. THE ENTIRE WORLD WILL CHANGE IN A BLINK, ROGERS...
... IT WILL BE AS IF THE NAZIS HAD WON WORLD WAR TWO... AND RULED THE EARTH.
AND THIS IS SOMETHING YOU WANT TO STOP?
HE DROPPED THE DICTATOR OF TOMORROW INTO A CUBE. YOU DON'T THIN HITLER WILL WANT PAYBACK?
BESIDES, HOW GOOD IS A NEW REICH TO THE SKULL IF HE'S NOT IN CHARGE?
LIKE IT OR NOT... THE SKULL IS THE DEVIL WE KNOW.

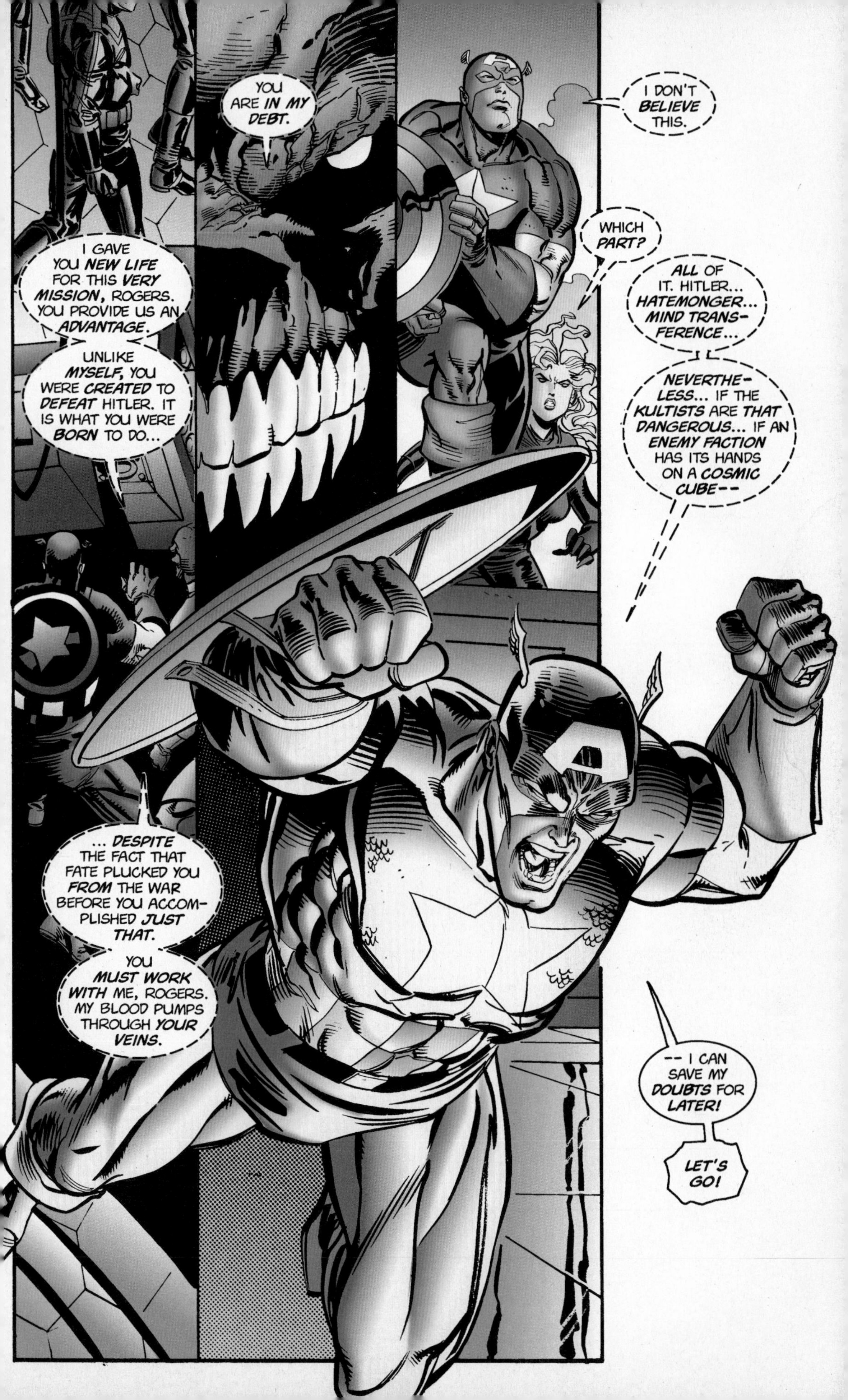

I GAVE YOU NEW LIFE FOR THIS VERY MISSION, ROGERS. YOU PROVIDE US AN ADVANTAGE.
UNLIKE MYSELF, YOU WERE CREATED TO DEFEAT HITLER. IT IS WHAT YOU WERE BORN TO DO...
YOU ARE IN MY DEBT.
I DON'T BELIEVE THIS.
WHICH PART?
ALL OF IT. HITLER... HATEMONGER... MIND TRANSFERENCE...
NEVERTHELESS... IF THE KULTISTS ARE THAT DANGEROUS... IF AN ENEMY FACTION HAS ITS HANDS ON A COSMIC CUBE--
... DESPITE THE FACT THAT FATE PLUCKED YOU FROM THE WAR BEFORE YOU ACCOMPLISHED JUST THAT.
YOU MUST WORK WITH ME, ROGERS. MY BLOOD PUMPS THROUGH YOUR VEINS.
-- I CAN SAVE MY DOUBTS FOR LATER!
LET'S GO!

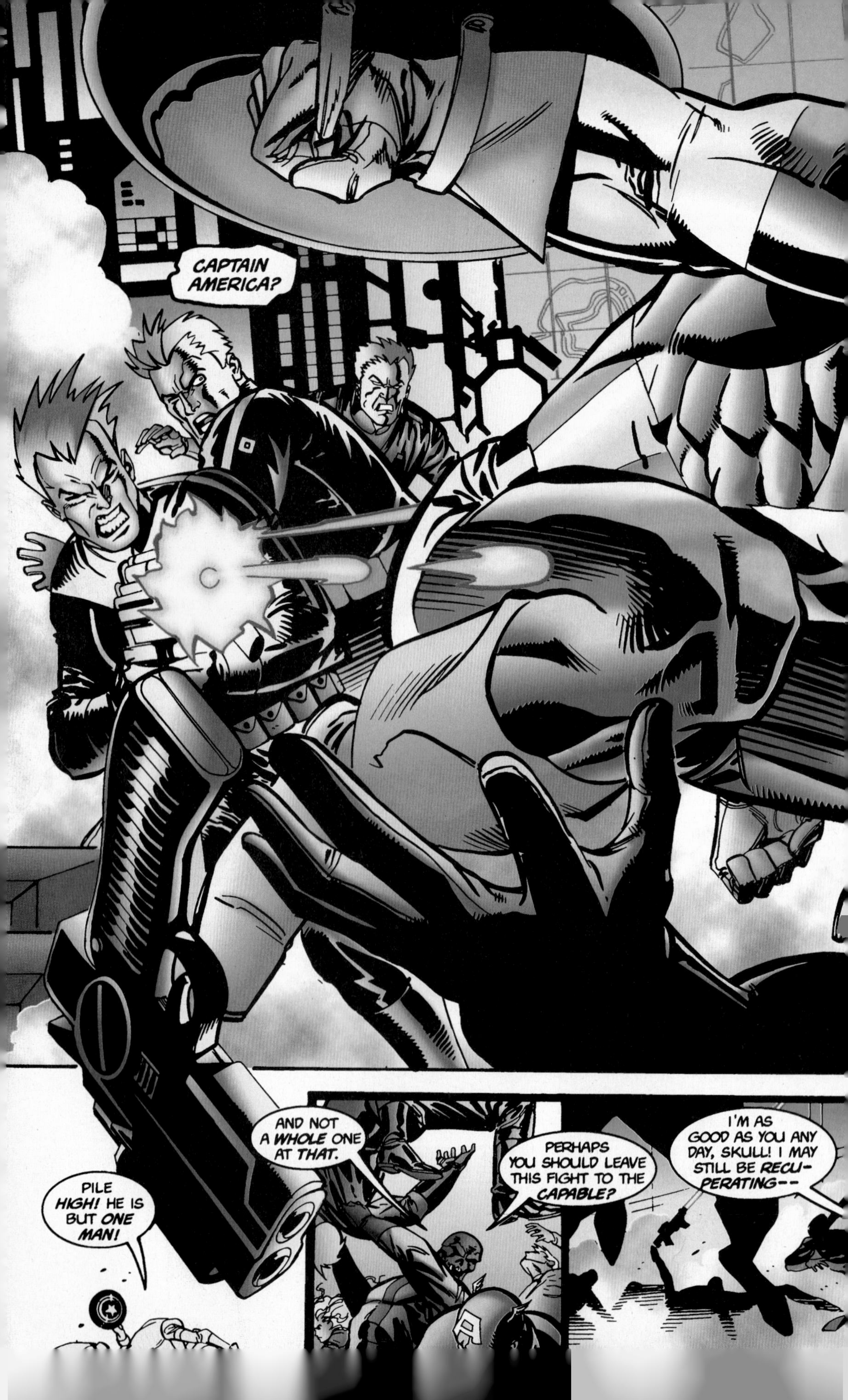
CAPTAIN AMERICA?
PILE HIGH! HE IS BUT ONE MAN!
AND NOT A WHOLE ONE AT THAT.
PERHAPS YOU SHOULD LEAVE THIS FIGHT TO THE CAPABLE?
I'M AS GOOD AS YOU ANY DAY, SKULL! I MAY STILL BE RECU-PERATING--

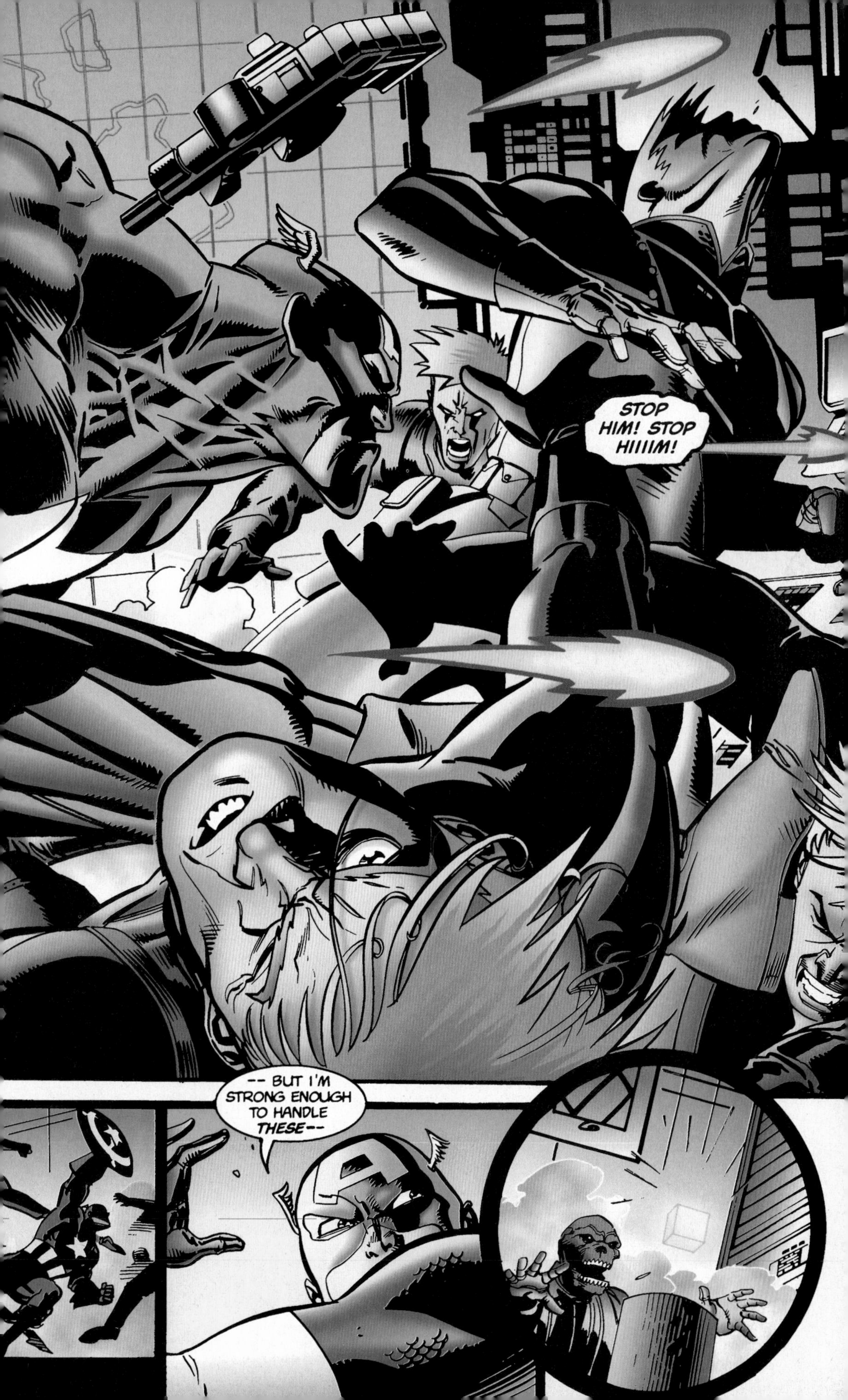
STOP HIM! STOP HIIIIM!
-- BUT I'M STRONG ENOUGH TO HANDLE THESE--

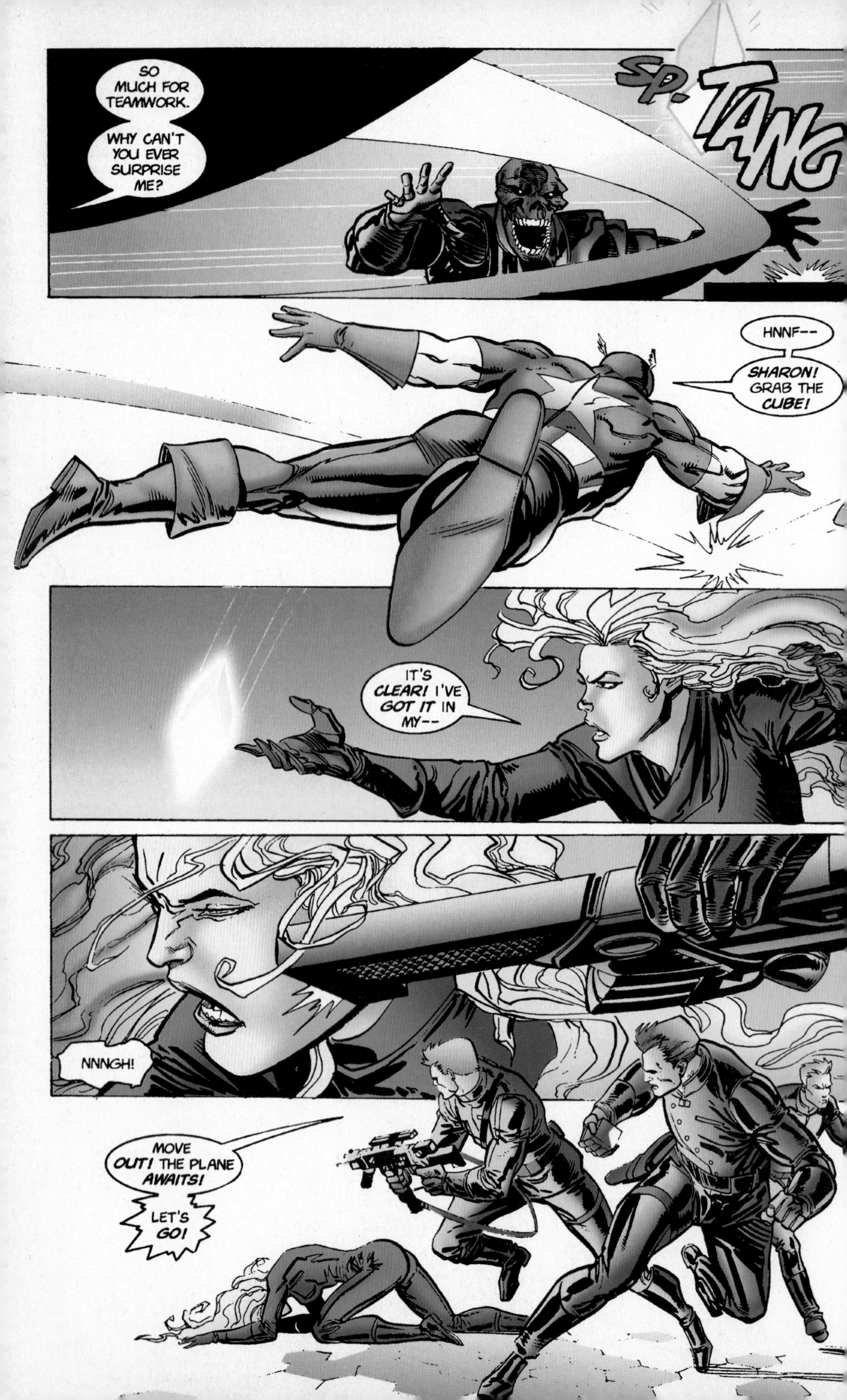
SO MUCH FOR TEAMWORK.
WHY CAN'T YOU EVER SURPRISE ME?
SP-TANG
HNNF--
SHARON! GRAB THE CUBE!
IT'S CLEAR! I'VE GOT IT IN MY--
NNNGH!
MOVE OUT! THE PLANE AWAITS!
LET'S GO!

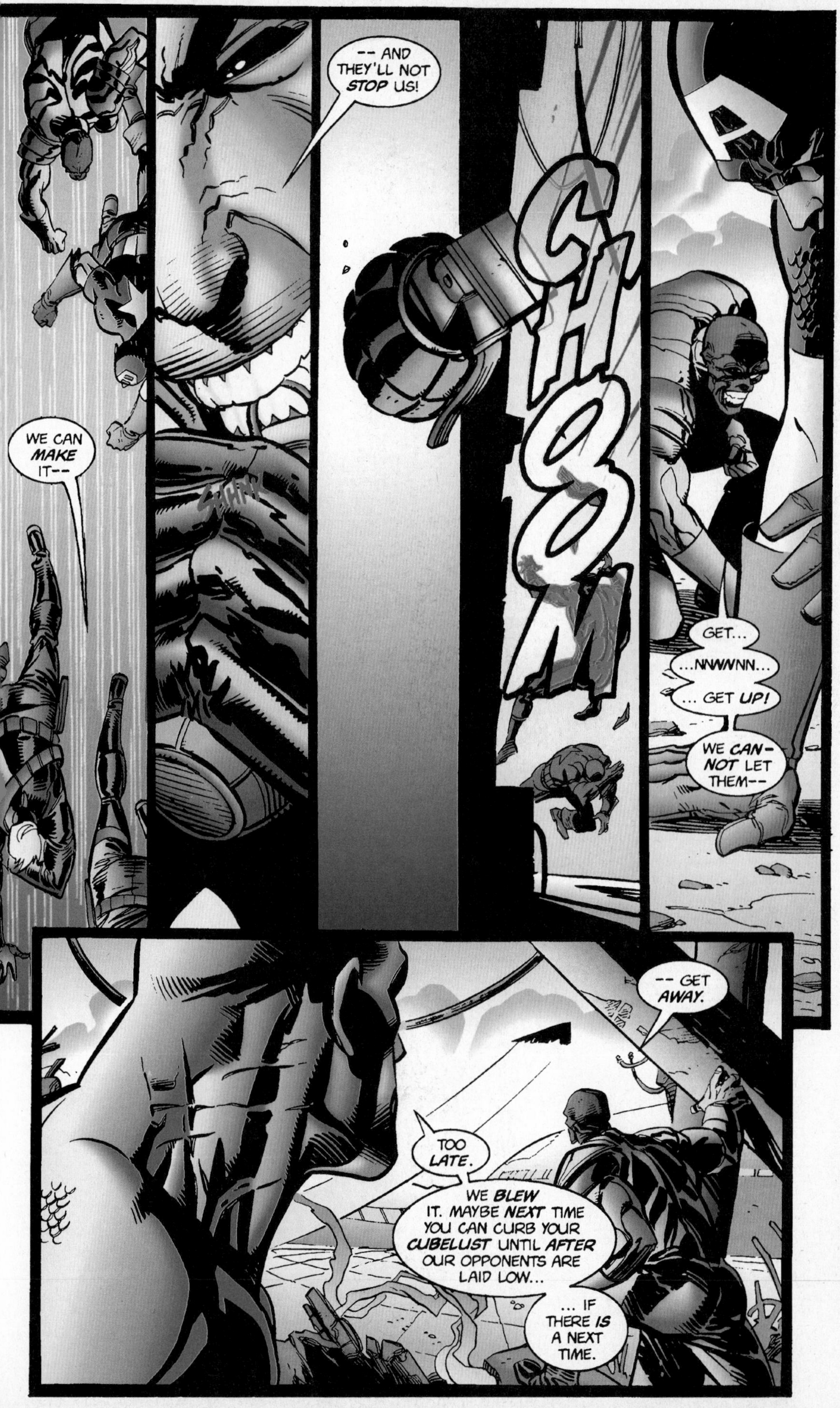
-- AND THEY'LL NOT STOP US!
WE CAN MAKE IT--
CHOOOM
GET...
...NNWNNN...
... GET UP!
WE CAN-NOT LET THEM--
-- GET AWAY.
TOO LATE.
WE BLEW IT. MAYBE NEXT TIME YOU CAN CURB YOUR CUBELUST UNTIL AFTER OUR OPPONENTS ARE LAID LOW...
... IF THERE IS A NEXT TIME.

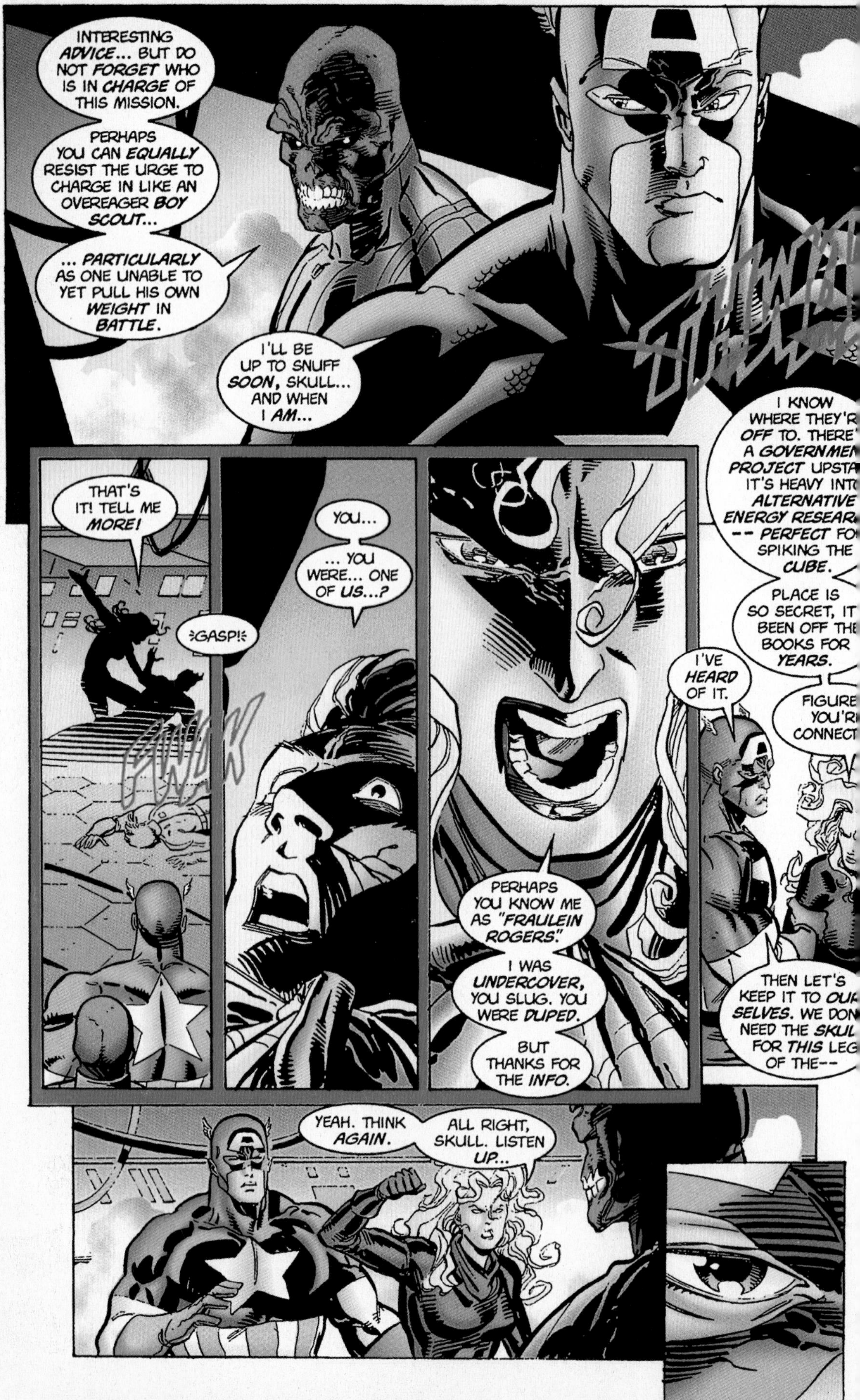

INTERESTING ADVICE... BUT DO NOT FORGET WHO IS IN CHARGE OF THIS MISSION.
PERHAPS YOU CAN EQUALLY RESIST THE URGE TO CHARGE IN LIKE AN OVEREAGER BOY SCOUT...
... PARTICULARLY AS ONE UNABLE TO YET PULL HIS OWN WEIGHT IN BATTLE.
I'LL BE UP TO SNUFF SOON, SKULL... AND WHEN I AM...
THAT'S IT! TELL ME MORE!
GASP!
YOU...
... YOU WERE... ONE OF US...?
PERHAPS YOU KNOW ME AS "FRAULEIN ROGERS."
I WAS UNDERCOVER, YOU SLUG. YOU WERE DUPED.
BUT THANKS FOR THE INFO.
I KNOW WHERE THEY'R OFF TO. THERE' A GOVERNMEN PROJECT UPSTA IT'S HEAVY INT ALTERNATIVE ENERGY RESEAR -- PERFECT FO SPIKING THE CUBE.
PLACE IS SO SECRET, IT BEEN OFF TH BOOKS FOR YEARS.
I'VE HEARD OF IT.
FIGURE YOU'R CONNECT
THEN LET'S KEEP IT TO OU SELVES. WE DON NEED THE SKUL FOR THIS LEG OF THE--
YEAH. THINK AGAIN.
ALL RIGHT, SKULL. LISTEN UP...

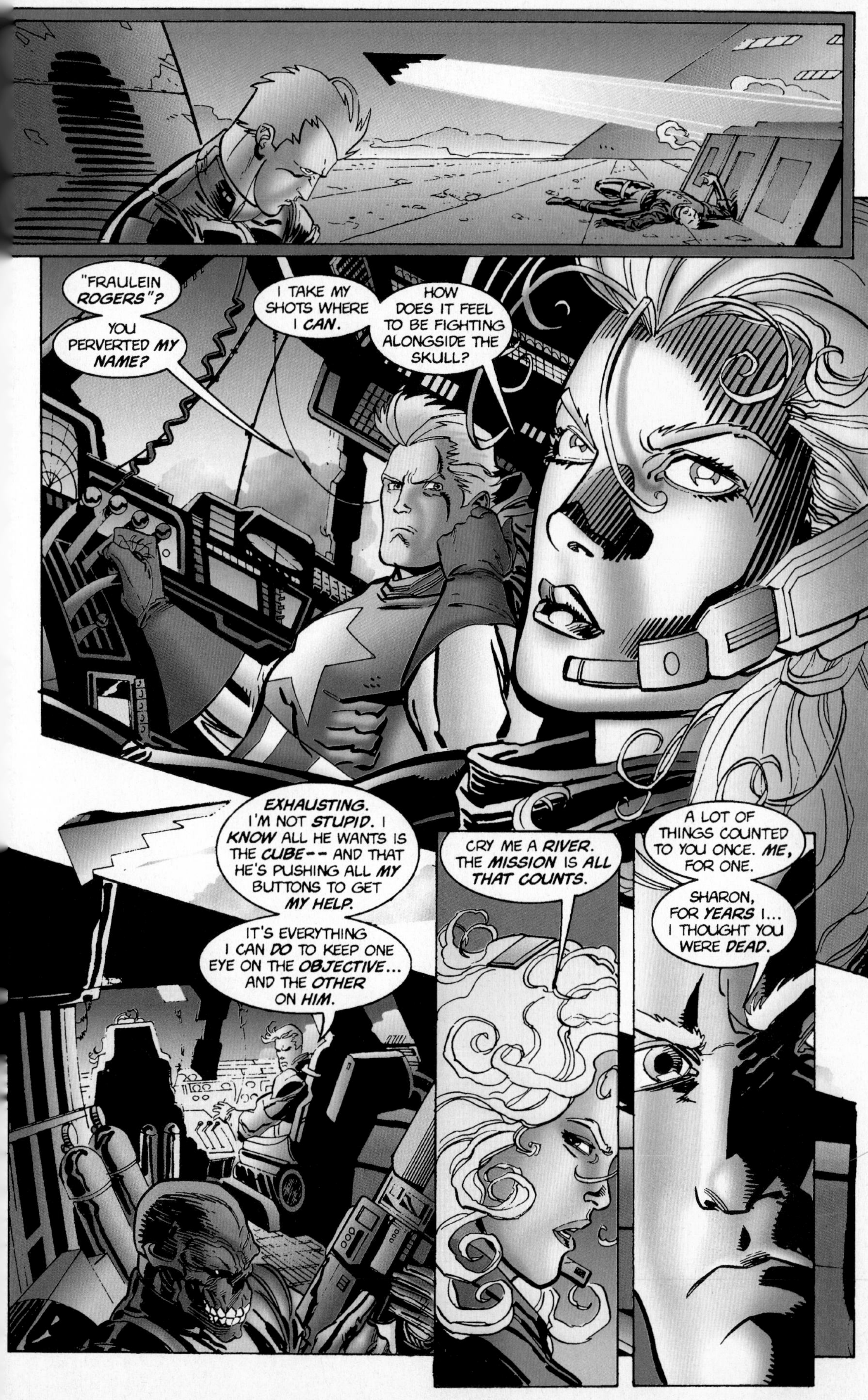
"FRAULEIN ROGERS"? YOU PERVERTED MY NAME?
I TAKE MY SHOTS WHERE I CAN.
HOW DOES IT FEEL TO BE FIGHTING ALONGSIDE THE SKULL?
EXHAUSTING. I'M NOT STUPID. I KNOW ALL HE WANTS IS THE CUBE-- AND THAT HE'S PUSHING ALL MY BUTTONS TO GET MY HELP.
IT'S EVERYTHING I CAN DO TO KEEP ONE EYE ON THE OBJECTIVE... AND THE OTHER ON HIM.
CRY ME A RIVER. THE MISSION IS ALL THAT COUNTS.
A LOT OF THINGS COUNTED TO YOU ONCE. ME, FOR ONE.
SHARON, FOR YEARS I... I THOUGHT YOU WERE DEAD.

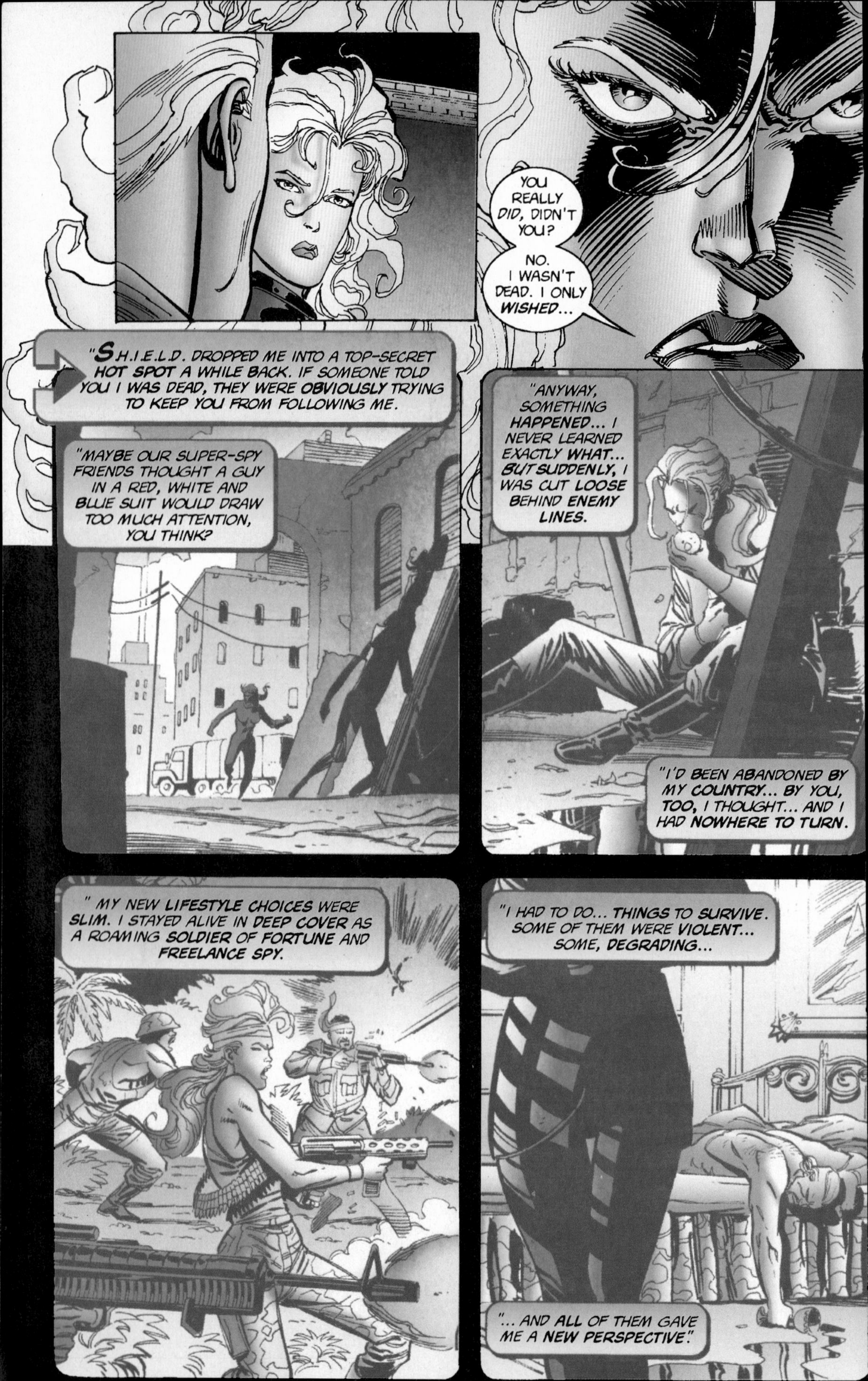

YOU REALLY DID, DIDN'T YOU?
NO. I WASN'T DEAD. I ONLY WISHED...
"S.H.I.E.L.D. DROPPED ME INTO A TOP-SECRET HOT SPOT A WHILE BACK. IF SOMEONE TOLD YOU I WAS DEAD, THEY WERE OBVIOUSLY TRYING TO KEEP YOU FROM FOLLOWING ME.
"MAYBE OUR SUPER-SPY FRIENDS THOUGHT A GUY IN A RED, WHITE AND BLUE SUIT WOULD DRAW TOO MUCH ATTENTION, YOU THINK?
"ANYWAY, SOMETHING HAPPENED... I NEVER LEARNED EXACTLY WHAT... BUT SUDDENLY, I WAS CUT LOOSE BEHIND ENEMY LINES.
"I'D BEEN ABANDONED BY MY COUNTRY... BY YOU, TOO, I THOUGHT... AND I HAD NOWHERE TO TURN.
" MY NEW LIFESTYLE CHOICES WERE SLIM. I STAYED ALIVE IN DEEP COVER AS A ROAMING SOLDIER OF FORTUNE AND FREELANCE SPY.
"I HAD TO DO... THINGS TO SURVIVE. SOME OF THEM WERE VIOLENT... SOME, DEGRADING...
"... AND ALL OF THEM GAVE ME A NEW PERSPECTIVE."

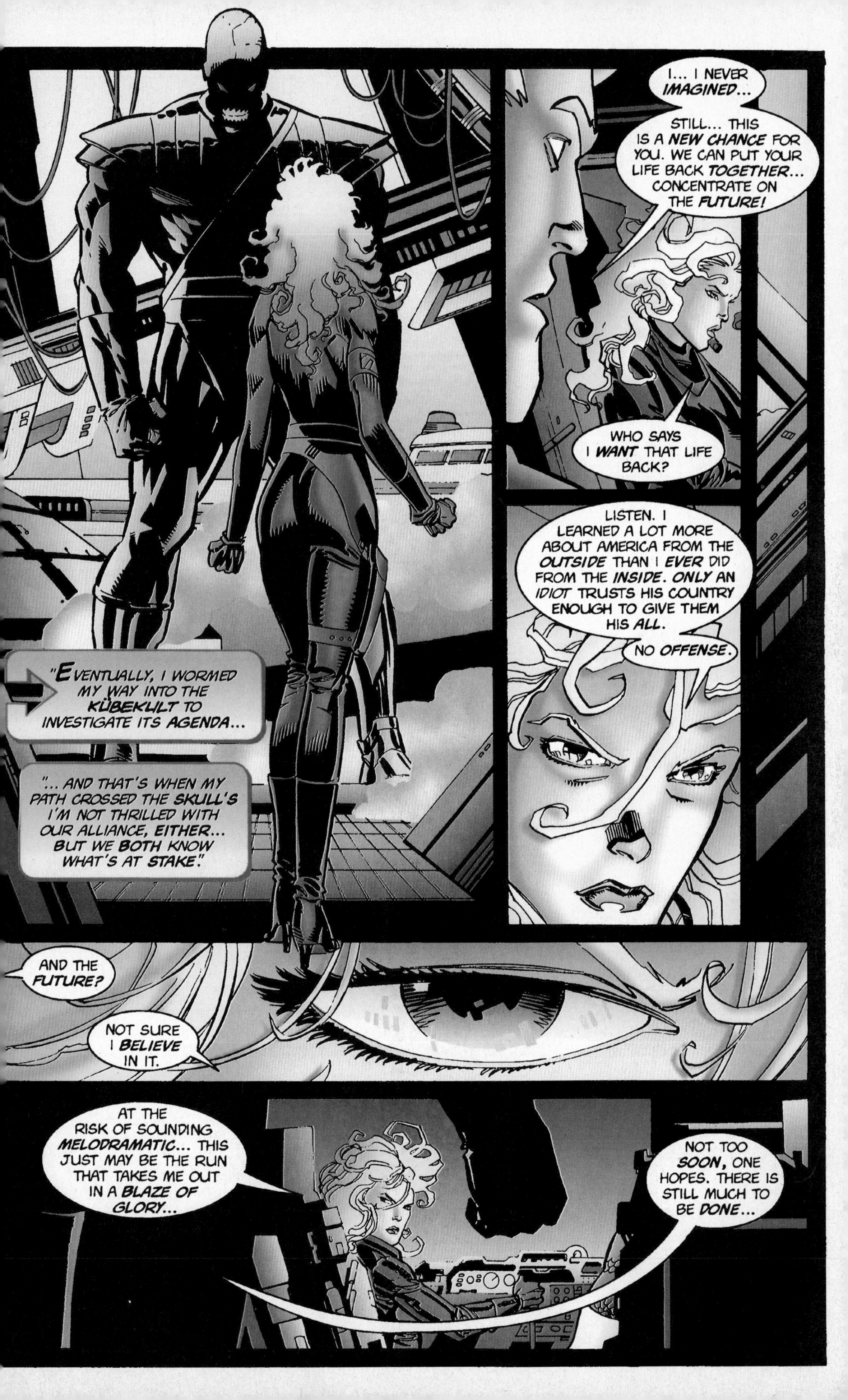
"EVENTUALLY, I WORMED MY WAY INTO THE KÜBEKULT TO INVESTIGATE ITS AGENDA...
"... AND THAT'S WHEN MY PATH CROSSED THE SKULL'S I'M NOT THRILLED WITH OUR ALLIANCE, EITHER... BUT WE BOTH KNOW WHAT'S AT STAKE."
I... I NEVER IMAGINED...
STILL... THIS IS A NEW CHANCE FOR YOU. WE CAN PUT YOUR LIFE BACK TOGETHER... CONCENTRATE ON THE FUTURE!
WHO SAYS I WANT THAT LIFE BACK?
LISTEN. I LEARNED A LOT MORE ABOUT AMERICA FROM THE OUTSIDE THAN I EVER DID FROM THE INSIDE. ONLY AN IDIOT TRUSTS HIS COUNTRY ENOUGH TO GIVE THEM HIS ALL.
NO OFFENSE.
AND THE FUTURE?
NOT SURE I BELIEVE IN IT.
AT THE RISK OF SOUNDING MELODRAMATIC... THIS JUST MAY BE THE RUN THAT TAKES ME OUT IN A BLAZE OF GLORY...
NOT TOO SOON, ONE HOPES. THERE IS STILL MUCH TO BE DONE...

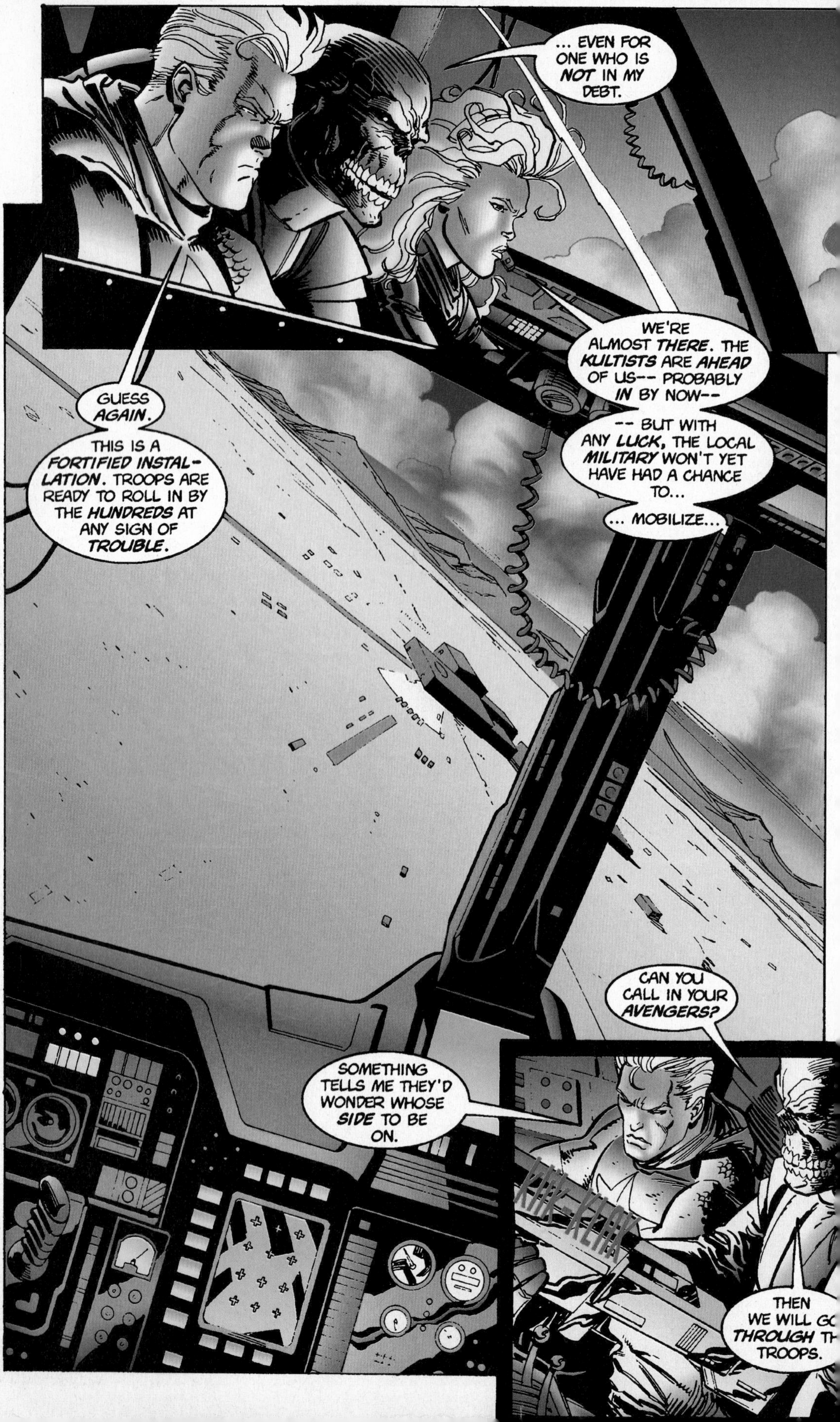
... EVEN FOR ONE WHO IS NOT IN MY DEBT.
GUESS AGAIN.
THIS IS A FORTIFIED INSTALLATION. TROOPS ARE READY TO ROLL IN BY THE HUNDREDS AT ANY SIGN OF TROUBLE.
WE'RE ALMOST THERE. THE KULTISTS ARE AHEAD OF US-- PROBABLY IN BY NOW--
-- BUT WITH ANY LUCK, THE LOCAL MILITARY WON'T YET HAVE HAD A CHANCE TO...
... MOBILIZE...
CAN YOU CALL IN YOUR AVENGERS?
SOMETHING TELLS ME THEY'D WONDER WHOSE SIDE TO BE ON.
KLIK-KLAK
THEN WE WILL GO THROUGH TH TROOPS.

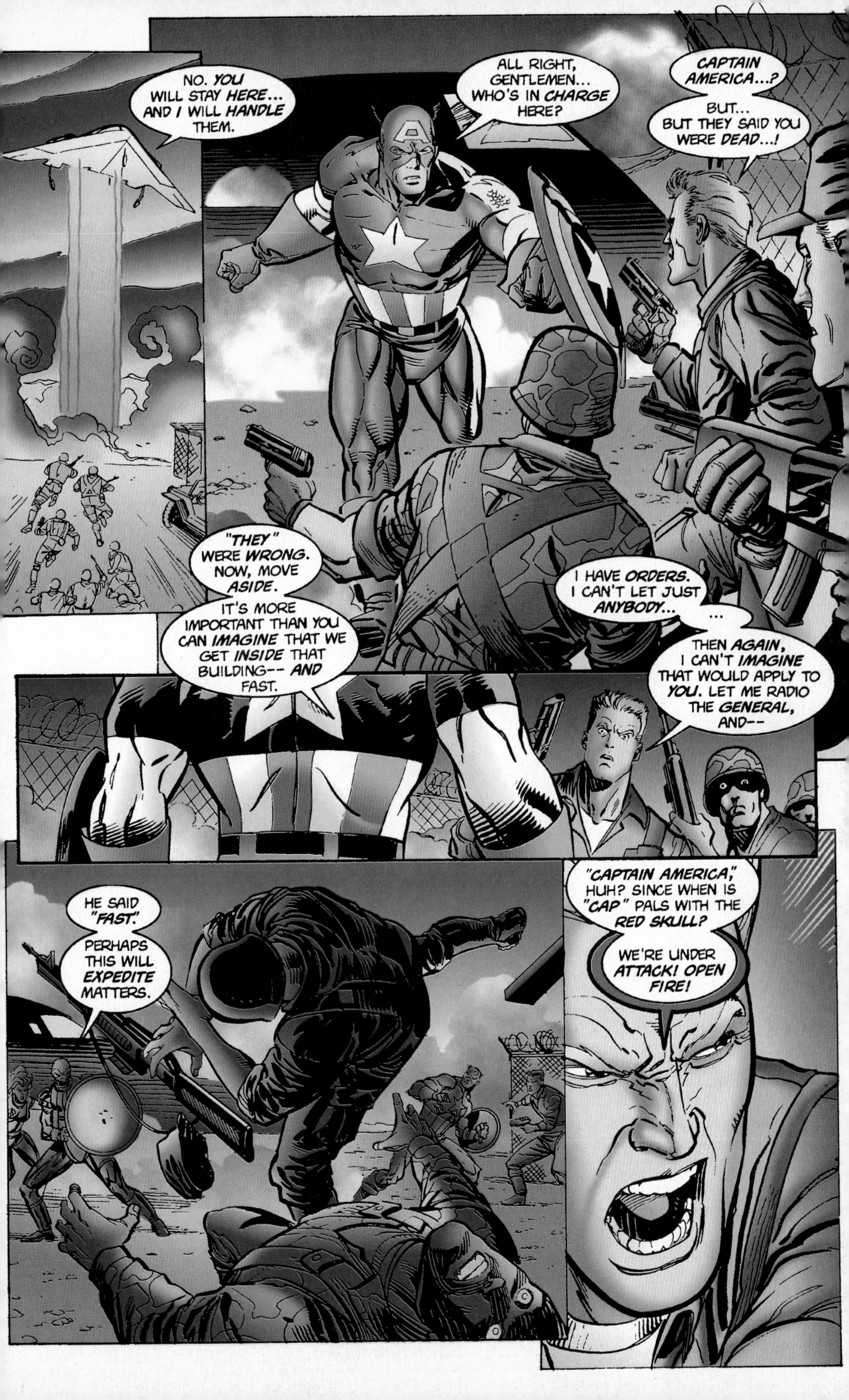
NO. YOU WILL STAY HERE... AND I WILL HANDLE THEM.
ALL RIGHT, GENTLEMEN... WHO'S IN CHARGE HERE?
CAPTAIN AMERICA...?
BUT... BUT THEY SAID YOU WERE DEAD...!
"THEY" WERE WRONG. NOW, MOVE ASIDE.
IT'S MORE IMPORTANT THAN YOU CAN IMAGINE THAT WE GET INSIDE THAT BUILDING-- AND FAST.
I HAVE ORDERS. I CAN'T LET JUST ANYBODY...
...
THEN AGAIN, I CAN'T IMAGINE THAT WOULD APPLY TO YOU. LET ME RADIO THE GENERAL, AND--
HE SAID "FAST."
PERHAPS THIS WILL EXPEDITE MATTERS.
"CAPTAIN AMERICA," HUH? SINCE WHEN IS "CAP" PALS WITH THE RED SKULL?
WE'RE UNDER ATTACK! OPEN FIRE!

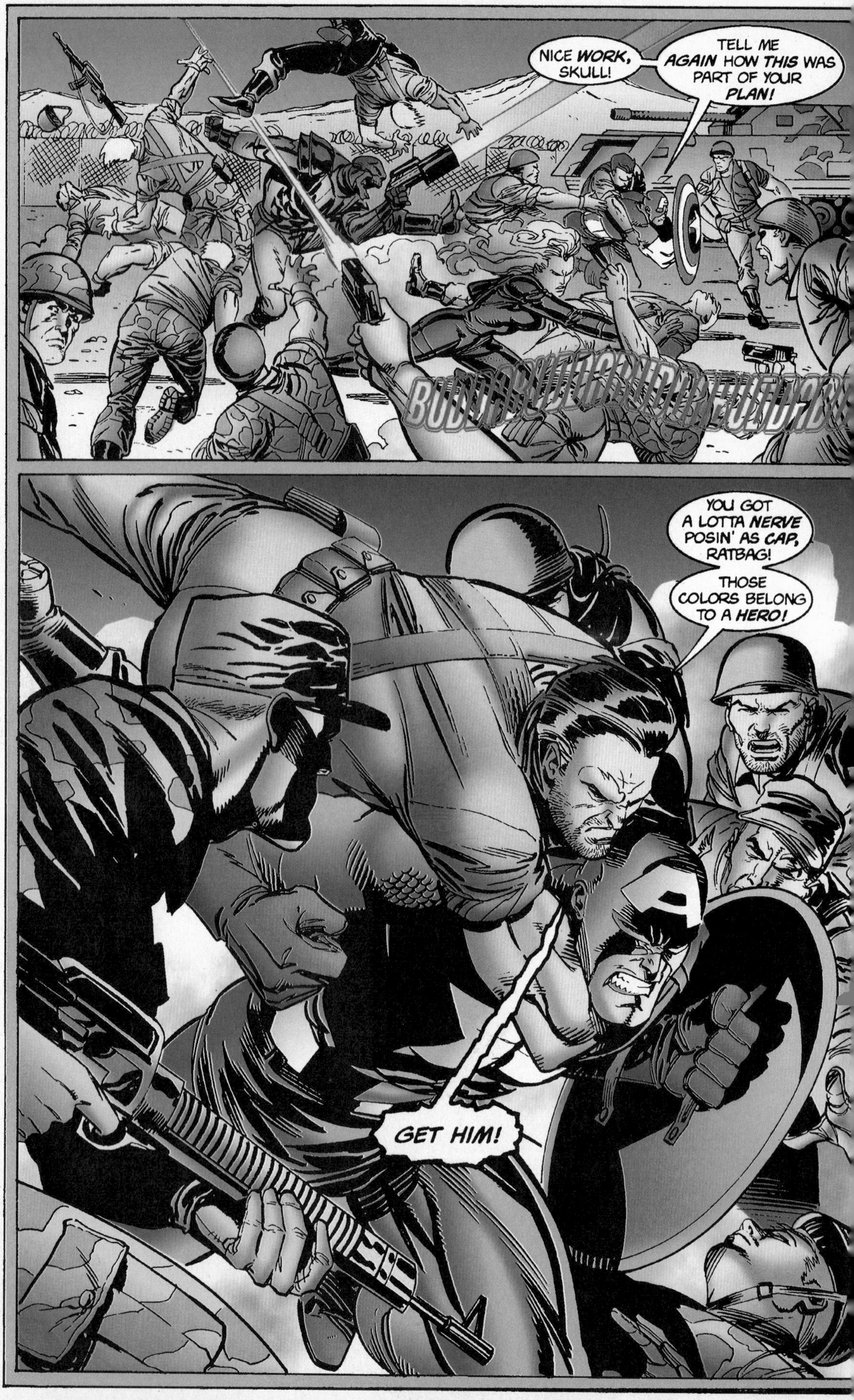
NICE WORK, SKULL!
TELL ME AGAIN HOW THIS WAS PART OF YOUR PLAN!
YOU GOT A LOTTA NERVE POSIN' AS CAP, RATBAG!
THOSE COLORS BELONG TO A HERO!
GET HIM!

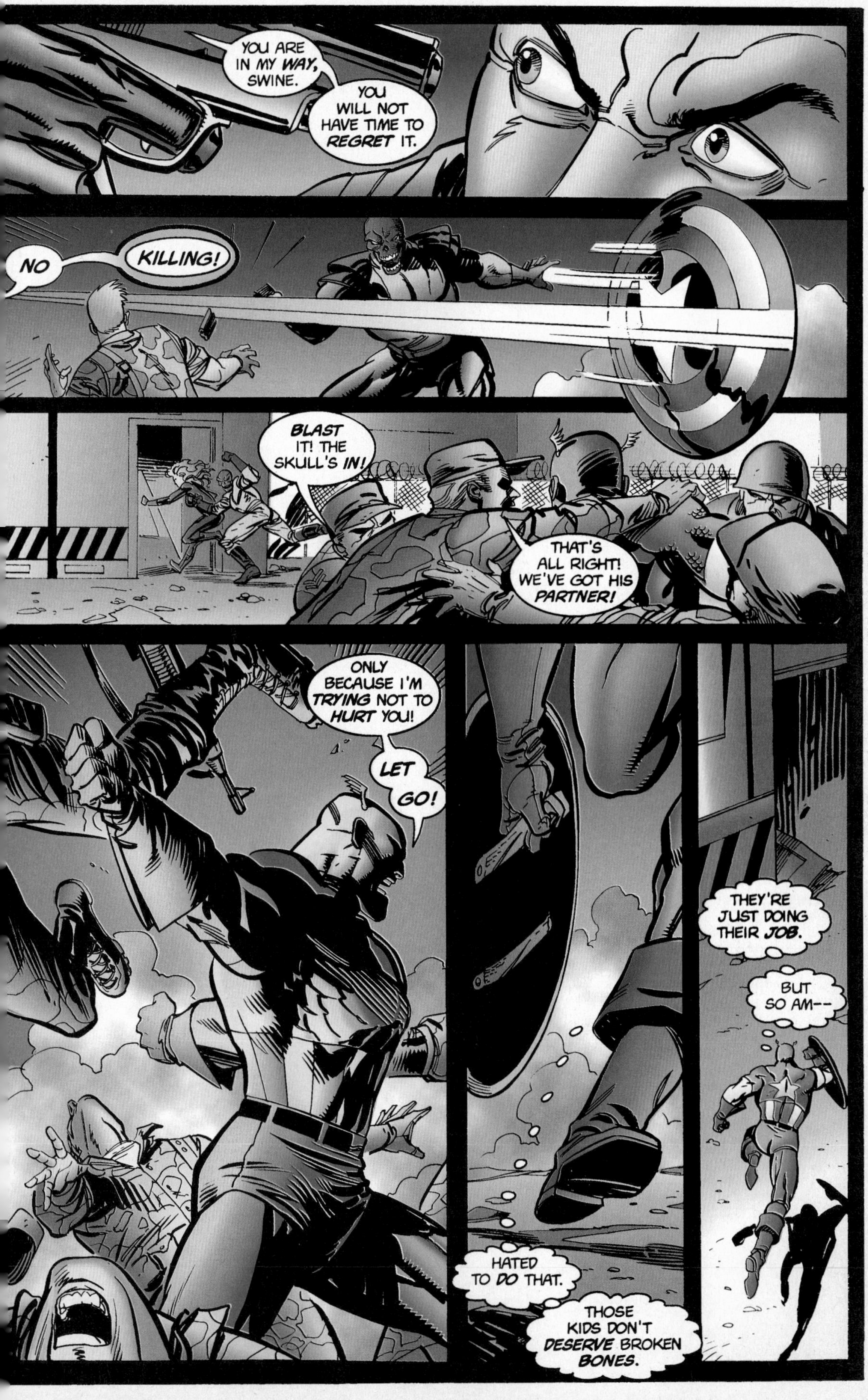
YOU ARE IN MY WAY, SWINE.
YOU WILL NOT HAVE TIME TO REGRET IT.
NO
KILLING!
BLAST IT! THE SKULL'S IN!
THAT'S ALL RIGHT! WE'VE GOT HIS PARTNER!
ONLY BECAUSE I'M TRYING NOT TO HURT YOU!
LET GO!
HATED TO DO THAT.
THOSE KIDS DON'T DESERVE BROKEN BONES.
THEY'RE JUST DOING THEIR JOB.
BUT SO AM--

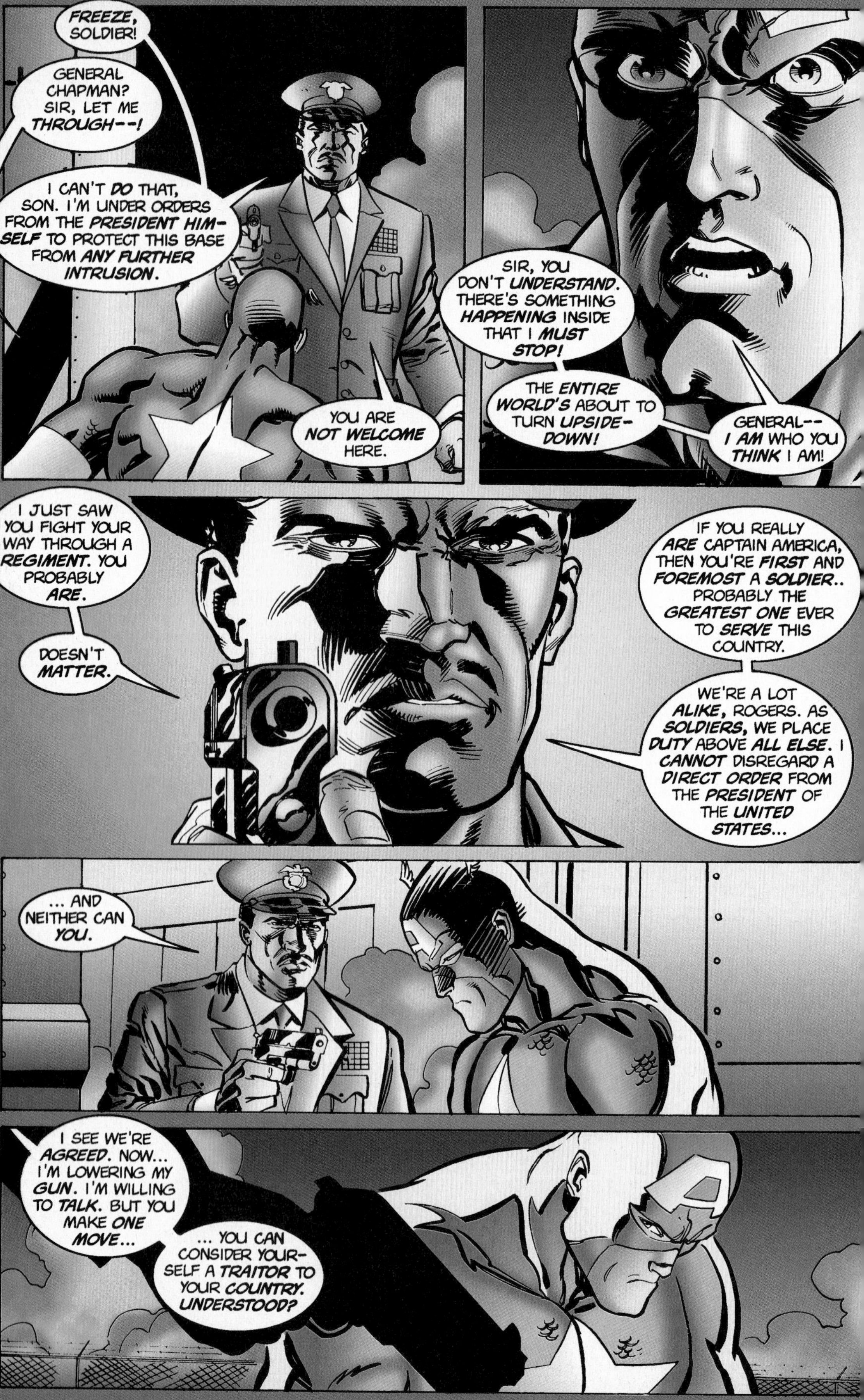
FREEZE, SOLDIER!
GENERAL CHAPMAN? SIR, LET ME THROUGH--!
I CAN'T DO THAT, SON. I'M UNDER ORDERS FROM THE PRESIDENT HIMSELF TO PROTECT THIS BASE FROM ANY FURTHER INTRUSION.
YOU ARE NOT WELCOME HERE.
SIR, YOU DON'T UNDERSTAND. THERE'S SOMETHING HAPPENING INSIDE THAT I MUST STOP!
THE ENTIRE WORLD'S ABOUT TO TURN UPSIDE-DOWN!
GENERAL-- I AM WHO YOU THINK I AM!
I JUST SAW YOU FIGHT YOUR WAY THROUGH A REGIMENT. YOU PROBABLY ARE.
DOESN'T MATTER.
IF YOU REALLY ARE CAPTAIN AMERICA, THEN YOU'RE FIRST AND FOREMOST A SOLDIER.. PROBABLY THE GREATEST ONE EVER TO SERVE THIS COUNTRY.
WE'RE A LOT ALIKE, ROGERS. AS SOLDIERS, WE PLACE DUTY ABOVE ALL ELSE. I CANNOT DISREGARD A DIRECT ORDER FROM THE PRESIDENT OF THE UNITED STATES...
... AND NEITHER CAN YOU.
I SEE WE'RE AGREED. NOW... I'M LOWERING MY GUN. I'M WILLING TO TALK. BUT YOU MAKE ONE MOVE...
... YOU CAN CONSIDER YOURSELF A TRAITOR TO YOUR COUNTRY. UNDERSTOOD?

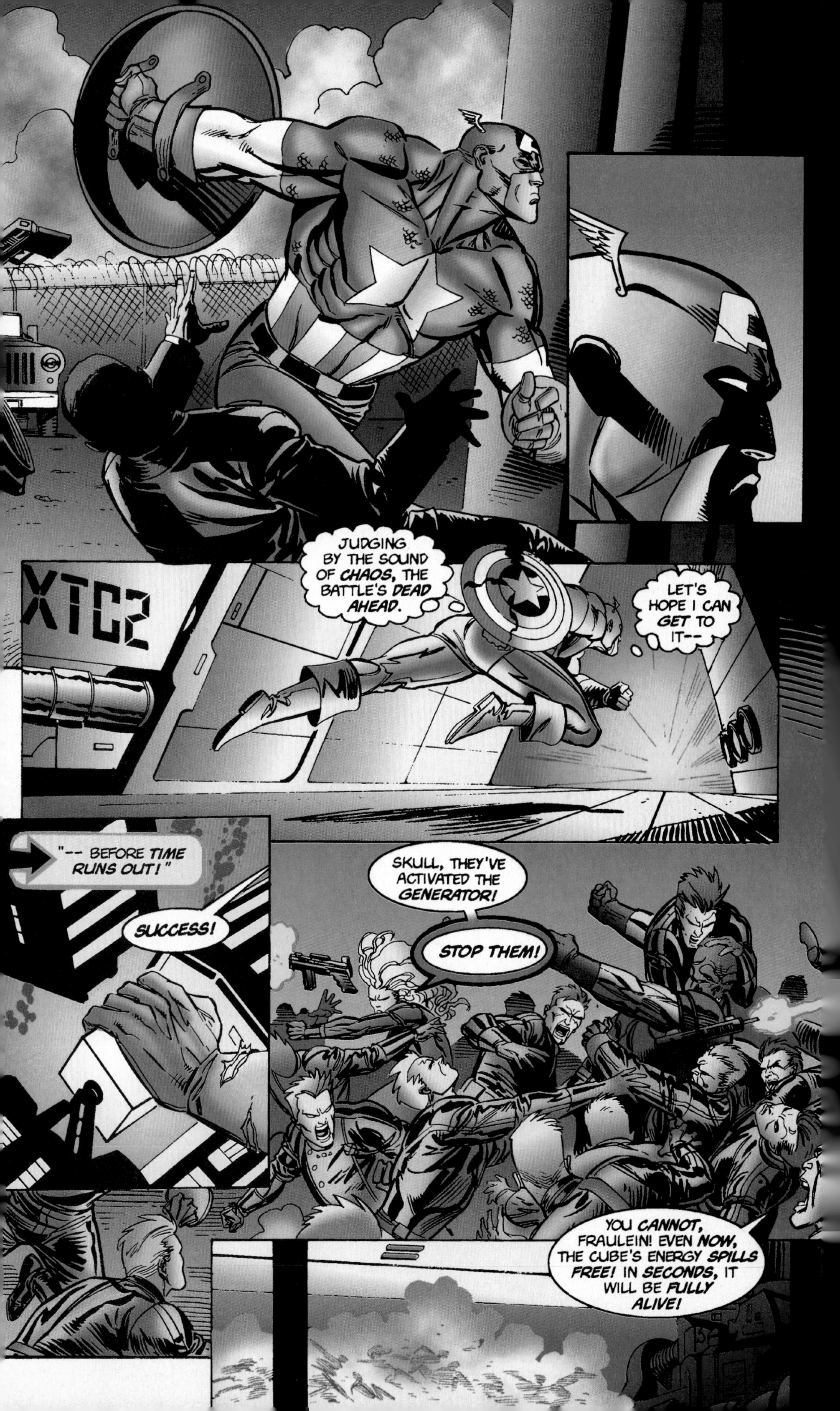
JUDGING BY THE SOUND OF CHAOS, THE BATTLE'S DEAD AHEAD.
LET'S HOPE I CAN GET TO IT--
XTC2
"-- BEFORE TIME RUNS OUT!"
SUCCESS!
SKULL, THEY'VE ACTIVATED THE GENERATOR!
STOP THEM!
YOU CANNOT, FRAULEIN! EVEN NOW, THE CUBE'S ENERGY SPILLS FREE! IN SECONDS, IT WILL BE FULLY ALIVE!

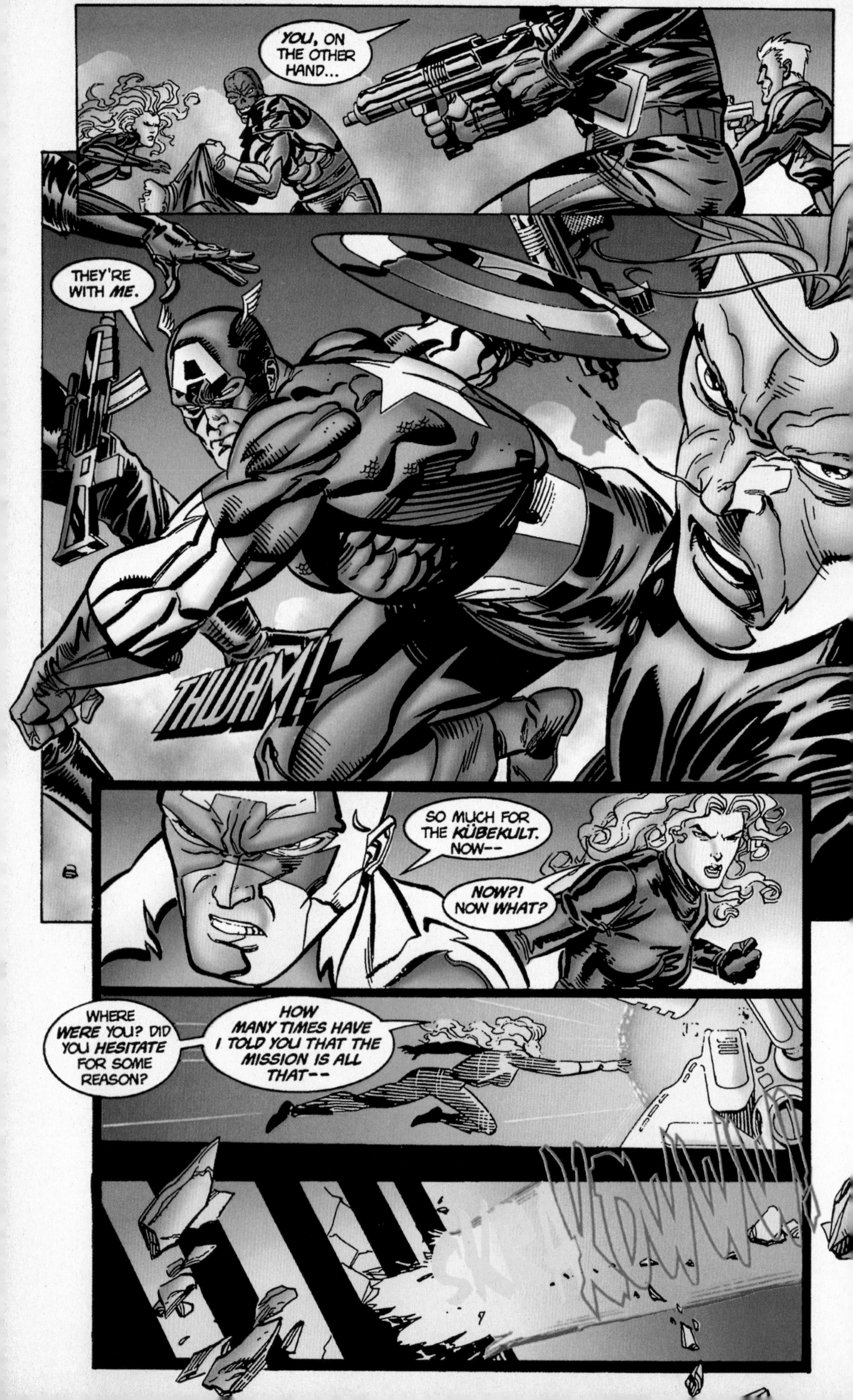

YOU, ON THE OTHER HAND...
THEY'RE WITH ME.
THWAM!
SO MUCH FOR THE KÜBEKULT. NOW--
NOW?! NOW WHAT?
WHERE WERE YOU? DID YOU HESITATE FOR SOME REASON?
HOW MANY TIMES HAVE I TOLD YOU THAT THE MISSION IS ALL THAT--

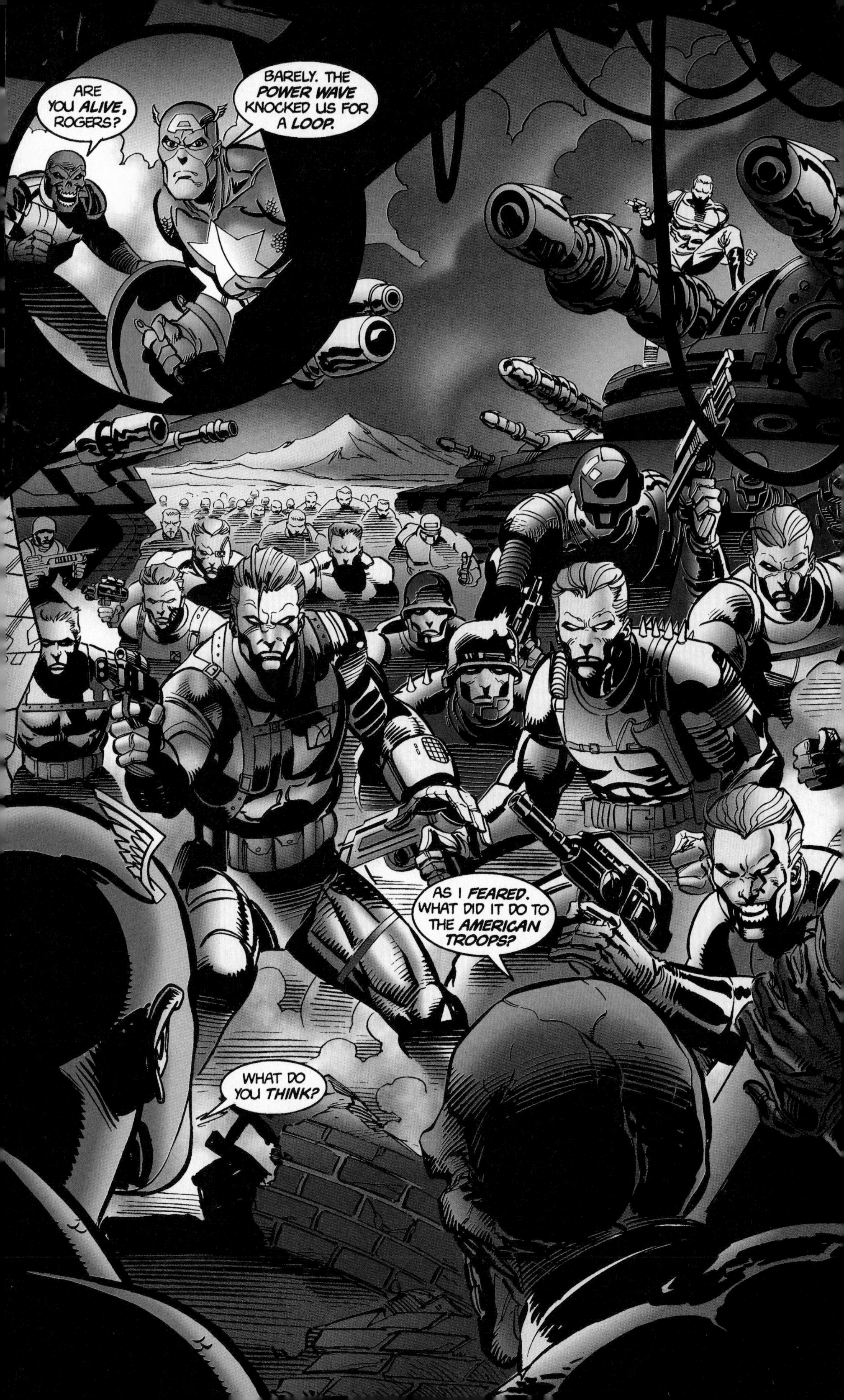
ARE YOU ALIVE, ROGERS?
BARELY. THE POWER WAVE KNOCKED US FOR A LOOP.
AS I FEARED. WHAT DID IT DO TO THE AMERICAN TROOPS?
WHAT DO YOU THINK?

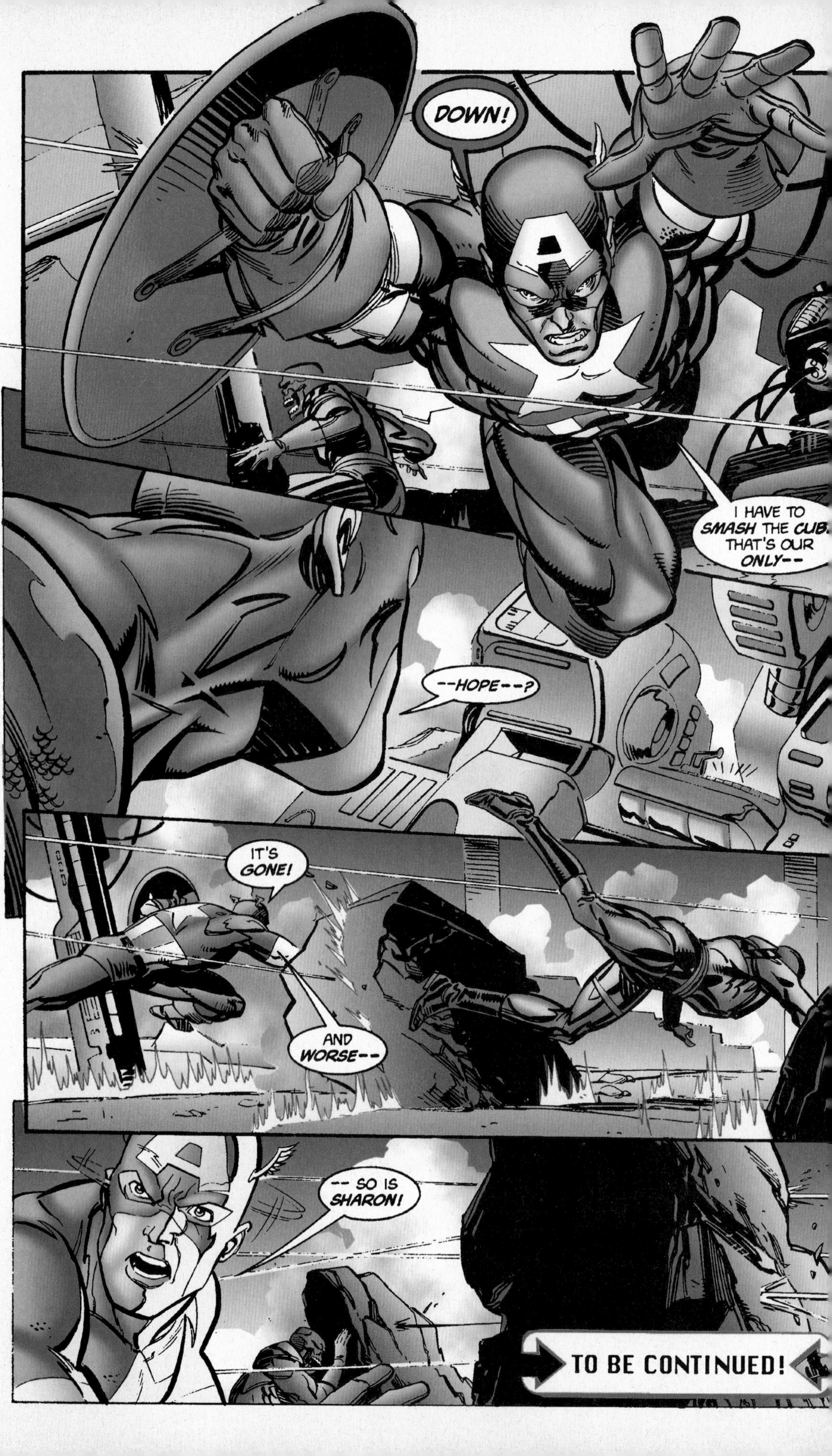
DOWN!
I HAVE TO SMASH THE CUB. THAT'S OUR ONLY--
--HOPE--?
IT'S GONE!
AND WORSE--
-- SO IS SHARON!
TO BE CONTINUED!

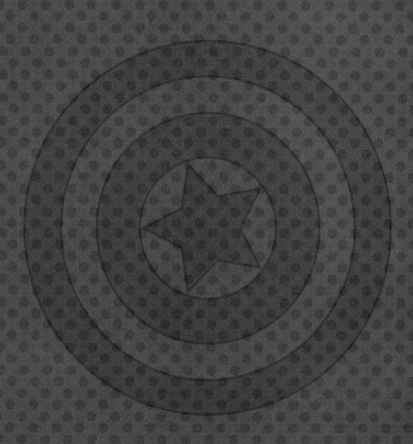

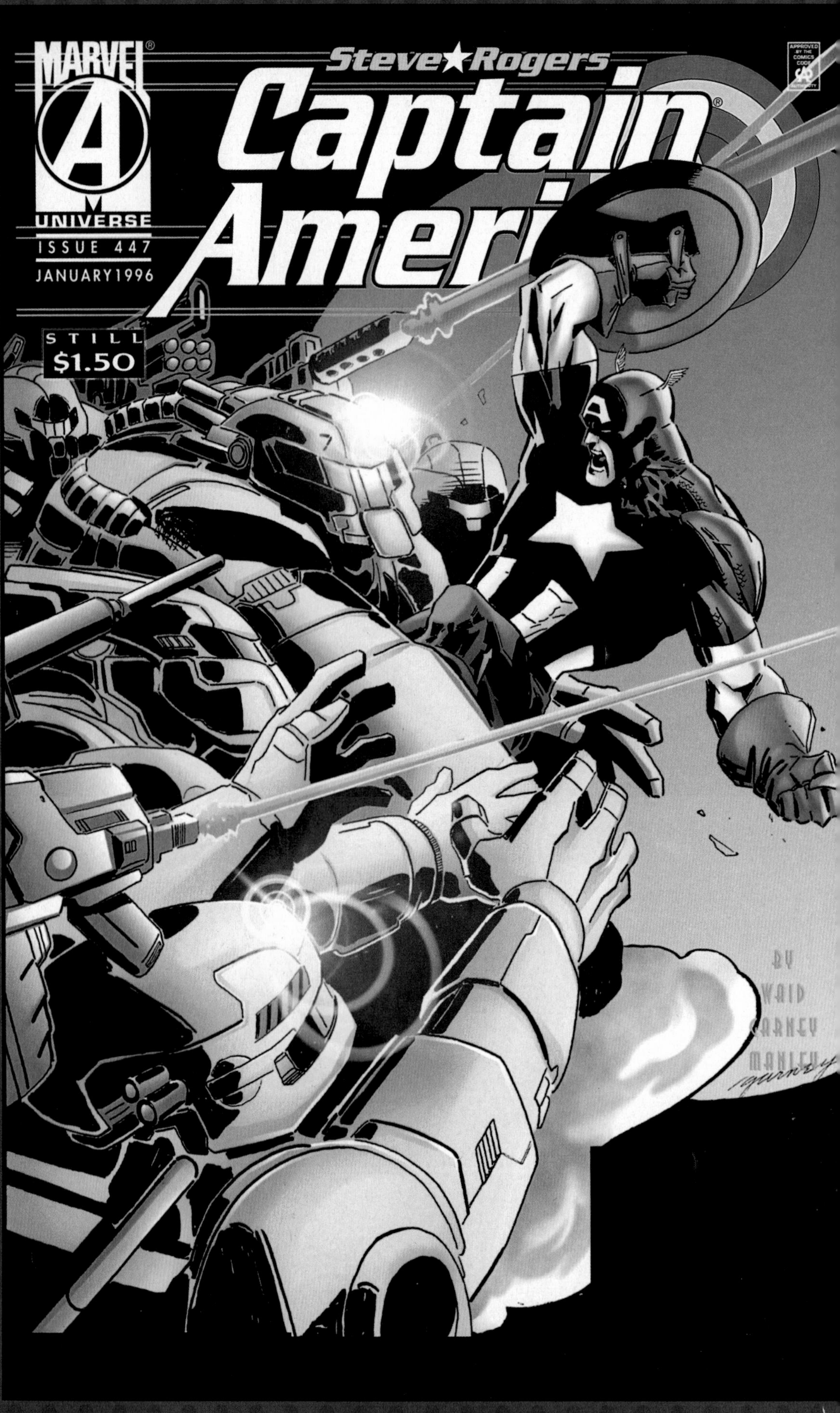
MARVEL
UNIVERSE
ISSUE 447
JANUARY 1996
STILL $1.50
Steve★Rogers
Captain America
BY
WAID
GARNEY
MANLEY

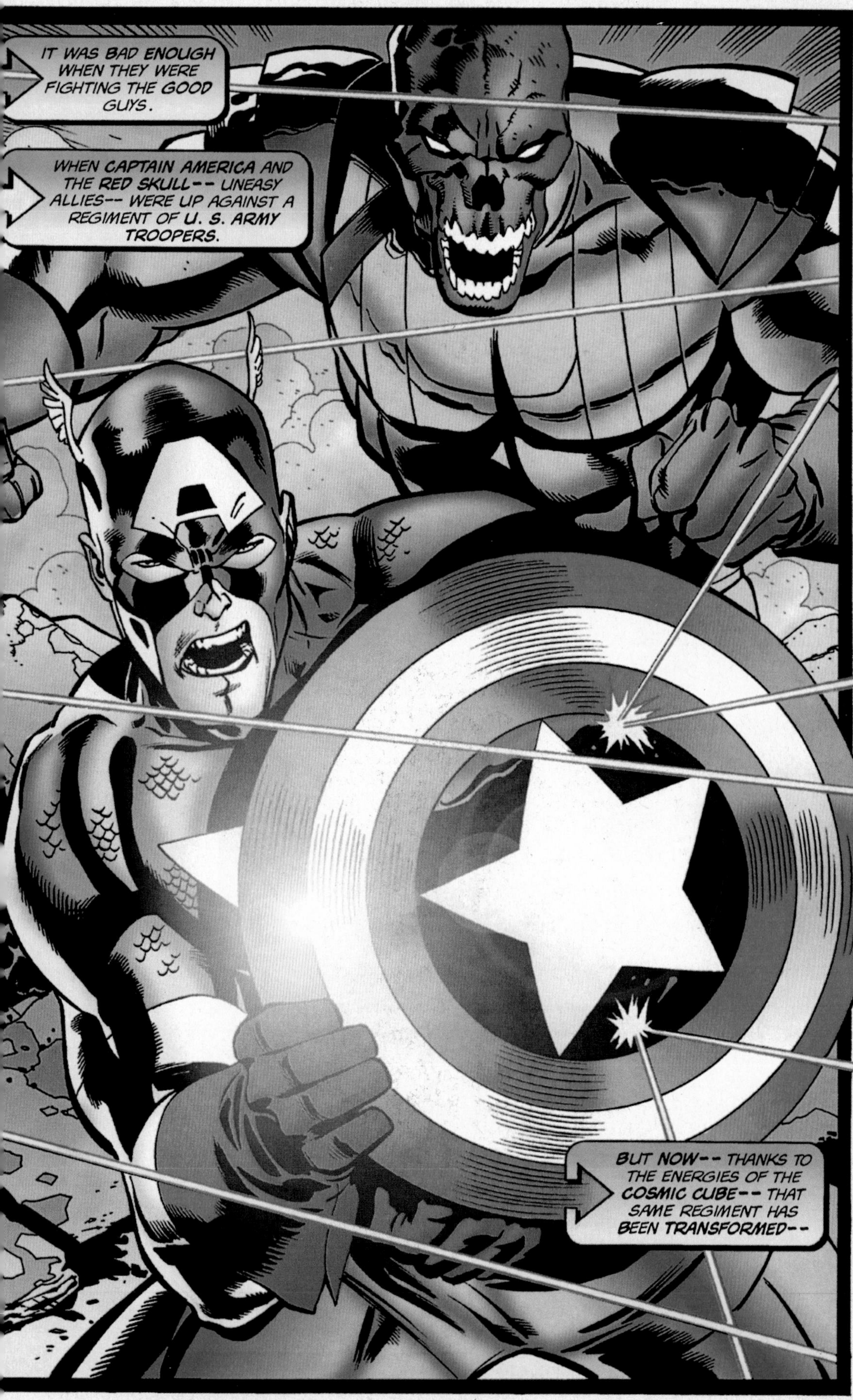
IT WAS BAD ENOUGH WHEN THEY WERE FIGHTING THE GOOD GUYS.
WHEN CAPTAIN AMERICA AND THE RED SKULL-- UNEASY ALLIES-- WERE UP AGAINST A REGIMENT OF U. S. ARMY TROOPERS.
BUT NOW-- THANKS TO THE ENERGIES OF THE COSMIC CUBE-- THAT SAME REGIMENT HAS BEEN TRANSFORMED--

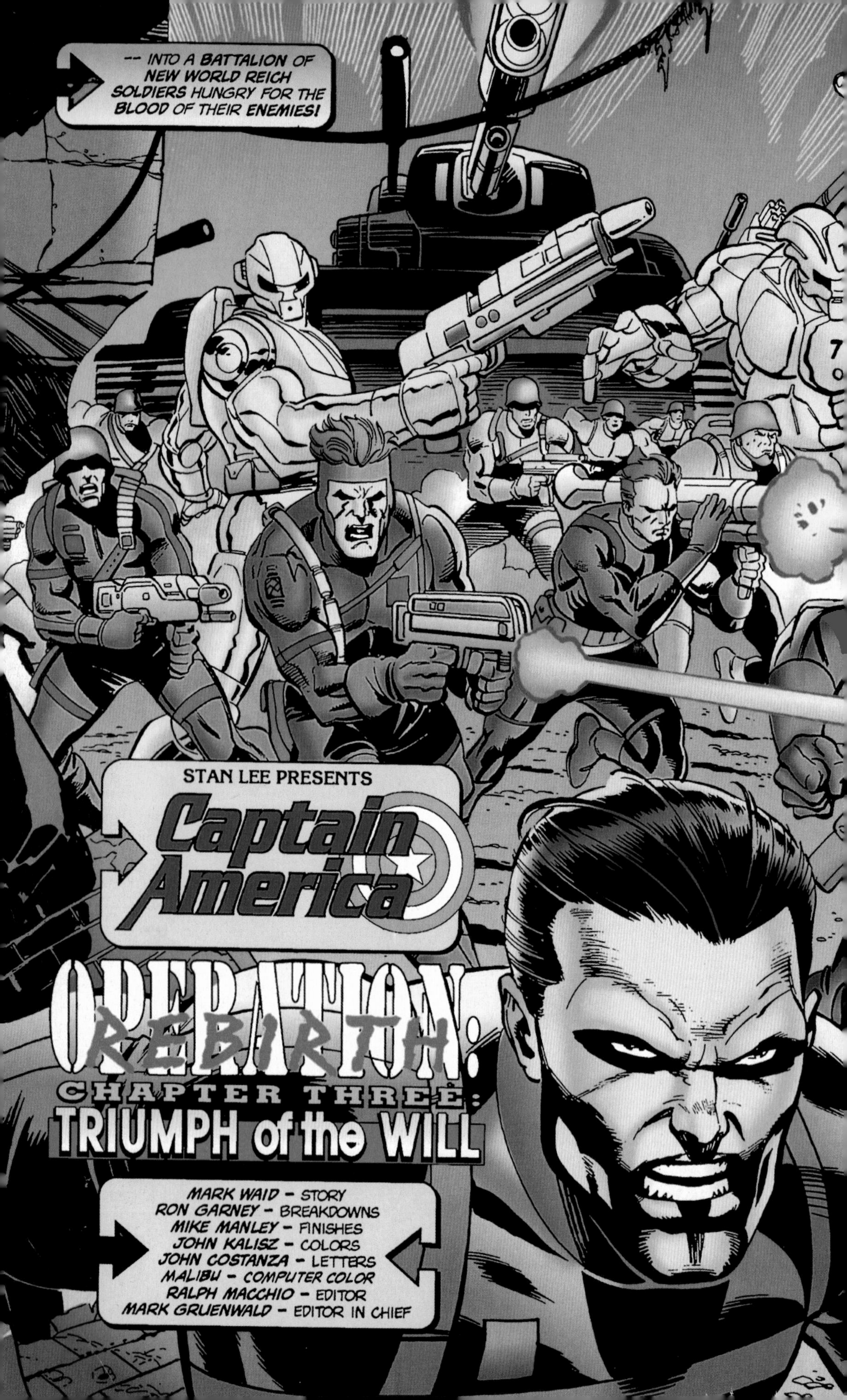
-- INTO A BATTALION OF NEW WORLD REICH SOLDIERS HUNGRY FOR THE BLOOD OF THEIR ENEMIES!
STAN LEE PRESENTS
Captain America
OPERATION: REBIRTH
CHAPTER THREE:
TRIUMPH of the WILL
MARK WAID - STORY
RON GARNEY - BREAKDOWNS
MIKE MANLEY - FINISHES
JOHN KALISZ - COLORS
JOHN COSTANZA - LETTERS
MALIBU - COMPUTER COLOR
RALPH MACCHIO - EDITOR
MARK GRUENWALD - EDITOR IN CHIEF

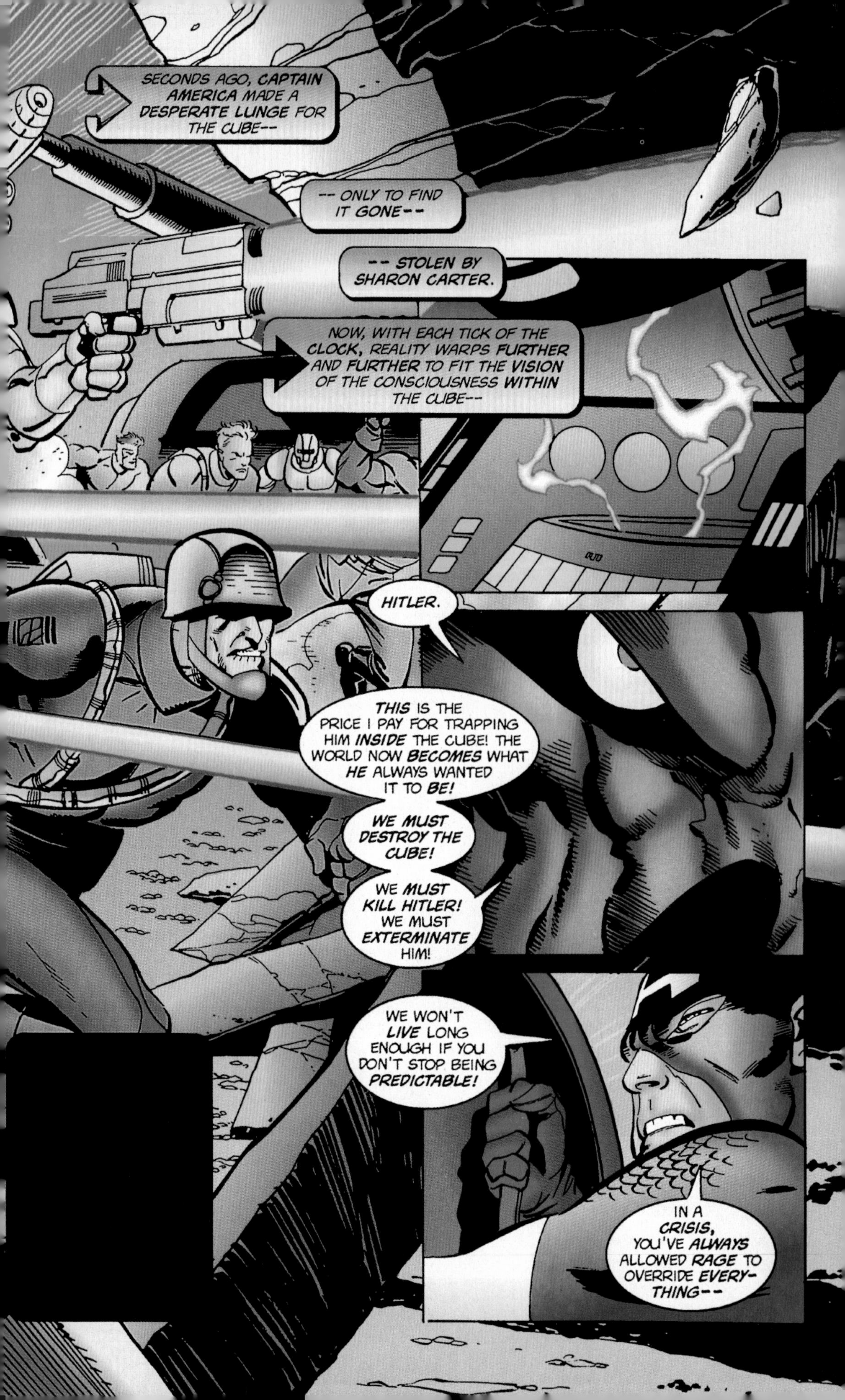

SECONDS AGO, CAPTAIN AMERICA MADE A DESPERATE LUNGE FOR THE CUBE--
-- ONLY TO FIND IT GONE--
-- STOLEN BY SHARON CARTER.
NOW, WITH EACH TICK OF THE CLOCK, REALITY WARPS FURTHER AND FURTHER TO FIT THE VISION OF THE CONSCIOUSNESS WITHIN THE CUBE--
HITLER.
THIS IS THE PRICE I PAY FOR TRAPPING HIM INSIDE THE CUBE! THE WORLD NOW BECOMES WHAT HE ALWAYS WANTED IT TO BE!
WE MUST DESTROY THE CUBE!
WE MUST KILL HITLER! WE MUST EXTERMINATE HIM!
WE WON'T LIVE LONG ENOUGH IF YOU DON'T STOP BEING PREDICTABLE!
IN A CRISIS, YOU'VE ALWAYS ALLOWED RAGE TO OVERRIDE EVERY-THING--

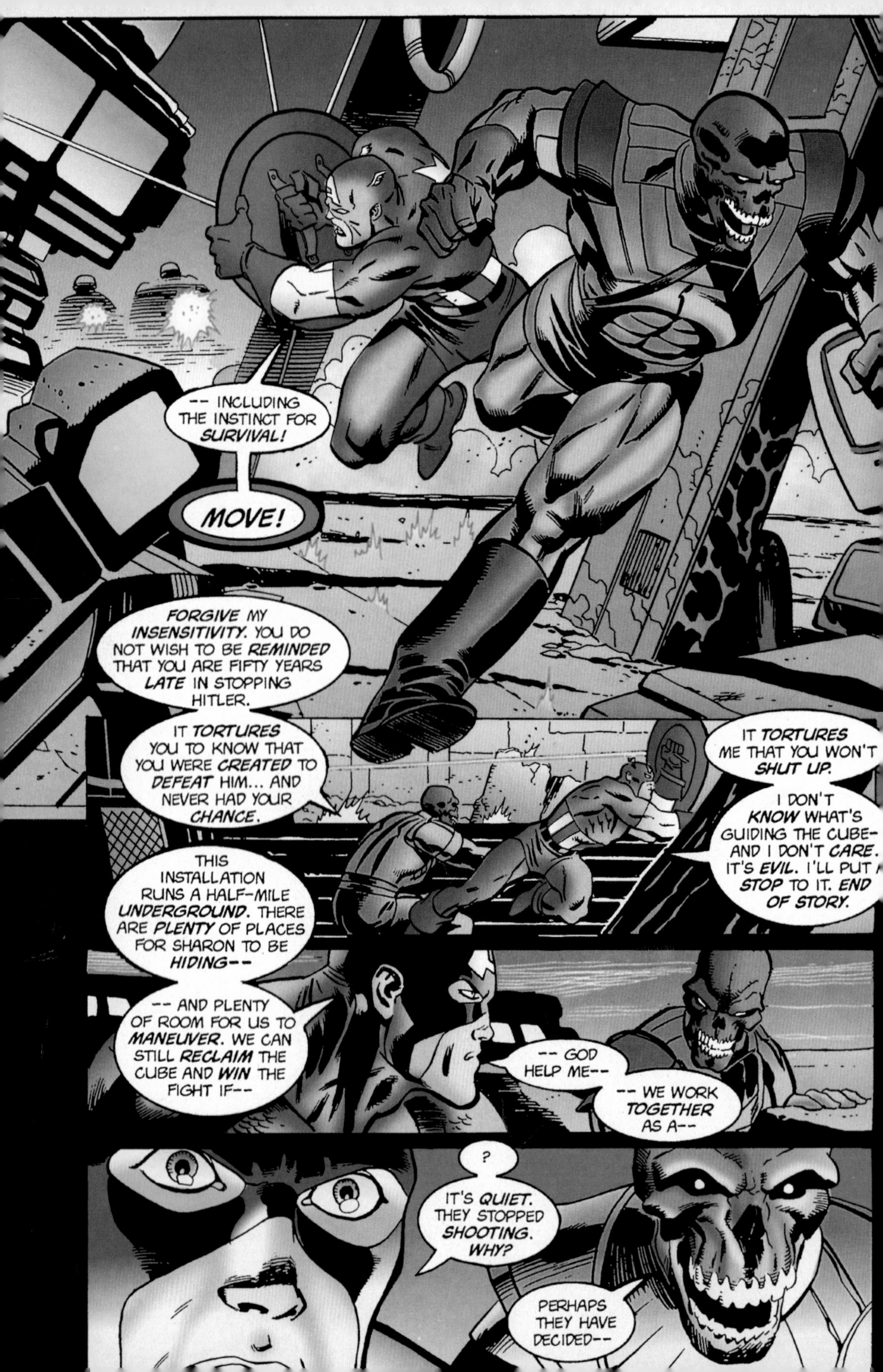
-- INCLUDING THE INSTINCT FOR SURVIVAL!
MOVE!
FORGIVE MY INSENSITIVITY. YOU DO NOT WISH TO BE REMINDED THAT YOU ARE FIFTY YEARS LATE IN STOPPING HITLER.
IT TORTURES YOU TO KNOW THAT YOU WERE CREATED TO DEFEAT HIM... AND NEVER HAD YOUR CHANCE.
IT TORTURES ME THAT YOU WON'T SHUT UP.
I DON'T KNOW WHAT'S GUIDING THE CUBE-- AND I DON'T CARE. IT'S EVIL. I'LL PUT A STOP TO IT. END OF STORY.
THIS INSTALLATION RUNS A HALF-MILE UNDERGROUND. THERE ARE PLENTY OF PLACES FOR SHARON TO BE HIDING--
-- AND PLENTY OF ROOM FOR US TO MANEUVER. WE CAN STILL RECLAIM THE CUBE AND WIN THE FIGHT IF--
-- GOD HELP ME--
-- WE WORK TOGETHER AS A--
?
IT'S QUIET. THEY STOPPED SHOOTING. WHY?
PERHAPS THEY HAVE DECIDED--

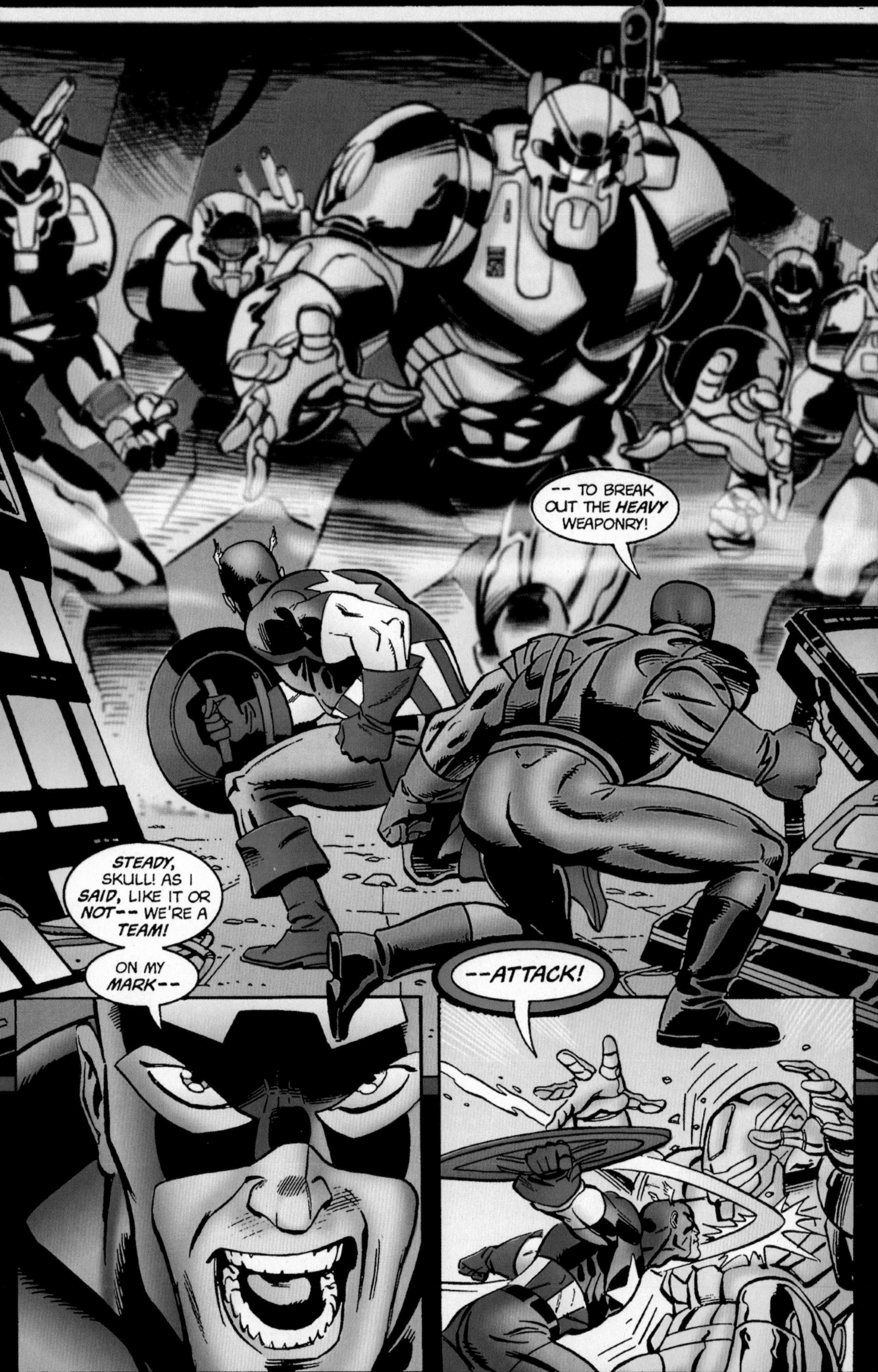

-- TO BREAK OUT THE HEAVY WEAPONRY!
STEADY, SKULL! AS I SAID, LIKE IT OR NOT-- WE'RE A TEAM!
ON MY MARK--
--ATTACK!

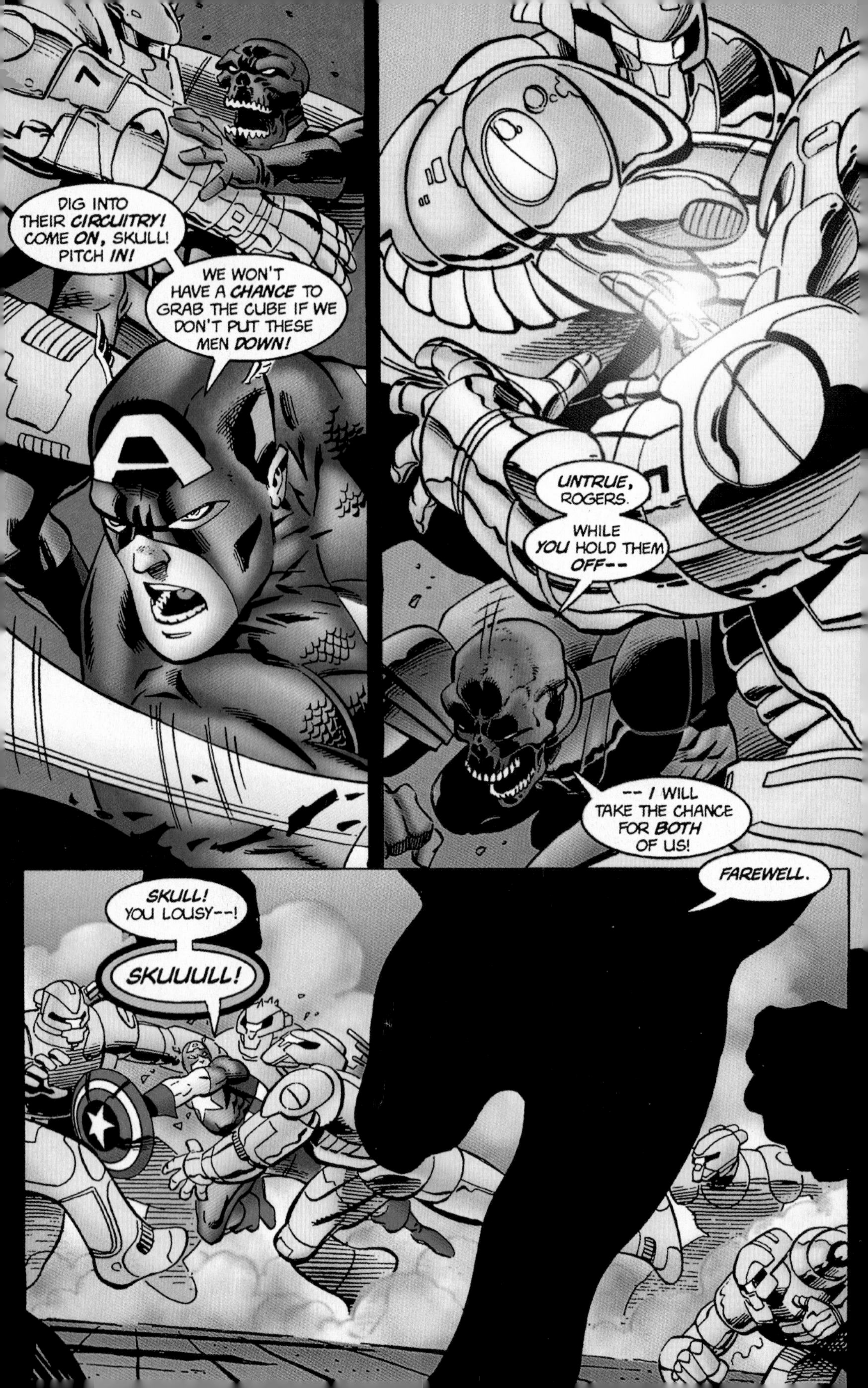
DIG INTO THEIR *CIRCUITRY!* COME *ON*, SKULL! PITCH *IN!*
WE WON'T HAVE A *CHANCE* TO GRAB THE CUBE IF WE DON'T PUT THESE MEN *DOWN!*
UNTRUE, ROGERS.
WHILE *YOU* HOLD THEM *OFF--*
-- *I* WILL TAKE THE CHANCE FOR *BOTH* OF US!
FAREWELL.
SKULL! YOU LOUSY--!
SKUUUULL!

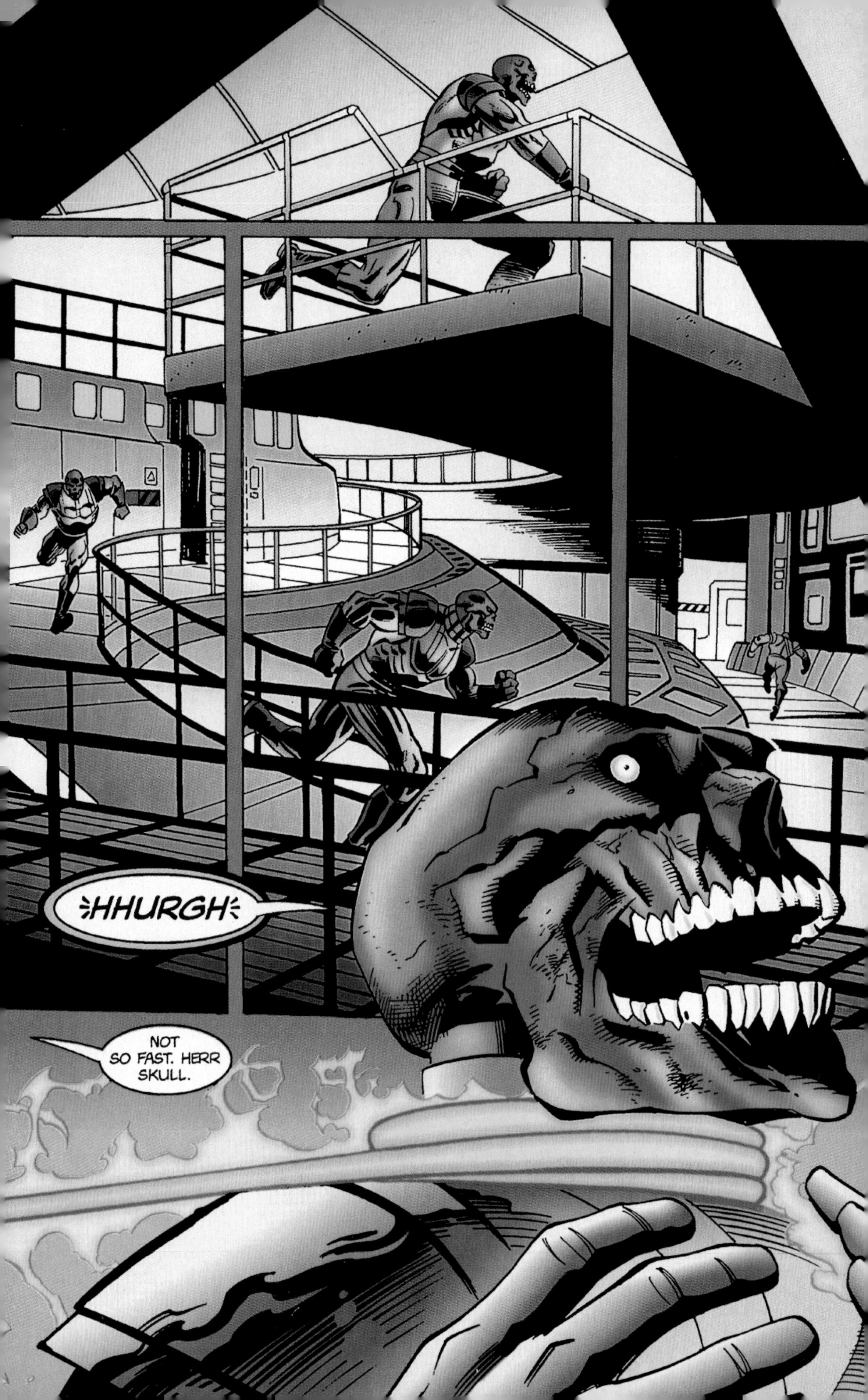
HHURGH
NOT SO FAST. HERR SKULL.

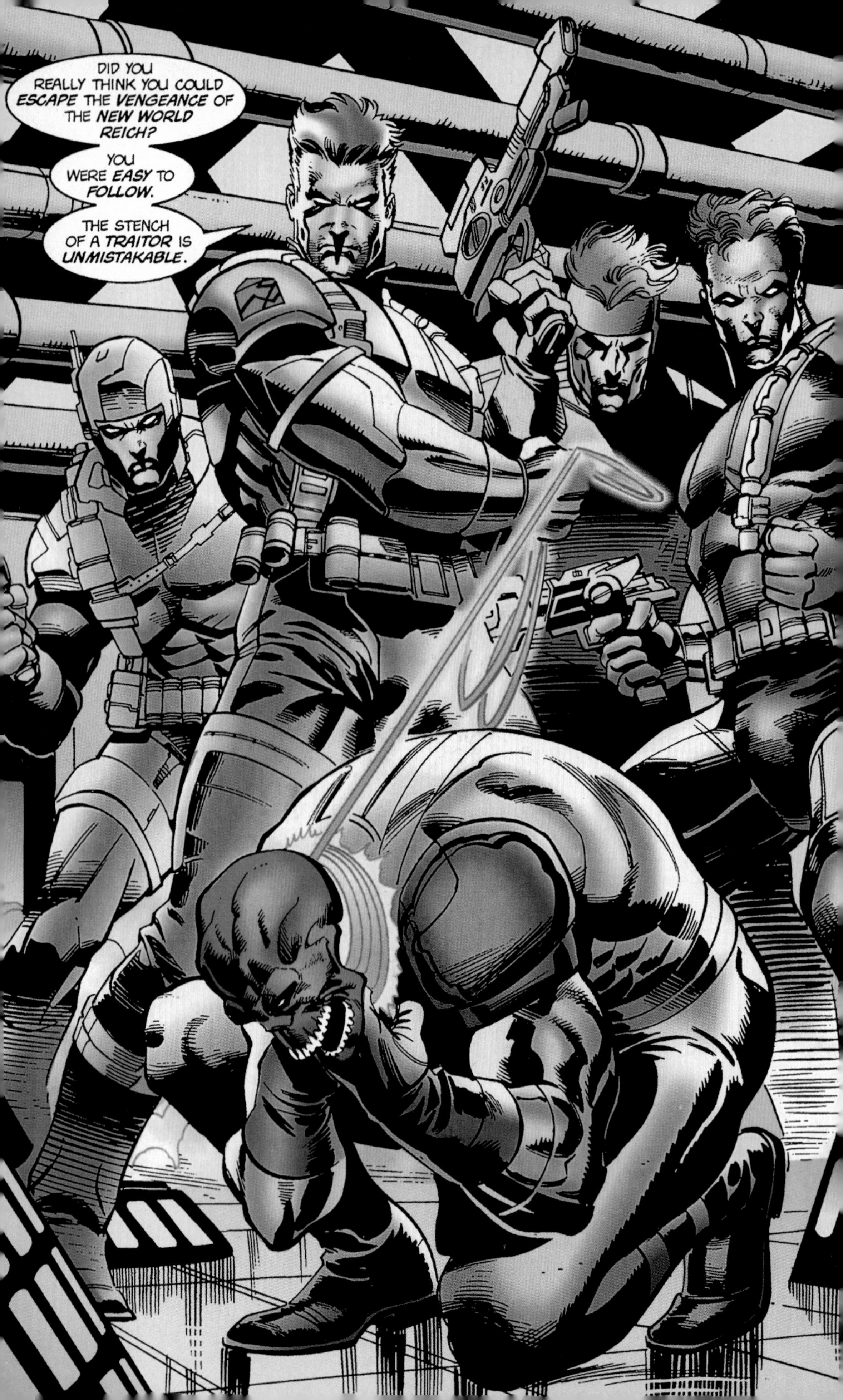

DID YOU REALLY THINK YOU COULD *ESCAPE* THE *VENGEANCE* OF THE *NEW WORLD REICH?*
YOU WERE *EASY* TO *FOLLOW.*
THE STENCH OF A *TRAITOR* IS *UNMISTAKABLE.*

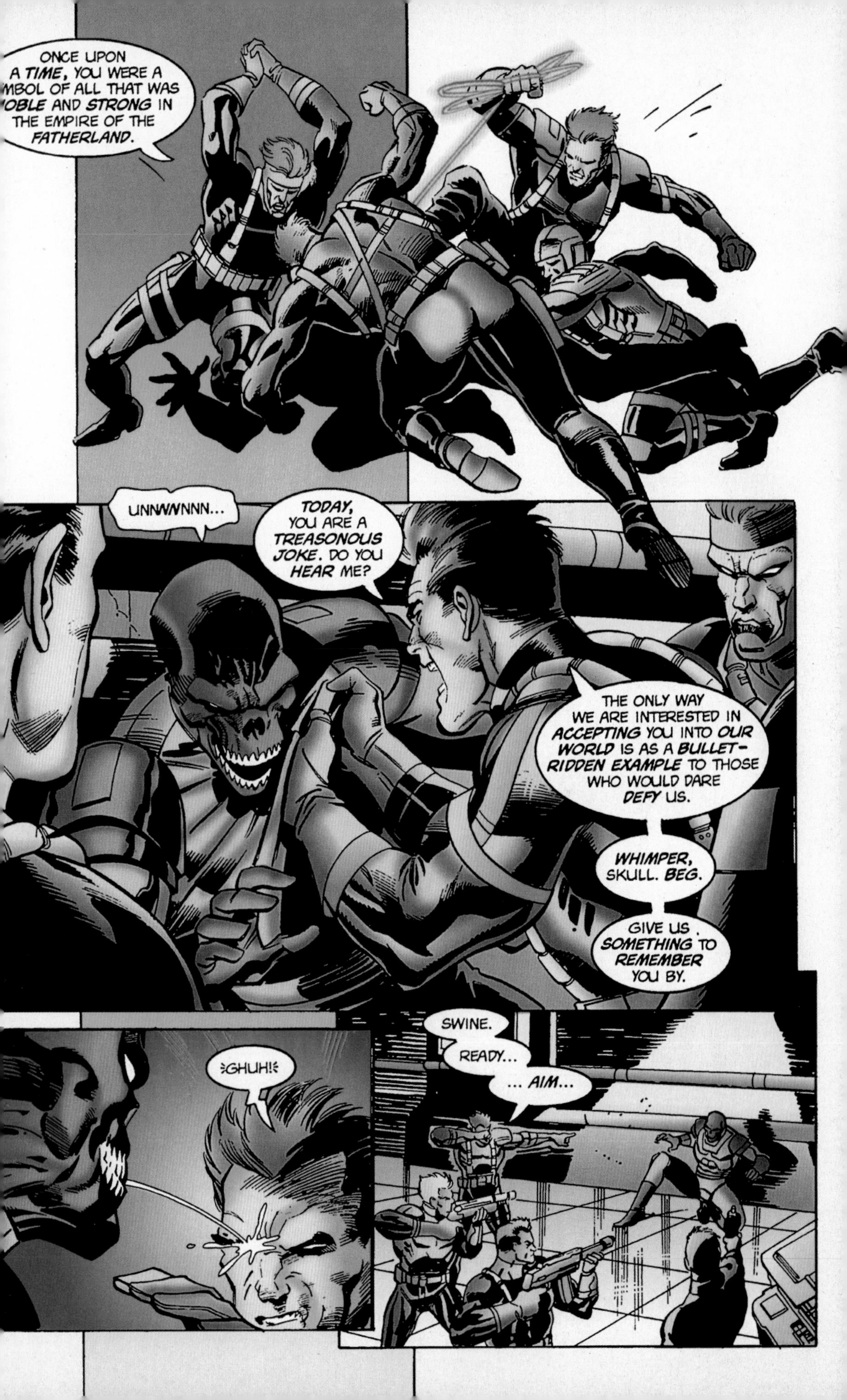
ONCE UPON A *TIME*, YOU WERE A MBOL OF ALL THAT WAS OBLE AND *STRONG* IN THE EMPIRE OF THE *FATHERLAND*.
UNNNNNNN...
TODAY, YOU ARE A *TREASONOUS JOKE*. DO YOU *HEAR* ME?
THE ONLY WAY WE ARE INTERESTED IN *ACCEPTING* YOU INTO *OUR WORLD* IS AS A *BULLET-RIDDEN EXAMPLE* TO THOSE WHO WOULD DARE *DEFY* US.
WHIMPER, SKULL. *BEG*.
GIVE US *SOMETHING* TO *REMEMBER* YOU BY.
GHUH!
SWINE.
READY...
... *AIM*...

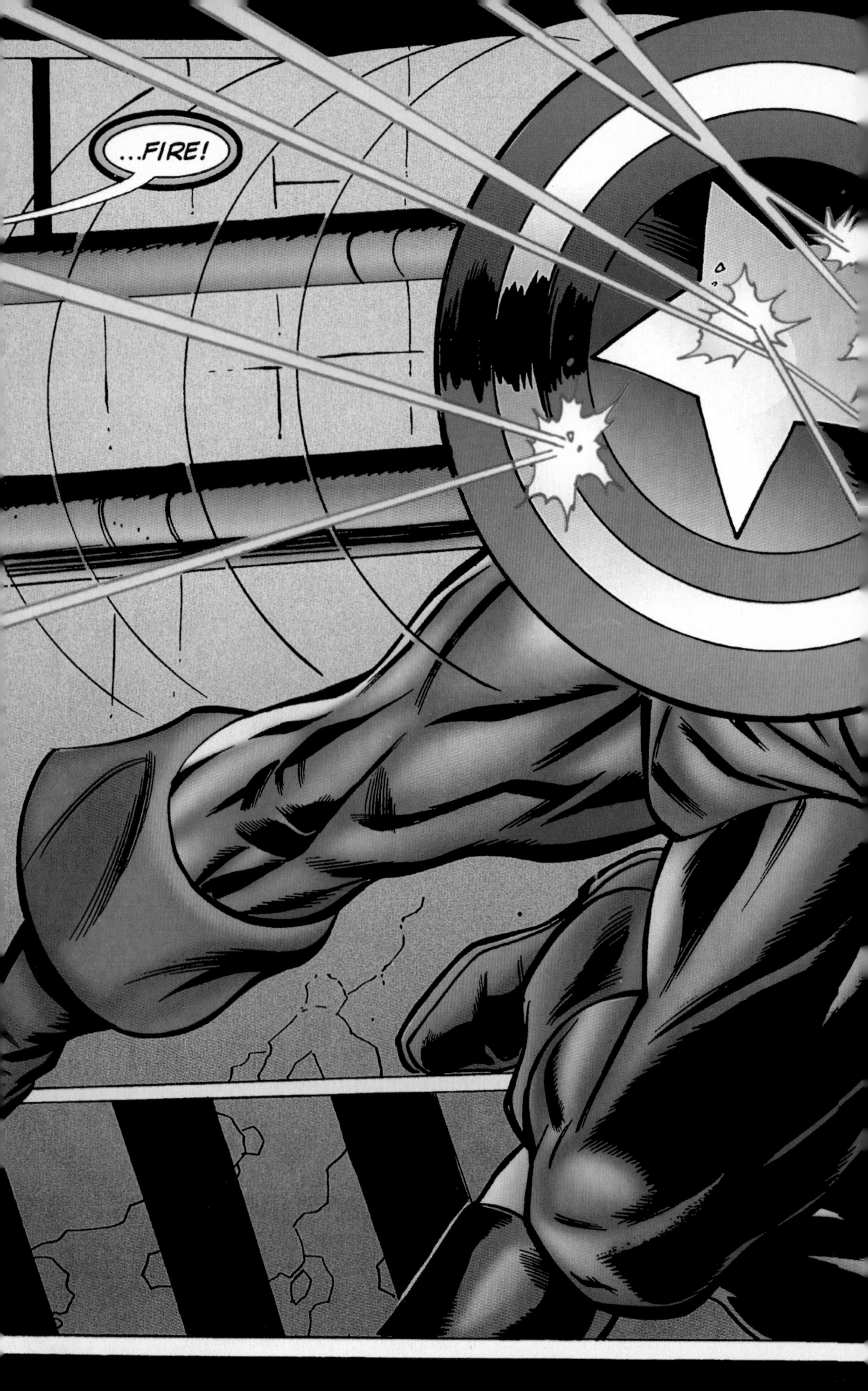
...FIRE!

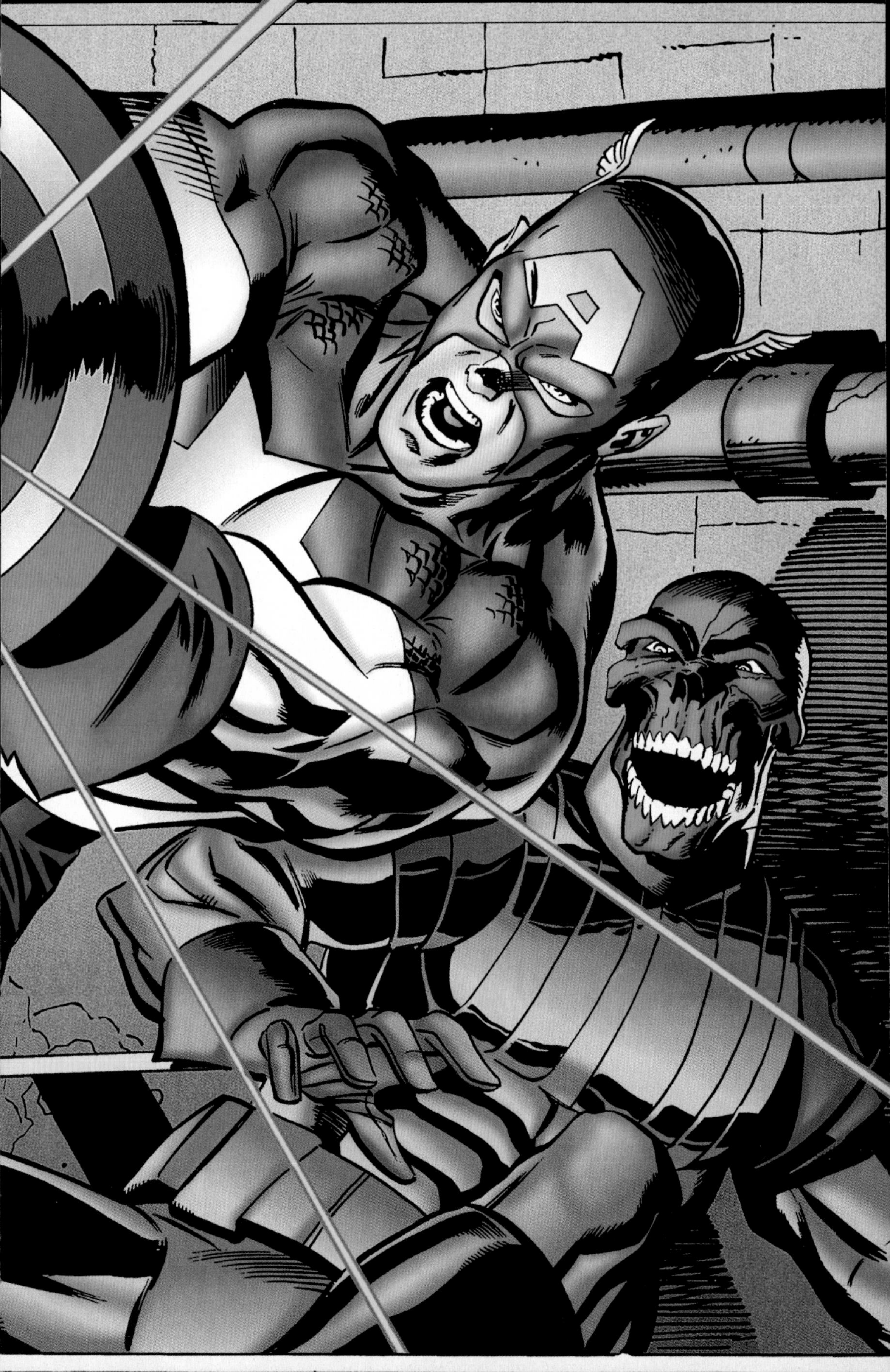

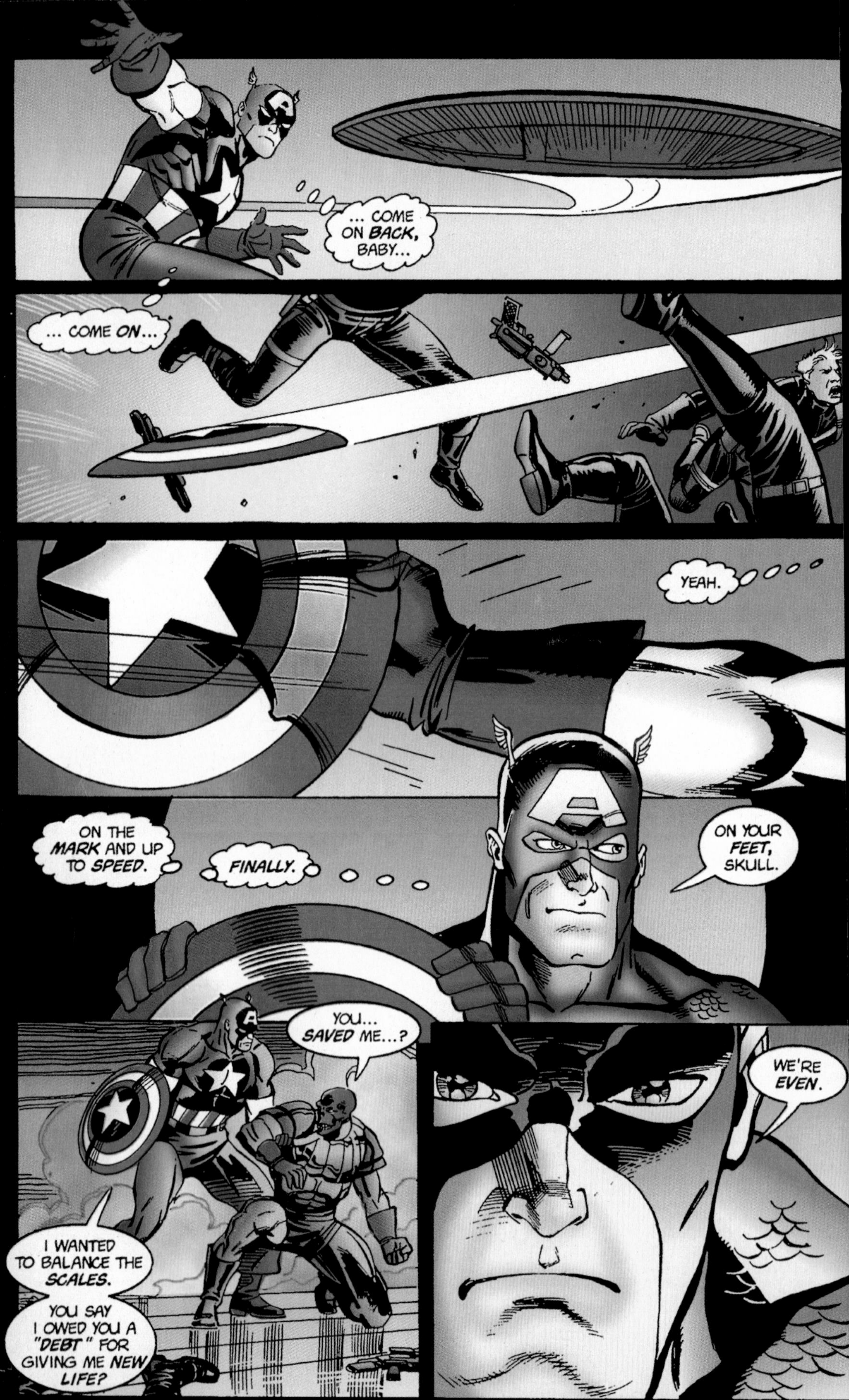
... COME ON BACK, BABY...
... COME ON...
YEAH.
ON THE MARK AND UP TO SPEED.
FINALLY.
ON YOUR FEET, SKULL.
YOU... SAVED ME...?
I WANTED TO BALANCE THE SCALES.
YOU SAY I OWED YOU A "DEBT" FOR GIVING ME NEW LIFE?
WE'RE EVEN.

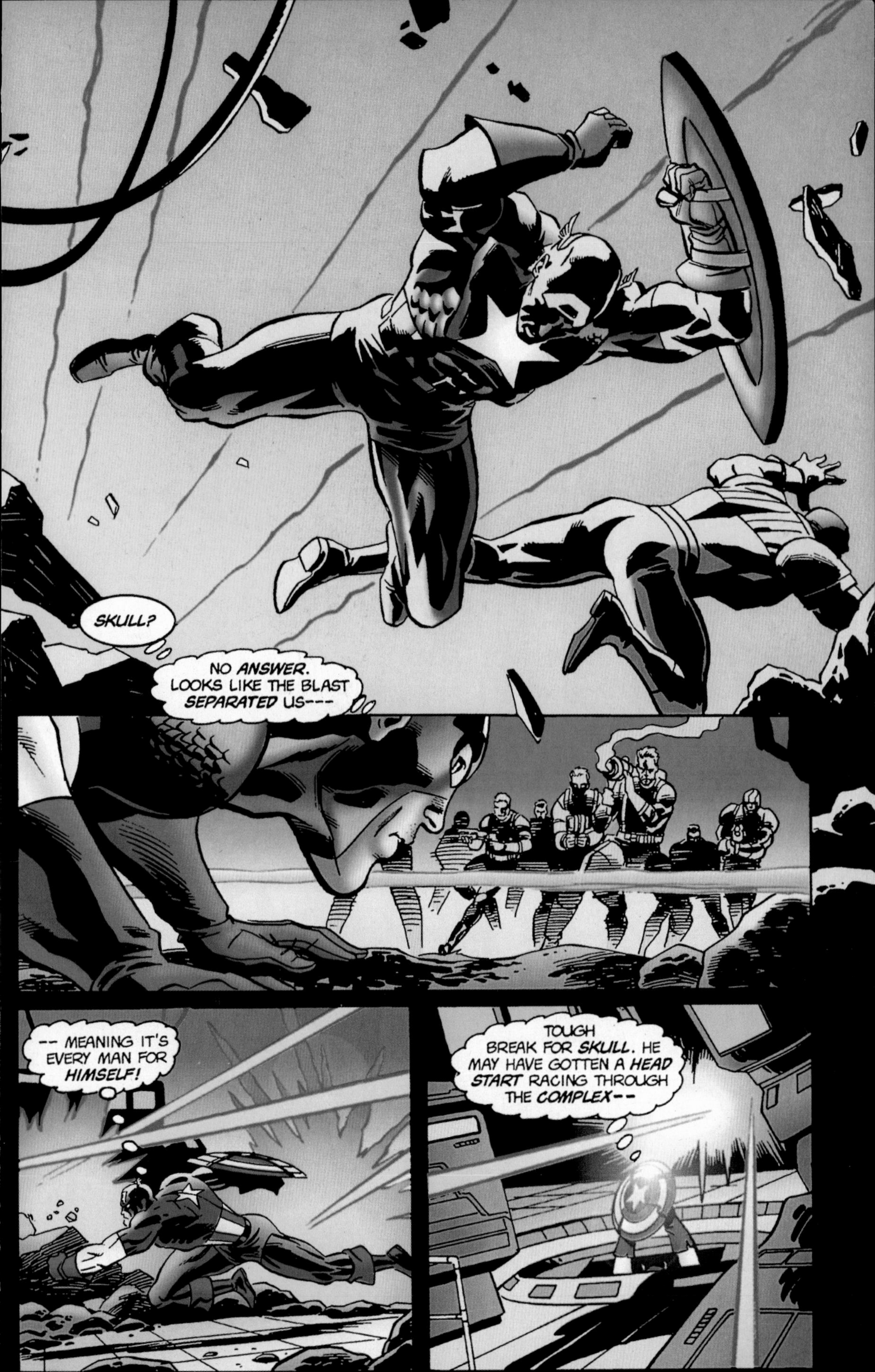
SKULL?
NO ANSWER. LOOKS LIKE THE BLAST SEPARATED US---
-- MEANING IT'S EVERY MAN FOR HIMSELF!
TOUGH BREAK FOR SKULL. HE MAY HAVE GOTTEN A HEAD START RACING THROUGH THE COMPLEX--

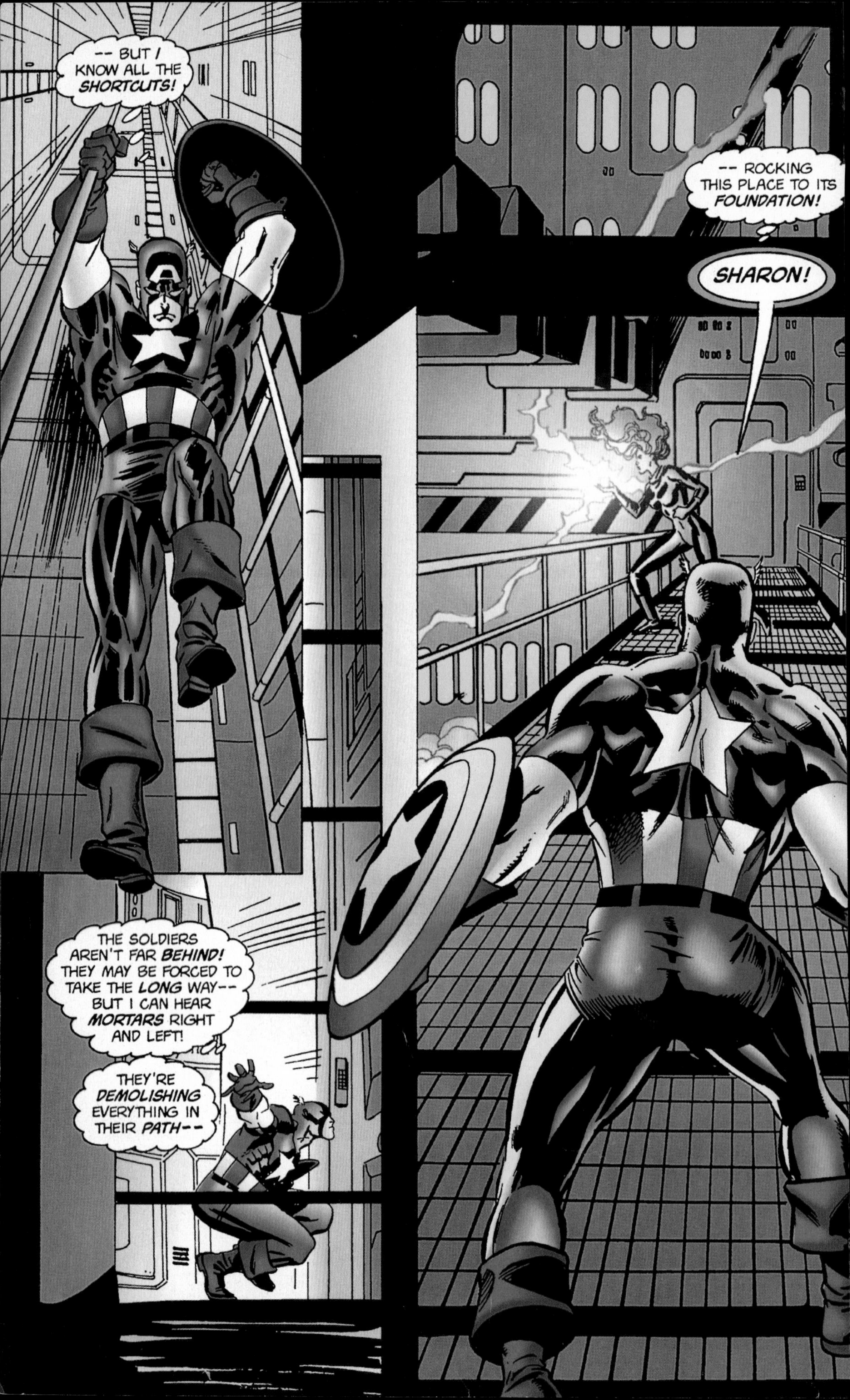

-- BUT I KNOW ALL THE *SHORTCUTS!*
THE SOLDIERS AREN'T FAR *BEHIND!* THEY MAY BE FORCED TO TAKE THE *LONG* WAY-- BUT I CAN HEAR *MORTARS* RIGHT AND LEFT!
THEY'RE *DEMOLISHING* EVERYTHING IN THEIR *PATH*--
-- ROCKING THIS PLACE TO ITS *FOUNDATION!*
SHARON!

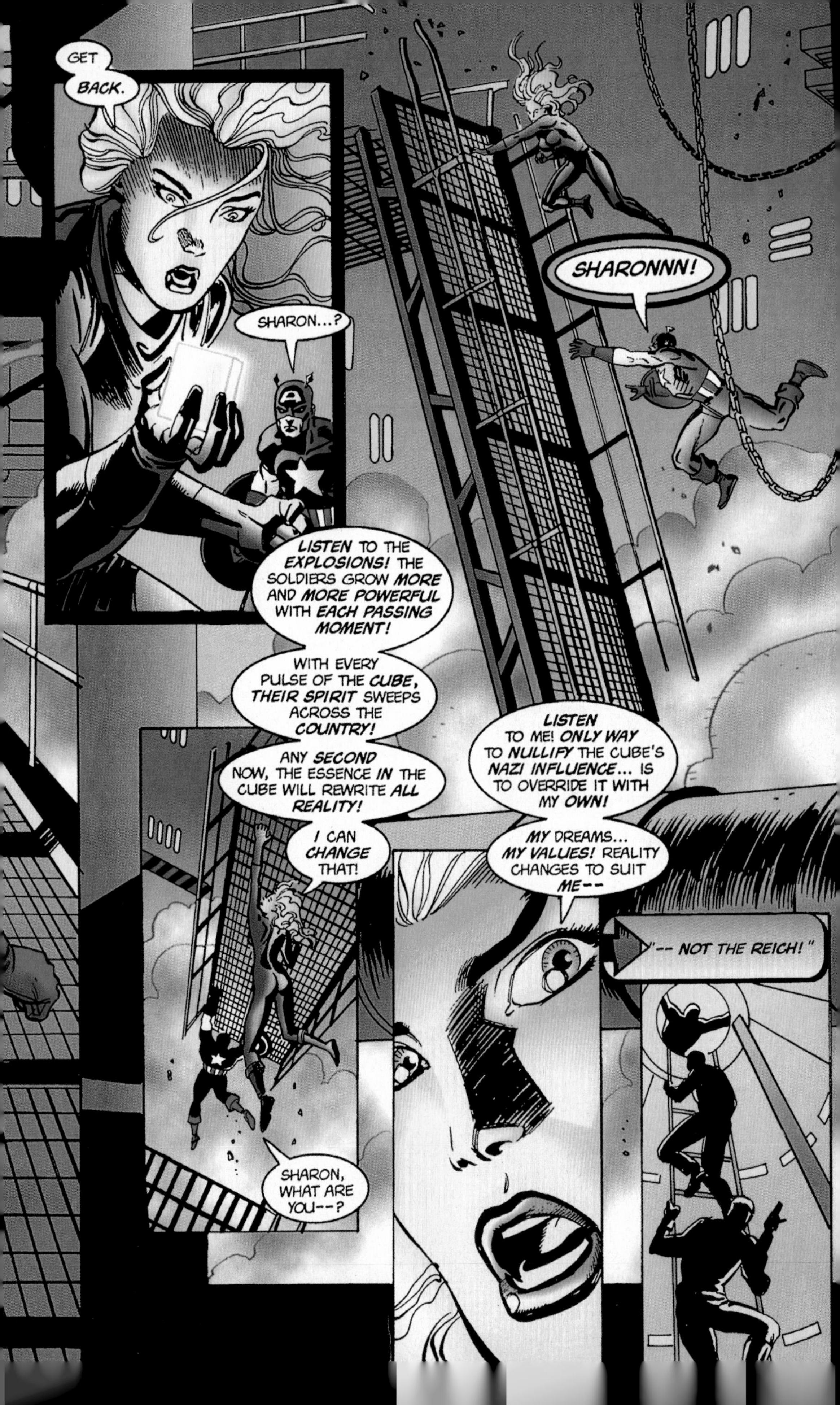

GET BACK.
SHARON...?
SHARONNN!
LISTEN TO THE EXPLOSIONS! THE SOLDIERS GROW MORE AND MORE POWERFUL WITH EACH PASSING MOMENT!
WITH EVERY PULSE OF THE CUBE, THEIR SPIRIT SWEEPS ACROSS THE COUNTRY!
ANY SECOND NOW, THE ESSENCE IN THE CUBE WILL REWRITE ALL REALITY!
I CAN CHANGE THAT!
SHARON, WHAT ARE YOU--?
LISTEN TO ME! ONLY WAY TO NULLIFY THE CUBE'S NAZI INFLUENCE... IS TO OVERRIDE IT WITH MY OWN!
MY DREAMS... MY VALUES! REALITY CHANGES TO SUIT ME--
"-- NOT THE REICH!"

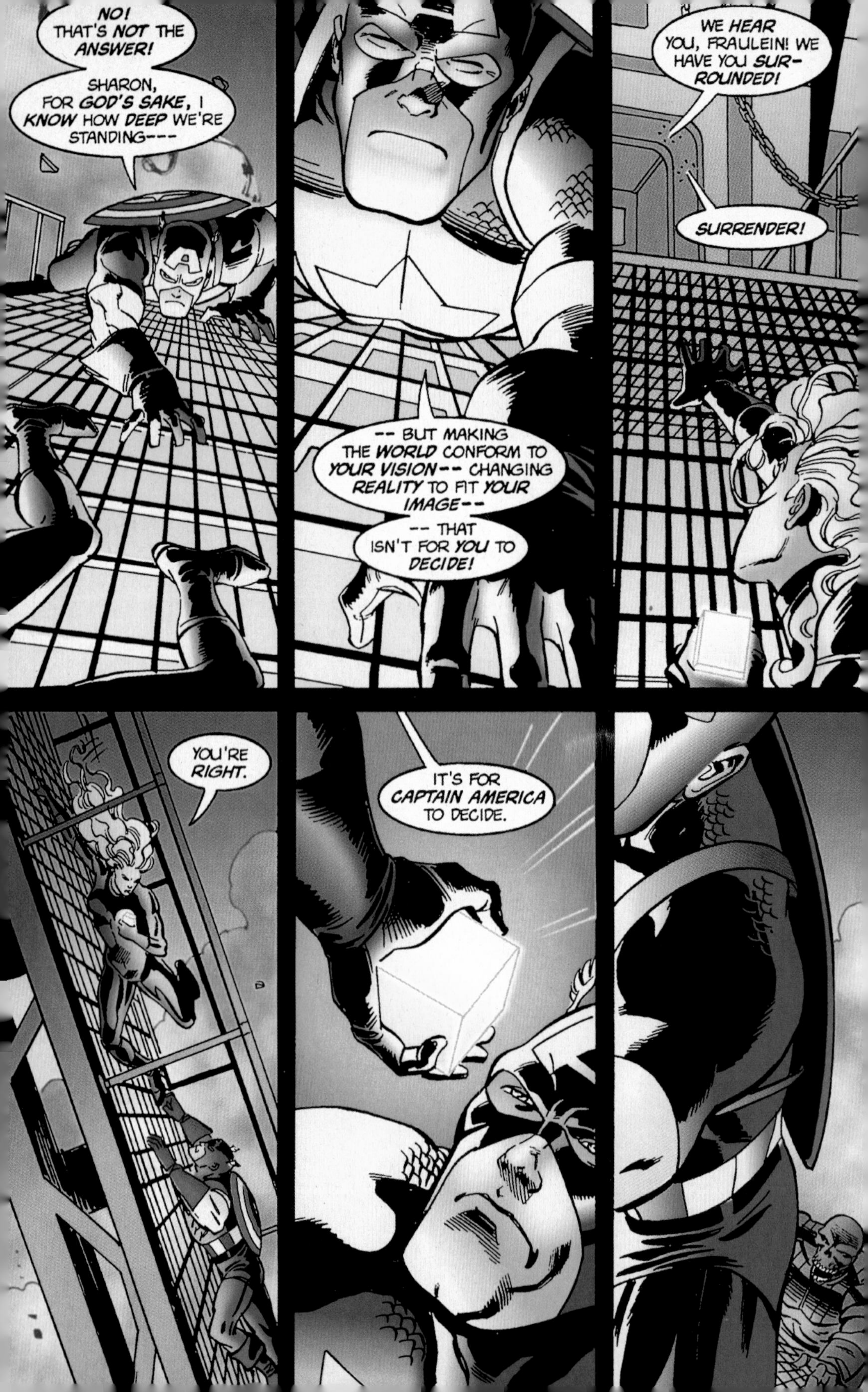
NO! THAT'S NOT THE ANSWER!
SHARON, FOR GOD'S SAKE, I KNOW HOW DEEP WE'RE STANDING---
-- BUT MAKING THE WORLD CONFORM TO YOUR VISION-- CHANGING REALITY TO FIT YOUR IMAGE--
-- THAT ISN'T FOR YOU TO DECIDE!
WE HEAR YOU, FRAULEIN! WE HAVE YOU SUR-ROUNDED!
SURRENDER!
YOU'RE RIGHT.
IT'S FOR CAPTAIN AMERICA TO DECIDE.

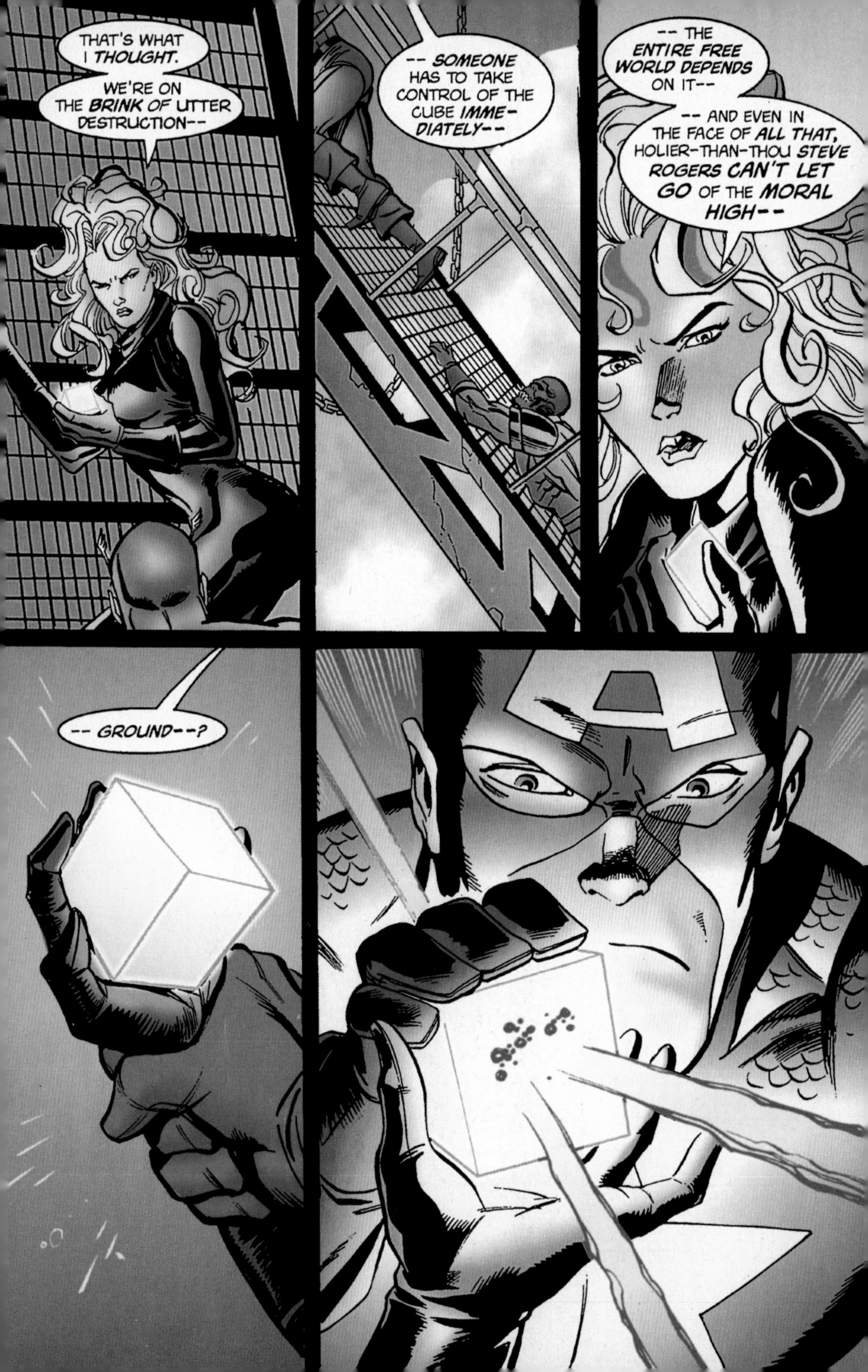
THAT'S WHAT I THOUGHT.
WE'RE ON THE BRINK OF UTTER DESTRUCTION--
-- SOMEONE HAS TO TAKE CONTROL OF THE CUBE IMME-DIATELY--
-- THE ENTIRE FREE WORLD DEPENDS ON IT--
-- AND EVEN IN THE FACE OF ALL THAT, HOLIER-THAN-THOU STEVE ROGERS CAN'T LET GO OF THE MORAL HIGH--
-- GROUND--?

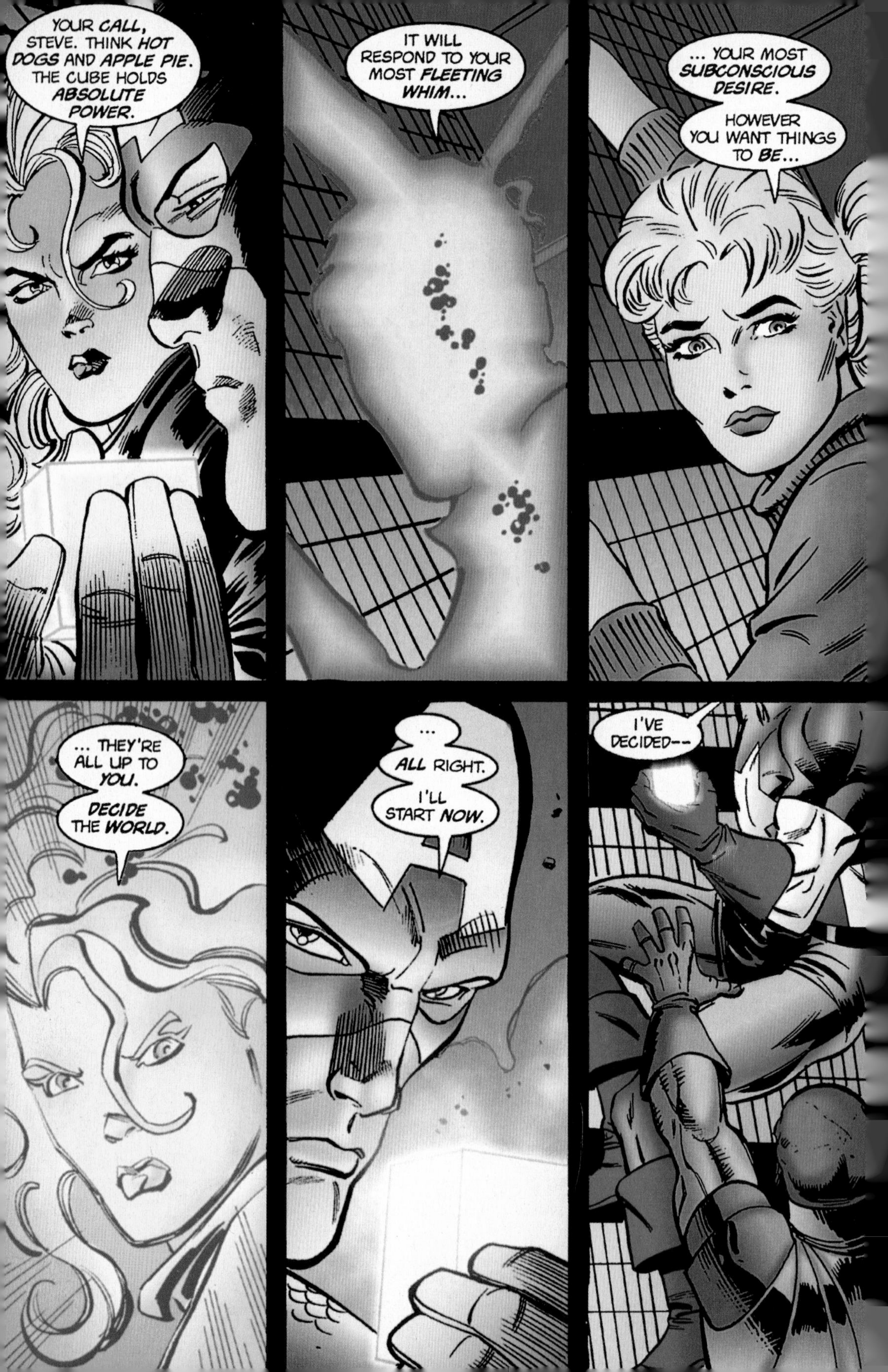
YOUR CALL, STEVE. THINK HOT DOGS AND APPLE PIE. THE CUBE HOLDS ABSOLUTE POWER.
IT WILL RESPOND TO YOUR MOST FLEETING WHIM...
... YOUR MOST SUBCONSCIOUS DESIRE.
HOWEVER YOU WANT THINGS TO BE...
... THEY'RE ALL UP TO YOU.
DECIDE THE WORLD.
...
ALL RIGHT.
I'LL START NOW.
I'VE DECIDED--

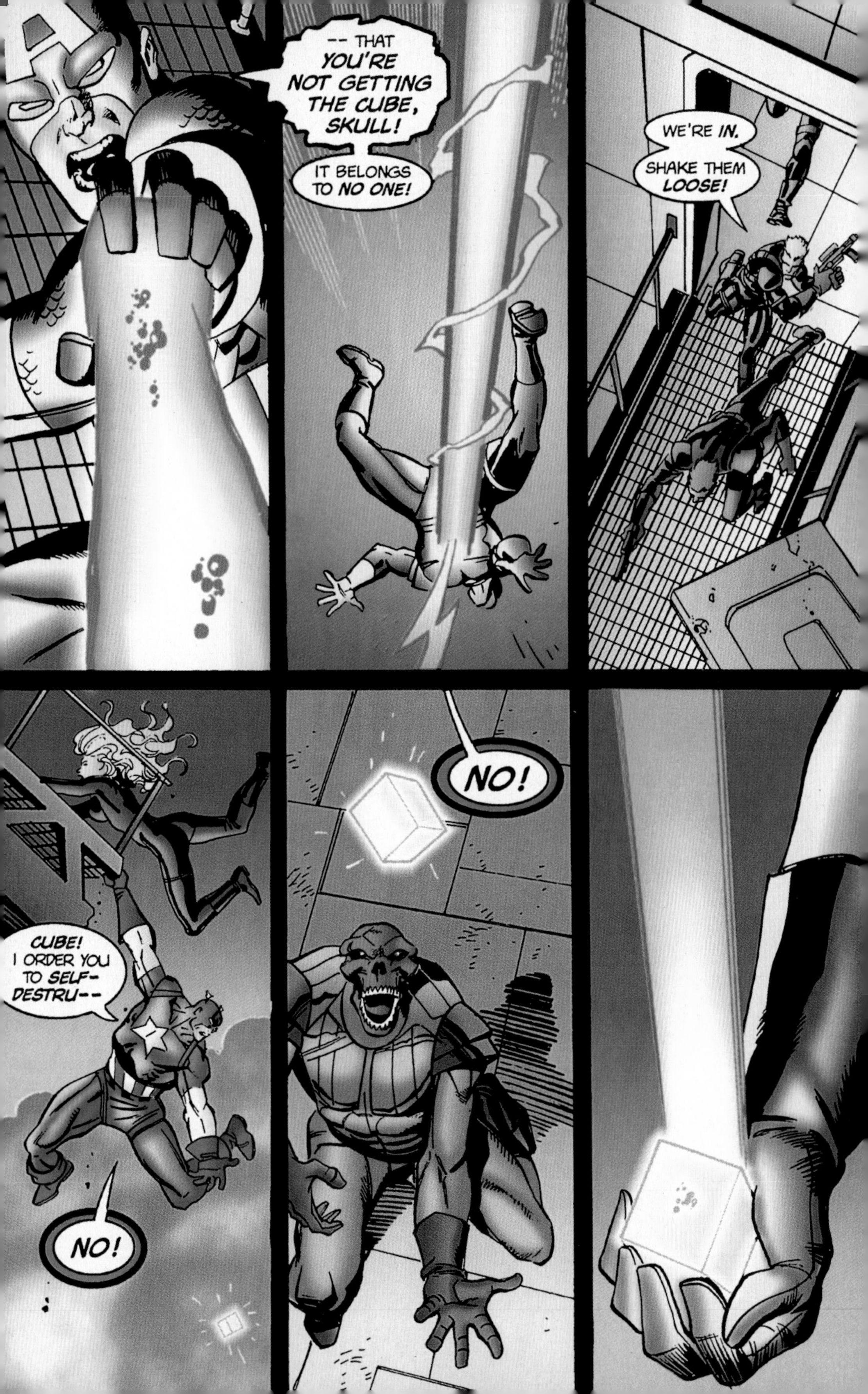
-- THAT YOU'RE NOT GETTING THE CUBE, SKULL!
IT BELONGS TO NO ONE!
WE'RE IN.
SHAKE THEM LOOSE!
CUBE! I ORDER YOU TO SELF-DESTRU--
NO!
NO!

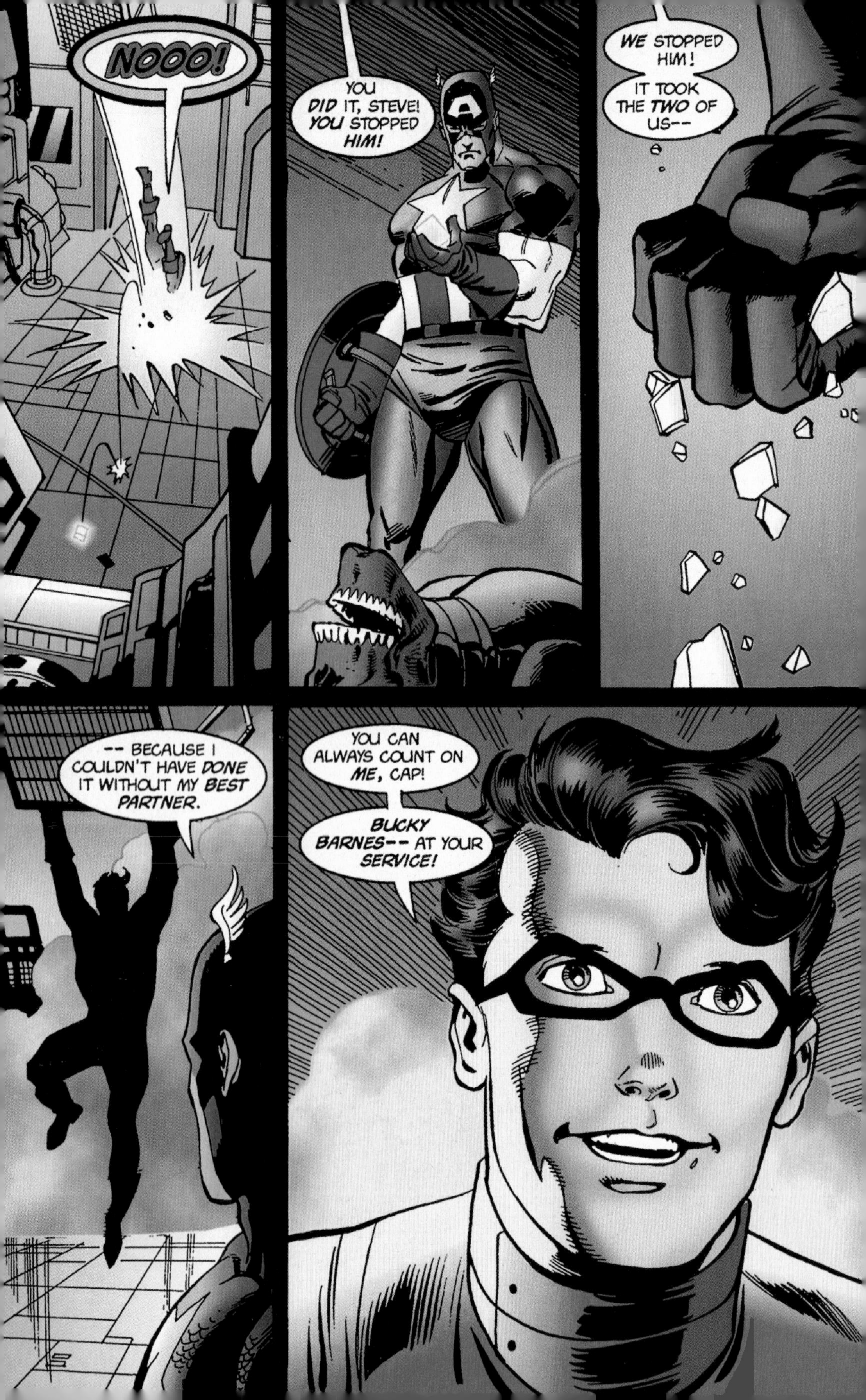
NOOO!
YOU DID IT, STEVE! YOU STOPPED HIM!
WE STOPPED HIM!
IT TOOK THE TWO OF US--
-- BECAUSE I COULDN'T HAVE DONE IT WITHOUT MY BEST PARTNER.
YOU CAN ALWAYS COUNT ON ME, CAP!
BUCKY BARNES-- AT YOUR SERVICE!

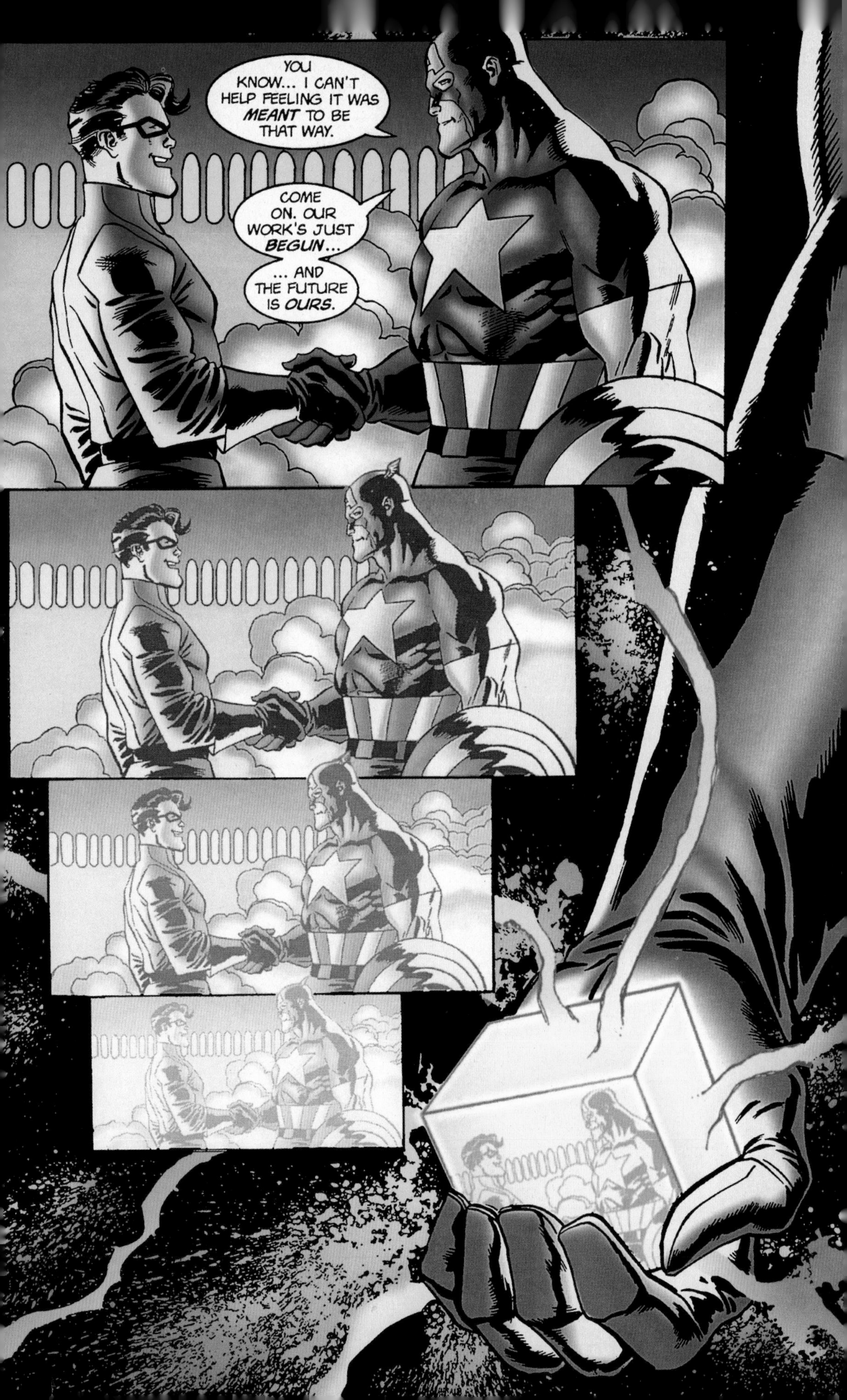
YOU KNOW... I CAN'T HELP FEELING IT WAS MEANT TO BE THAT WAY.
COME ON. OUR WORK'S JUST BEGUN...
... AND THE FUTURE IS OURS.

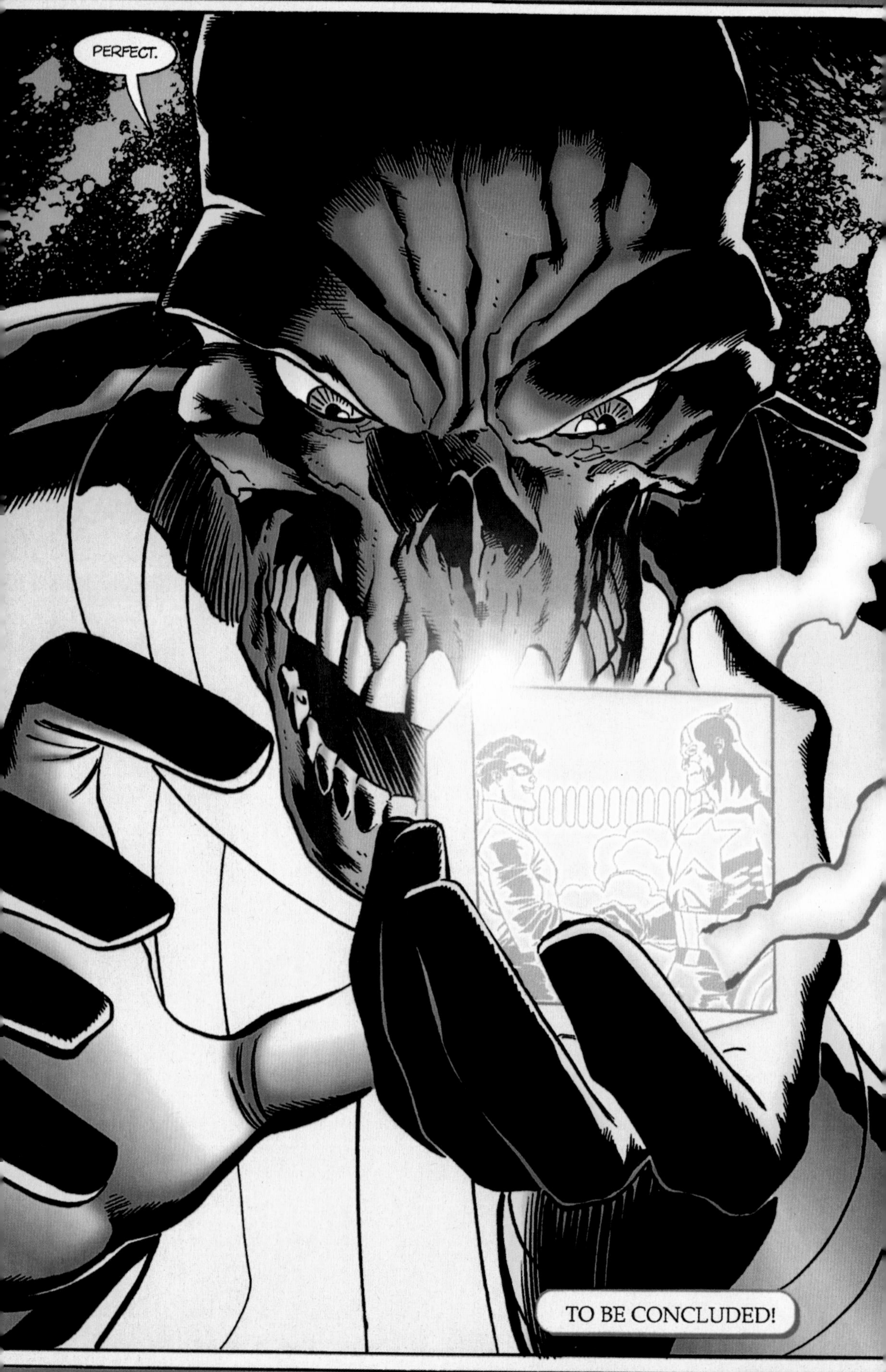
PERFECT.
TO BE CONCLUDED!

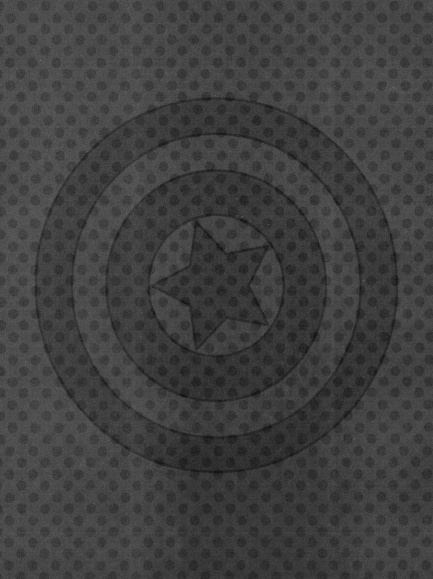

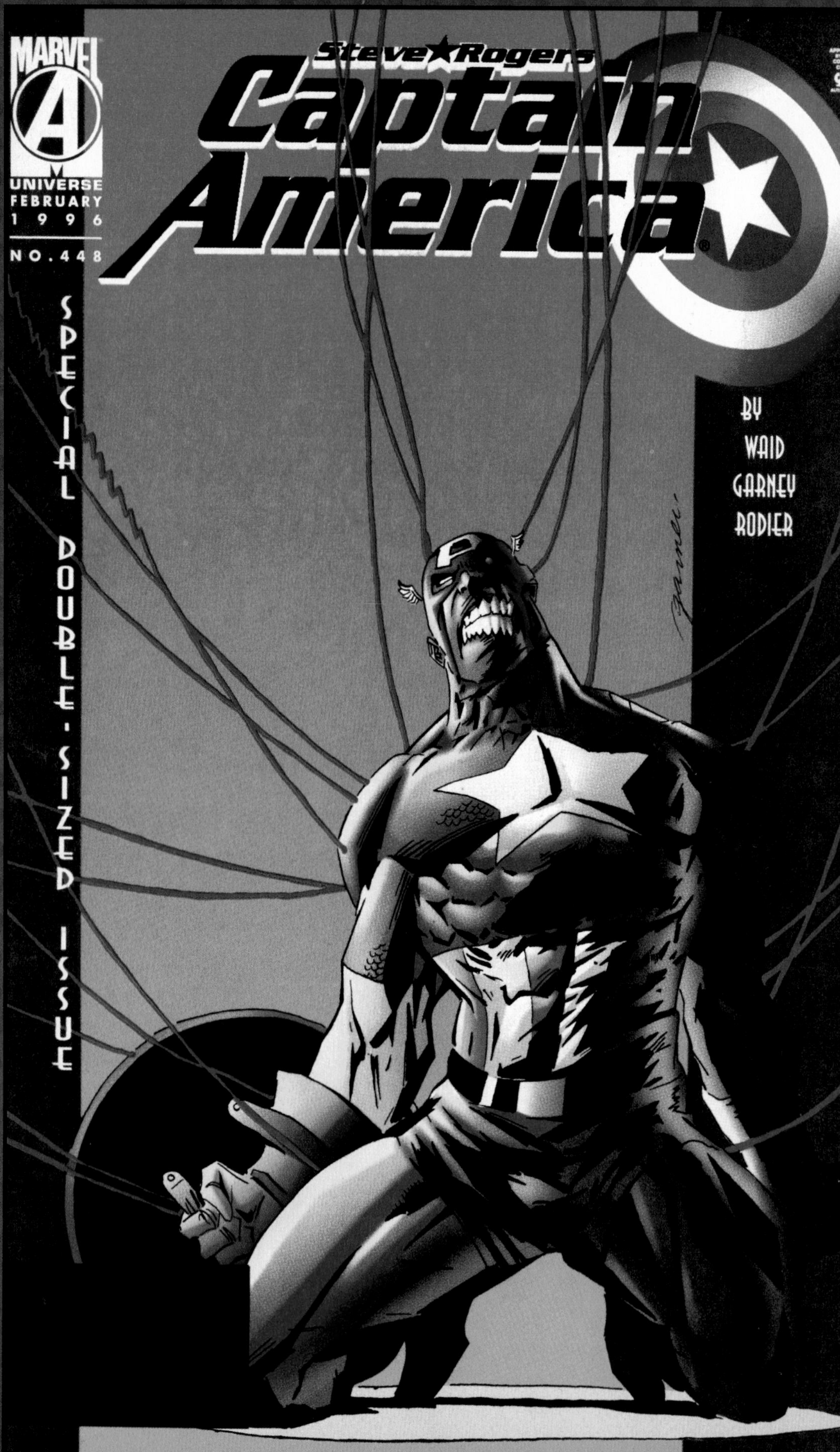

MARVEL
UNIVERSE
FEBRUARY
1996
NO.448
Steve★Rogers
Captain America
SPECIAL DOUBLE-SIZED ISSUE
BY
WAID
GARNEY
RODIER

STAN LEE PRESENTS

OPERATION: REBIRTH:

CONCLUSION

STARRING

CAPTAIN AMERICA

BY

MARK WAID

STORY

RON GARNEY

PENCILS

DENIS RODIER

INKS

JOHN KALISZ

COLORS

MALIBU

COLOR SEPARATIONS

JOHN COSTANZA

LETTERS

RALPH MACCHIO

EDITOR

MARK GRUENWALD

EDITOR IN CHIEF

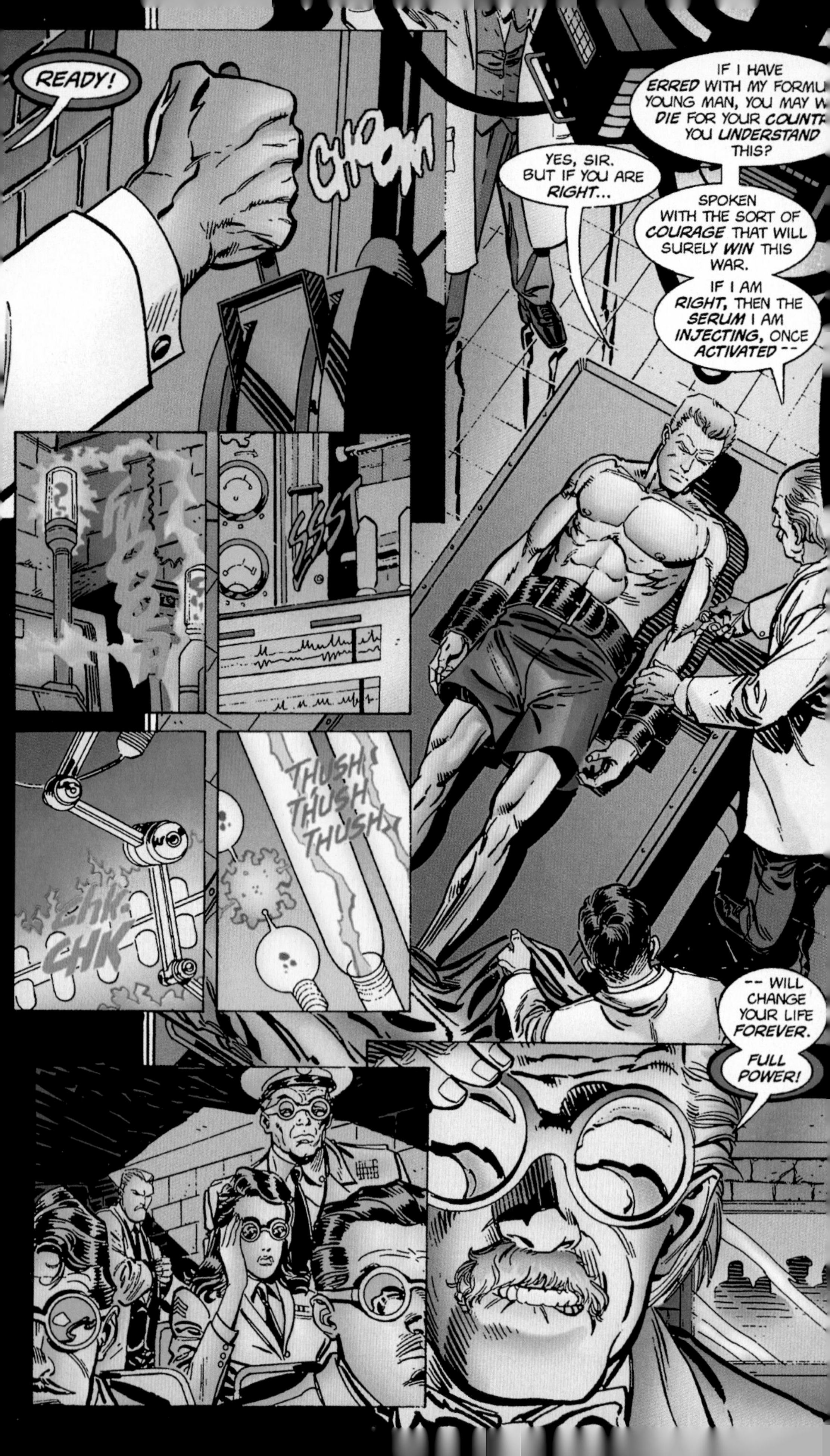
READY!
CHOOM
IF I HAVE ERRED WITH MY FORMU
YOUNG MAN, YOU MAY W
DIE FOR YOUR COUNTR
YOU UNDERSTAND THIS?
YES, SIR. BUT IF YOU ARE RIGHT...
SPOKEN WITH THE SORT OF COURAGE THAT WILL SURELY WIN THIS WAR.
IF I AM RIGHT, THEN THE SERUM I AM INJECTING, ONCE ACTIVATED --
SSST
CHK-CHK
THUSH THUSH THUSH
-- WILL CHANGE YOUR LIFE FOREVER.
FULL POWER!

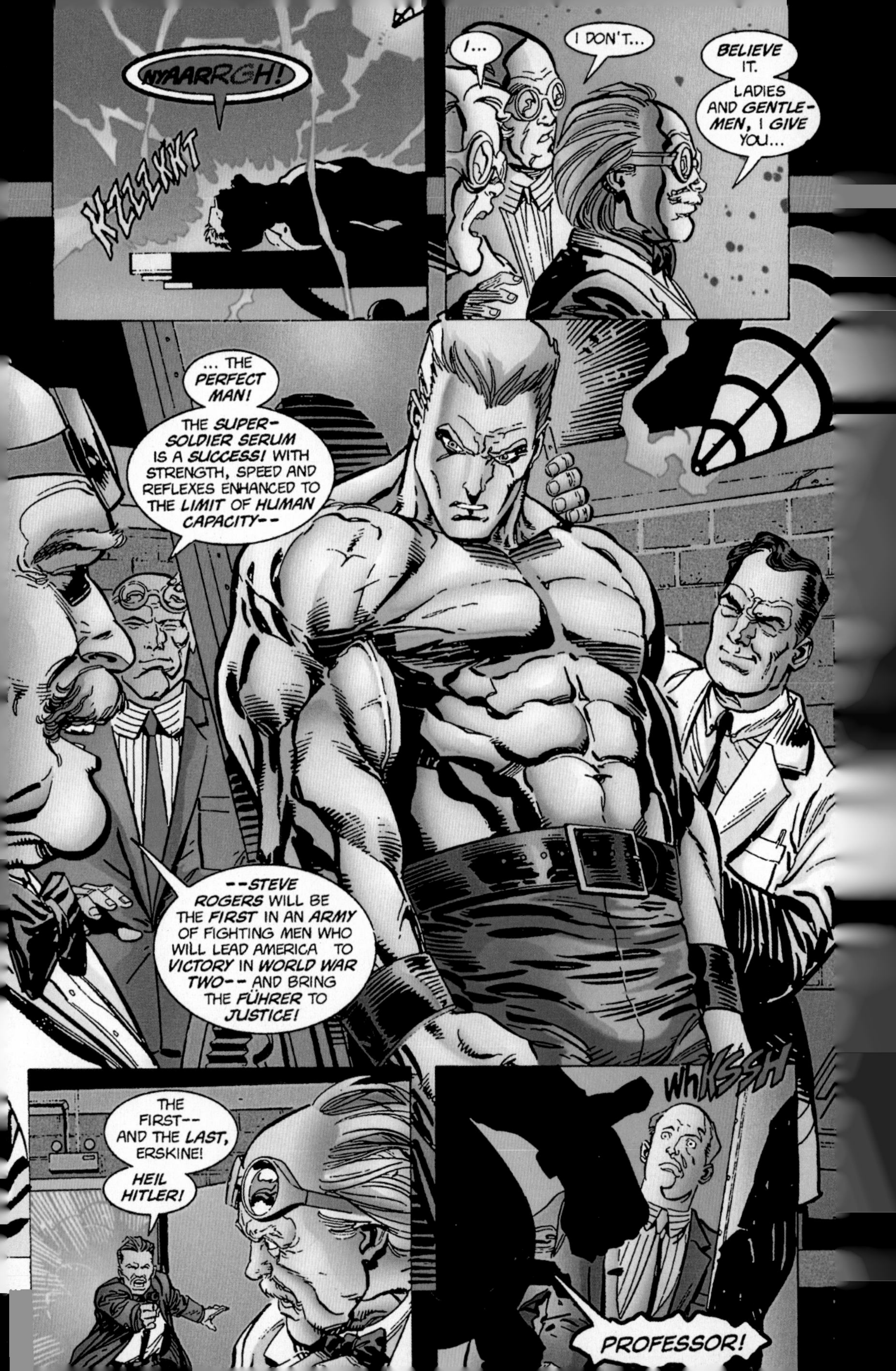
NYAARRGH!
KZZZLKKT
I...
I DON'T...
BELIEVE IT. LADIES AND GENTLEMEN, I GIVE YOU...
... THE PERFECT MAN!
THE SUPER-SOLDIER SERUM IS A SUCCESS! WITH STRENGTH, SPEED AND REFLEXES ENHANCED TO THE LIMIT OF HUMAN CAPACITY--
--STEVE ROGERS WILL BE THE FIRST IN AN ARMY OF FIGHTING MEN WHO WILL LEAD AMERICA TO VICTORY IN WORLD WAR TWO-- AND BRING THE FÜHRER TO JUSTICE!
THE FIRST-- AND THE LAST, ERSKINE!
HEIL HITLER!
WHKSSH
PROFESSOR!

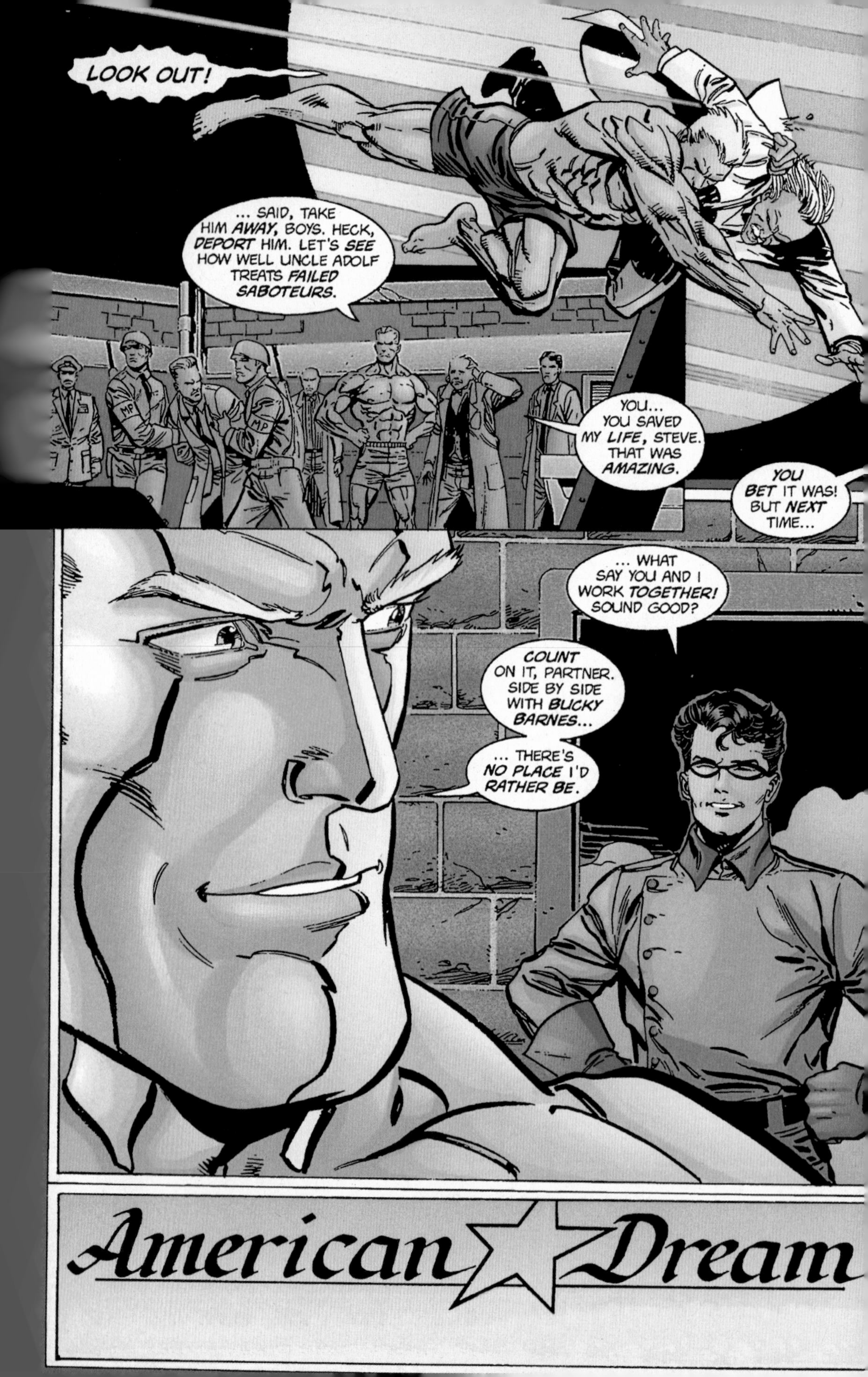
LOOK OUT!
... SAID, TAKE HIM AWAY, BOYS. HECK, DEPORT HIM. LET'S SEE HOW WELL UNCLE ADOLF TREATS FAILED SABOTEURS.
MP
MP
YOU... YOU SAVED MY LIFE, STEVE. THAT WAS AMAZING.
YOU BET IT WAS! BUT NEXT TIME...
... WHAT SAY YOU AND I WORK TOGETHER! SOUND GOOD?
COUNT ON IT, PARTNER. SIDE BY SIDE WITH BUCKY BARNES...
... THERE'S NO PLACE I'D RATHER BE.
American Dream

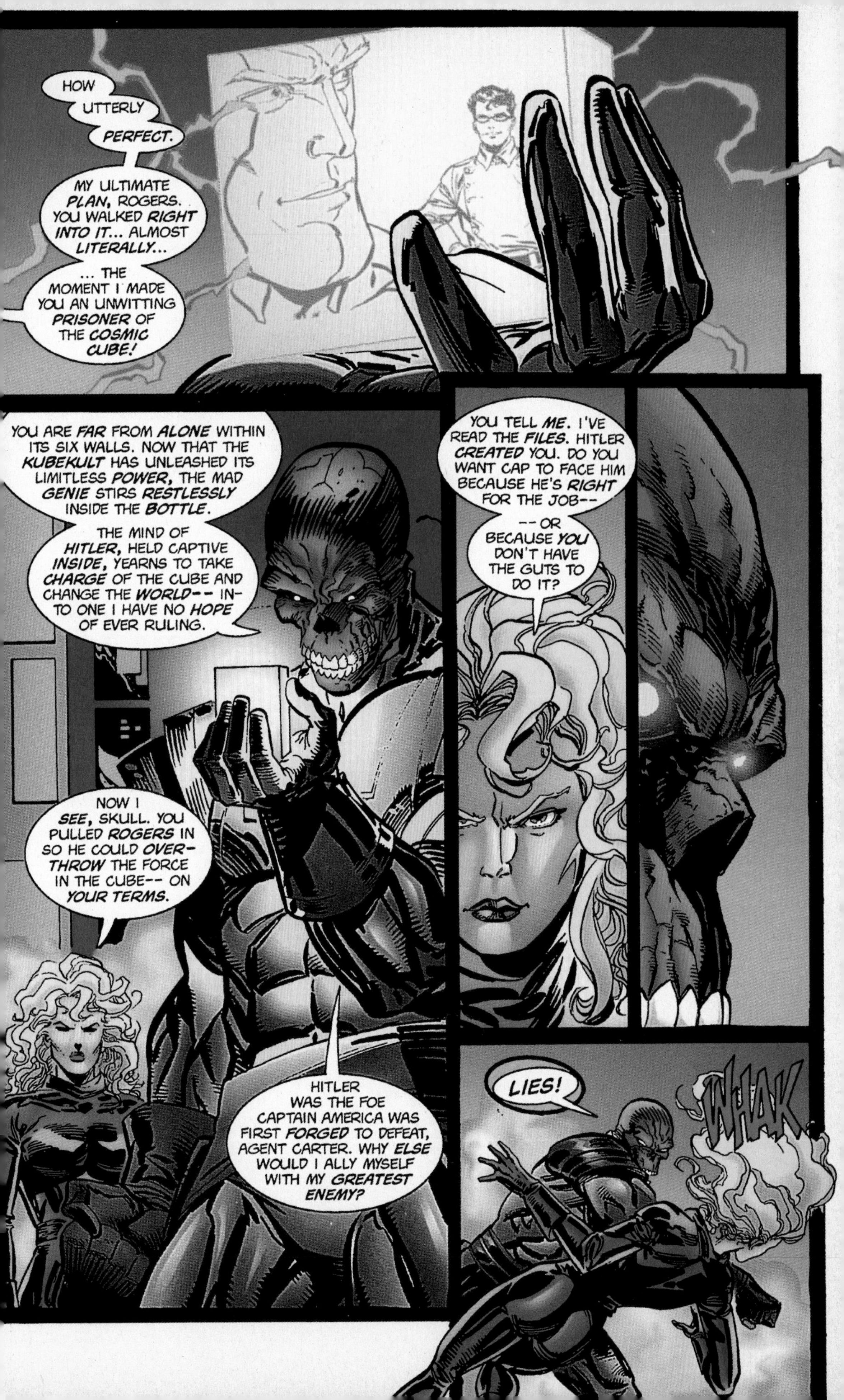
HOW UTTERLY PERFECT.
MY ULTIMATE PLAN, ROGERS. YOU WALKED RIGHT INTO IT... ALMOST LITERALLY...
... THE MOMENT I MADE YOU AN UNWITTING PRISONER OF THE COSMIC CUBE!
YOU ARE FAR FROM ALONE WITHIN ITS SIX WALLS. NOW THAT THE KUBEKULT HAS UNLEASHED ITS LIMITLESS POWER, THE MAD GENIE STIRS RESTLESSLY INSIDE THE BOTTLE.
THE MIND OF HITLER, HELD CAPTIVE INSIDE, YEARNS TO TAKE CHARGE OF THE CUBE AND CHANGE THE WORLD-- INTO ONE I HAVE NO HOPE OF EVER RULING.
NOW I SEE, SKULL. YOU PULLED ROGERS IN SO HE COULD OVERTHROW THE FORCE IN THE CUBE-- ON YOUR TERMS.
HITLER WAS THE FOE CAPTAIN AMERICA WAS FIRST FORGED TO DEFEAT, AGENT CARTER. WHY ELSE WOULD I ALLY MYSELF WITH MY GREATEST ENEMY?
YOU TELL ME. I'VE READ THE FILES. HITLER CREATED YOU. DO YOU WANT CAP TO FACE HIM BECAUSE HE'S RIGHT FOR THE JOB--
--OR BECAUSE YOU DON'T HAVE THE GUTS TO DO IT?
LIES!
WHAK

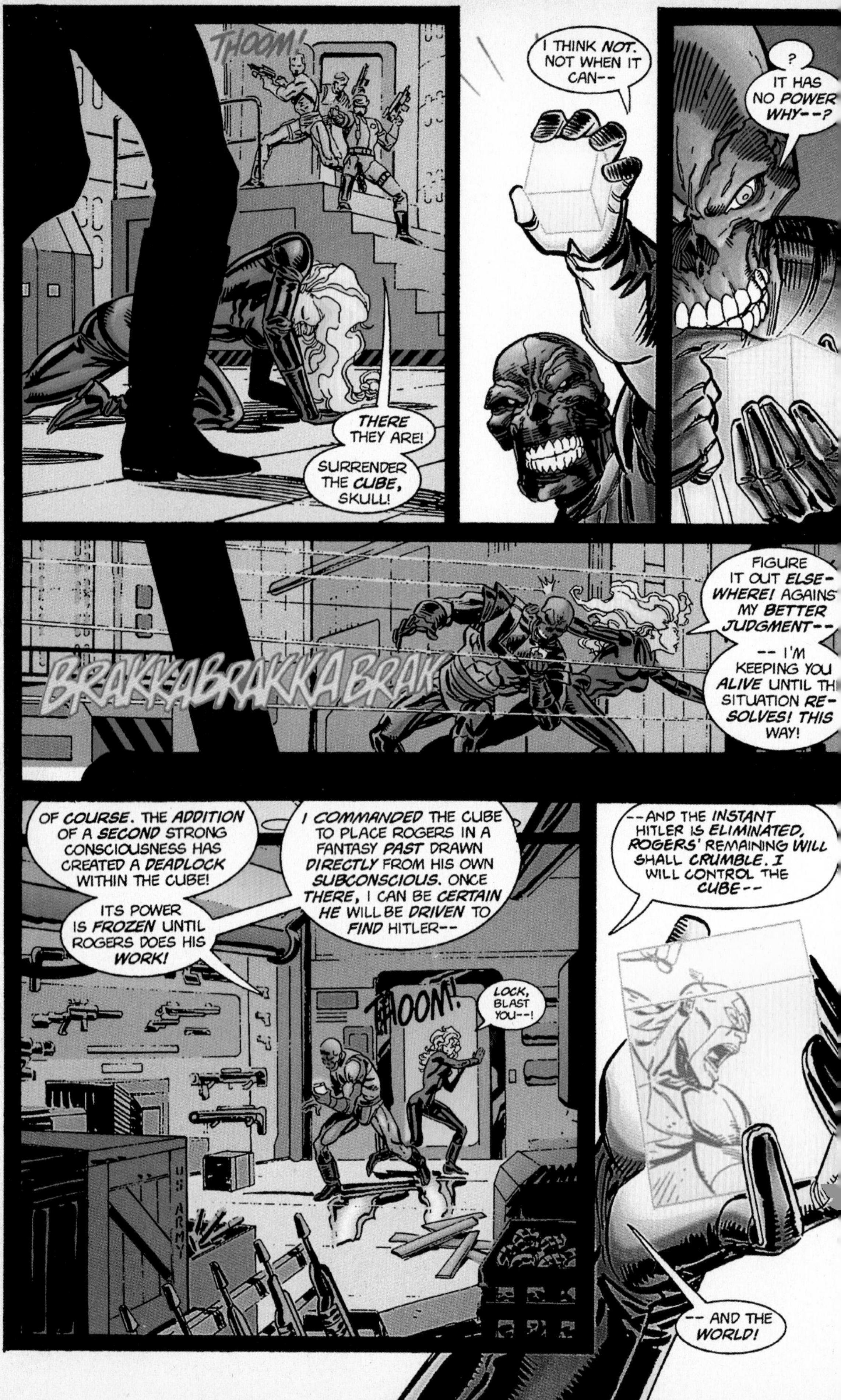
THOOM!
THERE THEY ARE!
SURRENDER THE CUBE, SKULL!
I THINK NOT. NOT WHEN IT CAN--
?
IT HAS NO POWER WHY--?
BRAKKABRAKKA BRAK
FIGURE IT OUT ELSE-WHERE! AGAINST MY BETTER JUDGMENT--
-- I'M KEEPING YOU ALIVE UNTIL TH SITUATION RE-SOLVES! THIS WAY!
OF COURSE. THE ADDITION OF A SECOND STRONG CONSCIOUSNESS HAS CREATED A DEADLOCK WITHIN THE CUBE!
ITS POWER IS FROZEN UNTIL ROGERS DOES HIS WORK!
I COMMANDED THE CUBE TO PLACE ROGERS IN A FANTASY PAST DRAWN DIRECTLY FROM HIS OWN SUBCONSCIOUS. ONCE THERE, I CAN BE CERTAIN HE WILL BE DRIVEN TO FIND HITLER--
THOOM!
LOCK, BLAST YOU--!
U.S. ARMY
--AND THE INSTANT HITLER IS ELIMINATED, ROGERS' REMAINING WILL SHALL CRUMBLE. I WILL CONTROL THE CUBE--
-- AND THE WORLD!

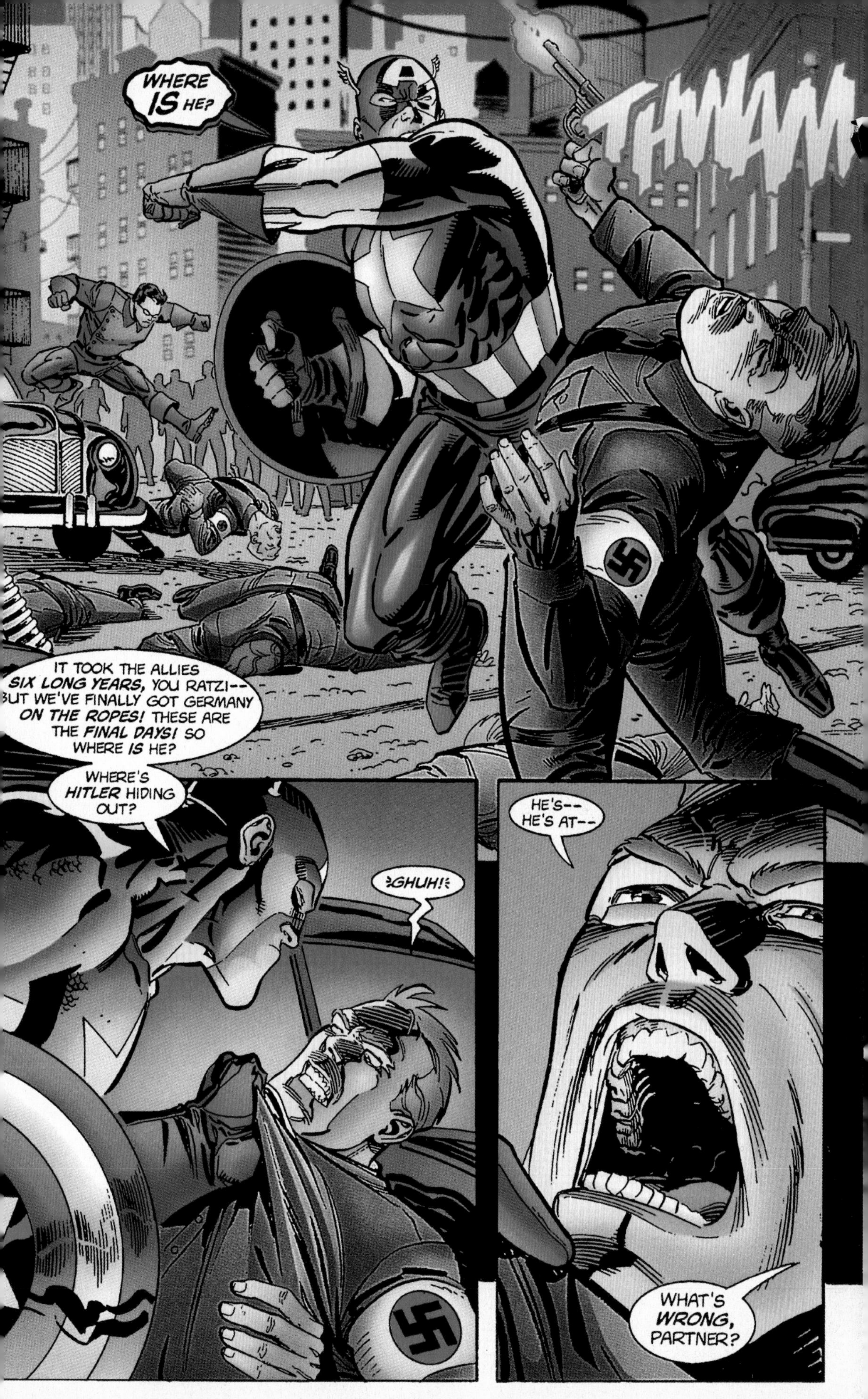

WHERE IS HE?
THWAM
IT TOOK THE ALLIES SIX LONG YEARS, YOU RATZI-- BUT WE'VE FINALLY GOT GERMANY ON THE ROPES! THESE ARE THE FINAL DAYS! SO WHERE IS HE?
WHERE'S HITLER HIDING OUT?
GHUH!
HE'S-- HE'S AT--
WHAT'S WRONG, PARTNER?

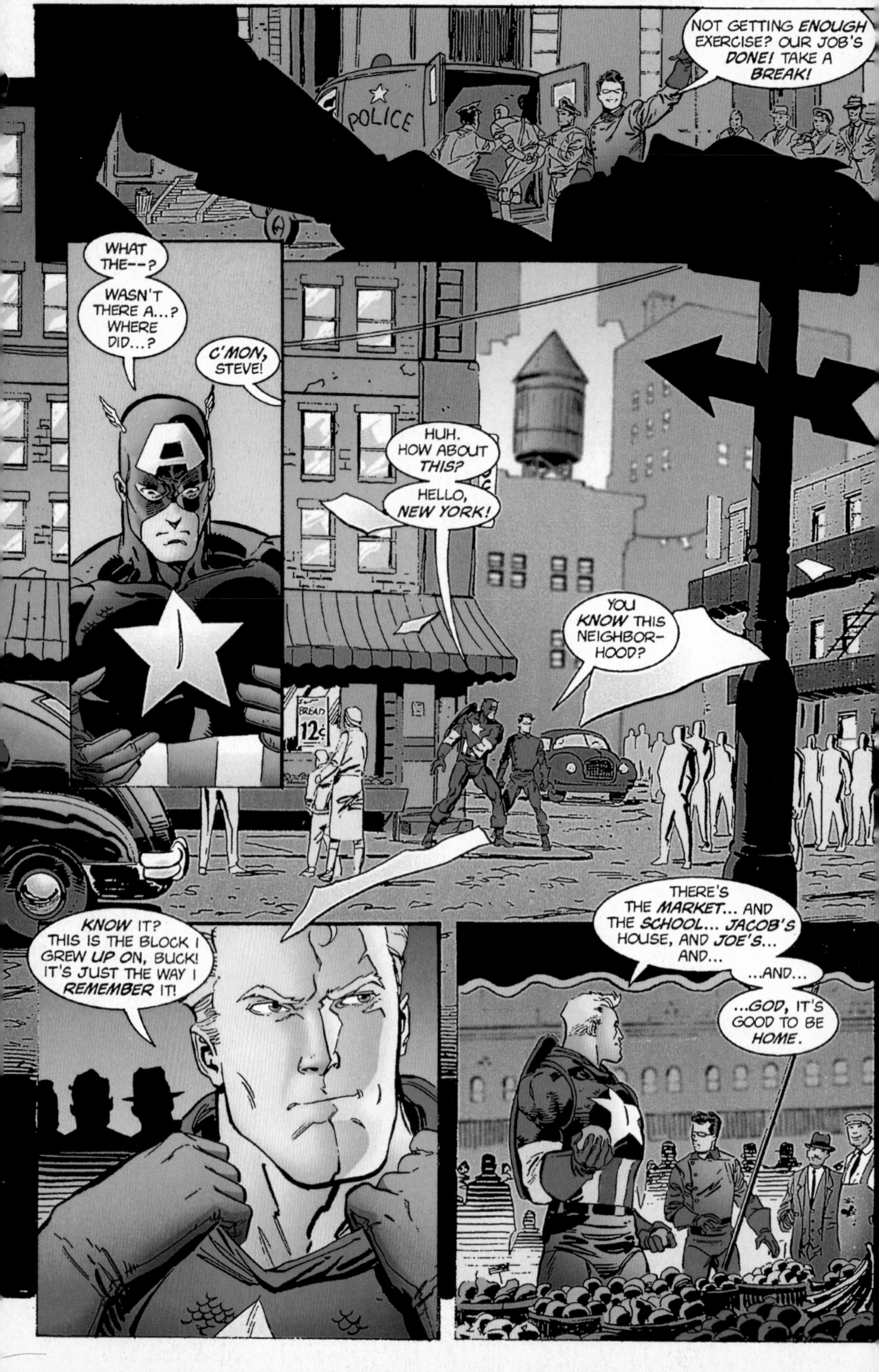
NOT GETTING ENOUGH EXERCISE? OUR JOB'S DONE! TAKE A BREAK!
POLICE
WHAT THE--?
WASN'T THERE A...? WHERE DID...?
C'MON, STEVE!
HUH. HOW ABOUT THIS?
HELLO, NEW YORK!
BREAD 12¢
YOU KNOW THIS NEIGHBOR-HOOD?
KNOW IT? THIS IS THE BLOCK I GREW UP ON, BUCK! IT'S JUST THE WAY I REMEMBER IT!
THERE'S THE MARKET... AND THE SCHOOL... JACOB'S HOUSE, AND JOE'S... AND...
...AND...
...GOD, IT'S GOOD TO BE HOME.

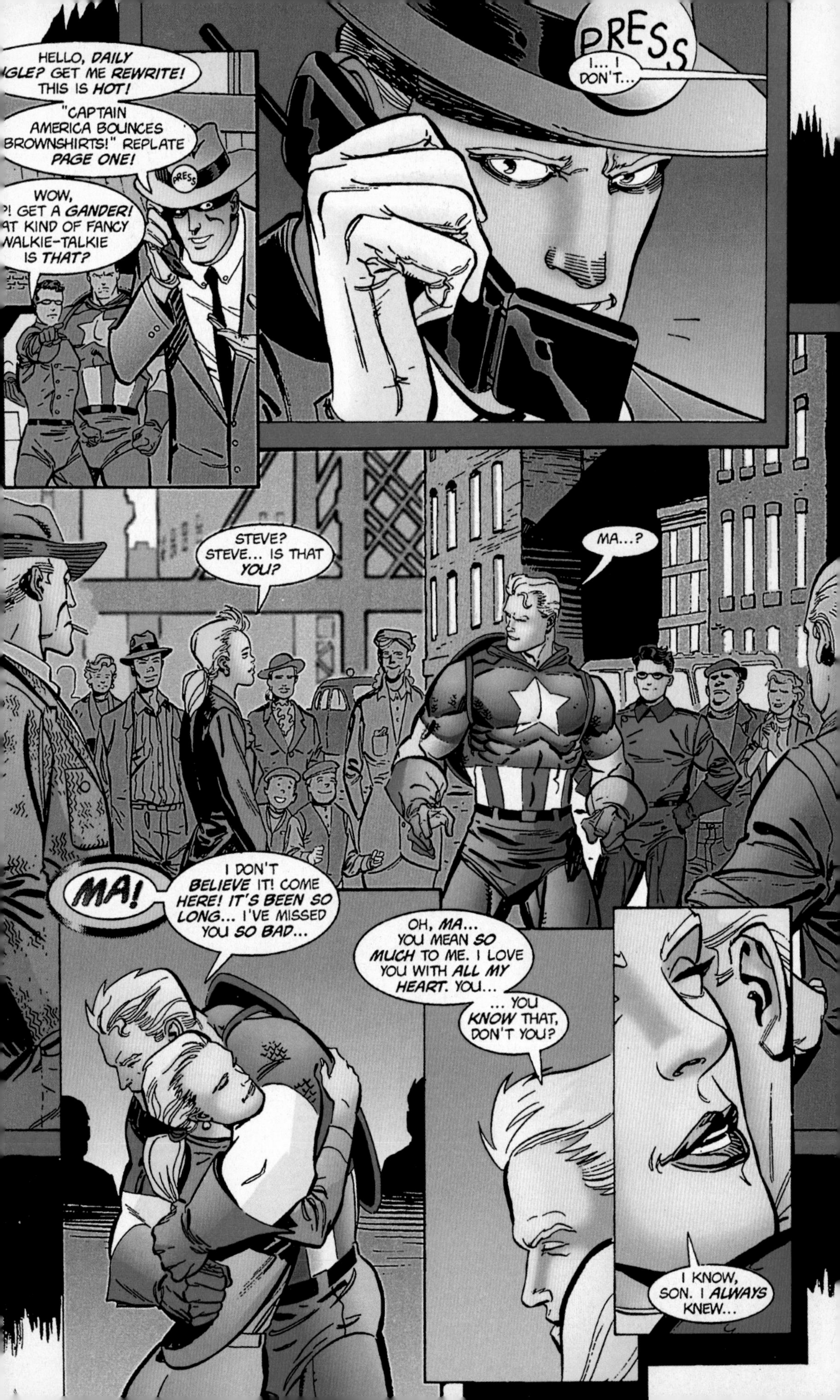
HELLO, DAILY
...GLE? GET ME REWRITE! THIS IS HOT!
"CAPTAIN AMERICA BOUNCES BROWNSHIRTS!" REPLATE PAGE ONE!
PRESS
WOW,
...! GET A GANDER! ...AT KIND OF FANCY ...ALKIE-TALKIE IS THAT?
PRESS
I... I DON'T...
STEVE? STEVE... IS THAT YOU?
MA...?
MA!
I DON'T BELIEVE IT! COME HERE! IT'S BEEN SO LONG... I'VE MISSED YOU SO BAD...
OH, MA... YOU MEAN SO MUCH TO ME. I LOVE YOU WITH ALL MY HEART. YOU...
... YOU KNOW THAT, DON'T YOU?
I KNOW, SON. I ALWAYS KNEW...

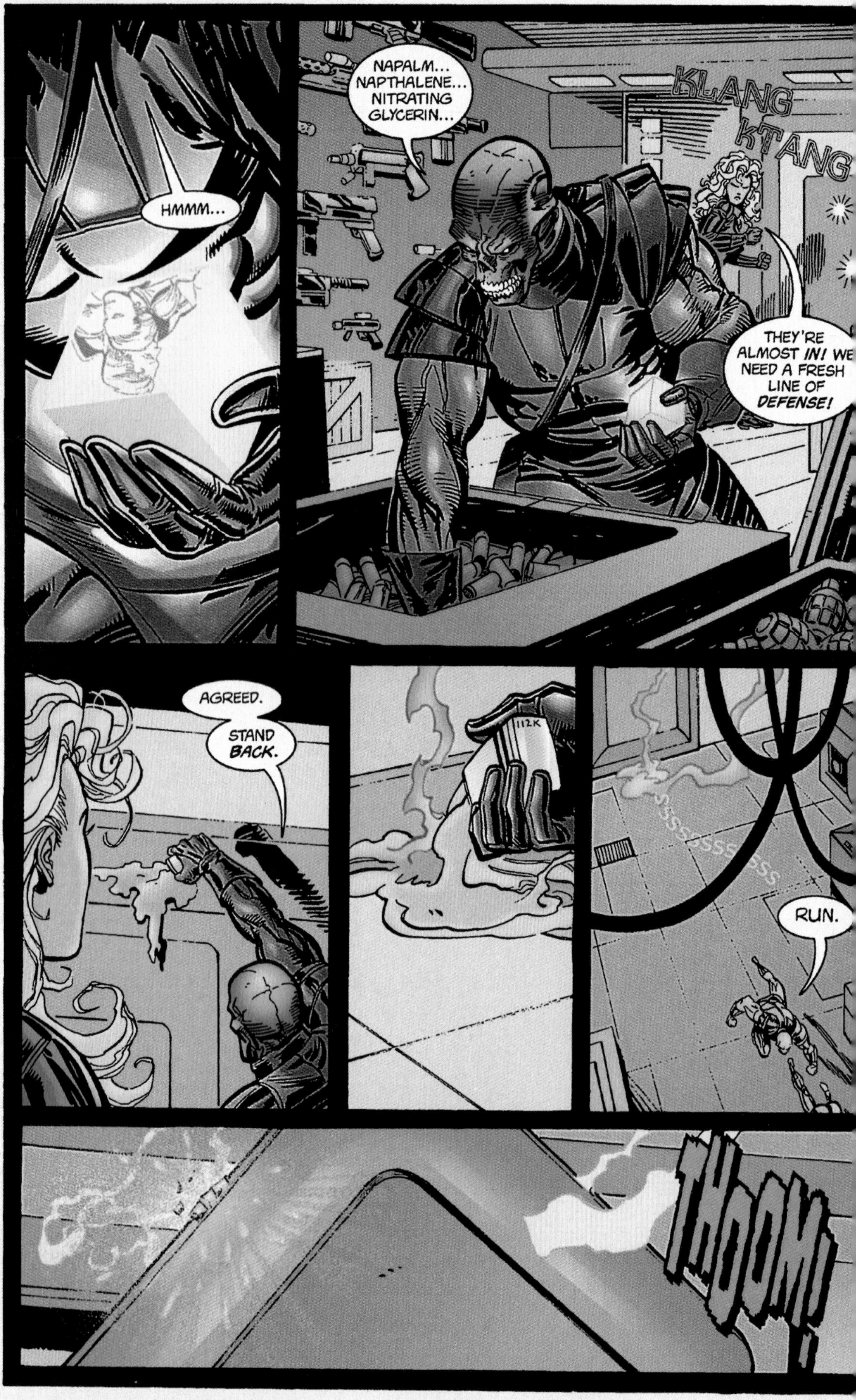
HMMM...
NAPALM... NAPTHALENE... NITRATING GLYCERIN...
KLANG
KTANG
THEY'RE ALMOST *IN!* WE NEED A FRESH LINE OF *DEFENSE!*
AGREED.
STAND *BACK.*
112K
SSSSSSSSSSSS
RUN.
THOOM!

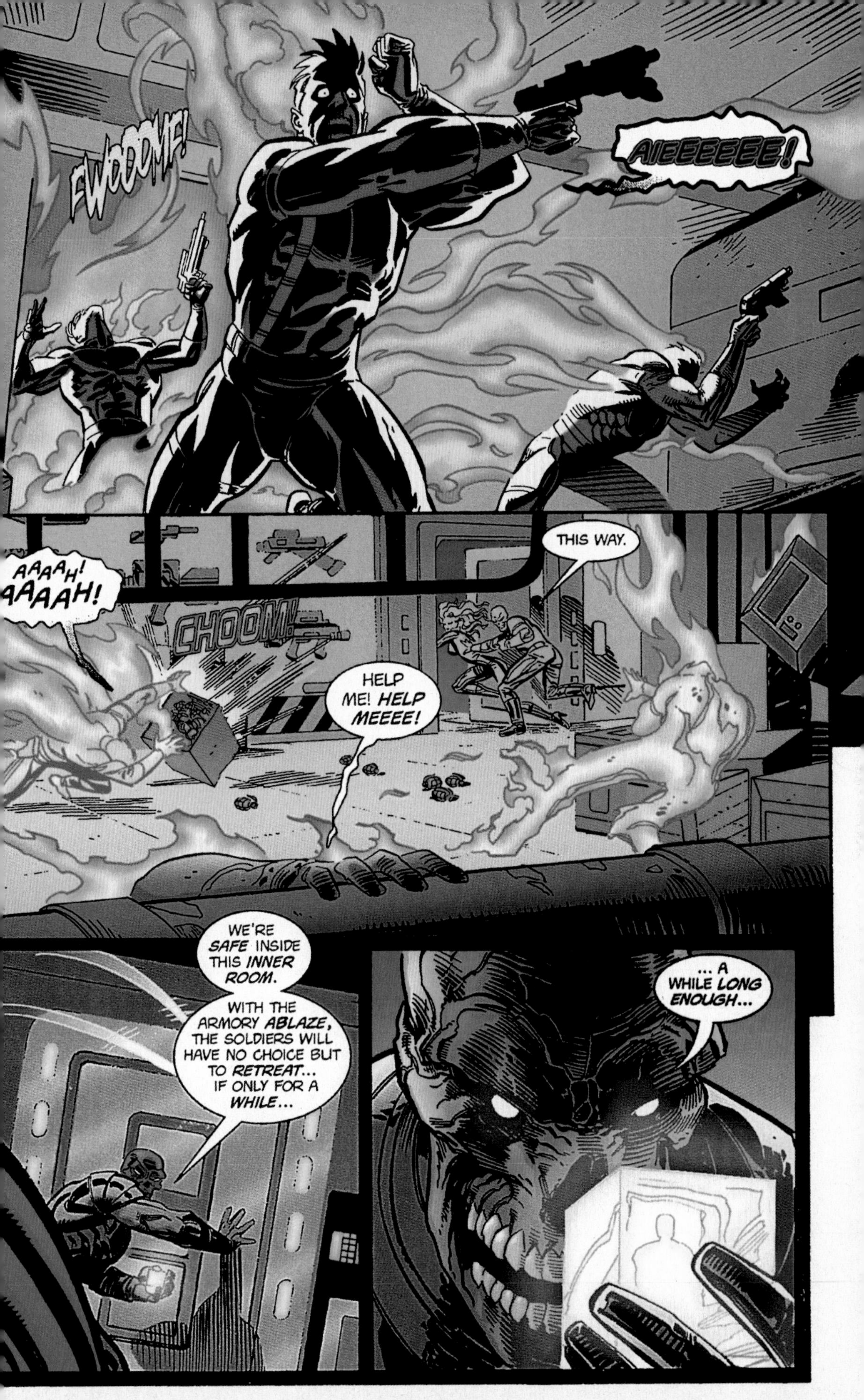
FWOOOMF!
AIEEEEEEE!
AAAAH! AAAAH!
CHOOM!
THIS WAY.
HELP ME! HELP MEEEE!
WE'RE SAFE INSIDE THIS INNER ROOM.
WITH THE ARMORY ABLAZE, THE SOLDIERS WILL HAVE NO CHOICE BUT TO RETREAT... IF ONLY FOR A WHILE...
... A WHILE LONG ENOUGH...

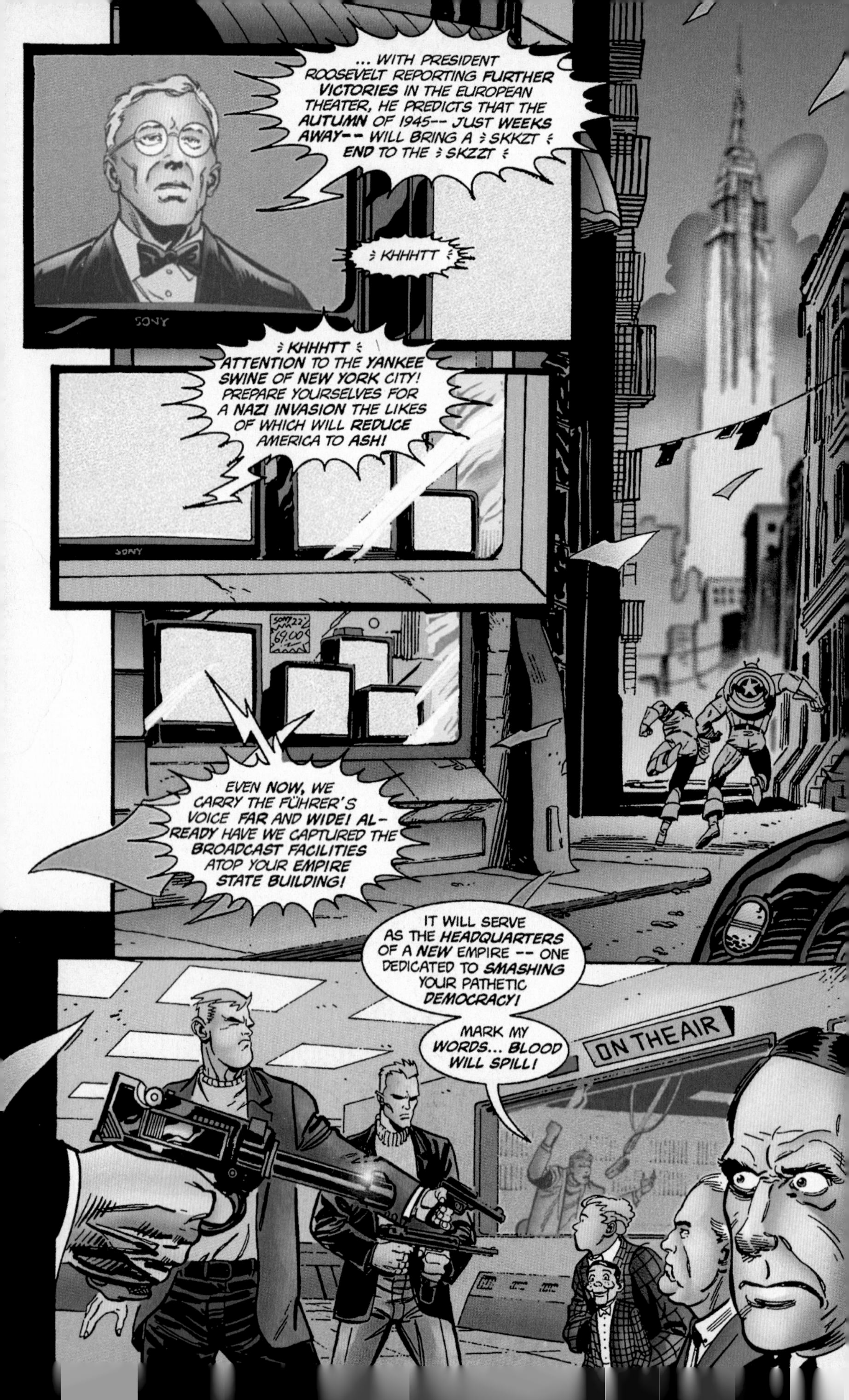

... WITH PRESIDENT ROOSEVELT REPORTING FURTHER VICTORIES IN THE EUROPEAN THEATER, HE PREDICTS THAT THE AUTUMN OF 1945-- JUST WEEKS AWAY-- WILL BRING A SKKZT END TO THE SKZZT
SONY
KHHHTT
KHHHTT ATTENTION TO THE YANKEE SWINE OF NEW YORK CITY! PREPARE YOURSELVES FOR A NAZI INVASION THE LIKES OF WHICH WILL REDUCE AMERICA TO ASH!
SONY
SONY 22 69.00
EVEN NOW, WE CARRY THE FÜHRER'S VOICE FAR AND WIDE! ALREADY HAVE WE CAPTURED THE BROADCAST FACILITIES ATOP YOUR EMPIRE STATE BUILDING!
IT WILL SERVE AS THE HEADQUARTERS OF A NEW EMPIRE -- ONE DEDICATED TO SMASHING YOUR PATHETIC DEMOCRACY!
MARK MY WORDS... BLOOD WILL SPILL!
ON THE AIR

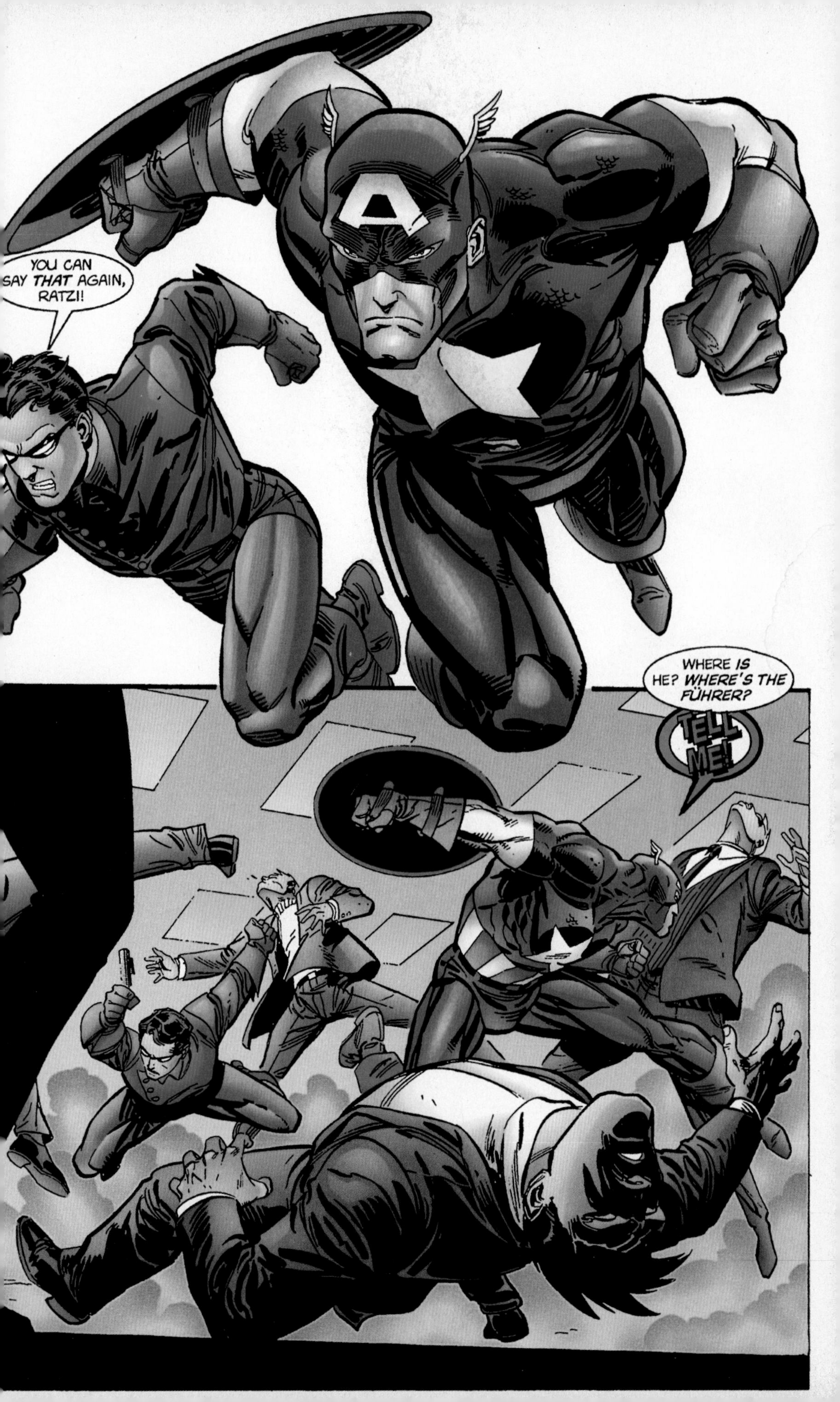
YOU CAN SAY *THAT* AGAIN, RATZI!
WHERE *IS* HE? *WHERE'S THE FÜHRER?*
TELL ME!

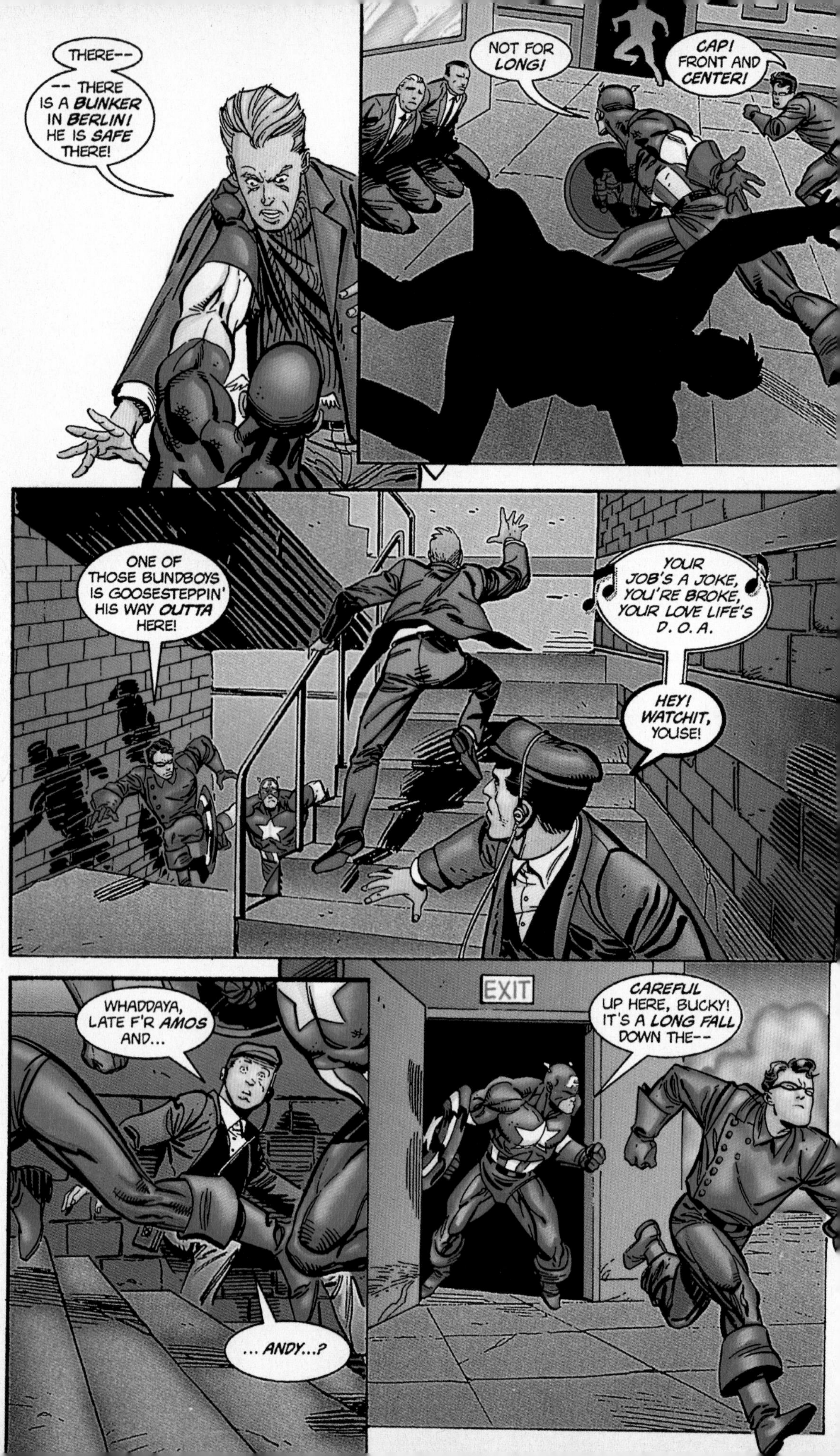
THERE--
-- THERE IS A BUNKER IN BERLIN! HE IS SAFE THERE!
NOT FOR LONG!
CAP! FRONT AND CENTER!
ONE OF THOSE BUNDBOYS IS GOOSESTEPPIN' HIS WAY OUTTA HERE!
YOUR JOB'S A JOKE, YOU'RE BROKE, YOUR LOVE LIFE'S D. O. A.
HEY! WATCHIT, YOUSE!
WHADDAYA, LATE F'R AMOS AND...
... ANDY...?
EXIT
CAREFUL UP HERE, BUCKY! IT'S A LONG FALL DOWN THE--

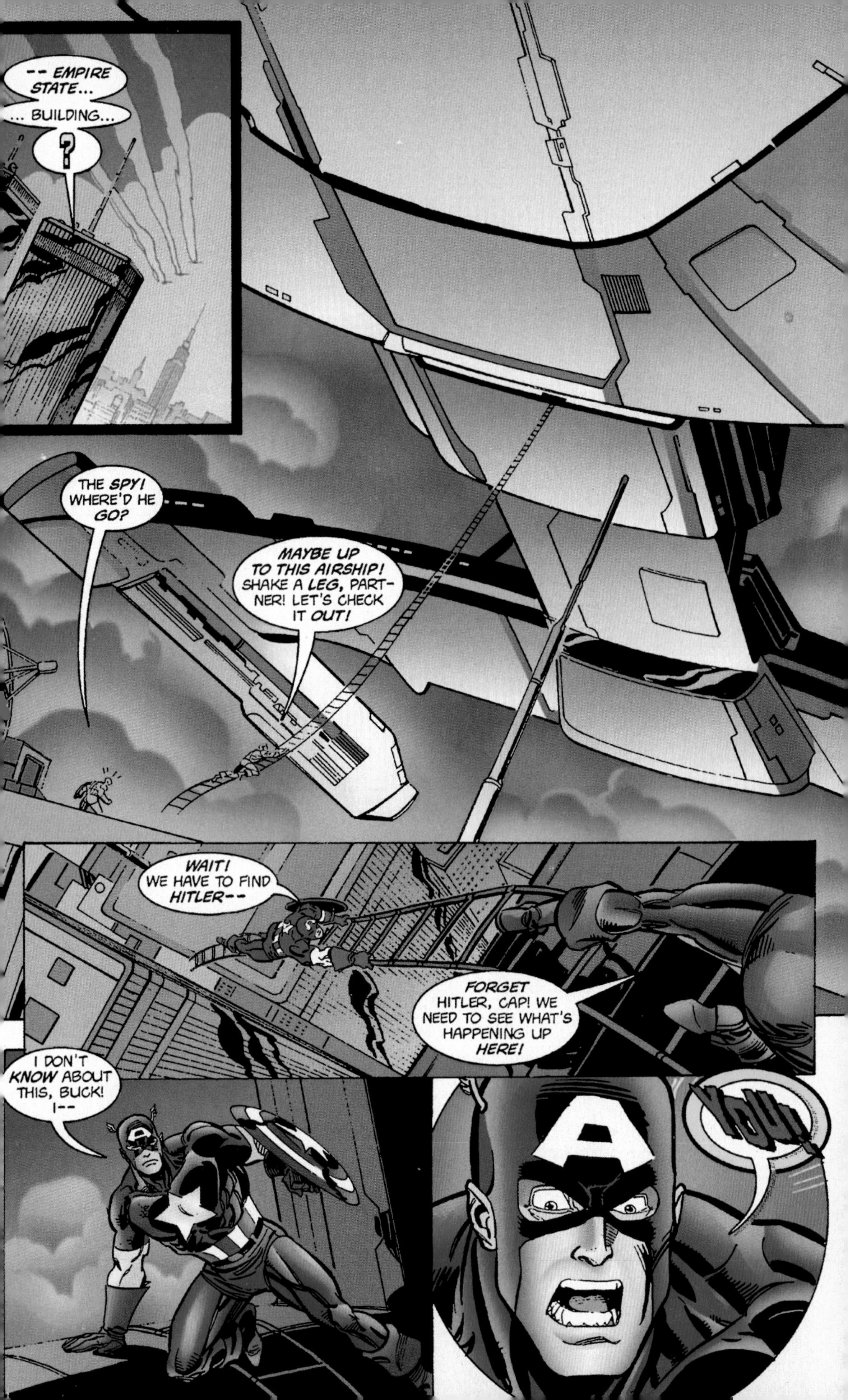
-- EMPIRE STATE...
... BUILDING...
?
THE SPY! WHERE'D HE GO?
MAYBE UP TO THIS AIRSHIP! SHAKE A LEG, PARTNER! LET'S CHECK IT OUT!
WAIT! WE HAVE TO FIND HITLER--
FORGET HITLER, CAP! WE NEED TO SEE WHAT'S HAPPENING UP HERE!
I DON'T KNOW ABOUT THIS, BUCK! I--
YOU!

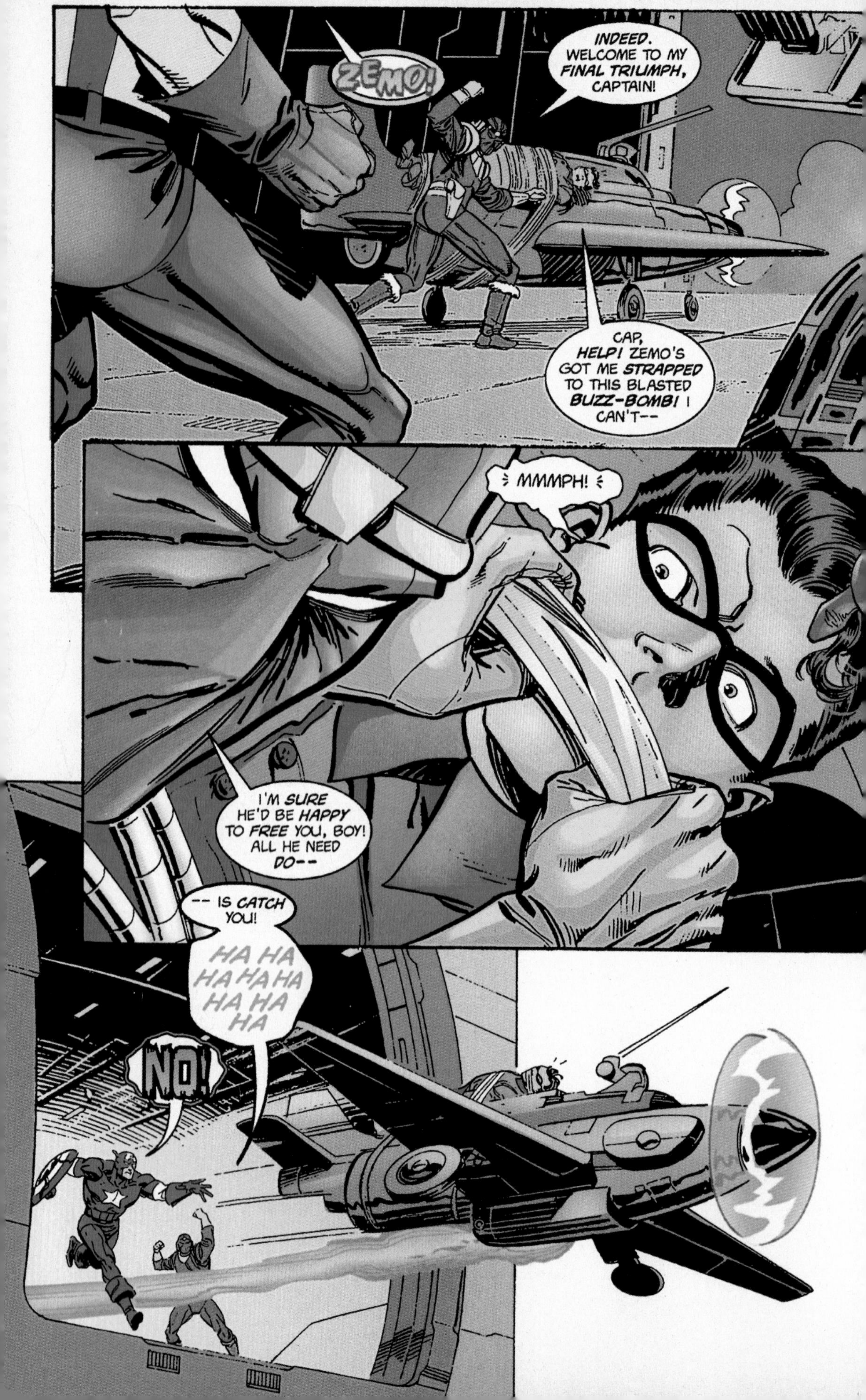
ZEMO!
INDEED. WELCOME TO MY FINAL TRIUMPH, CAPTAIN!
CAP, HELP! ZEMO'S GOT ME STRAPPED TO THIS BLASTED BUZZ-BOMB! I CAN'T--
MMMPH!
I'M SURE HE'D BE HAPPY TO FREE YOU, BOY! ALL HE NEED DO--
-- IS CATCH YOU!
HA HA HA HA HA HA HA HA HA
NO!

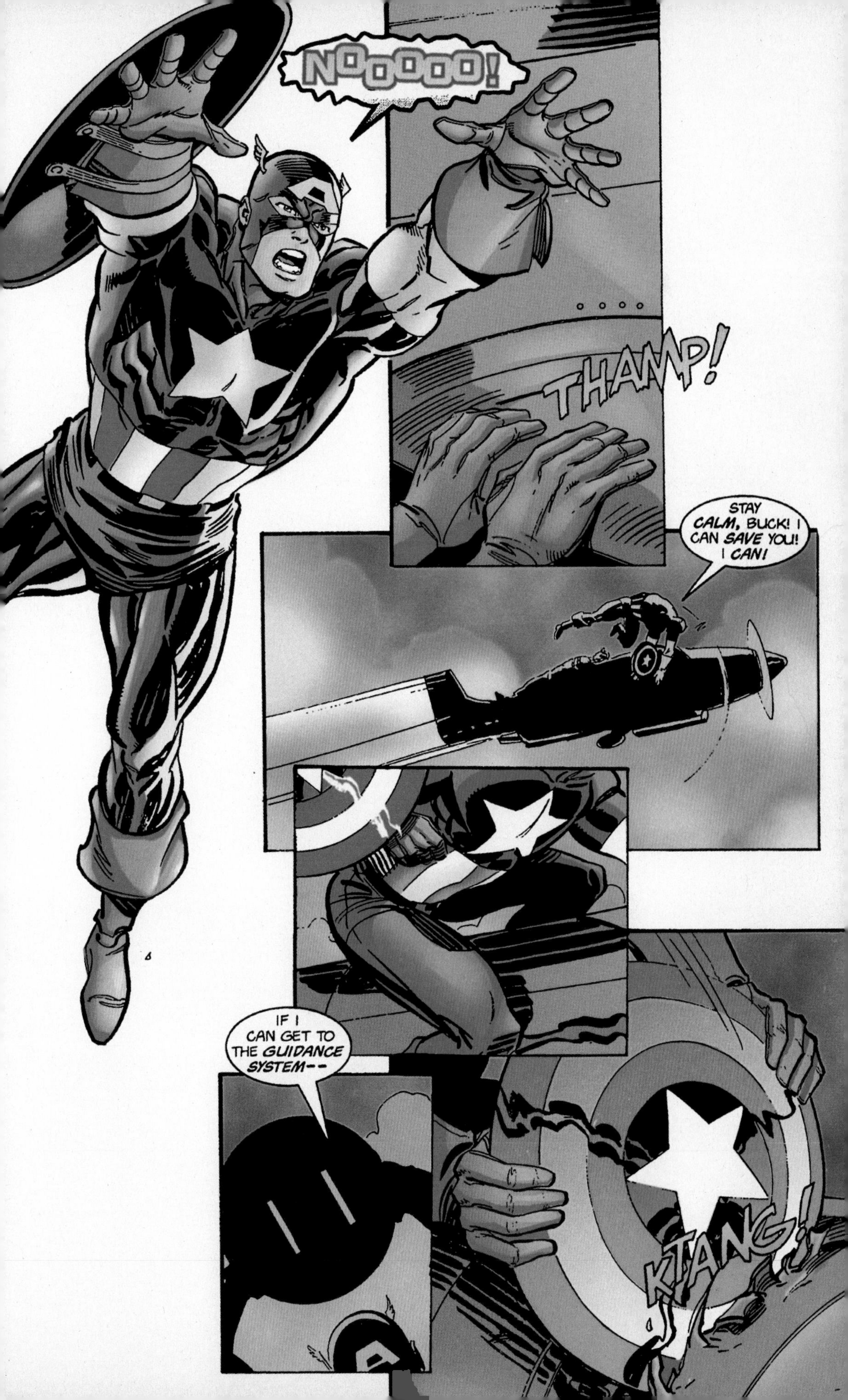
NOOOOOO!
THAMP!
STAY CALM, BUCK! I CAN SAVE YOU! I CAN!
IF I CAN GET TO THE GUIDANCE SYSTEM--
KTANG!

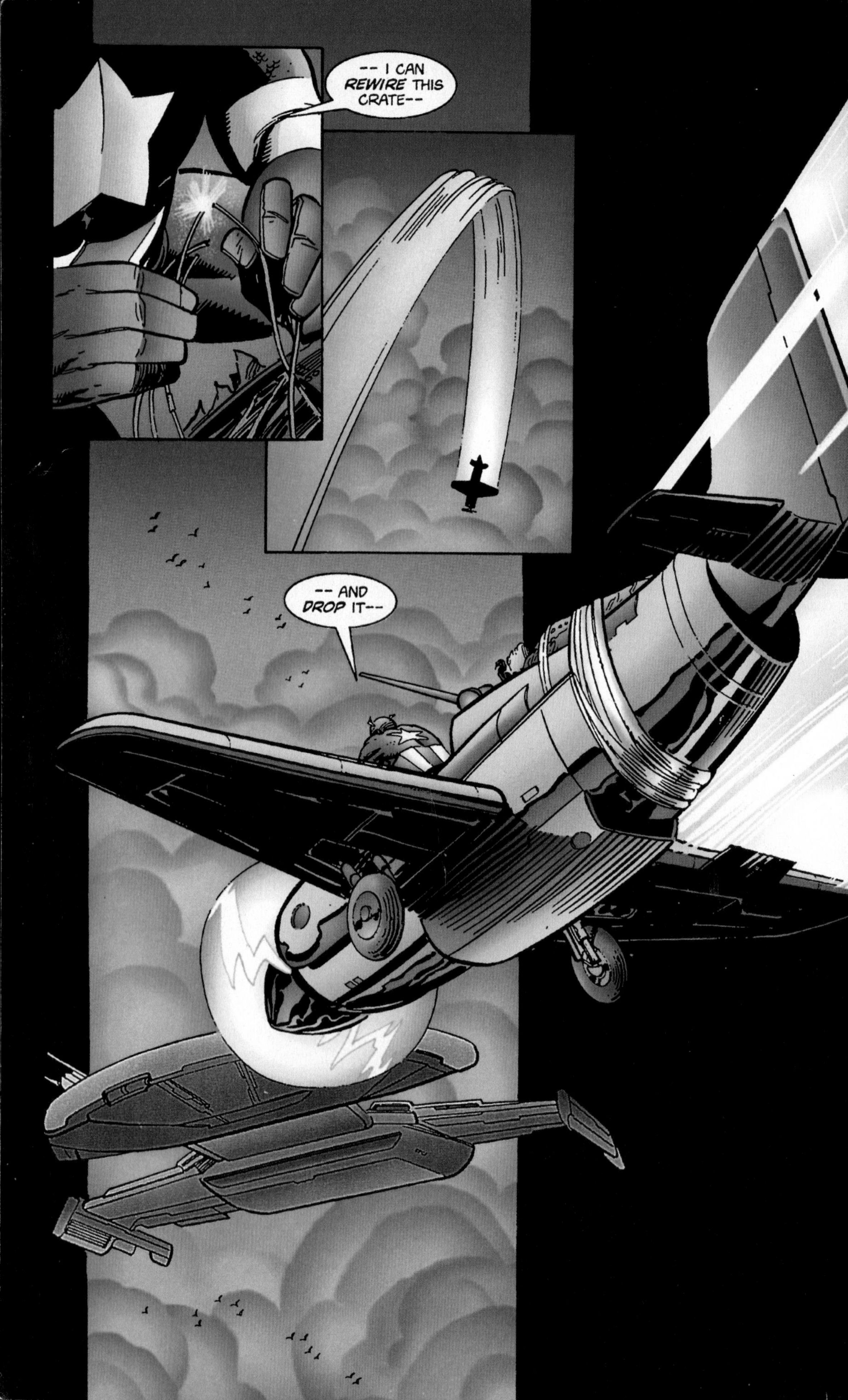
-- I CAN REWIRE THIS CRATE--
-- AND DROP IT--

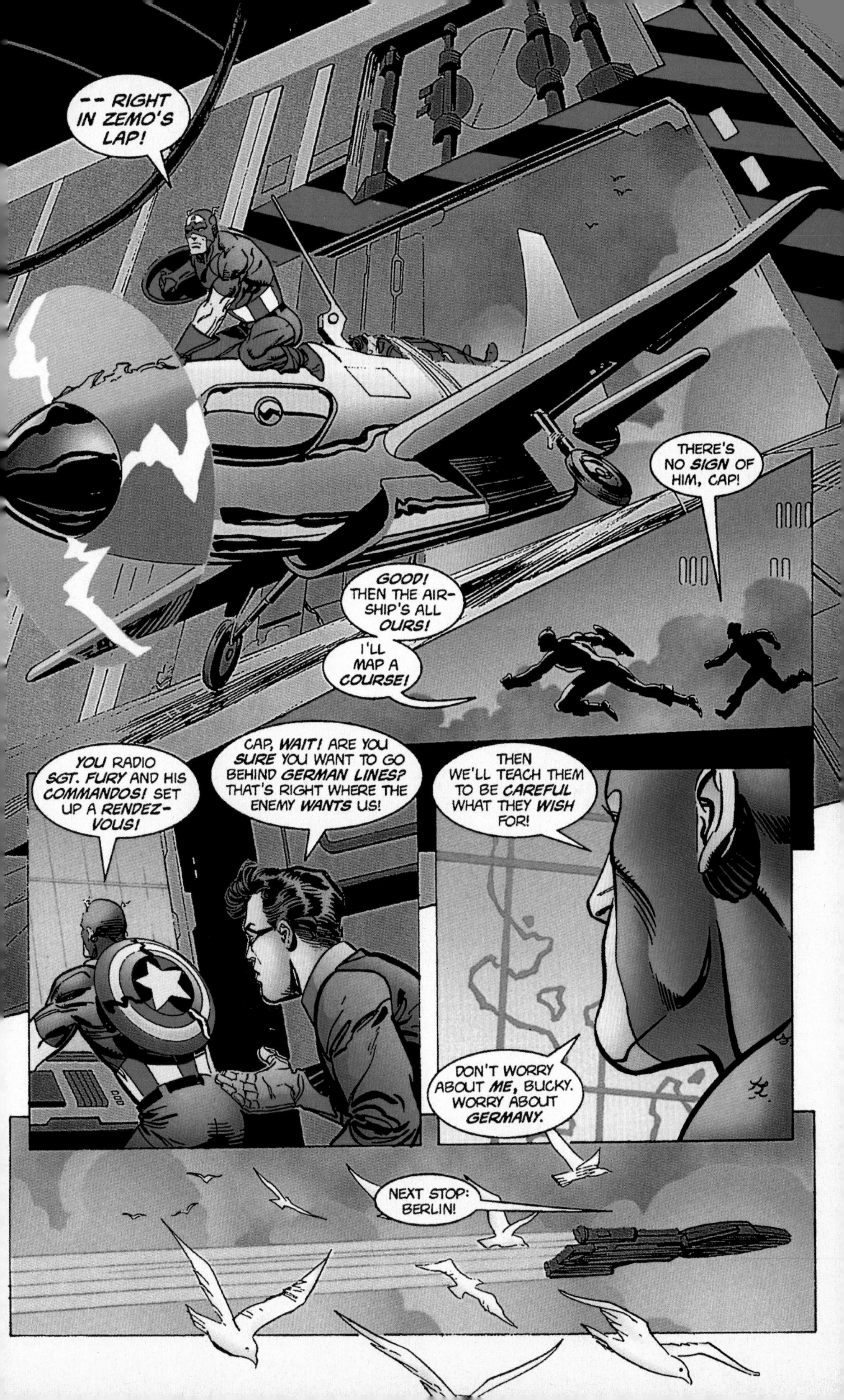
-- RIGHT IN ZEMO'S LAP!
THERE'S NO SIGN OF HIM, CAP!
GOOD! THEN THE AIR-SHIP'S ALL OURS!
I'LL MAP A COURSE!
YOU RADIO SGT. FURY AND HIS COMMANDOS! SET UP A RENDEZ-VOUS!
CAP, WAIT! ARE YOU SURE YOU WANT TO GO BEHIND GERMAN LINES? THAT'S RIGHT WHERE THE ENEMY WANTS US!
THEN WE'LL TEACH THEM TO BE CAREFUL WHAT THEY WISH FOR!
DON'T WORRY ABOUT ME, BUCKY. WORRY ABOUT GERMANY.
NEXT STOP: BERLIN!

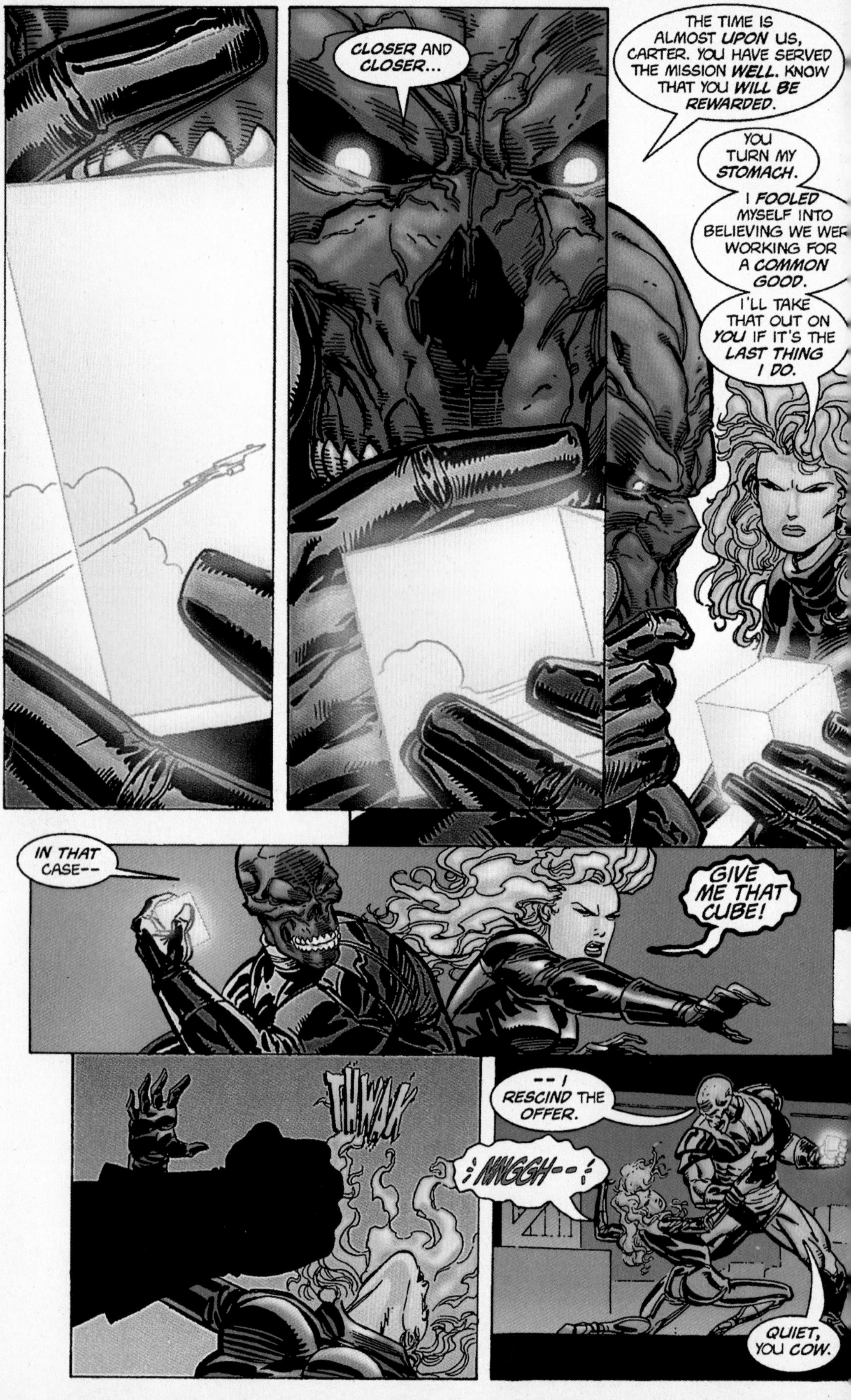
CLOSER AND CLOSER...
THE TIME IS ALMOST UPON US, CARTER. YOU HAVE SERVED THE MISSION WELL. KNOW THAT YOU WILL BE REWARDED.
YOU TURN MY STOMACH.
I FOOLED MYSELF INTO BELIEVING WE WER WORKING FOR A COMMON GOOD.
I'LL TAKE THAT OUT ON YOU IF IT'S THE LAST THING I DO.
IN THAT CASE--
GIVE ME THAT CUBE!
THWAK
--I RESCIND THE OFFER.
NNGGH--
QUIET, YOU COW.

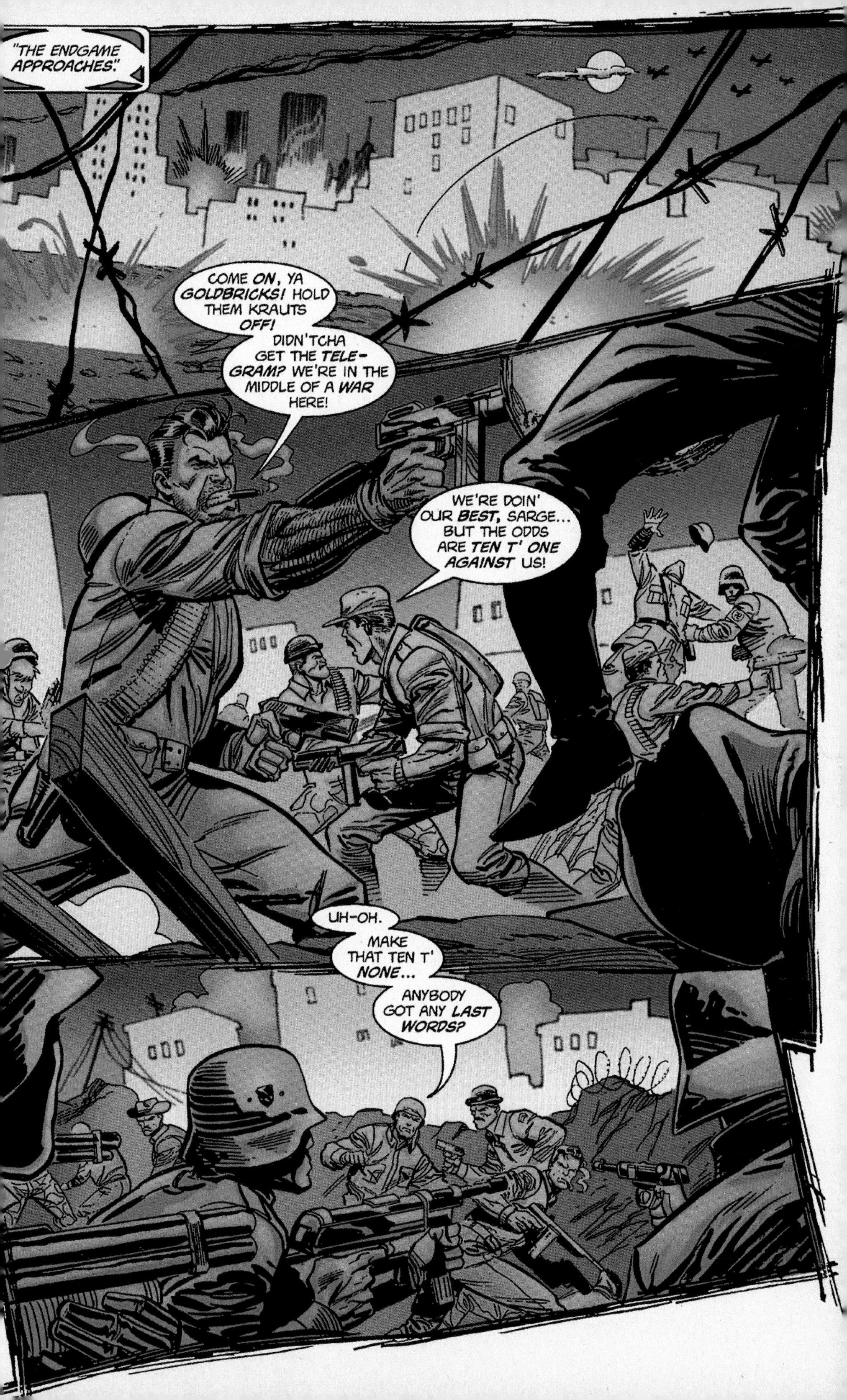
"THE ENDGAME APPROACHES."
COME ON, YA GOLDBRICKS! HOLD THEM KRAUTS OFF!
DIDN'TCHA GET THE TELE-GRAM? WE'RE IN THE MIDDLE OF A WAR HERE!
WE'RE DOIN' OUR BEST, SARGE... BUT THE ODDS ARE TEN T' ONE AGAINST US!
UH-OH.
MAKE THAT TEN T' NONE...
ANYBODY GOT ANY LAST WORDS?

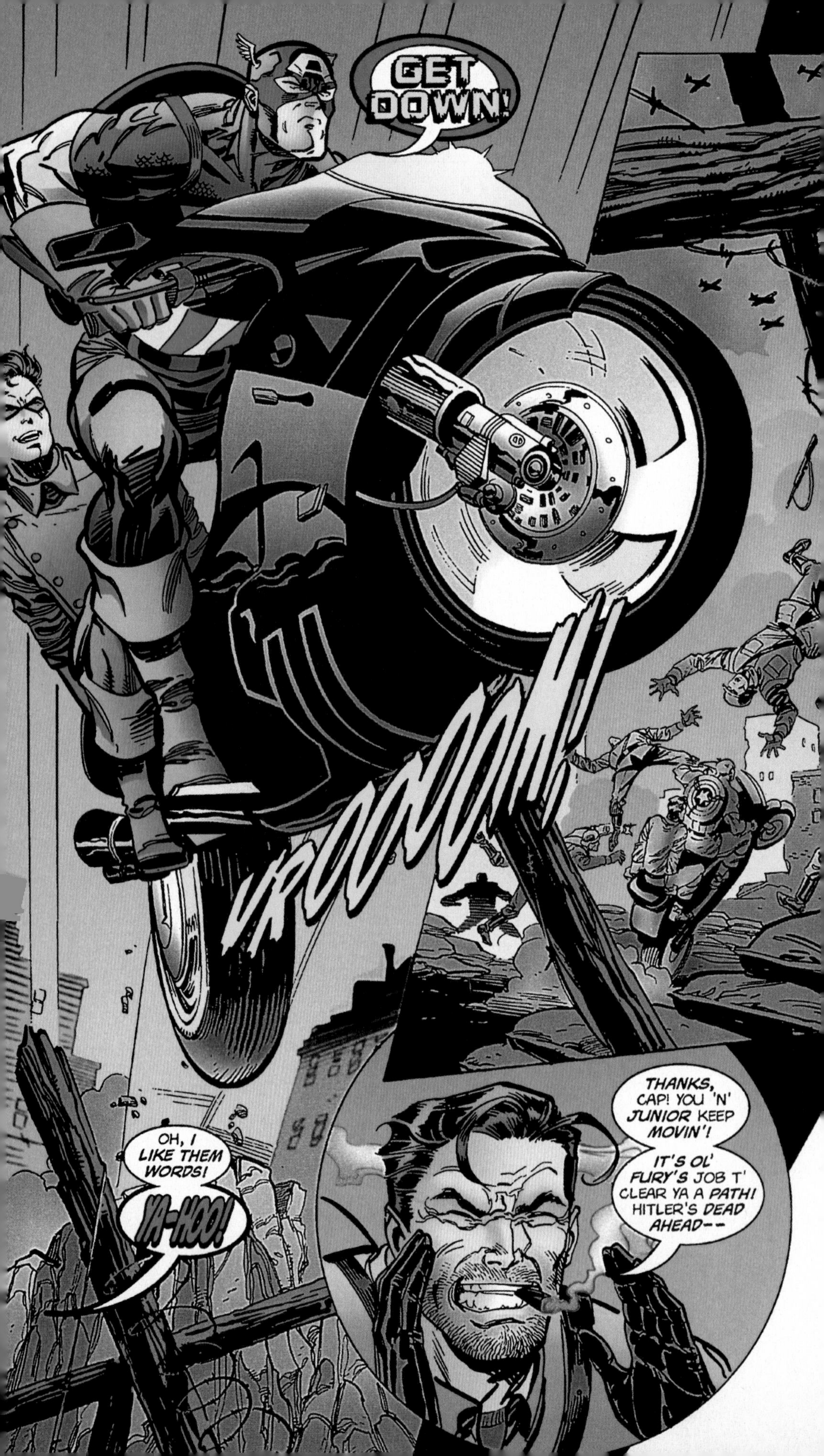
GET DOWN!
VROOOOM!
OH, I LIKE THEM WORDS!
YA-HOO!
THANKS, CAP! YOU 'N' JUNIOR KEEP MOVIN'!
IT'S OL' FURY'S JOB T' CLEAR YA A PATH! HITLER'S DEAD AHEAD--

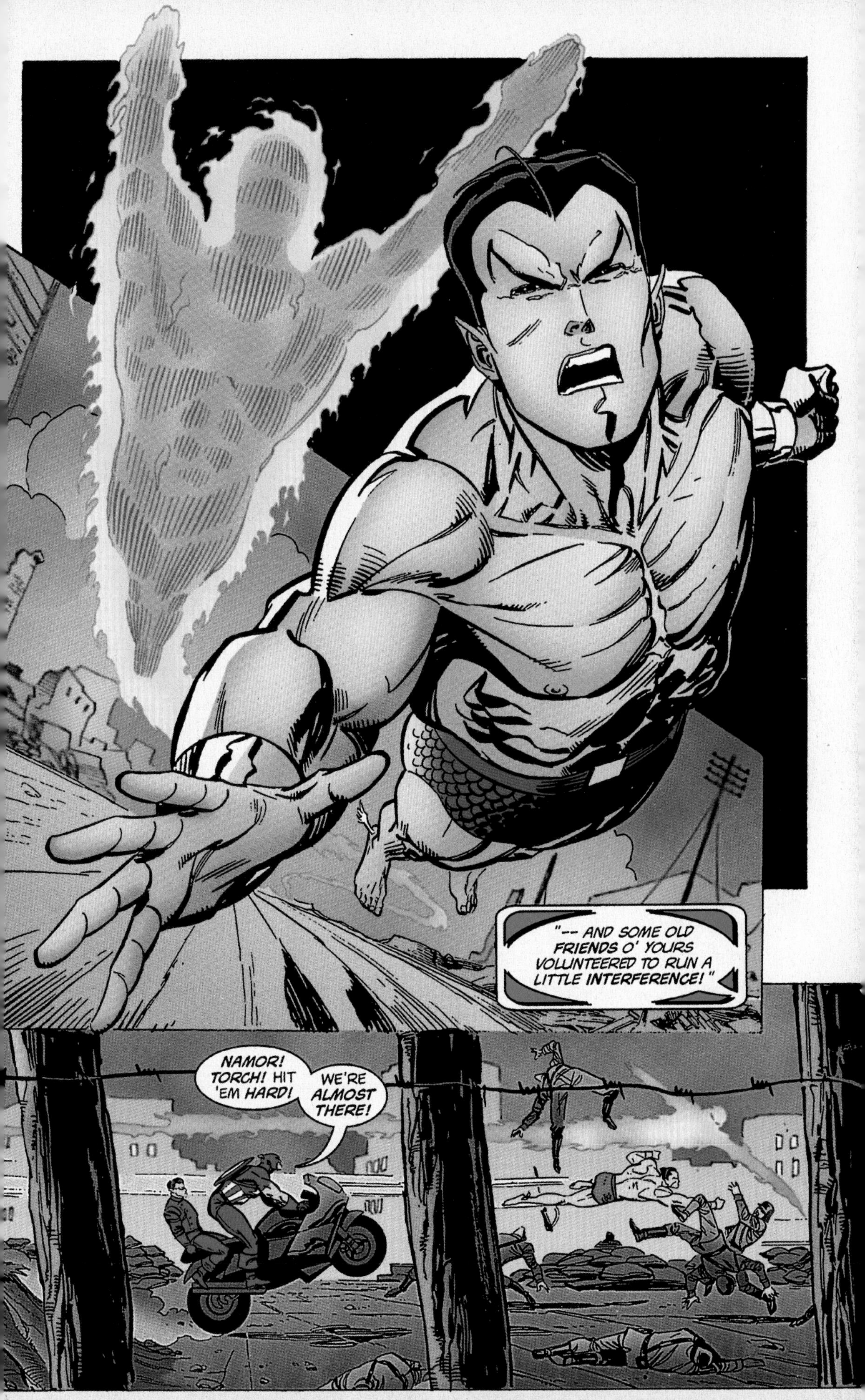
"-- AND SOME OLD FRIENDS O' YOURS VOLUNTEERED TO RUN A LITTLE INTERFERENCE!"
NAMOR! TORCH! HIT 'EM HARD!
WE'RE ALMOST THERE!

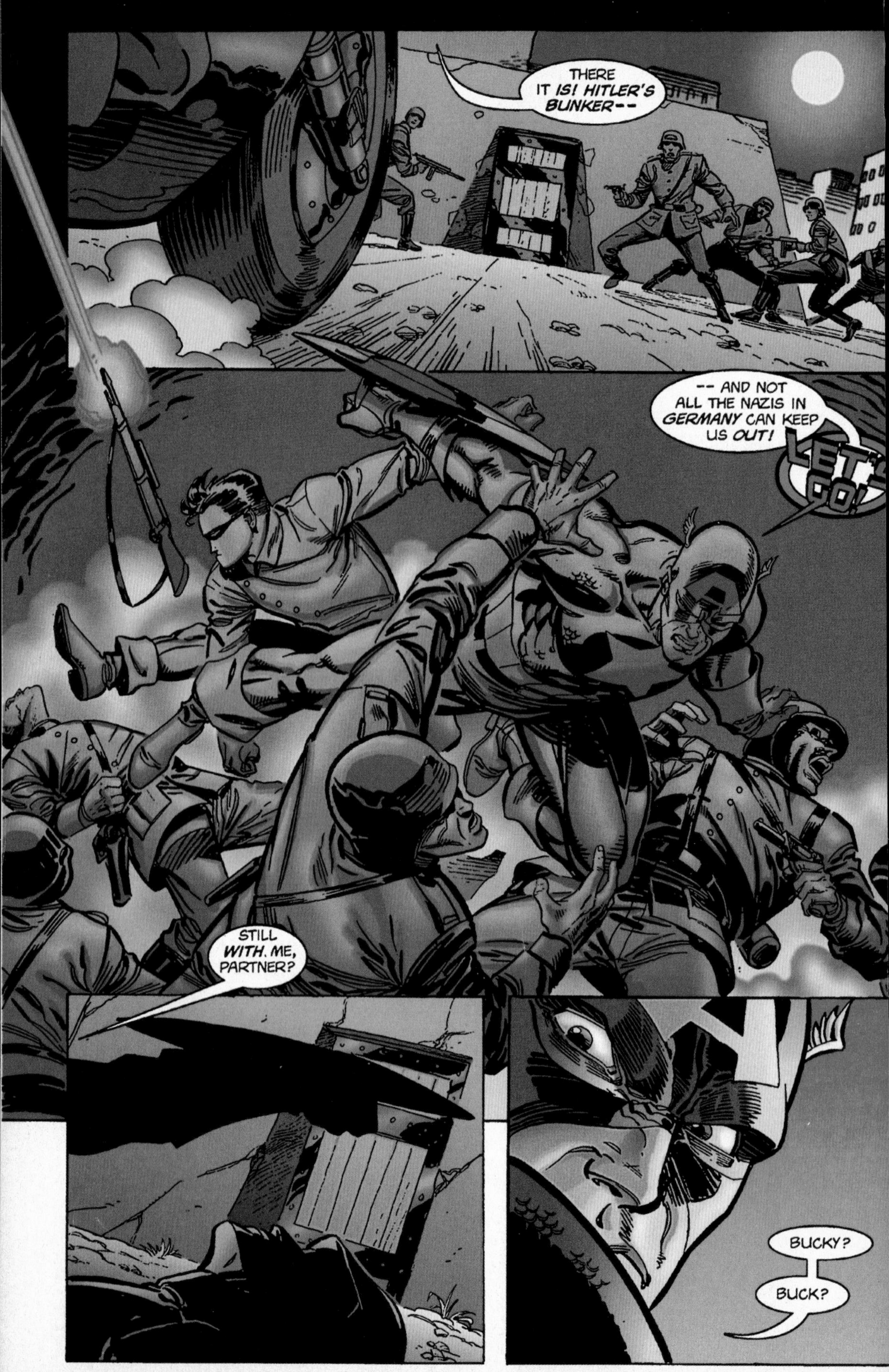
THERE IT IS! HITLER'S BUNKER--
-- AND NOT ALL THE NAZIS IN GERMANY CAN KEEP US OUT!
LET'S GO!
STILL WITH ME, PARTNER?
BUCKY?
BUCK?

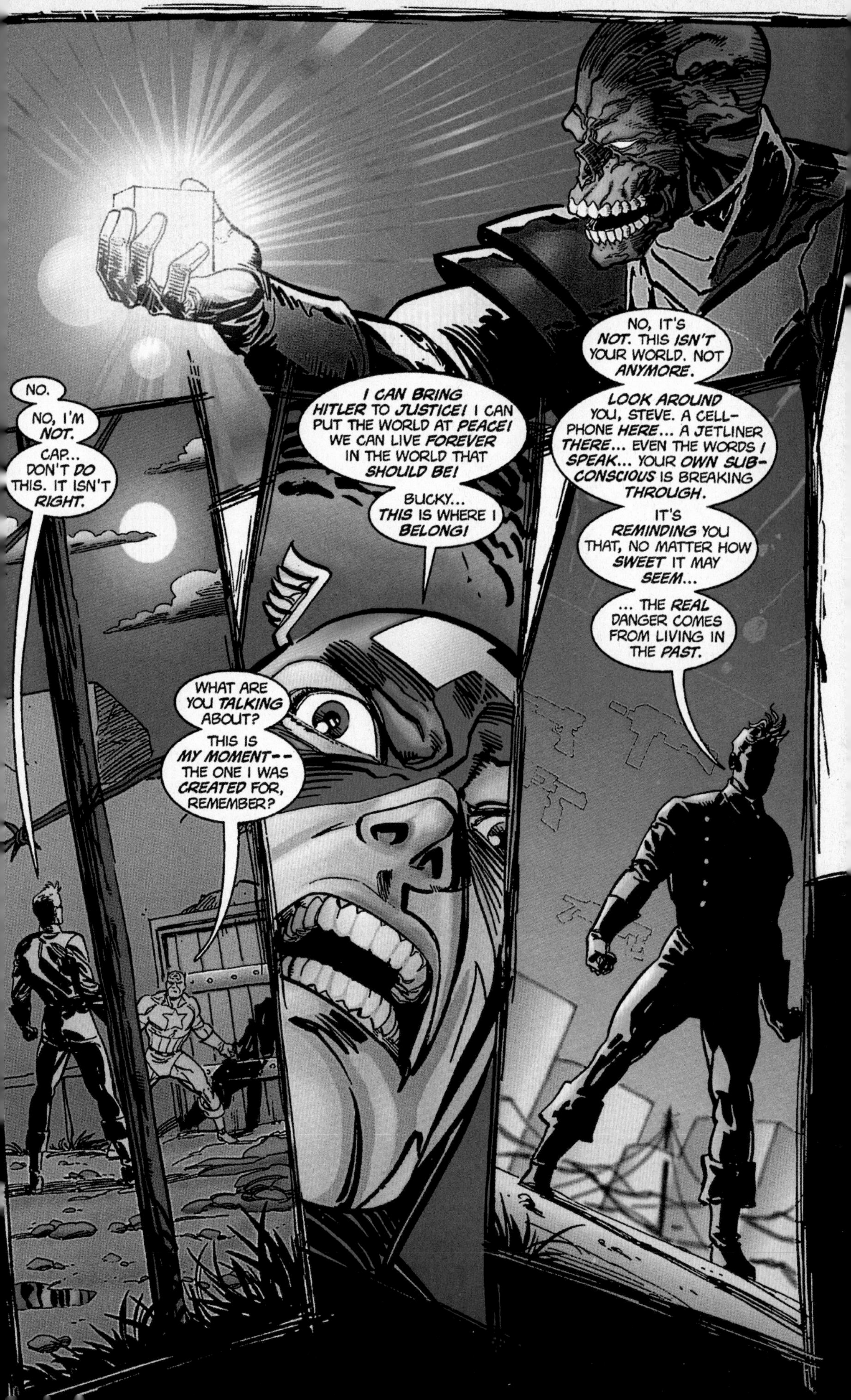

NO.
NO, I'M NOT.
CAP... DON'T DO THIS. IT ISN'T RIGHT.
I CAN BRING HITLER TO JUSTICE! I CAN PUT THE WORLD AT PEACE! WE CAN LIVE FOREVER IN THE WORLD THAT SHOULD BE!
BUCKY... THIS IS WHERE I BELONG!
WHAT ARE YOU TALKING ABOUT?
THIS IS MY MOMENT-- THE ONE I WAS CREATED FOR, REMEMBER?
NO, IT'S NOT. THIS ISN'T YOUR WORLD. NOT ANYMORE.
LOOK AROUND YOU, STEVE. A CELL-PHONE HERE... A JETLINER THERE... EVEN THE WORDS I SPEAK... YOUR OWN SUB-CONSCIOUS IS BREAKING THROUGH.
IT'S REMINDING YOU THAT, NO MATTER HOW SWEET IT MAY SEEM...
... THE REAL DANGER COMES FROM LIVING IN THE PAST.

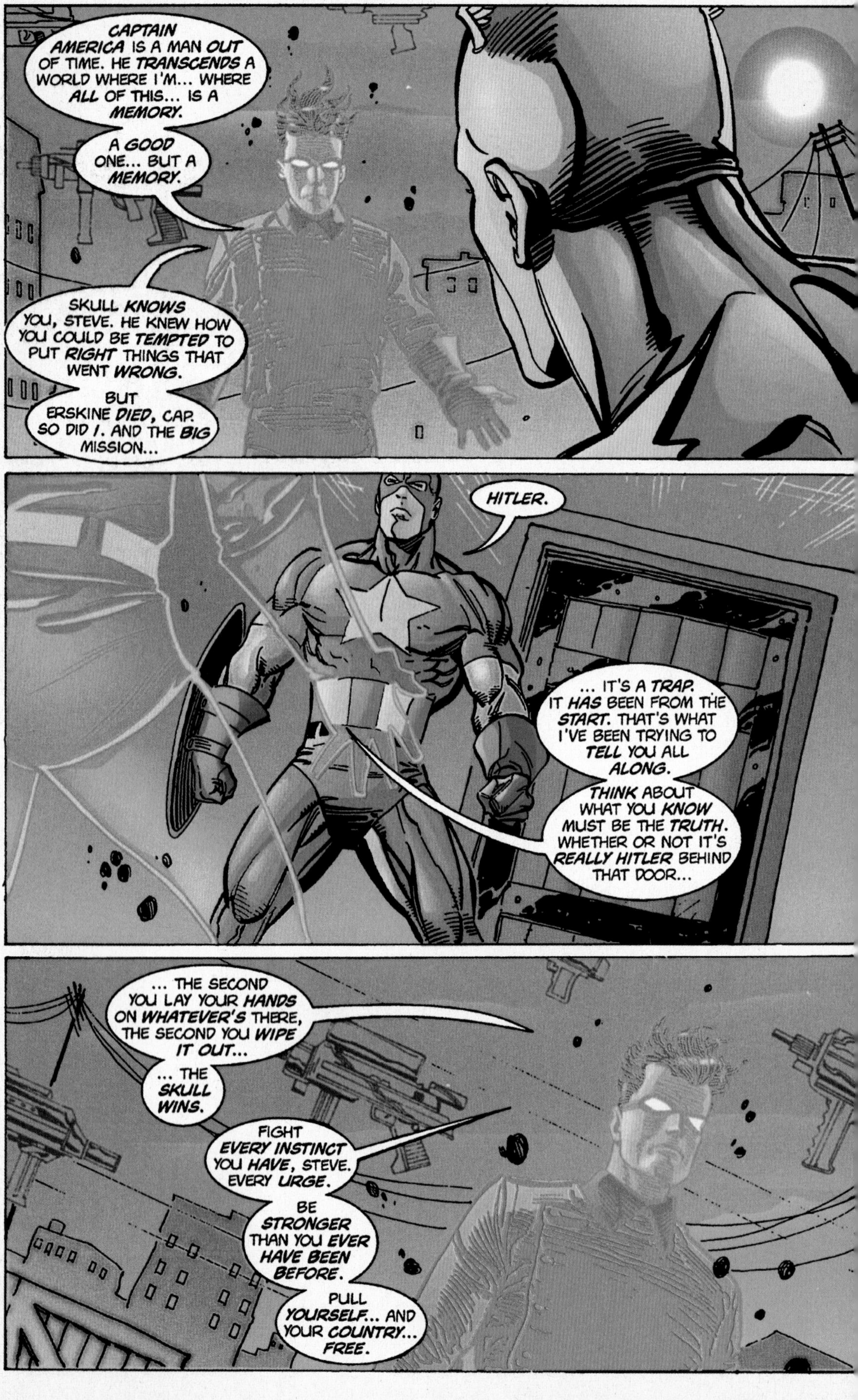
CAPTAIN AMERICA IS A MAN OUT OF TIME. HE TRANSCENDS A WORLD WHERE I'M... WHERE ALL OF THIS... IS A MEMORY.
A GOOD ONE... BUT A MEMORY.
SKULL KNOWS YOU, STEVE. HE KNEW HOW YOU COULD BE TEMPTED TO PUT RIGHT THINGS THAT WENT WRONG.
BUT ERSKINE DIED, CAP. SO DID I. AND THE BIG MISSION...
HITLER.
... IT'S A TRAP. IT HAS BEEN FROM THE START. THAT'S WHAT I'VE BEEN TRYING TO TELL YOU ALL ALONG.
THINK ABOUT WHAT YOU KNOW MUST BE THE TRUTH. WHETHER OR NOT IT'S REALLY HITLER BEHIND THAT DOOR...
... THE SECOND YOU LAY YOUR HANDS ON WHATEVER'S THERE, THE SECOND YOU WIPE IT OUT...
... THE SKULL WINS.
FIGHT EVERY INSTINCT YOU HAVE, STEVE. EVERY URGE.
BE STRONGER THAN YOU EVER HAVE BEEN BEFORE.
PULL YOURSELF... AND YOUR COUNTRY... FREE.

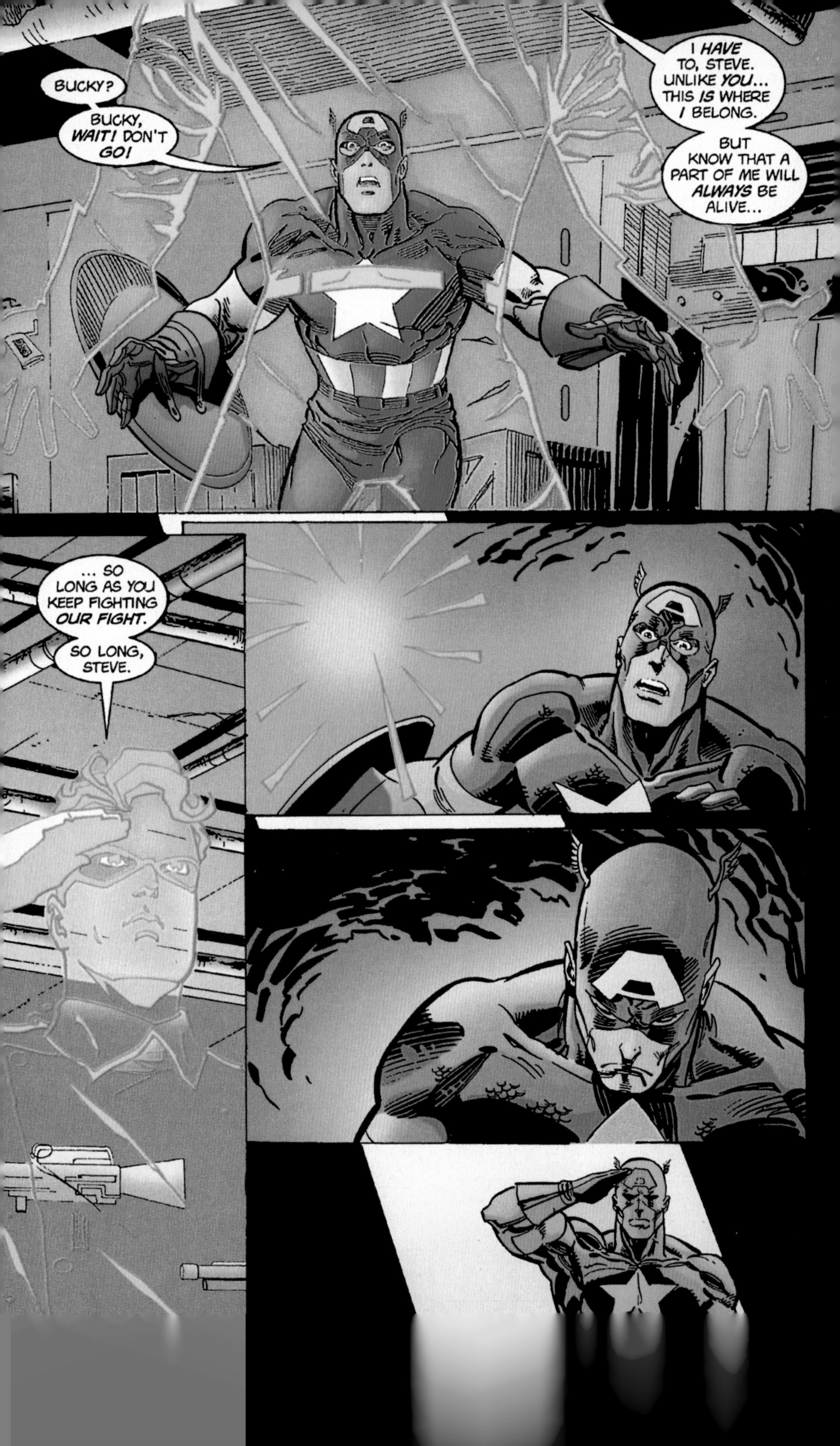
BUCKY?
BUCKY, WAIT! DON'T GO!
I HAVE TO, STEVE. UNLIKE YOU... THIS IS WHERE I BELONG.
BUT KNOW THAT A PART OF ME WILL ALWAYS BE ALIVE...
... SO LONG AS YOU KEEP FIGHTING OUR FIGHT.
SO LONG, STEVE.

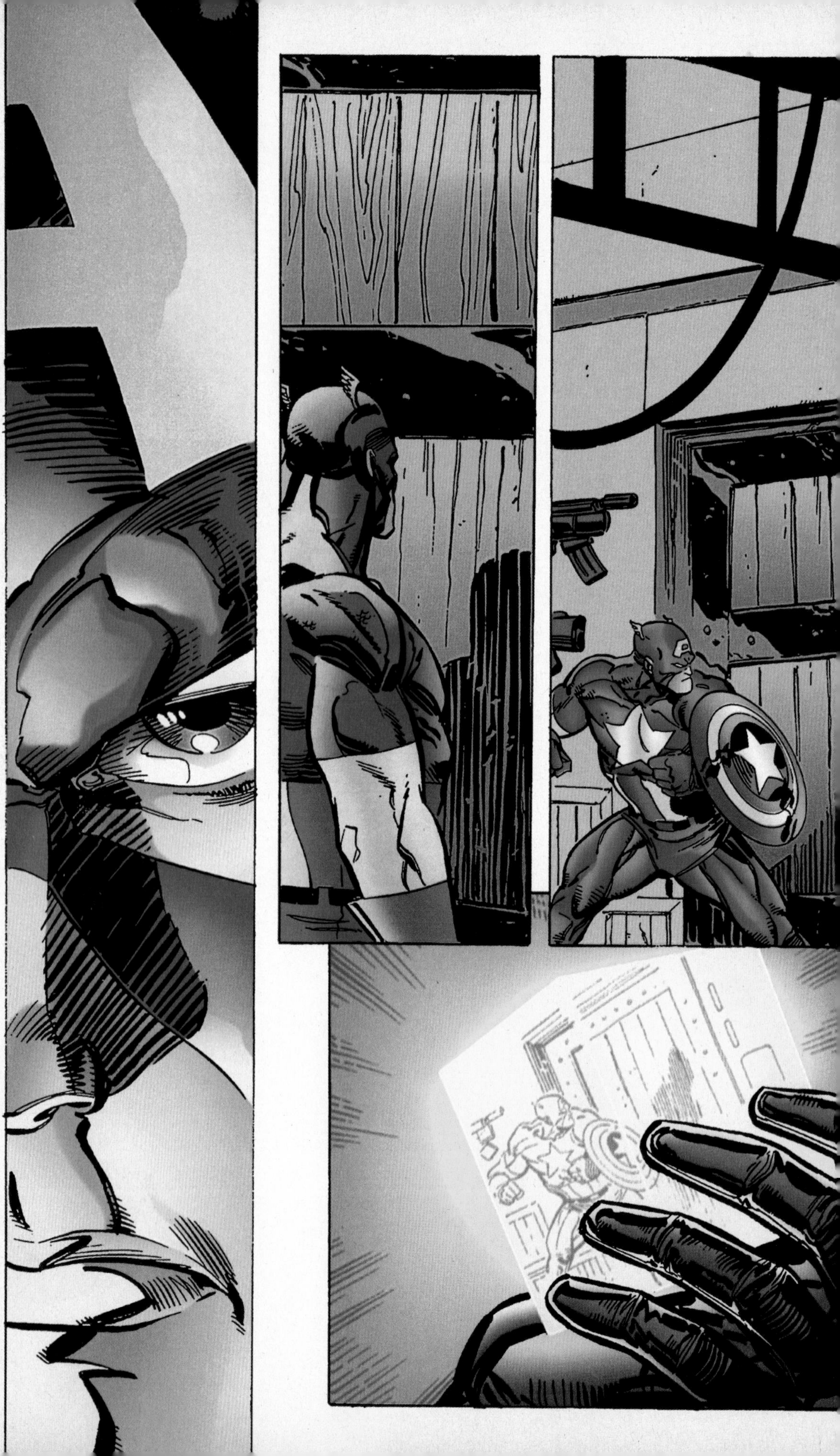

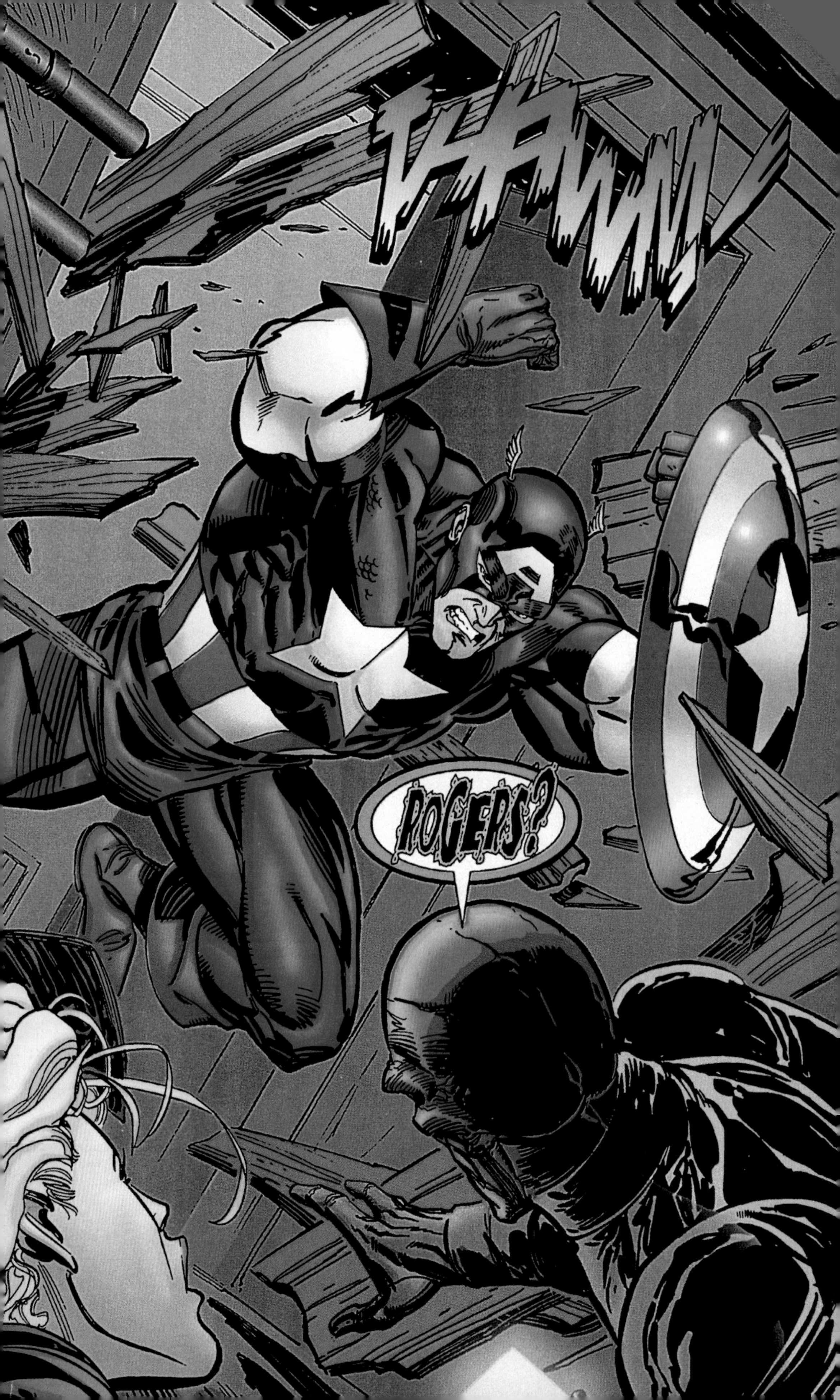
ROGERS?

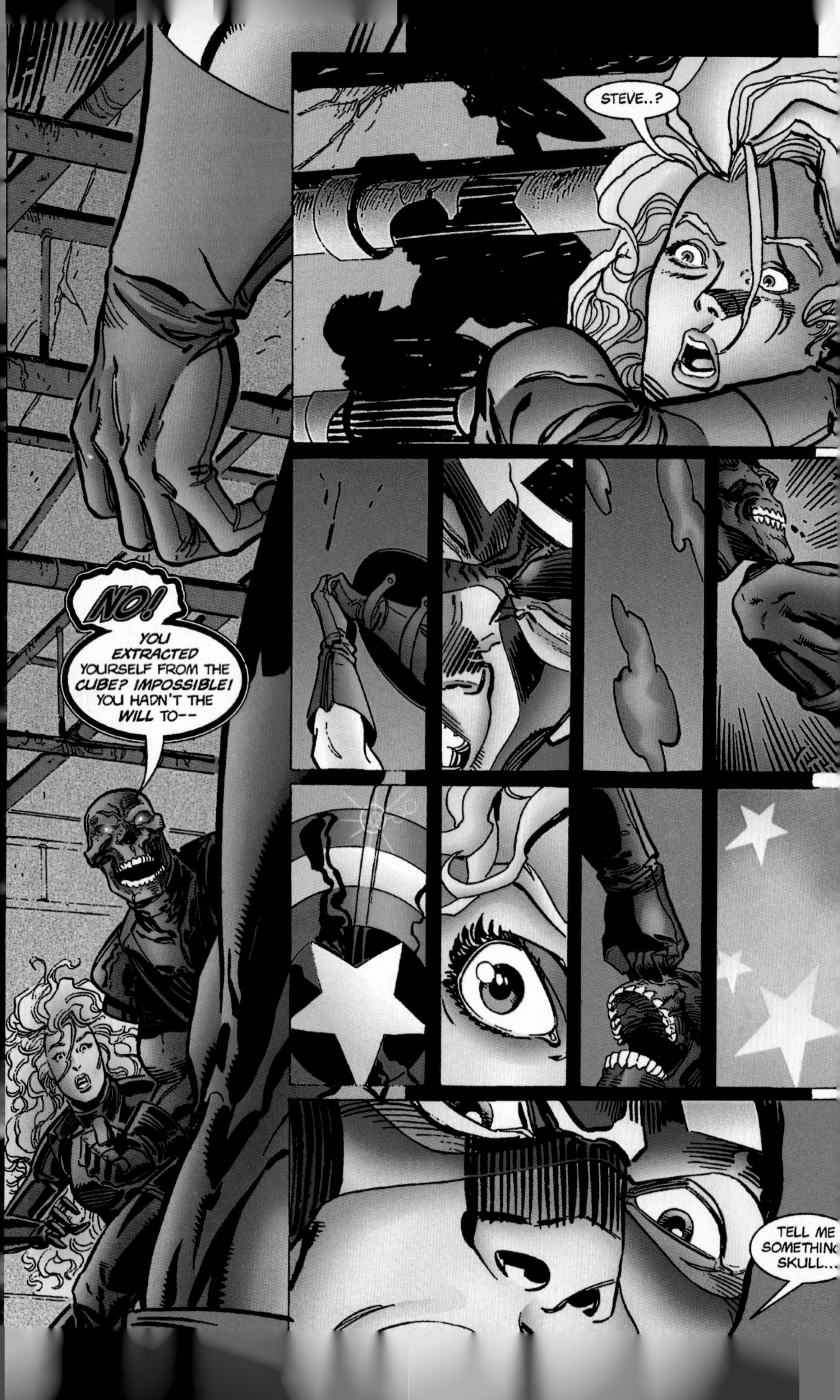
STEVE..?
NO! YOU EXTRACTED YOURSELF FROM THE CUBE? IMPOSSIBLE! YOU HADN'T THE WILL TO--
TELL ME SOMETHIN SKULL...

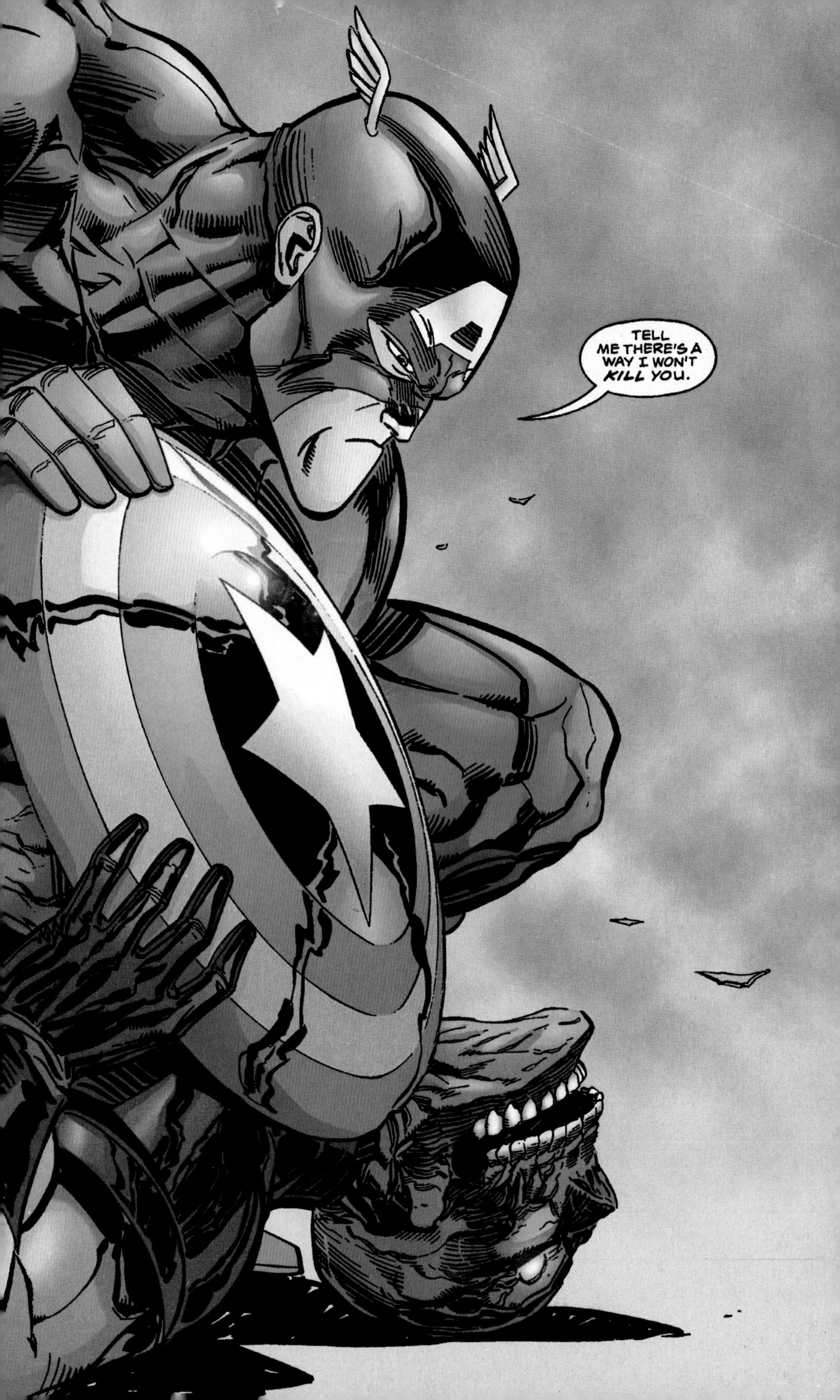
TELL ME THERE'S A WAY I WON'T *KILL* YOU.

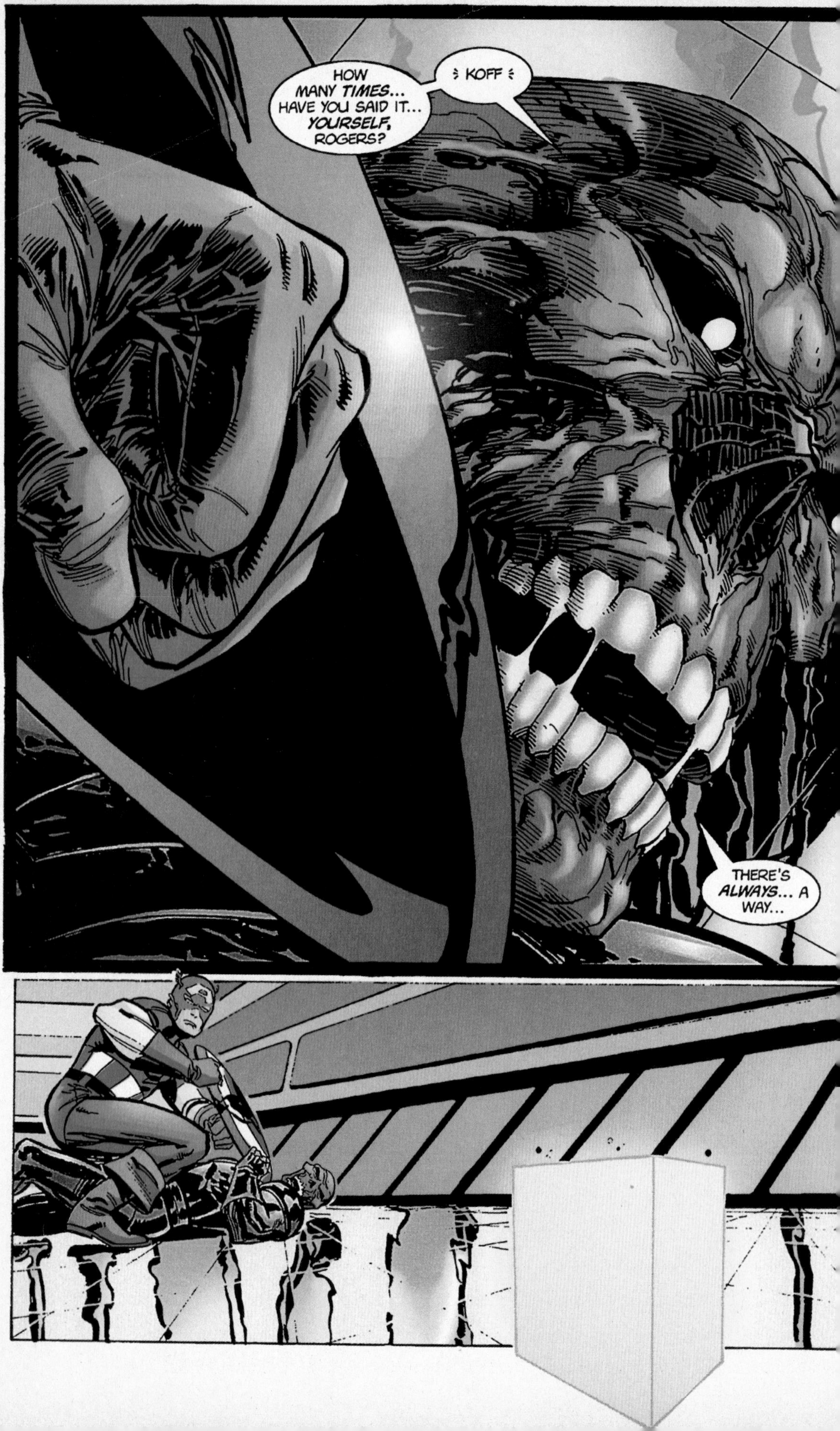
HOW MANY TIMES... HAVE YOU SAID IT... YOURSELF, ROGERS?
⁑ KOFF ⁑
THERE'S ALWAYS... A WAY...

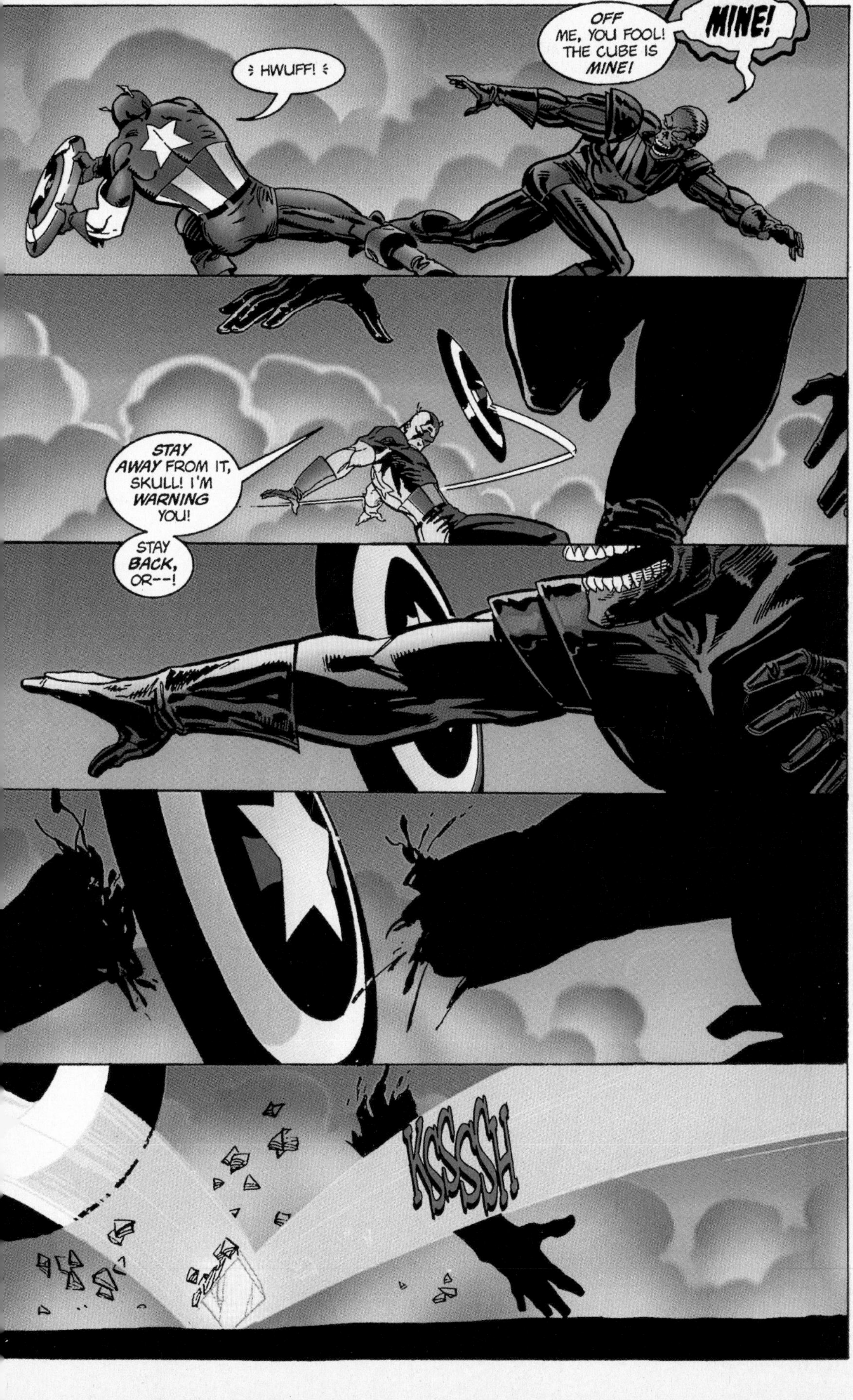
HWUFF!
OFF ME, YOU FOOL! THE CUBE IS MINE!
MINE!
STAY AWAY FROM IT, SKULL! I'M WARNING YOU!
STAY BACK, OR--!
KSSSSH

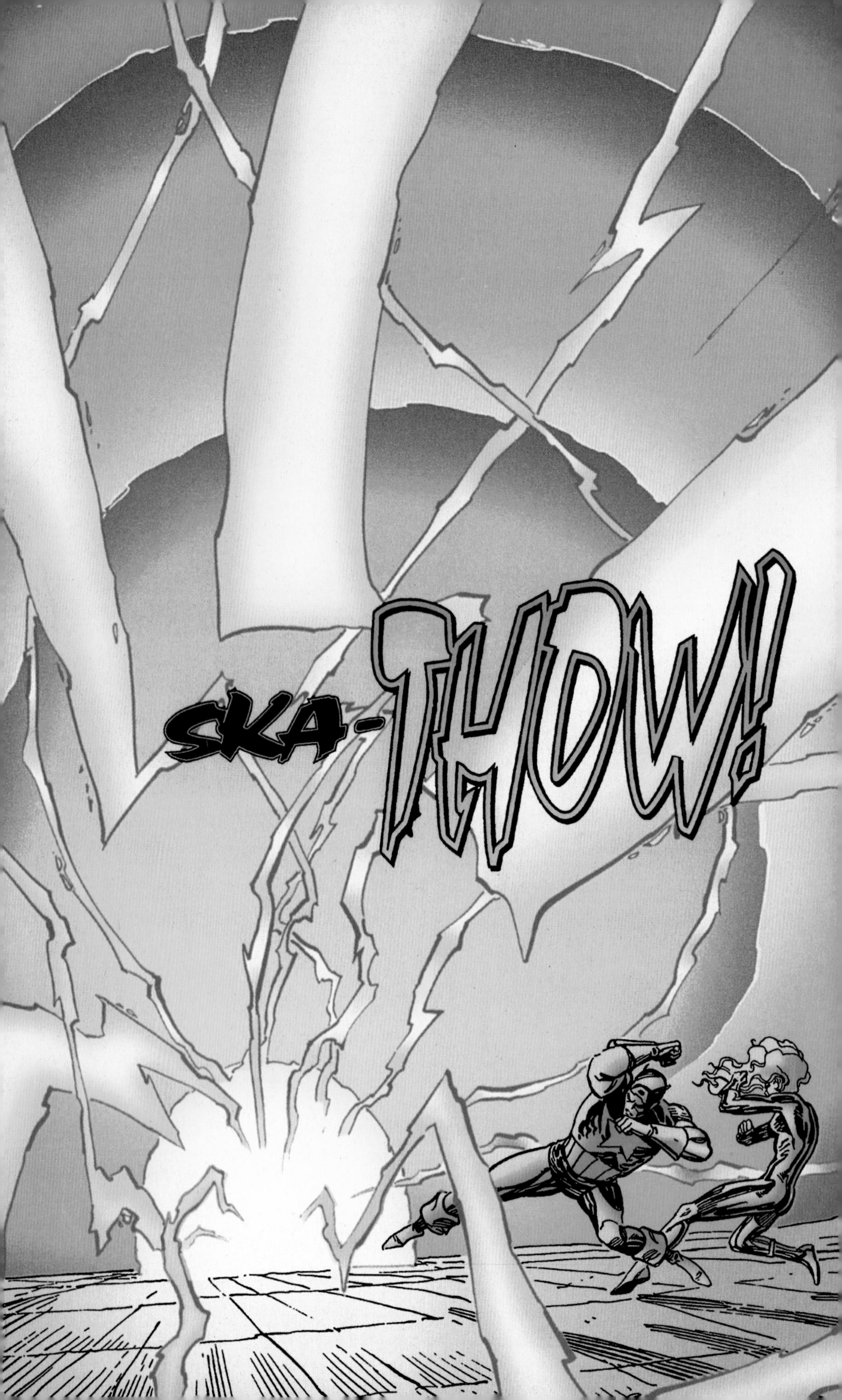
SKA-THOOM!

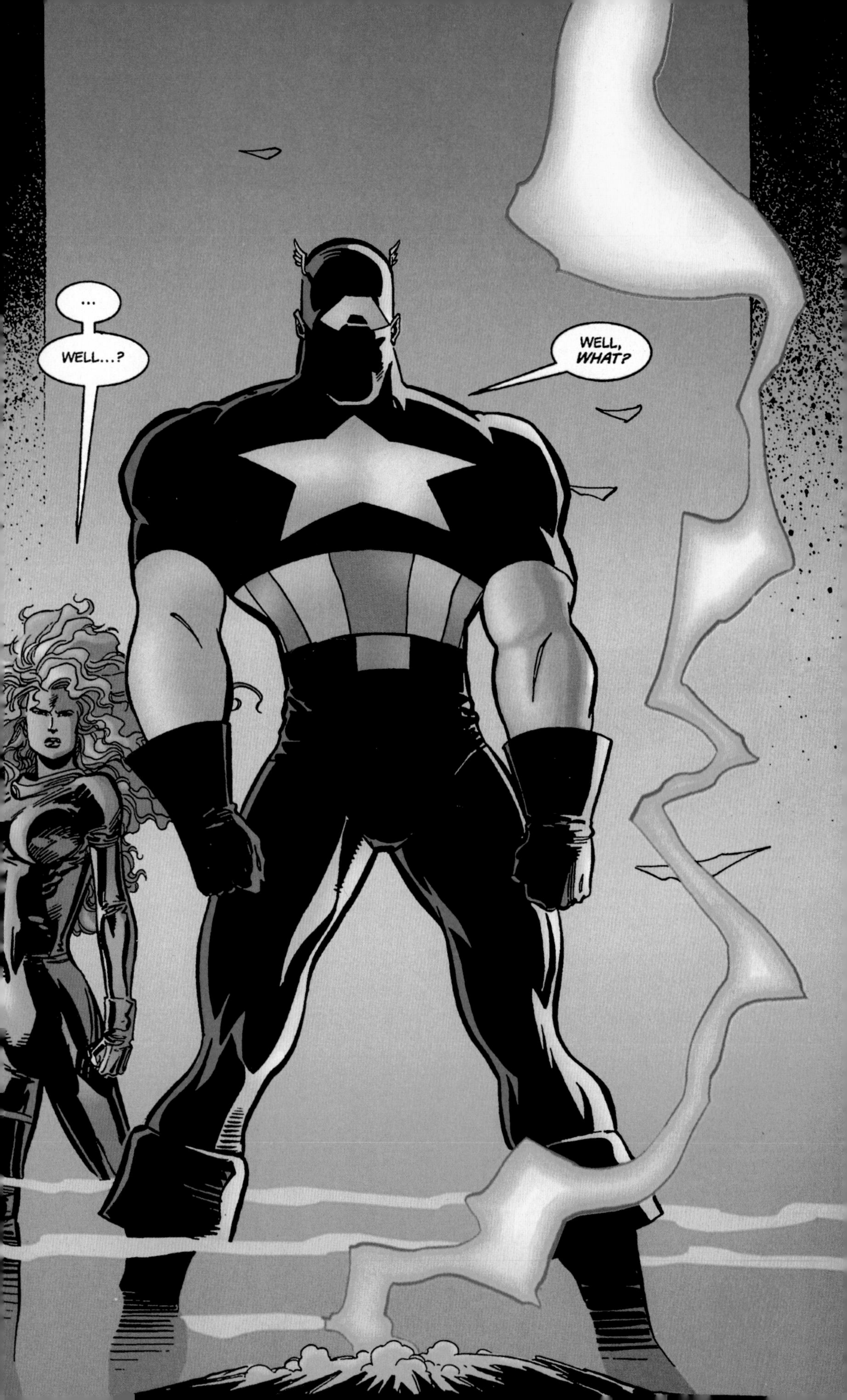
...
WELL...?
WELL, WHAT?

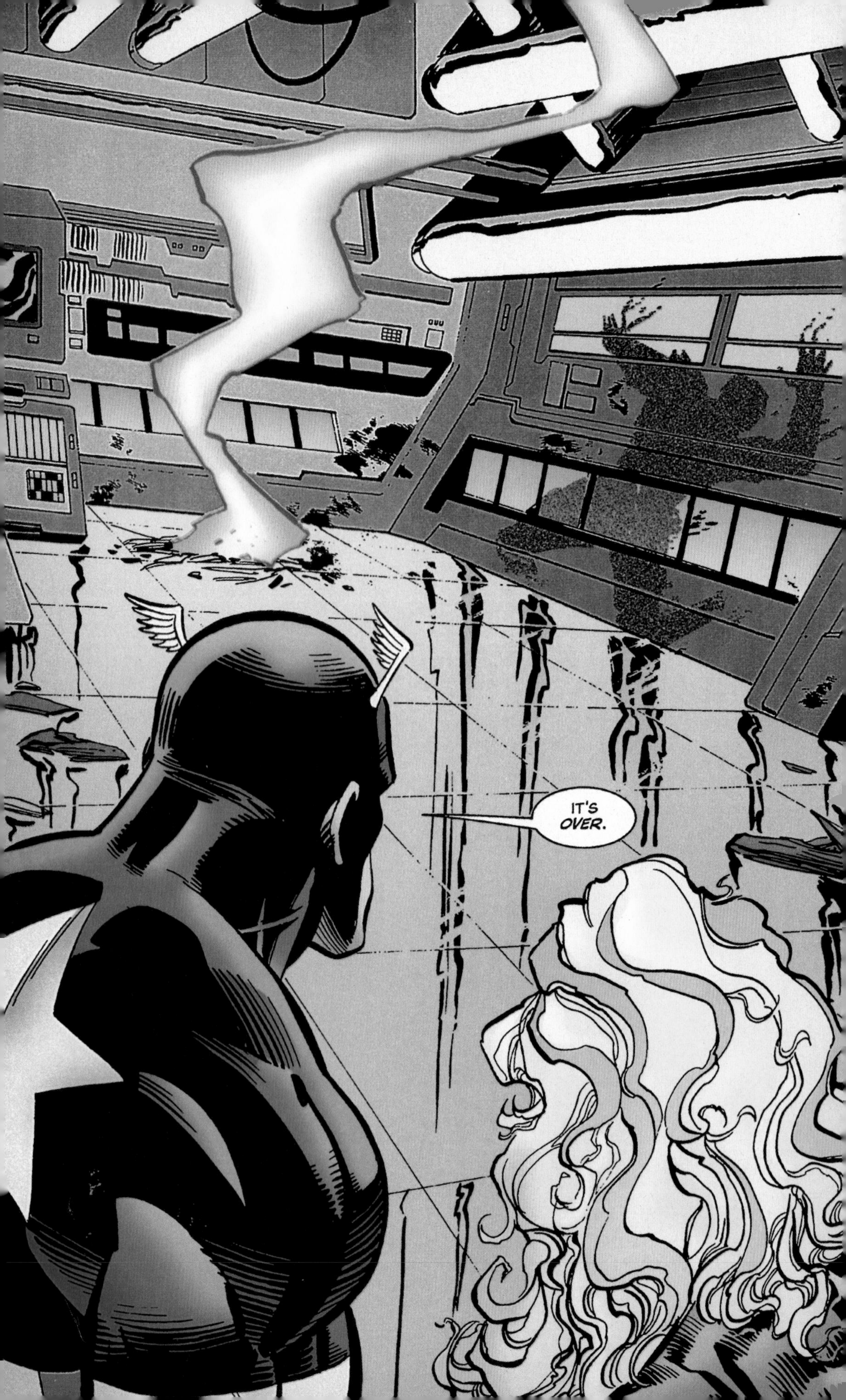
IT'S OVER.

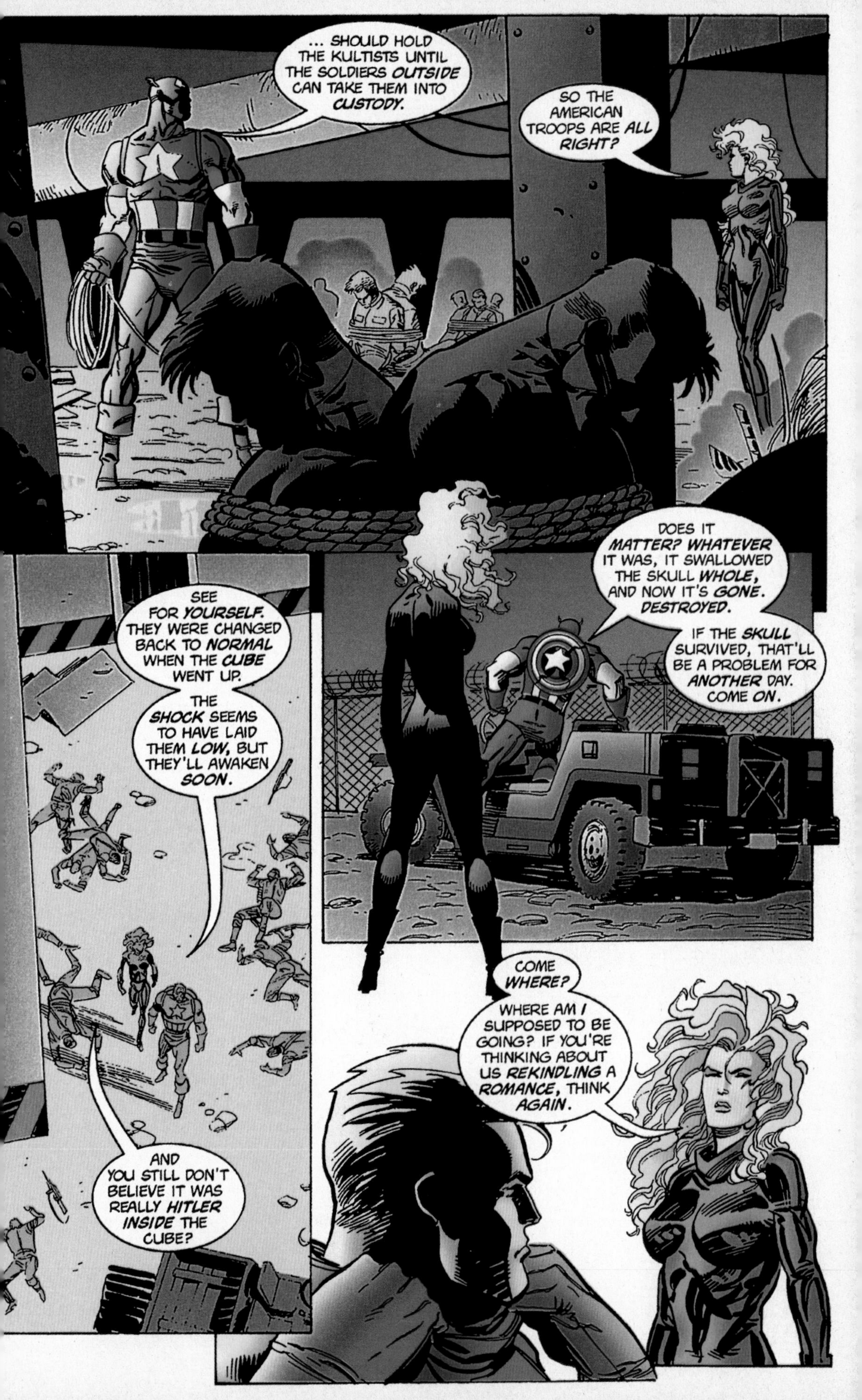

... SHOULD HOLD THE KULTISTS UNTIL THE SOLDIERS OUTSIDE CAN TAKE THEM INTO CUSTODY.
SO THE AMERICAN TROOPS ARE ALL RIGHT?
SEE FOR YOURSELF. THEY WERE CHANGED BACK TO NORMAL WHEN THE CUBE WENT UP.
THE SHOCK SEEMS TO HAVE LAID THEM LOW, BUT THEY'LL AWAKEN SOON.
AND YOU STILL DON'T BELIEVE IT WAS REALLY HITLER INSIDE THE CUBE?
DOES IT MATTER? WHATEVER IT WAS, IT SWALLOWED THE SKULL WHOLE, AND NOW IT'S GONE. DESTROYED.
IF THE SKULL SURVIVED, THAT'LL BE A PROBLEM FOR ANOTHER DAY. COME ON.
COME WHERE?
WHERE AM I SUPPOSED TO BE GOING? IF YOU'RE THINKING ABOUT US REKINDLING A ROMANCE, THINK AGAIN.

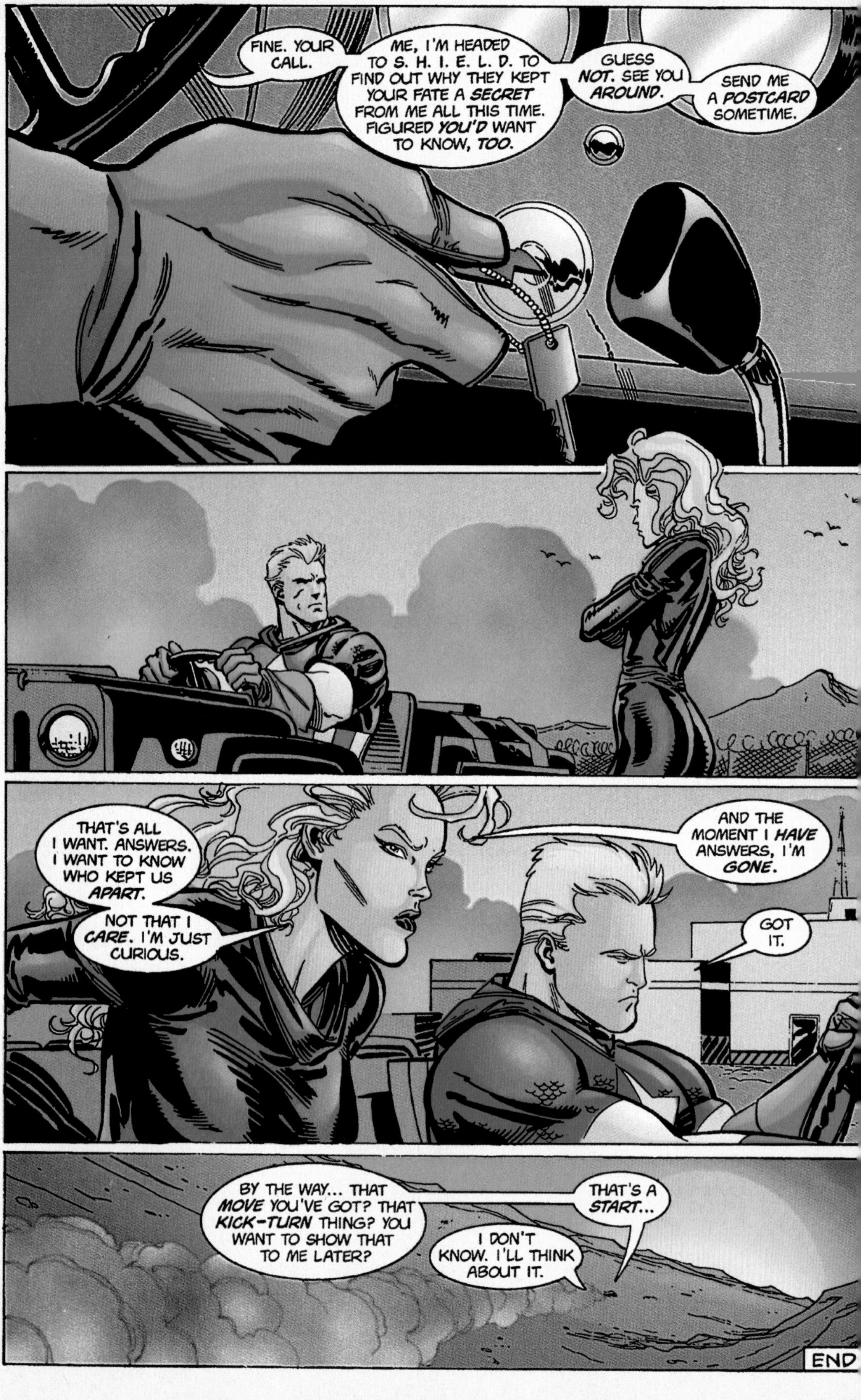
FINE. YOUR CALL.
ME, I'M HEADED TO S. H. I. E. L. D. TO FIND OUT WHY THEY KEPT YOUR FATE A SECRET FROM ME ALL THIS TIME. FIGURED YOU'D WANT TO KNOW, TOO.
GUESS NOT. SEE YOU AROUND.
SEND ME A POSTCARD SOMETIME.
THAT'S ALL I WANT. ANSWERS. I WANT TO KNOW WHO KEPT US APART.
NOT THAT I CARE. I'M JUST CURIOUS.
AND THE MOMENT I HAVE ANSWERS, I'M GONE.
GOT IT.
BY THE WAY... THAT MOVE YOU'VE GOT? THAT KICK-TURN THING? YOU WANT TO SHOW THAT TO ME LATER?
I DON'T KNOW. I'LL THINK ABOUT IT.
THAT'S A START...
END

FIRST SIGN

Even as Steve Rogers begins to reclaim his life as Captain America, a brush with his old friends in the Avengers discloses the massive changes in their ranks.

CAPTAIN AMERICA #449

Cap and Sharon visit SHIELD hoping that Nick Fury holds the answers behind Sharon's abandonment in the field – only to hear that Fury has been assassinated by the Punisher. Heading into Manhattan, Cap is trapped behind an energy barrier generated by a team of fanatics called the Zodiac. With electrical power in Manhattan shut down by the barrier, Cap heads to his old friend Thor for aid. Reaching Thor's apartment, he has two surprises in store: first, Thor is now romantically entwined with his old foe the Enchantress; second, he has lost his powers!

THOR #496

The Enchantress discerns that the Zodiac are entering Manhattan through a portal and directs Cap and Thor to its location. The two heroes must cross a veritable war zone of fires and looters before reaching the location and Thor's lack of superhuman power impedes him. They finally reach the portal, only to find the Zodiac's forces arriving en masse!

IRON MAN #326

At this time Tony Stark is dead and the mantle of Iron Man has been assumed by a college-aged Tony Stark from an alternate reality. Although his armor is still incomplete, Tony sees the effects of the barrier and sets out to help Cap and Thor, arriving just as they engage the Zodiac's armies. Tony destroys the Zodiac's portal and hotwires their technology to broadcast a distress message to the Avengers trapped outside the barrier. He has already discerned a means to momentarily breach the barrier – but it would cost him all the power in his life-preserving chestplate!

AVENGERS #396

Tony lifts the barrier long enough to allow the other Avengers in, nearly killing himself in the process. The Zodiac's command base soon reveals itself: a massive aircraft carrier full of soldiers and led by a mysterious figure named Libra who grapples with the full might of the Avengers! Giant-Man is able to find and destroy the generator powering the barrier, freeing Manhattan from imprisonment. Libra retaliates by killing all of his men then vanishes, warning that he will return when the rest of his allies are prepared.

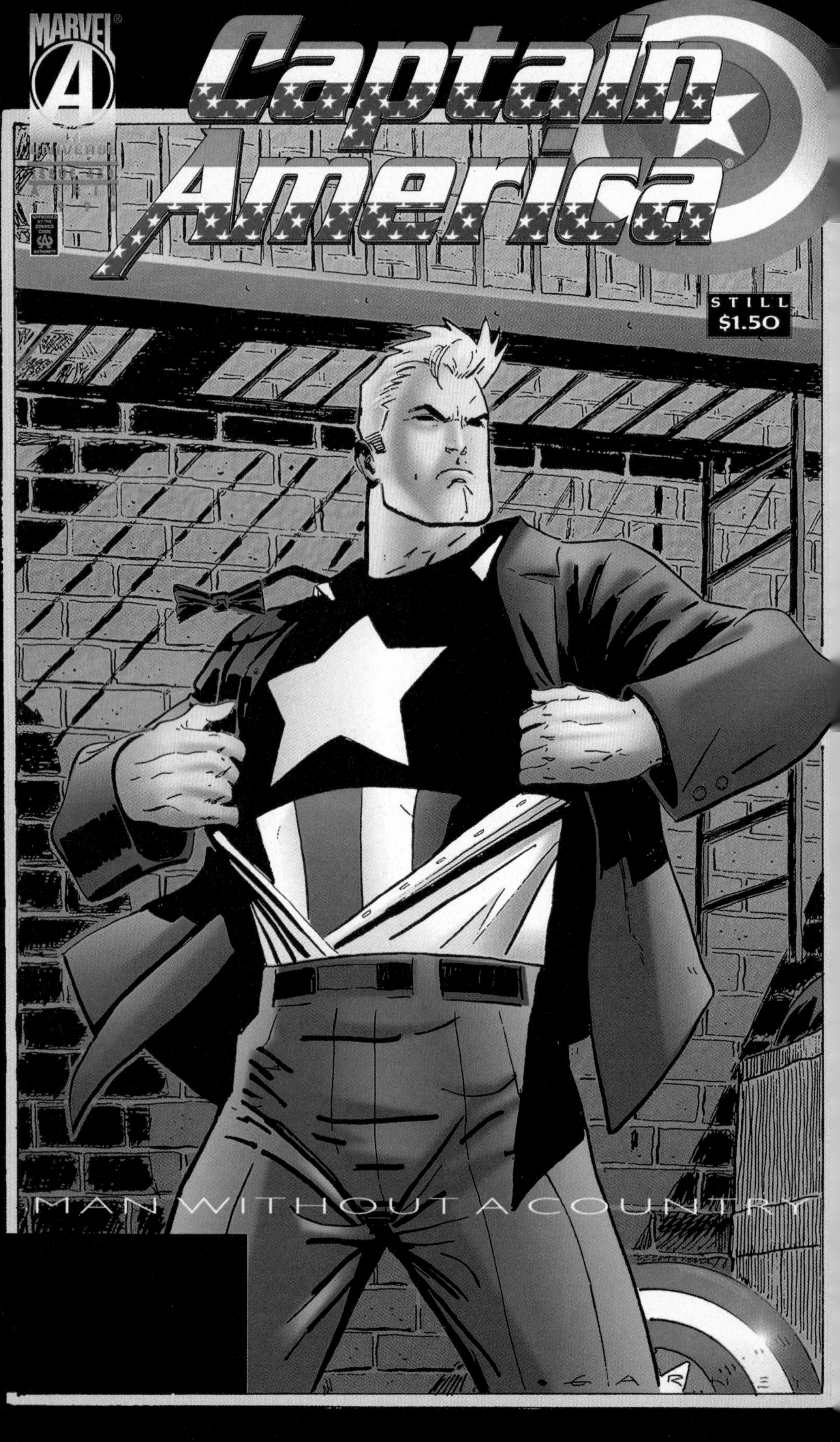
MARVEL
Captain America
STILL $1.50
MAN WITHOUT A COUNTRY

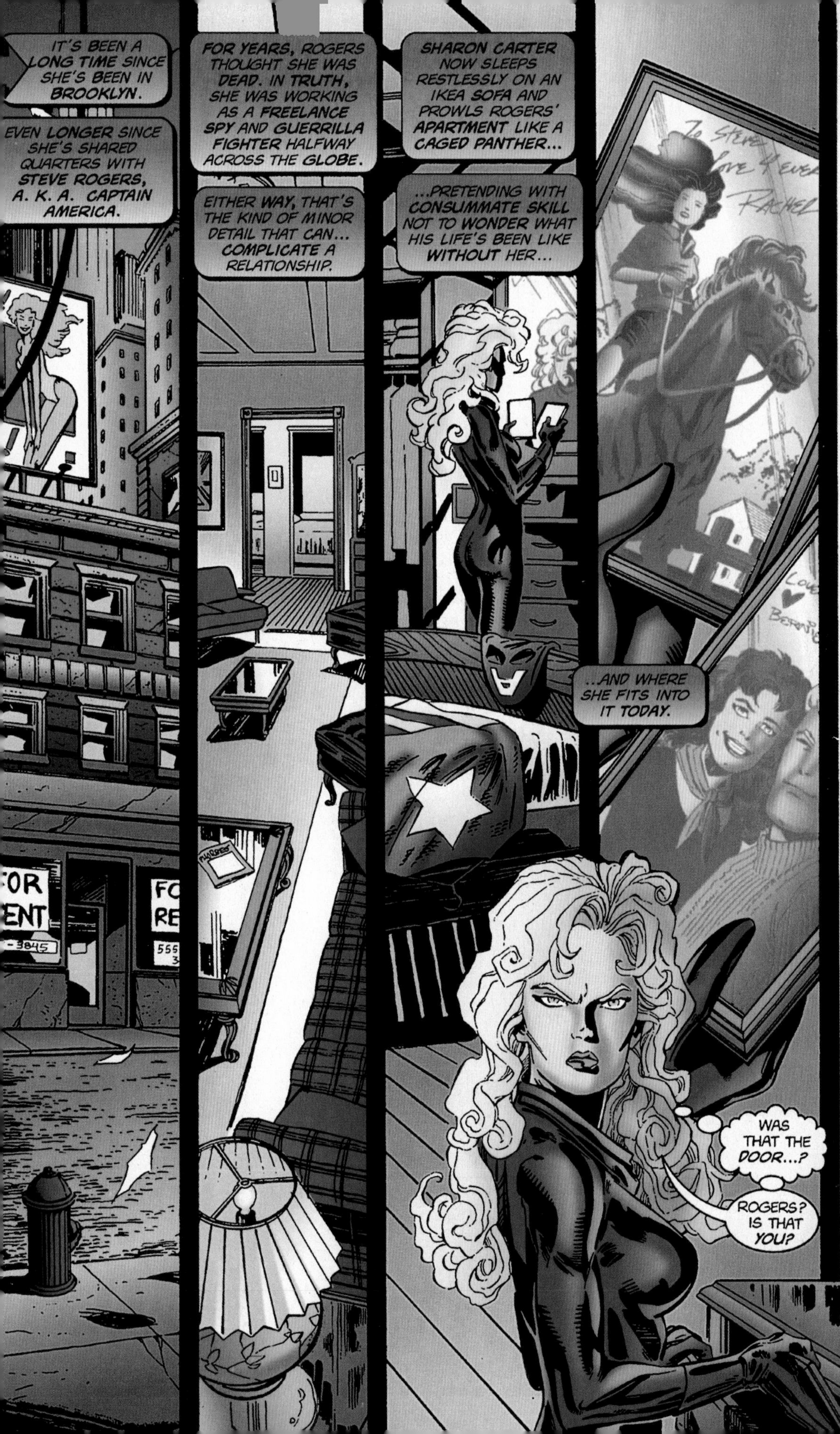
IT'S BEEN A LONG TIME SINCE SHE'S BEEN IN BROOKLYN.
EVEN LONGER SINCE SHE'S SHARED QUARTERS WITH STEVE ROGERS, A. K. A. CAPTAIN AMERICA.
FOR YEARS, ROGERS THOUGHT SHE WAS DEAD. IN TRUTH, SHE WAS WORKING AS A FREELANCE SPY AND GUERRILLA FIGHTER HALFWAY ACROSS THE GLOBE.
EITHER WAY, THAT'S THE KIND OF MINOR DETAIL THAT CAN... COMPLICATE A RELATIONSHIP.
SHARON CARTER NOW SLEEPS RESTLESSLY ON AN IKEA SOFA AND PROWLS ROGERS' APARTMENT LIKE A CAGED PANTHER...
...PRETENDING WITH CONSUMMATE SKILL NOT TO WONDER WHAT HIS LIFE'S BEEN LIKE WITHOUT HER...
...AND WHERE SHE FITS INTO IT TODAY.
WAS THAT THE DOOR...?
ROGERS? IS THAT YOU?
FOR RENT
-3845
To Steve Love 4 ever Rachel

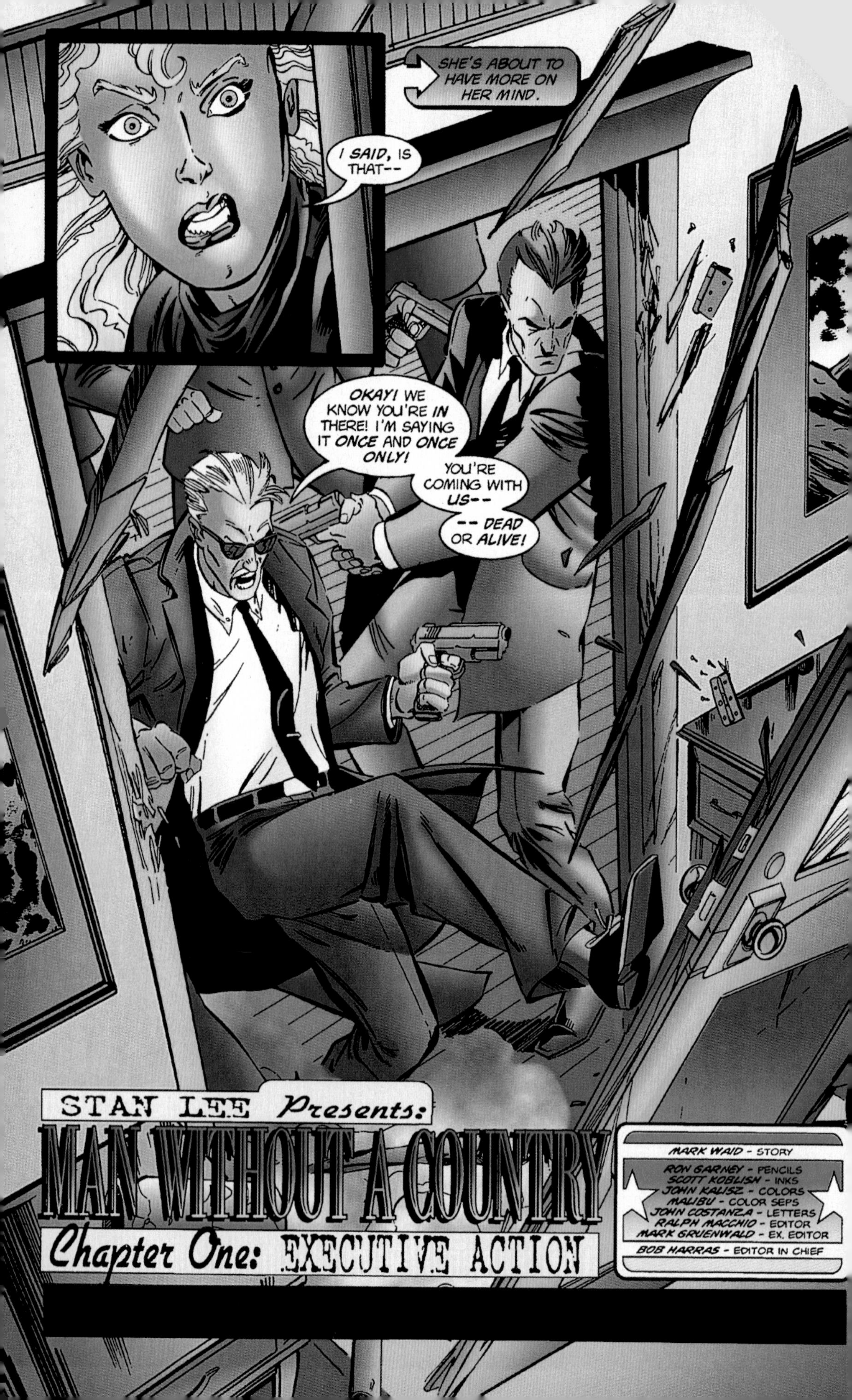
SHE'S ABOUT TO HAVE MORE ON HER MIND.
I SAID, IS THAT--
OKAY! WE KNOW YOU'RE IN THERE! I'M SAYING IT ONCE AND ONCE ONLY!
YOU'RE COMING WITH US--
-- DEAD OR ALIVE!
STAN LEE Presents:
MAN WITHOUT A COUNTRY
Chapter One: EXECUTIVE ACTION
MARK WAID - STORY
RON GARNEY - PENCILS
SCOTT KOBLISH - INKS
JOHN KALISZ - COLORS
MALIBU - COLOR SEPS
JOHN COSTANZA - LETTERS
RALPH MACCHIO - EDITOR
MARK GRUENWALD - EX. EDITOR
BOB HARRAS - EDITOR IN CHIEF

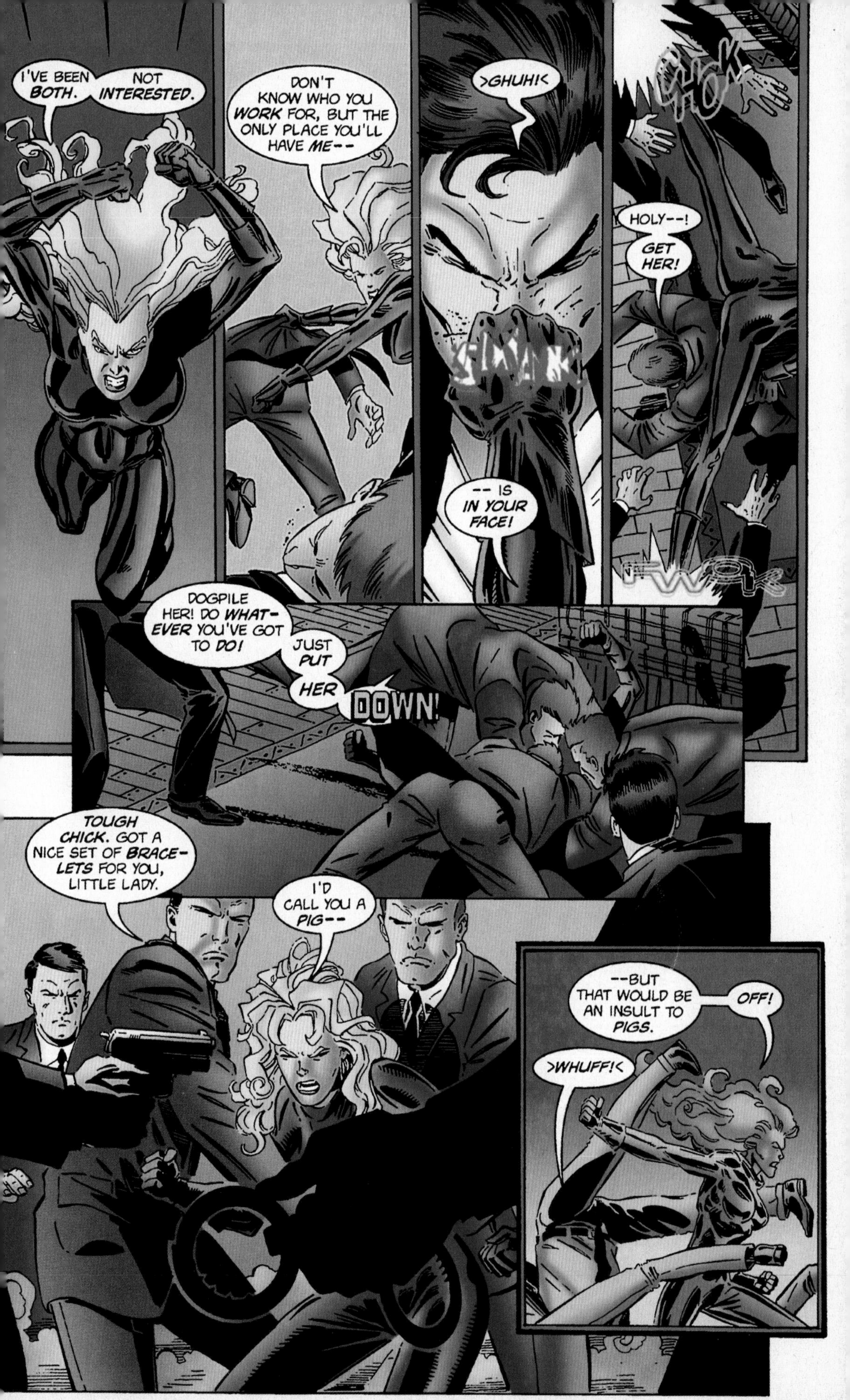
I'VE BEEN BOTH.
NOT INTERESTED.
DON'T KNOW WHO YOU WORK FOR, BUT THE ONLY PLACE YOU'LL HAVE ME--
>GHUH!<
-- IS IN YOUR FACE!
HOLY--!
GET HER!
DOGPILE HER! DO WHAT-EVER YOU'VE GOT TO DO!
JUST PUT
HER
DOWN!
TOUGH CHICK. GOT A NICE SET OF BRACE-LETS FOR YOU, LITTLE LADY.
I'D CALL YOU A PIG--
--BUT THAT WOULD BE AN INSULT TO PIGS.
OFF!
>WHUFF!<

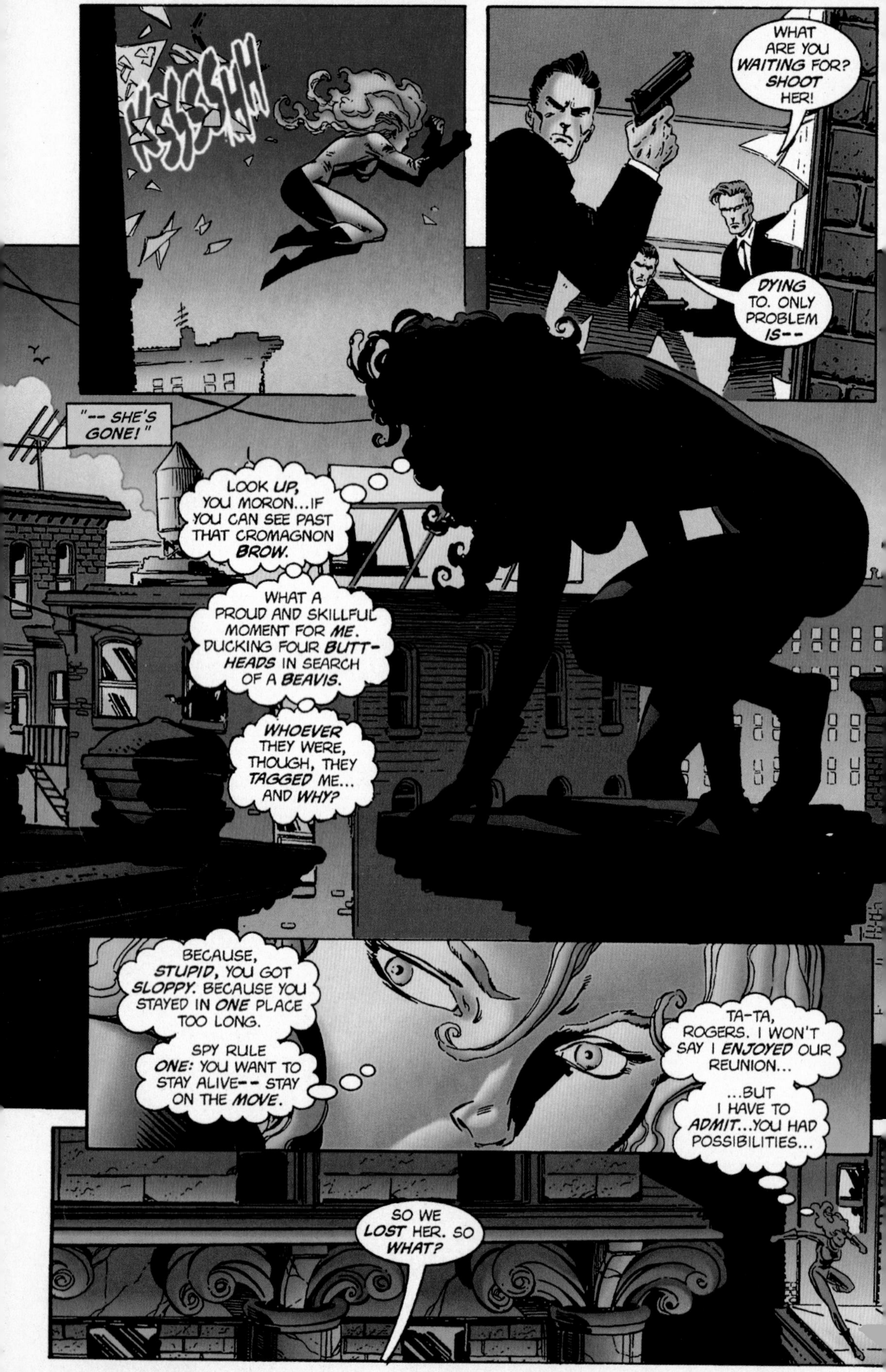
KSSSHH
WHAT ARE YOU WAITING FOR? SHOOT HER!
DYING TO. ONLY PROBLEM IS--
"-- SHE'S GONE!"
LOOK UP, YOU MORON...IF YOU CAN SEE PAST THAT CROMAGNON BROW.
WHAT A PROUD AND SKILLFUL MOMENT FOR ME. DUCKING FOUR BUTT-HEADS IN SEARCH OF A BEAVIS.
WHOEVER THEY WERE, THOUGH, THEY TAGGED ME... AND WHY?
BECAUSE, STUPID, YOU GOT SLOPPY. BECAUSE YOU STAYED IN ONE PLACE TOO LONG.
SPY RULE ONE: YOU WANT TO STAY ALIVE-- STAY ON THE MOVE.
TA-TA, ROGERS. I WON'T SAY I ENJOYED OUR REUNION...
...BUT I HAVE TO ADMIT...YOU HAD POSSIBILITIES...
SO WE LOST HER. SO WHAT?

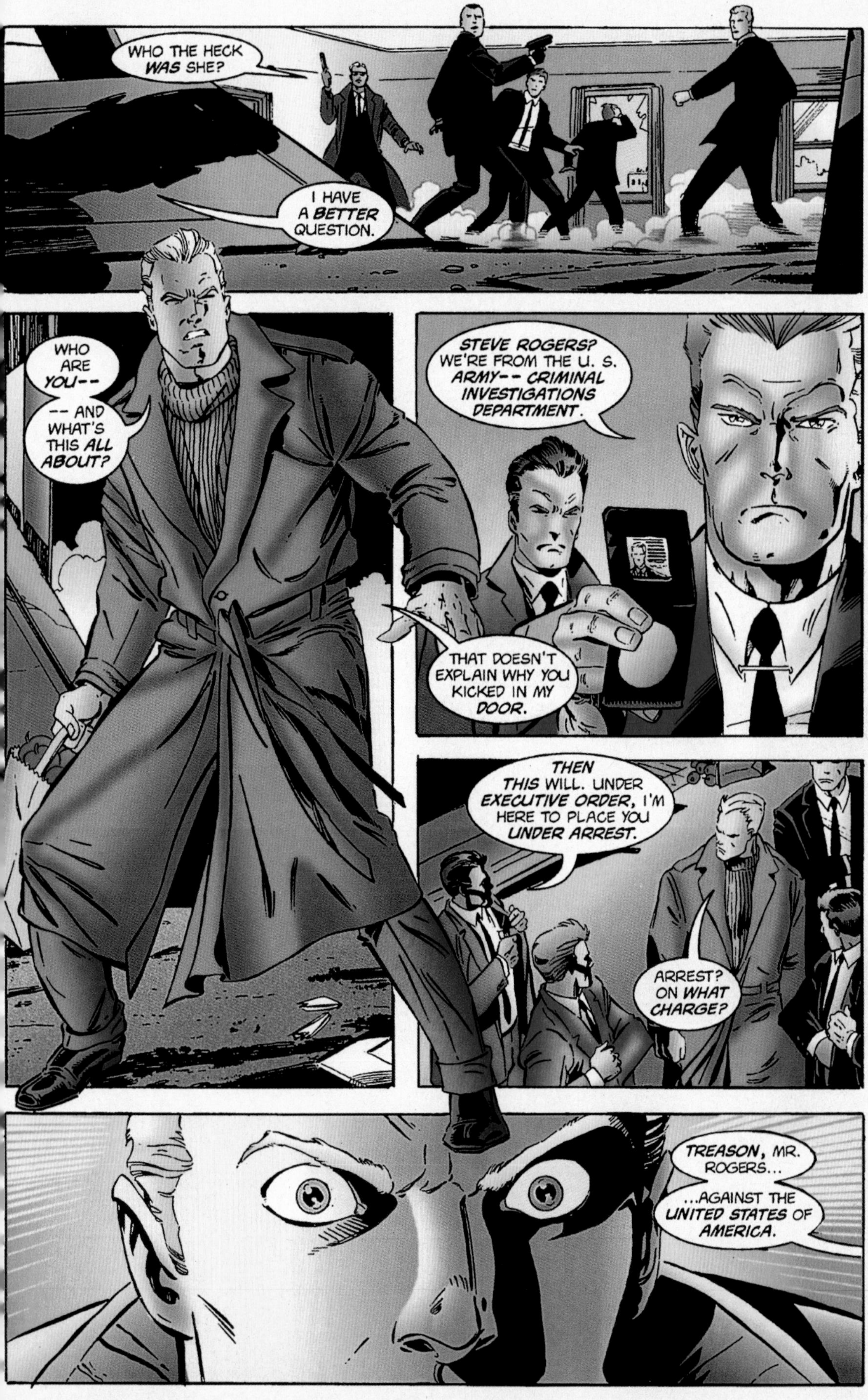
WHO THE HECK WAS SHE?
I HAVE A BETTER QUESTION.
WHO ARE YOU--
-- AND WHAT'S THIS ALL ABOUT?
STEVE ROGERS? WE'RE FROM THE U. S. ARMY-- CRIMINAL INVESTIGATIONS DEPARTMENT.
THAT DOESN'T EXPLAIN WHY YOU KICKED IN MY DOOR.
THEN THIS WILL. UNDER EXECUTIVE ORDER, I'M HERE TO PLACE YOU UNDER ARREST.
ARREST? ON WHAT CHARGE?
TREASON, MR. ROGERS...
...AGAINST THE UNITED STATES OF AMERICA.

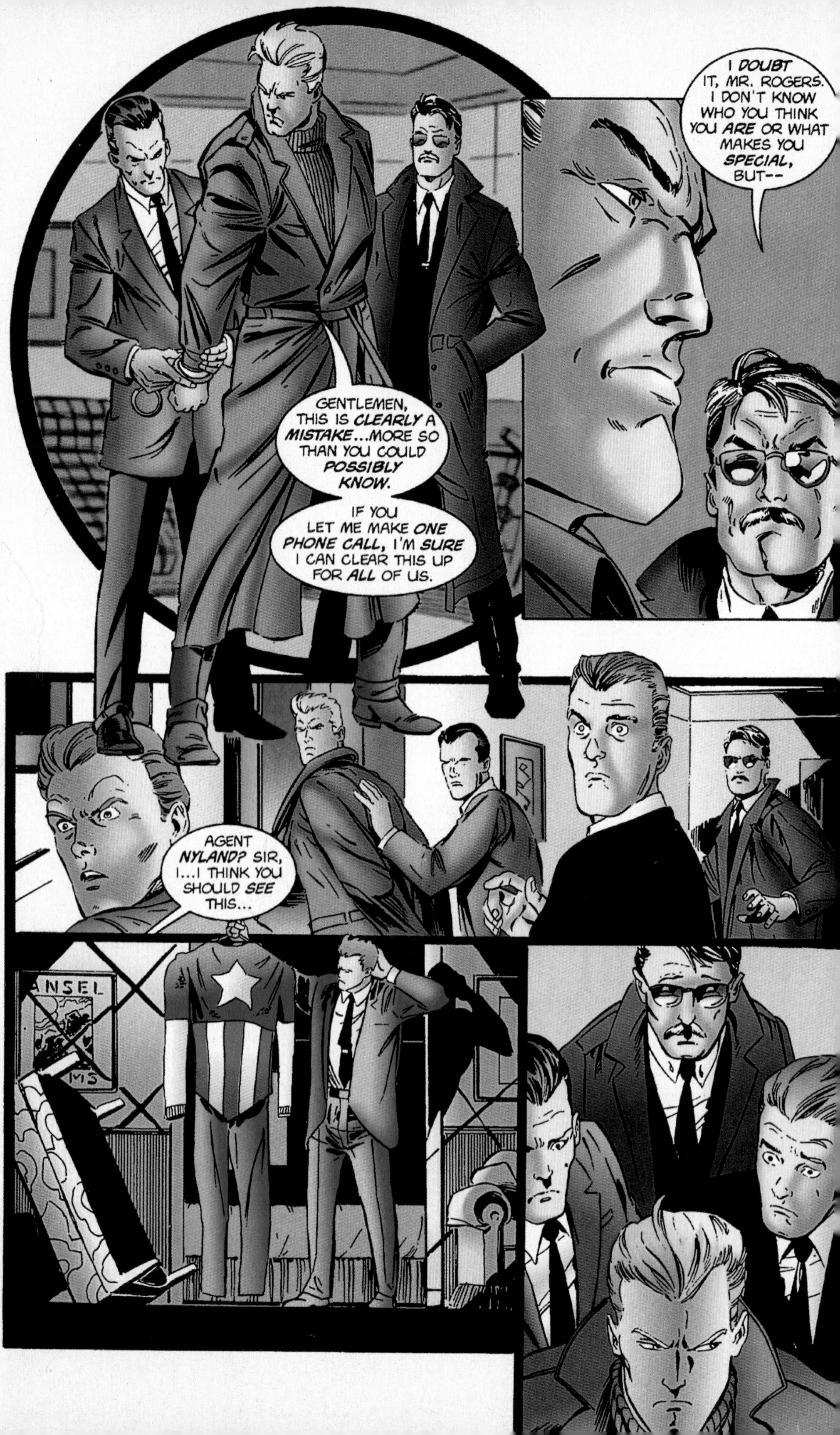
GENTLEMEN, THIS IS CLEARLY A MISTAKE...MORE SO THAN YOU COULD POSSIBLY KNOW.
IF YOU LET ME MAKE ONE PHONE CALL, I'M SURE I CAN CLEAR THIS UP FOR ALL OF US.
I DOUBT IT, MR. ROGERS. I DON'T KNOW WHO YOU THINK YOU ARE OR WHAT MAKES YOU SPECIAL, BUT--
AGENT NYLAND? SIR, I...I THINK YOU SHOULD SEE THIS...
ANSEL
MS

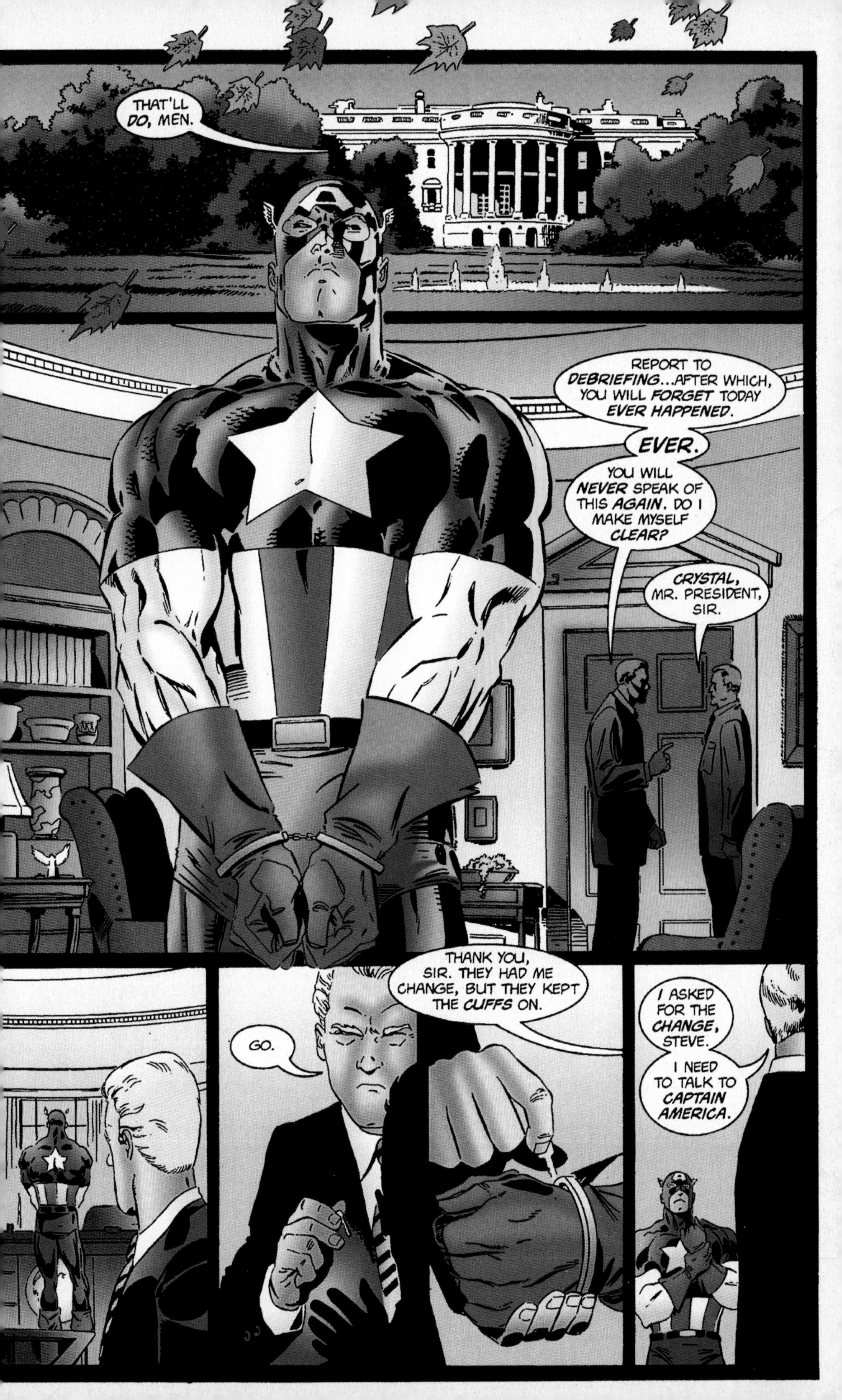
THAT'LL DO, MEN.
REPORT TO DEBRIEFING...AFTER WHICH, YOU WILL FORGET TODAY EVER HAPPENED.
EVER.
YOU WILL NEVER SPEAK OF THIS AGAIN. DO I MAKE MYSELF CLEAR?
CRYSTAL, MR. PRESIDENT, SIR.
GO.
THANK YOU, SIR. THEY HAD ME CHANGE, BUT THEY KEPT THE CUFFS ON.
I ASKED FOR THE CHANGE, STEVE.
I NEED TO TALK TO CAPTAIN AMERICA.

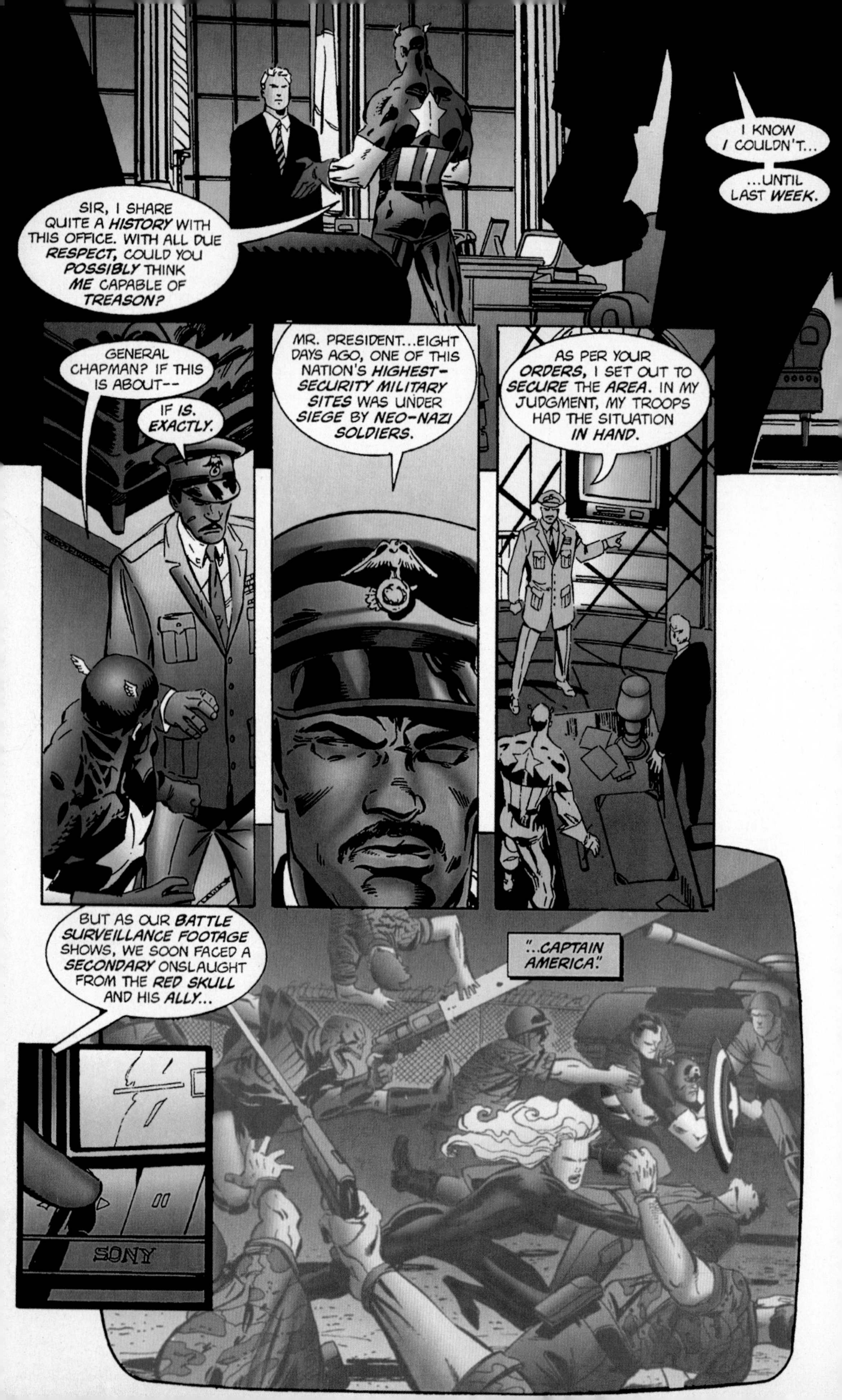
SIR, I SHARE QUITE A HISTORY WITH THIS OFFICE. WITH ALL DUE RESPECT, COULD YOU POSSIBLY THINK ME CAPABLE OF TREASON?
I KNOW I COULDN'T...
...UNTIL LAST WEEK.
GENERAL CHAPMAN? IF THIS IS ABOUT--
IF IS. EXACTLY.
MR. PRESIDENT...EIGHT DAYS AGO, ONE OF THIS NATION'S HIGHEST-SECURITY MILITARY SITES WAS UNDER SIEGE BY NEO-NAZI SOLDIERS.
AS PER YOUR ORDERS, I SET OUT TO SECURE THE AREA. IN MY JUDGMENT, MY TROOPS HAD THE SITUATION IN HAND.
BUT AS OUR BATTLE SURVEILLANCE FOOTAGE SHOWS, WE SOON FACED A SECONDARY ONSLAUGHT FROM THE RED SKULL AND HIS ALLY...
"...CAPTAIN AMERICA."
SONY

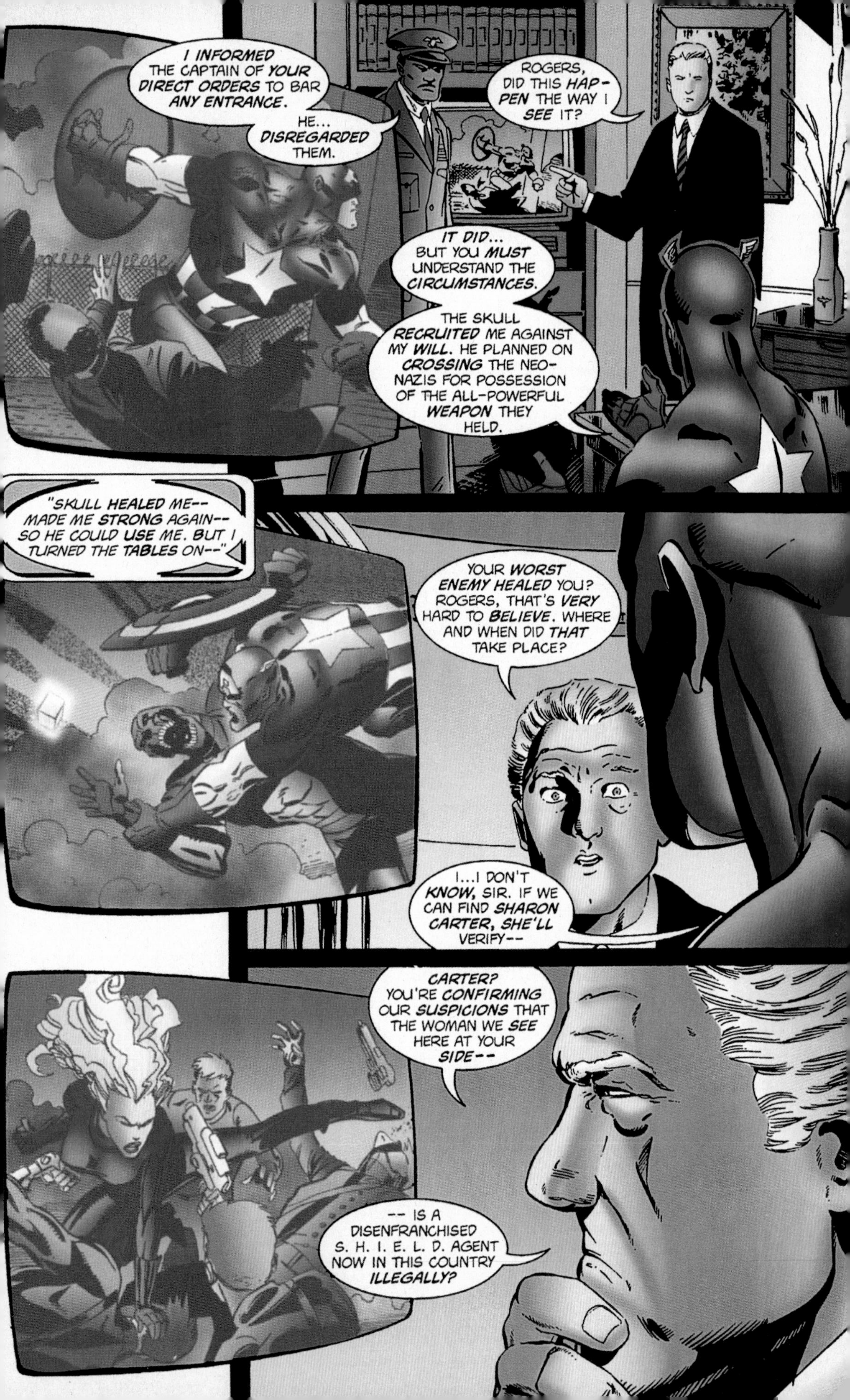
I INFORMED THE CAPTAIN OF YOUR DIRECT ORDERS TO BAR ANY ENTRANCE.
HE... DISREGARDED THEM.
ROGERS, DID THIS HAPPEN THE WAY I SEE IT?
IT DID... BUT YOU MUST UNDERSTAND THE CIRCUMSTANCES.
THE SKULL RECRUITED ME AGAINST MY WILL. HE PLANNED ON CROSSING THE NEO-NAZIS FOR POSSESSION OF THE ALL-POWERFUL WEAPON THEY HELD.
"SKULL HEALED ME--MADE ME STRONG AGAIN--SO HE COULD USE ME. BUT I TURNED THE TABLES ON--"
YOUR WORST ENEMY HEALED YOU? ROGERS, THAT'S VERY HARD TO BELIEVE. WHERE AND WHEN DID THAT TAKE PLACE?
I...I DON'T KNOW, SIR. IF WE CAN FIND SHARON CARTER, SHE'LL VERIFY--
CARTER? YOU'RE CONFIRMING OUR SUSPICIONS THAT THE WOMAN WE SEE HERE AT YOUR SIDE--
-- IS A DISENFRANCHISED S. H. I. E. L. D. AGENT NOW IN THIS COUNTRY ILLEGALLY?

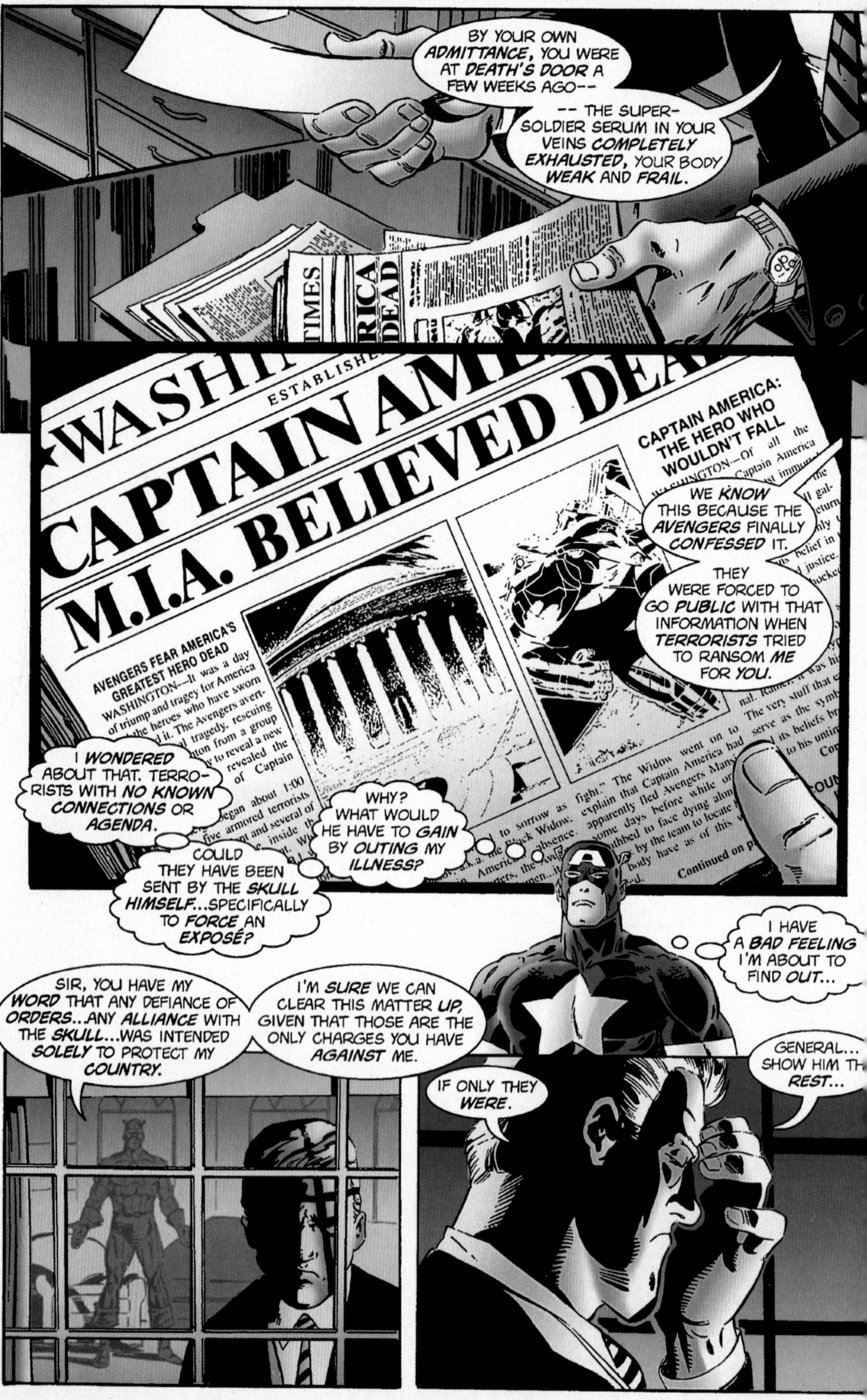
BY YOUR OWN ADMITTANCE, YOU WERE AT DEATH'S DOOR A FEW WEEKS AGO--
-- THE SUPER-SOLDIER SERUM IN YOUR VEINS COMPLETELY EXHAUSTED, YOUR BODY WEAK AND FRAIL.
TIMES
RICA
DEAD
WASHI
ESTABLISHE
CAPTAIN AME
M.I.A. BELIEVED DEA
CAPTAIN AMERICA: THE HERO WHO WOULDN'T FALL
AVENGERS FEAR AMERICA'S GREATEST HERO DEAD
WE KNOW THIS BECAUSE THE AVENGERS FINALLY CONFESSED IT.
THEY WERE FORCED TO GO PUBLIC WITH THAT INFORMATION WHEN TERRORISTS TRIED TO RANSOM ME FOR YOU.
I WONDERED ABOUT THAT. TERRORISTS WITH NO KNOWN CONNECTIONS OR AGENDA.
COULD THEY HAVE BEEN SENT BY THE SKULL HIMSELF...SPECIFICALLY TO FORCE AN EXPOSÉ?
WHY? WHAT WOULD HE HAVE TO GAIN BY OUTING MY ILLNESS?
Continued on p
I HAVE A BAD FEELING I'M ABOUT TO FIND OUT...
SIR, YOU HAVE MY WORD THAT ANY DEFIANCE OF ORDERS...ANY ALLIANCE WITH THE SKULL...WAS INTENDED SOLELY TO PROTECT MY COUNTRY.
I'M SURE WE CAN CLEAR THIS MATTER UP, GIVEN THAT THOSE ARE THE ONLY CHARGES YOU HAVE AGAINST ME.
IF ONLY THEY WERE.
GENERAL... SHOW HIM TH REST...

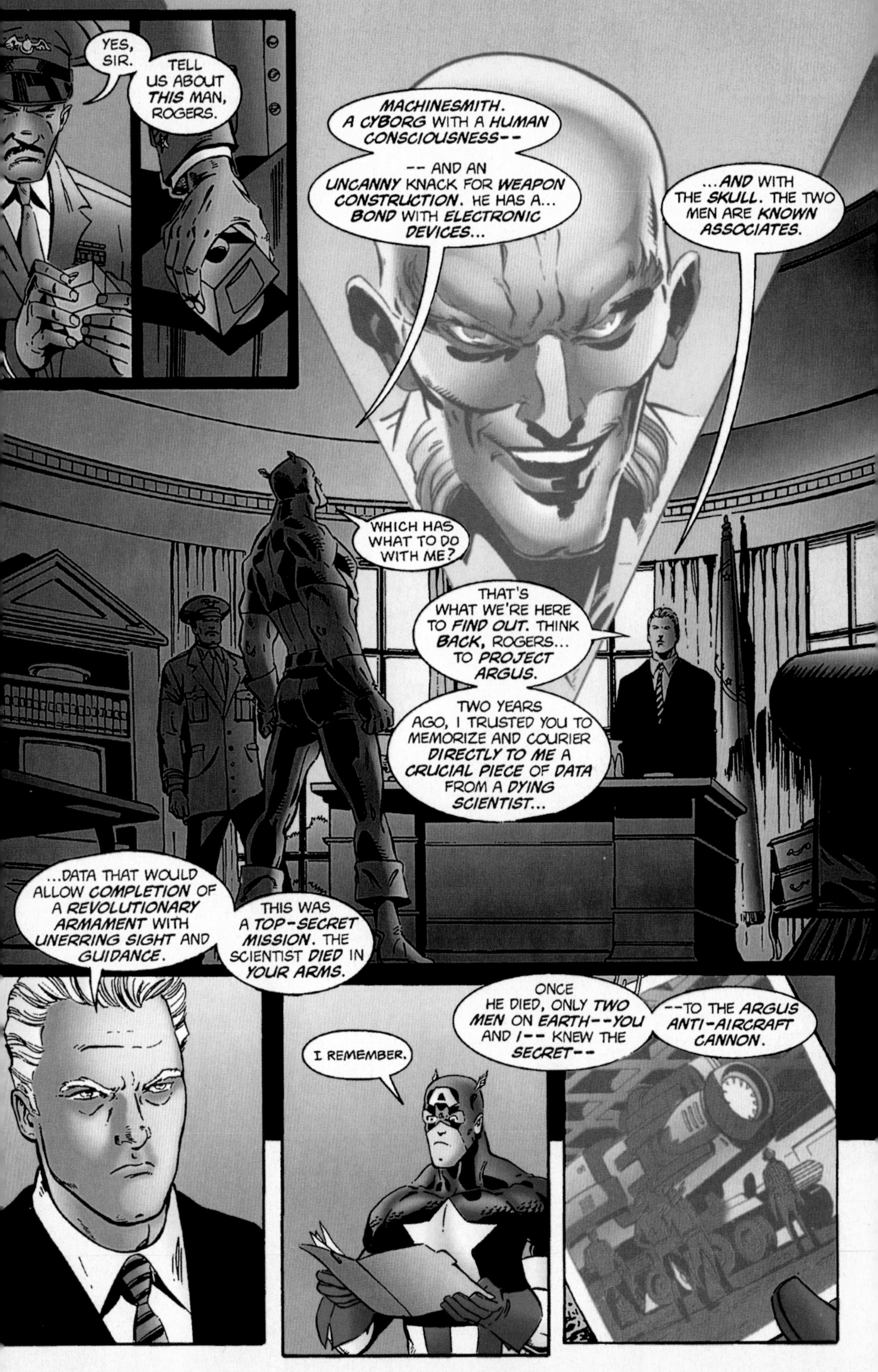
YES, SIR.
TELL US ABOUT THIS MAN, ROGERS.
MACHINESMITH. A CYBORG WITH A HUMAN CONSCIOUSNESS--
-- AND AN UNCANNY KNACK FOR WEAPON CONSTRUCTION. HE HAS A... BOND WITH ELECTRONIC DEVICES...
...AND WITH THE SKULL. THE TWO MEN ARE KNOWN ASSOCIATES.
WHICH HAS WHAT TO DO WITH ME?
THAT'S WHAT WE'RE HERE TO FIND OUT. THINK BACK, ROGERS... TO PROJECT ARGUS.
TWO YEARS AGO, I TRUSTED YOU TO MEMORIZE AND COURIER DIRECTLY TO ME A CRUCIAL PIECE OF DATA FROM A DYING SCIENTIST...
...DATA THAT WOULD ALLOW COMPLETION OF A REVOLUTIONARY ARMAMENT WITH UNERRING SIGHT AND GUIDANCE.
THIS WAS A TOP-SECRET MISSION. THE SCIENTIST DIED IN YOUR ARMS.
I REMEMBER.
ONCE HE DIED, ONLY TWO MEN ON EARTH--YOU AND I-- KNEW THE SECRET--
--TO THE ARGUS ANTI-AIRCRAFT CANNON.

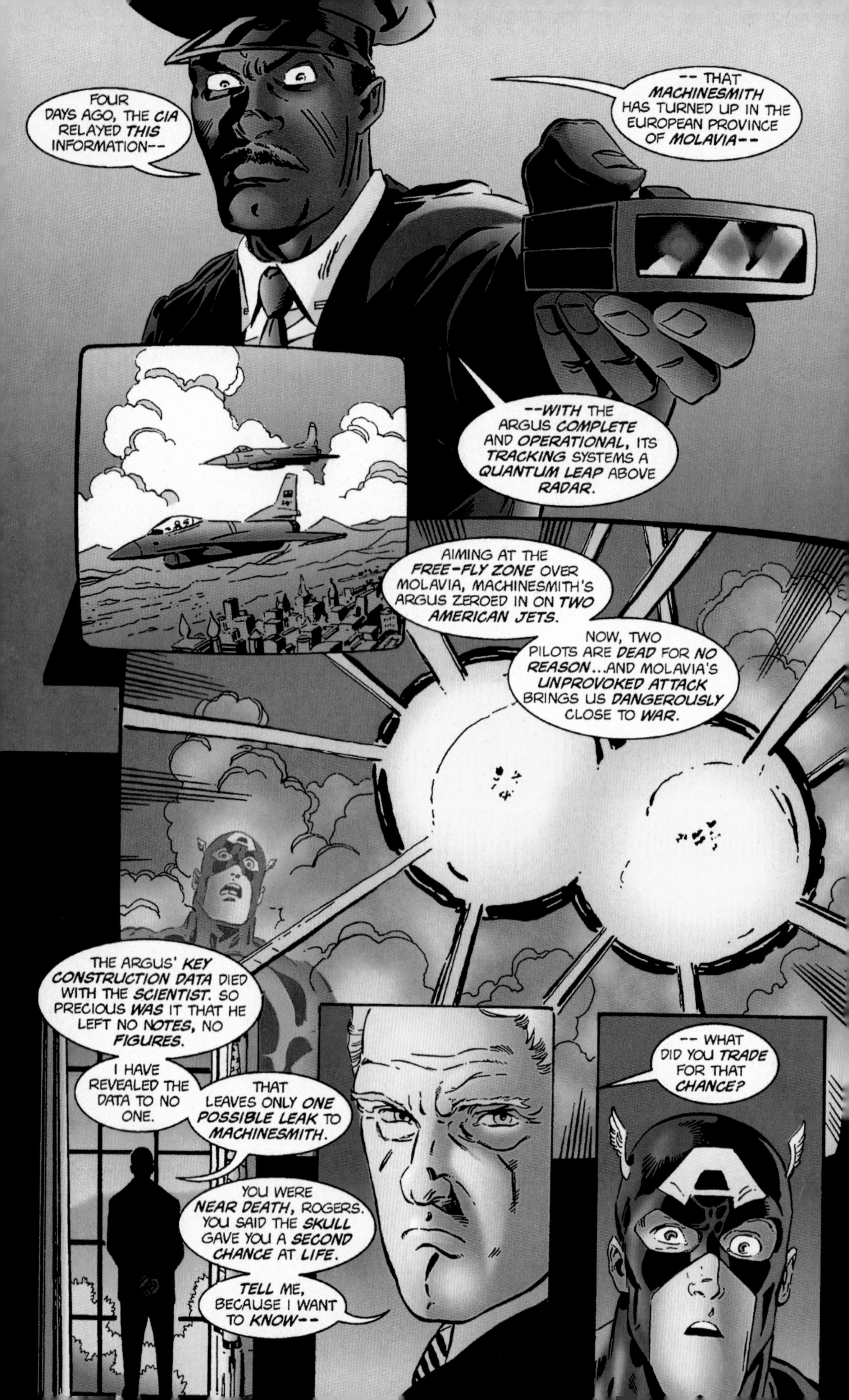
FOUR DAYS AGO, THE CIA RELAYED THIS INFORMATION--
-- THAT MACHINESMITH HAS TURNED UP IN THE EUROPEAN PROVINCE OF MOLAVIA--
--WITH THE ARGUS COMPLETE AND OPERATIONAL, ITS TRACKING SYSTEMS A QUANTUM LEAP ABOVE RADAR.
AIMING AT THE FREE-FLY ZONE OVER MOLAVIA, MACHINESMITH'S ARGUS ZEROED IN ON TWO AMERICAN JETS.
NOW, TWO PILOTS ARE DEAD FOR NO REASON...AND MOLAVIA'S UNPROVOKED ATTACK BRINGS US DANGEROUSLY CLOSE TO WAR.
THE ARGUS' KEY CONSTRUCTION DATA DIED WITH THE SCIENTIST. SO PRECIOUS WAS IT THAT HE LEFT NO NOTES, NO FIGURES.
I HAVE REVEALED THE DATA TO NO ONE.
THAT LEAVES ONLY ONE POSSIBLE LEAK TO MACHINESMITH.
YOU WERE NEAR DEATH, ROGERS. YOU SAID THE SKULL GAVE YOU A SECOND CHANCE AT LIFE.
TELL ME, BECAUSE I WANT TO KNOW--
-- WHAT DID YOU TRADE FOR THAT CHANCE?

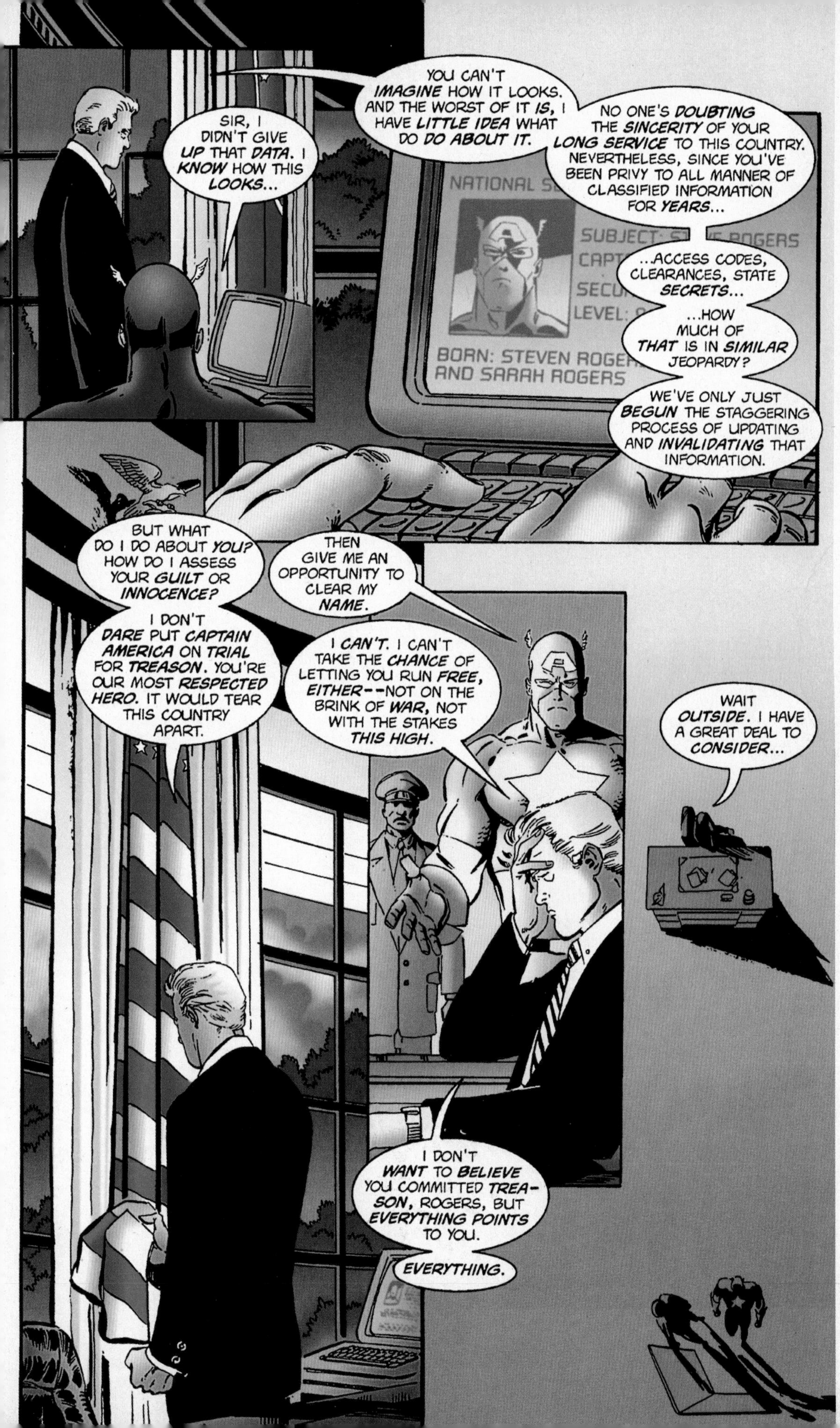
SIR, I DIDN'T GIVE UP THAT DATA. I KNOW HOW THIS LOOKS...
YOU CAN'T IMAGINE HOW IT LOOKS. AND THE WORST OF IT IS, I HAVE LITTLE IDEA WHAT DO DO ABOUT IT.
NO ONE'S DOUBTING THE SINCERITY OF YOUR LONG SERVICE TO THIS COUNTRY. NEVERTHELESS, SINCE YOU'VE BEEN PRIVY TO ALL MANNER OF CLASSIFIED INFORMATION FOR YEARS...
...ACCESS CODES, CLEARANCES, STATE SECRETS...
...HOW MUCH OF THAT IS IN SIMILAR JEOPARDY?
WE'VE ONLY JUST BEGUN THE STAGGERING PROCESS OF UPDATING AND INVALIDATING THAT INFORMATION.
BUT WHAT DO I DO ABOUT YOU? HOW DO I ASSESS YOUR GUILT OR INNOCENCE?
THEN GIVE ME AN OPPORTUNITY TO CLEAR MY NAME.
I DON'T DARE PUT CAPTAIN AMERICA ON TRIAL FOR TREASON. YOU'RE OUR MOST RESPECTED HERO. IT WOULD TEAR THIS COUNTRY APART.
I CAN'T. I CAN'T TAKE THE CHANCE OF LETTING YOU RUN FREE, EITHER--NOT ON THE BRINK OF WAR, NOT WITH THE STAKES THIS HIGH.
I DON'T WANT TO BELIEVE YOU COMMITTED TREA-SON, ROGERS, BUT EVERYTHING POINTS TO YOU.
EVERYTHING.
WAIT OUTSIDE. I HAVE A GREAT DEAL TO CONSIDER...

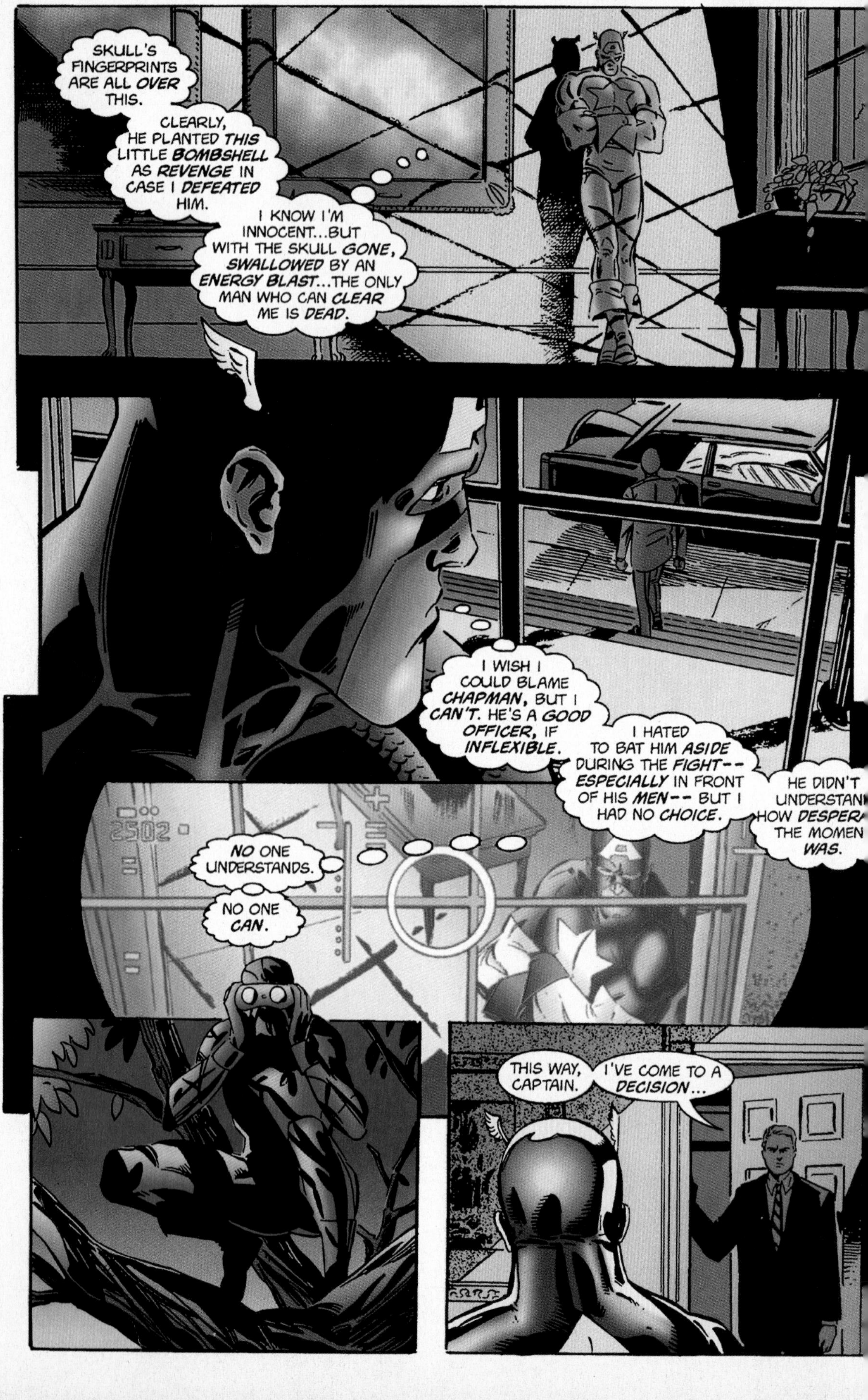
SKULL'S FINGERPRINTS ARE ALL OVER THIS.
CLEARLY, HE PLANTED THIS LITTLE BOMBSHELL AS REVENGE IN CASE I DEFEATED HIM.
I KNOW I'M INNOCENT...BUT WITH THE SKULL GONE, SWALLOWED BY AN ENERGY BLAST...THE ONLY MAN WHO CAN CLEAR ME IS DEAD.
I WISH I COULD BLAME CHAPMAN, BUT I CAN'T. HE'S A GOOD OFFICER, IF INFLEXIBLE.
I HATED TO BAT HIM ASIDE DURING THE FIGHT-- ESPECIALLY IN FRONT OF HIS MEN-- BUT I HAD NO CHOICE.
HE DIDN'T UNDERSTAN HOW DESPER THE MOMEN WAS.
2502
NO ONE UNDERSTANDS.
NO ONE CAN.
THIS WAY, CAPTAIN.
I'VE COME TO A DECISION...

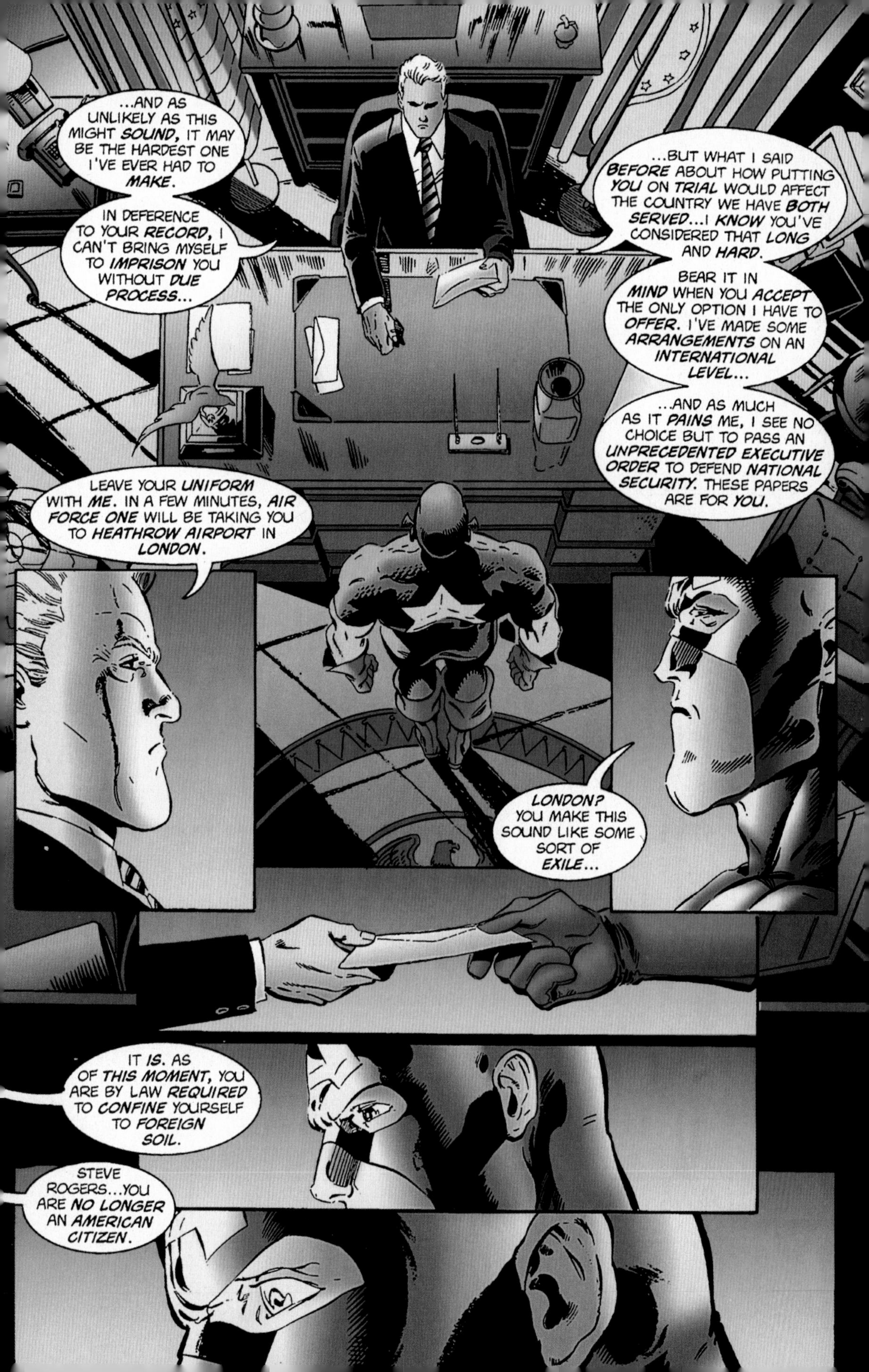
...AND AS UNLIKELY AS THIS MIGHT SOUND, IT MAY BE THE HARDEST ONE I'VE EVER HAD TO MAKE.
IN DEFERENCE TO YOUR RECORD, I CAN'T BRING MYSELF TO IMPRISON YOU WITHOUT DUE PROCESS...
...BUT WHAT I SAID BEFORE ABOUT HOW PUTTING YOU ON TRIAL WOULD AFFECT THE COUNTRY WE HAVE BOTH SERVED...I KNOW YOU'VE CONSIDERED THAT LONG AND HARD.
BEAR IT IN MIND WHEN YOU ACCEPT THE ONLY OPTION I HAVE TO OFFER. I'VE MADE SOME ARRANGEMENTS ON AN INTERNATIONAL LEVEL...
...AND AS MUCH AS IT PAINS ME, I SEE NO CHOICE BUT TO PASS AN UNPRECEDENTED EXECUTIVE ORDER TO DEFEND NATIONAL SECURITY. THESE PAPERS ARE FOR YOU.
LEAVE YOUR UNIFORM WITH ME. IN A FEW MINUTES, AIR FORCE ONE WILL BE TAKING YOU TO HEATHROW AIRPORT IN LONDON.
LONDON? YOU MAKE THIS SOUND LIKE SOME SORT OF EXILE...
IT IS. AS OF THIS MOMENT, YOU ARE BY LAW REQUIRED TO CONFINE YOURSELF TO FOREIGN SOIL.
STEVE ROGERS...YOU ARE NO LONGER AN AMERICAN CITIZEN.

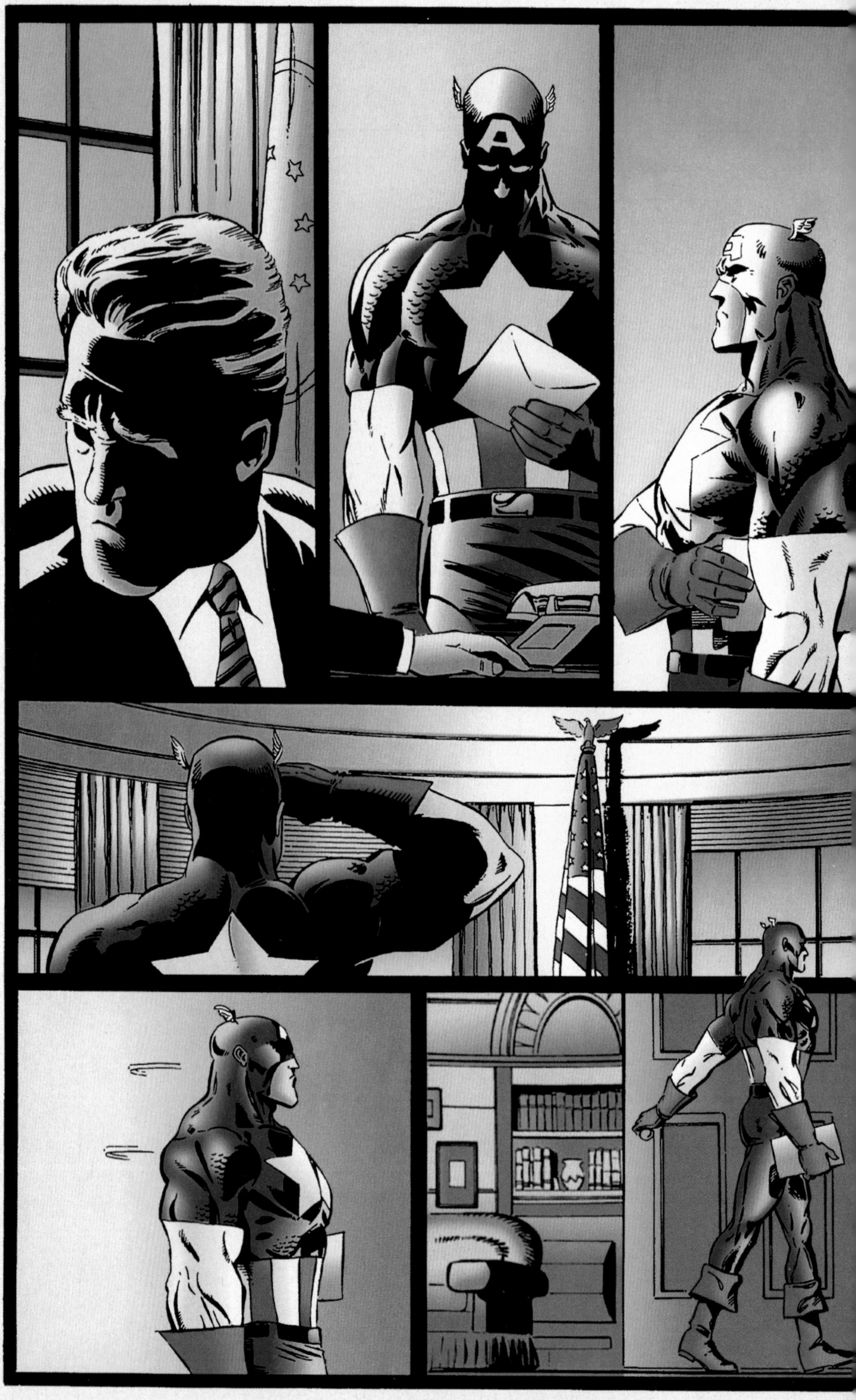

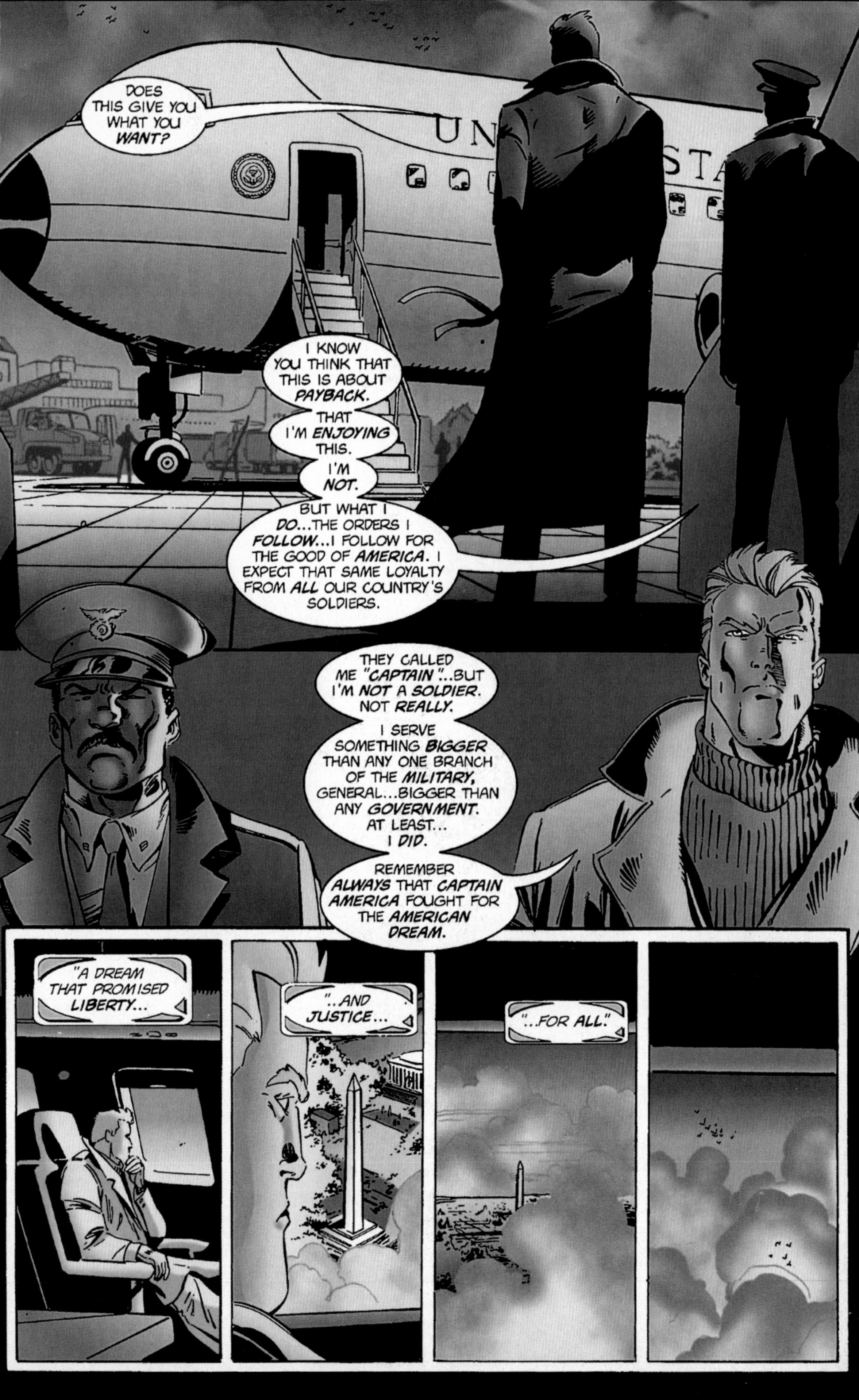
DOES THIS GIVE YOU WHAT YOU WANT?
I KNOW YOU THINK THAT THIS IS ABOUT PAYBACK.
THAT I'M ENJOYING THIS.
I'M NOT.
BUT WHAT I DO...THE ORDERS I FOLLOW...I FOLLOW FOR THE GOOD OF AMERICA. I EXPECT THAT SAME LOYALTY FROM ALL OUR COUNTRY'S SOLDIERS.
THEY CALLED ME "CAPTAIN"...BUT I'M NOT A SOLDIER. NOT REALLY.
I SERVE SOMETHING BIGGER THAN ANY ONE BRANCH OF THE MILITARY, GENERAL...BIGGER THAN ANY GOVERNMENT. AT LEAST... I DID.
REMEMBER ALWAYS THAT CAPTAIN AMERICA FOUGHT FOR THE AMERICAN DREAM.
"A DREAM THAT PROMISED LIBERTY...
"...AND JUSTICE...
"...FOR ALL."

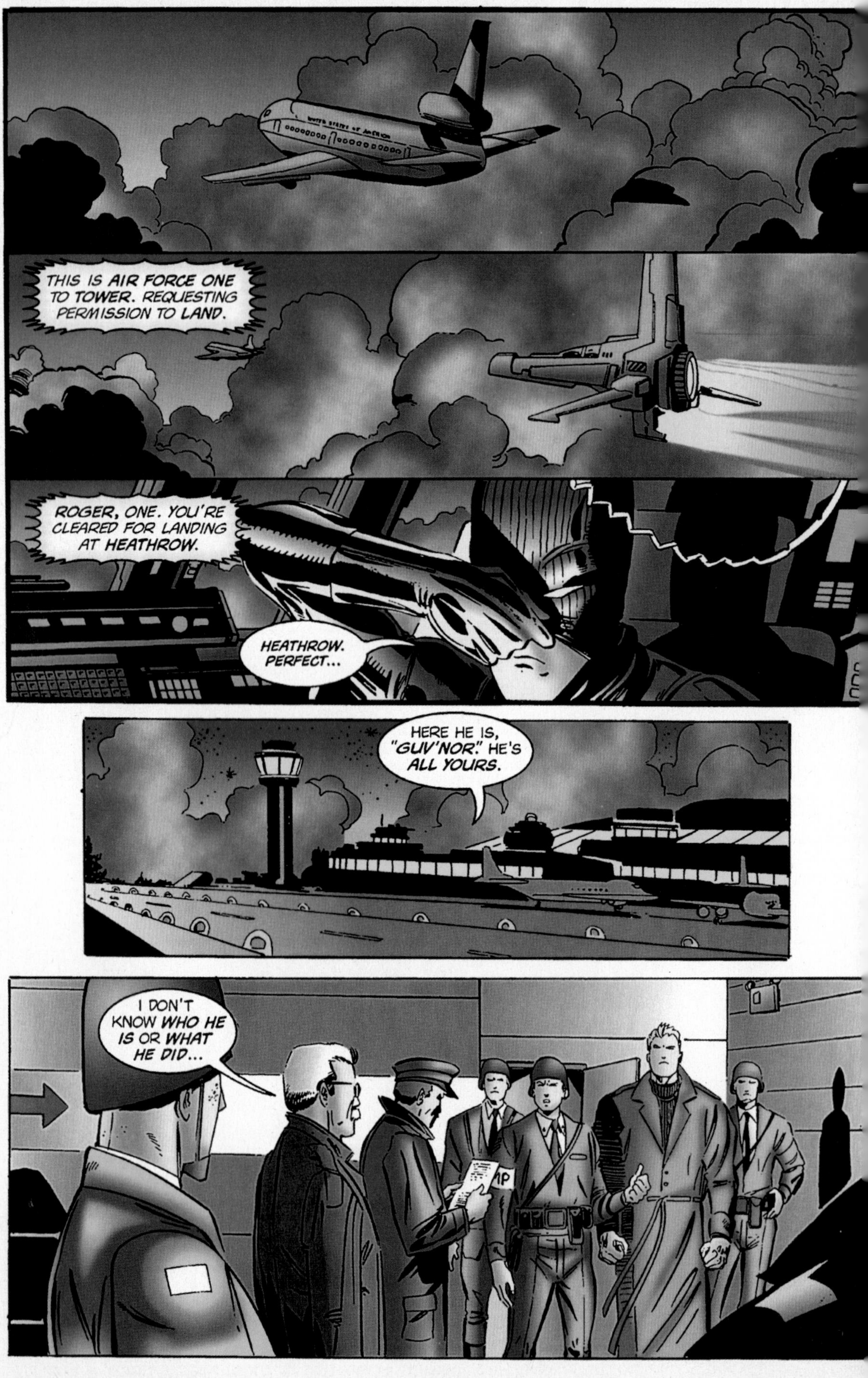
UNITED STATES OF AMERICA
THIS IS AIR FORCE ONE TO TOWER. REQUESTING PERMISSION TO LAND.
ROGER, ONE. YOU'RE CLEARED FOR LANDING AT HEATHROW.
HEATHROW. PERFECT...
HERE HE IS, "GUV'NOR." HE'S ALL YOURS.
I DON'T KNOW WHO HE IS OR WHAT HE DID...

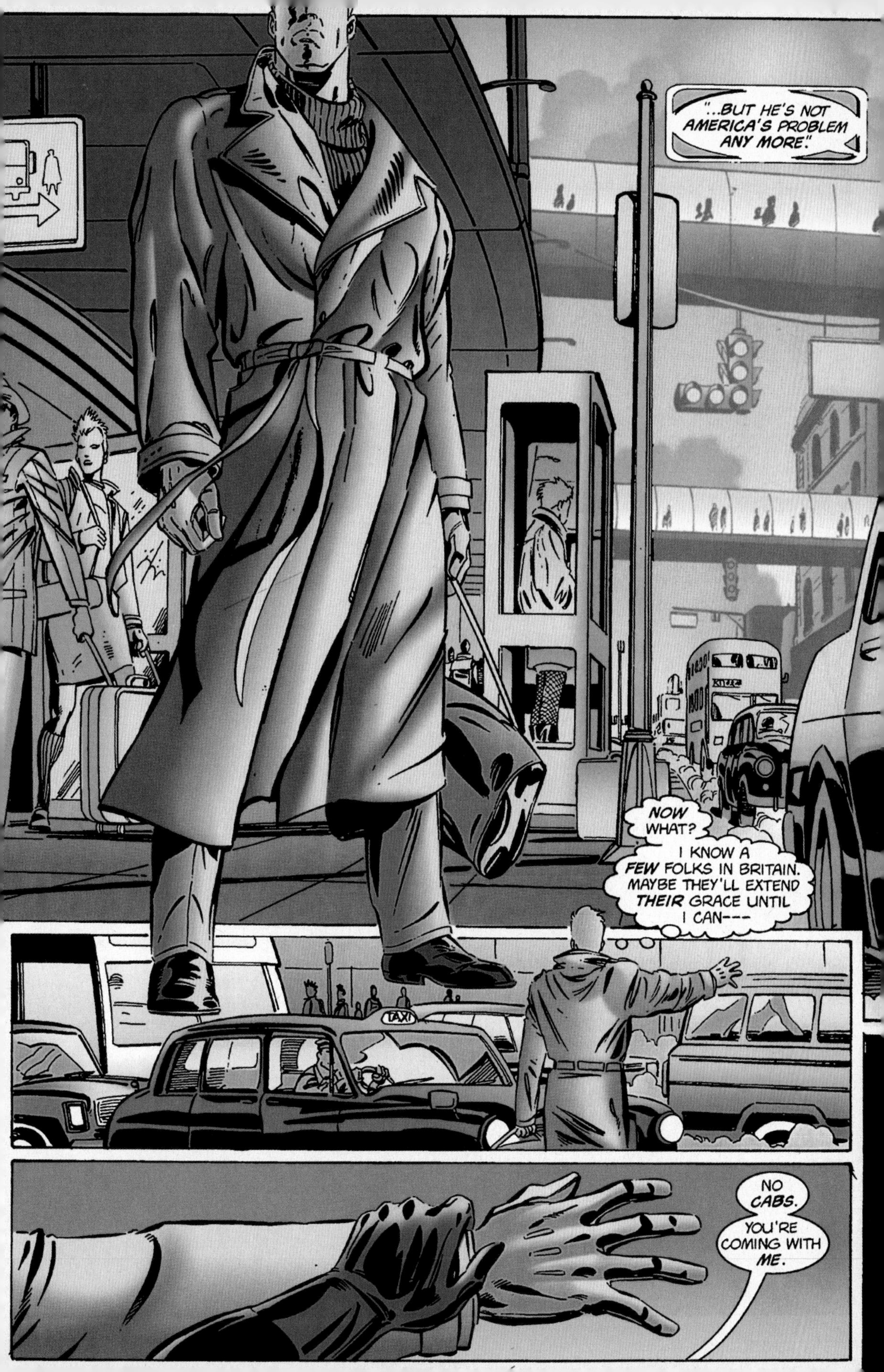
"...BUT HE'S NOT AMERICA'S PROBLEM ANY MORE."
NOW WHAT?
I KNOW A FEW FOLKS IN BRITAIN. MAYBE THEY'LL EXTEND THEIR GRACE UNTIL I CAN---
TAXI
NO CABS.
YOU'RE COMING WITH ME.

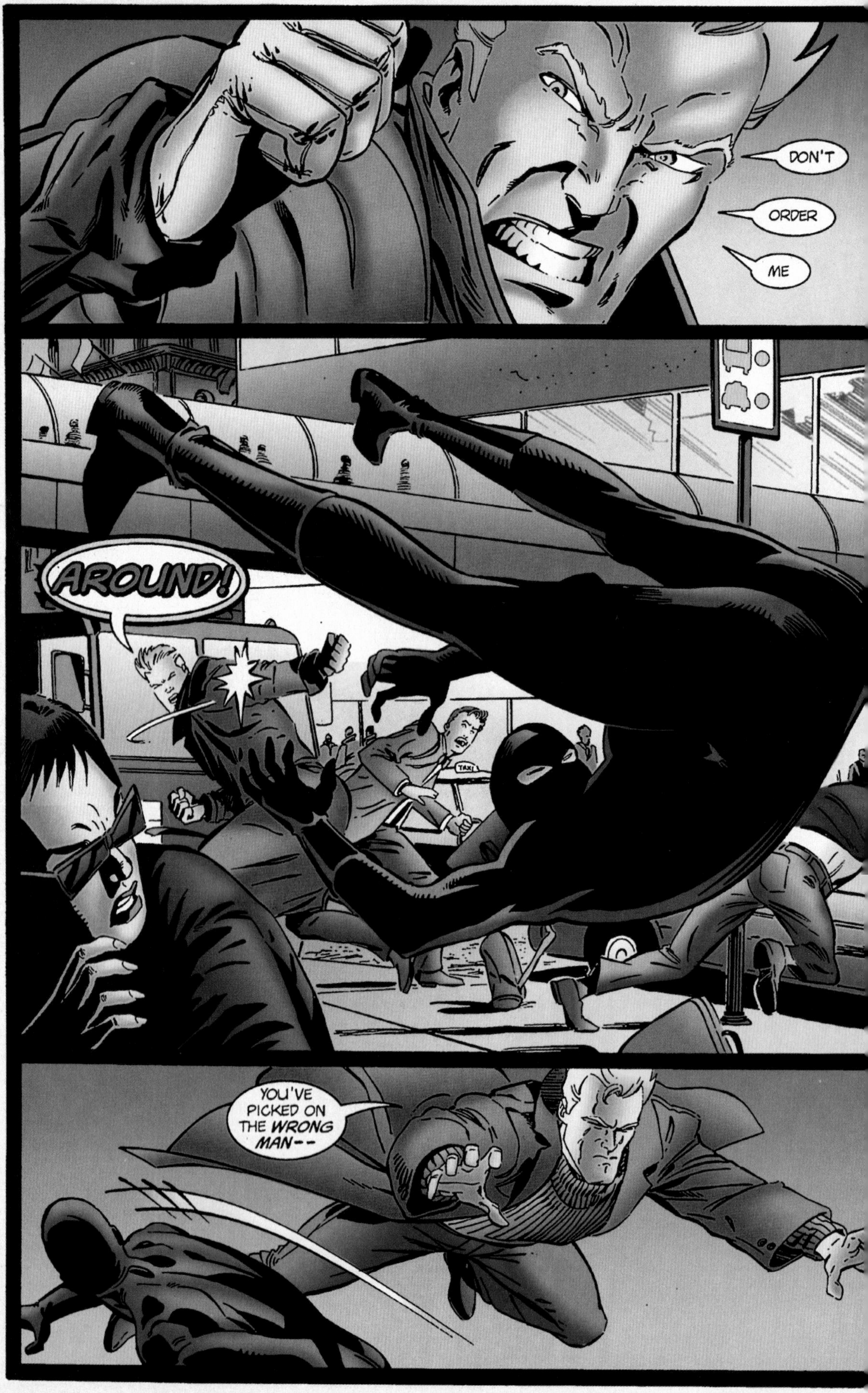
DON'T
ORDER
ME
AROUND!
YOU'VE PICKED ON THE WRONG MAN--
TAXI

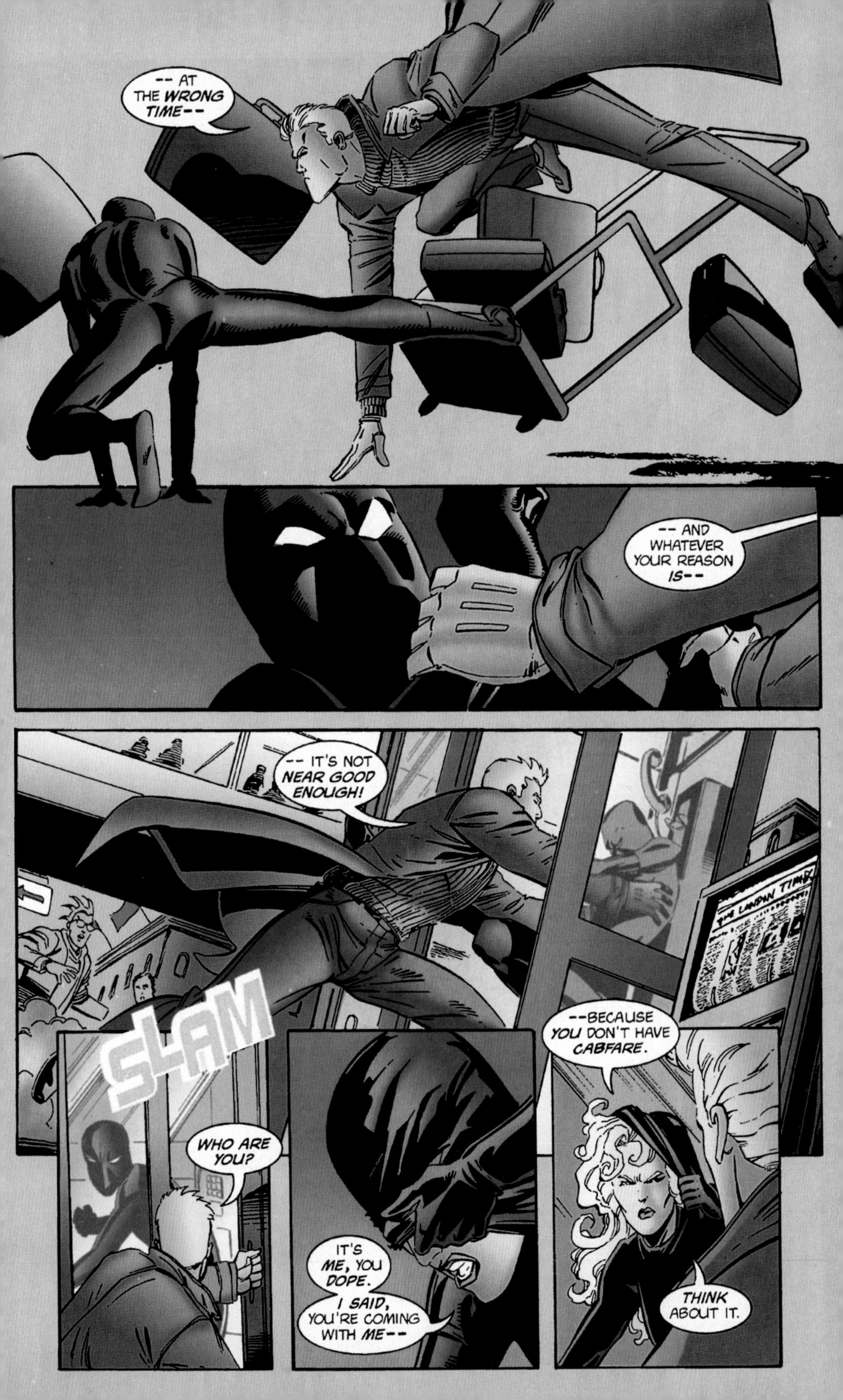

-- AT THE WRONG TIME--
-- AND WHATEVER YOUR REASON IS--
-- IT'S NOT NEAR GOOD ENOUGH!
SLAM
WHO ARE YOU?
IT'S ME, YOU DOPE. I SAID, YOU'RE COMING WITH ME--
--BECAUSE YOU DON'T HAVE CABFARE.
THINK ABOUT IT.

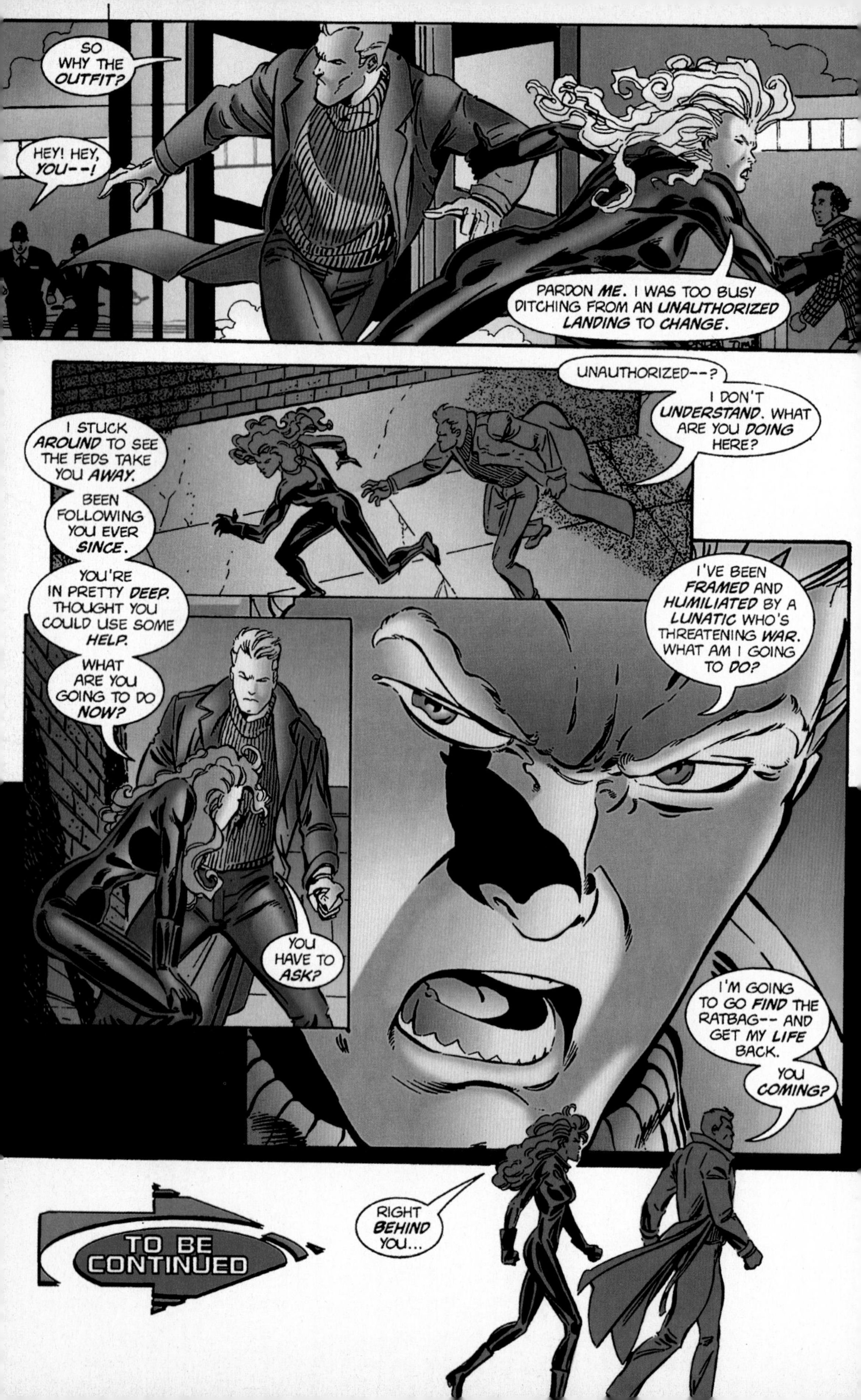
SO WHY THE OUTFIT?
HEY! HEY, YOU--!
PARDON ME. I WAS TOO BUSY DITCHING FROM AN UNAUTHORIZED LANDING TO CHANGE.
UNAUTHORIZED--?
I DON'T UNDERSTAND. WHAT ARE YOU DOING HERE?
I STUCK AROUND TO SEE THE FEDS TAKE YOU AWAY.
BEEN FOLLOWING YOU EVER SINCE.
YOU'RE IN PRETTY DEEP. THOUGHT YOU COULD USE SOME HELP.
WHAT ARE YOU GOING TO DO NOW?
I'VE BEEN FRAMED AND HUMILIATED BY A LUNATIC WHO'S THREATENING WAR. WHAT AM I GOING TO DO?
YOU HAVE TO ASK?
I'M GOING TO GO FIND THE RATBAG-- AND GET MY LIFE BACK.
YOU COMING?
RIGHT BEHIND YOU...
TO BE CONTINUED

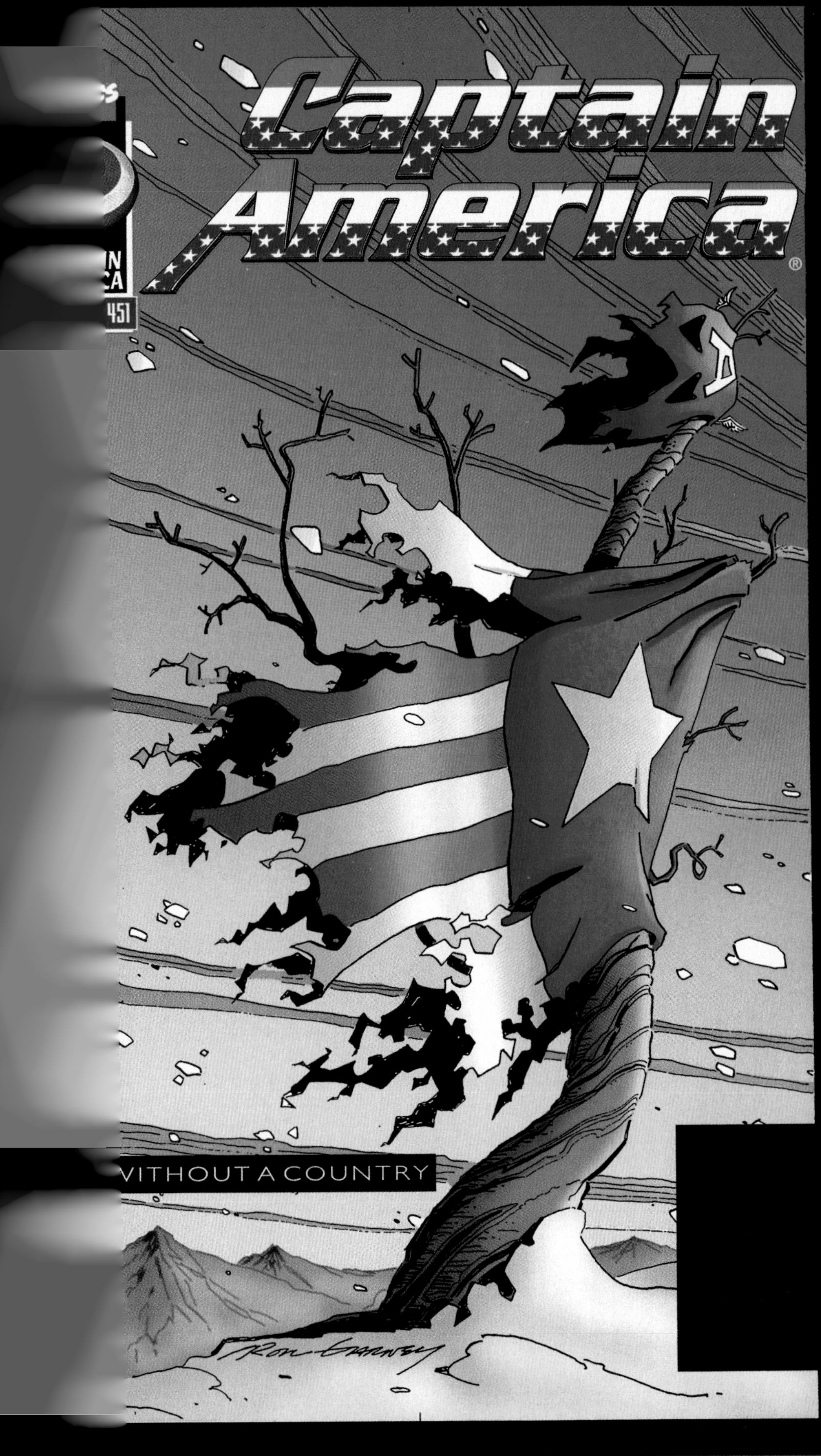
Captain America
451
VITHOUT A COUNTRY

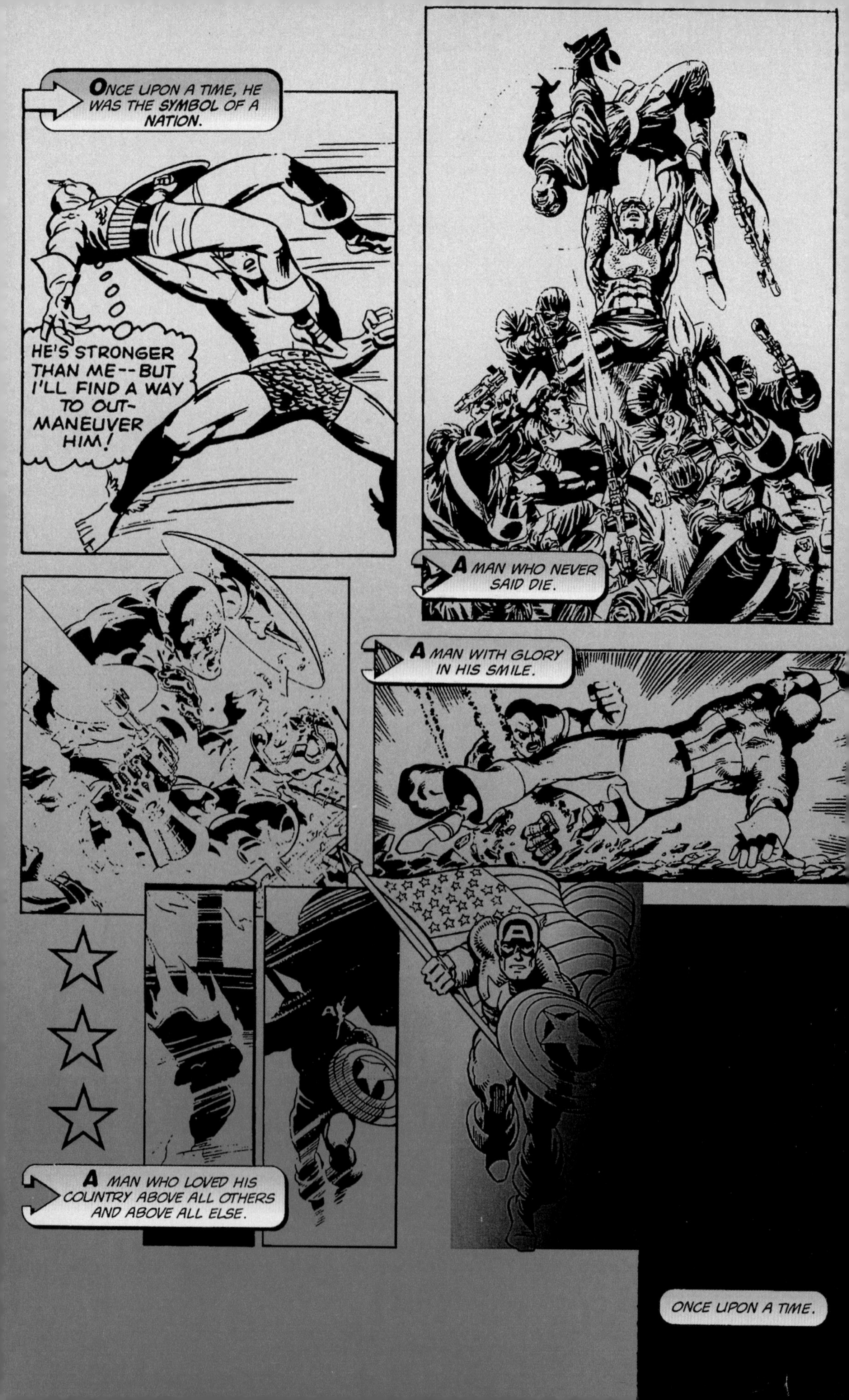
ONCE UPON A TIME, HE WAS THE SYMBOL OF A NATION.
HE'S STRONGER THAN ME--BUT I'LL FIND A WAY TO OUT-MANEUVER HIM!
A MAN WHO NEVER SAID DIE.
A MAN WITH GLORY IN HIS SMILE.
A MAN WHO LOVED HIS COUNTRY ABOVE ALL OTHERS AND ABOVE ALL ELSE.
ONCE UPON A TIME.

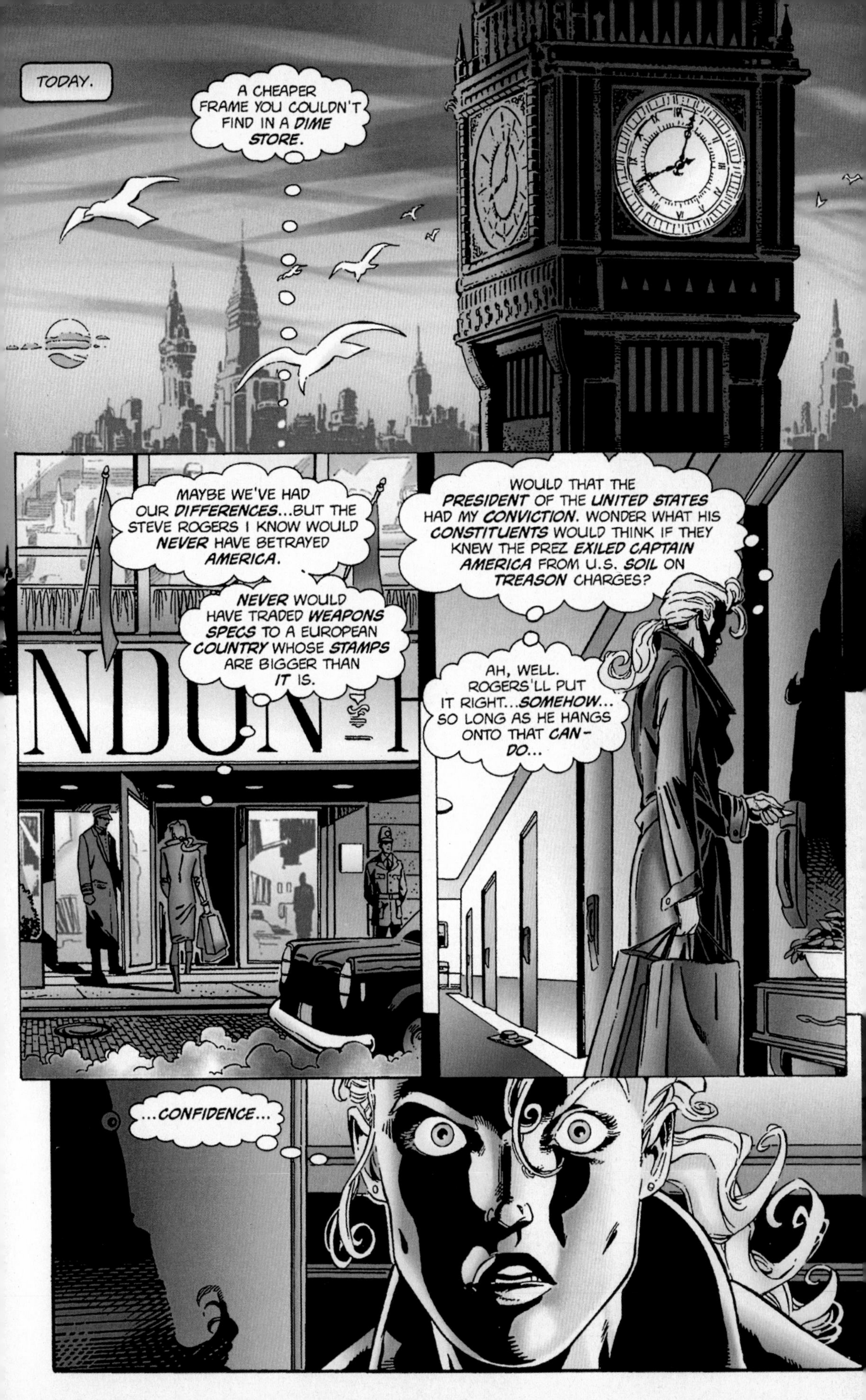
TODAY.
A CHEAPER FRAME YOU COULDN'T FIND IN A DIME STORE.
MAYBE WE'VE HAD OUR DIFFERENCES...BUT THE STEVE ROGERS I KNOW WOULD NEVER HAVE BETRAYED AMERICA.
NEVER WOULD HAVE TRADED WEAPONS SPECS TO A EUROPEAN COUNTRY WHOSE STAMPS ARE BIGGER THAN IT IS.
NDON H
WOULD THAT THE PRESIDENT OF THE UNITED STATES HAD MY CONVICTION. WONDER WHAT HIS CONSTITUENTS WOULD THINK IF THEY KNEW THE PREZ EXILED CAPTAIN AMERICA FROM U.S. SOIL ON TREASON CHARGES?
AH, WELL. ROGERS'LL PUT IT RIGHT...SOMEHOW... SO LONG AS HE HANGS ONTO THAT CAN-DO...
...CONFIDENCE...

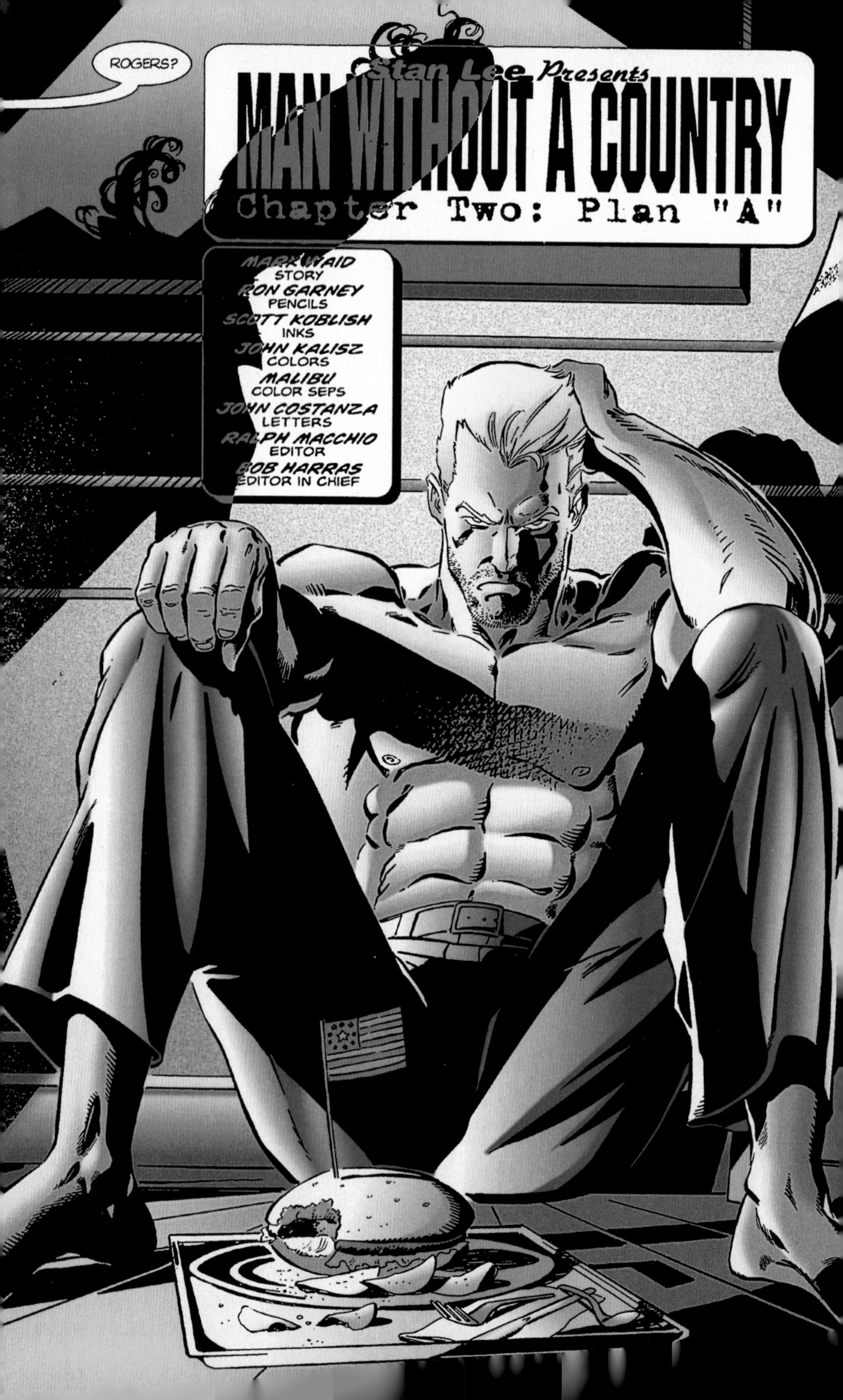

ROGERS?
Stan Lee Presents
MAN WITHOUT A COUNTRY
Chapter Two: Plan "A"
MARK WAID
STORY
RON GARNEY
PENCILS
SCOTT KOBLISH
INKS
JOHN KALISZ
COLORS
MALIBU
COLOR SEPS
JOHN COSTANZA
LETTERS
RALPH MACCHIO
EDITOR
BOB HARRAS
EDITOR IN CHIEF

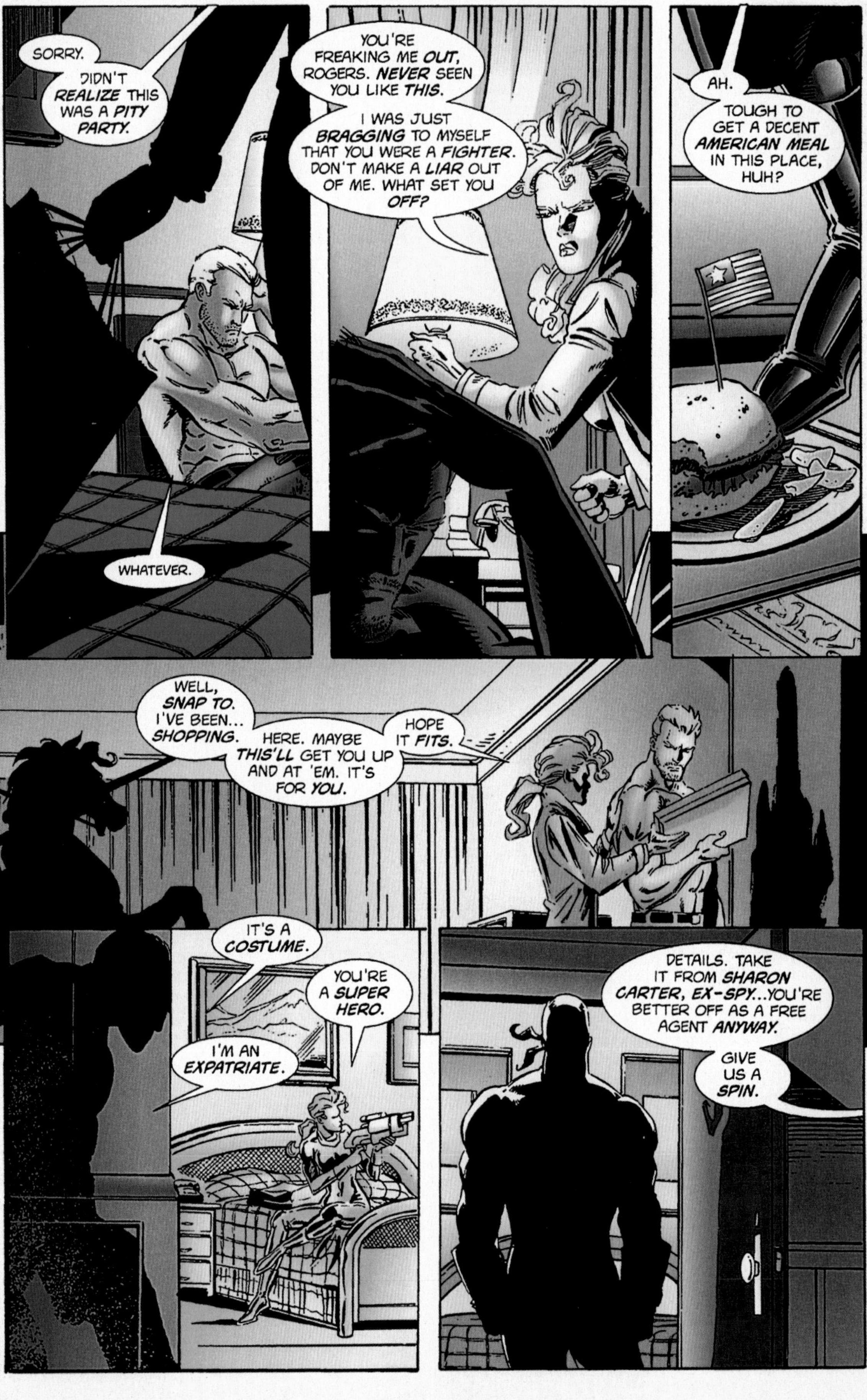
SORRY.
DIDN'T REALIZE THIS WAS A PITY PARTY.
WHATEVER.
YOU'RE FREAKING ME OUT, ROGERS. NEVER SEEN YOU LIKE THIS.
I WAS JUST BRAGGING TO MYSELF THAT YOU WERE A FIGHTER. DON'T MAKE A LIAR OUT OF ME. WHAT SET YOU OFF?
AH.
TOUGH TO GET A DECENT AMERICAN MEAL IN THIS PLACE, HUH?
WELL, SNAP TO. I'VE BEEN... SHOPPING.
HERE. MAYBE THIS'LL GET YOU UP AND AT 'EM. IT'S FOR YOU.
HOPE IT FITS.
IT'S A COSTUME.
I'M AN EXPATRIATE.
YOU'RE A SUPER HERO.
DETAILS. TAKE IT FROM SHARON CARTER, EX-SPY...YOU'RE BETTER OFF AS A FREE AGENT ANYWAY.
GIVE US A SPIN.

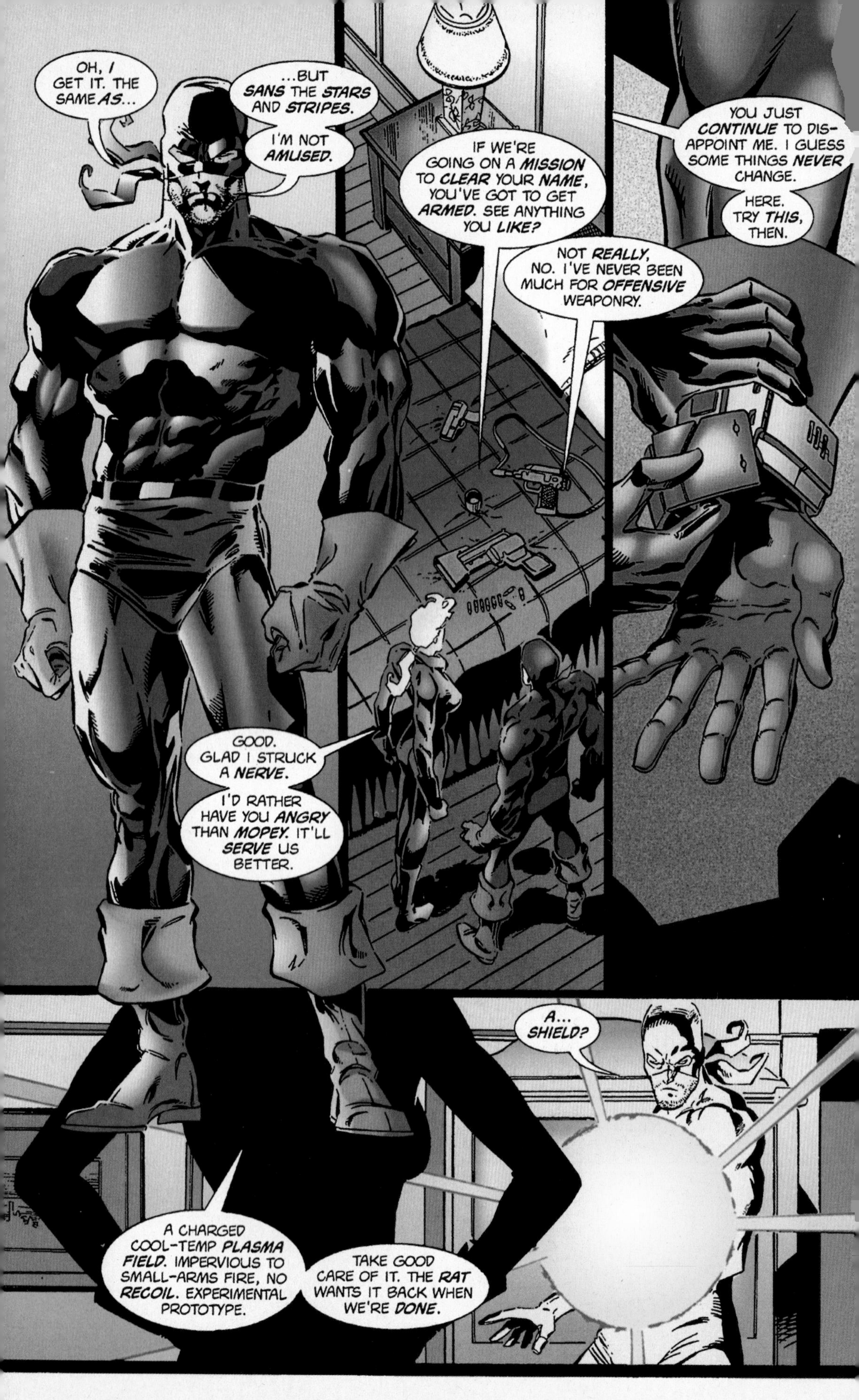
OH, I GET IT. THE SAME AS...
...BUT SANS THE STARS AND STRIPES.
I'M NOT AMUSED.
GOOD. GLAD I STRUCK A NERVE.
I'D RATHER HAVE YOU ANGRY THAN MOPEY. IT'LL SERVE US BETTER.
IF WE'RE GOING ON A MISSION TO CLEAR YOUR NAME, YOU'VE GOT TO GET ARMED. SEE ANYTHING YOU LIKE?
NOT REALLY, NO. I'VE NEVER BEEN MUCH FOR OFFENSIVE WEAPONRY.
YOU JUST CONTINUE TO DISAPPOINT ME. I GUESS SOME THINGS NEVER CHANGE.
HERE. TRY THIS, THEN.
A... SHIELD?
A CHARGED COOL-TEMP PLASMA FIELD. IMPERVIOUS TO SMALL-ARMS FIRE, NO RECOIL. EXPERIMENTAL PROTOTYPE.
TAKE GOOD CARE OF IT. THE RAT WANTS IT BACK WHEN WE'RE DONE.

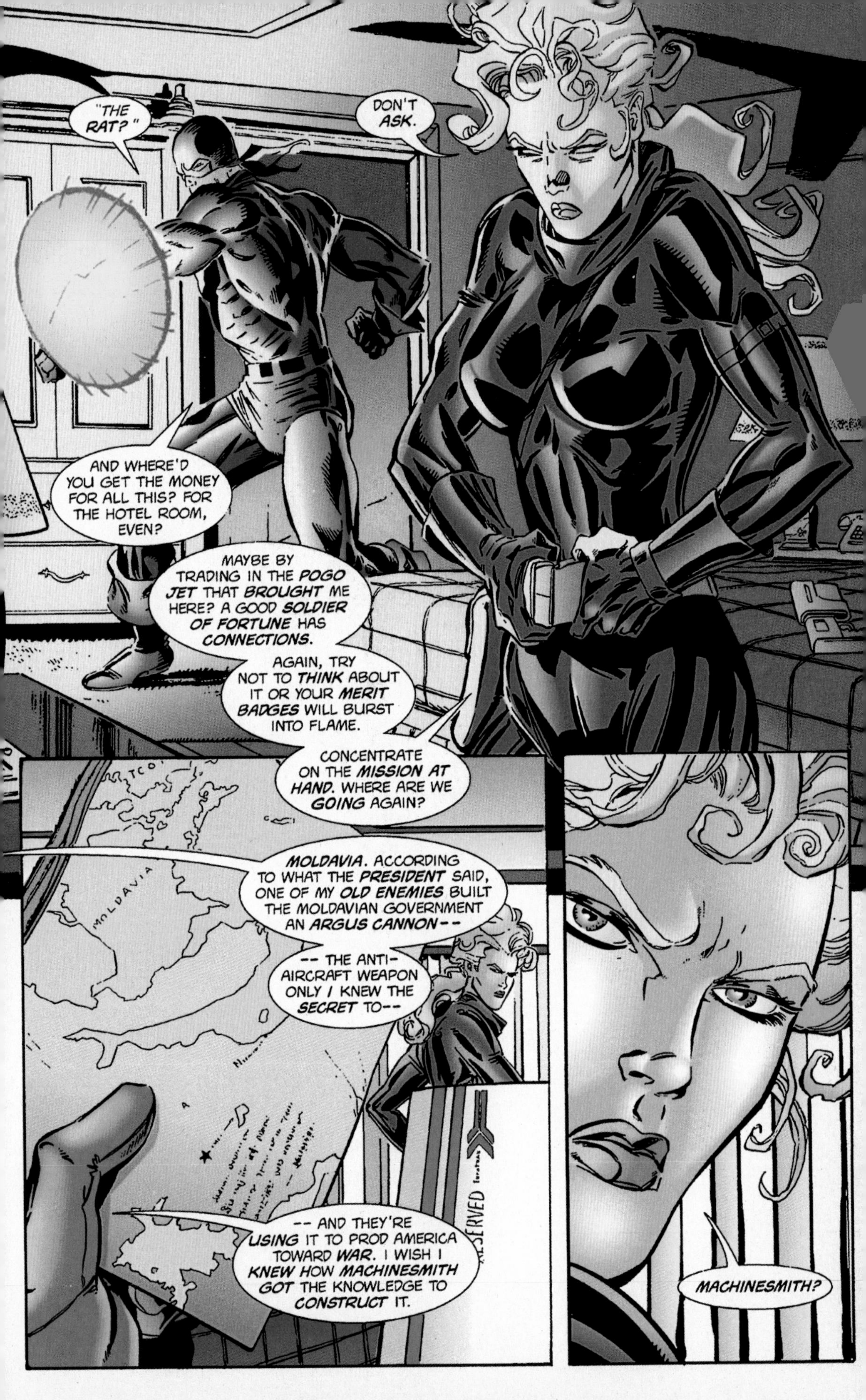
"THE RAT?"
DON'T ASK.
AND WHERE'D YOU GET THE MONEY FOR ALL THIS? FOR THE HOTEL ROOM, EVEN?
MAYBE BY TRADING IN THE POGO JET THAT BROUGHT ME HERE? A GOOD SOLDIER OF FORTUNE HAS CONNECTIONS.
AGAIN, TRY NOT TO THINK ABOUT IT OR YOUR MERIT BADGES WILL BURST INTO FLAME.
CONCENTRATE ON THE MISSION AT HAND. WHERE ARE WE GOING AGAIN?
MOLDAVIA
MOLDAVIA. ACCORDING TO WHAT THE PRESIDENT SAID, ONE OF MY OLD ENEMIES BUILT THE MOLDAVIAN GOVERNMENT AN ARGUS CANNON--
-- THE ANTI-AIRCRAFT WEAPON ONLY I KNEW THE SECRET TO--
-- AND THEY'RE USING IT TO PROD AMERICA TOWARD WAR. I WISH I KNEW HOW MACHINESMITH GOT THE KNOWLEDGE TO CONSTRUCT IT.
MACHINESMITH?

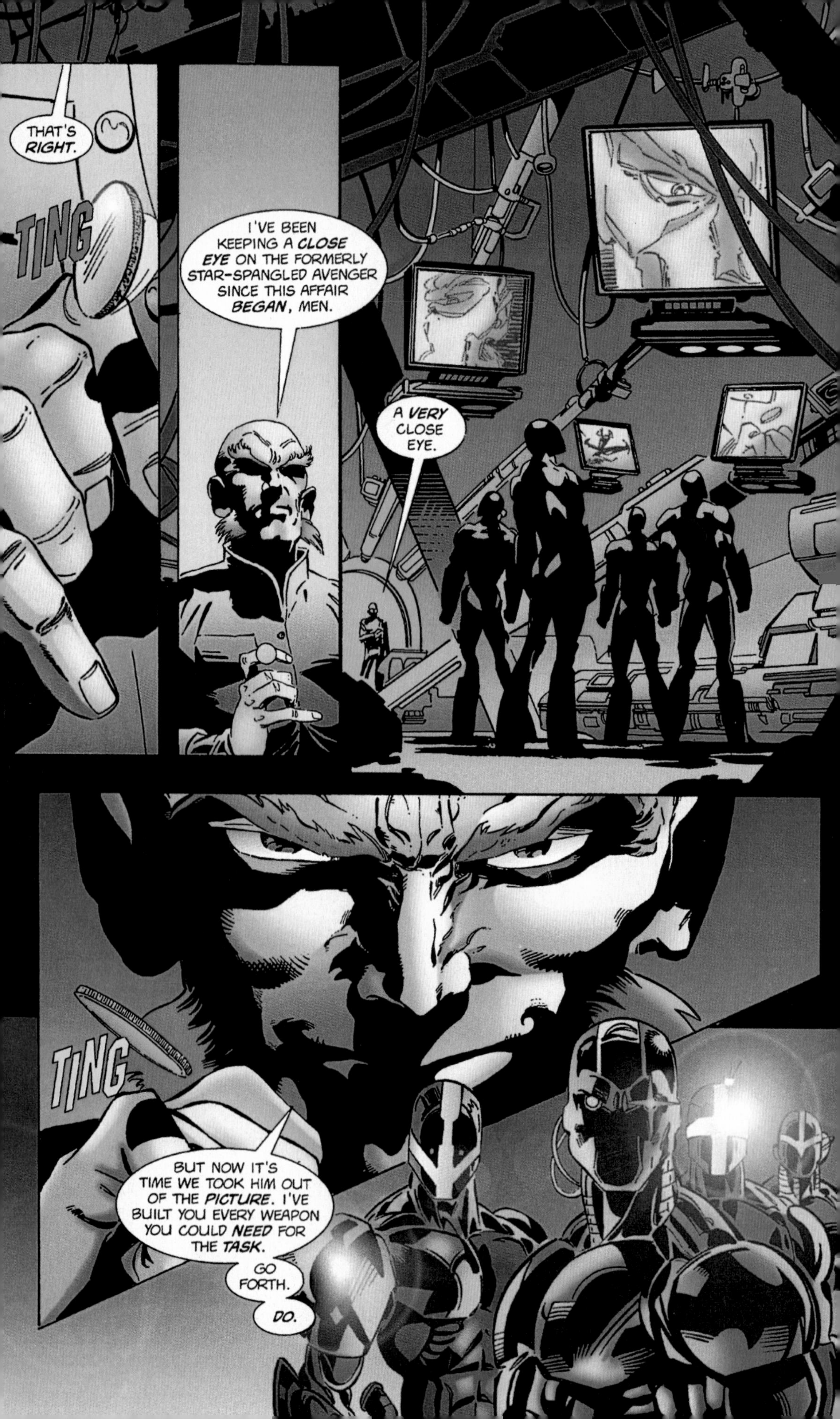
THAT'S RIGHT.
TING
I'VE BEEN KEEPING A CLOSE EYE ON THE FORMERLY STAR-SPANGLED AVENGER SINCE THIS AFFAIR BEGAN, MEN.
A VERY CLOSE EYE.
TING
BUT NOW IT'S TIME WE TOOK HIM OUT OF THE PICTURE. I'VE BUILT YOU EVERY WEAPON YOU COULD NEED FOR THE TASK.
GO FORTH.
DO.

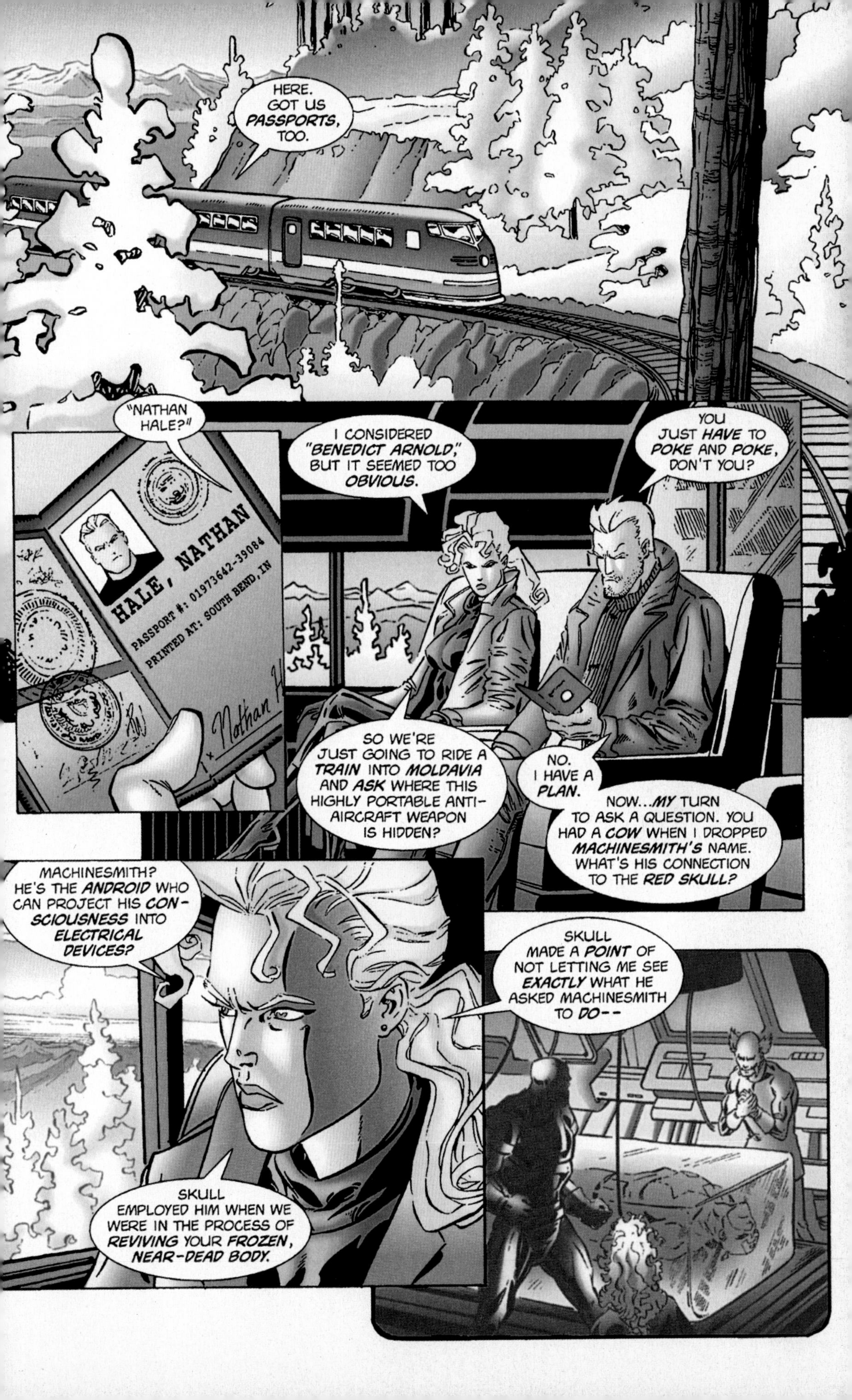
HERE. GOT US PASSPORTS, TOO.
"NATHAN HALE?"
HALE, NATHAN
PASSPORT #: 01973642-39084
PRINTED AT: SOUTH BEND, IN
I CONSIDERED "BENEDICT ARNOLD," BUT IT SEEMED TOO OBVIOUS.
YOU JUST HAVE TO POKE AND POKE, DON'T YOU?
SO WE'RE JUST GOING TO RIDE A TRAIN INTO MOLDAVIA AND ASK WHERE THIS HIGHLY PORTABLE ANTI-AIRCRAFT WEAPON IS HIDDEN?
NO. I HAVE A PLAN.
NOW...MY TURN TO ASK A QUESTION. YOU HAD A COW WHEN I DROPPED MACHINESMITH'S NAME. WHAT'S HIS CONNECTION TO THE RED SKULL?
MACHINESMITH? HE'S THE ANDROID WHO CAN PROJECT HIS CONSCIOUSNESS INTO ELECTRICAL DEVICES?
SKULL EMPLOYED HIM WHEN WE WERE IN THE PROCESS OF REVIVING YOUR FROZEN, NEAR-DEAD BODY.
SKULL MADE A POINT OF NOT LETTING ME SEE EXACTLY WHAT HE ASKED MACHINESMITH TO DO--

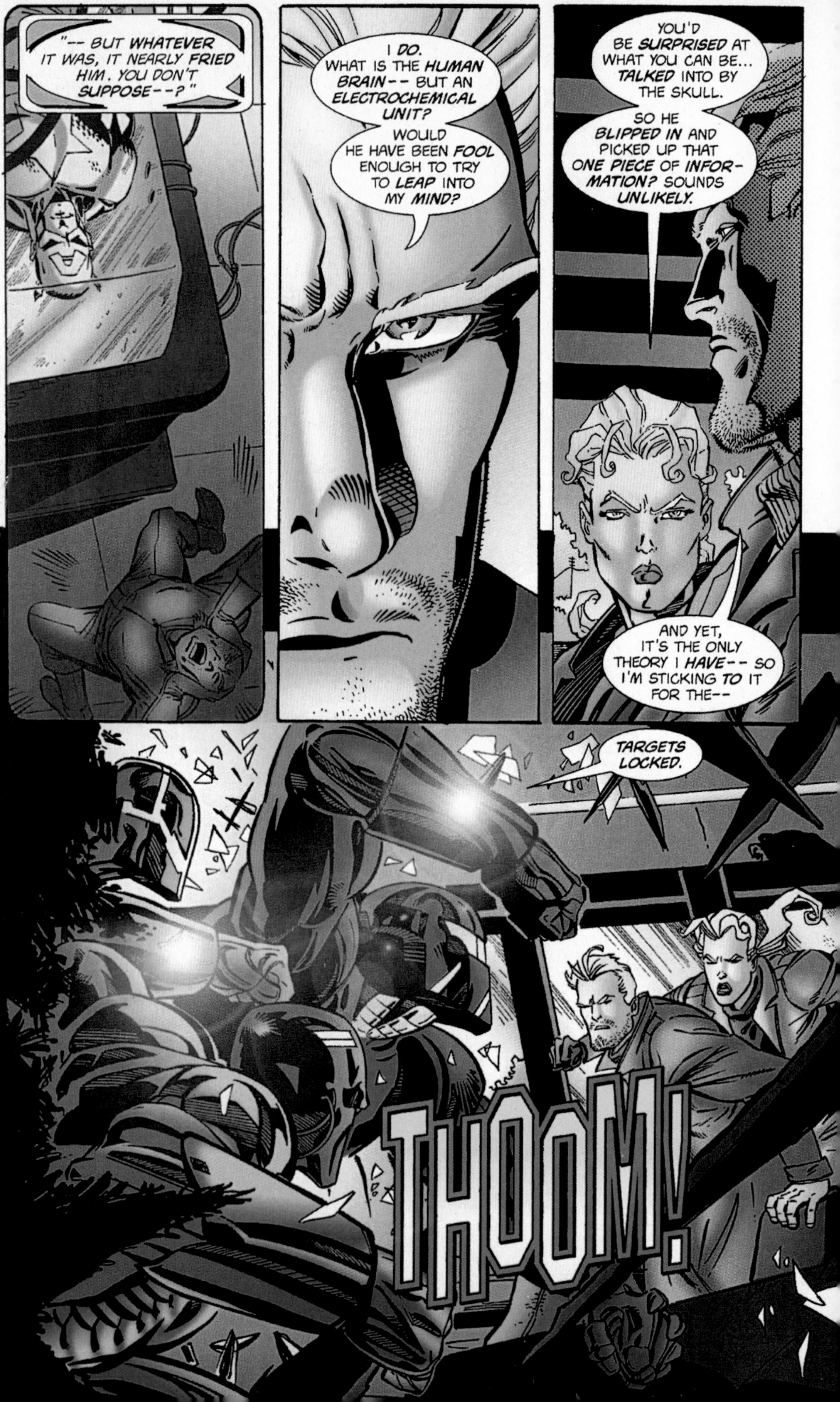
"-- BUT WHATEVER IT WAS, IT NEARLY FRIED HIM. YOU DON'T SUPPOSE--?"
I DO. WHAT IS THE HUMAN BRAIN-- BUT AN ELECTROCHEMICAL UNIT?
WOULD HE HAVE BEEN FOOL ENOUGH TO TRY TO LEAP INTO MY MIND?
YOU'D BE SURPRISED AT WHAT YOU CAN BE... TALKED INTO BY THE SKULL.
SO HE BLIPPED IN AND PICKED UP THAT ONE PIECE OF INFORMATION? SOUNDS UNLIKELY.
AND YET, IT'S THE ONLY THEORY I HAVE-- SO I'M STICKING TO IT FOR THE--
TARGETS LOCKED.
THOOM!

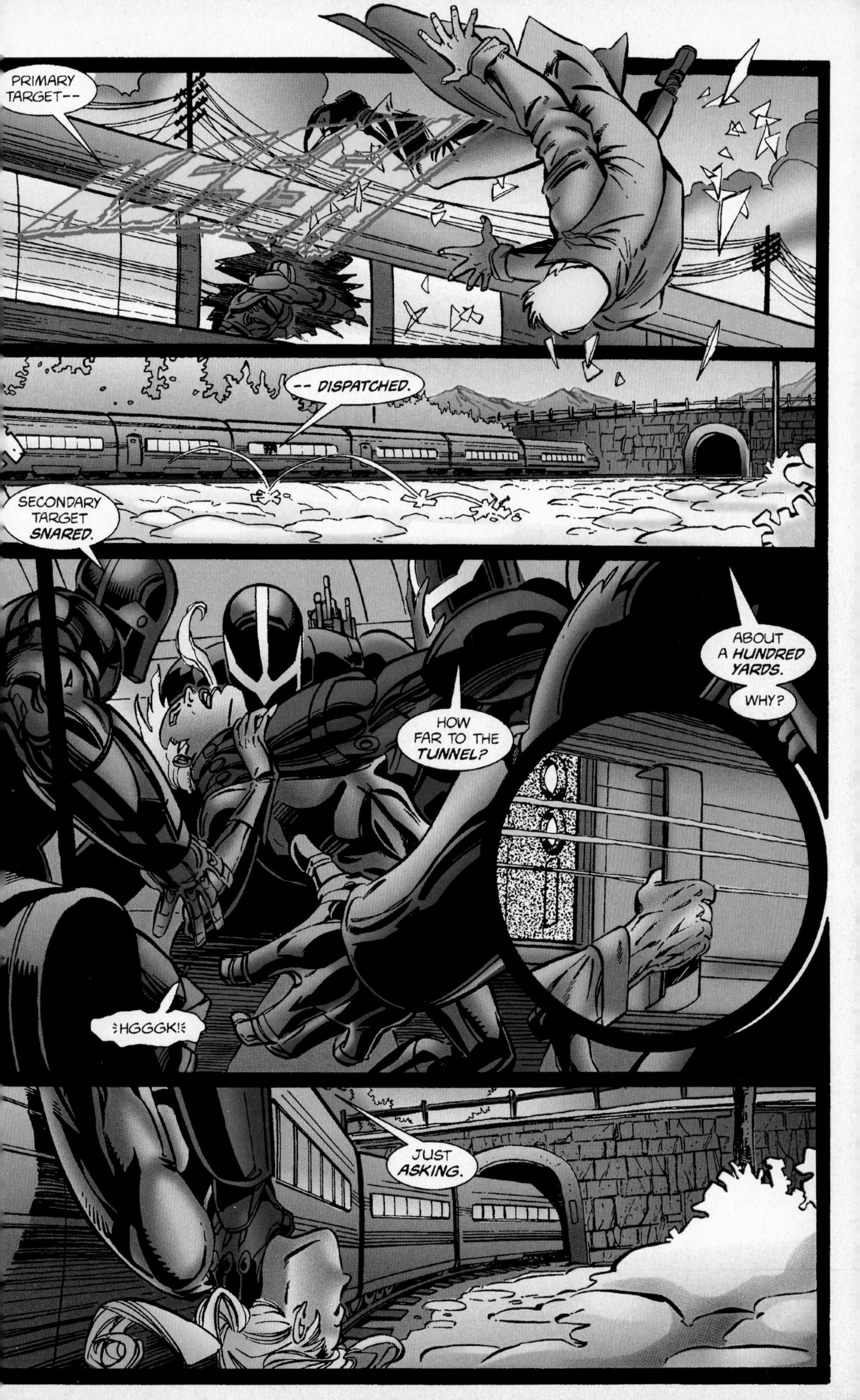
PRIMARY TARGET--
-- DISPATCHED.
SECONDARY TARGET SNARED.
HOW FAR TO THE TUNNEL?
ABOUT A HUNDRED YARDS.
WHY?
HGGGK!
JUST ASKING.

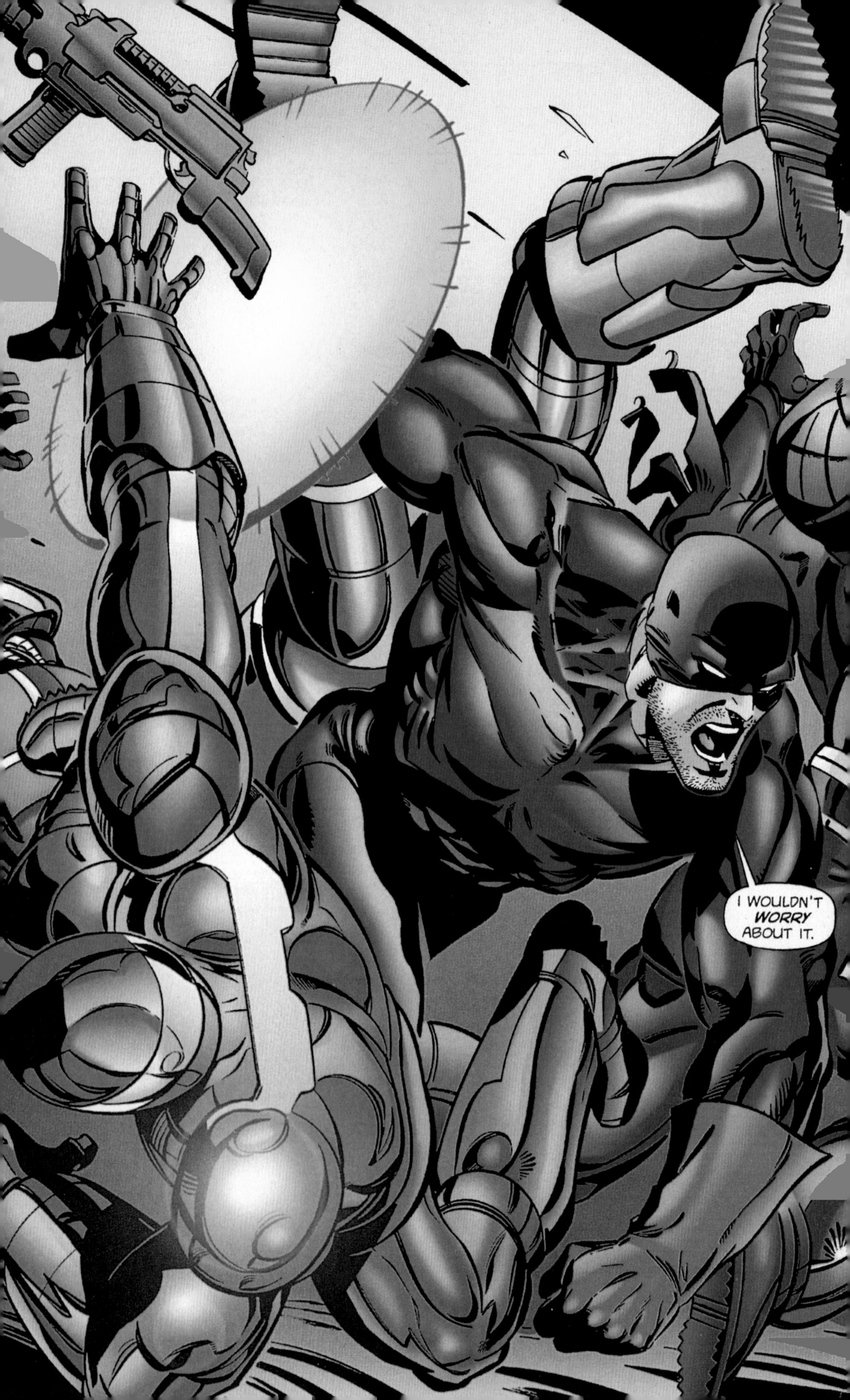
I WOULDN'T WORRY ABOUT IT.

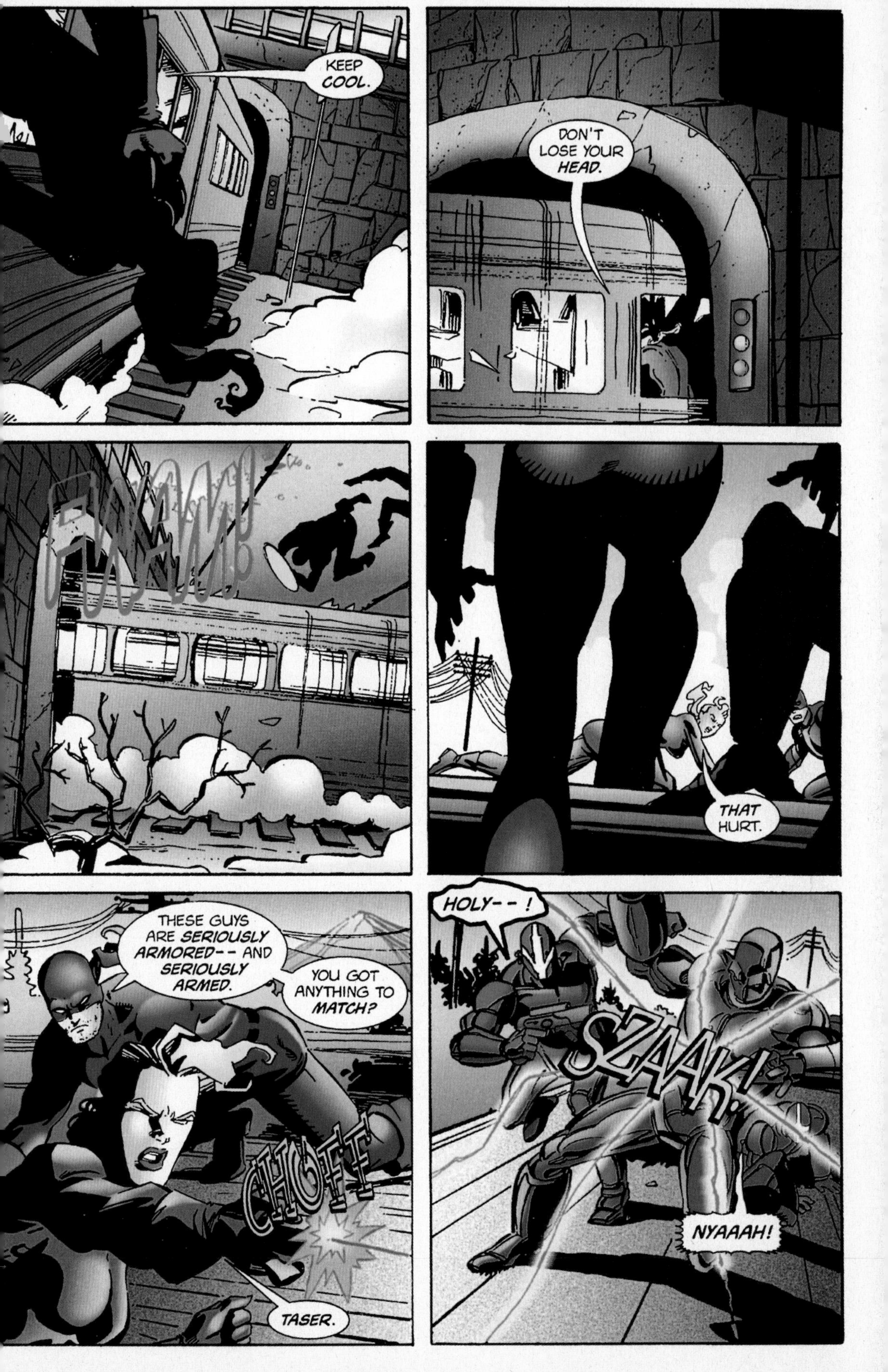
KEEP COOL.
DON'T LOSE YOUR HEAD.
THAT HURT.
THESE GUYS ARE SERIOUSLY ARMORED-- AND SERIOUSLY ARMED.
YOU GOT ANYTHING TO MATCH?
CHOFF
TASER.
HOLY-- !
SZAAK!
NYAAAH!

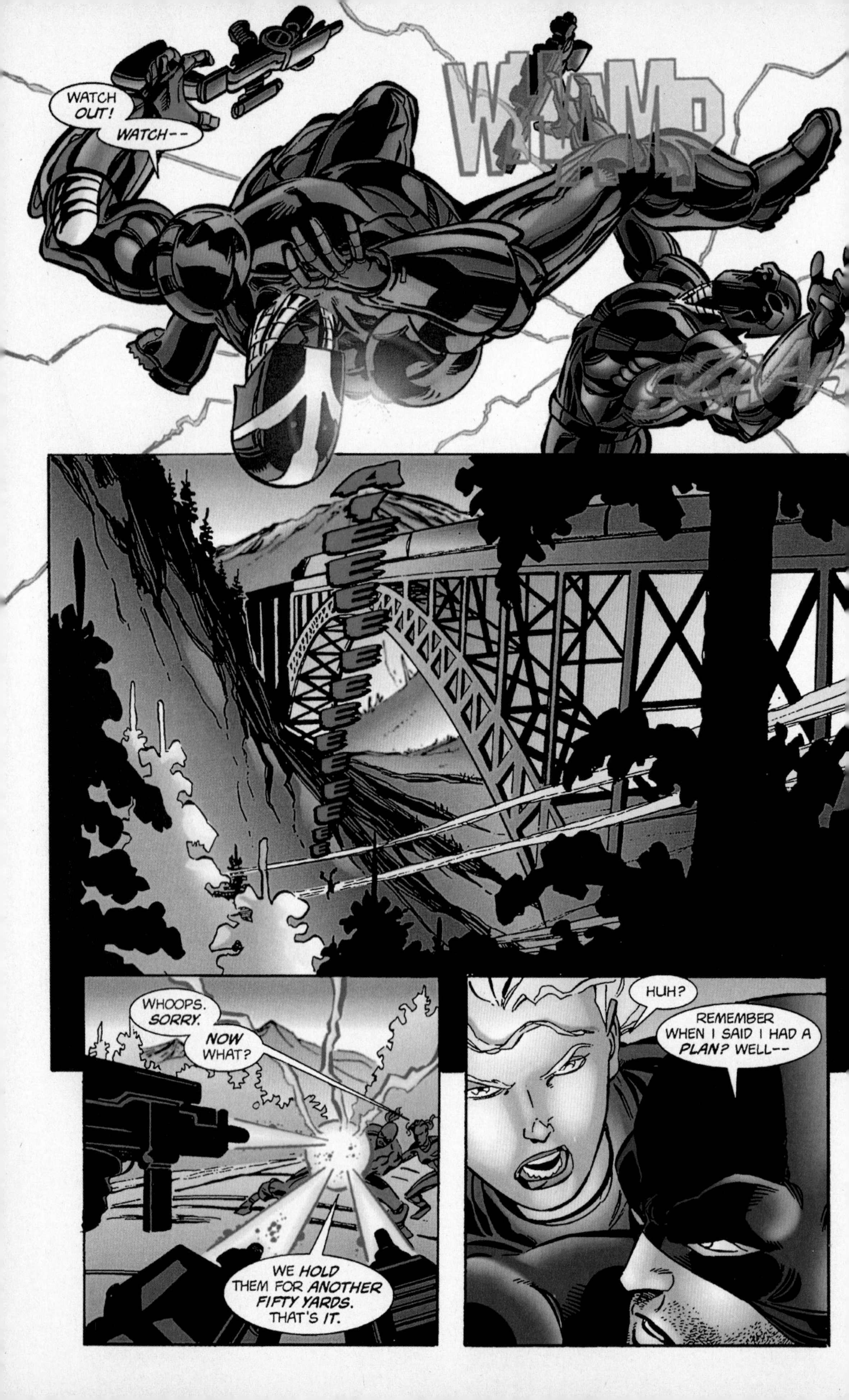
WATCH OUT!
WATCH--
WHOOPS. SORRY.
NOW WHAT?
WE HOLD THEM FOR ANOTHER FIFTY YARDS. THAT'S IT.
HUH?
REMEMBER WHEN I SAID I HAD A PLAN? WELL--

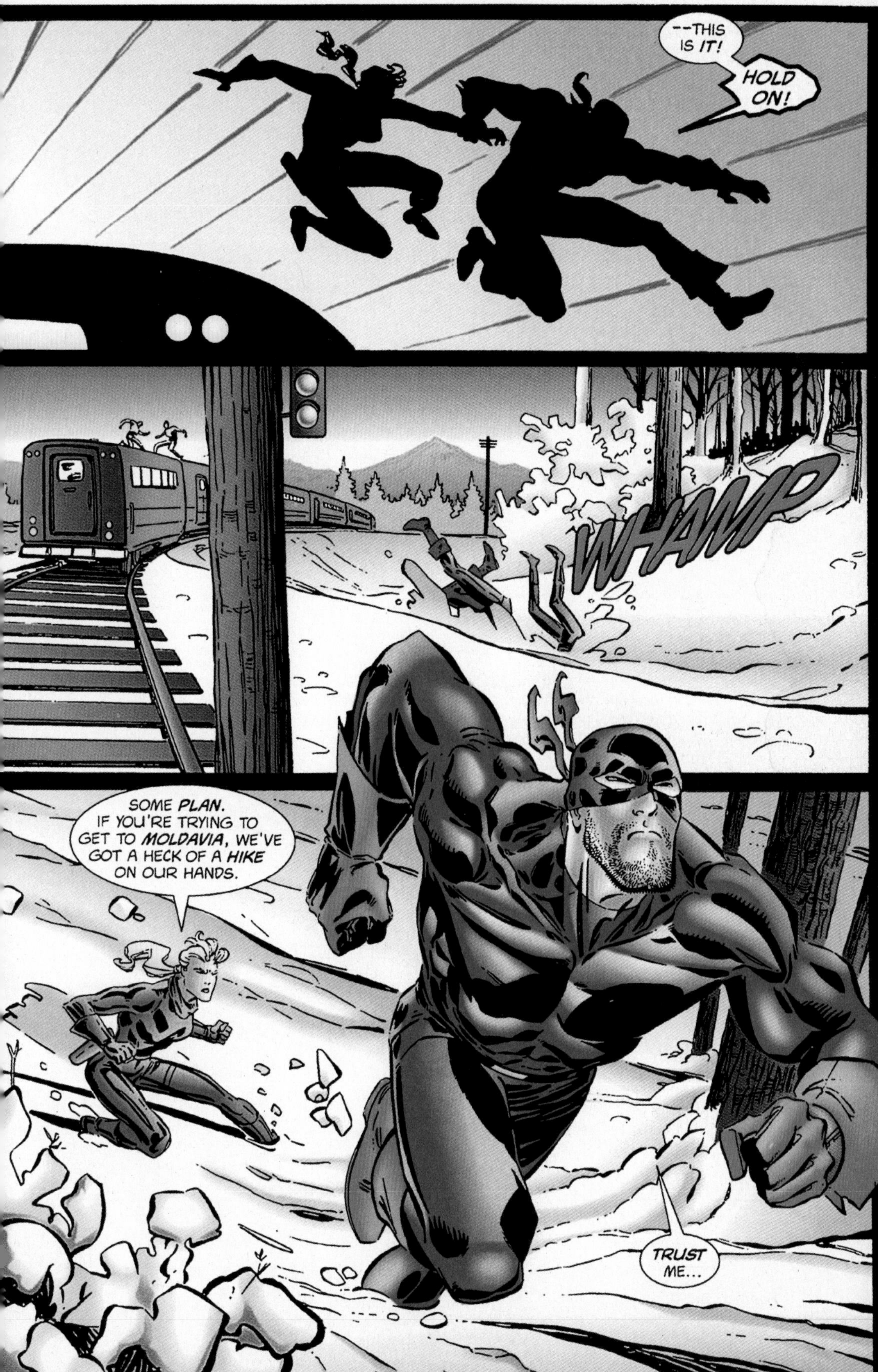
--THIS IS IT!
HOLD ON!
WHAMP
SOME PLAN. IF YOU'RE TRYING TO GET TO MOLDAVIA, WE'VE GOT A HECK OF A HIKE ON OUR HANDS.
TRUST ME...

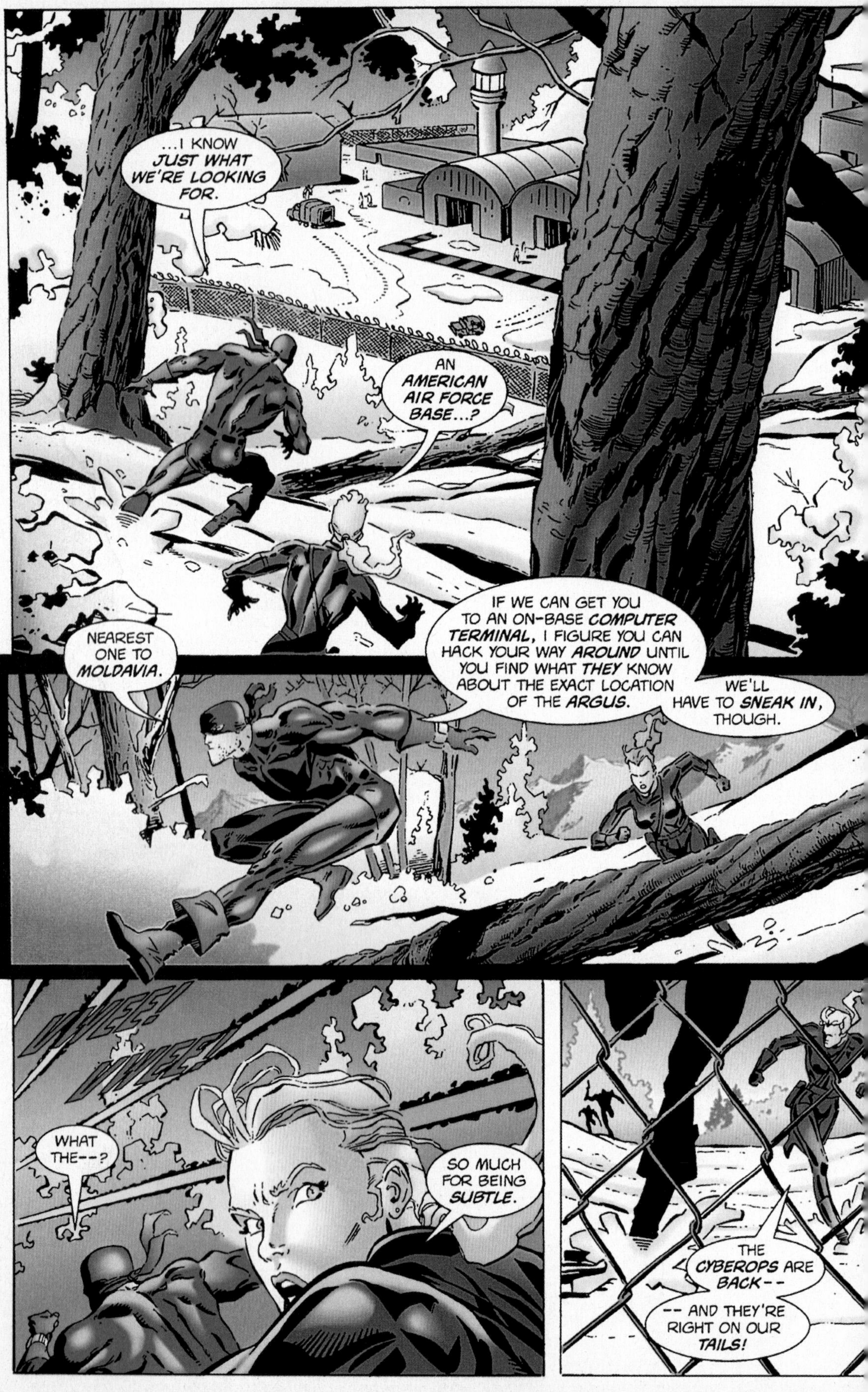
...I KNOW JUST WHAT WE'RE LOOKING FOR.
AN AMERICAN AIR FORCE BASE...?
NEAREST ONE TO MOLDAVIA.
IF WE CAN GET YOU TO AN ON-BASE COMPUTER TERMINAL, I FIGURE YOU CAN HACK YOUR WAY AROUND UNTIL YOU FIND WHAT THEY KNOW ABOUT THE EXACT LOCATION OF THE ARGUS.
WE'LL HAVE TO SNEAK IN, THOUGH.
WHAT THE--?
SO MUCH FOR BEING SUBTLE.
THE CYBEROPS ARE BACK--
-- AND THEY'RE RIGHT ON OUR TAILS!

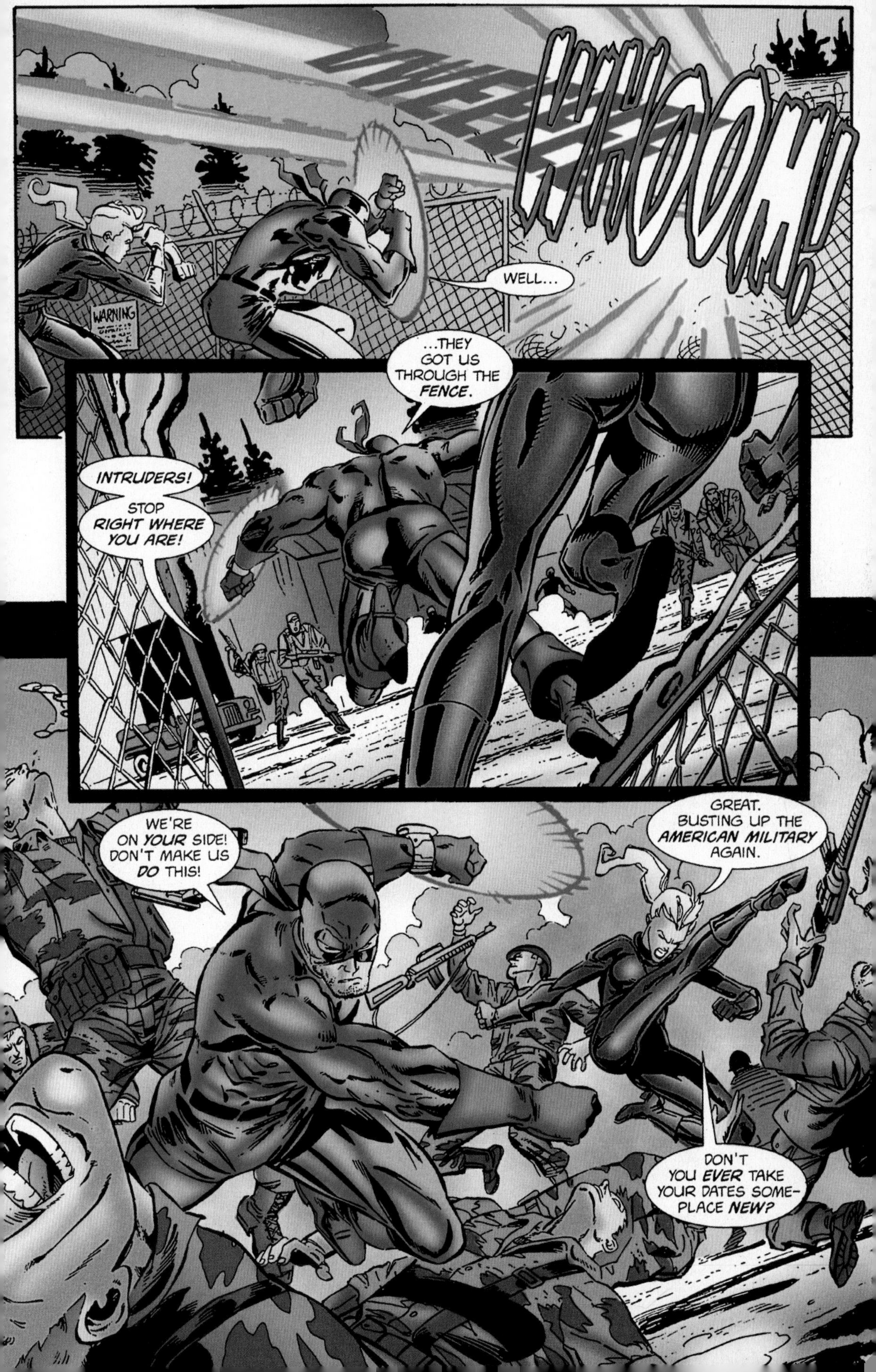
WHOOOM!
WELL...
...THEY GOT US THROUGH THE FENCE.
INTRUDERS! STOP RIGHT WHERE YOU ARE!
WE'RE ON YOUR SIDE! DON'T MAKE US DO THIS!
GREAT. BUSTING UP THE AMERICAN MILITARY AGAIN.
DON'T YOU EVER TAKE YOUR DATES SOME-PLACE NEW?

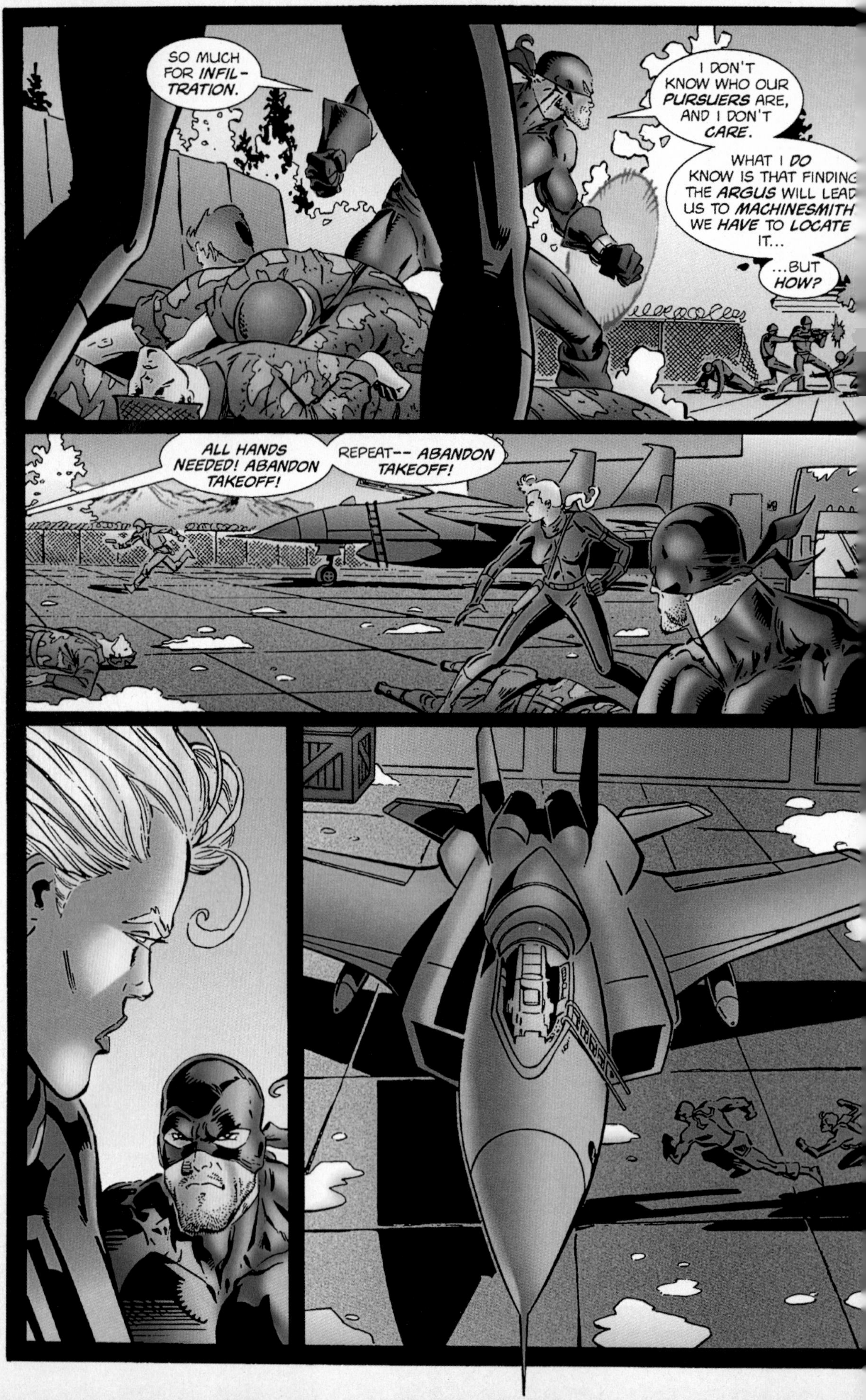
SO MUCH FOR INFIL-TRATION.
I DON'T KNOW WHO OUR PURSUERS ARE, AND I DON'T CARE.
WHAT I DO KNOW IS THAT FINDING THE ARGUS WILL LEAD US TO MACHINESMITH. WE HAVE TO LOCATE IT...
...BUT HOW?
ALL HANDS NEEDED! ABANDON TAKEOFF!
REPEAT-- ABANDON TAKEOFF!

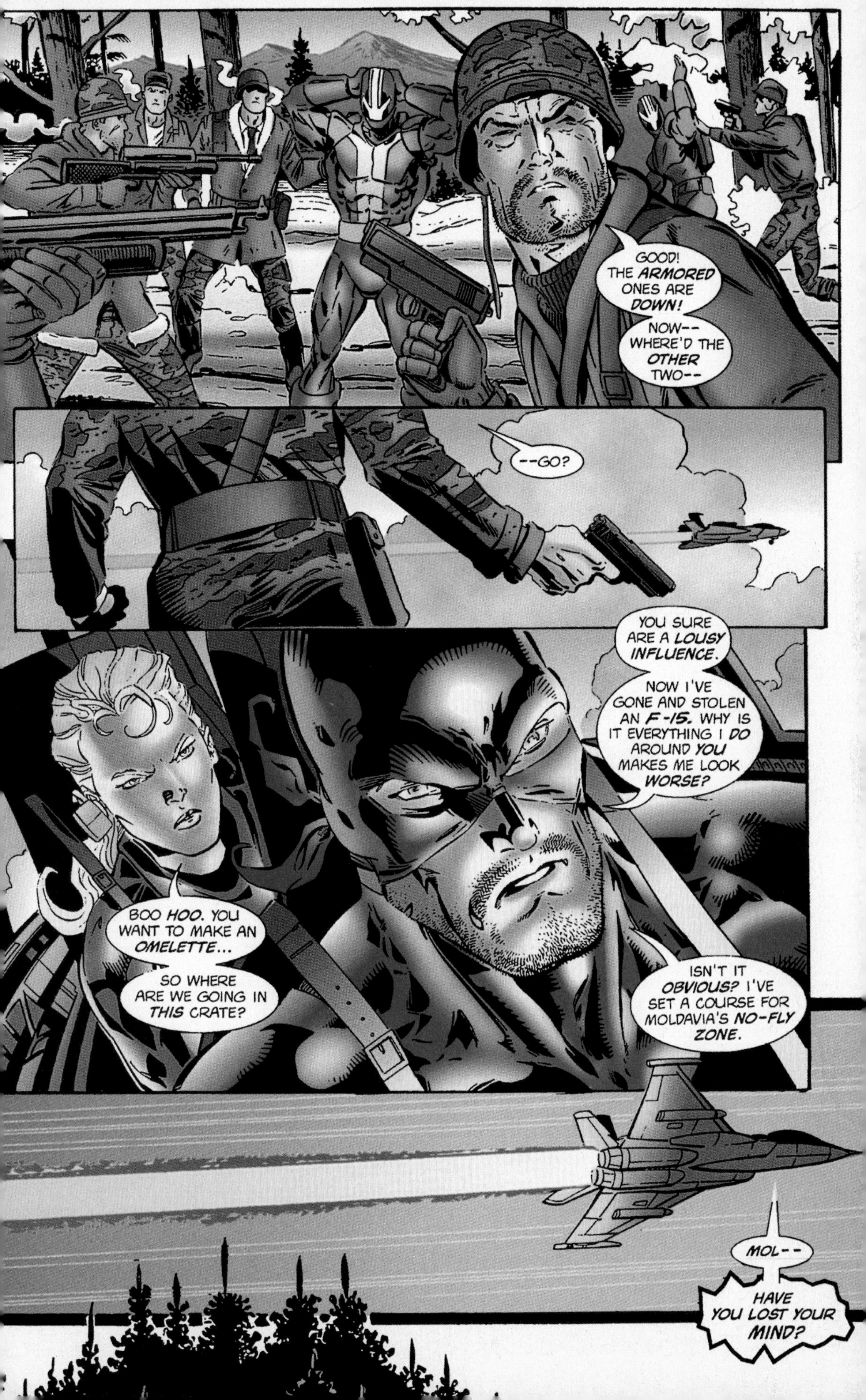
GOOD! THE ARMORED ONES ARE DOWN!
NOW-- WHERE'D THE OTHER TWO--
--GO?
YOU SURE ARE A LOUSY INFLUENCE.
NOW I'VE GONE AND STOLEN AN F-15. WHY IS IT EVERYTHING I DO AROUND YOU MAKES ME LOOK WORSE?
BOO HOO. YOU WANT TO MAKE AN OMELETTE...
SO WHERE ARE WE GOING IN THIS CRATE?
ISN'T IT OBVIOUS? I'VE SET A COURSE FOR MOLDAVIA'S NO-FLY ZONE.
MOL--
HAVE YOU LOST YOUR MIND?

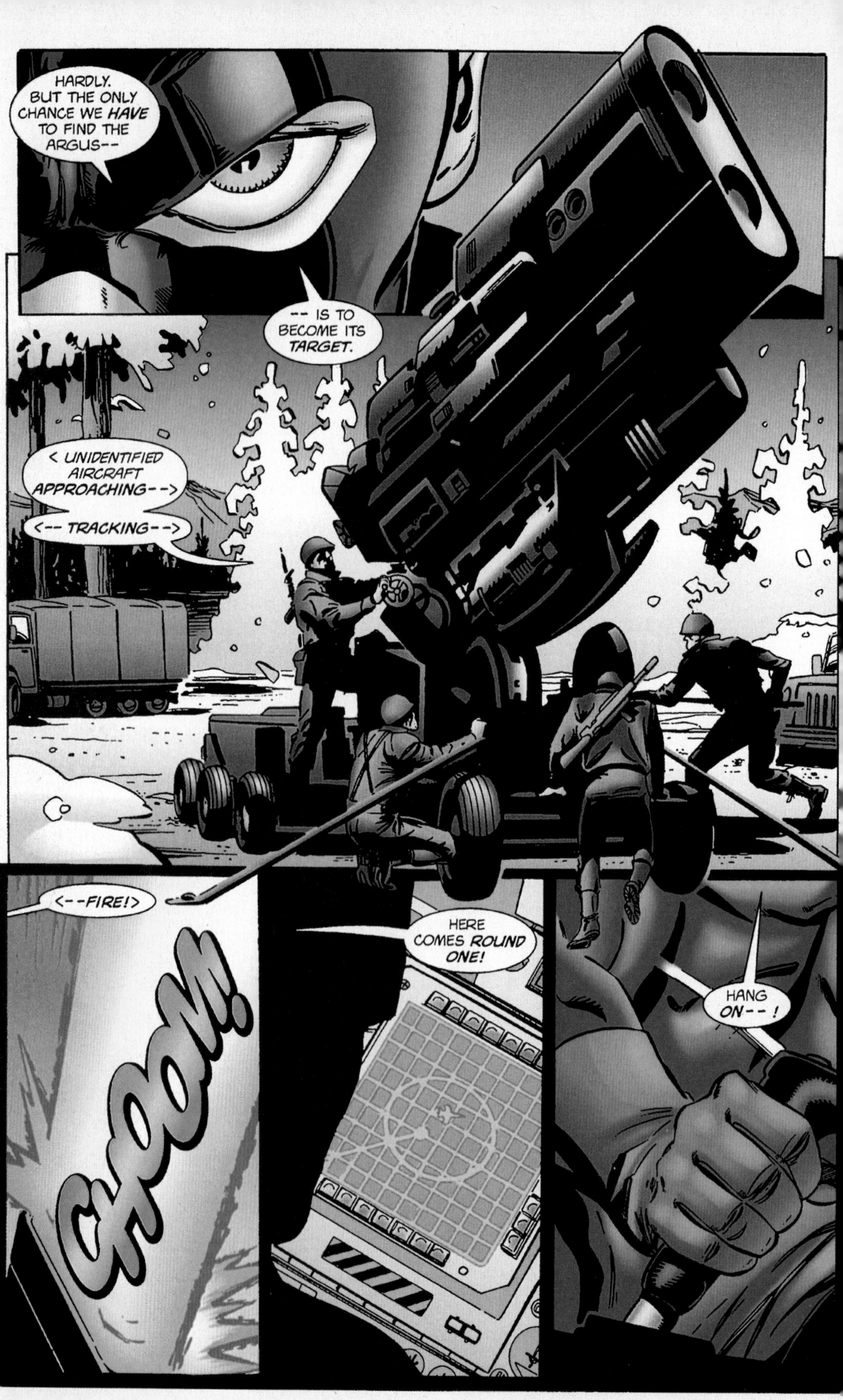

HARDLY. BUT THE ONLY CHANCE WE *HAVE* TO FIND THE ARGUS--
-- IS TO BECOME ITS *TARGET*.
< UNIDENTIFIED AIRCRAFT *APPROACHING*-->
<-- *TRACKING*-->
<--*FIRE!*>
CHOOM!
HERE COMES *ROUND ONE!*
HANG *ON*--!

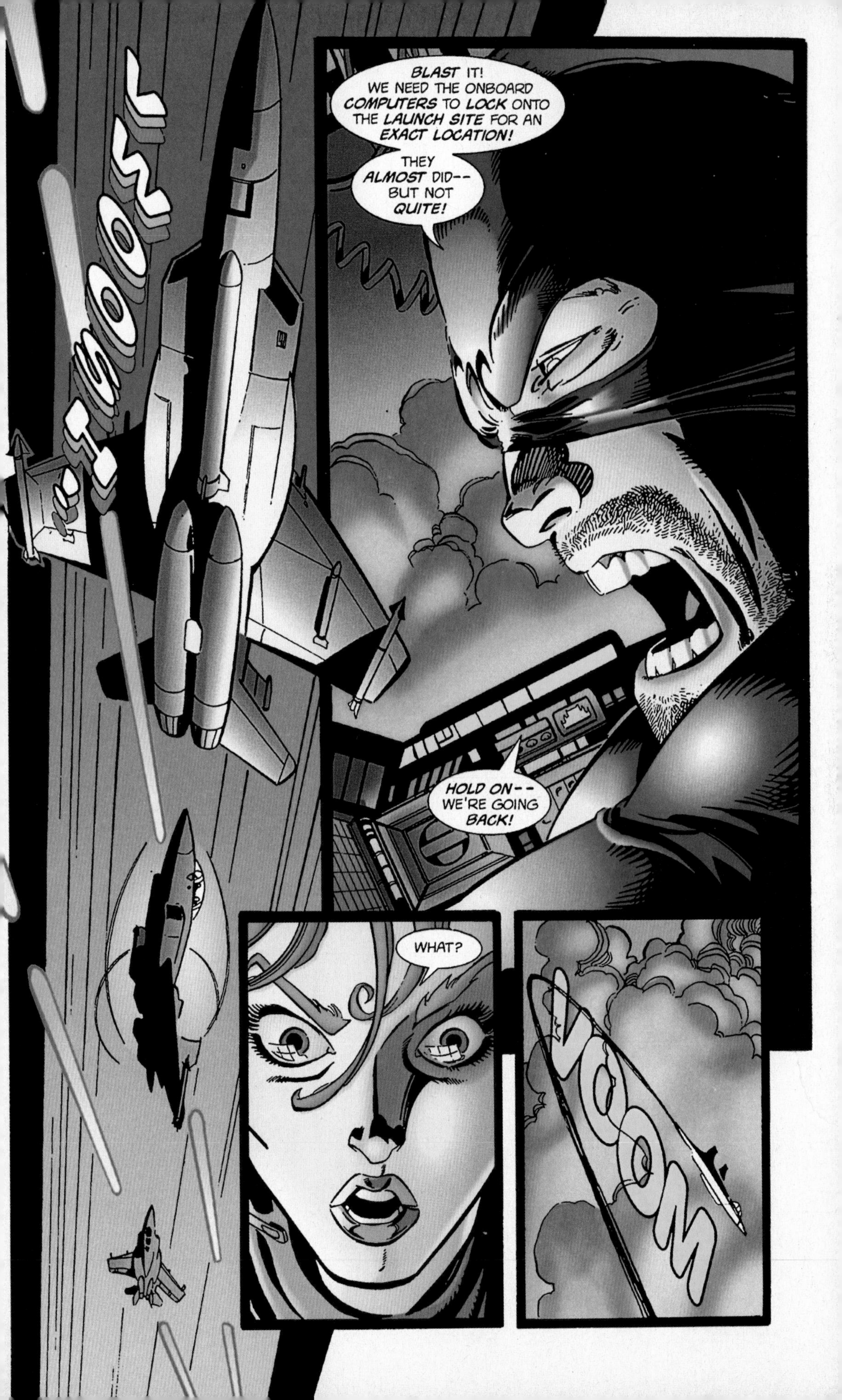
WHOOSH
BLAST IT! WE NEED THE ONBOARD COMPUTERS TO LOCK ONTO THE LAUNCH SITE FOR AN EXACT LOCATION!
THEY ALMOST DID-- BUT NOT QUITE!
HOLD ON-- WE'RE GOING BACK!
WHAT?
VOOOM

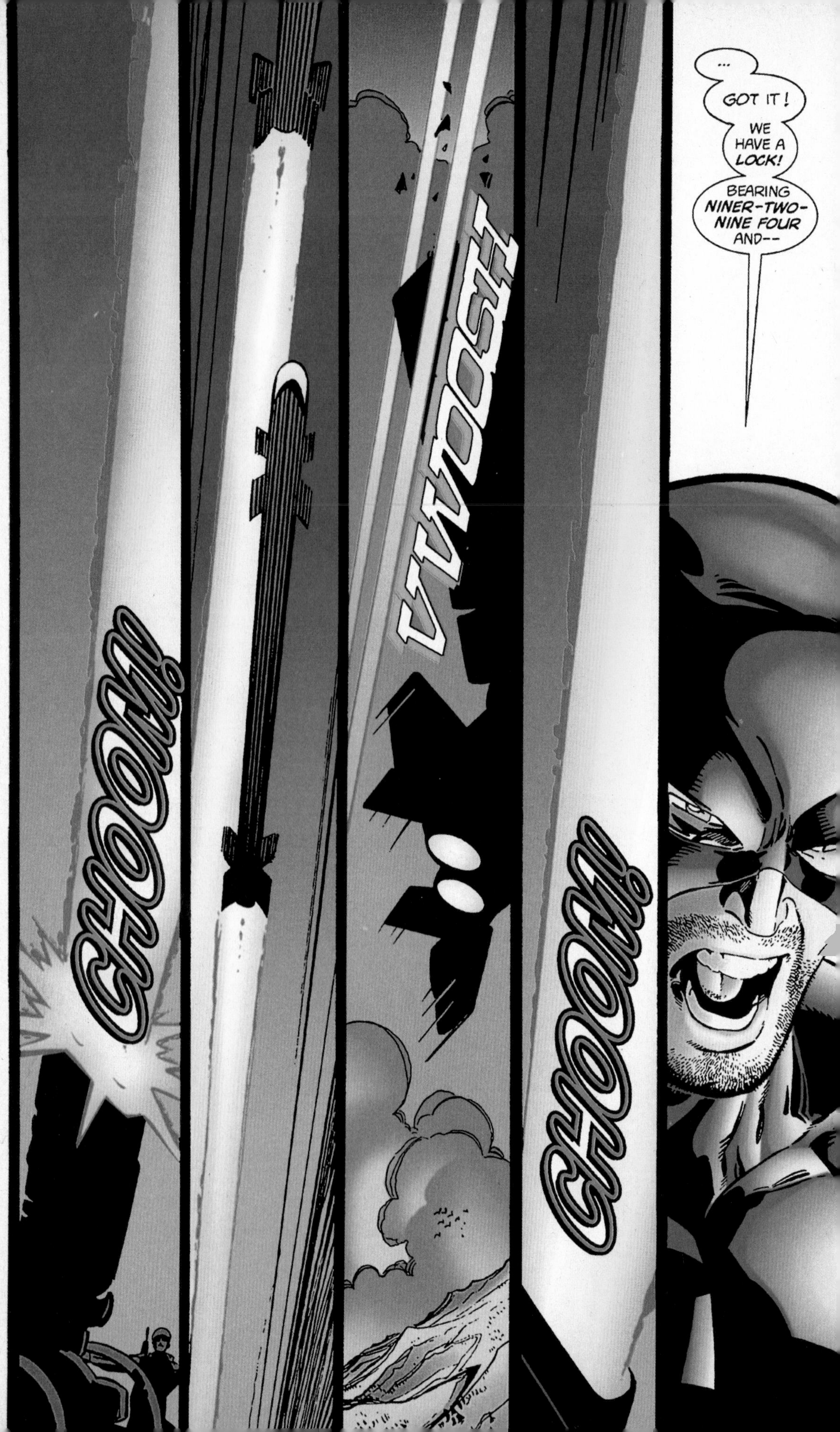
CHOOM!
VWOOSH
CHOOM!
...
GOT IT!
WE HAVE A LOCK!
BEARING NINER-TWO-NINE FOUR AND--

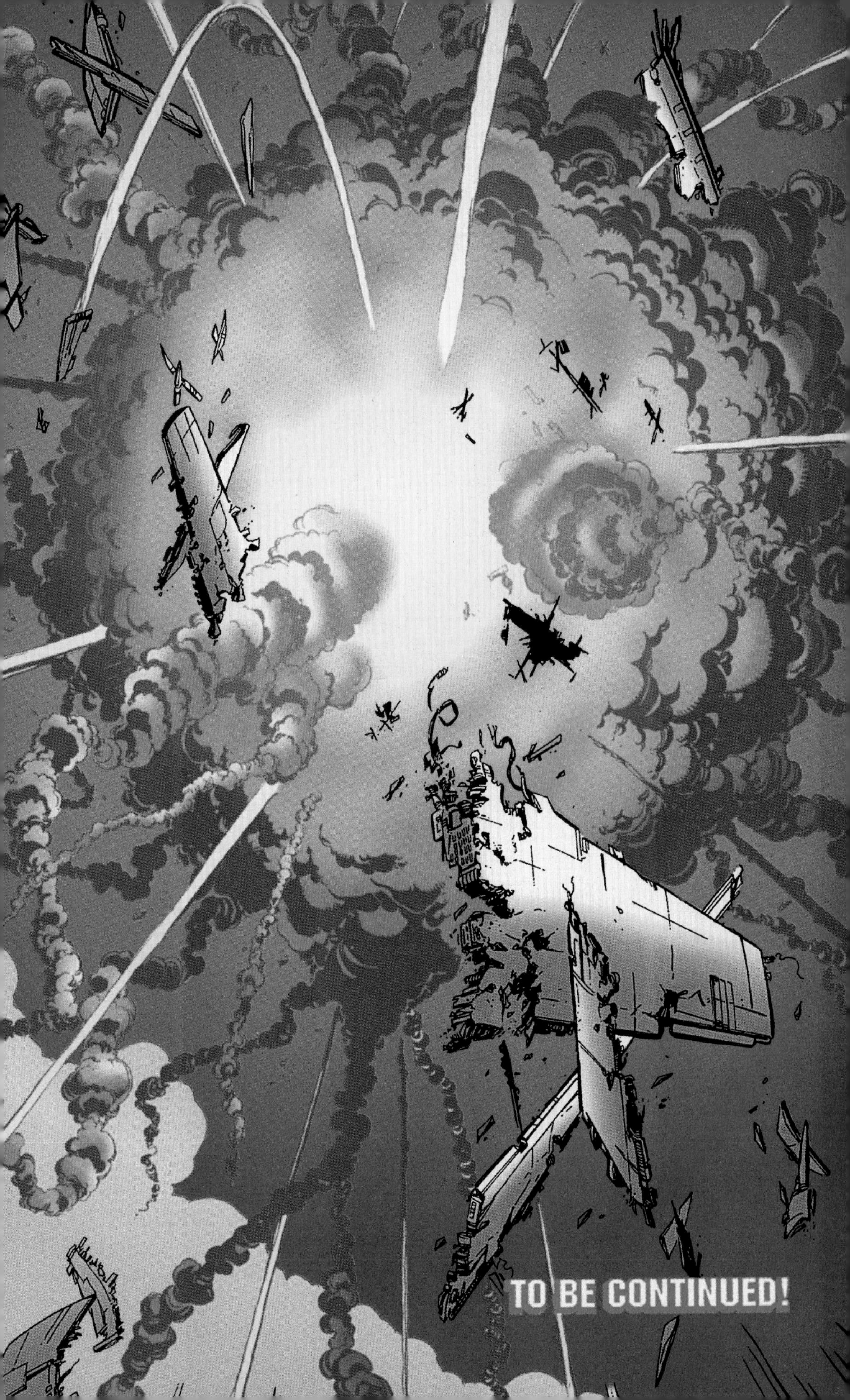
TO BE CONTINUED!

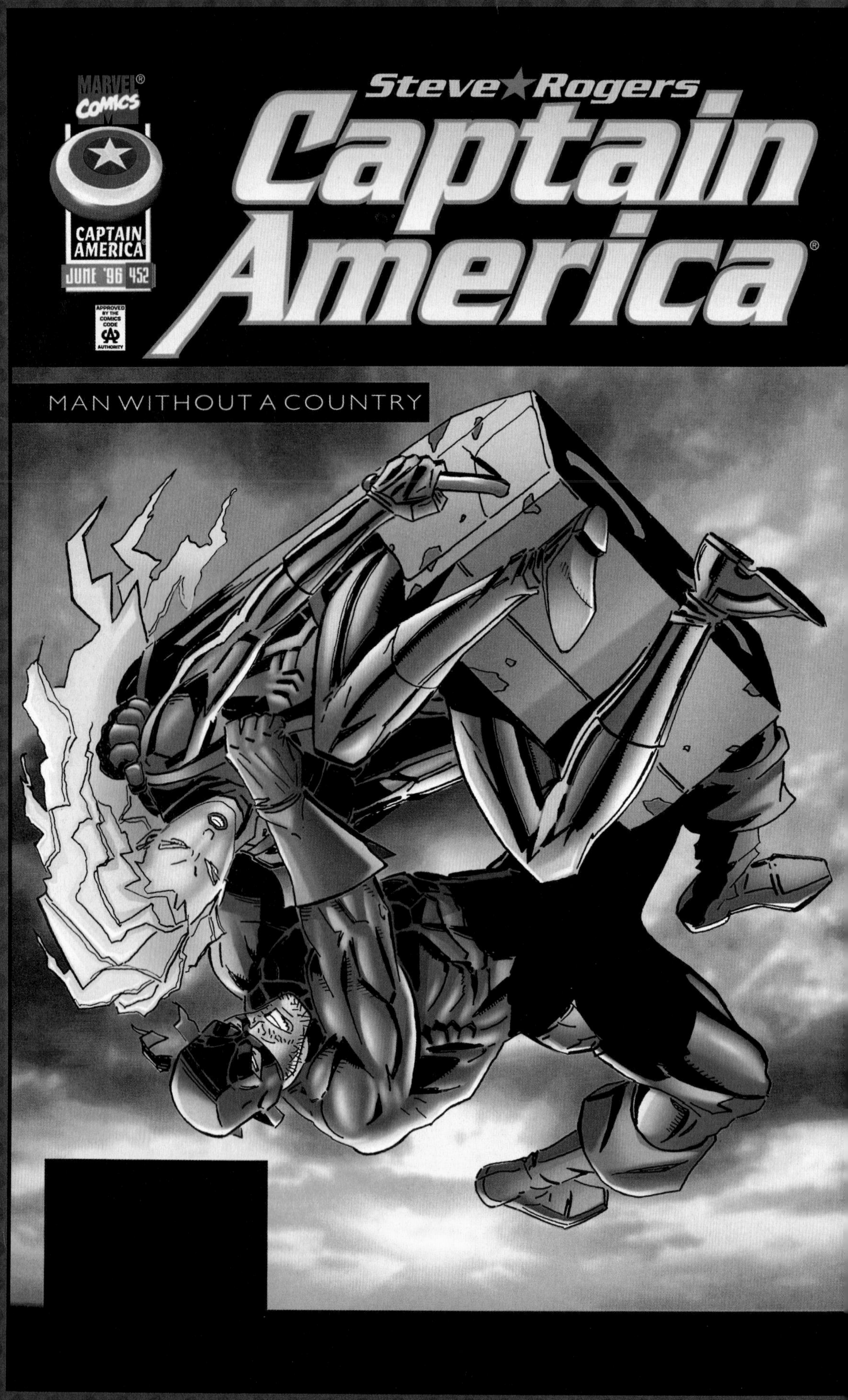
MARVEL® COMICS
CAPTAIN AMERICA
JUNE '96 452
APPROVED BY THE COMICS CODE AUTHORITY
Steve★Rogers
Captain America®
MAN WITHOUT A COUNTRY

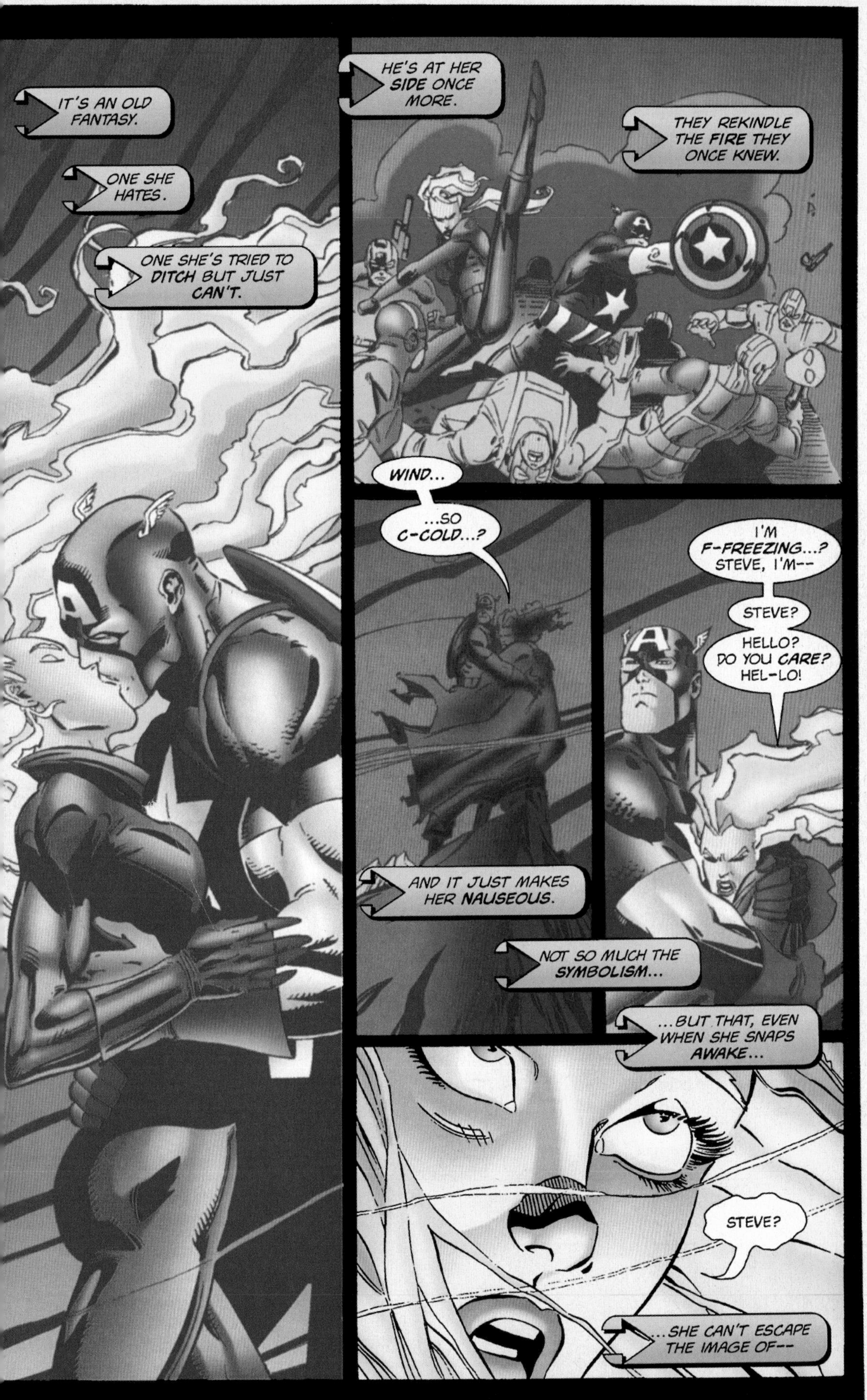
IT'S AN OLD FANTASY.
ONE SHE HATES.
ONE SHE'S TRIED TO DITCH BUT JUST CAN'T.
HE'S AT HER SIDE ONCE MORE.
THEY REKINDLE THE FIRE THEY ONCE KNEW.
WIND...
...SO C-COLD...?
AND IT JUST MAKES HER NAUSEOUS.
I'M F-FREEZING...? STEVE, I'M--
STEVE?
HELLO? DO YOU CARE? HEL-LO!
NOT SO MUCH THE SYMBOLISM...
...BUT THAT, EVEN WHEN SHE SNAPS AWAKE...
STEVE?
...SHE CAN'T ESCAPE THE IMAGE OF--

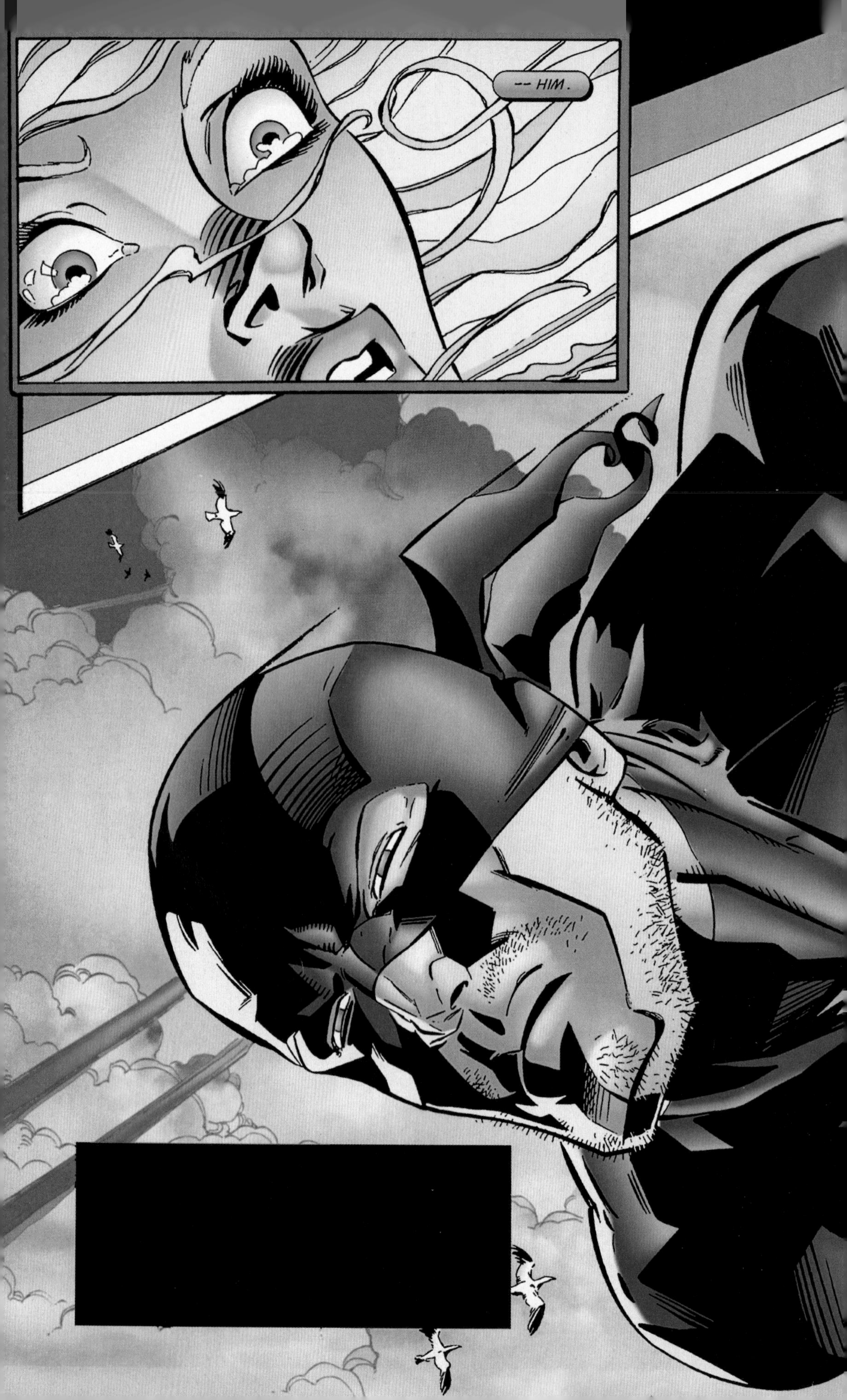
-- HIM.
[redacted]

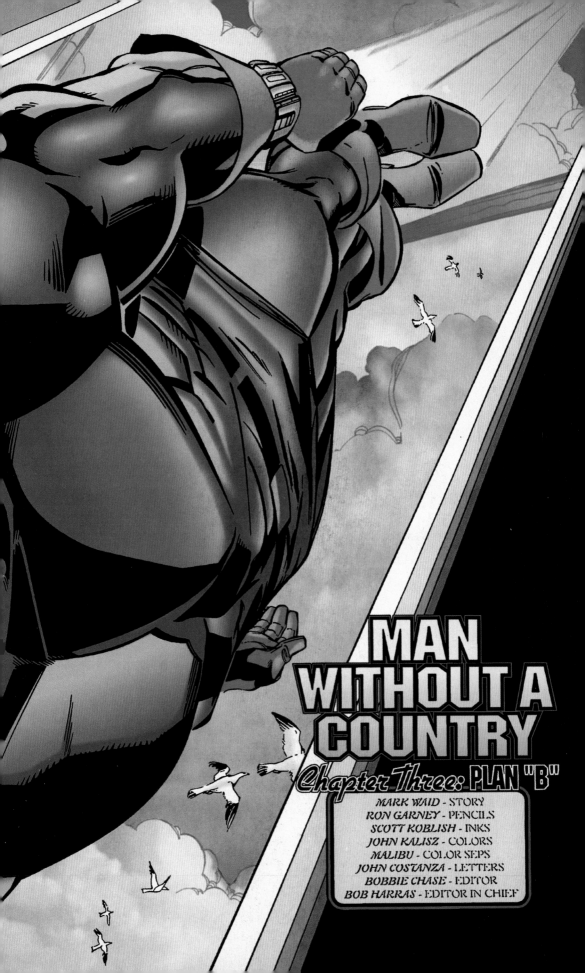

MAN WITHOUT A COUNTRY

Chapter Three: PLAN "B"

MARK WAID - STORY
RON GARNEY - PENCILS
SCOTT KOBLISH - INKS
JOHN KALISZ - COLORS
MALIBU - COLOR SEPS
JOHN COSTANZA - LETTERS
BOBBIE CHASE - EDITOR
BOB HARRAS - EDITOR IN CHIEF

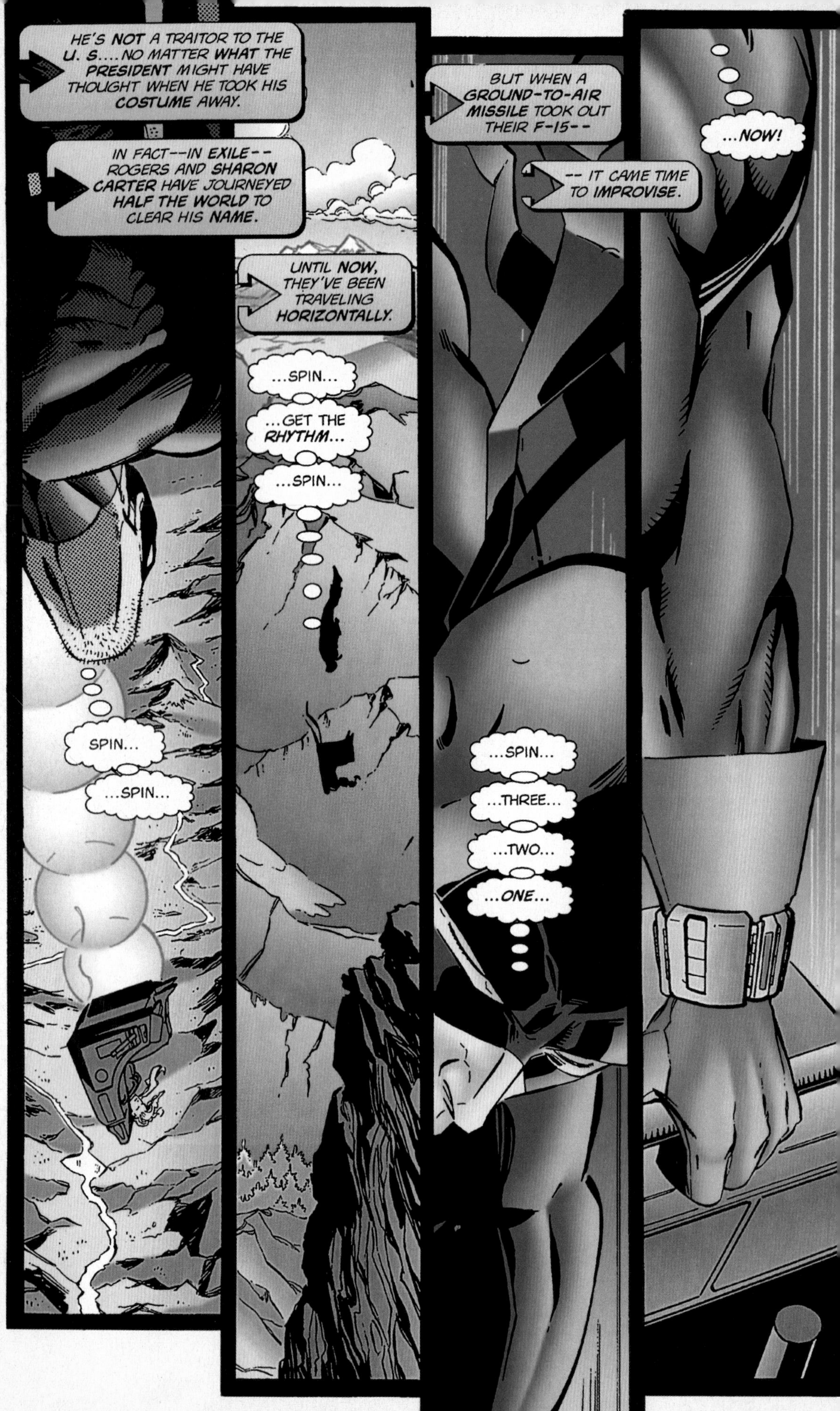

HE'S NOT A TRAITOR TO THE U. S.... NO MATTER WHAT THE PRESIDENT MIGHT HAVE THOUGHT WHEN HE TOOK HIS COSTUME AWAY.
IN FACT--IN EXILE--ROGERS AND SHARON CARTER HAVE JOURNEYED HALF THE WORLD TO CLEAR HIS NAME.
SPIN...
...SPIN...
UNTIL NOW, THEY'VE BEEN TRAVELING HORIZONTALLY.
...SPIN...
...GET THE RHYTHM...
...SPIN...
BUT WHEN A GROUND-TO-AIR MISSILE TOOK OUT THEIR F-15--
-- IT CAME TIME TO IMPROVISE.
...SPIN...
...THREE...
...TWO...
...ONE...
...NOW!

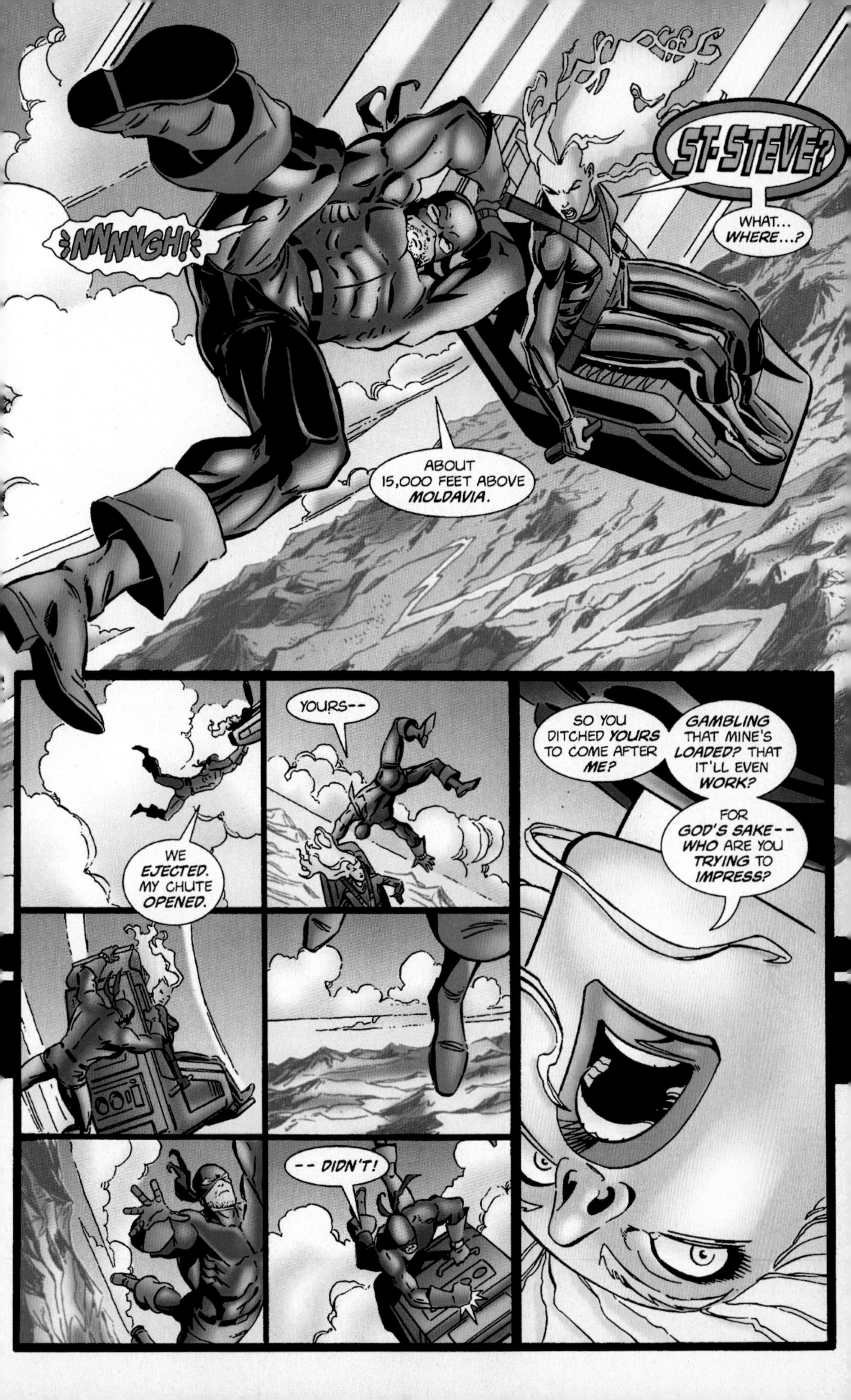
ST-STEVE?
WHAT... WHERE...?
NNNNGH!
ABOUT 15,000 FEET ABOVE MOLDAVIA.
WE EJECTED. MY CHUTE OPENED.
YOURS--
SO YOU DITCHED YOURS TO COME AFTER ME?
GAMBLING THAT MINE'S LOADED? THAT IT'LL EVEN WORK?
FOR GOD'S SAKE-- WHO ARE YOU TRYING TO IMPRESS?
-- DIDN'T!

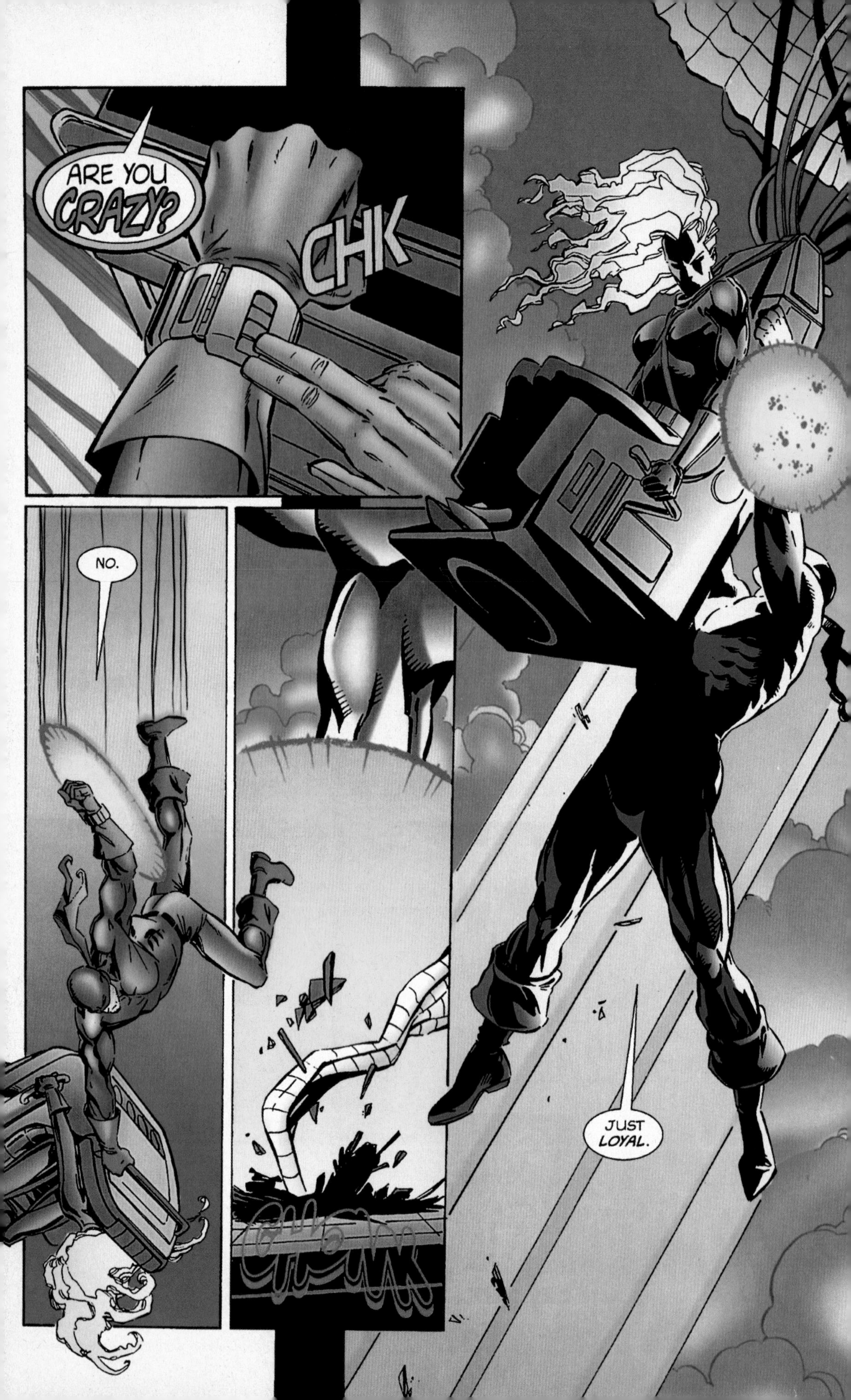
ARE YOU CRAZY?
CHK
NO.
JUST LOYAL.

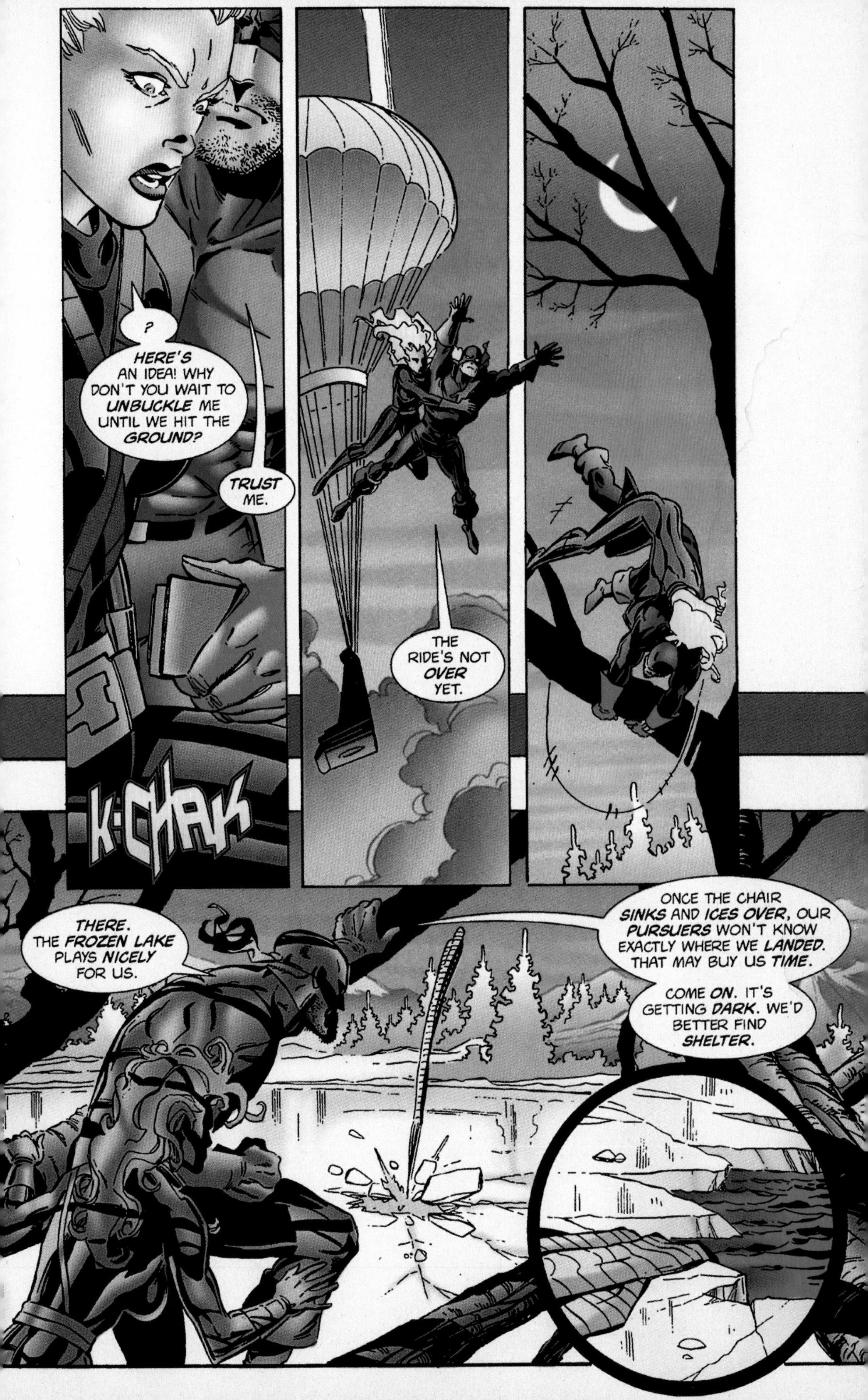
?
HERE'S AN IDEA! WHY DON'T YOU WAIT TO UNBUCKLE ME UNTIL WE HIT THE GROUND?
TRUST ME.
K-CHAK
THE RIDE'S NOT OVER YET.
THERE. THE FROZEN LAKE PLAYS NICELY FOR US.
ONCE THE CHAIR SINKS AND ICES OVER, OUR PURSUERS WON'T KNOW EXACTLY WHERE WE LANDED. THAT MAY BUY US TIME.
COME ON. IT'S GETTING DARK. WE'D BETTER FIND SHELTER.

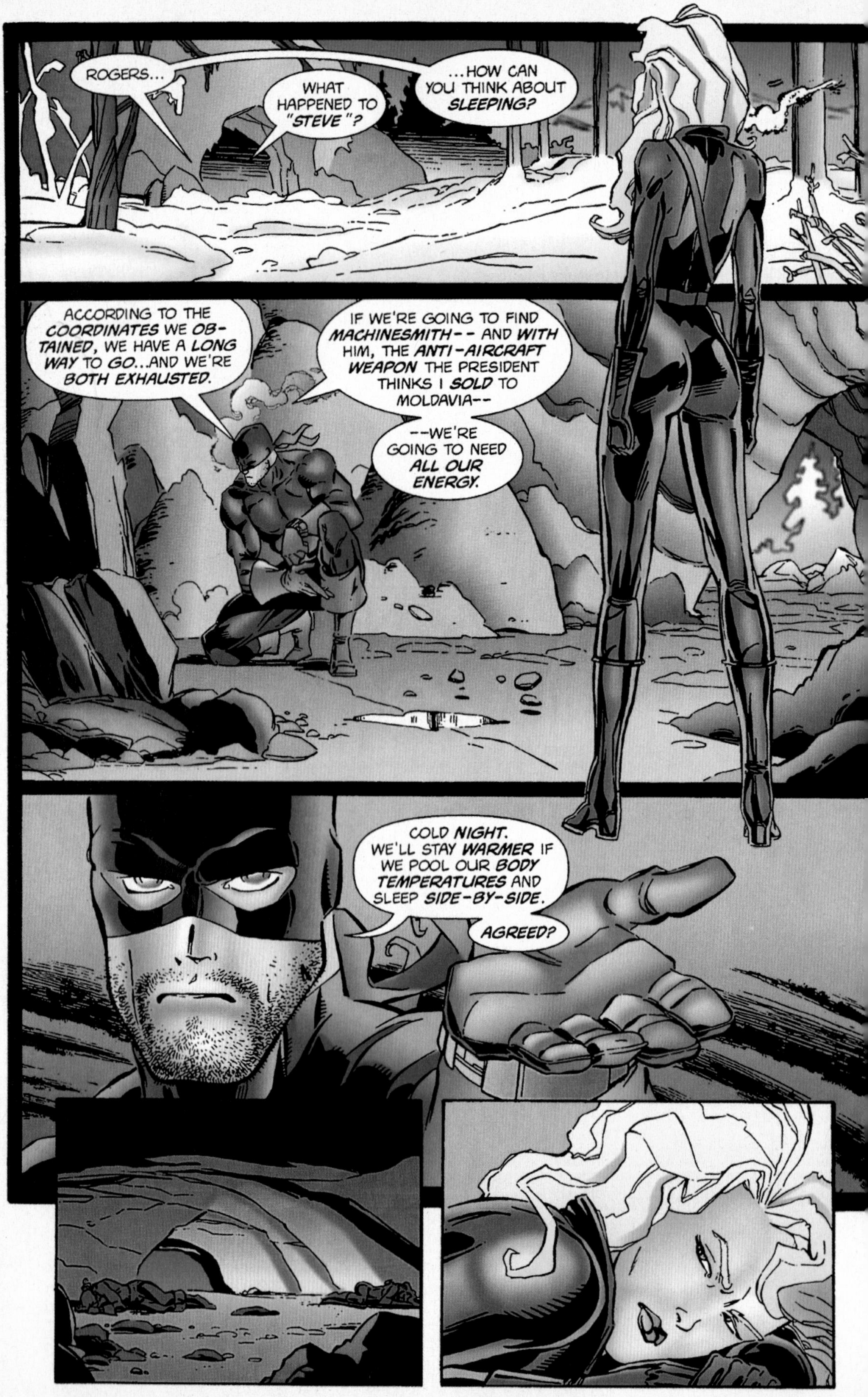

ROGERS...
...HOW CAN YOU THINK ABOUT SLEEPING?
WHAT HAPPENED TO "STEVE"?
ACCORDING TO THE COORDINATES WE OBTAINED, WE HAVE A LONG WAY TO GO...AND WE'RE BOTH EXHAUSTED.
IF WE'RE GOING TO FIND MACHINESMITH-- AND WITH HIM, THE ANTI-AIRCRAFT WEAPON THE PRESIDENT THINKS I SOLD TO MOLDAVIA--
--WE'RE GOING TO NEED ALL OUR ENERGY.
COLD NIGHT. WE'LL STAY WARMER IF WE POOL OUR BODY TEMPERATURES AND SLEEP SIDE-BY-SIDE.
AGREED?

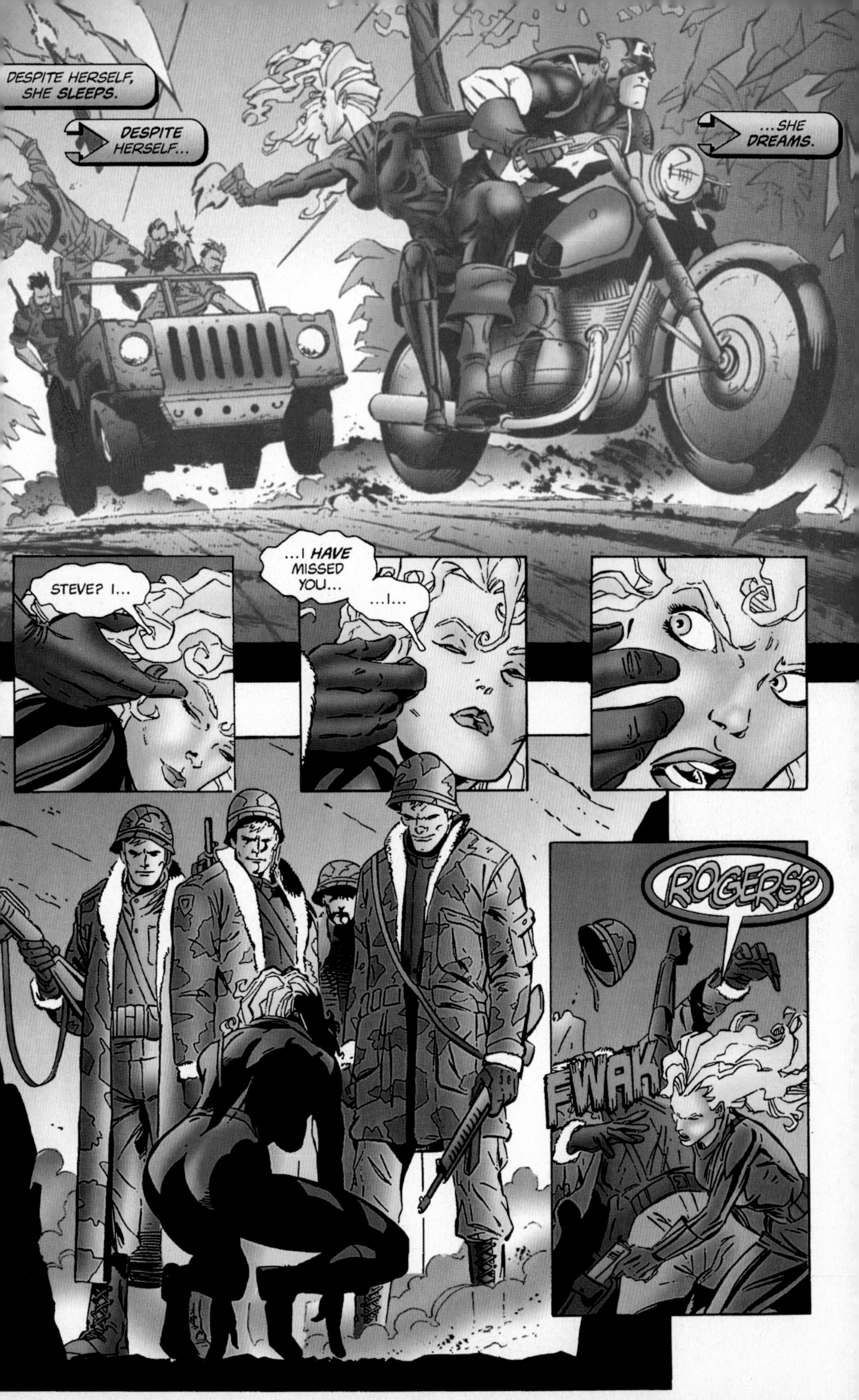
DESPITE HERSELF, SHE SLEEPS.
DESPITE HERSELF...
...SHE DREAMS.
STEVE? I...
...I HAVE MISSED YOU...
...I...
ROGERS?
FWAK

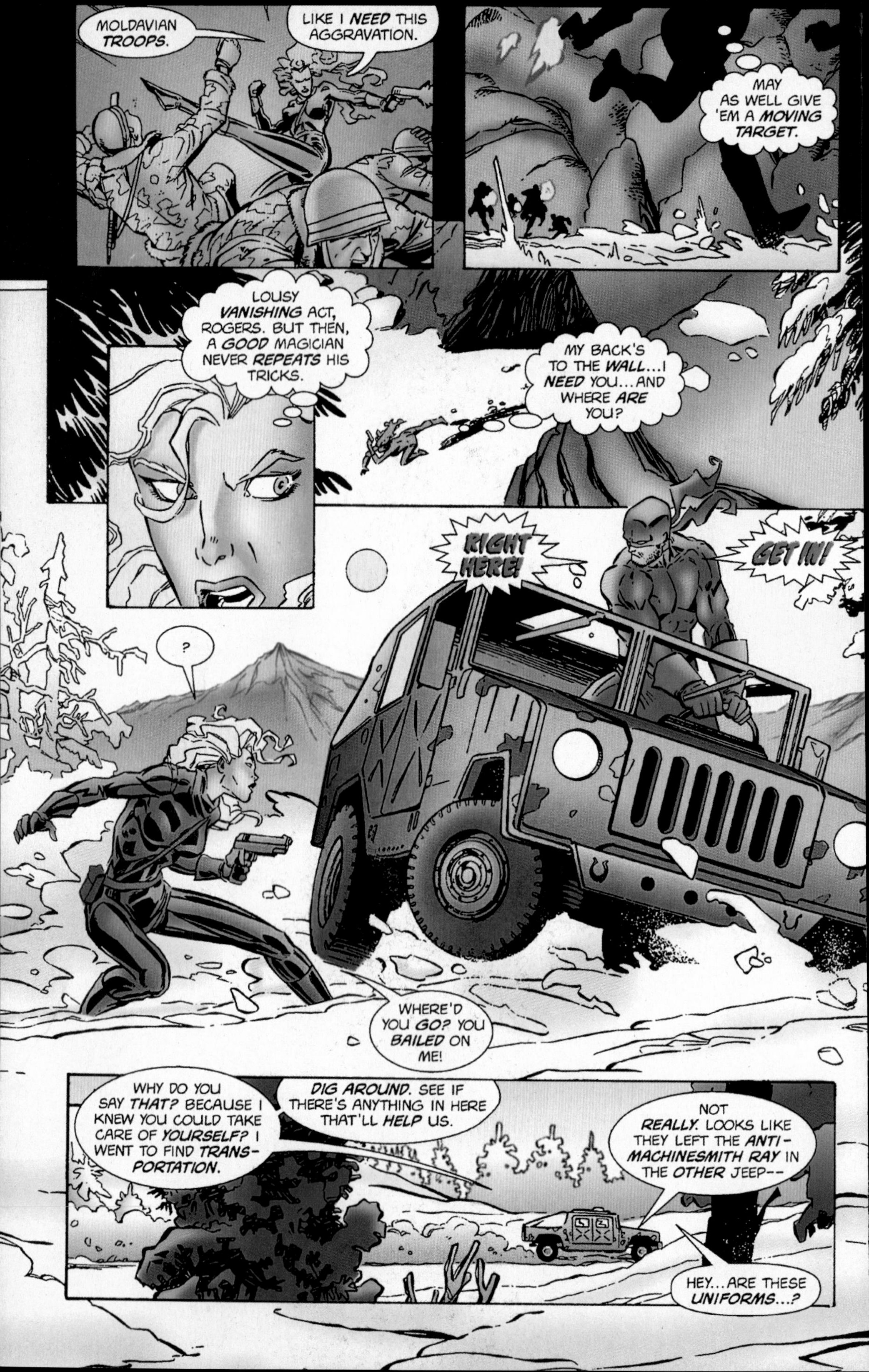
MOLDAVIAN TROOPS.
LIKE I NEED THIS AGGRAVATION.
MAY AS WELL GIVE 'EM A MOVING TARGET.
LOUSY VANISHING ACT, ROGERS. BUT THEN, A GOOD MAGICIAN NEVER REPEATS HIS TRICKS.
MY BACK'S TO THE WALL...I NEED YOU...AND WHERE ARE YOU?
RIGHT HERE!
GET IN!
?
WHERE'D YOU GO? YOU BAILED ON ME!
WHY DO YOU SAY THAT? BECAUSE I KNEW YOU COULD TAKE CARE OF YOURSELF? I WENT TO FIND TRANS-PORTATION.
DIG AROUND. SEE IF THERE'S ANYTHING IN HERE THAT'LL HELP US.
NOT REALLY. LOOKS LIKE THEY LEFT THE ANTI-MACHINESMITH RAY IN THE OTHER JEEP--
HEY...ARE THESE UNIFORMS...?

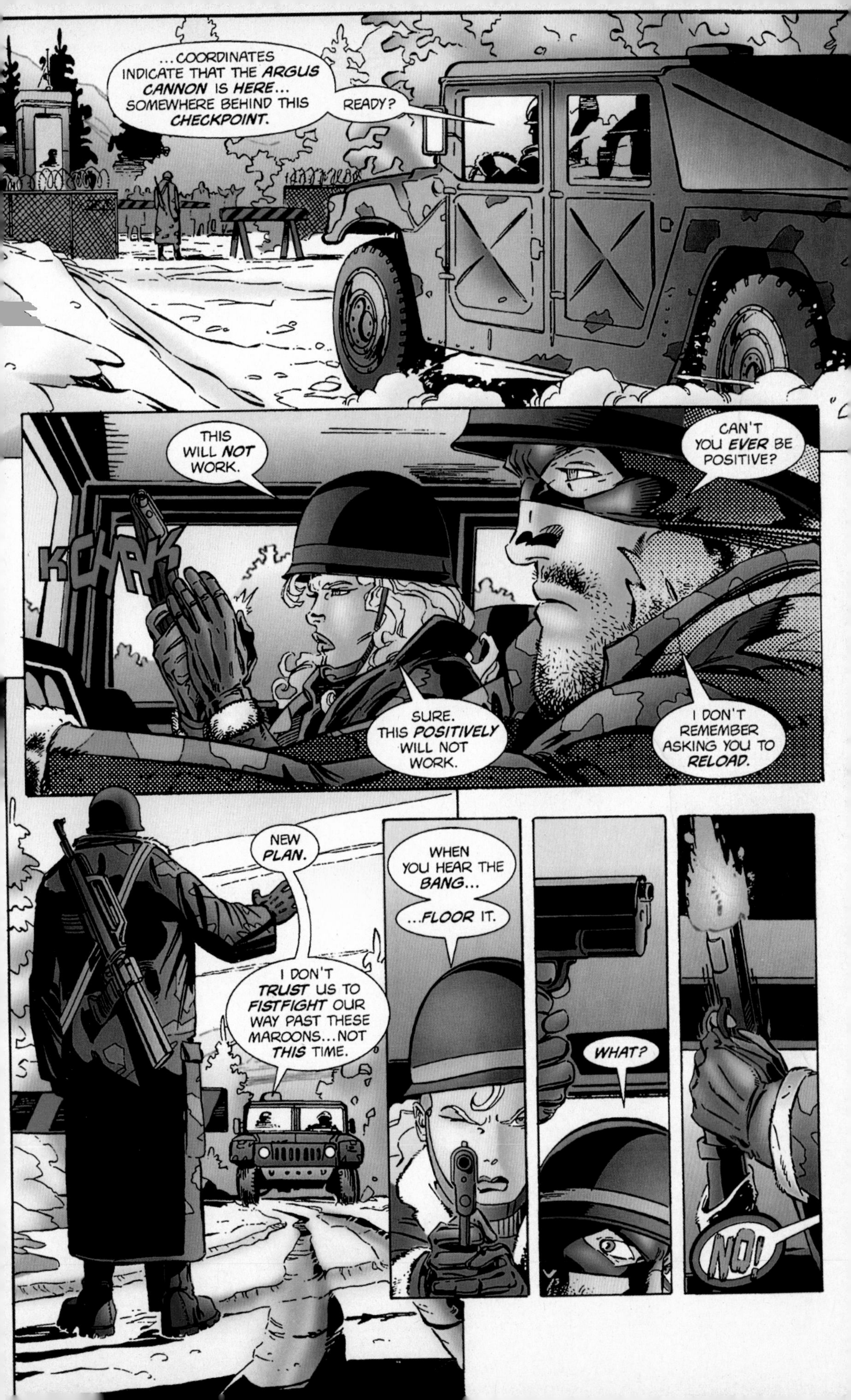
...COORDINATES INDICATE THAT THE ARGUS CANNON IS HERE... SOMEWHERE BEHIND THIS CHECKPOINT.
READY?
THIS WILL NOT WORK.
CAN'T YOU EVER BE POSITIVE?
KCHAK
SURE. THIS POSITIVELY WILL NOT WORK.
I DON'T REMEMBER ASKING YOU TO RELOAD.
NEW PLAN.
I DON'T TRUST US TO FISTFIGHT OUR WAY PAST THESE MAROONS...NOT THIS TIME.
WHEN YOU HEAR THE BANG...
...FLOOR IT.
WHAT?
NO!

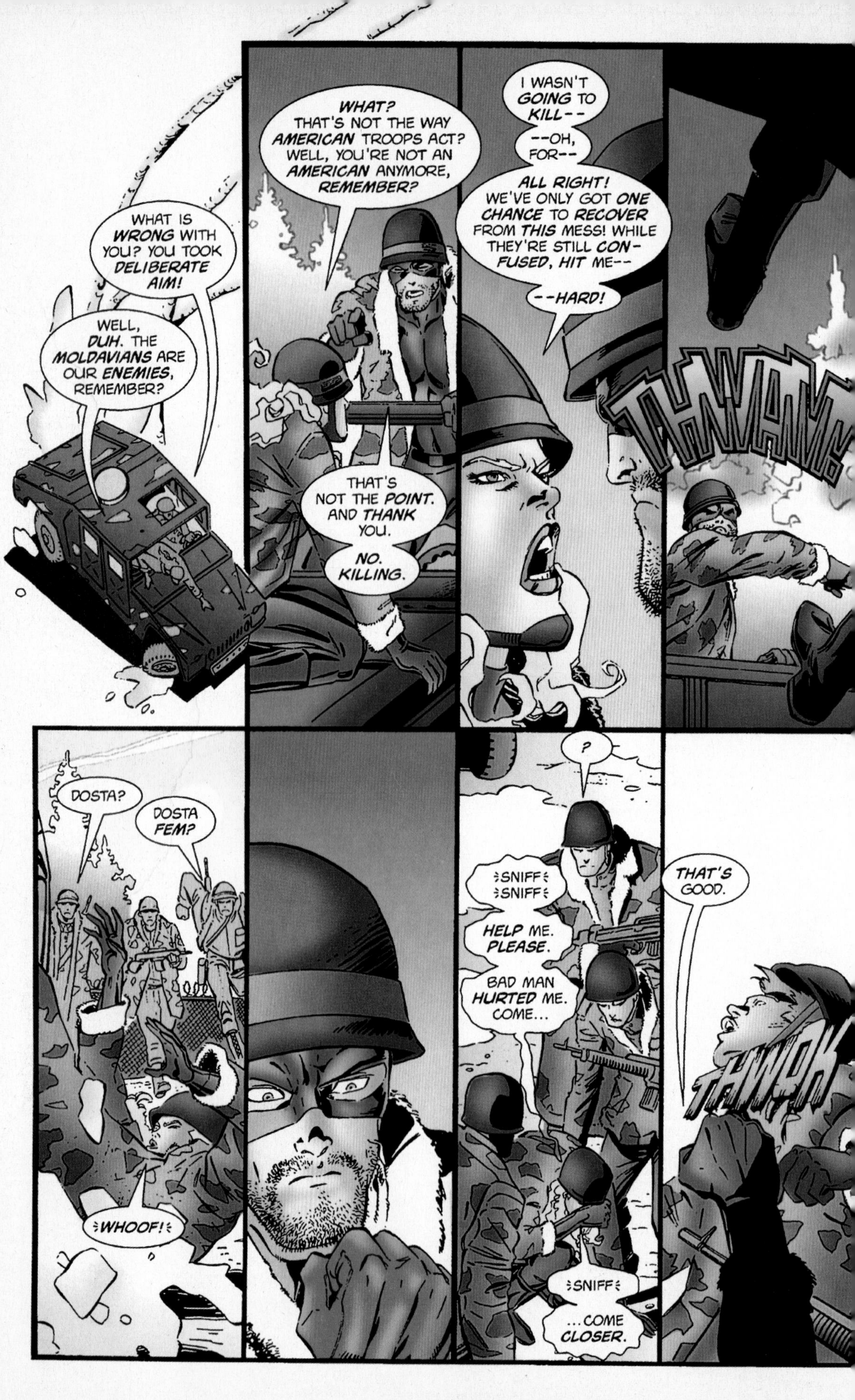
WHAT IS WRONG WITH YOU? YOU TOOK DELIBERATE AIM!
WELL, DUH. THE MOLDAVIANS ARE OUR ENEMIES, REMEMBER?
WHAT? THAT'S NOT THE WAY AMERICAN TROOPS ACT? WELL, YOU'RE NOT AN AMERICAN ANYMORE, REMEMBER?
THAT'S NOT THE POINT. AND THANK YOU.
NO. KILLING.
I WASN'T GOING TO KILL--
--OH, FOR--
ALL RIGHT! WE'VE ONLY GOT ONE CHANCE TO RECOVER FROM THIS MESS! WHILE THEY'RE STILL CON-FUSED, HIT ME--
--HARD!
THWAM!
DOSTA?
DOSTA FEM?
WHOOF!
?
SNIFF SNIFF
HELP ME. PLEASE.
BAD MAN HURTED ME. COME...
SNIFF
...COME CLOSER.
THAT'S GOOD.
THWOK!

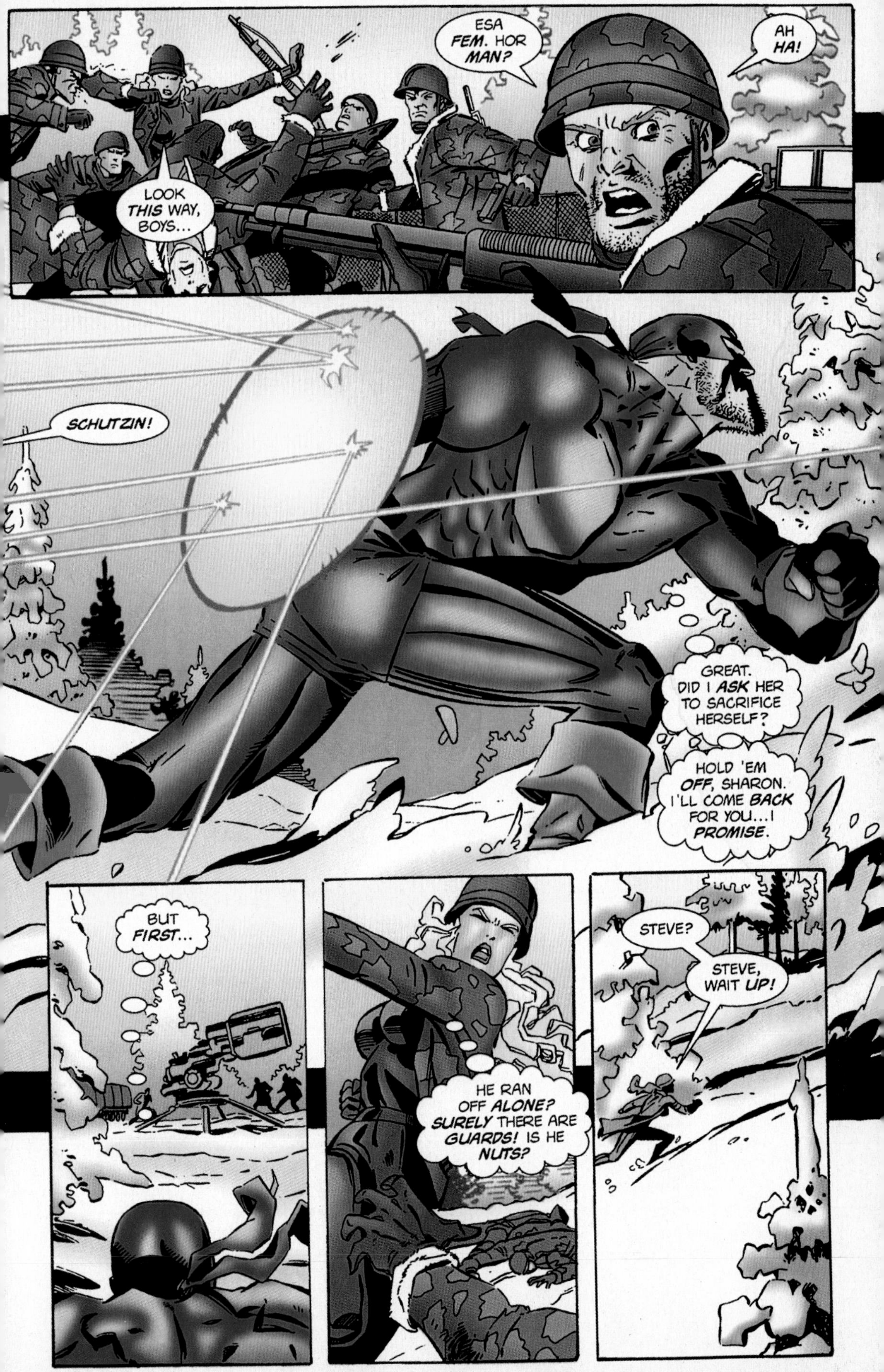

ESA FEM. HOR MAN?
AH HA!
LOOK THIS WAY, BOYS...
SCHUTZIN!
GREAT. DID I ASK HER TO SACRIFICE HERSELF?
HOLD 'EM OFF, SHARON. I'LL COME BACK FOR YOU...I PROMISE.
BUT FIRST...
HE RAN OFF ALONE? SURELY THERE ARE GUARDS! IS HE NUTS?
STEVE?
STEVE, WAIT UP!

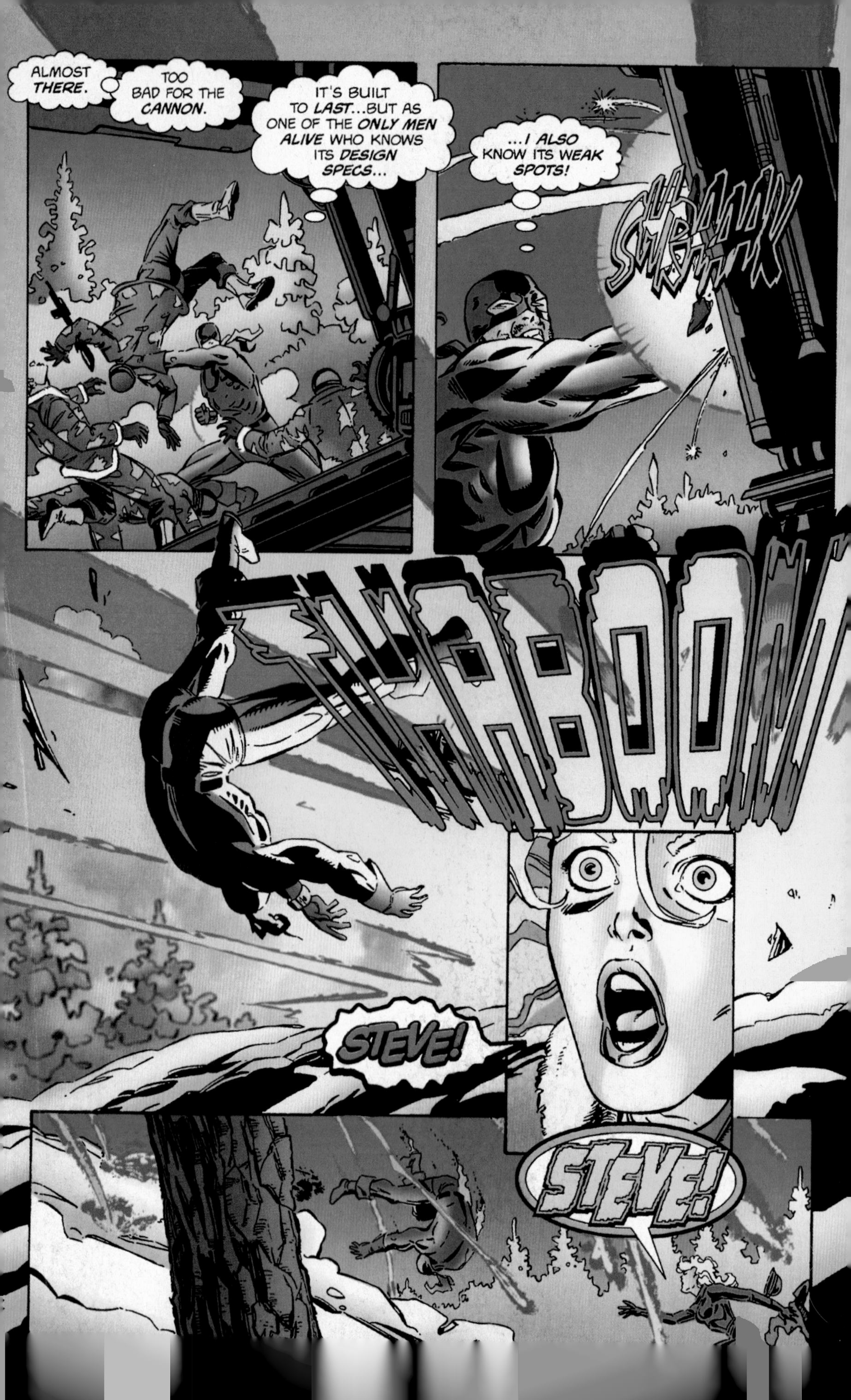

ALMOST THERE.
TOO BAD FOR THE CANNON.
IT'S BUILT TO LAST...BUT AS ONE OF THE ONLY MEN ALIVE WHO KNOWS ITS DESIGN SPECS...
...I ALSO KNOW ITS WEAK SPOTS!
SHRAAAK
THRA-BOOM
STEVE!
STEVE!

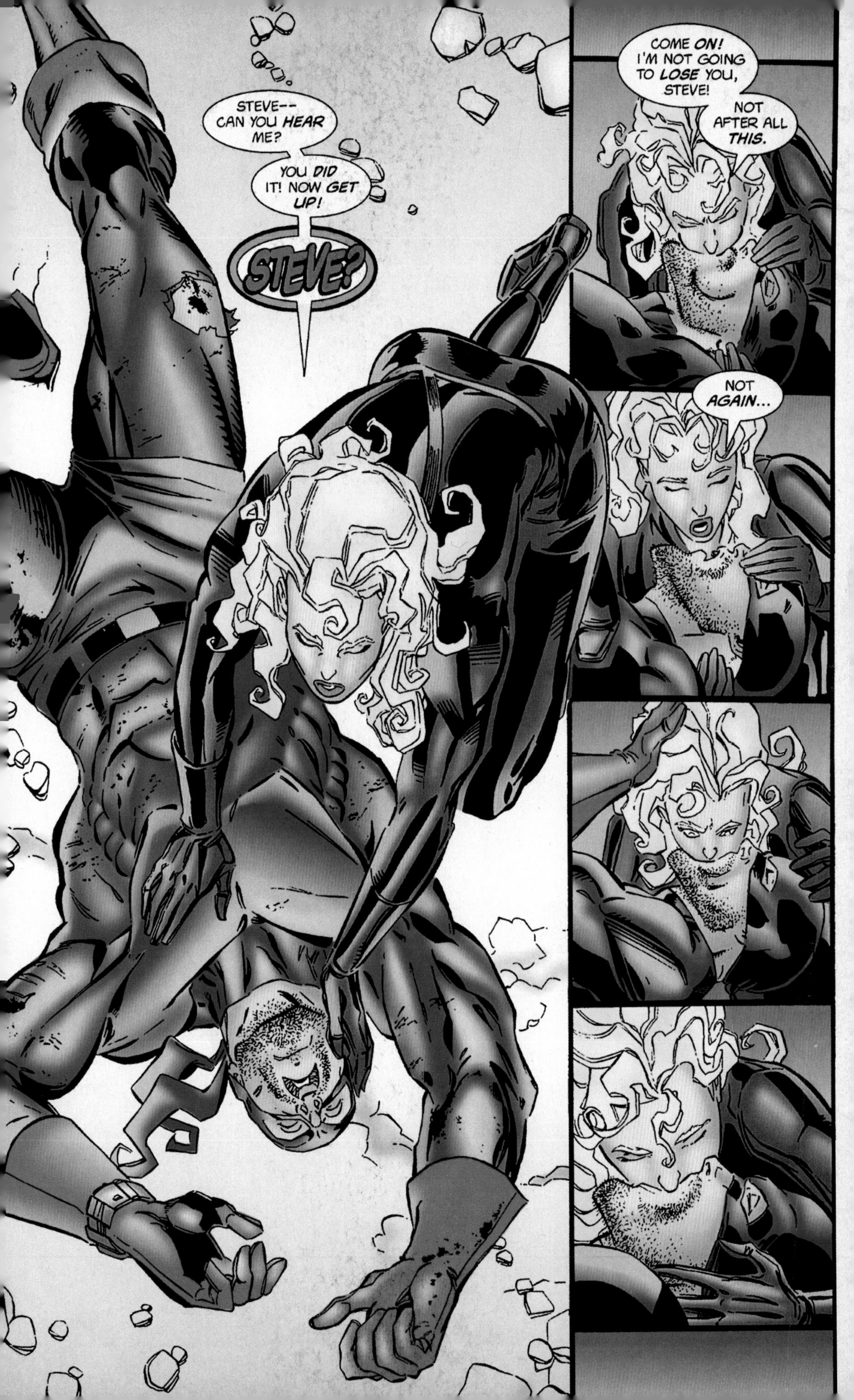
STEVE-- CAN YOU HEAR ME?
YOU DID IT! NOW GET UP!
STEVE?
COME ON! I'M NOT GOING TO LOSE YOU, STEVE!
NOT AFTER ALL THIS.
NOT AGAIN...

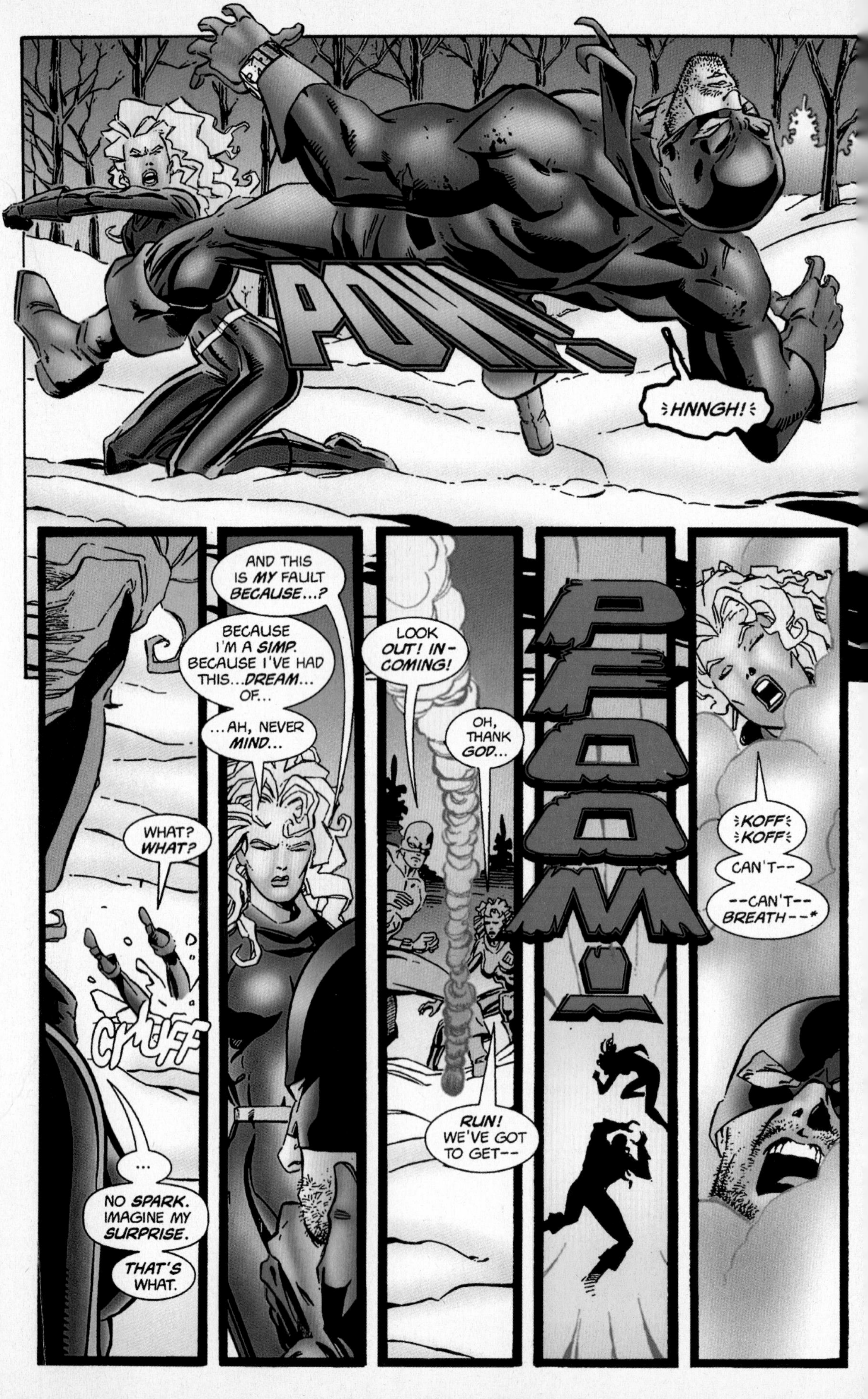
POW!!
HNNGH!
WHAT? WHAT?
CRUFF
...
NO SPARK. IMAGINE MY SURPRISE.
THAT'S WHAT.
AND THIS IS MY FAULT BECAUSE...?
BECAUSE I'M A SIMP. BECAUSE I'VE HAD THIS...DREAM... OF...
...AH, NEVER MIND...
LOOK OUT! IN-COMING!
OH, THANK GOD...
RUN! WE'VE GOT TO GET--
PFOOM!
KOFF KOFF
CAN'T--
--CAN'T-- BREATH--*

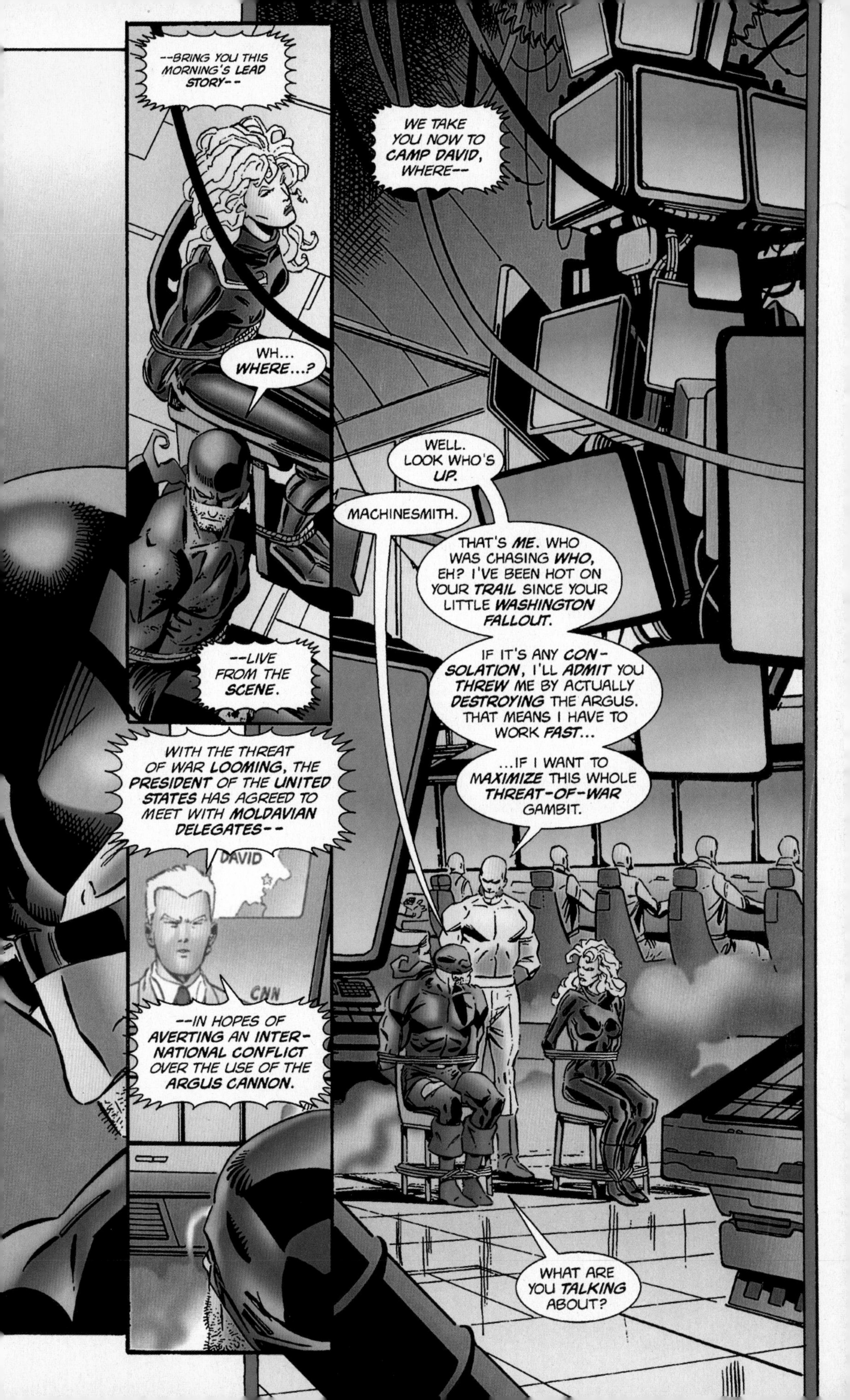
--BRING YOU THIS MORNING'S LEAD STORY--
WE TAKE YOU NOW TO CAMP DAVID, WHERE--
WH... WHERE...?
--LIVE FROM THE SCENE.
WITH THE THREAT OF WAR LOOMING, THE PRESIDENT OF THE UNITED STATES HAS AGREED TO MEET WITH MOLDAVIAN DELEGATES--
DAVID
CNN
--IN HOPES OF AVERTING AN INTERNATIONAL CONFLICT OVER THE USE OF THE ARGUS CANNON.
WELL. LOOK WHO'S UP.
MACHINESMITH.
THAT'S ME. WHO WAS CHASING WHO, EH? I'VE BEEN HOT ON YOUR TRAIL SINCE YOUR LITTLE WASHINGTON FALLOUT.
IF IT'S ANY CONSOLATION, I'LL ADMIT YOU THREW ME BY ACTUALLY DESTROYING THE ARGUS. THAT MEANS I HAVE TO WORK FAST...
...IF I WANT TO MAXIMIZE THIS WHOLE THREAT-OF-WAR GAMBIT.
WHAT ARE YOU TALKING ABOUT?

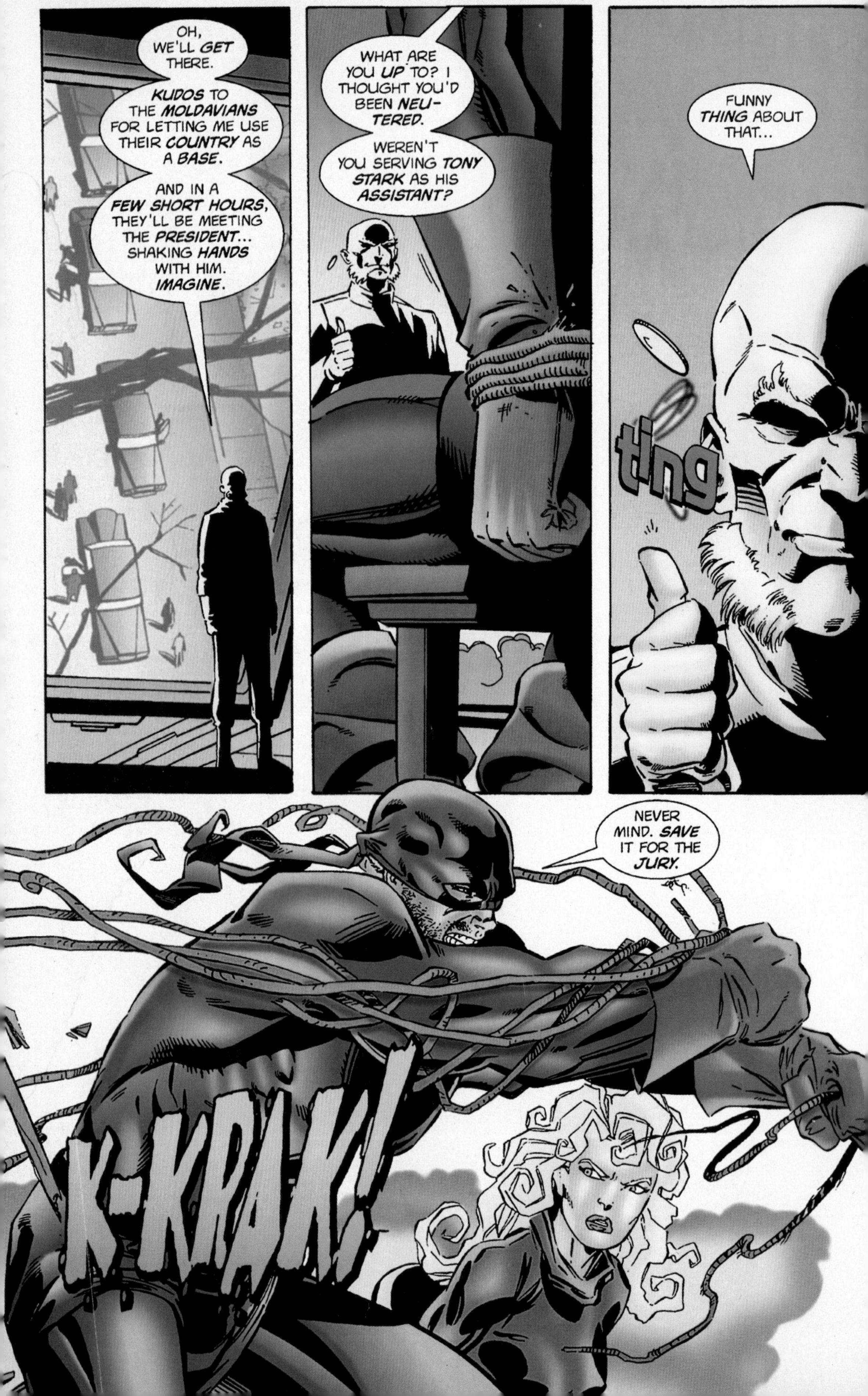
OH, WE'LL GET THERE.
KUDOS TO THE MOLDAVIANS FOR LETTING ME USE THEIR COUNTRY AS A BASE.
AND IN A FEW SHORT HOURS, THEY'LL BE MEETING THE PRESIDENT... SHAKING HANDS WITH HIM. IMAGINE.
WHAT ARE YOU UP TO? I THOUGHT YOU'D BEEN NEU-TERED.
WEREN'T YOU SERVING TONY STARK AS HIS ASSISTANT?
FUNNY THING ABOUT THAT...
ting
NEVER MIND. SAVE IT FOR THE JURY.
K-KRAK!

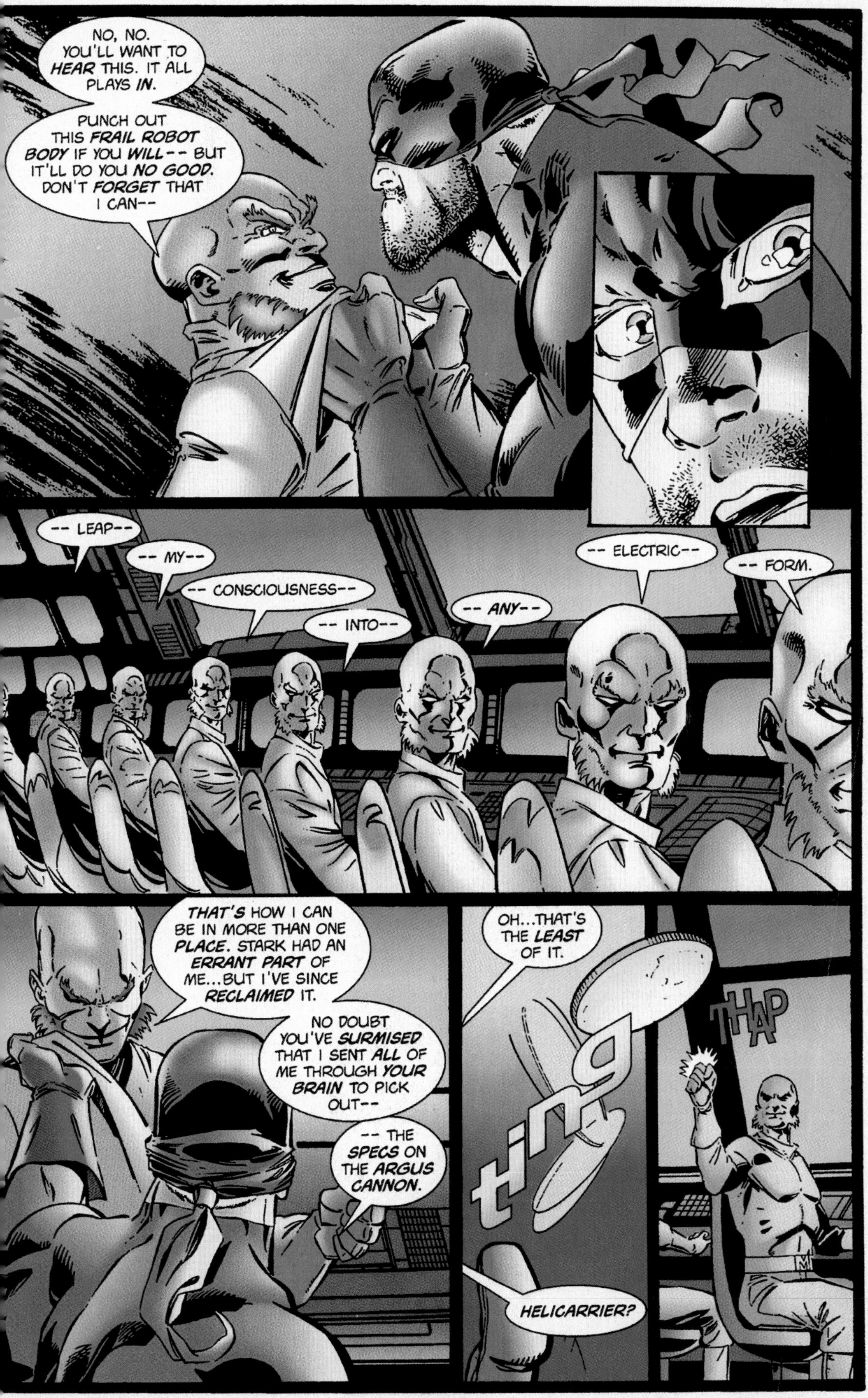
NO, NO. YOU'LL WANT TO HEAR THIS. IT ALL PLAYS IN.
PUNCH OUT THIS FRAIL ROBOT BODY IF YOU WILL-- BUT IT'LL DO YOU NO GOOD. DON'T FORGET THAT I CAN--
-- LEAP--
-- MY--
-- CONSCIOUSNESS--
-- INTO--
-- ANY--
-- ELECTRIC--
-- FORM.
THAT'S HOW I CAN BE IN MORE THAN ONE PLACE. STARK HAD AN ERRANT PART OF ME...BUT I'VE SINCE RECLAIMED IT.
NO DOUBT YOU'VE SURMISED THAT I SENT ALL OF ME THROUGH YOUR BRAIN TO PICK OUT--
-- THE SPECS ON THE ARGUS CANNON.
OH...THAT'S THE LEAST OF IT.
ting
THAP
HELICARRIER?

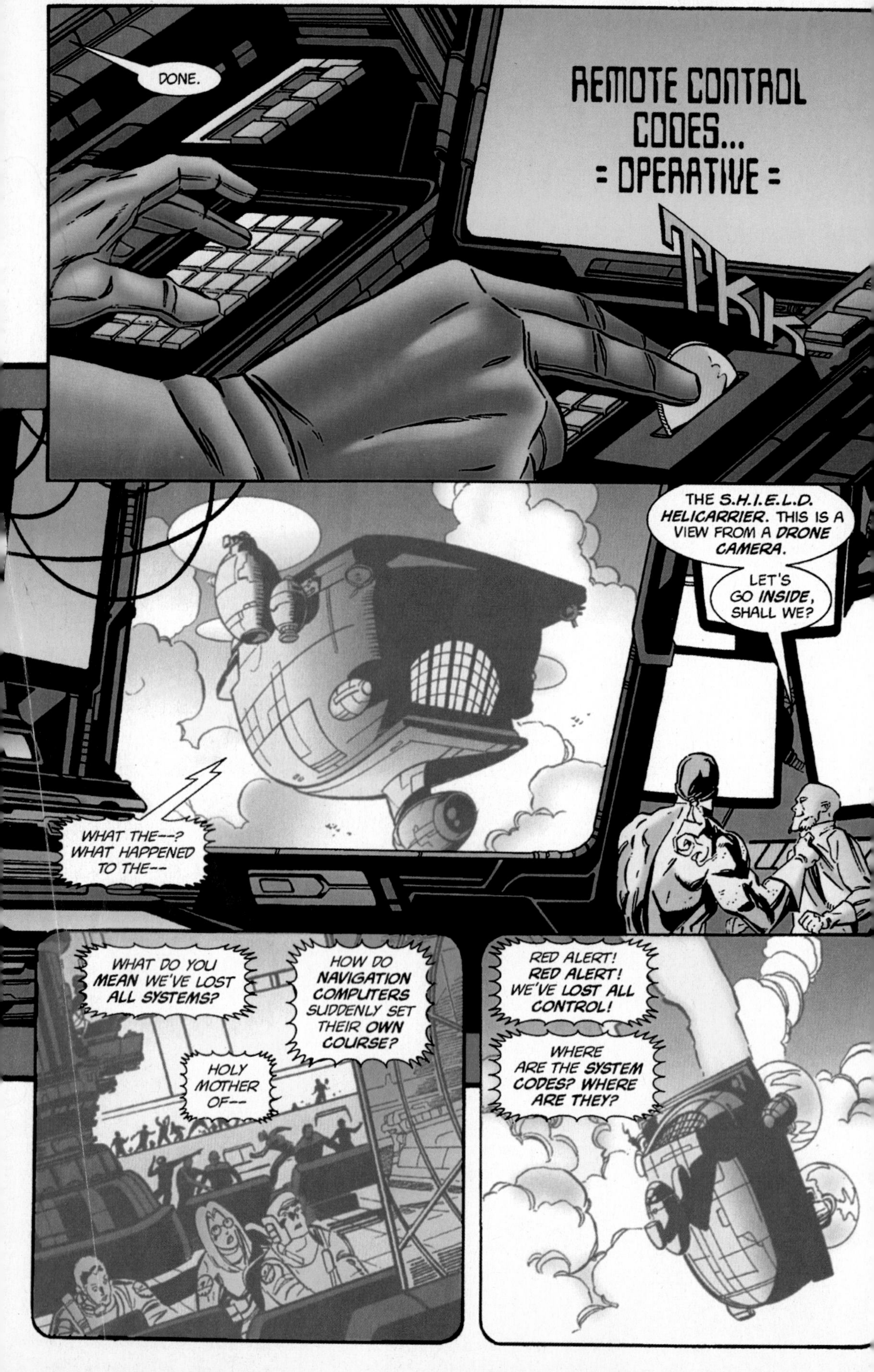
DONE.
REMOTE CONTROL CODES... = OPERATIVE =
TKK
THE S.H.I.E.L.D. HELICARRIER. THIS IS A VIEW FROM A DRONE CAMERA.
LET'S GO INSIDE, SHALL WE?
WHAT THE--? WHAT HAPPENED TO THE--
WHAT DO YOU MEAN WE'VE LOST ALL SYSTEMS?
HOW DO NAVIGATION COMPUTERS SUDDENLY SET THEIR OWN COURSE?
HOLY MOTHER OF--
RED ALERT! RED ALERT! WE'VE LOST ALL CONTROL!
WHERE ARE THE SYSTEM CODES? WHERE ARE THEY?

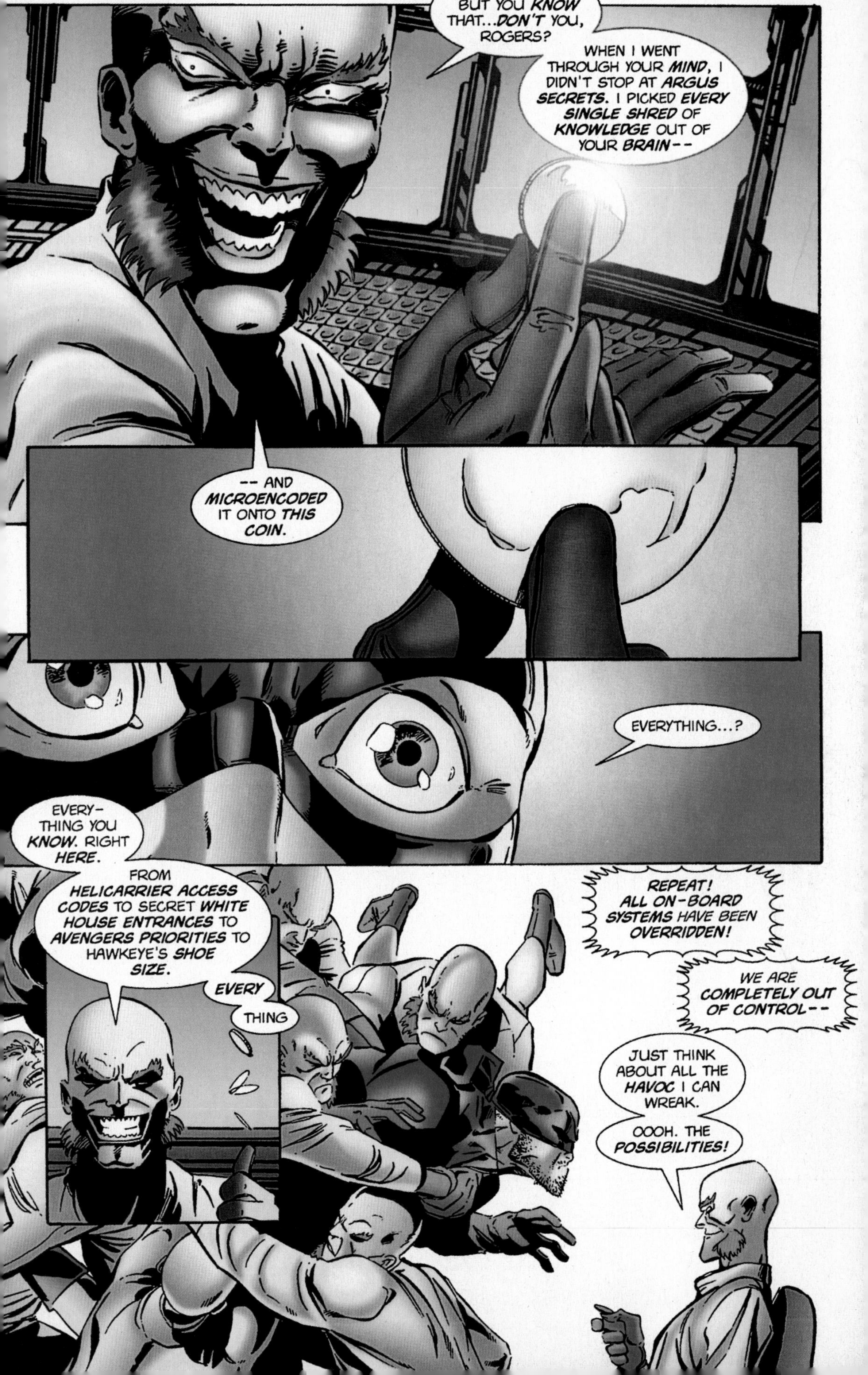
RIGHT HERE. BUT YOU KNOW THAT...DON'T YOU, ROGERS?
WHEN I WENT THROUGH YOUR MIND, I DIDN'T STOP AT ARGUS SECRETS. I PICKED EVERY SINGLE SHRED OF KNOWLEDGE OUT OF YOUR BRAIN--
-- AND MICROENCODED IT ONTO THIS COIN.
EVERYTHING...?
EVERY-THING YOU KNOW. RIGHT HERE.
FROM HELICARRIER ACCESS CODES TO SECRET WHITE HOUSE ENTRANCES TO AVENGERS PRIORITIES TO HAWKEYE'S SHOE SIZE.
EVERY
THING
REPEAT! ALL ON-BOARD SYSTEMS HAVE BEEN OVERRIDDEN!
WE ARE COMPLETELY OUT OF CONTROL--
JUST THINK ABOUT ALL THE HAVOC I CAN WREAK.
OOOH. THE POSSIBILITIES!

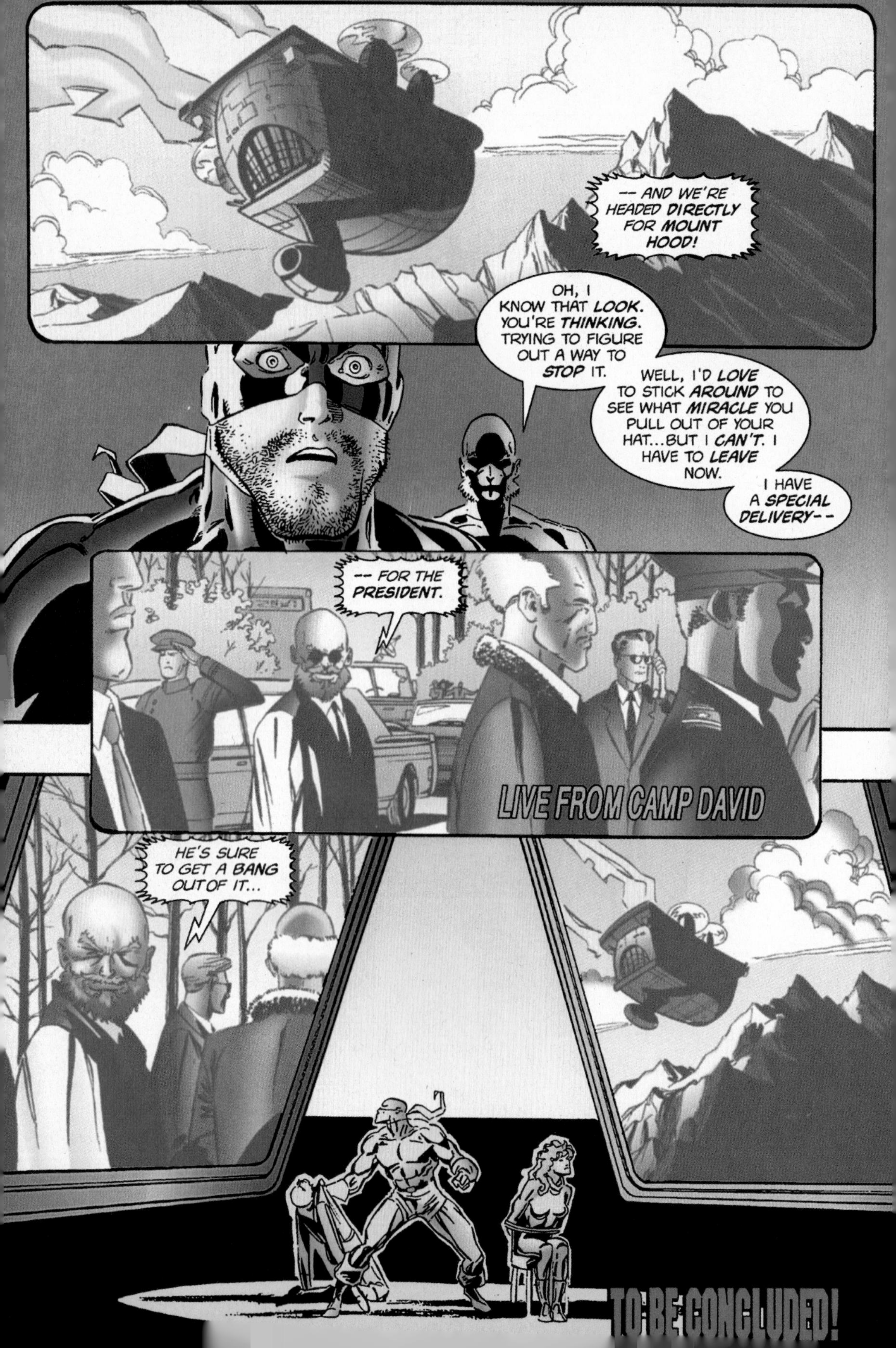
-- AND WE'RE HEADED DIRECTLY FOR MOUNT HOOD!
OH, I KNOW THAT LOOK. YOU'RE THINKING. TRYING TO FIGURE OUT A WAY TO STOP IT.
WELL, I'D LOVE TO STICK AROUND TO SEE WHAT MIRACLE YOU PULL OUT OF YOUR HAT...BUT I CAN'T. I HAVE TO LEAVE NOW.
I HAVE A SPECIAL DELIVERY--
-- FOR THE PRESIDENT.
LIVE FROM CAMP DAVID
HE'S SURE TO GET A BANG OUT OF IT...
TO BE CONCLUDED!

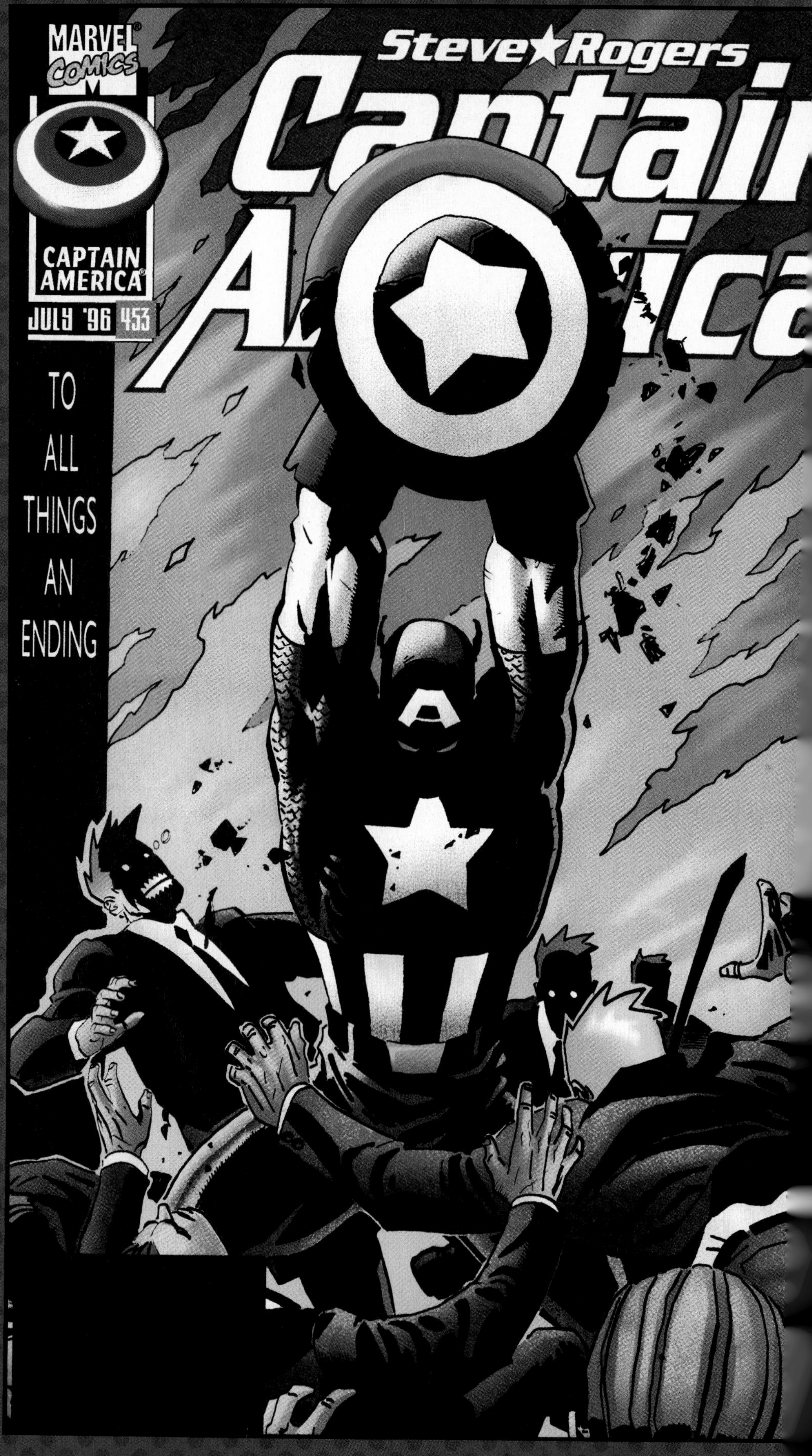
MARVEL COMICS
Steve★Rogers
Captain America
CAPTAIN AMERICA
JULY '96 453
TO ALL THINGS AN ENDING

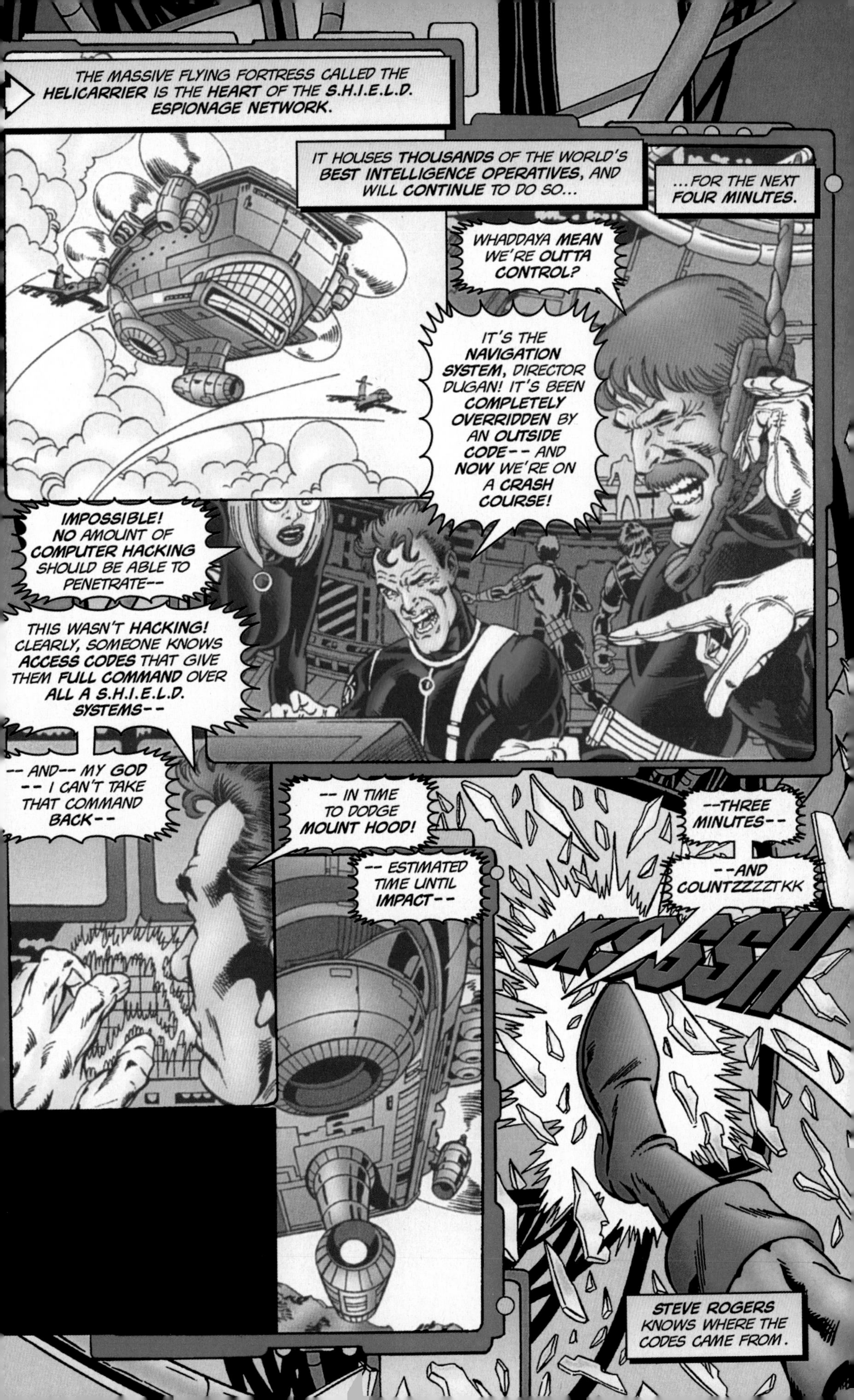
THE MASSIVE FLYING FORTRESS CALLED THE HELICARRIER IS THE HEART OF THE S.H.I.E.L.D. ESPIONAGE NETWORK.
IT HOUSES THOUSANDS OF THE WORLD'S BEST INTELLIGENCE OPERATIVES, AND WILL CONTINUE TO DO SO...
...FOR THE NEXT FOUR MINUTES.
WHADDAYA MEAN WE'RE OUTTA CONTROL?
IT'S THE NAVIGATION SYSTEM, DIRECTOR DUGAN! IT'S BEEN COMPLETELY OVERRIDDEN BY AN OUTSIDE CODE-- AND NOW WE'RE ON A CRASH COURSE!
IMPOSSIBLE! NO AMOUNT OF COMPUTER HACKING SHOULD BE ABLE TO PENETRATE--
THIS WASN'T HACKING! CLEARLY, SOMEONE KNOWS ACCESS CODES THAT GIVE THEM FULL COMMAND OVER ALL A S.H.I.E.L.D. SYSTEMS--
-- AND-- MY GOD -- I CAN'T TAKE THAT COMMAND BACK--
-- IN TIME TO DODGE MOUNT HOOD!
-- ESTIMATED TIME UNTIL IMPACT--
--THREE MINUTES--
--AND COUNTZZZZTKK
KSSSH
STEVE ROGERS KNOWS WHERE THE CODES CAME FROM.

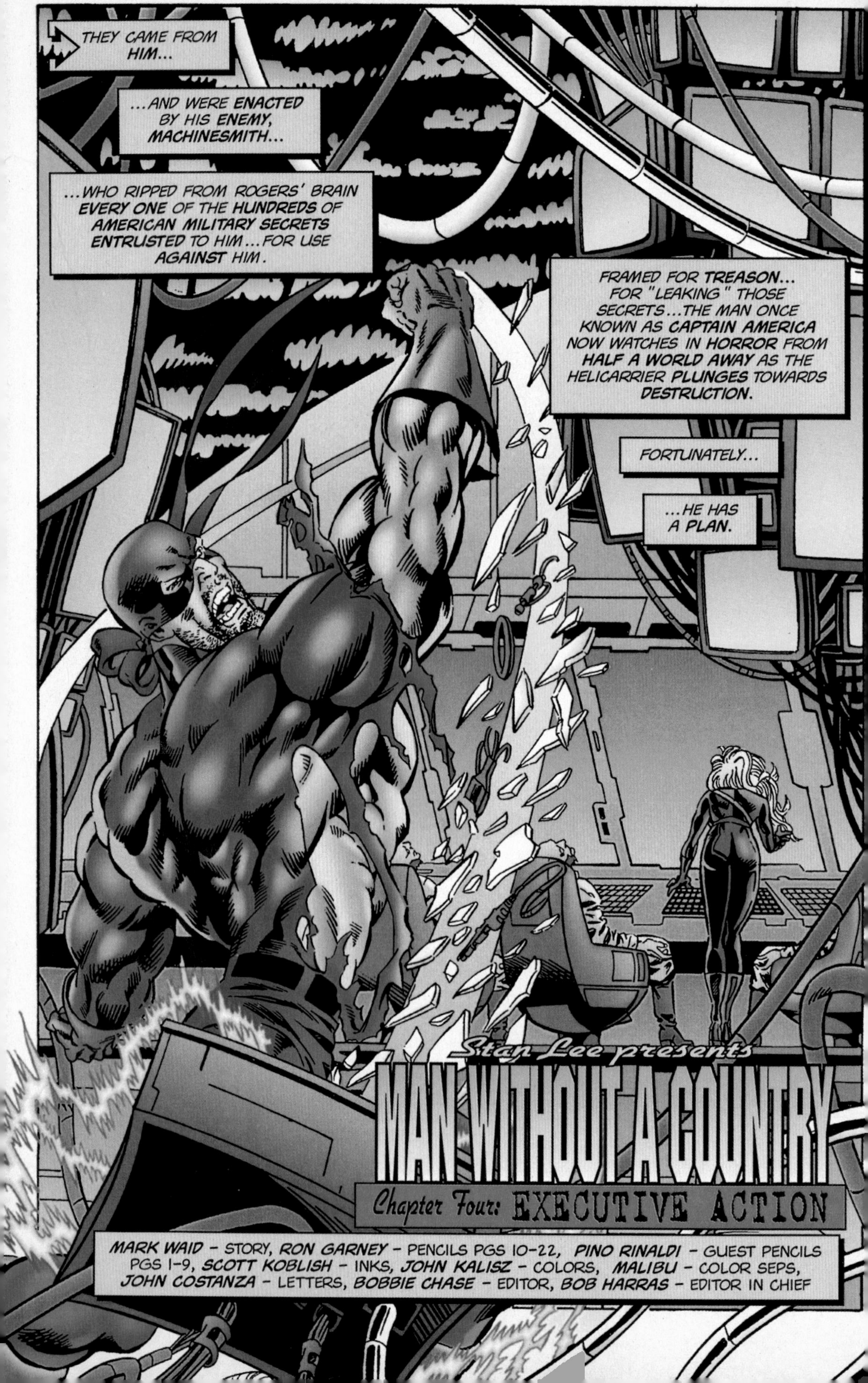
THEY CAME FROM HIM...
...AND WERE ENACTED BY HIS ENEMY, MACHINESMITH...
...WHO RIPPED FROM ROGERS' BRAIN EVERY ONE OF THE HUNDREDS OF AMERICAN MILITARY SECRETS ENTRUSTED TO HIM...FOR USE AGAINST HIM.
FRAMED FOR TREASON... FOR "LEAKING" THOSE SECRETS...THE MAN ONCE KNOWN AS CAPTAIN AMERICA NOW WATCHES IN HORROR FROM HALF A WORLD AWAY AS THE HELICARRIER PLUNGES TOWARDS DESTRUCTION.
FORTUNATELY...
...HE HAS A PLAN.
Stan Lee presents
MAN WITHOUT A COUNTRY
Chapter Four: EXECUTIVE ACTION
MARK WAID - STORY, RON GARNEY - PENCILS PGS 10-22, PINO RINALDI - GUEST PENCILS PGS 1-9, SCOTT KOBLISH - INKS, JOHN KALISZ - COLORS, MALIBU - COLOR SEPS, JOHN COSTANZA - LETTERS, BOBBIE CHASE - EDITOR, BOB HARRAS - EDITOR IN CHIEF

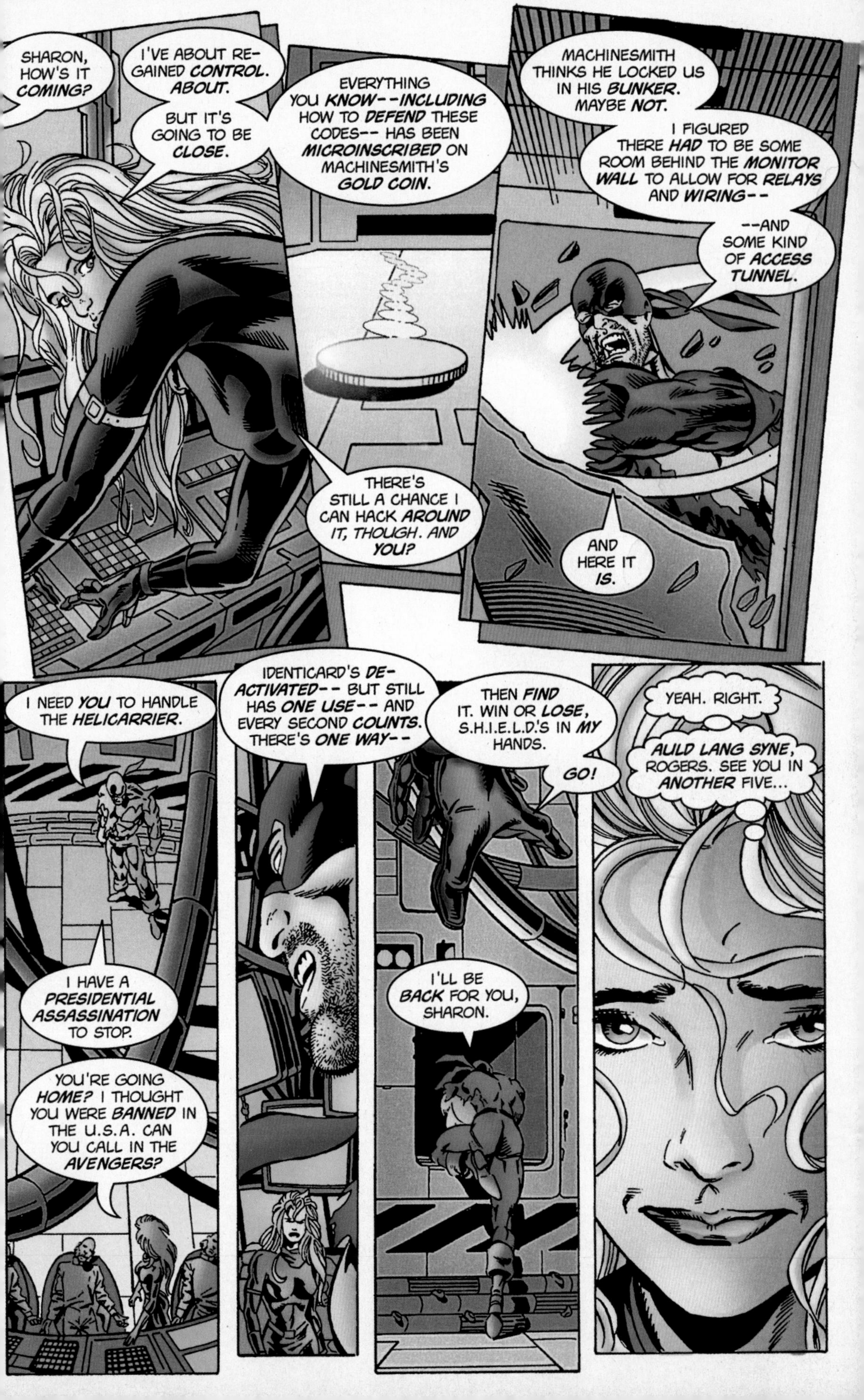
SHARON, HOW'S IT COMING?
I'VE ABOUT RE-GAINED CONTROL. ABOUT.
BUT IT'S GOING TO BE CLOSE.
EVERYTHING YOU KNOW--INCLUDING HOW TO DEFEND THESE CODES-- HAS BEEN MICROINSCRIBED ON MACHINESMITH'S GOLD COIN.
THERE'S STILL A CHANCE I CAN HACK AROUND IT, THOUGH. AND YOU?
MACHINESMITH THINKS HE LOCKED US IN HIS BUNKER. MAYBE NOT.
I FIGURED THERE HAD TO BE SOME ROOM BEHIND THE MONITOR WALL TO ALLOW FOR RELAYS AND WIRING--
--AND SOME KIND OF ACCESS TUNNEL.
AND HERE IT IS.
I NEED YOU TO HANDLE THE HELICARRIER.
I HAVE A PRESIDENTIAL ASSASSINATION TO STOP.
YOU'RE GOING HOME? I THOUGHT YOU WERE BANNED IN THE U.S.A. CAN YOU CALL IN THE AVENGERS?
IDENTICARD'S DE-ACTIVATED-- BUT STILL HAS ONE USE-- AND EVERY SECOND COUNTS. THERE'S ONE WAY--
THEN FIND IT. WIN OR LOSE, S.H.I.E.L.D.'S IN MY HANDS.
GO!
I'LL BE BACK FOR YOU, SHARON.
YEAH. RIGHT.
AULD LANG SYNE, ROGERS. SEE YOU IN ANOTHER FIVE...

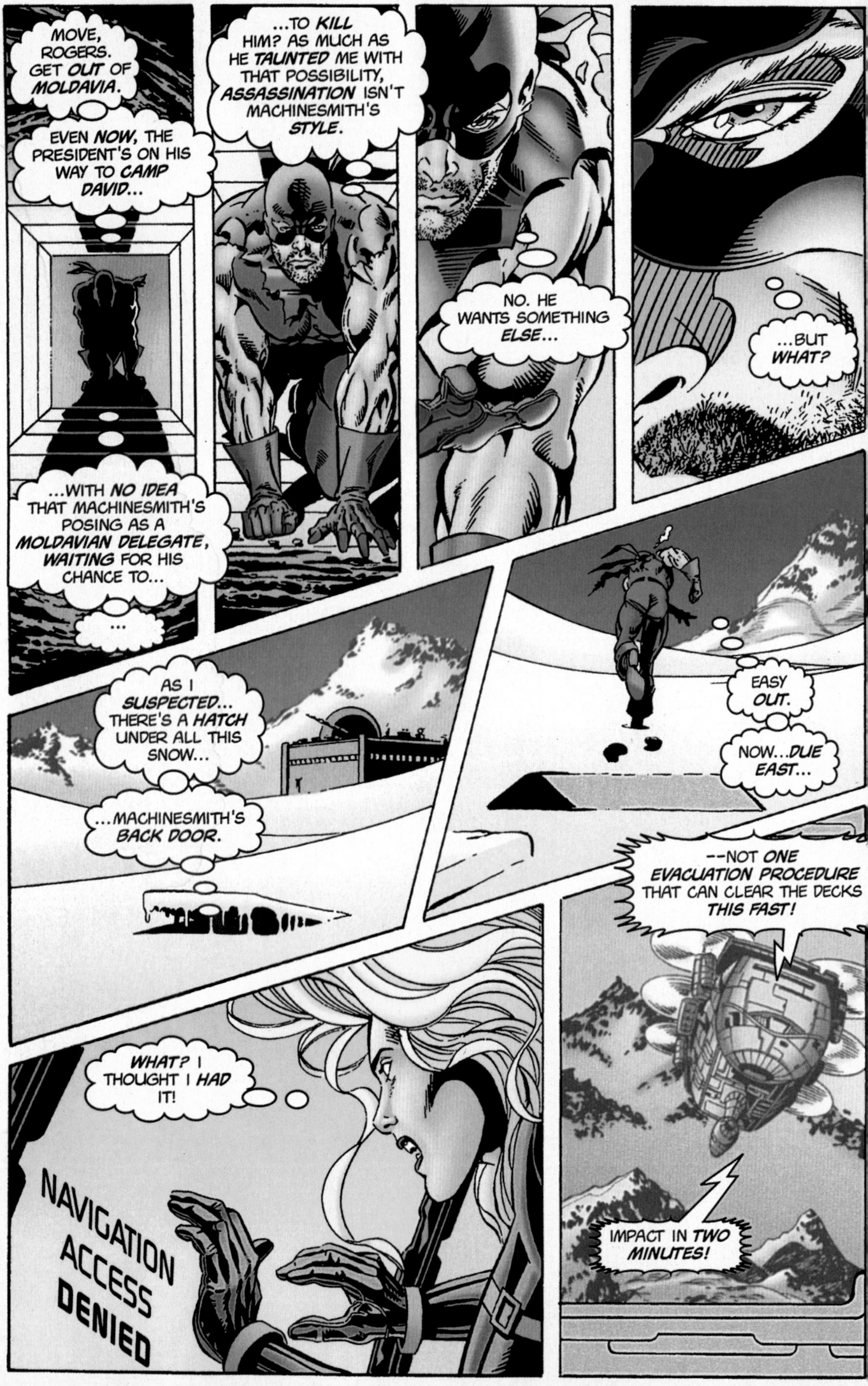
MOVE, ROGERS. GET OUT OF MOLDAVIA.
EVEN NOW, THE PRESIDENT'S ON HIS WAY TO CAMP DAVID...
...WITH NO IDEA THAT MACHINESMITH'S POSING AS A MOLDAVIAN DELEGATE, WAITING FOR HIS CHANCE TO...
...
...TO KILL HIM? AS MUCH AS HE TAUNTED ME WITH THAT POSSIBILITY, ASSASSINATION ISN'T MACHINESMITH'S STYLE.
NO. HE WANTS SOMETHING ELSE...
...BUT WHAT?
AS I SUSPECTED... THERE'S A HATCH UNDER ALL THIS SNOW...
...MACHINESMITH'S BACK DOOR.
EASY OUT.
NOW...DUE EAST...
WHAT? I THOUGHT I HAD IT!
NAVIGATION ACCESS DENIED
--NOT ONE EVACUATION PROCEDURE THAT CAN CLEAR THE DECKS THIS FAST!
IMPACT IN TWO MINUTES!

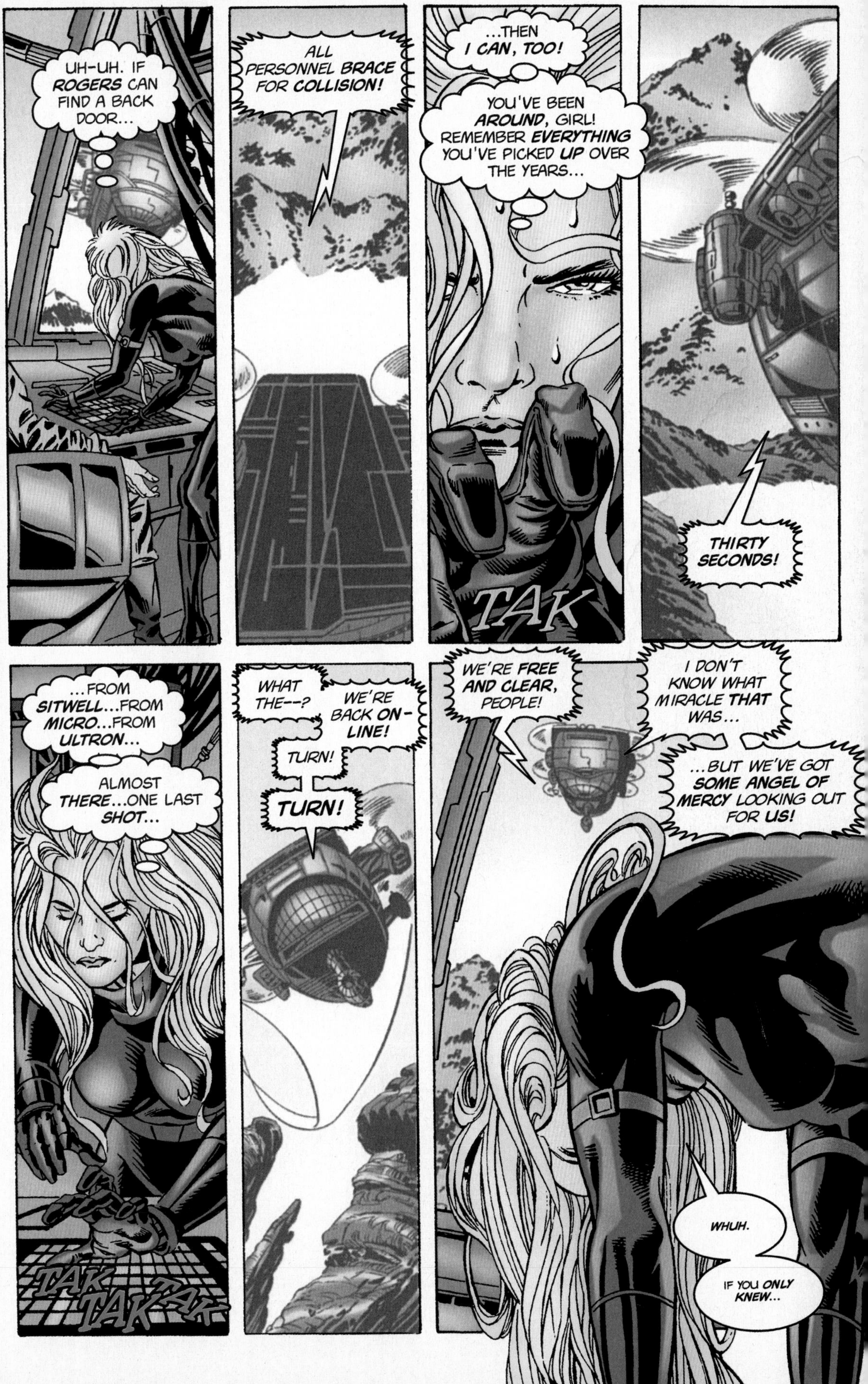
UH-UH. IF ROGERS CAN FIND A BACK DOOR...
ALL PERSONNEL BRACE FOR COLLISION!
...THEN I CAN, TOO!
YOU'VE BEEN AROUND, GIRL! REMEMBER EVERYTHING YOU'VE PICKED UP OVER THE YEARS...
TAK
THIRTY SECONDS!
...FROM SITWELL...FROM MICRO...FROM ULTRON...
ALMOST THERE...ONE LAST SHOT...
TAK TAK TAK
WHAT THE--?
WE'RE BACK ON-LINE!
TURN!
TURN!
WE'RE FREE AND CLEAR, PEOPLE!
I DON'T KNOW WHAT MIRACLE THAT WAS...
...BUT WE'VE GOT SOME ANGEL OF MERCY LOOKING OUT FOR US!
WHUH.
IF YOU ONLY KNEW...

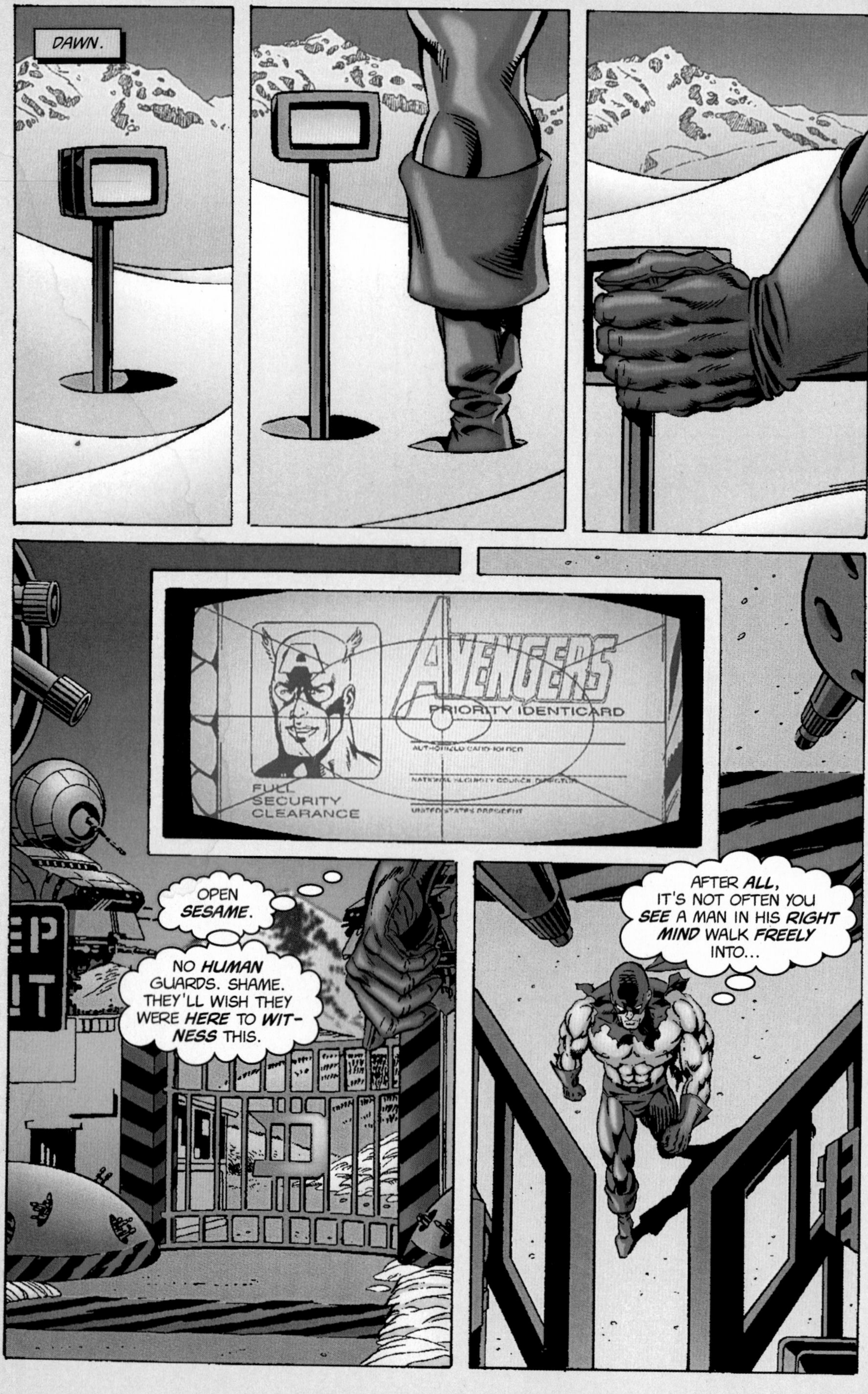
DAWN.
AVENGERS
PRIORITY IDENTICARD
FULL SECURITY CLEARANCE
OPEN SESAME.
NO HUMAN GUARDS. SHAME. THEY'LL WISH THEY WERE HERE TO WITNESS THIS.
AFTER ALL, IT'S NOT OFTEN YOU SEE A MAN IN HIS RIGHT MIND WALK FREELY INTO...

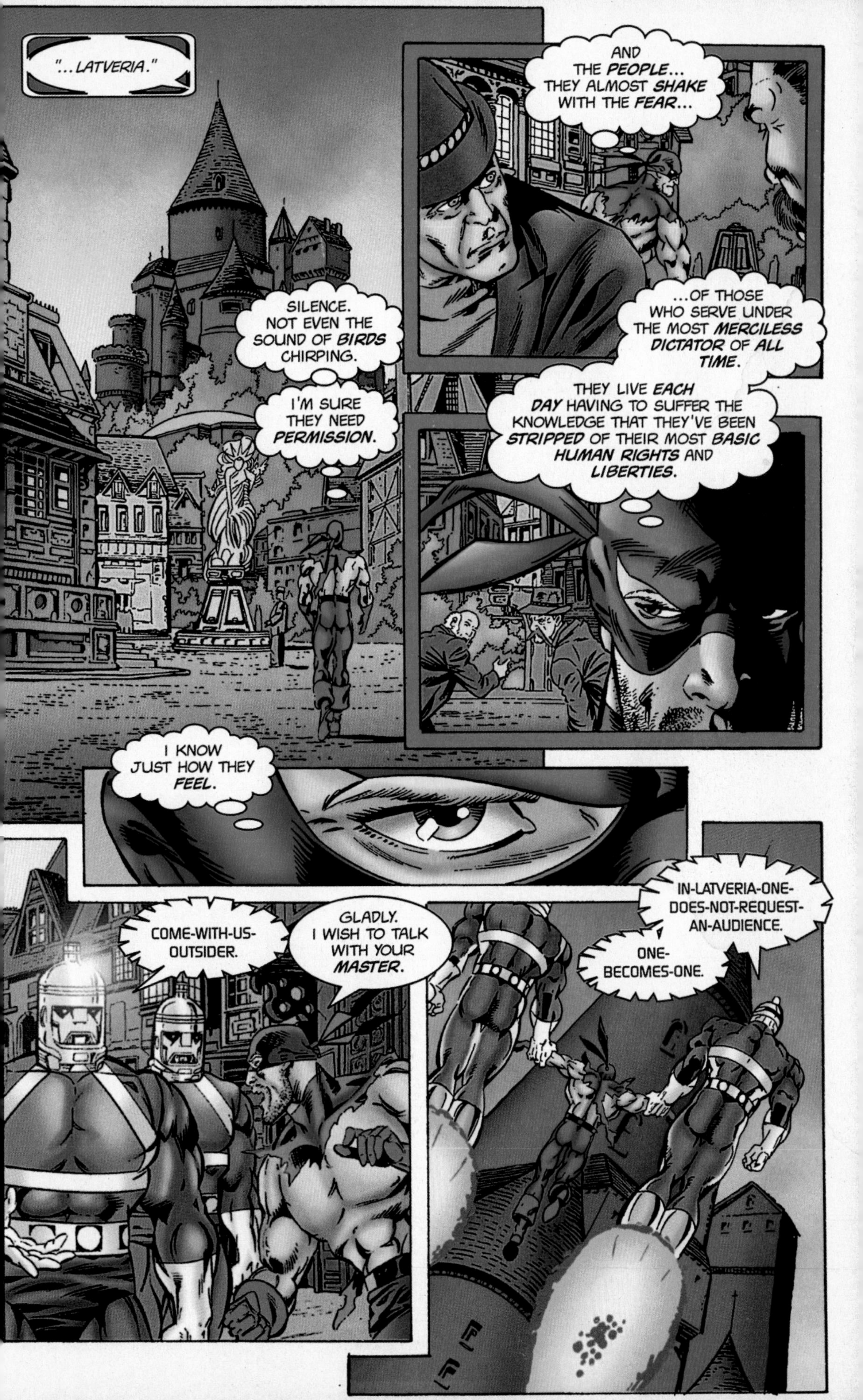
"...LATVERIA."
SILENCE. NOT EVEN THE SOUND OF BIRDS CHIRPING.
I'M SURE THEY NEED PERMISSION.
AND THE PEOPLE... THEY ALMOST SHAKE WITH THE FEAR...
...OF THOSE WHO SERVE UNDER THE MOST MERCILESS DICTATOR OF ALL TIME.
THEY LIVE EACH DAY HAVING TO SUFFER THE KNOWLEDGE THAT THEY'VE BEEN STRIPPED OF THEIR MOST BASIC HUMAN RIGHTS AND LIBERTIES.
I KNOW JUST HOW THEY FEEL.
COME-WITH-US-OUTSIDER.
GLADLY. I WISH TO TALK WITH YOUR MASTER.
IN-LATVERIA-ONE-DOES-NOT-REQUEST-AN-AUDIENCE.
ONE-BECOMES-ONE.

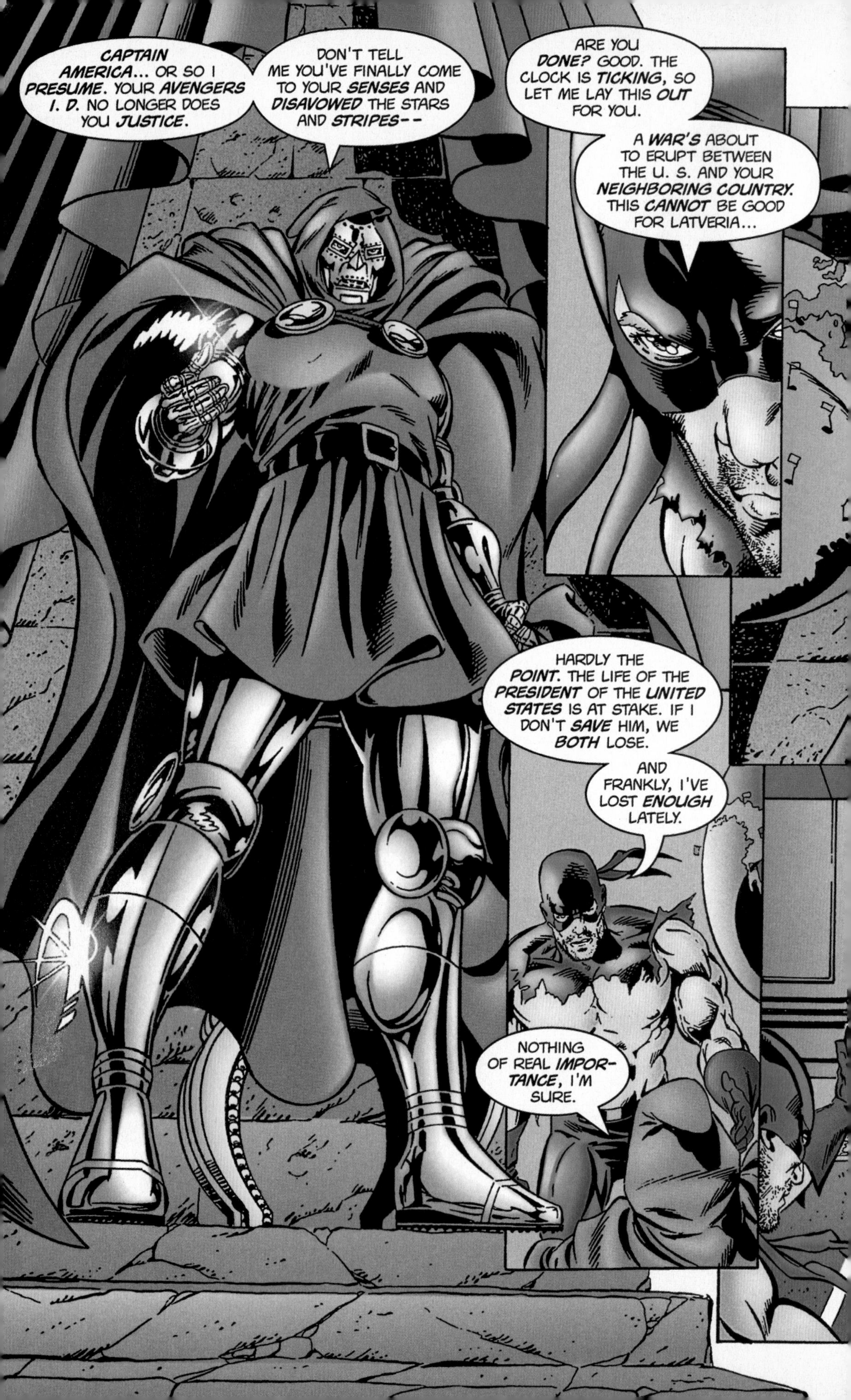
CAPTAIN AMERICA... OR SO I PRESUME. YOUR AVENGERS I. D. NO LONGER DOES YOU JUSTICE.
DON'T TELL ME YOU'VE FINALLY COME TO YOUR SENSES AND DISAVOWED THE STARS AND STRIPES--
ARE YOU DONE? GOOD. THE CLOCK IS TICKING, SO LET ME LAY THIS OUT FOR YOU.
A WAR'S ABOUT TO ERUPT BETWEEN THE U. S. AND YOUR NEIGHBORING COUNTRY. THIS CANNOT BE GOOD FOR LATVERIA...
HARDLY THE POINT. THE LIFE OF THE PRESIDENT OF THE UNITED STATES IS AT STAKE. IF I DON'T SAVE HIM, WE BOTH LOSE.
AND FRANKLY, I'VE LOST ENOUGH LATELY.
NOTHING OF REAL IMPORTANCE, I'M SURE.

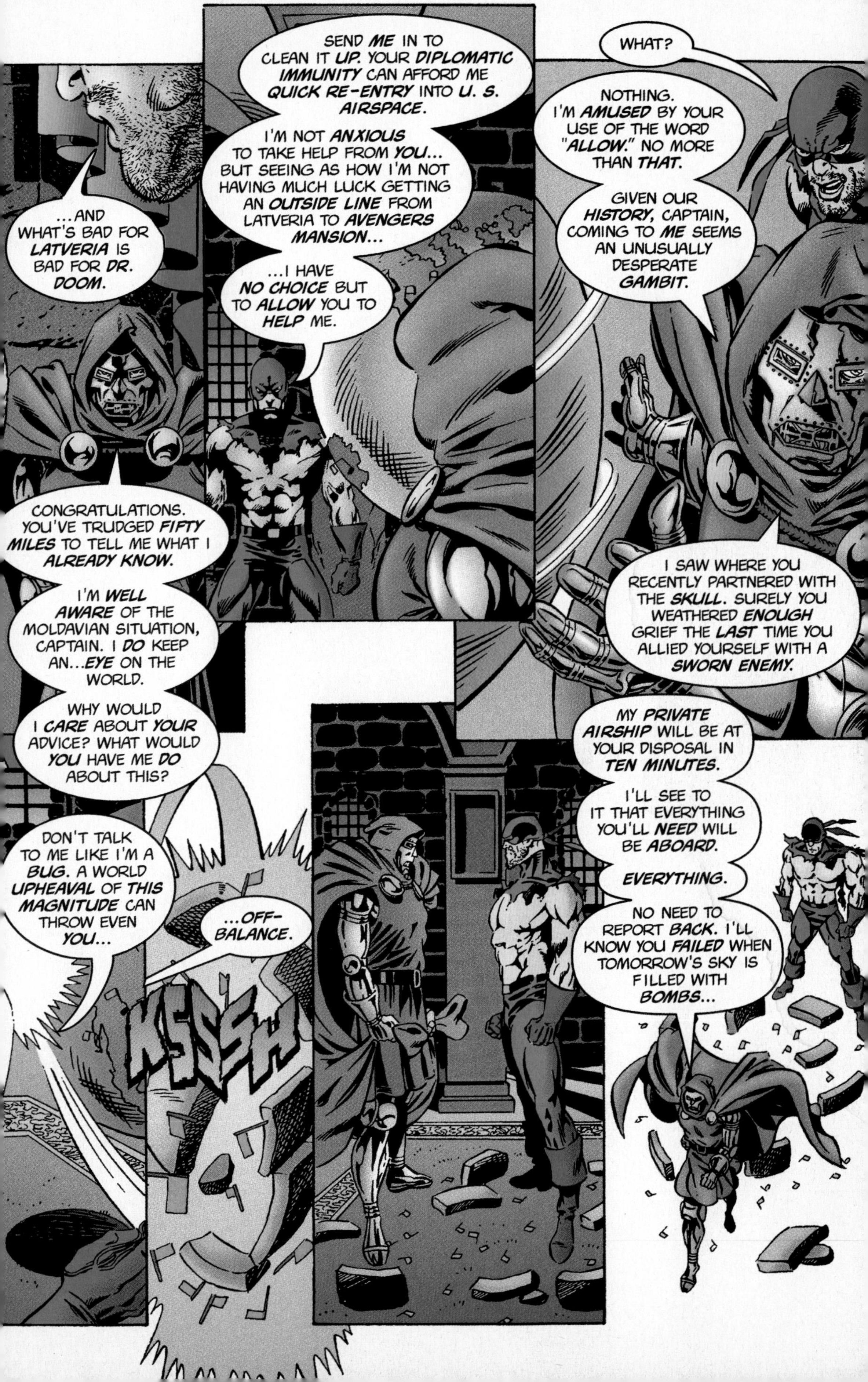
...AND WHAT'S BAD FOR LATVERIA IS BAD FOR DR. DOOM.
SEND ME IN TO CLEAN IT UP. YOUR DIPLOMATIC IMMUNITY CAN AFFORD ME QUICK RE-ENTRY INTO U. S. AIRSPACE.
I'M NOT ANXIOUS TO TAKE HELP FROM YOU... BUT SEEING AS HOW I'M NOT HAVING MUCH LUCK GETTING AN OUTSIDE LINE FROM LATVERIA TO AVENGERS MANSION...
...I HAVE NO CHOICE BUT TO ALLOW YOU TO HELP ME.
WHAT?
NOTHING. I'M AMUSED BY YOUR USE OF THE WORD "ALLOW." NO MORE THAN THAT.
GIVEN OUR HISTORY, CAPTAIN, COMING TO ME SEEMS AN UNUSUALLY DESPERATE GAMBIT.
CONGRATULATIONS. YOU'VE TRUDGED FIFTY MILES TO TELL ME WHAT I ALREADY KNOW.
I'M WELL AWARE OF THE MOLDAVIAN SITUATION, CAPTAIN. I DO KEEP AN...EYE ON THE WORLD.
WHY WOULD I CARE ABOUT YOUR ADVICE? WHAT WOULD YOU HAVE ME DO ABOUT THIS?
I SAW WHERE YOU RECENTLY PARTNERED WITH THE SKULL. SURELY YOU WEATHERED ENOUGH GRIEF THE LAST TIME YOU ALLIED YOURSELF WITH A SWORN ENEMY.
DON'T TALK TO ME LIKE I'M A BUG. A WORLD UPHEAVAL OF THIS MAGNITUDE CAN THROW EVEN YOU...
...OFF-BALANCE.
KSSH
MY PRIVATE AIRSHIP WILL BE AT YOUR DISPOSAL IN TEN MINUTES.
I'LL SEE TO IT THAT EVERYTHING YOU'LL NEED WILL BE ABOARD.
EVERYTHING.
NO NEED TO REPORT BACK. I'LL KNOW YOU FAILED WHEN TOMORROW'S SKY IS FILLED WITH BOMBS...

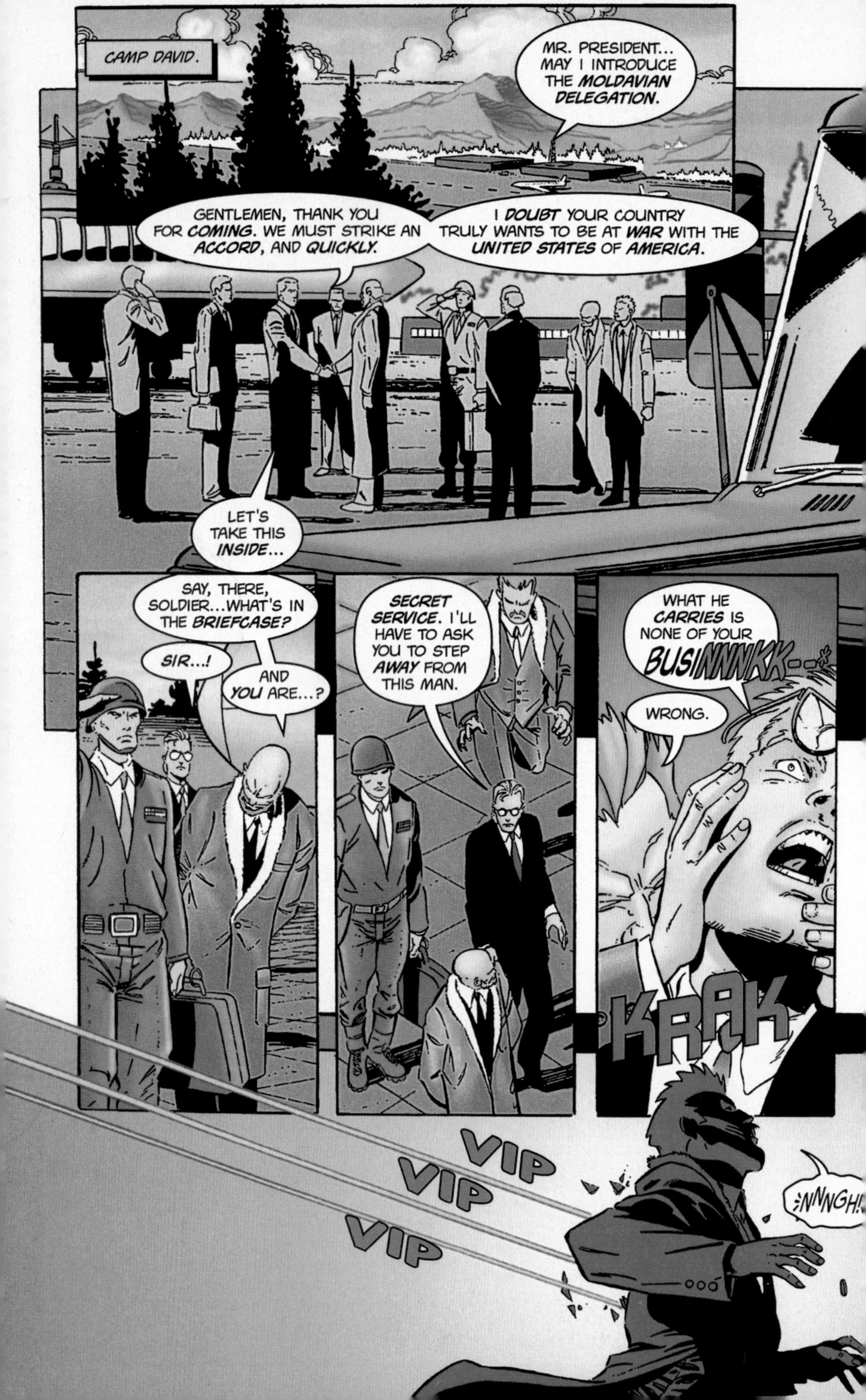
CAMP DAVID.
MR. PRESIDENT... MAY I INTRODUCE THE MOLDAVIAN DELEGATION.
GENTLEMEN, THANK YOU FOR COMING. WE MUST STRIKE AN ACCORD, AND QUICKLY.
I DOUBT YOUR COUNTRY TRULY WANTS TO BE AT WAR WITH THE UNITED STATES OF AMERICA.
LET'S TAKE THIS INSIDE...
SAY, THERE, SOLDIER...WHAT'S IN THE BRIEFCASE?
SIR...!
AND YOU ARE...?
SECRET SERVICE. I'LL HAVE TO ASK YOU TO STEP AWAY FROM THIS MAN.
WHAT HE CARRIES IS NONE OF YOUR BUSINNNKK--
WRONG.
KRAK
VIP
VIP
VIP
NNNGH!

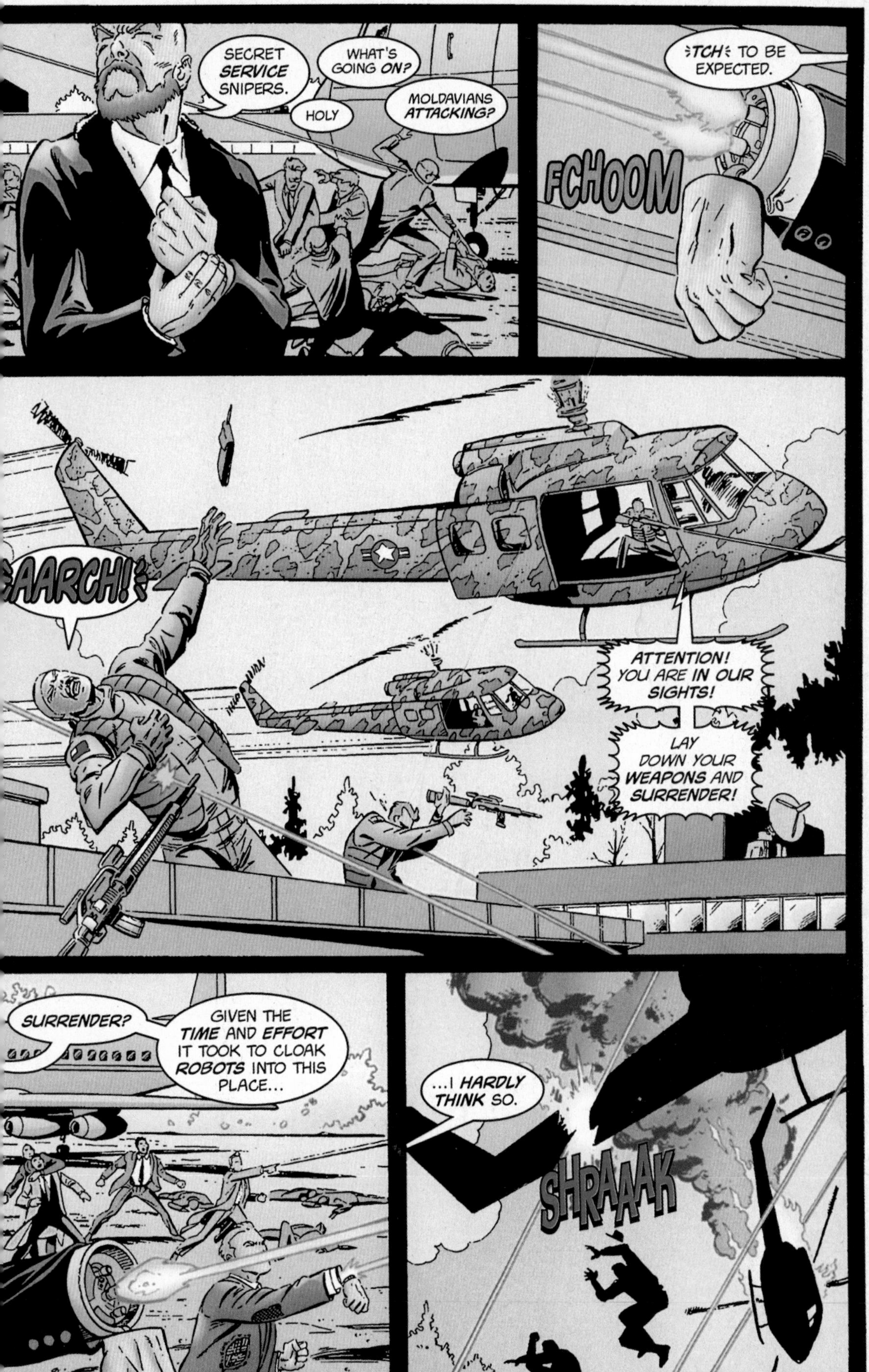
SECRET SERVICE SNIPERS.
WHAT'S GOING ON?
HOLY
MOLDAVIANS ATTACKING?
TCH TO BE EXPECTED.
FCHOOM
AARCH!
ATTENTION! YOU ARE IN OUR SIGHTS!
LAY DOWN YOUR WEAPONS AND SURRENDER!
SURRENDER?
GIVEN THE TIME AND EFFORT IT TOOK TO CLOAK ROBOTS INTO THIS PLACE...
...I HARDLY THINK SO.
SHRAAAK

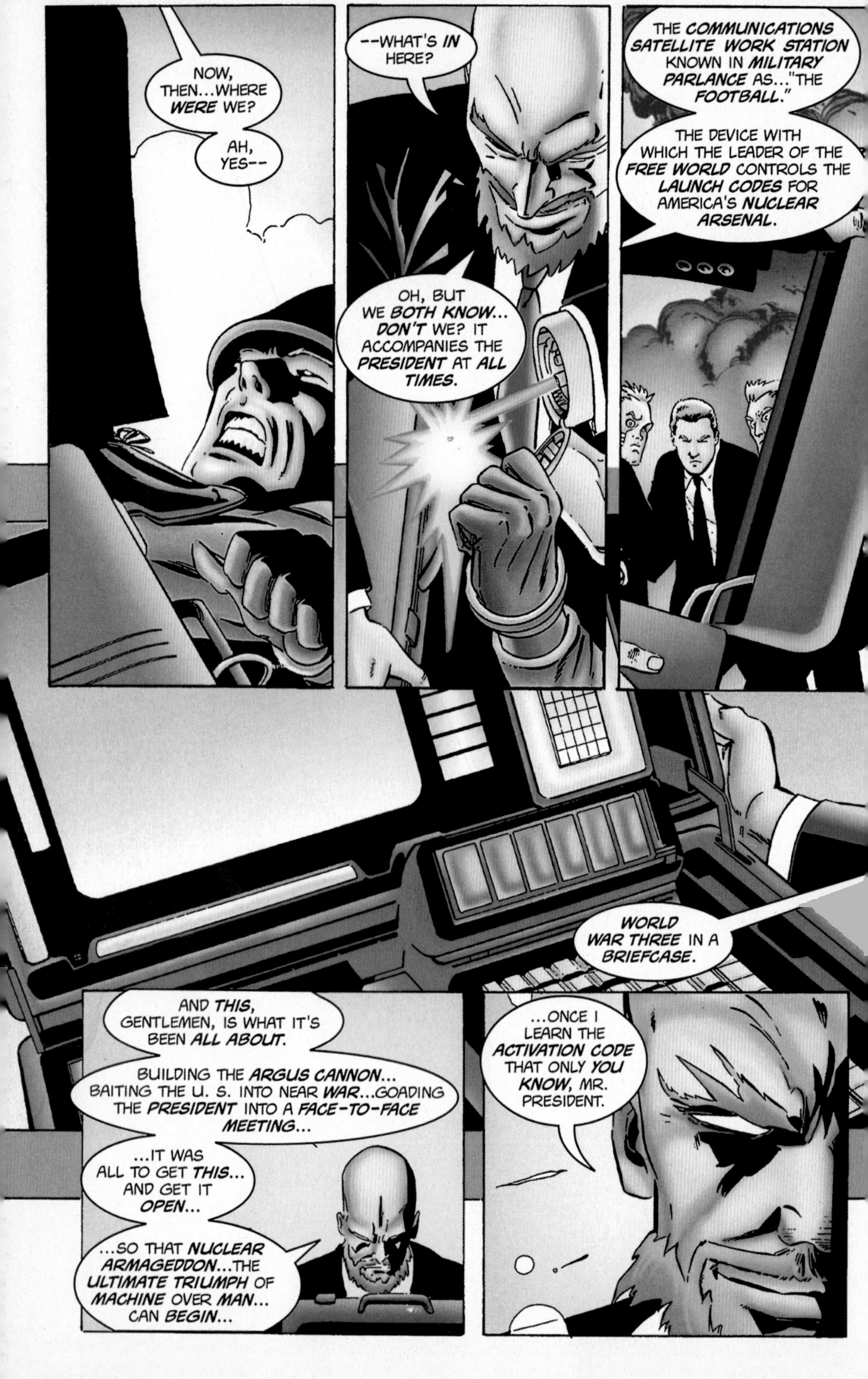
NOW, THEN...WHERE WERE WE?
AH, YES--
--WHAT'S IN HERE?
OH, BUT WE BOTH KNOW... DON'T WE? IT ACCOMPANIES THE PRESIDENT AT ALL TIMES.
THE COMMUNICATIONS SATELLITE WORK STATION KNOWN IN MILITARY PARLANCE AS..."THE FOOTBALL."
THE DEVICE WITH WHICH THE LEADER OF THE FREE WORLD CONTROLS THE LAUNCH CODES FOR AMERICA'S NUCLEAR ARSENAL.
WORLD WAR THREE IN A BRIEFCASE.
AND THIS, GENTLEMEN, IS WHAT IT'S BEEN ALL ABOUT.
BUILDING THE ARGUS CANNON... BAITING THE U. S. INTO NEAR WAR...GOADING THE PRESIDENT INTO A FACE-TO-FACE MEETING...
...IT WAS ALL TO GET THIS... AND GET IT OPEN...
...SO THAT NUCLEAR ARMAGEDDON...THE ULTIMATE TRIUMPH OF MACHINE OVER MAN... CAN BEGIN...
...ONCE I LEARN THE ACTIVATION CODE THAT ONLY YOU KNOW, MR. PRESIDENT.

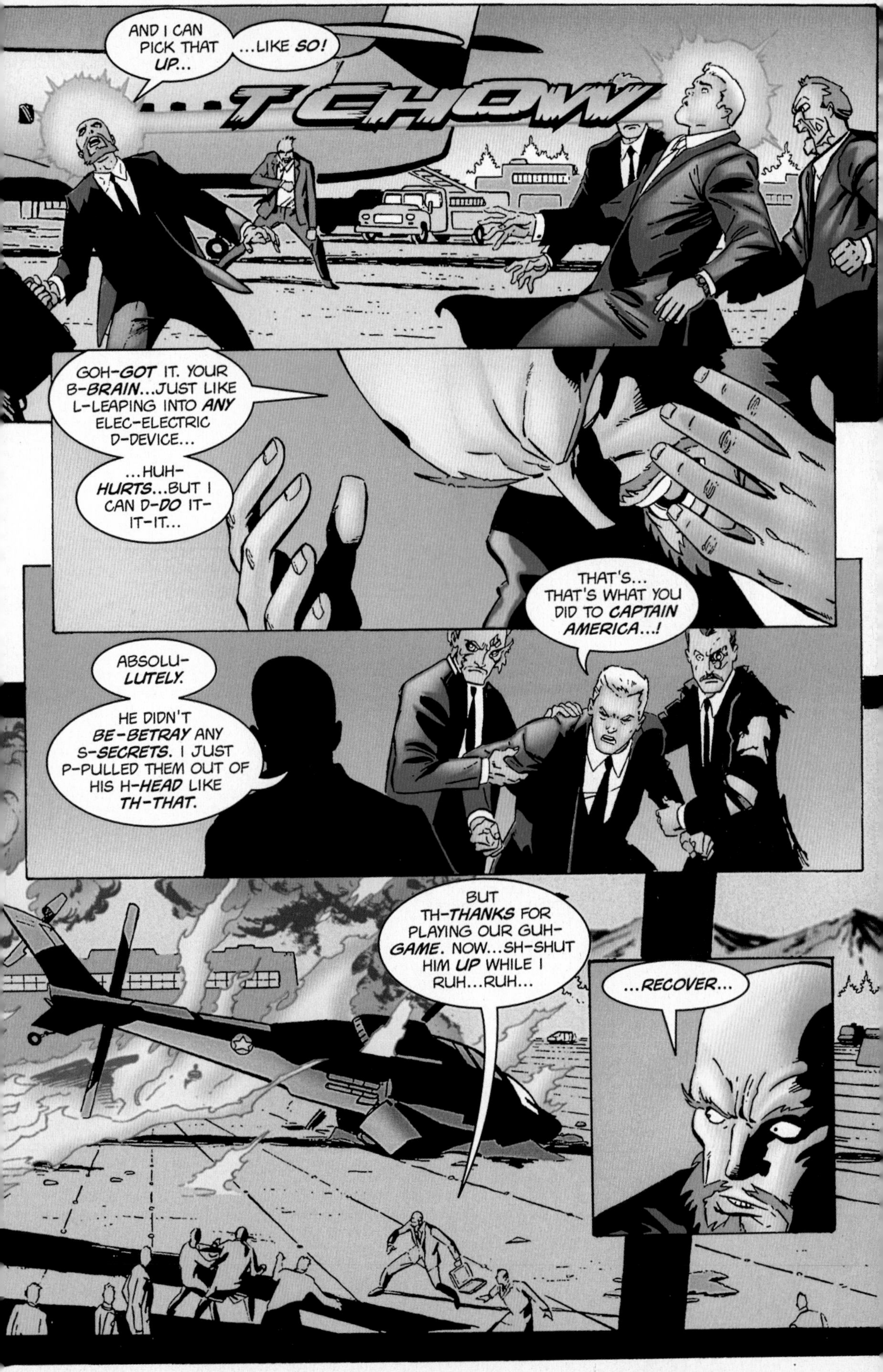
AND I CAN PICK THAT UP...
...LIKE SO!
...TCHOW
GOH-GOT IT. YOUR B-BRAIN...JUST LIKE L-LEAPING INTO ANY ELEC-ELECTRIC D-DEVICE...
...HUH-HURTS...BUT I CAN D-DO IT-IT-IT...
THAT'S... THAT'S WHAT YOU DID TO CAPTAIN AMERICA...!
ABSOLU-LUTELY.
HE DIDN'T BE-BETRAY ANY S-SECRETS. I JUST P-PULLED THEM OUT OF HIS H-HEAD LIKE TH-THAT.
BUT TH-THANKS FOR PLAYING OUR GUH-GAME. NOW...SH-SHUT HIM UP WHILE I RUH...RUH...
...RECOVER...

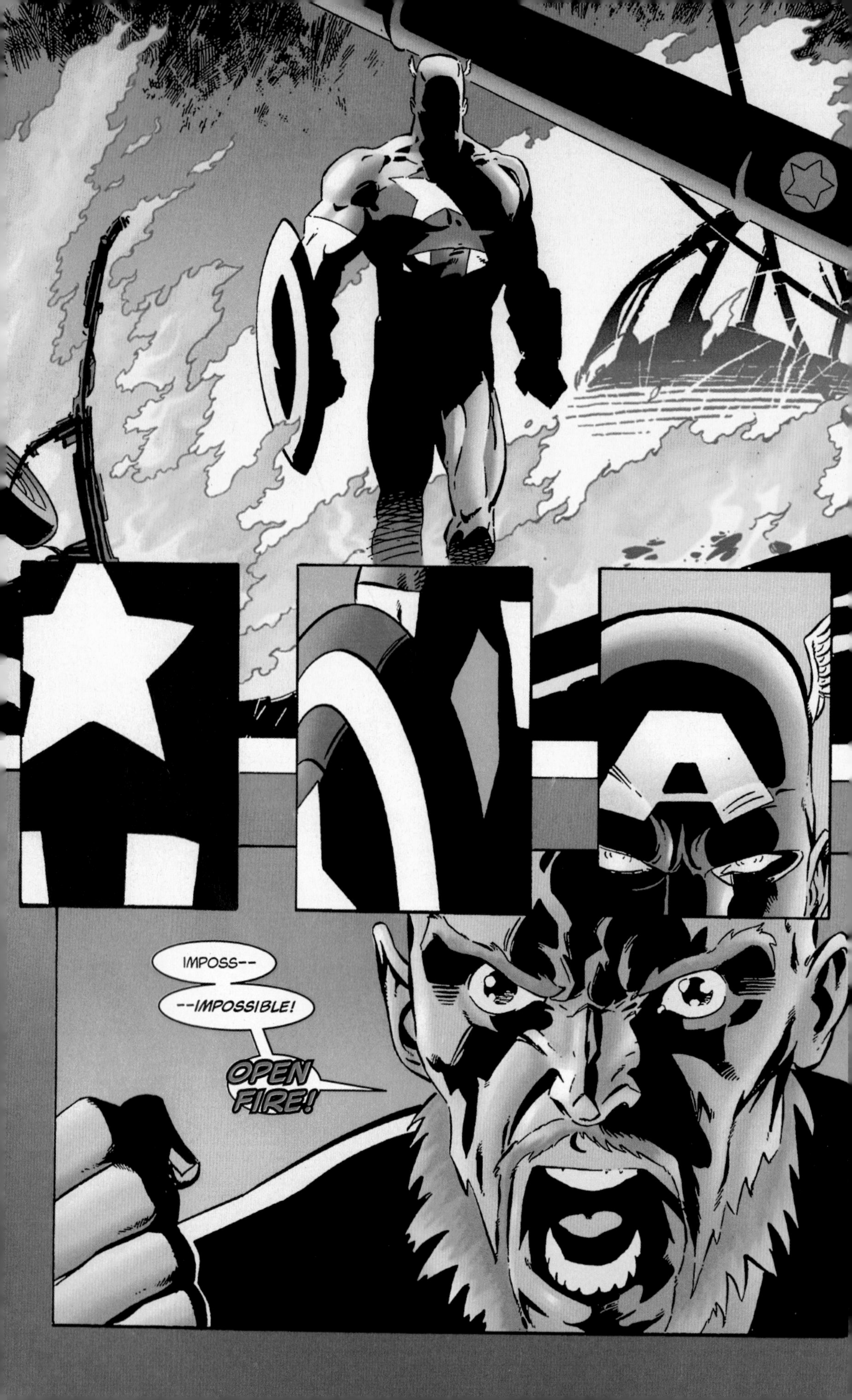
IMPOSS--
--IMPOSSIBLE!
OPEN FIRE!

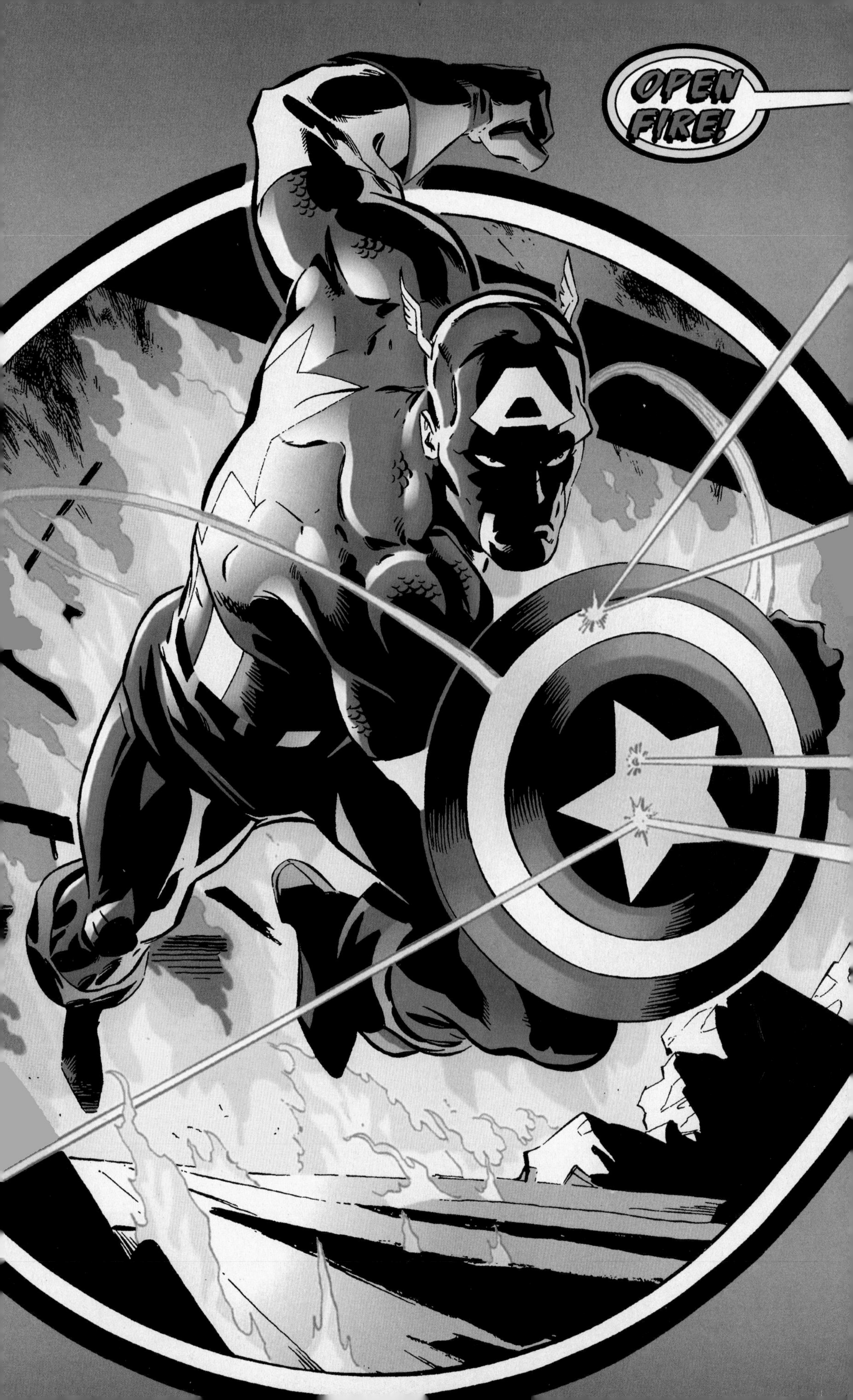
OPEN FIRE!

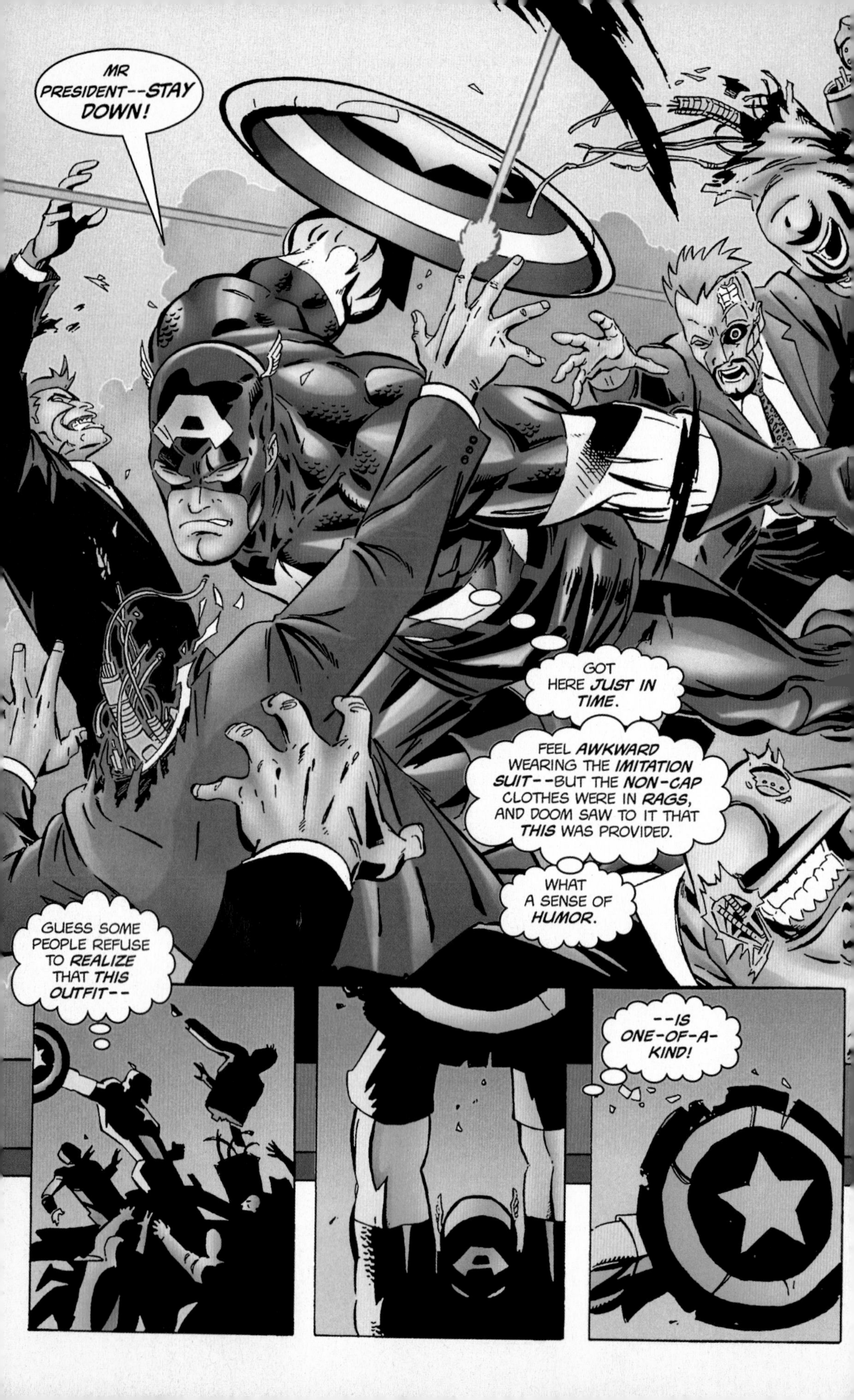
MR PRESIDENT--STAY DOWN!
GOT HERE JUST IN TIME.
FEEL AWKWARD WEARING THE IMITATION SUIT--BUT THE NON-CAP CLOTHES WERE IN RAGS, AND DOOM SAW TO IT THAT THIS WAS PROVIDED.
WHAT A SENSE OF HUMOR.
GUESS SOME PEOPLE REFUSE TO REALIZE THAT THIS OUTFIT--
--IS ONE-OF-A-KIND!

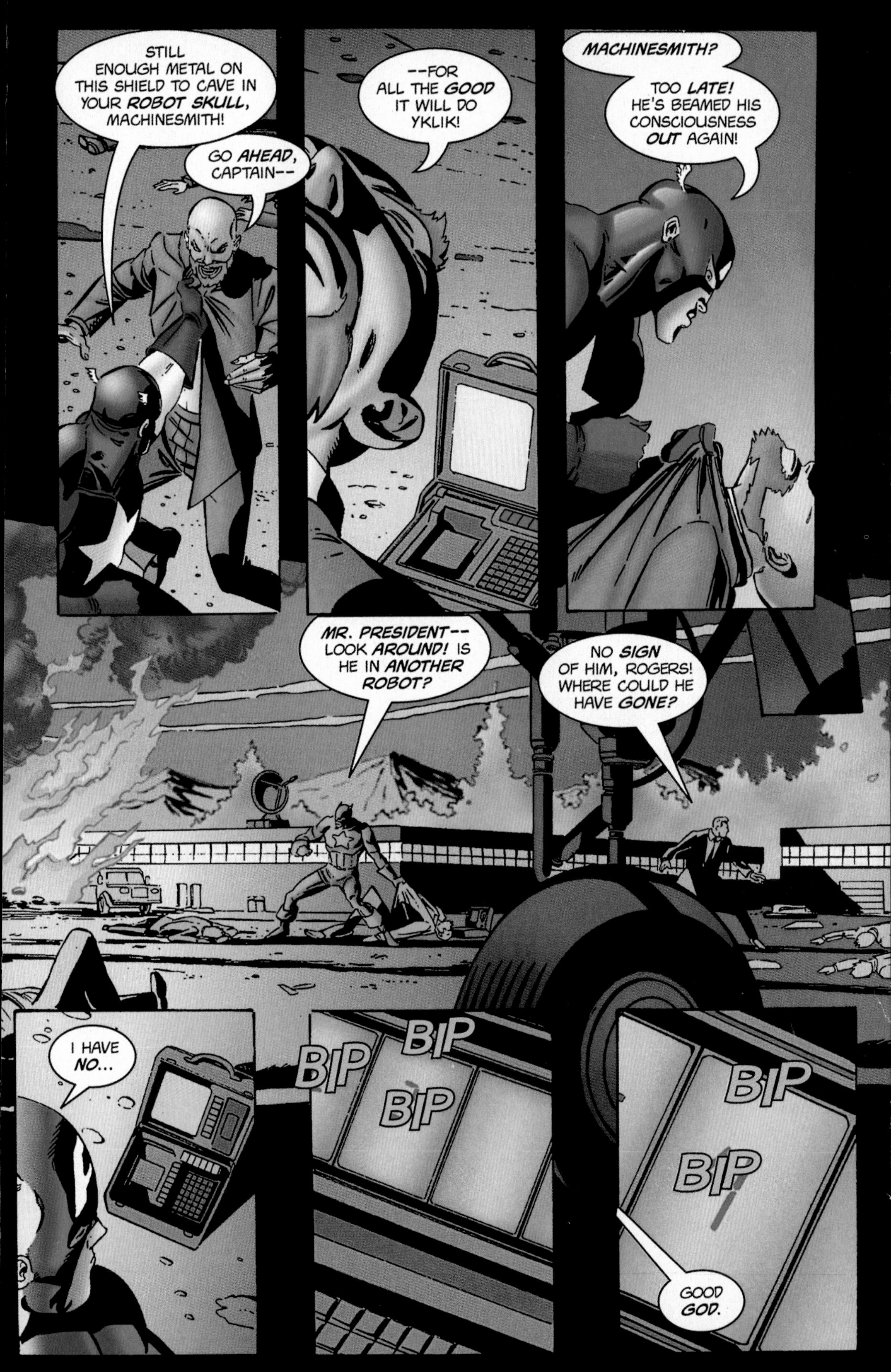
STILL ENOUGH METAL ON THIS SHIELD TO CAVE IN YOUR ROBOT SKULL, MACHINESMITH!
GO AHEAD, CAPTAIN--
--FOR ALL THE GOOD IT WILL DO YKLIK!
MACHINESMITH?
TOO LATE! HE'S BEAMED HIS CONSCIOUSNESS OUT AGAIN!
MR. PRESIDENT--LOOK AROUND! IS HE IN ANOTHER ROBOT?
NO SIGN OF HIM, ROGERS! WHERE COULD HE HAVE GONE?
I HAVE NO...
BIP
BIP
BIP
BIP
BIP
GOOD GOD.

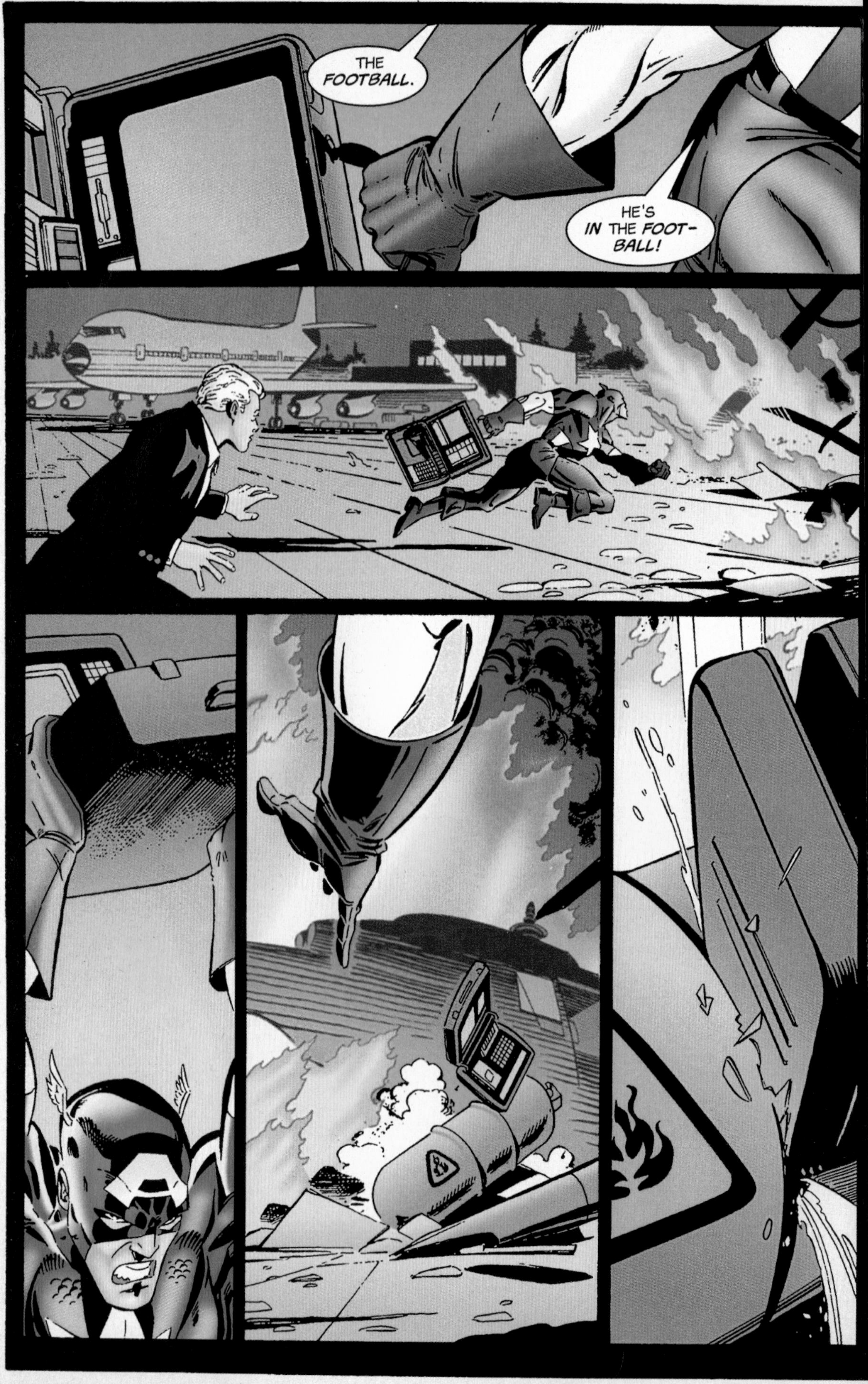
THE FOOTBALL.
HE'S IN THE FOOT-BALL!

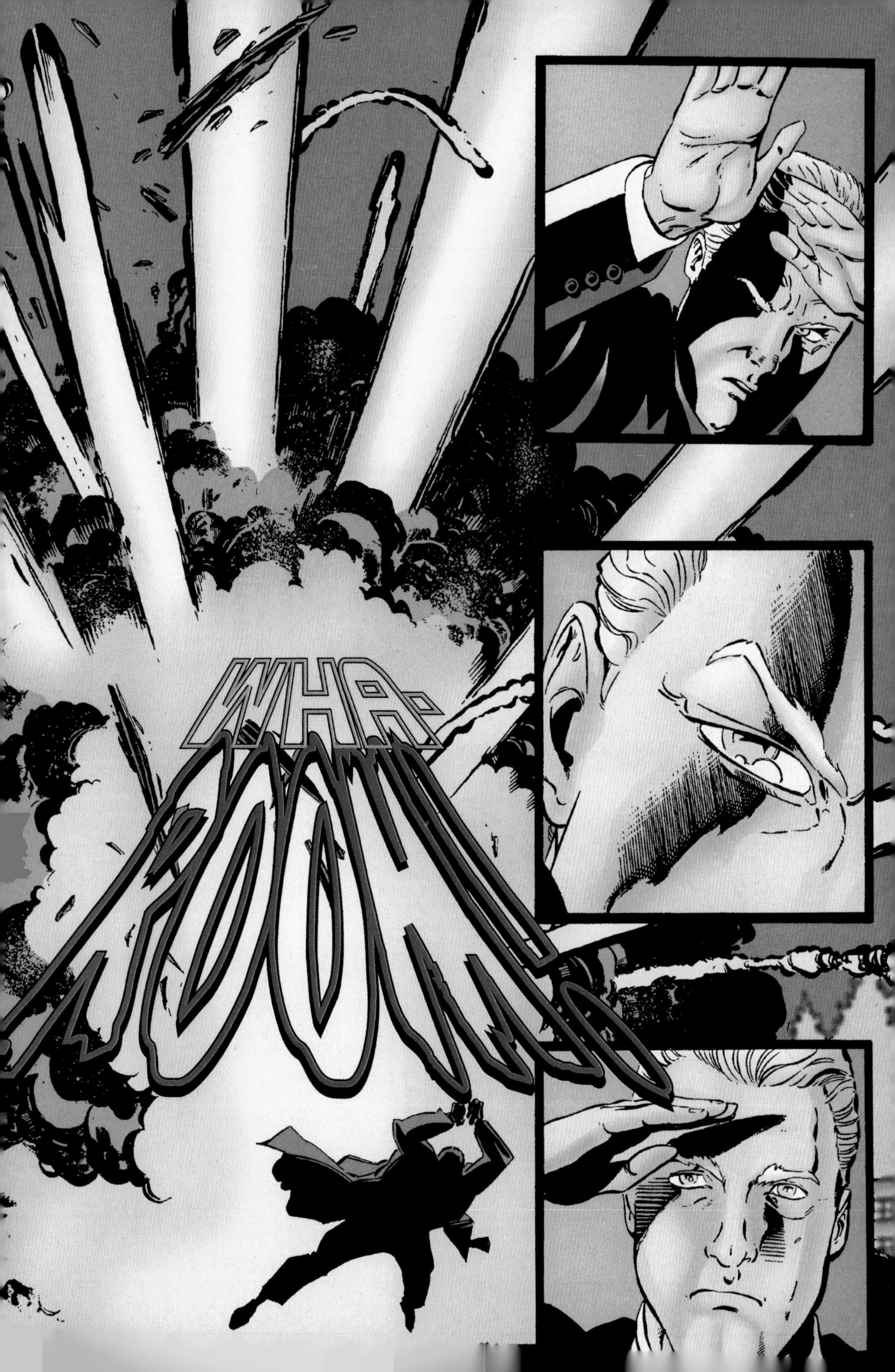
WHA-
BOOM!

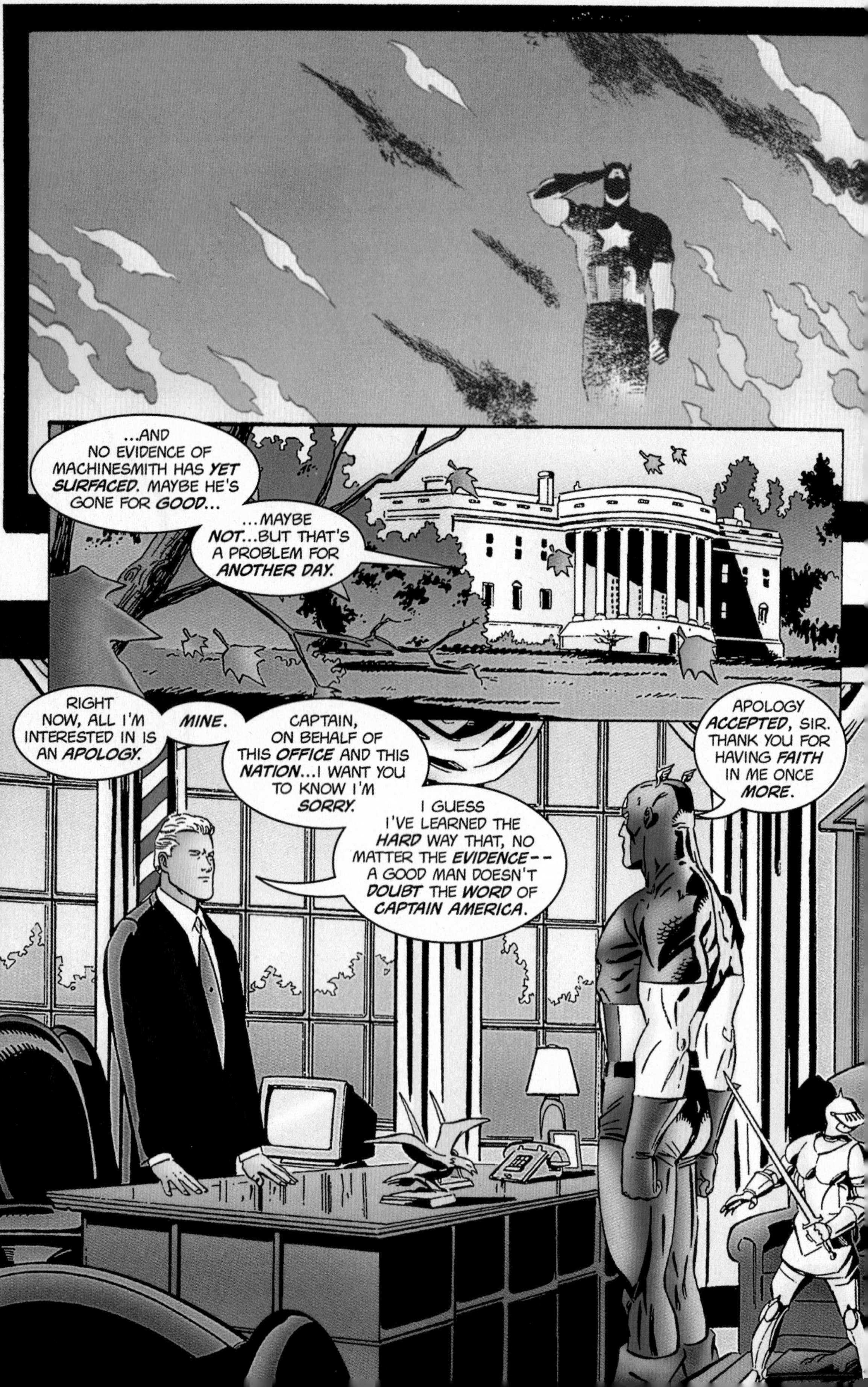
...AND NO EVIDENCE OF MACHINESMITH HAS YET SURFACED. MAYBE HE'S GONE FOR GOOD...
...MAYBE NOT...BUT THAT'S A PROBLEM FOR ANOTHER DAY.
RIGHT NOW, ALL I'M INTERESTED IN IS AN APOLOGY.
MINE.
CAPTAIN, ON BEHALF OF THIS OFFICE AND THIS NATION...I WANT YOU TO KNOW I'M SORRY.
I GUESS I'VE LEARNED THE HARD WAY THAT, NO MATTER THE EVIDENCE-- A GOOD MAN DOESN'T DOUBT THE WORD OF CAPTAIN AMERICA.
APOLOGY ACCEPTED, SIR. THANK YOU FOR HAVING FAITH IN ME ONCE MORE.

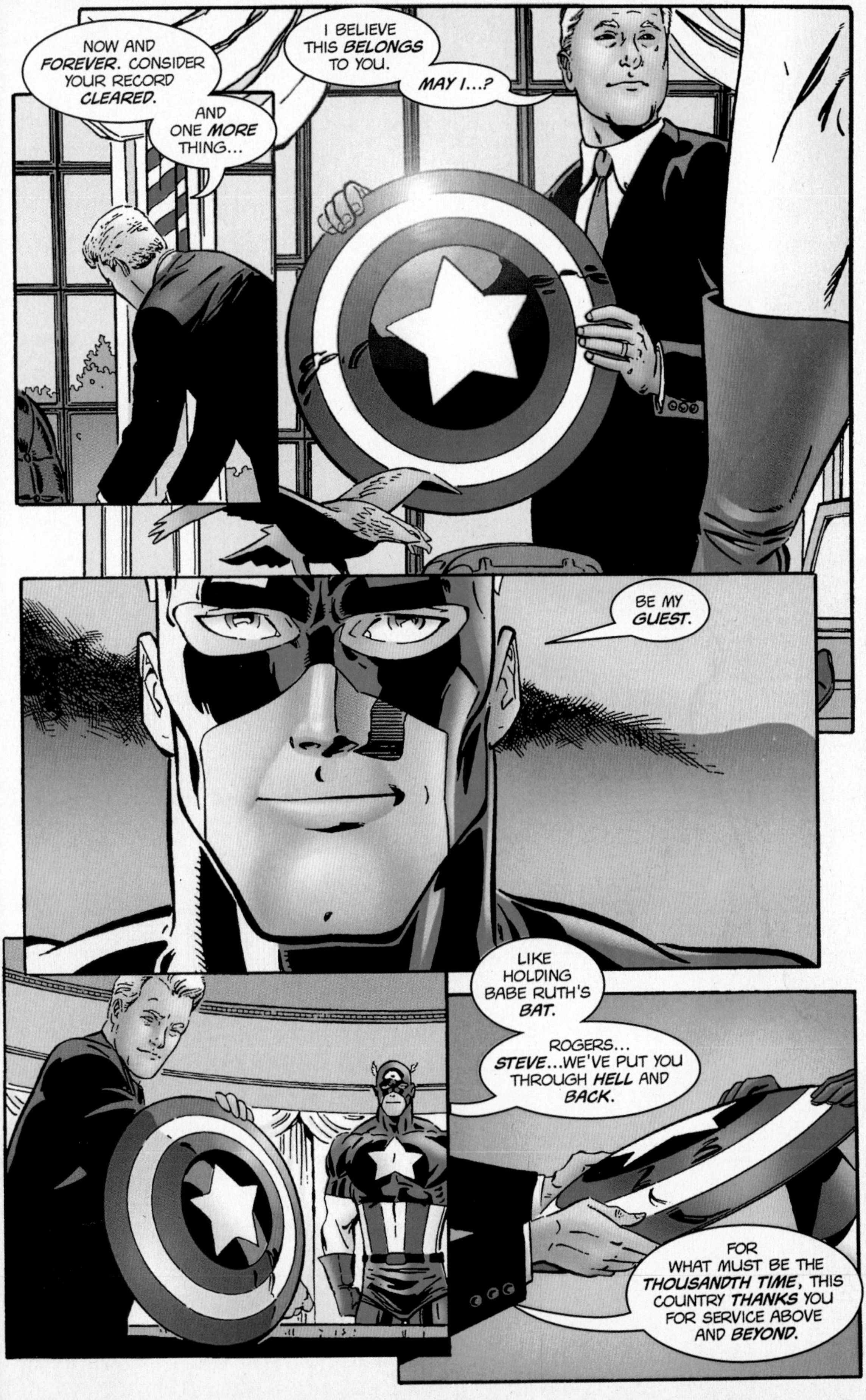
NOW AND FOREVER. CONSIDER YOUR RECORD CLEARED.
AND ONE MORE THING...
I BELIEVE THIS BELONGS TO YOU.
MAY I...?
BE MY GUEST.
LIKE HOLDING BABE RUTH'S BAT.
ROGERS... STEVE...WE'VE PUT YOU THROUGH HELL AND BACK.
FOR WHAT MUST BE THE THOUSANDTH TIME, THIS COUNTRY THANKS YOU FOR SERVICE ABOVE AND BEYOND.

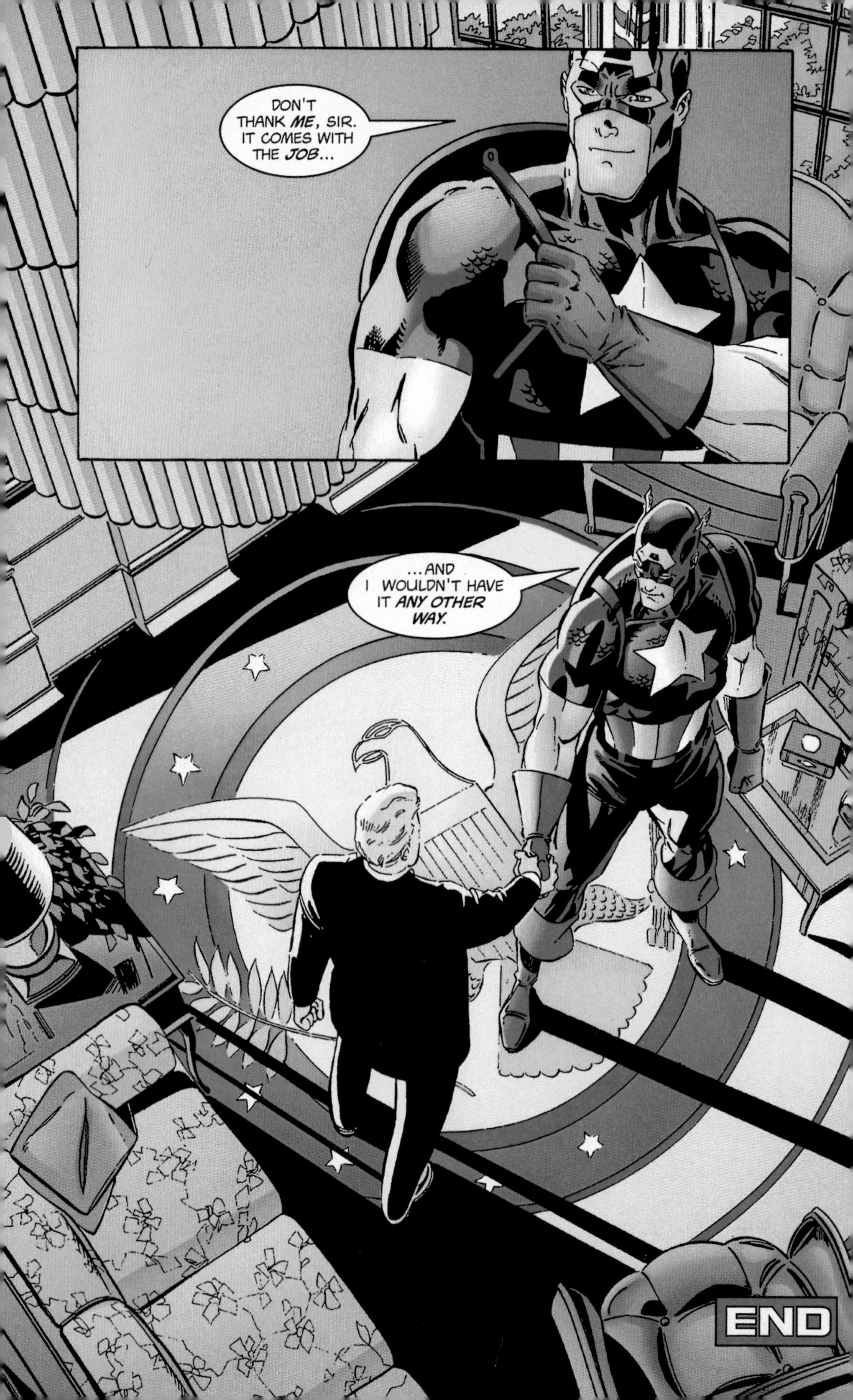
DON'T THANK *ME*, SIR. IT COMES WITH THE *JOB*...
...AND I WOULDN'T HAVE IT *ANY OTHER WAY*.
END

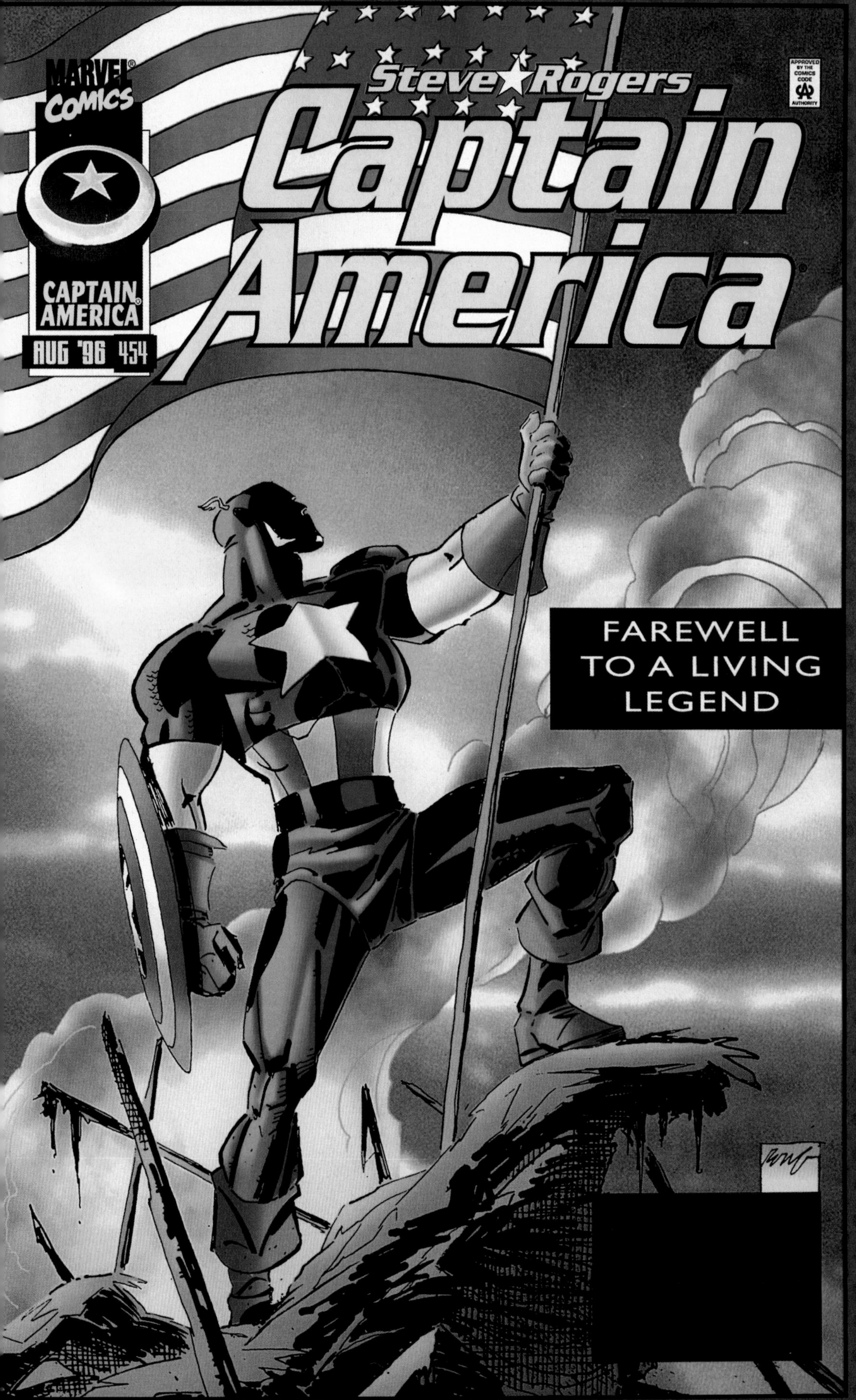

MARVEL COMICS
CAPTAIN AMERICA
AUG '96 454
Steve Rogers
Captain America
APPROVED BY THE COMICS CODE AUTHORITY
FAREWELL TO A LIVING LEGEND

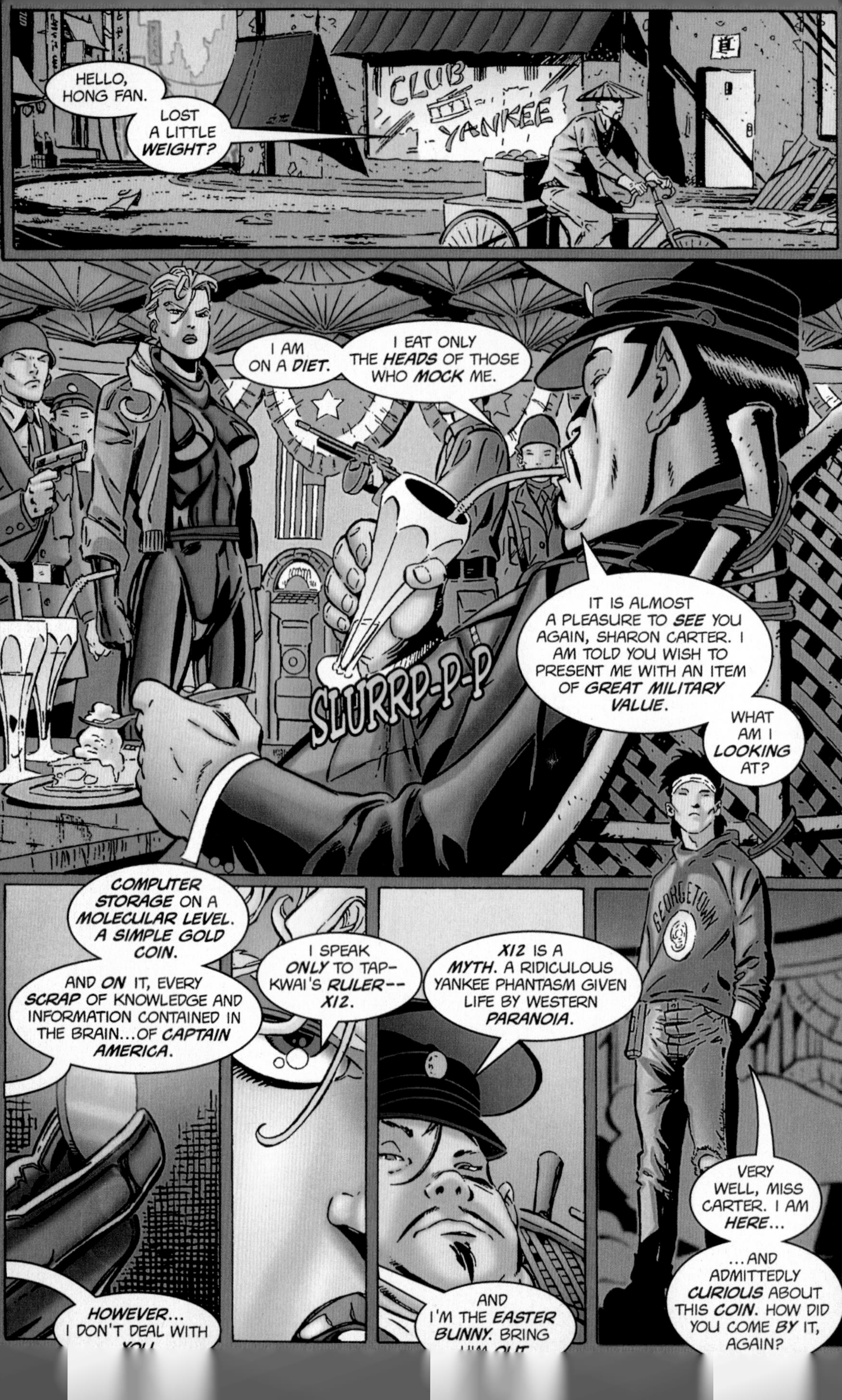
HELLO, HONG FAN.
LOST A LITTLE WEIGHT?
CLUB YANKEE
I AM ON A DIET.
I EAT ONLY THE HEADS OF THOSE WHO MOCK ME.
SLURRP-P-P
IT IS ALMOST A PLEASURE TO SEE YOU AGAIN, SHARON CARTER. I AM TOLD YOU WISH TO PRESENT ME WITH AN ITEM OF GREAT MILITARY VALUE.
WHAT AM I LOOKING AT?
COMPUTER STORAGE ON A MOLECULAR LEVEL. A SIMPLE GOLD COIN.
AND ON IT, EVERY SCRAP OF KNOWLEDGE AND INFORMATION CONTAINED IN THE BRAIN...OF CAPTAIN AMERICA.
HOWEVER... I DON'T DEAL WITH
I SPEAK ONLY TO TAP-KWAI'S RULER--X12.
X12 IS A MYTH. A RIDICULOUS YANKEE PHANTASM GIVEN LIFE BY WESTERN PARANOIA.
AND I'M THE EASTER BUNNY. BRING
GEORGETOWN
VERY WELL, MISS CARTER. I AM HERE...
...AND ADMITTEDLY CURIOUS ABOUT THIS COIN. HOW DID YOU COME BY IT, AGAIN?

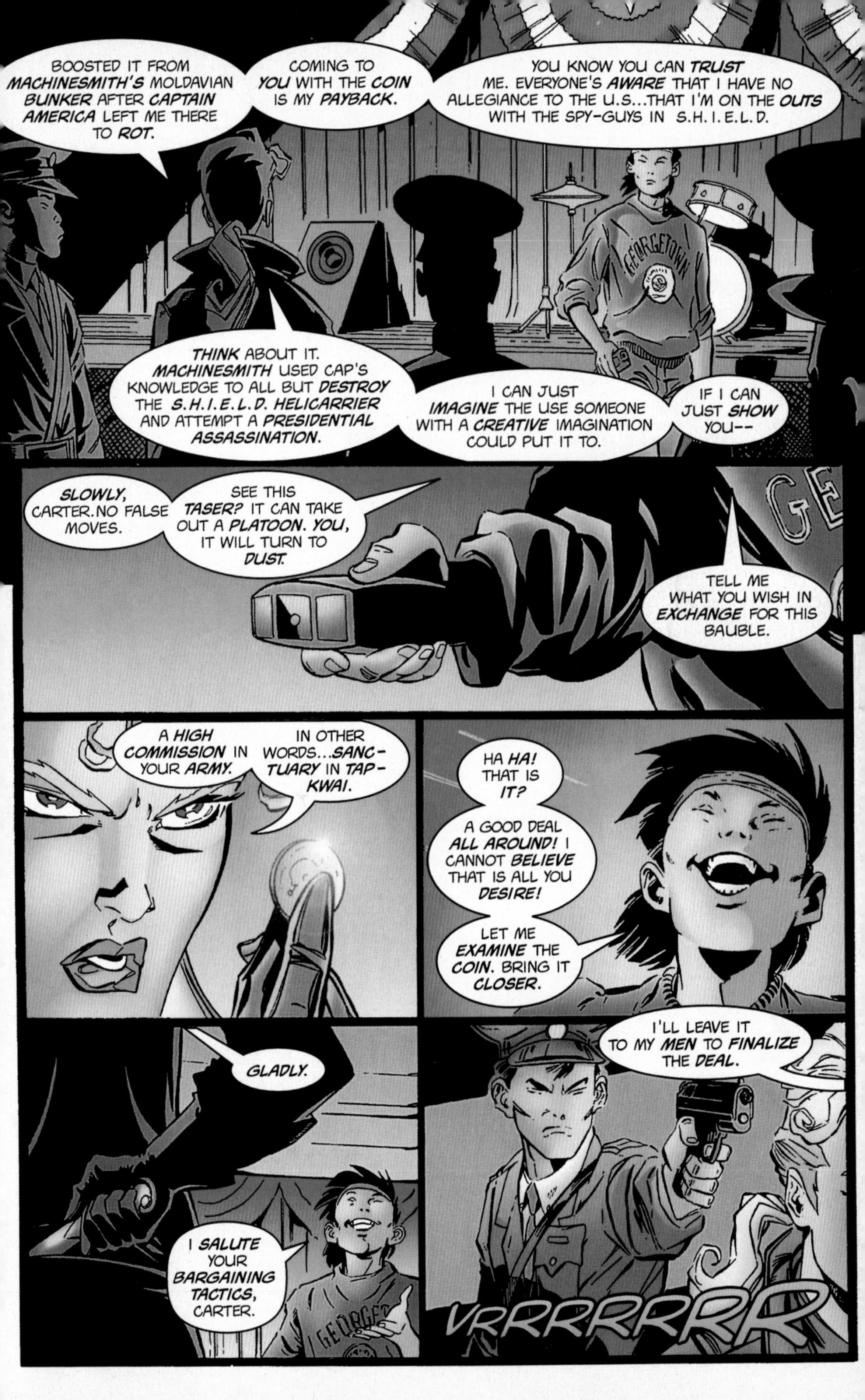
BOOSTED IT FROM MACHINESMITH'S MOLDAVIAN BUNKER AFTER CAPTAIN AMERICA LEFT ME THERE TO ROT.
COMING TO YOU WITH THE COIN IS MY PAYBACK.
YOU KNOW YOU CAN TRUST ME. EVERYONE'S AWARE THAT I HAVE NO ALLEGIANCE TO THE U.S...THAT I'M ON THE OUTS WITH THE SPY-GUYS IN S.H.I.E.L.D.
THINK ABOUT IT. MACHINESMITH USED CAP'S KNOWLEDGE TO ALL BUT DESTROY THE S.H.I.E.L.D. HELICARRIER AND ATTEMPT A PRESIDENTIAL ASSASSINATION.
I CAN JUST IMAGINE THE USE SOMEONE WITH A CREATIVE IMAGINATION COULD PUT IT TO.
IF I CAN JUST SHOW YOU--
SLOWLY, CARTER. NO FALSE MOVES.
SEE THIS TASER? IT CAN TAKE OUT A PLATOON. YOU, IT WILL TURN TO DUST.
TELL ME WHAT YOU WISH IN EXCHANGE FOR THIS BAUBLE.
A HIGH COMMISSION IN YOUR ARMY.
IN OTHER WORDS...SANCTUARY IN TAP-KWAI.
HA HA! THAT IS IT?
A GOOD DEAL ALL AROUND! I CANNOT BELIEVE THAT IS ALL YOU DESIRE!
LET ME EXAMINE THE COIN. BRING IT CLOSER.
GLADLY.
I SALUTE YOUR BARGAINING TACTICS, CARTER.
I'LL LEAVE IT TO MY MEN TO FINALIZE THE DEAL.
VRRRRRRRR

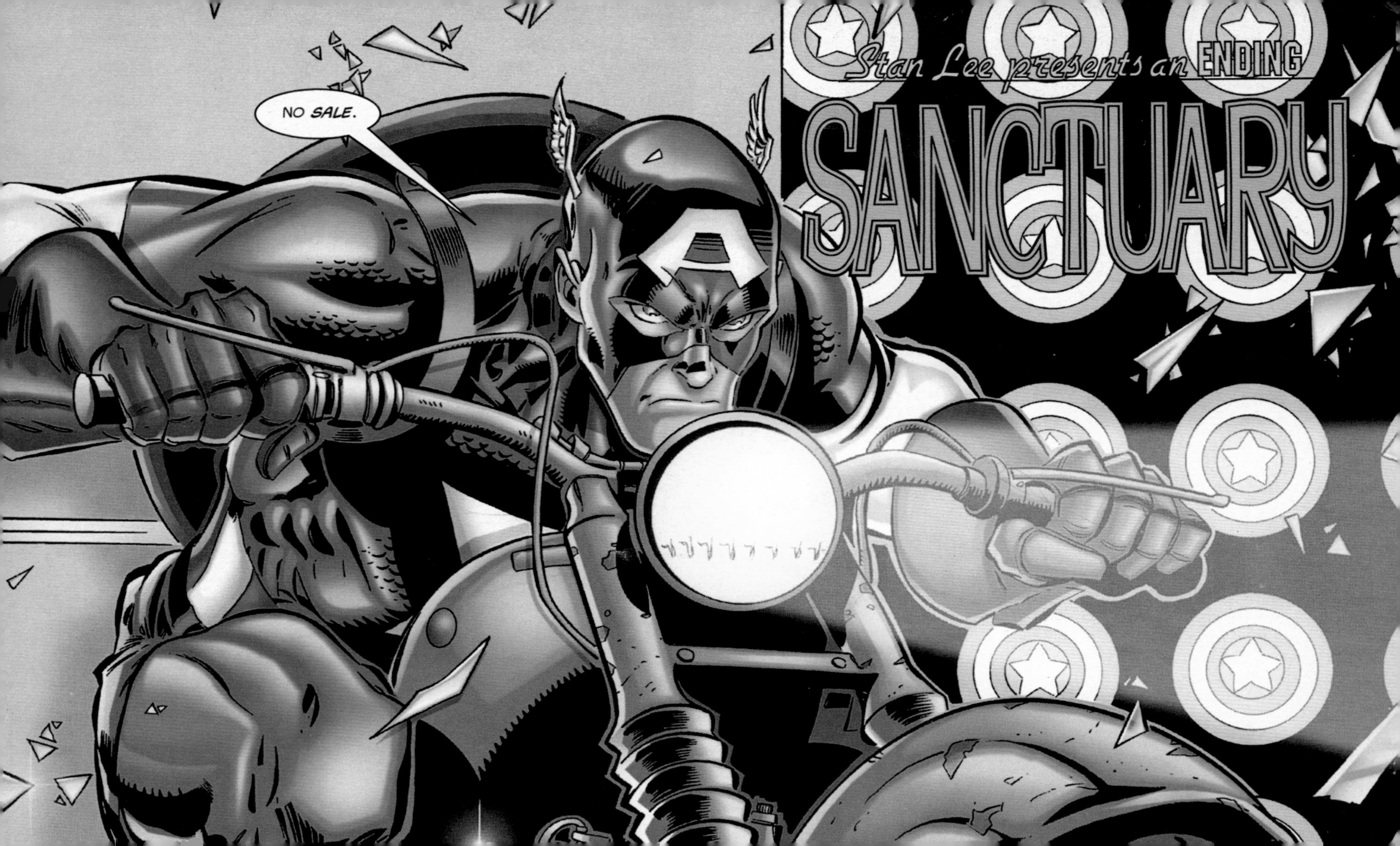
NO SALE.
Stan Lee presents an ENDING
SANCTUARY

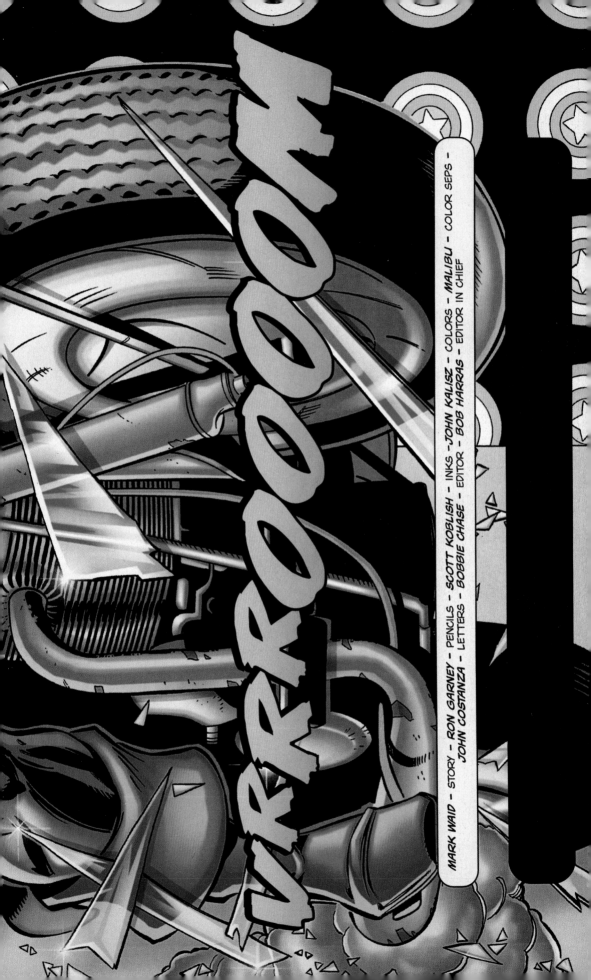

VRRRROOOOOM

MARK WAID – STORY – RON GARNEY – PENCILS – SCOTT KOBLISH – INKS –JOHN KALISZ – COLORS – MALIBU – COLOR SEPS – JOHN COSTANZA – LETTERS – BOBBIE CHASE – EDITOR – BOB HARRAS – EDITOR IN CHIEF –

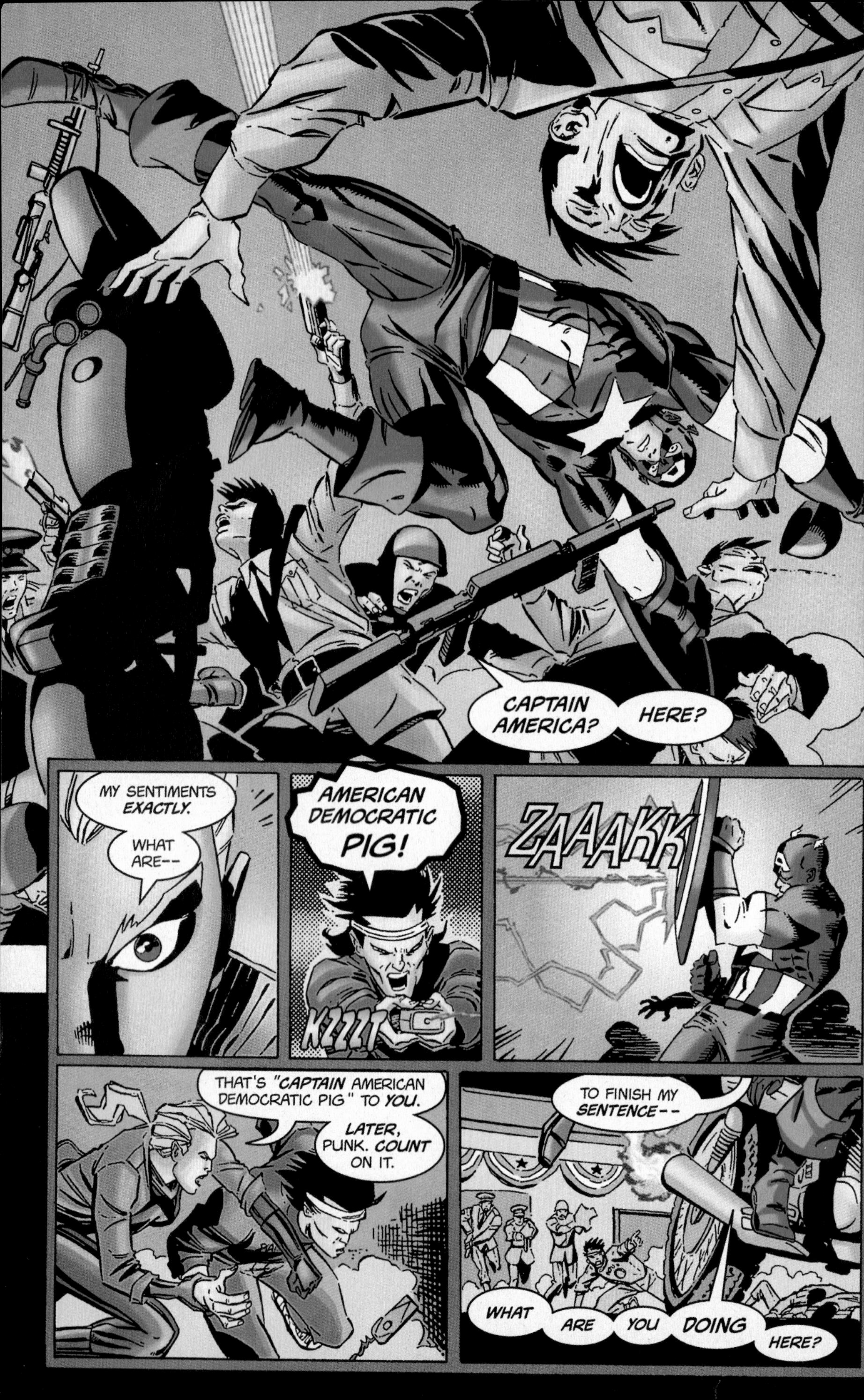
CAPTAIN AMERICA?
HERE?
MY SENTIMENTS EXACTLY.
WHAT ARE--
AMERICAN DEMOCRATIC PIG!
KZZZT
ZAAAKK
THAT'S "CAPTAIN AMERICAN DEMOCRATIC PIG" TO YOU.
LATER, PUNK. COUNT ON IT.
TO FINISH MY SENTENCE--
WHAT
ARE
YOU
DOING
HERE?

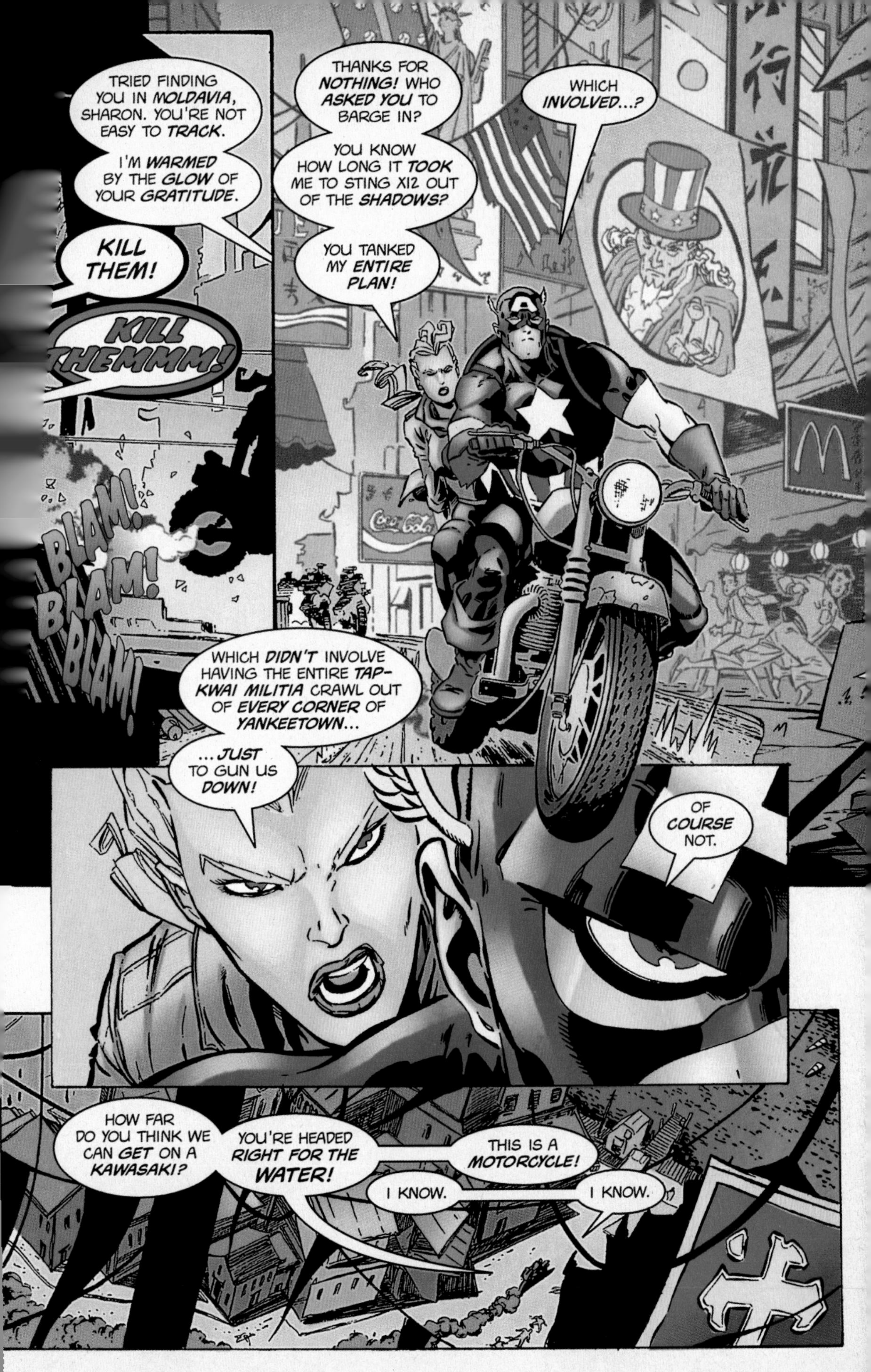
TRIED FINDING YOU IN MOLDAVIA, SHARON. YOU'RE NOT EASY TO TRACK.
I'M WARMED BY THE GLOW OF YOUR GRATITUDE.
KILL THEM!
KILL THEMMMM!
THANKS FOR NOTHING! WHO ASKED YOU TO BARGE IN?
YOU KNOW HOW LONG IT TOOK ME TO STING XI2 OUT OF THE SHADOWS?
YOU TANKED MY ENTIRE PLAN!
WHICH INVOLVED...?
BLAM! BLAM! BLAM!
WHICH DIDN'T INVOLVE HAVING THE ENTIRE TAP-KWAI MILITIA CRAWL OUT OF EVERY CORNER OF YANKEETOWN...
...JUST TO GUN US DOWN!
OF COURSE NOT.
HOW FAR DO YOU THINK WE CAN GET ON A KAWASAKI?
YOU'RE HEADED RIGHT FOR THE WATER!
THIS IS A MOTORCYCLE!
I KNOW.
I KNOW.

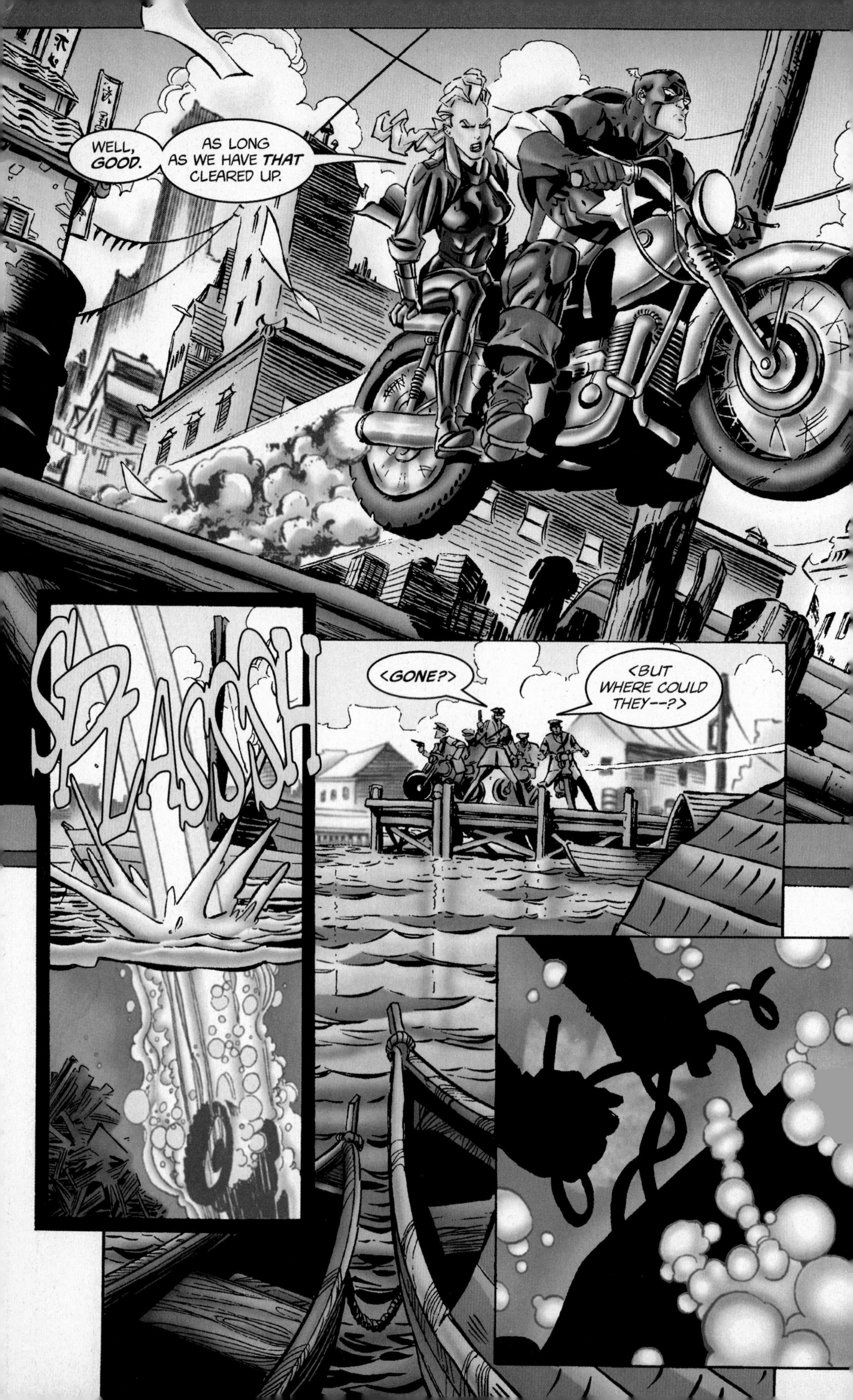
WELL, GOOD.
AS LONG AS WE HAVE THAT CLEARED UP.
SPLASSSH
<GONE?>
<BUT WHERE COULD THEY--?>

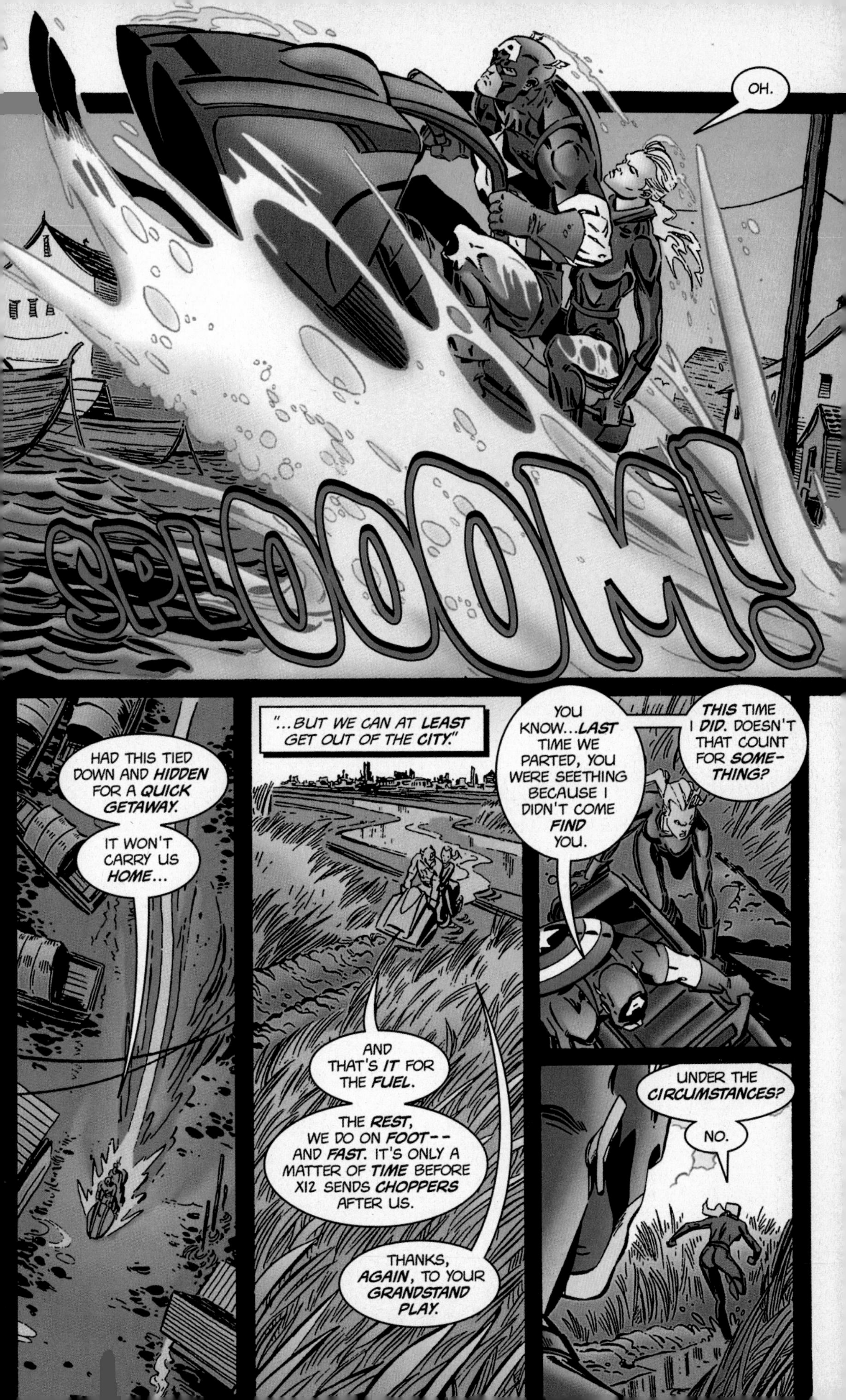
OH.
SPLOOOM!
HAD THIS TIED DOWN AND HIDDEN FOR A QUICK GETAWAY.
IT WON'T CARRY US HOME...
"...BUT WE CAN AT LEAST GET OUT OF THE CITY."
AND THAT'S IT FOR THE FUEL.
THE REST, WE DO ON FOOT-- AND FAST. IT'S ONLY A MATTER OF TIME BEFORE XI2 SENDS CHOPPERS AFTER US.
THANKS, AGAIN, TO YOUR GRANDSTAND PLAY.
YOU KNOW...LAST TIME WE PARTED, YOU WERE SEETHING BECAUSE I DIDN'T COME FIND YOU.
THIS TIME I DID. DOESN'T THAT COUNT FOR SOME-THING?
UNDER THE CIRCUMSTANCES?
NO.

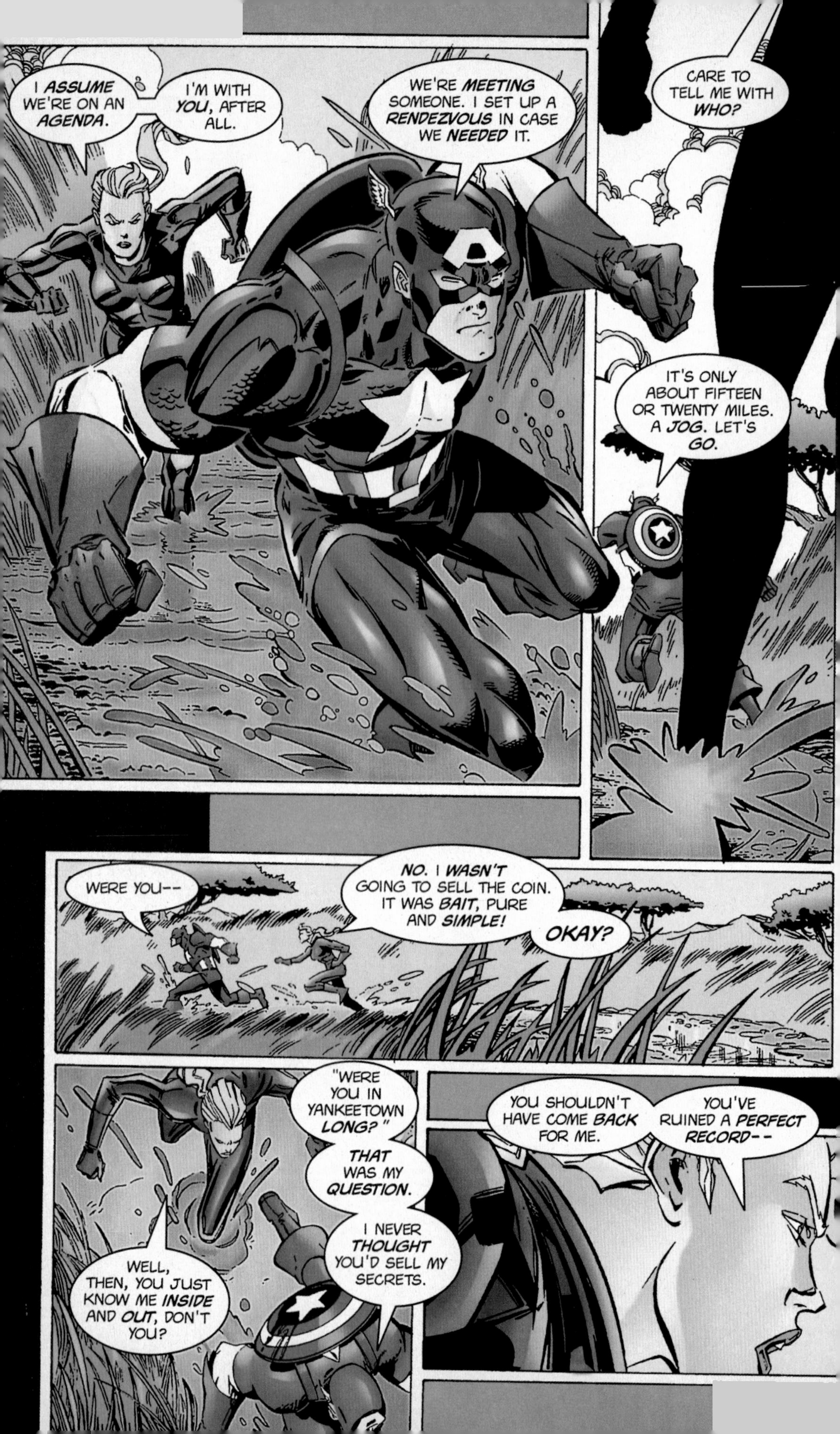
I ASSUME WE'RE ON AN AGENDA.
I'M WITH YOU, AFTER ALL.
WE'RE MEETING SOMEONE. I SET UP A RENDEZVOUS IN CASE WE NEEDED IT.
CARE TO TELL ME WITH WHO?
IT'S ONLY ABOUT FIFTEEN OR TWENTY MILES. A JOG. LET'S GO.
WERE YOU--
NO. I WASN'T GOING TO SELL THE COIN. IT WAS BAIT, PURE AND SIMPLE!
OKAY?
"WERE YOU IN YANKEETOWN LONG?"
THAT WAS MY QUESTION.
I NEVER THOUGHT YOU'D SELL MY SECRETS.
WELL, THEN, YOU JUST KNOW ME INSIDE AND OUT, DON'T YOU?
YOU SHOULDN'T HAVE COME BACK FOR ME.
YOU'VE RUINED A PERFECT RECORD--

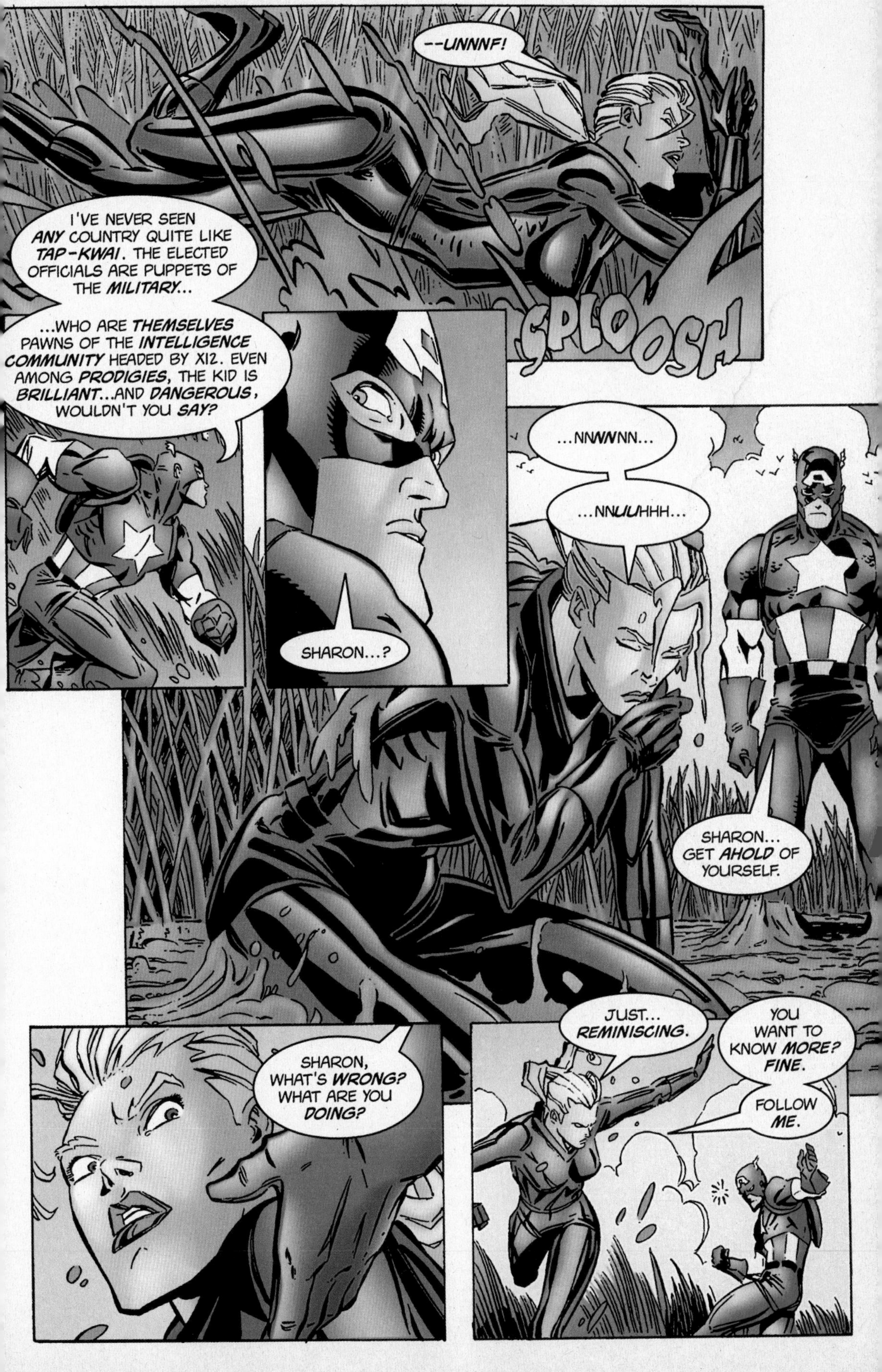
--UNNNF!
SPLOOSH
I'VE NEVER SEEN ANY COUNTRY QUITE LIKE TAP-KWAI. THE ELECTED OFFICIALS ARE PUPPETS OF THE MILITARY...
...WHO ARE THEMSELVES PAWNS OF THE INTELLIGENCE COMMUNITY HEADED BY XI2. EVEN AMONG PRODIGIES, THE KID IS BRILLIANT...AND DANGEROUS, WOULDN'T YOU SAY?
SHARON...?
...NNNNNN...
...NNUUHHH...
SHARON... GET AHOLD OF YOURSELF.
SHARON, WHAT'S WRONG? WHAT ARE YOU DOING?
JUST... REMINISCING.
YOU WANT TO KNOW MORE? FINE.
FOLLOW ME.

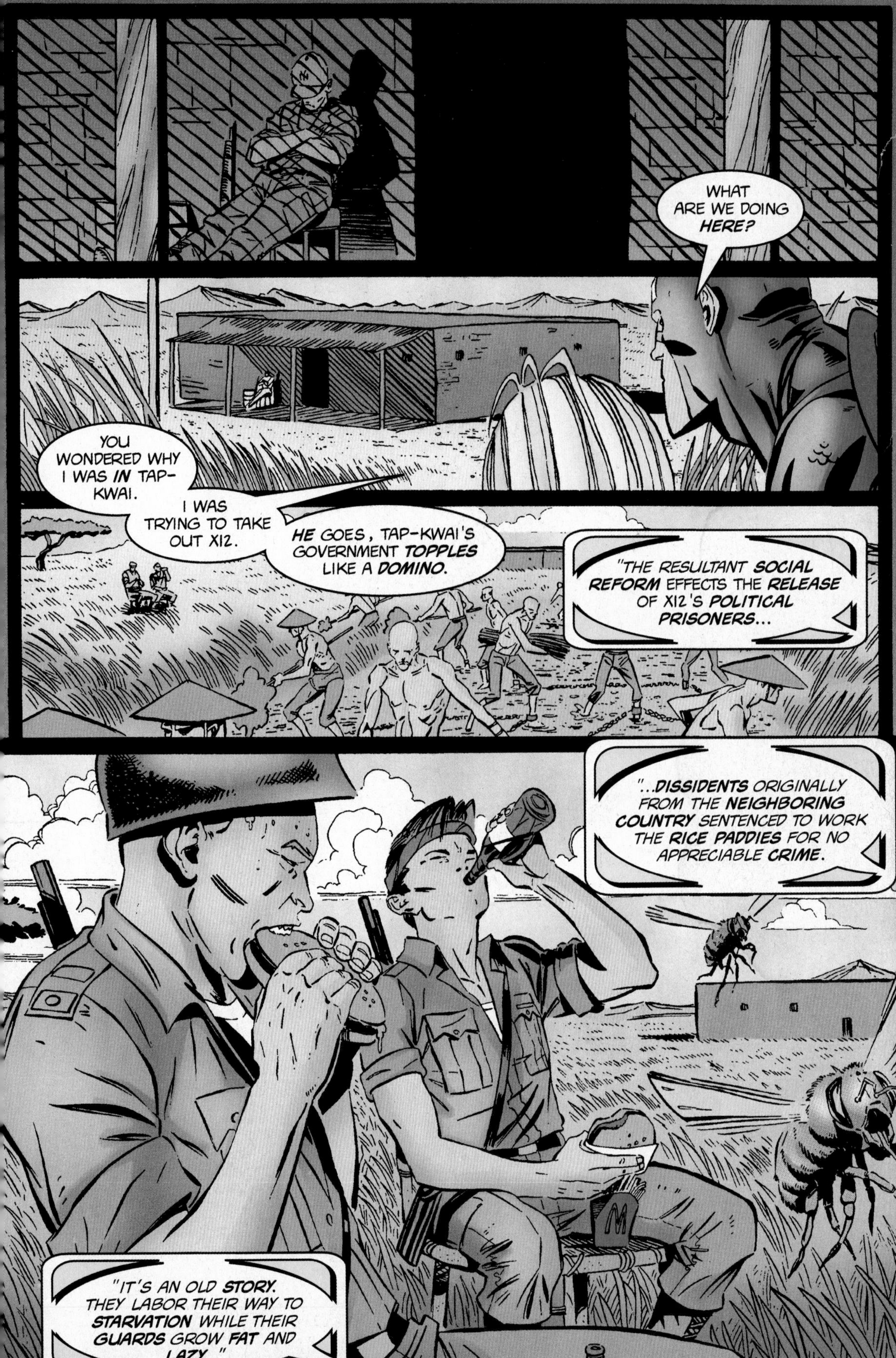
WHAT ARE WE DOING HERE?
YOU WONDERED WHY I WAS IN TAP-KWAI.
I WAS TRYING TO TAKE OUT X12.
HE GOES, TAP-KWAI'S GOVERNMENT TOPPLES LIKE A DOMINO.
"THE RESULTANT SOCIAL REFORM EFFECTS THE RELEASE OF X12'S POLITICAL PRISONERS...
"...DISSIDENTS ORIGINALLY FROM THE NEIGHBORING COUNTRY SENTENCED TO WORK THE RICE PADDIES FOR NO APPRECIABLE CRIME.
"IT'S AN OLD STORY. THEY LABOR THEIR WAY TO STARVATION WHILE THEIR GUARDS GROW FAT AND LAZY..."

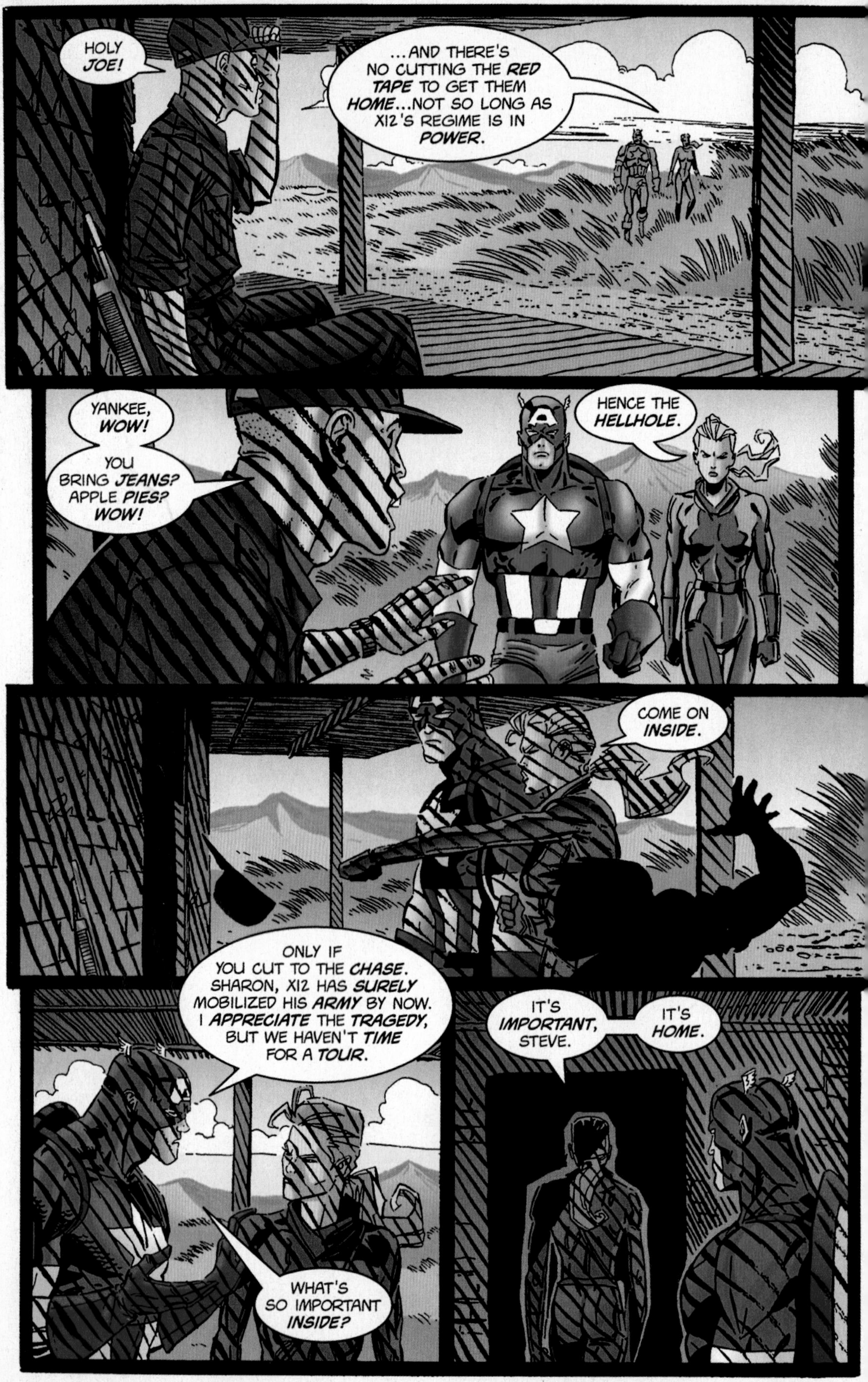
HOLY JOE!
...AND THERE'S NO CUTTING THE RED TAPE TO GET THEM HOME...NOT SO LONG AS XI2'S REGIME IS IN POWER.
YANKEE, WOW!
YOU BRING JEANS? APPLE PIES? WOW!
HENCE THE HELLHOLE.
COME ON INSIDE.
ONLY IF YOU CUT TO THE CHASE. SHARON, XI2 HAS SURELY MOBILIZED HIS ARMY BY NOW. I APPRECIATE THE TRAGEDY, BUT WE HAVEN'T TIME FOR A TOUR.
WHAT'S SO IMPORTANT INSIDE?
IT'S IMPORTANT, STEVE.
IT'S HOME.

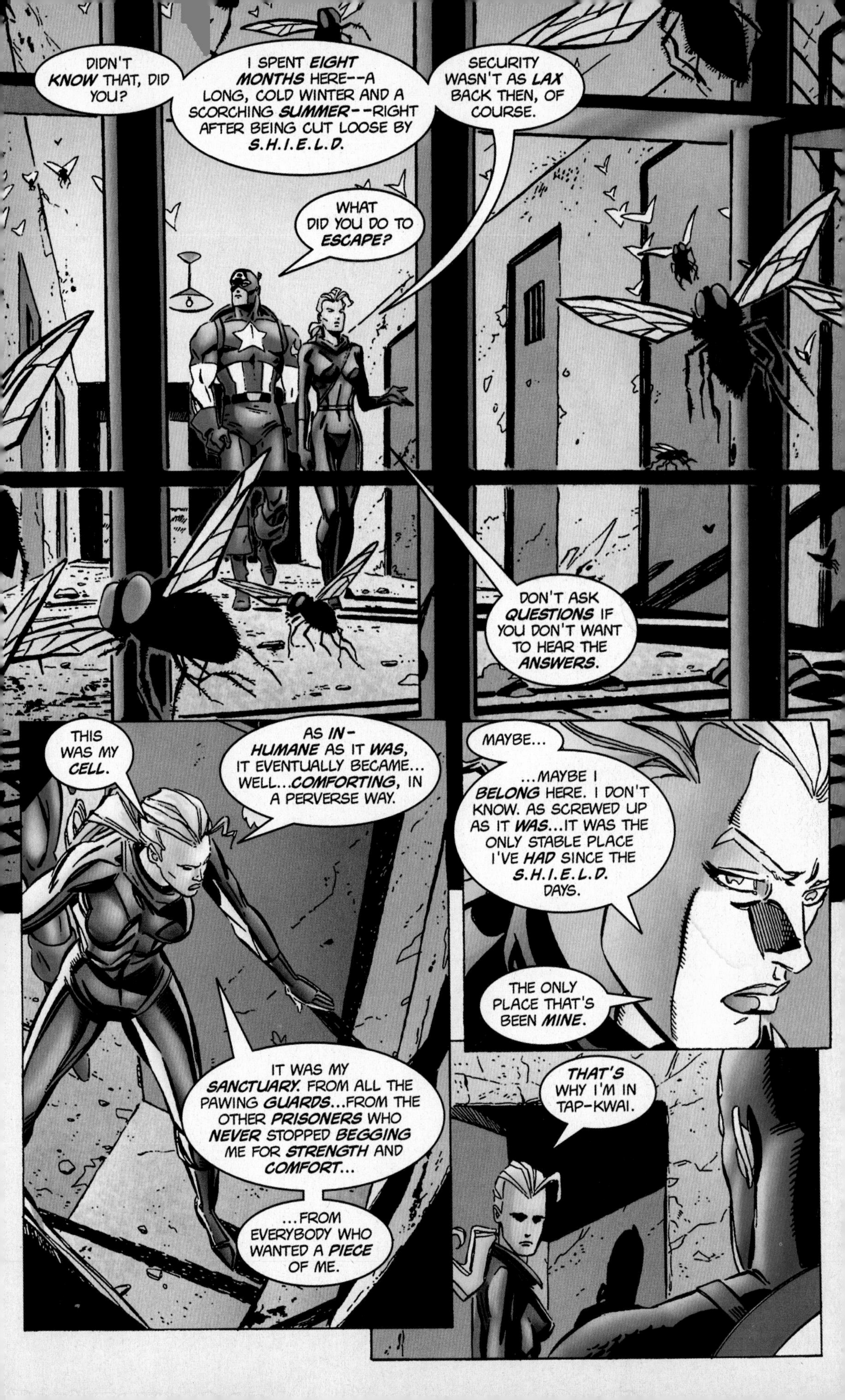
DIDN'T KNOW THAT, DID YOU?
I SPENT EIGHT MONTHS HERE--A LONG, COLD WINTER AND A SCORCHING SUMMER--RIGHT AFTER BEING CUT LOOSE BY S.H.I.E.L.D.
SECURITY WASN'T AS LAX BACK THEN, OF COURSE.
WHAT DID YOU DO TO ESCAPE?
DON'T ASK QUESTIONS IF YOU DON'T WANT TO HEAR THE ANSWERS.
THIS WAS MY CELL.
AS IN-HUMANE AS IT WAS, IT EVENTUALLY BECAME... WELL...COMFORTING, IN A PERVERSE WAY.
IT WAS MY SANCTUARY. FROM ALL THE PAWING GUARDS...FROM THE OTHER PRISONERS WHO NEVER STOPPED BEGGING ME FOR STRENGTH AND COMFORT...
...FROM EVERYBODY WHO WANTED A PIECE OF ME.
MAYBE...
...MAYBE I BELONG HERE. I DON'T KNOW. AS SCREWED UP AS IT WAS...IT WAS THE ONLY STABLE PLACE I'VE HAD SINCE THE S.H.I.E.L.D. DAYS.
THE ONLY PLACE THAT'S BEEN MINE.
THAT'S WHY I'M IN TAP-KWAI.

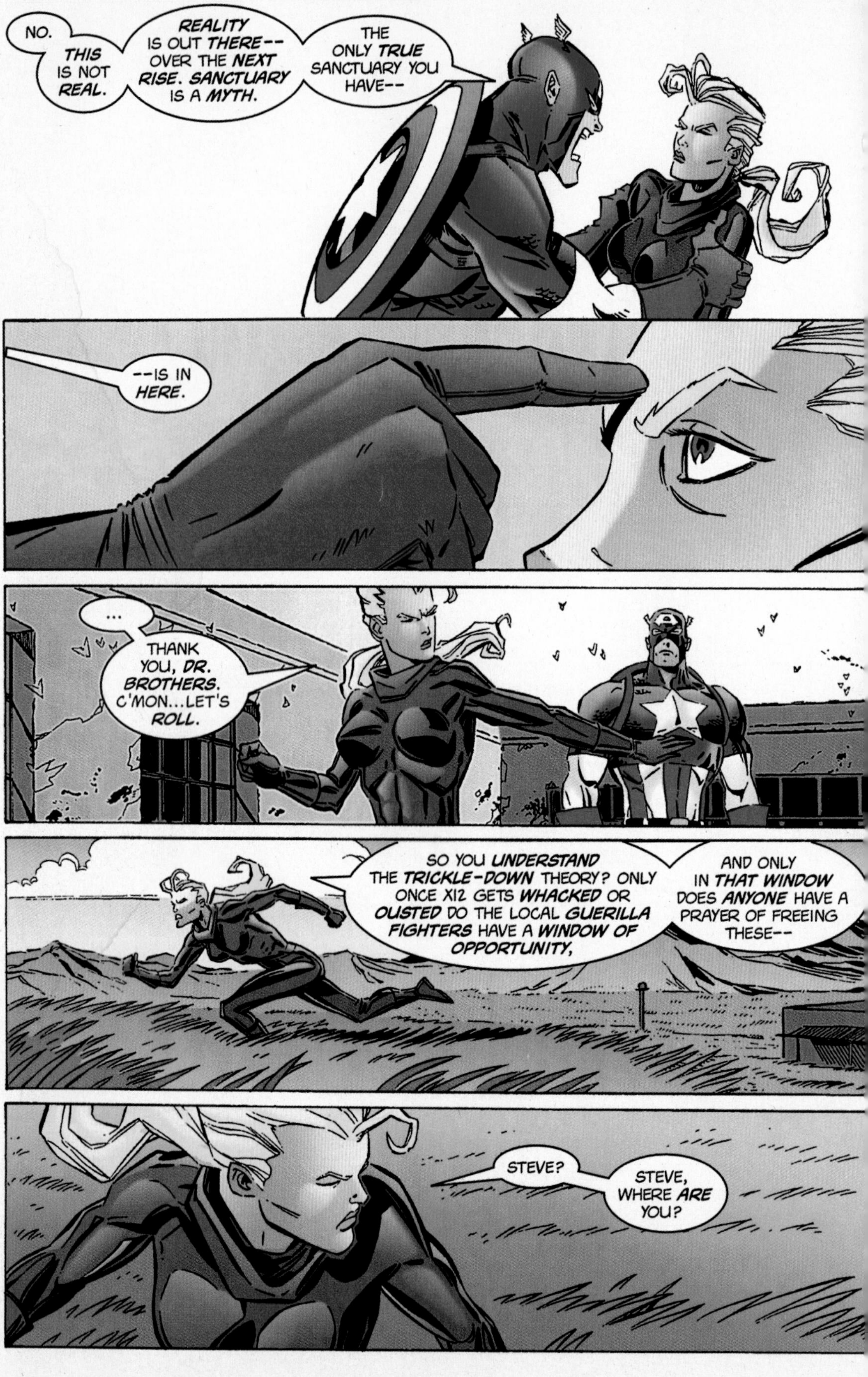
NO.
THIS IS NOT REAL.
REALITY IS OUT THERE-- OVER THE NEXT RISE. SANCTUARY IS A MYTH.
THE ONLY TRUE SANCTUARY YOU HAVE--
--IS IN HERE.
...
THANK YOU, DR. BROTHERS. C'MON...LET'S ROLL.
SO YOU UNDERSTAND THE TRICKLE-DOWN THEORY? ONLY ONCE XI2 GETS WHACKED OR OUSTED DO THE LOCAL GUERILLA FIGHTERS HAVE A WINDOW OF OPPORTUNITY,
AND ONLY IN THAT WINDOW DOES ANYONE HAVE A PRAYER OF FREEING THESE--
STEVE?
STEVE, WHERE ARE YOU?

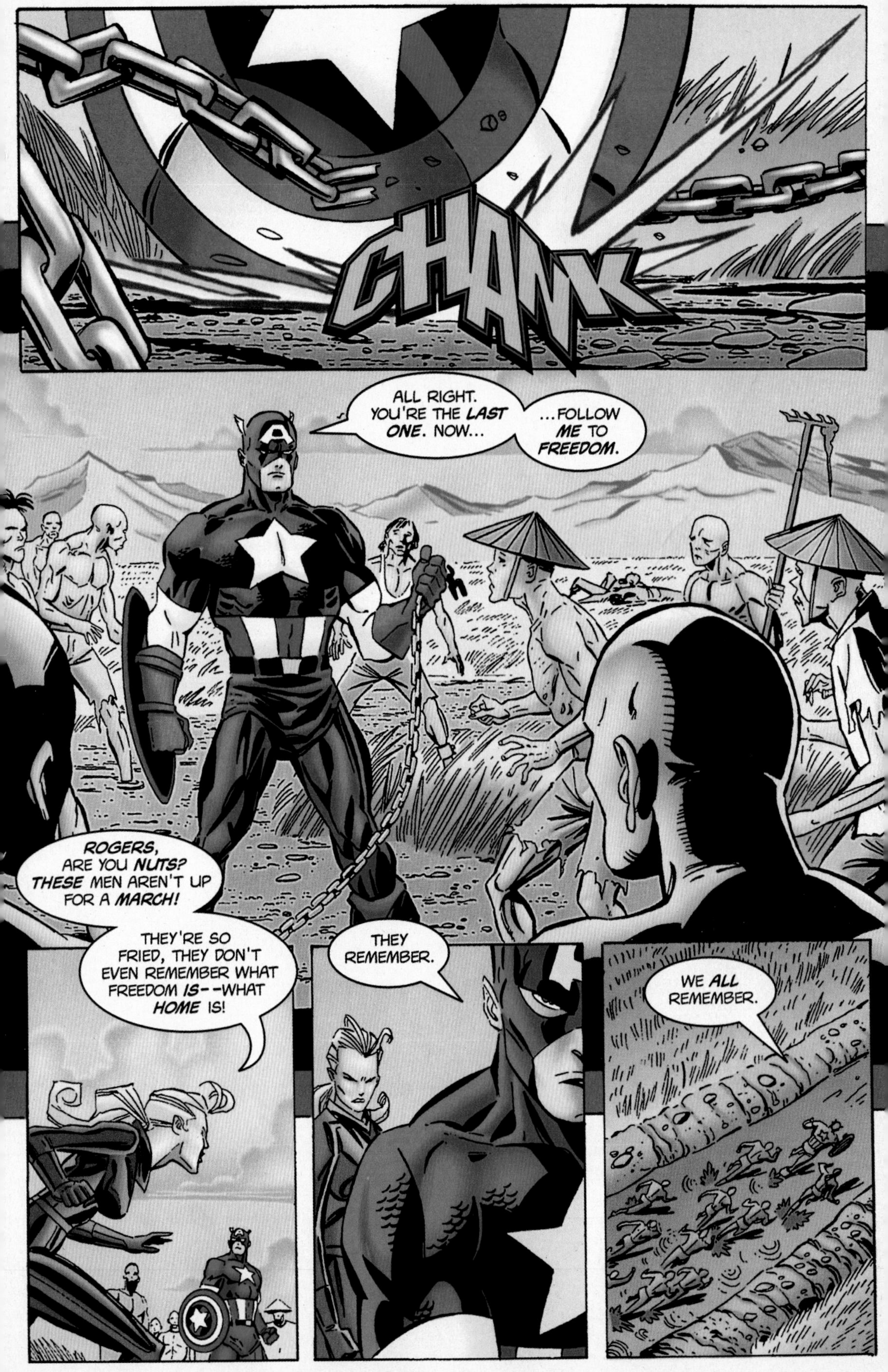
CHANK
ALL RIGHT. YOU'RE THE LAST ONE. NOW...
...FOLLOW ME TO FREEDOM.
ROGERS, ARE YOU NUTS? THESE MEN AREN'T UP FOR A MARCH!
THEY'RE SO FRIED, THEY DON'T EVEN REMEMBER WHAT FREEDOM IS--WHAT HOME IS!
THEY REMEMBER.
WE ALL REMEMBER.

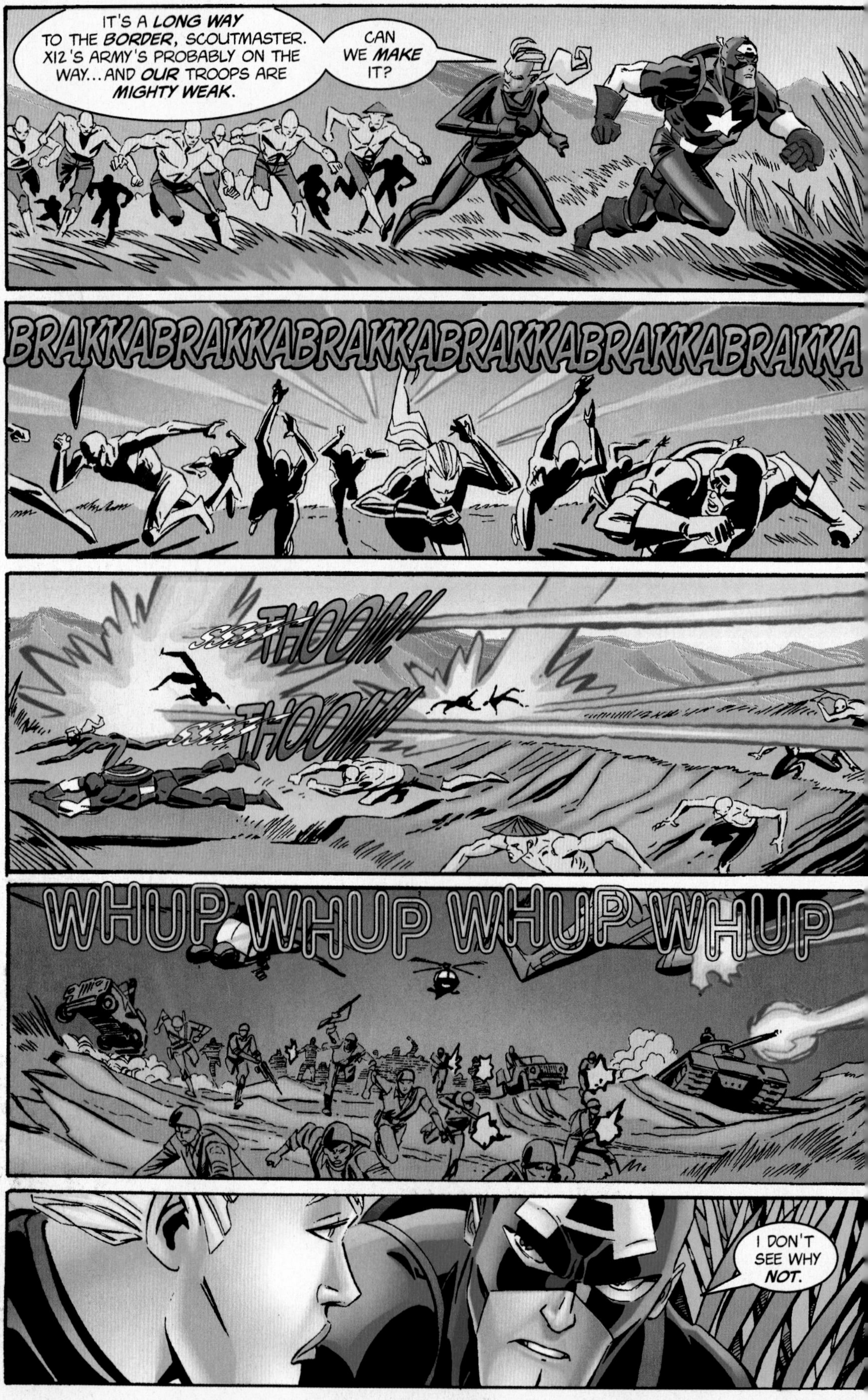
IT'S A LONG WAY TO THE BORDER, SCOUTMASTER. XI2'S ARMY'S PROBABLY ON THE WAY...AND OUR TROOPS ARE MIGHTY WEAK.
CAN WE MAKE IT?
BRAKKABRAKKABRAKKABRAKKABRAKKABRAKKA
SSSTHOOM!
SSSTHOOM!
WHUP WHUP WHUP WHUP
I DON'T SEE WHY NOT.

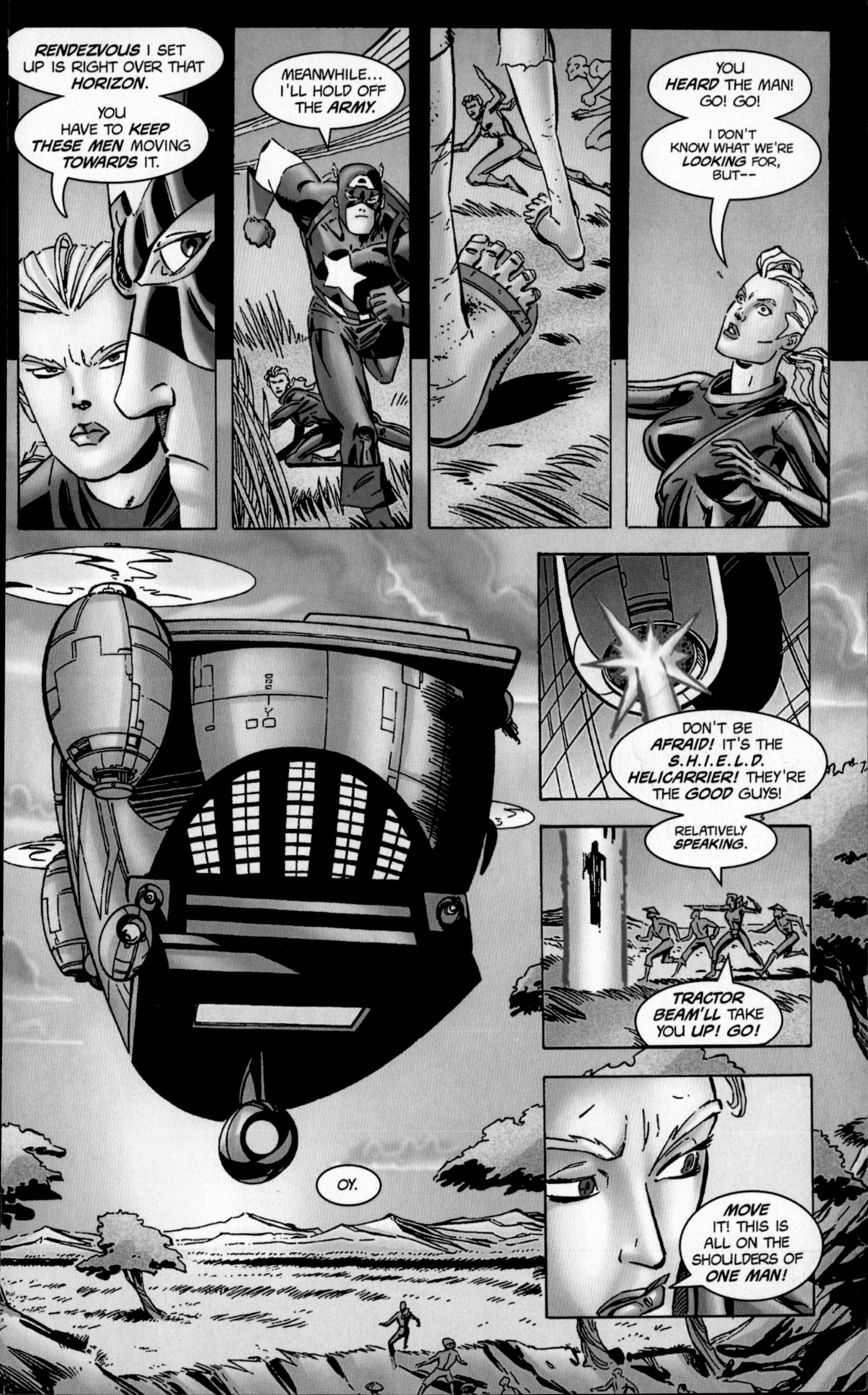
RENDEZVOUS I SET UP IS RIGHT OVER THAT HORIZON.
YOU HAVE TO KEEP THESE MEN MOVING TOWARDS IT.
MEANWHILE... I'LL HOLD OFF THE ARMY.
YOU HEARD THE MAN! GO! GO!
I DON'T KNOW WHAT WE'RE LOOKING FOR, BUT--
DON'T BE AFRAID! IT'S THE S.H.I.E.L.D. HELICARRIER! THEY'RE THE GOOD GUYS!
RELATIVELY SPEAKING.
TRACTOR BEAM'LL TAKE YOU UP! GO!
OY.
MOVE IT! THIS IS ALL ON THE SHOULDERS OF ONE MAN!

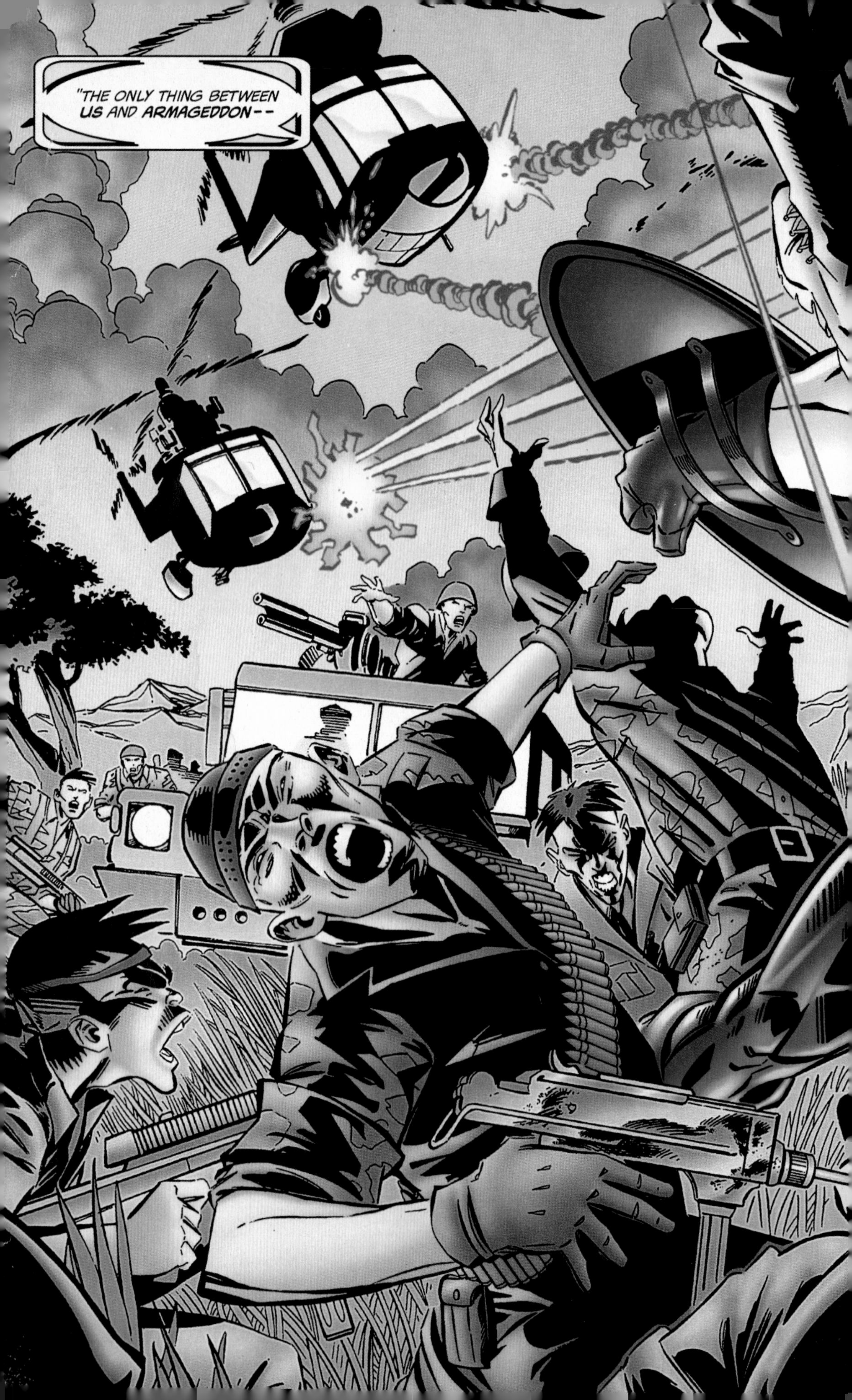
"THE ONLY THING BETWEEN US AND ARMAGEDDON--

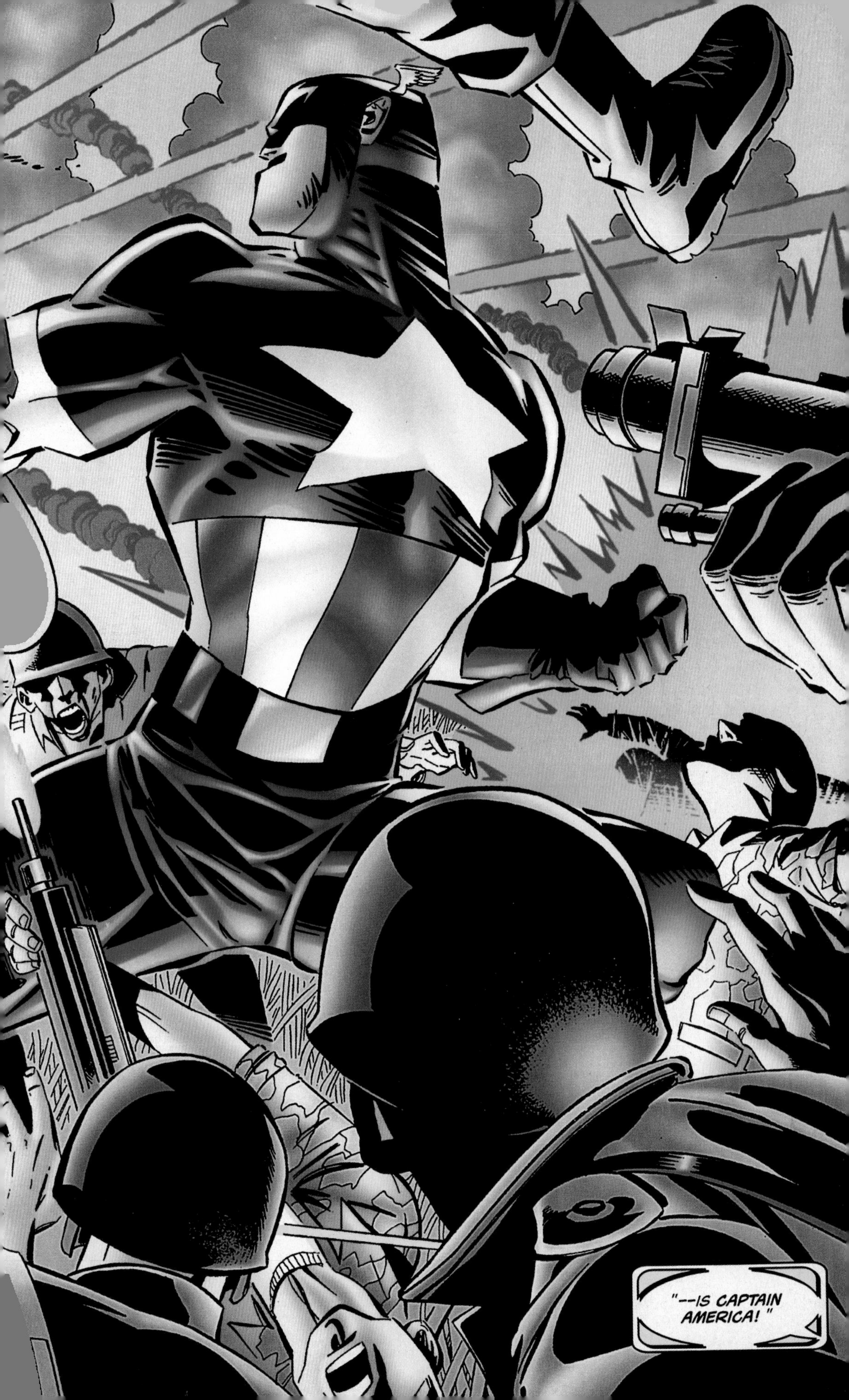
"--IS CAPTAIN AMERICA!"

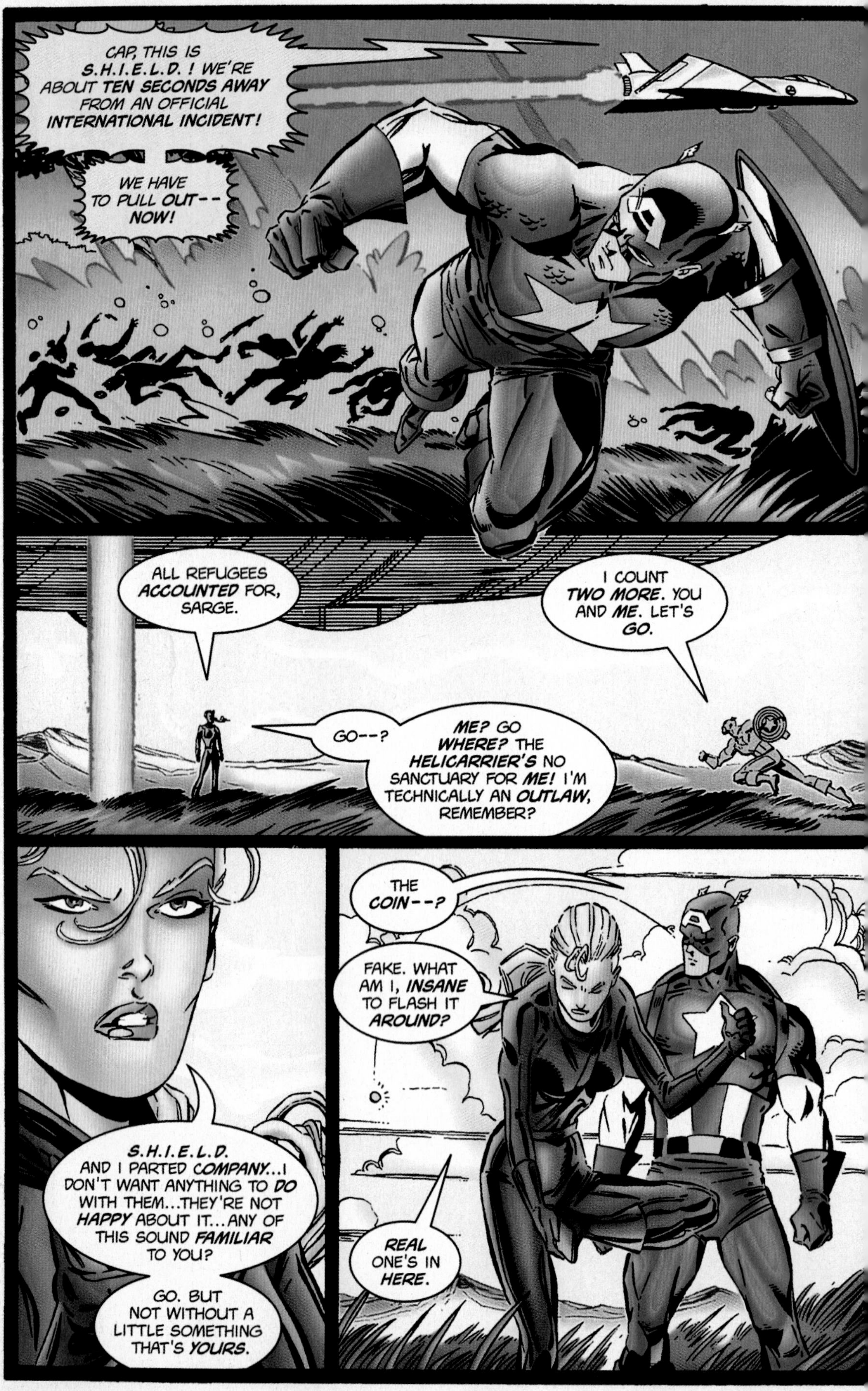
CAP, THIS IS S.H.I.E.L.D. ! WE'RE ABOUT TEN SECONDS AWAY FROM AN OFFICIAL INTERNATIONAL INCIDENT!
WE HAVE TO PULL OUT-- NOW!
ALL REFUGEES ACCOUNTED FOR, SARGE.
I COUNT TWO MORE. YOU AND ME. LET'S GO.
GO--?
ME? GO WHERE? THE HELICARRIER'S NO SANCTUARY FOR ME! I'M TECHNICALLY AN OUTLAW, REMEMBER?
S.H.I.E.L.D. AND I PARTED COMPANY...I DON'T WANT ANYTHING TO DO WITH THEM...THEY'RE NOT HAPPY ABOUT IT...ANY OF THIS SOUND FAMILIAR TO YOU?
GO. BUT NOT WITHOUT A LITTLE SOMETHING THAT'S YOURS.
THE COIN--?
FAKE. WHAT AM I, INSANE TO FLASH IT AROUND?
REAL ONE'S IN HERE.

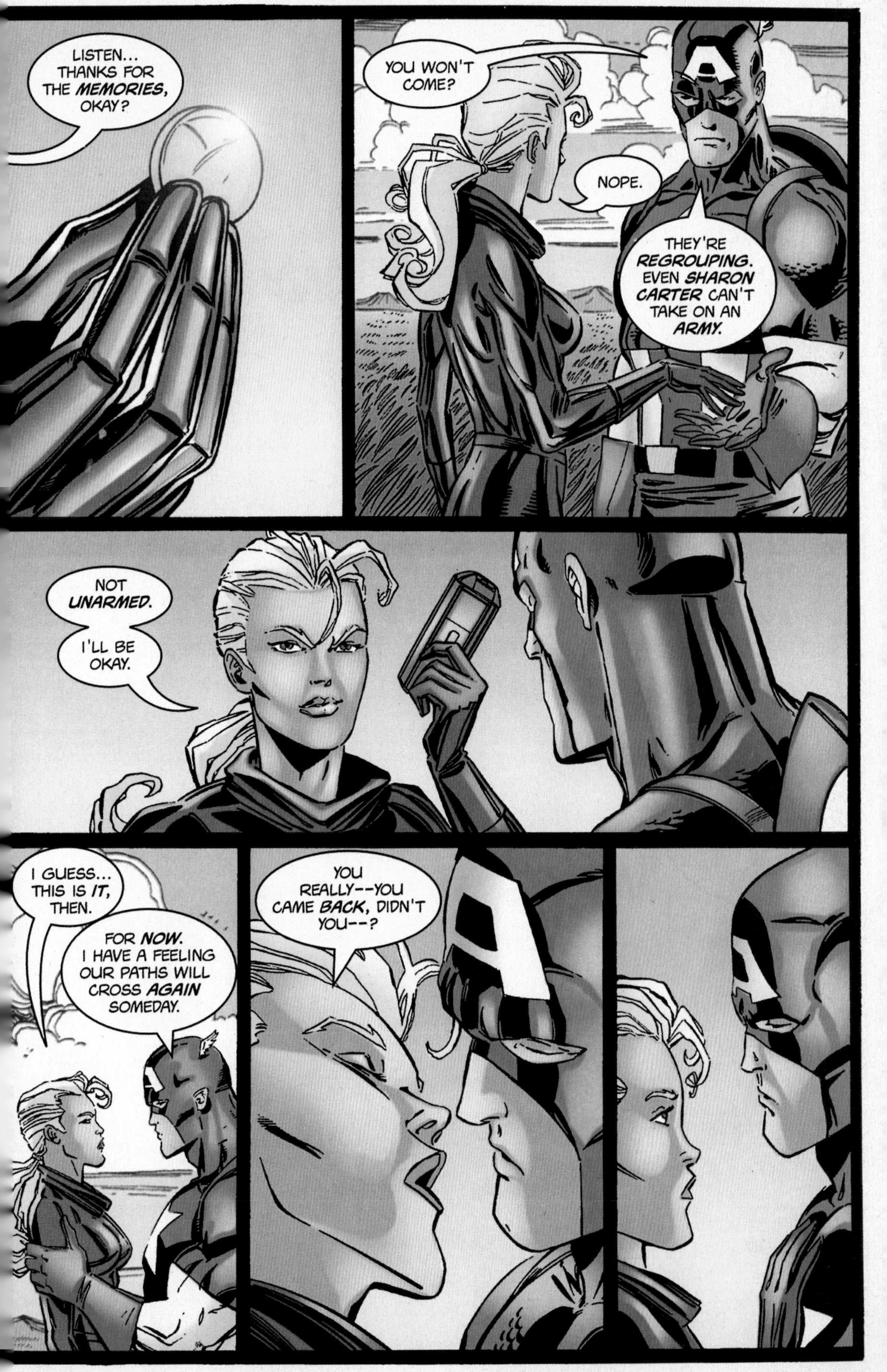
LISTEN... THANKS FOR THE *MEMORIES*, OKAY?
YOU WON'T COME?
NOPE.
THEY'RE *REGROUPING*. EVEN *SHARON CARTER* CAN'T TAKE ON AN *ARMY*.
NOT *UNARMED*.
I'LL BE OKAY.
I GUESS... THIS IS *IT*, THEN.
FOR *NOW*. I HAVE A FEELING OUR PATHS WILL CROSS *AGAIN* SOMEDAY.
YOU REALLY--YOU CAME *BACK*, DIDN'T YOU--?

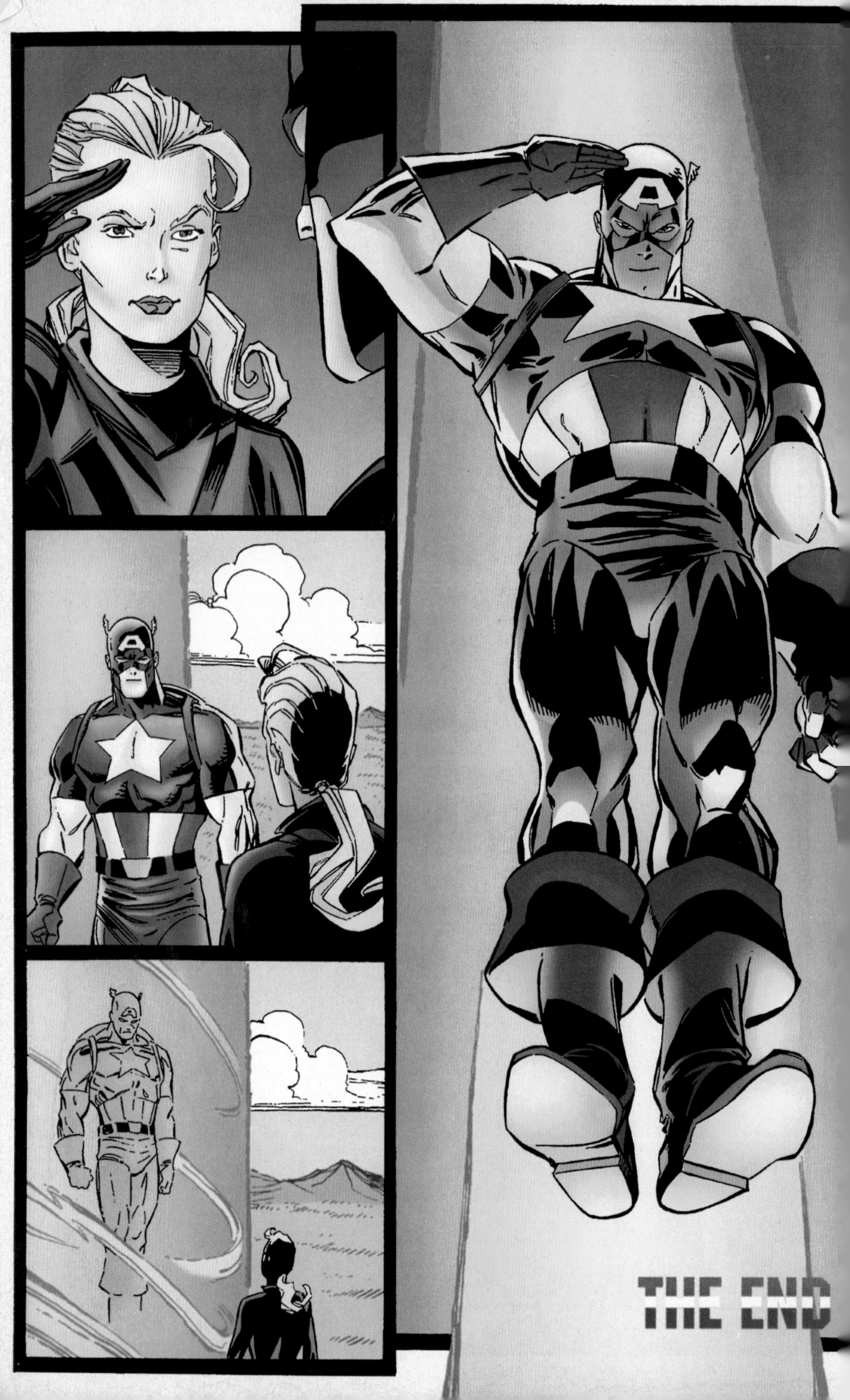
THE END

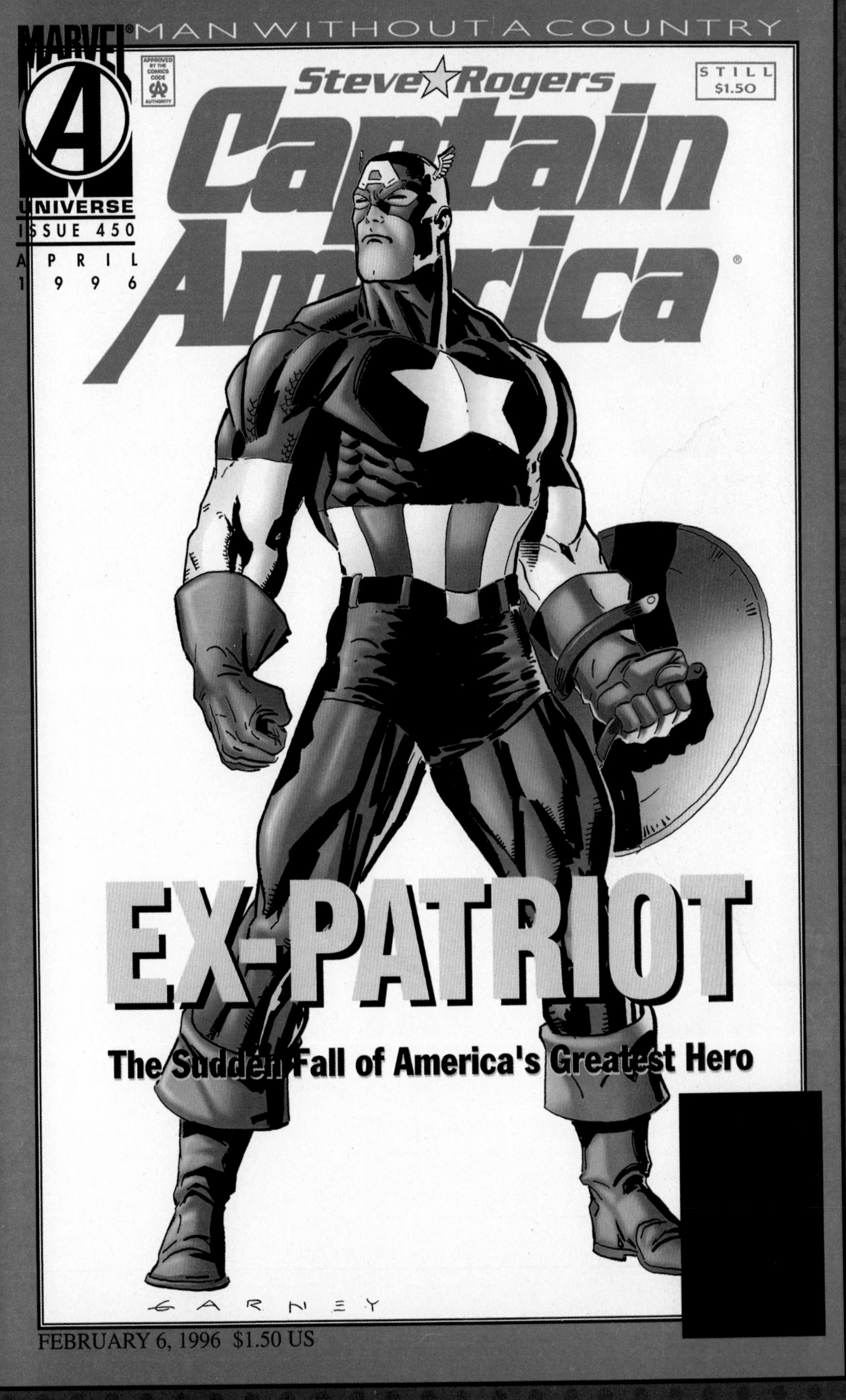

MARVEL
UNIVERSE
ISSUE 450
APRIL
1996
MAN WITHOUT A COUNTRY
APPROVED BY THE COMICS CODE AUTHORITY
STILL
$1.50
Steve Rogers
Captain America
EX-PATRIOT
The Sudden Fall of America's Greatest Hero
GARNEY
FEBRUARY 6, 1996 $1.50 US

Cover to Captain America: Man Without A Country TPB (1998)

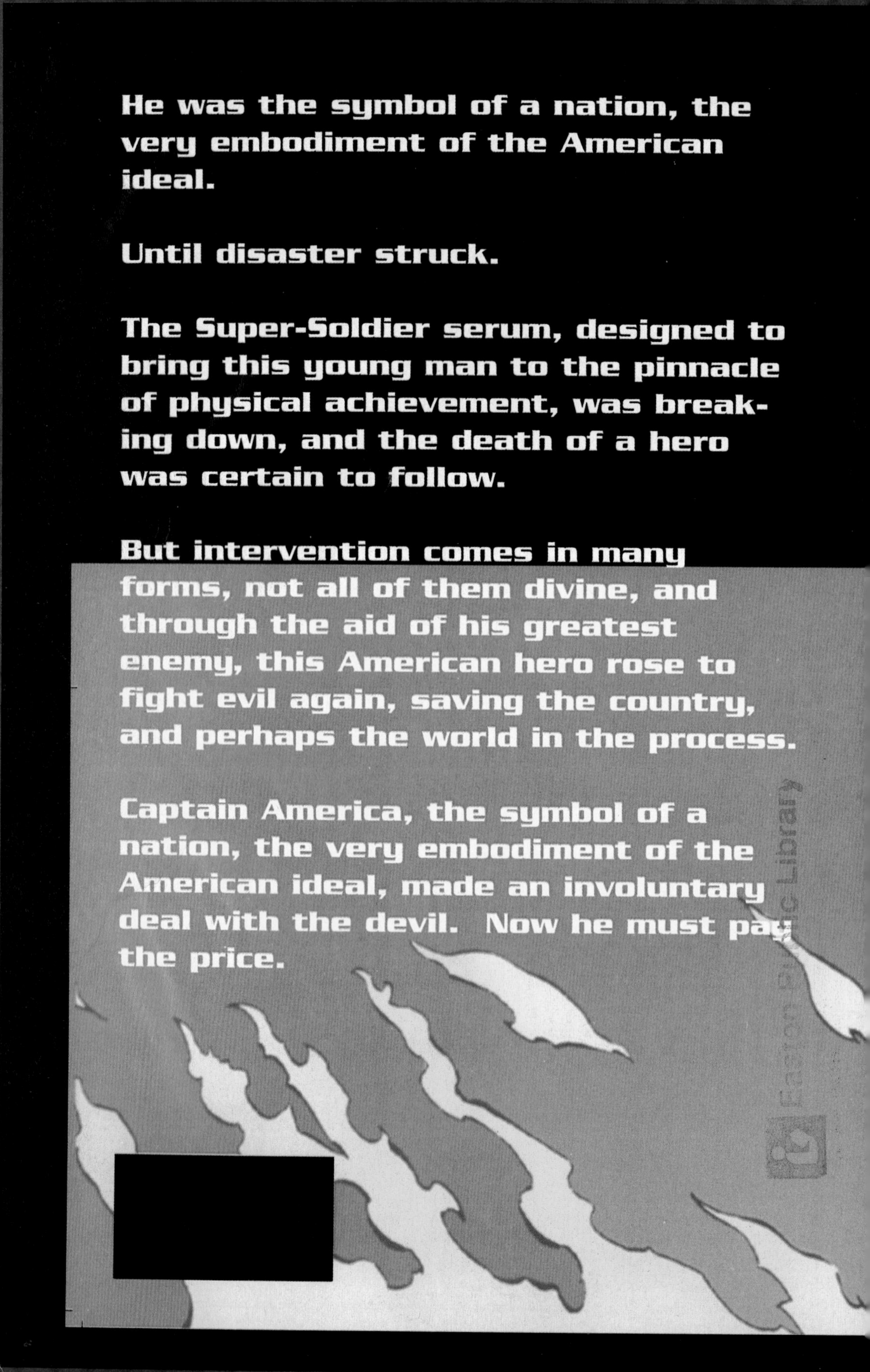

He was the symbol of a nation, the very embodiment of the American ideal.

Until disaster struck.

The Super-Soldier serum, designed to bring this young man to the pinnacle of physical achievement, was breaking down, and the death of a hero was certain to follow.

But intervention comes in many forms, not all of them divine, and through the aid of his greatest enemy, this American hero rose to fight evil again, saving the country, and perhaps the world in the process.

Captain America, the symbol of a nation, the very embodiment of the American ideal, made an involuntary deal with the devil. Now he must pay the price.

[redacted]